D1116660

The Reel Middle Ages

THE REEL MIDDLE AGES

*AMERICAN, WESTERN
AND EASTERN EUROPEAN,
MIDDLE EASTERN AND ASIAN FILMS
ABOUT MEDIEVAL EUROPE*

by KEVIN J. HARTY

McFarland & Company, Inc., Publishers
Jefferson, North Carolina, and London

Frontispiece: Margarete Schön as the vengeful
Kriemhild in Fritz Lang's 1924 film *Die Nibelungen*
(Still courtesy of the British Film Institute)

British Library Cataloguing-in-Publication data are available

Library of Congress Cataloguing-in-Publication Data

Harty, Kevin J.
    The reel Middle Ages : American, western and eastern
European, Middle Eastern, and Asian films about medieval
Europe / by Kevin J. Harty.
       p.   cm.
    Includes bibliographical references and index.
    ISBN 0-7864-0541-4 (library binding : 50# alkaline paper) ∞
    1. Middle Ages in motion pictures.   2. Motion pictures —
Catalogs. I. Title.
PN1995.9.M52H37   1999
791.43'658 — dc21   98-29385
                                           CIP

Manufactured in the United States of America

*McFarland & Company, Inc., Publishers
  Box 611, Jefferson, North Carolina 28640*

For

Rick Fisher and Cornelius Kelly,
who put me up,

and

the staff of the British Film Institute,
who put up with me,
while I was researching this book.

CONTENTS

PREFACE

The Reel Middle Ages is the first comprehensive survey of cinematic depictions of the Middle Ages. What follows is a record of nearly 600 films (plus alternate titles) that represent a hundred years of cinema, from the first of Georges Méliès's several films about Joan of Arc in 1897 to Rob Cohen's *Dragonheart*, Sean McNamara's *Galgameth* and Gary Trousdale's animated *The Hunchback of Notre Dame*— all released in 1996. In compiling materials for this volume, I have defined the Middle Ages as running roughly from the early fifth to the late fifteenth centuries, but time periods — historical, literary or even cinematic — are rarely very neat. Readers will therefore find included here films that recount events as early as St. Patrick's conversion of Ireland to Christianity, a process generally thought to have begun after 432, and films that recount events as late as John of Austria's defeat of Turkish forces at the Battle of Lepanto in 1571.

I have excluded any films based directly on the plays of William Shakespeare, since such films have been the subject of a number of previous studies. On the other hand, films that tell stories also told by Shakespeare but do so in a different way are included in this volume.

Finally, I have defined the medieval only in terms of the Occident. As a result, I have excluded films from Japan and India dealing with those nations' "medieval" eras, which are differently defined. I do, however, include Chinese films that recount the journeys of Marco Polo and Arabic or Islamic films that are set during the Crusades.

The arrangement of films in this volume is alphabetical by title with abundant cross references to alternate film titles. Each title is followed by the date of a film's production or release, the country of origin, the director, the production or releasing company, any alternate titles and the cast. (Unfortunately, for some early films, full production details could not be found.) I then provide a brief synopsis and commentary on each film. The synopsis and commentary are followed by a list of reviews and other discussions, including screenplays, scholarly evaluations, promotional materials and book-length analyses. Reviews and shorter materials are drawn from film journals, trade publications and newspapers of record.

The completion of this study would have been impossible without the help, generosity and kindness of a great number of people. The dedication of this volume records my greatest debts. Again, I am happy to thank Rick Fisher and Cornelius Kelly for providing me with a place to hang my hat in London, where I conducted most of the research for this book. Time and again, they proved the best of hosts, and I only hope I did not manage to wear out my welcome over the past several years. I am also greatly indebted to the staff of the British Film Institute for their assistance and kindness. All of them, from the staff in reception to those in the library and archives, went out of their way to make me feel at home, and members of the staff in the library and archives responded cheerfully by post, E-mail, fax and telephone to the many questions that invariably arose two days after I returned each time to Philadelphia from London. In particular, I am happy to acknowledge my continuing debt to Simon Baker and Olwen Terris in the National Film and Television Archive and to David Sharp and his coworkers in the BFI Library, most especially Lira Fernandes, Tony Mechele, Pat Daniels, Fiona Bolt, Anastasia Kerameos, Stephen Pearson, Janet Moat, Janice Headland and

Jackie Madden. My thanks, too, to the staff in the Stills and Viewing Services Departments of the British Film Institute. While I was in London, I also benefited from the encouragement and friendship of David Barrable and Simon Cunniffe, Judith Greenwood, Sheena Napier and Gary Yershon.

Closer to home, I am especially grateful to Madeline F. Matz at the Library of Congress for her continuing assistance on this and other projects. In San Francisco, I owe several kinds of debts to Matt McCabe and Charlie Wilson, who clipped film reviews for me and provided me with yet another place to hang my hat. For their help and good company while I was in San Francisco, I am also grateful to Richard Meiss, Peter Rudy, Nanette Miller and Eleanore Samarzes. Dan Mansiere in Santa Barbara also clipped film reviews and provided me with room and board. My thanks, too, to Nancy Goldman and the staff of the Pacific Film Archive in Berkeley and to the staff of the San Francisco Public Library for their assistance.

Kenneth Kaukola (of the Toronto Kaukolas) proved a valuable source of film information and good cheer when I conducted research at the Cinémathèque Ontario, to whose staff I also extend my thanks. In New York City, I am grateful to the staffs of the New York Public Library at Lincoln Center and of the libraries at the Museum of Broadcasting and the Museum of Modern Art. I am also happy once again to thank Geraldine Duclow and the staff of the Theatre and Film Collection at the Free Library of Philadelphia. My thanks, too, to Donald Burns for helping me maintain my sanity while I worked on this project. My sister, Kathleen Harty, was kind enough to scan newspapers in the Chicago area and clip film reviews for me. I am also grateful to the staff of the Boston Public Library, and for assistance and hospitality to Michael Schwartz, Jeff Knudsen, Reed Woodhouse and Charlie Rockwell.

For responding to various queries, I am happy to thank Richard Abel, Henri Bousquet, Hrafn Gunnlaugsson, Elias Savada and the staffs of Walt Disney Pictures, the Family Channel, Filmeffekt A/S Iceland, the Nederlands Filmmuseum, Norsk Film AS and Vine International Pictures Ltd.

La Salle University was kind enough to award me two research leaves to allow time to complete this project, and I have been buoyed in my research by the help of my friends and colleagues Brother Gabriel Fagan, F.S.C., John Keenan, John Kleis, Francine Lottier, Linda Merians and Helena White. My former chair, Jim Butler, and my former provost, Brother Emery Mollenhauer, F.S.C., supported me in every way possible and proved they were as good colleagues as administrators in doing so. George Stow and Bill Wine, my colleagues in the History and Communication departments, kindly agreed to write in support of my grant applications. My research would have been impossible without the help of the librarians at La Salle, and I am especially grateful to Eithne Bearden, Stephen Breedlove and Nancy Tresnan, whom I deluged with research requests, all of which they quickly and cheerfully (!?) filled.

I owe a special debt to Gary Kuris for his support for this and earlier projects and his continuing friendship. In addition, I am happy to acknowledge the help and encouragement of so many fellow medievalists, especially Ruth J. Dean, Jacquie de Weever, Jackie Jenkins, Norris J. Lacy, Barbara and Alan Lupack, Debra Mancoff, Michael Salda, Elizabeth Sklar, Bonnie Wheeler and Charles T. Wood.

Finally, I note as always with continuing thanks the past support and encouragement of James P. Ricciardelli and James D. Stobaugh—"ch'io non avrei mai creduto/che morte tanta n'avesse disfatta."

KEVIN J. HARTY
La Salle University
Philadelphia

Introduction

Two great principles divide the world, and contend for the mastery, antiquity and the middle ages. These are the two civilizations that have preceded us, the two elements of which ours is composed. All political as well as religious questions reduce themselves practically to this. This is the great dualism that runs through our society. —Lord Acton

Humanity does not pass through phases as a train passes through stations: being alive, it has the privilege of always moving yet never leaving anything behind. Whatever we have been, in some sort we are still. Neither the form nor the sentiment of this old [medieval love] poetry has passed away without leaving indelible traces on our minds. We shall understand our present, and perhaps even our future, the better if we can succeed, by an effort of historical imagination, in reconstructing that long-lost state of mind for which the allegorical love poem was a natural mode of expression. —C.S. Lewis

It seems that people like the Middle Ages. —Umberto Eco

For a century, filmmakers have regularly turned to medieval subjects as a source for movie plots. The hundreds of what, for lack of a better term, might be called "medieval films" do not, however, constitute a cinematic genre along the same lines as film noir, or the Western, or the road picture. Rather, these films are more properly a genre of "medievalism," a continuing process of creating and recreating ideas of the medieval that began almost as soon as the Middle Ages had come to an end. As John Simons notes, "Medievalism is the process by which the Middle Ages is transformed into a useful discourse out of which can be produced ideologies and practices which comment upon or contest other contemporary beliefs" (5). Medievalism takes a long view in which the present and the future can be studied in light of the past and the past can be reimagined in light of the present and the future.

Medieval people did not, of course, think of themselves as living in the middle of anything. They saw themselves at the end of time, not at some juncture between ancient and modern. For them, the world was on the brink of apocalypse, not of rebirth. But no sooner had the Western imagination freed itself from the medieval when the past began to inspire new imaginative responses. Sir Thomas Malory's *Le Morte Darthur*— the great English synthesis of the legend of Arthur — is certainly a pivotal example of medievalism. Written during the ninth year of Edward IV's reign (1470) in the last days of medieval England, but first published by William Caxton 15 years later in the first year of the reign of Henry VII, Malory's work provides a ready bridge between the late medieval and the early modern.[1]

Others soon followed in Malory's — and Caxton's — footsteps. Early in the sixteenth century, chroniclers such as Polydore Vergil and John Leland debated anew the merits of Geoffrey of Monmouth's twelfth-century depiction of Arthur. Later in the same century, Aristo in Italy and Spenser in England combined allegory with the epic to produce works that were both medieval and Renaissance, or more properly medieval as understood in Renaissance terms. No less a literary light than Milton first considered, but then rejected, the idea of producing an Arthurian epic. The medieval also haunts the works of such diverse writers as Tasso and Cervantes.

The great surge of medievalism occurred, however, in the nineteenth century in the English Gothic Revival, which was responsible for rescuing Malory from two centuries of obscurity, and which redefined chivalry as a model for contemporary behavior. From the mid–nineteenth century on, all forms of Victorian art embraced the medieval in general and the Arthurian in particular. In France, the medieval similarly influenced the decorative arts; and in Germany, thanks to Wagner, the medieval was canonized as the inspiration for music in its highest and most sublime form. And just as the Gothic Revival began to wane at the end of the nineteenth century, the growing popularity of a new art form, the motion picture, assured the continued return to the medieval in a now century-old tradition.

Film had its birth early in 1895 when the Lumière brothers, Auguste and Louis, shot their first film, *Workers Leaving the Lumière Factory*. In March of that same year, the Lumières began regular private showings of their films; public screenings began in the basement of a Paris café at year's end. Soon films began to tell stories (both historical and fictional). This expansion in cinematic subject matter coincided with the first examples of medieval film, the earliest of which were also French. In 1897, the pioneering filmmaker Georges Méliès presented the first of his several cinematic retellings of the life of Joan of Arc. Georges Hatot followed Méliès's lead a year later with his *Jeanne d'Arc* for Pathé. In 1899, Méliès presented a second film about Joan consisting of 12 tableaux, featuring a cast of 500 in elaborate costume, and running 15 minutes. These films not only inaugurated film as a genre of medievalism, but also began a rich tradition of film treatments of the legend of the Maid of Orleans that continues the debate in France over Joan's sometimes conflicting roles as mother of a nation and saint of the Church. In this tradition, Joan has been seen as simple peasant girl, wily politician, androgyne, woman, doubting sinner, representative of a nation and self-assured saint.[2]

Early medieval film was not solely the provenance of the French. In America, Edwin J. Porter directed a film version of Wagner's *Parsifal* for Thomas Edison in 1904. Five years later, using Tennyson as his source, Charles Kent directed *Launcelot and Elaine* for Vitagraph; in the same year, Albert Capellani directed *Tristan et Yseult* from the opera by Wagner for Pathé.[3] In 1910, probably using Malory as a source, Giuseppe de Liguoro directed *Il Re Artù e i cavalieri della tavola rotonda* for Milano Films.[4] In 1916, the pioneer maker of epic films, D.W. Griffith, announced plans for a film based on the famous Grail murals by Edwin Austin Abbey that decorate the second floor delivery room of the Boston Public Library ("Film Flashes" 16), although the project was never realized for reasons that remain unclear.

Medieval film follows the lead of popular culture in what Umberto Eco calls the "messing up" of the Middle Ages "in order to meet the vital requirements of different periods" (68). Eco has gone on to argue that when we reimagine — or "dream"— the medieval, we do so in at least ten ways (68–72), each of which finds an expression in medieval film: (1) For filmmakers, as for others, the medieval can simply be "a pretext ... a mythological stage on which to place contemporary characters." (2) Medieval film can be a way of ironically revisiting the Middle Ages "in order to speculate about our infancy, but also about the illusion of our senility." (3) Medieval film can allow us to visit a "barbaric age, a land of elementary and outlaw feelings." (4) Medieval film offers a window to a romantic world of "stormy castles and their ghosts." (5) Medieval film reflects the "neo–Thomism" that underlies contemporary "speculative and systematic approaches ... such as structuralism." (6) Medieval film becomes a way of enshrining "national identities." (7) Medieval film allows further opportunities for us to dabble in "decadentism." (8) Medieval film goes hand in hand with "philosophical reconstruction[s]" of the medieval that help us "to criticize all the other Middle Ages that at one time or another arouse our enthusiasm." (9) Medieval film is part of our (at times misguided) sense of tradition. (10) Medieval film ties in, especially in the late 1990s, with our expectations of the millennium.

Medieval films show, however, that Eco's ten "dreams" of the Middle Ages are not necessarily mutually exclusive; they may at times overlap. Gustav Ucicky's *Das Mädchen Johanna* (1935) — a Nazi appropriation of France's national symbol made on the eve of World War II with the blessings, if not the actual participation, of Goebbels[5] — clearly on one level represents the medieval as pretext. The film's hero is not Joan but the dauphin, a visionary leader (and stand-in for Hitler) intent upon defending his country's interests and righting past wrongs. At the same time, *Mädchen* has affinities with more benign films such as Fritz Lang's masterpiece *Die Nibelungen* (1924) in examining the roots of Teutonic identity. But while Lang's film presents the medieval under the guise of cinematic art, Ucicky's film perverts the medieval in the service of cinematic propaganda. It makes a darker use of the medieval than Lang's film in an attempt to enshrine National Socialism's (mis)use of tradition.[6]

Less troubling are the reflections of the contemporary — at least in part — in a number of medieval films drawn from a variety of cinematic traditions. On the surface, Marcel Carné's *Les Visiteurs du soir* (1942) tells a tale of demonic interference in a courtly love affair. But Jacques Prévert, who penned the film's screenplay, has suggested that the Devil could represent Hitler and that the medieval setting was simply a way of avoiding possible Nazi censorship.[7] In the same way, Leopold Lindtberg's *Landamann Stauffacher* (1941) — recounting as it does the Swiss struggle during the Middle Ages for independence from Austria — could not help having a contemporary political subtext with Nazi troops amassed along the Swiss border.

The reception of medieval films can even unexpectedly be at the mercy of contemporary concerns. S.M. Eisenstein's *Alexander Nevsky* (1938) opened to praise in Stalinist Russia, only to be withdrawn the following year in light of the Nazi-Soviet Non-aggression Pact. After Hitler invaded Russia in 1941, the film was rereleased as part of the patriotic effort to rally Russians to the defense of their homeland.

Pseudo-medieval films like John Milius's *Conan the Barbarian* and George Lucas's *Star Wars* trilogy — which are not the subject of this study — provide good examples of how film can speculate ironically about the infancy and senility of the modern. But films more readily identifiable with the medieval can do the same. Eco himself cites the example of *Monty Python and the Holy Grail* (69). Similar attempts to visit a period without necessarily believing in it can be seen in such widely different films as Giorgio Simonelli's inane comedy *Robin Hood e i pirati* (1960), Chi Kuan-chun's kung fu adventure *Marco Polo* (1975), Sam Raimi's "gorefest" *Army of Darkness* (1992), Gary Trousdale's animated *The Hunchback of Notre Dame* (1996) and Sean McNamara's science fiction fantasy *Galgameth* (1996).

The use of the Middle Ages as a means to enter a barbaric world also takes many forms in medieval film. Ingmar Bergman's *The Virgin Spring* (1959) retells a medieval Swedish ballad about rape, murder and parental retribution that finally gives way to redemption when the title spring appears at the site of the initial rape and murder. Rowland V. Lee's *Tower of London* (1939) so effectively uses lingering camera shots to emphasize the brutality of a series of murders that the 1962 remake by the acknowledged king of the B-movies, Roger Corman, pales in comparison. Paul Verhoeven's *Flesh and Blood* (1985) — like Raimi's *Army of Darkness* — avoids any notion of redemption. Both films are content to offer two of the bloodiest and least romanticized cinematic depictions of the Middle Ages. Walerian Borowczyk's *Blanche* (1971) and Bernard Tavernier's *La Passion Béatrice* (1987) may be less prurient and voyeuristic than Verhoeven and Raimi's films, but they are nonetheless unflinching in the view of the brutality of the Middle Ages that they present.

The use of medieval film to provide a window to a Gothic or romantic world of "stormy castles and their ghosts" dates back more than 90 years. W.R. Booth's *Magic Sword* (1901) used trick photography to tell a tale involving a 15-foot-tall ogre, a knight with a flaming sword, a witch and a damsel in distress. Georges Méliès's *La Fée carabosse* (1906) offered a fascinating array of monsters, witches, gnomes and other creatures. Benjamin Christensen's *Häxan* (1921) showed nude flagellants, the excesses of the Inquisition and scenes from a witch-craze-induced mass hysteria. More recently, dragons and monsters — malevolent and otherwise — have taken to the screen in Alexander Stitt's *Grendel Grendel Grendel* (1981), Matthew Robbins's *Dragonslayer* (1981), Joao César Montiero's *Silvestre* (1981), Rob Cohen's *Dragonheart* (1996) and Sean McNamara's *Galgameth*— while the continuing series of cinematic remakes of Victor Hugo's *The Hunchback of Notre Dame* offers a view of the grotesque, although Quasimodo obviously haunts a Gothic cathedral rather than a castle.

More philosophical approaches to the Middle Ages inform a number of medieval films. Ingmar Bergman's *The Seventh Seal* (1957) is in part concerned with the possibility of nuclear holocaust while at the same time it reflects an existential response to human nature. Robert Bresson's *The Trail of Joan of Arc* (1962) and *Lancelot du lac* (1974) both seek spiritual solace in the medieval for a modern world devoid, as far as the director is concerned, of any spirituality. And Jean-Jacques Annaud's *The Name of the Rose* (1986) — from Umberto Eco's novel of the same title — attempts, with decidedly mixed results, to examine semiotics from a combined medieval and modern perspective.

Medieval films have regularly been used to enshrine national identities. For European (unlike American) directors, such films can record actual events in a nation or people's history — or what is perceived as their history. The myth of the Grail and the more general legend of King Arthur — examples of perceived history — are recounted cinematically in dozens of films. Other films take pages from real history. The solidification of Polish national identity informs Alexsander Ford's *Knights of the Teutonic Order* (1960), Witold Lesiewicz's *King Boleslaus the Bold* (1971) and Ewa and Czeslaw Petelski's *Casimir the Great* (1975). The Christian origins of Bohemia and Hungary are recorded in Michael Tuchner's *Good King Wenceslas* (1994) and Gabor Koltay's *Istvan, a Kiraly* (1984), as are the differing medieval origins of Albania in Mary Antjapardize's *Skanderbeg* (1953), of Georgia in Sergei Paradzhanov's *The Legend of Suram Fortress* (1984), of Iceland in Hrafn Gunnlaugsson's *The White Viking* (1991), of Russia in Kai Hansen's *Dimitry Donskoy* (1909), of Serbia in Vatroslav Mimica's *Banovic Strahinja* (1981) and of Uzbekistan in Kamil Yaramatov's *Alisher Navoi* (1947).

Medieval films readily offer entrée into the decadent. Medieval films that flirt with soft-core pornography include Richard Kanter's *The Ribald Tales of Robin Hood* (1969), in which "fly-jabbing" is the primary activity for both merry men and merry women; Adrian Hoven's *The Erotic Adventures of Siegfried* (1971), which was alternately entitled *The Long Swift Sword of Siegfried* so as to be perfectly clear about its take on the saga of the Nibelungs; and Bitto Albertini's *Metti lo diavolo tuo ne le mio inferno* (1972), whose title is a slang phrase in Italian for coitus. Decadence on a higher level informs Pier Paolo Pasolini's so-called "trilogy of life": *The Decameron* (1971), *The Canterbury Tales* (1971) and *The Arabian Nights* (1974). The success of *The Decameron* had, however, the unintended effect of spawning a cottage industry in soft-core, generally Italian, and often very poorly made codpiece comedies all alleging a source in Boccaccio. In these films, all women wish to be deflowered or raped, and all husbands deserve to be cuckolded. Such films include Gian Paolo Callegari's *Le Calde notti del Decamerone* (1971), Franco Rosetti's *Una Cavalla tutta nuda* (1972), Mino Guerrini's *Decameron n. 2* (1971), Italo Alfaro's *Decameron n. 3* (1972), Paolo Bianchini's *Decameron n. 4* (1972),

Franco Martinelli's *Il Decamerone probitissimo* (1972), Carlo Infascelli's *Il Decamerone proibito* (1972), Mario Sequi's *Fratello homo, sorella bona* (1973) and Sam Phillips's *Love Boccaccio Style* (1977). Chaucer's *Canterbury Tales* suffered a similar fate in two films: Mino Guerrini's *Gli Altri racconti di Canterbury* (1972) and Lucio Dandolo's *Lusty Wives of Canterbury* (1972).

Medieval film is also capable of being self-reflective. *Monty Python and the Holy Grail* is not so much a send-up of the Arthurian legend as it is a send-up of other film versions of that legend, especially Bresson's bleak *Lancelot du lac*. In addition, whenever later filmmakers return to a medieval plot, they at least unconsciously reflect upon the previous films in the cinematic tradition they seek to continue.

Comparisons are also eventually inevitable. Twain's *A Connecticut Yankee in King Arthur's Court* offers an interesting example of ongoing medieval reflection. The novel is based in part on Malory. It first came to the screen in Emmett J. Flynn's *A Connecticut Yankee at King Arthur's Court* (1920). The success of this film inspired first a Rodgers and Hart musical, *A Connecticut Yankee* (1927), and a second film, David Butler's *A Connecticut Yankee* (1931). The 1940s saw a revival of the musical and a musical film (not based on Rodgers and Hart), Tay Garnett's *A Connecticut Yankee in King Arthur's Court* (1949). The 1950s and 1960s produced nearly a half dozen television versions, one based on Rodgers and Hart; more recently, in yet another twist to the pattern, we have had three film versions that change the Yankee into a child, in one case into an African American school girl (Mel Damski's *A Connecticut Yankee in King Arthur's Court* [1989]).

The rich cinematic tradition of Robin Hood offers a further example of medieval self-reflection, imitation and parody.[8] The screen legend had its beginnings long before Allan Dwan's *Robin Hood* (1922), which defined the swashbuckler as a silent film genre. Michael Curtiz's *The Adventures of Robin Hood* (1938) did the same for the

talkies and inspired a series of would-be sequels of decidedly uneven critical merit. In each case, though, these sequels continued a pattern where the name Robin Hood was associated with deeds of derring-do. Richard Lester's *Robin and Marian* (1976) offered a commentary on all this cinematic (mis)adventuring by suggesting that swashbuckling derring-do has its limits. But Robin Hood then returned to the screen twice in 1991 in films that seem clearly intent upon reestablishing the value of derring-do. John Irvin's *Robin Hood* featured a no-nonsense 1990s Maid Marian and a Robin who seemed to delight in getting into trouble for trouble's sake. Kevin Reynolds's *Robin Hood, Prince of Thieves* consciously attempted to name Kevin Costner successor to Douglas Fairbanks's 1922 and Errol Flynn's 1938 Robins; the Sherwood Forest hero ended up the butt of an elaborate joke in Mel Brooks's *Robin Hood, Men in Tights* (1993) in which Cary Elwes's Robin could, unlike Costner's, boast of a genuine (and consistent) British accent.

Ucicky's *Das Mädchen Johanna* is not the only example of cinematic medievalism offering a sense (at times misguided) of tradition. A clearly fascist agenda lies behind Alessandro Blasetti's *Ettore Fieramosca* (1938) and *La Corona di ferro* (1940). Official concerns about their failure to reflect Communist orthodoxy hindered the release of Paradzhanov's *The Legend of Suram Fortress* and Andrei Tarkovsky's *Andrei Rublev* (1966). Paco Lucio's *El Aliento del diablo* (1993) seems in part a commentary on contemporary Spanish-Basque relations.

Finally, the connection between the millennial and the medieval becomes apparent in a number of films. In Jean-Dominique de la Rochefoucald's *L'An mil* (1985), the inhabitants of a remote village in the Pyrenees await the end of the world. A now-lost 1910 Gaumont film with the same title seems to have told a similar story. Bergman's *The Seventh Seal* nods in the direction of the possibility of nuclear annihilation, as does Vincent Ward's *Navigator* (1988), which also finds a link between the Black Plague of the mid–fourteenth century and the present AIDS pandemic. That link also informs Meredith Monk's *Book of Days* (1988). Derek Jarman's *Edward II* (1991) sees in Christopher Marlowe's play a lesson for contemporary battles over issues of sexual preference, the religious right and AIDS.

While Eco's ten "dreams" of the Middle Ages readily find expression in medieval films, we can also look for less philosophical explanations for the continuing cinematic fascination with the Middle Ages. As cinema has changed over the last century, the medieval has offered a continuing source of storylines rich in possible swordplay and spectacle to match anything Greek, Roman or Biblical. The Middle Ages easily presented all the elements of a good film story: love, friendship, intrigue, passion and war. Such a broad-based appeal explains in part American film fascination with the medieval. A comment by Jeff Rider and his students about King Arthur films has some relevance here for medieval film in general:

> In Anglo-American culture, the Arthurian legend has served as a means of quasi-historical reflection since the early Middle Ages. For a modern English-speaking audience, every treatment of the Arthurian legend, in whatever medium and however patently fictitious or inaccurate, refers to a dim, mythological past, and is thus a statement about the ways things were or the way they might have been, or should have been — and is also, therefore, a statement about the way present-day Anglo-American culture is, might be, or should be.
>
> The Arthurian legend plays an altogether different role in France. The past to which modern French treatments of the legend refer is not shadowy and mythological but datable and literary. The principal referent is not a pseudo-historical recollection of archaic military glory and political ascendancy but some of the greatest works of medieval literature. (42–43)

The model in American medieval films is often the Western, a reflection of the complicated interrelationship between film and American culture. Almost 20 years ago, Frank O'Connell convincingly argued that the American Western was the heir and analogue to the Arthurian legends in whatever version they appeared (3–20 and passim). In a curious reversal, medieval films in the 1950s and 1960s became little more than cowboy pictures in which the good guys wore white armor, or at least white plumes. Tay Garnett's *The Black Knight* (1954) offered a reverse take on the tradition by having the title hero wear black.

As Alan Lupack has pointed out, *The Black Knight* could be a medieval Western while also carrying a contemporary political subtext: Lupack sees the film as "an allegory for the triumph of American values over a Communist threat" (38). A similar concern may underlie the anti–Semitic hysteria in Richard Thorpe's *Ivanhoe* (1952), and would link at least these two medieval films from the 1950s with 1980s and 1990s medieval films in having a political subtext — though the latter films, such as Jarman's *Edward II*, are usually less discreet in advancing those subtexts.[9] But by and large, American medieval films share with the Italian screen spectacles of the late 1950s and the 1960s a love for "panoramic widescreen and luscious color" and a simple moral world where "political and social behavior are reduced to manageable opposites — good and evil — where characters are clearly revealed as heroes and villains, and where notions of ideal moral behavior always triumph." (Lucanio 2)

Or maybe filmmakers, American and otherwise, have simply taken another page from Umberto Eco: "It seems that people like the Middle Ages" (61); and in their search for profits, they know enough to continue to give people what they like. In 1895, audiences shrieked and ducked when the Lumière brothers showed their *L'Arrivée d'un train en gare*. Today, we shriek and applaud when a very 1990s, post–*Iron John* Lancelot defeats Malagant in Jerry Zucker's *First Knight* (1995).

Notes

1. The new historicists have come to prefer the term *early modern* to *Renaissance*, in part because it is

more egalitarian and less hierarchical. For my purposes, it is also a more useful term to suggest the continuity that underlies reworkings of the medieval. But the term *early modern* has, as Marcus points out (41–43), been more readily accepted by scholars outside the field of literature.

2. On the complicated cinematic treatment of Joan of Arc, see Blaetz passim; Harty, "Jeanne au cinéma"; and Margolis 393–406.

3. For an overview of cinematic treatments of King Arthur, see Harty, "The Arthurian Legends on Film."

4. The film was released in England under the title *King Arthur; or The Knights of the Round Table.* The film, now lost, was based, D'Heur and De Groeve suggest (423), on Malory.

5. What we today can readily see as the film's Nazi subtext seems to have escaped reviewers in England and the United States when *Das Mädchen Johanna* was released outside of Germany. See Harty, "The Nazis, Joan of Arc, and Medievalism Gone Awry."

6. After the fact, the Nazi propaganda machine was, of course, more than willing to pervert Lang's film to its own means as Goebbels's own assessment of the film makes clear: "Here is an epic film of our time, and yet so modern, so contemporary, so typical, that even the stalwarts of the National Socialist movement were deeply moved" (quoted by Lesier 10–11). Moreover, in the case of Ucicky's film, Goebbels may have actually helped write the screenplay (Steinberg 55).

7. For insightful commentary on the film's contemporary resonances, see the clippings file on *Les Visiteurs du soir* in the Billy Rose Collection at the New York Public Library, Lincoln Center. The file contains a series of handouts that accompanied showings of the film by various American film societies in the 1950s.

8. On the screen history of Robin Hood, see Behlmer 91–102, Knight 218–61, Richards 187–216, and Turner passim.

9. Biblical epics may also have Cold War subtexts; see Nadel 415–30.

Works Cited

Behlmer, Rudy. "Robin Hood on the Screen." *Films in Review* 16 (February 1965): 91–102.

Blaetz, Robin J. "Strategies of Containment: Joan of Arc in Film." Ph.D. dissertation, New York University, 1989.

D'Heur, J.M., and J. De Groeve. "Arthur, Excalibur and the Enchanter Boorman." In *Studia in honorem prof. M. de Riquer III.* Barcelona: Quaderns Crema, 1988.

Eco, Umberto. *Travels in Hyperreality.* William Weaver, trans. San Diego: Harvest, 1986.

"Film Flashes." *Variety* 28 May 1915: 6.

Harty, Kevin J. "The Arthurian Legends on Film: An Overview." In Kevin J. Harty, ed. *Cinema Arthuriana: Essays on Arthurian Film.* New York: Garland, 1991.

_____. "Jeanne au cinéma." In Bonnie Wheeler and Charles T. Wood, eds. *Fresh Verdicts on Joan of Arc.* New York: Garland, 1996.

_____. "The Nazis, Joan of Arc, and Medievalism Gone Awry." In [the Centenary College Department of English, ed.] *Rationality and the Liberal Spirit, A Festschrift Honoring Ira Lee Morgan.* Shreveport: Centenary Publications, 1997.

Knight, Stephen. *Robin Hood, A Complete Study of the Outlaw.* Oxford: Blackwell, 1994.

Lesier, Erwin. *Nazi Cinema.* Gertrud Mander and David Wilson, trans. London: Secker & Warburg, 1974.

Lucanio, Patrick. *With Fire and Sword, Italian Spectacles on American Screens 1958–1968.* Metuchen, N.J.: Scarecrow, 1994.

Lupack, Alan. "An Enemy in Our Midst, *The Black Knight* and the American Dream." In Kevin J. Harty, ed. *Cinema Arthuriana: Essays on Arthurian Film.* New York: Garland, 1991.

Marcus, Leah. "Renaissance/Early Modern Studies." In Stephen Greenblatt and Giles Gunn, eds. *Redrawing the Boundaries, The Transformation of English and American Literary Studies.* New York: Modern Language Association, 1992.

Nadel, Alan. "God's Law and the Wide Screen: *The Ten Commandments* as Cold War 'Epic.'" *PMLA* 108 (May 1993): 415–30.

O'Connell, Frank. *Storytelling & Mythmaking, Images from Film and Literature.* New York: Oxford University Press, 1979.

Richards, Jeffrey. *Swordsmen of the Screen from Douglas Fairbanks to Michael York.* London: Routledge & Kegan Paul, 1977.

Rider, Jeff, Richard Hull, and Christopher Smith. "The Arthurian Legend in French Cinema: *Lancelot du lac* and *Perceval le Gallois*." In Kevin J. Harty, ed. *Cinema Arthuriana: Essays on Arthurian Film.* New York: Garland, 1991.

Simons, John. "Medievalism as Cultural Process in Pre-industrial Popular Literature." In Leslie J. Workman and Kathleen Verduin, eds. *Medievalism in England II.* Studies in Medievalism VII. Cambridge, Eng.: D.S. Brewer, 1995.

Steinberg, Heniz. "*Das Mädchen Johanna,* de Gustav Ucicky [sic] or Jeanne et Goebbels." *Etudes cinématographique* 18–19 (Autumn 1962): 53–57.

Turner, David. *Robin of the Movies.* Kingswinford, Eng.: Yeoman Press, 1989.

THE FILMS

Abu Rayhan Biruni (1974) see *Abu Reikhan Biruni* (1974)

1. *Abu Reikhan Biruni* (1974)

Soviet Union; dir. Shurat Abasov; Uzbek Films.

ALTERNATE TITLE: *Abu Rayhan Biruni.*

CAST: Sovetbek Jumadilov, Dilorom Kambarova, Razzak Khamraev, Pulat Saidkasymov, Bikhtiar Shukurov, Bimbulat Vatayev.

Gifted even in childhood and destined to marry the daughter of the Shah and serve as his vizier, Abu Reikhan Biruni turns instead to science and its application to the needs of the poor. His devotion to knowledge makes him a favorite of a series of rulers; his devotion to the welfare of others, often those suffering under the tyranny of these same rulers, leads him into conflict with his would-be patrons.

Emphasizing his commitment to truth and justice, even in the face of persecution and death, this film offers a reverential biography of Abu Reikhan Biruni (973–1048), the noted Islamic mathematician, physician and philosopher, whom some Soviet film commentators compared to Galileo.

REVIEW: *Variety* 18 June 1980: 24.

ADDITIONAL DISCUSSIONS:

Birkos, Alexander S. *Soviet Cinema.* Hamden, Conn.: Archon, 1976.

Lipkov, Alexander. "Immortal Tales." *Soviet Film* 6 (1975): 21–23.

Radvanyi, Jean, ed. *Le Cinéma d'asie centrale sovietique.* Paris: Centre Georges Pompidou, 1991.

Salikova, Neila. "Abu Reikhan Biruni." *Soviet Film* 2 (1974): 36–37.

Vartanov, A. "Fakty, legendy, vymysel." *Iskusstvo kino* 8 (1975): 35–51.

The Abyss (1988) see *L' Œuvre au noir* (1988)

2. *The Adventures of Boccaccio* (1910)

Great Britain; New Agency Film Company.

In medieval Florence, a lover invents an elaborate subterfuge to dupe a jealous husband.

With the notable exception of Pasolini's 1971 film *The Decameron*, Boccaccio has not fared well at the hands of filmmakers. This early film unknowingly establishes a pattern where the works of Boccaccio become synonymous with sexploitative or codpiece comedies.

REVIEW: *Bioscope* 4 August 1910: 27.

3. *The Adventures of Marco Polo* (1938)

United States; dir. Archie Mayo; Samuel Goldwyn.

CAST: Gary Cooper, Sigrid Gurie, Alan Hale, Basil Rathbone, Lana Turner.

Sent by his father to thirteenth century China on a trade mission, the Venetian Marco Polo has a series of adventures before becoming an advisor to Kublai Khan, whose court he introduces to the Western custom of kissing. Later he arranges peace between the Khan and his enemies and rescues the Khan from an assassination attempt. In the film's final sequence, Marco Polo accompanies the Khan's daughter, Princess Kukachin, on a trip to Persia, where the film suggests they will marry.

The screenplay by Robert Sherwood suggests a more tongue-in-cheek approach to the life of Marco Polo (1254–1324) than the film actually shows. The final product, despite a stellar cast, is at times majestic, especially in its settings, and at times ridiculous, especially in its dialogue, plot and characterization. Marco Polo left Italy in the company of his father and uncle in 1271. Four years later, he entered the service of Kublai Khan, first as a government inspector and then as a provincial governor. In 1292, Marco Polo accompanied a Mongol princess on a journey to Persia where she was to marry that country's ruler. He then returned to Venice in 1295, after a 24-year absence. In 1298, he commanded a ship in the Venetian war against Genoa and was taken prisoner. Confined to jail for a year, he dictated a journal of his exploits to Rusticiano of Pisa, with whom he shared a prison cell.

REVIEWS: *Film Daily* 15 February 1938: 8. *Film Weekly* 3 September 1938: 21, 30. *Great Britain and the East* 51 (22 September 1938): 323–24. *Harrison's Reports* 19 March 1938: 47. *Hollywood Reporter* 12 February 1938: 3. *Kinematograph Weekly* 23 June 1938: 26; 29 March 1945: 25. *Motion Picture Daily* 15 February 1993: 4. *Motion Picture Herald* 19 February 1938: 38. *Motion Picture Review Digest* 3 (4 April 1938): 2–3; 3 (27 June 1938): 2. *Monthly Film Bulletin* 5 (June 1938): 155–56. *New York Times* 8 April 1938: 17. *Photoplay* 52 (April 1938): 53. *Picturegoer Weekly* 9 April 1938: 12–13. *Picture Show* 19 November 1938: 16–17. *Rob Wagner's Script* 16 April 1938: 9. *Times* [London] 5 September 1938: 10. *To-day's Cinema* 27 March 1945: 10. *Variety* 16 February 1938: 15. *World Film News* 3 (May-June 1938): 58–59, 87; 3 (October 1938): 267–68.

ADDITIONAL DISCUSSIONS:
"Adventures Ahead." *Hollywood Reporter* 4 April 1938: 9–19.
Dickens, Homer. *The Films of Gary Cooper.* New York: Citadel, 1970.
Druxman, Michael B. *Basil Rathbone, His Life and His Films.* New York: A.S. Barnes, 1975.
Fetrow, Alan G. *Sound Films, 1927–1939.* Jefferson, N.C.: McFarland, 1992.
Hanson, Patricia King, ed. *The American Film Institute Catalog of Motion Pictures Produced in the United States: Feature Films, 1931–1940.* Berkeley: University of California Press, 1993.
Nash, Jay Robert, and Stanley Ralph Ross. *The Motion Picture Guide, A–B, 1927–1983.* Chicago: Cinebooks, 1985.
Sherwood, Robert E. "Marco Polo." In Frances Marion. *How to Write and Sell Film Stories.* New York: Covici Friede, 1937. [Screenplay.]
Valentino, Lou. *The Films of Lana Turner.* Secaucus, N.J.: Citadel, 1976.

The Adventures of Quentin Durward (1955) see *Quentin Durward* (1955)

4. *The Adventures of Robin Hood* (1938)

United States; dir. Michael Curtiz and William Keighley; Warner Bros.

CAST: Melville Cooper, Olivia de Havilland, Errol Flynn, Alan Hale, Ian Hunter, Patric Knowles, Montagu Love, Herbert Mundin, Una O'Connor, Eugene Pallette, Claude Rains, Basil Rathbone.

After England's Richard I is taken prisoner and held for ransom in Austria, his brother Prince John usurps the throne and plots with the Sheriff of Nottingham and Sir Guy of Gisbourne to tax the people for the ransom, which they plan to keep for themselves. Opposing Prince John, Sir Guy and their soldiers is Robin of Locksley, leader of a band of forest outlaws. Prince John also intends to marry off Richard's ward, Lady Marian Fitzwalter, to Gisbourne. One day, while robbing the Sheriff and Gisbourne, Locksley also kidnaps Maid Marian. She is at first his reluctant guest until she learns the truth about the Norman tyranny and joins with Locksley against Prince John, the Sheriff and Gisbourne. When they become aware of her shift in loyalties, the villainous trio decide to use Marian as bait in a trap set to capture Locksley. Locksley rescues Marian, defeats Prince John and the Sheriff, kills Gisbourne in a famous swordfight on a spiral staircase and secures the throne for Richard, who returns to make Locksley Earl of Sherwood and Nottingham and to bless his marriage to Marian.

The Adventures of Robin Hood redefined a film genre, the swashbuckler, for audiences of talking films in much the same way that Allan Dwan's 1922 *Robin Hood* starring Douglas Fairbanks had done for those of silent films. Curtiz's film won Academy Awards for art direction, music and editing and was also nominated as Best Picture. It remains unmatched, despite numerous attempts to better or remake it, most recently in 1991 by John Irvin, with Patrick Bergin in the title role, and by Kevin Reynolds, with Kevin Costner in the title role.

REVIEWS: *Films in Review* 40 (May 1989): 315–17. *Harrison's Reports* 7 May 1938: 74. *Hollywood Reporter* 26 April 1938: 3. *Hollywood Spectator* 7 May 1939: 6. *Kinematograph Weekly* 23 June 1938: 45; 26 August 1943: 54. *Monthly Film Bulletin* 5 (June 1938): 156. *Motion Picture Daily* 27 April 1938: 1–2. *Motion Picture Herald* 30 April 1938: 44. *Motion Picture Review Digest* 3 (27 June 1938): 2–3. *New York Times* 13 May 1938: 17. *Photoplay* 52 (June 1938): 53; 52 (July 1938): 23. *Rob Wagner's Script* 19 (14 May 1938): 8. *Times* [London] 10 October 1938: 12. *Variety* 27 April 1938: 22. *World Film News* 3 (August 1938): 172; 3 (November 1938): 313.

ADDITIONAL DISCUSSIONS:
"The Adventures of Robin Hood." *Hollywood Reporter* 7 May 1938: 5–12.
The Adventures of Robin Hood. London: Ward, Lock [1938]. [Novelization.]
Behlmer, Rudy, ed. *The Adventures of Robin Hood.* Madison: University of Wisconsin Press, 1979. [Screenplay.]
_____. *America's Favorite Movies.* New York: Ungar, 1982.
_____. "Robin Hood on Record." *Cue Sheet* 1 (January 1984): 5–7.

Errol Flynn in the title role in Michael Curtiz's *The Adventures of Robin Hood* (1938).

_____. "Robin Hood on the Screen." *Films in Review* 16 (February 1965): 91–102.

_____. "Swordplay on the Screen." *Films in Review* 16 (June-July 1965): 362–75.

Callenbach, Ernest. "Comparative Anatomy of Folk-Myth Films: Robin Hood and *Antonio das Mortes*." *Film Quarterly* 23 (Winter 1969-70): 42–47.

Druxman, Michael B. *Basil Rathbone, His Life and His Films.* New York: A.S. Barnes, 1975.

Fetrow, Alan G. *Sound Films, 1927–1939.* Jefferson, N.C.: McFarland, 1992.

Garbicz, Adam, and Jacek Klinowski. *Cinema, The Magic Vehicle.* Metuchen, N.J.: Scarecrow, 1975.

Hanson, Patricia King, ed. *The American Film Institute Catalog of Motion Pictures Produced in the United States: Feature Films, 1931–1940.* Berkeley: University of California Press, 1993.

Hark, Ina Rae. "The Visual Politics of *The Adventures of Robin Hood*." *Journal of Popular Film* 5.1 (1976): 3–17.

Huiskamp, Verna. "Historical Approach: The Political Implications of *The Adventures of Robin Hood* (Michael Curtiz, 1938)." In Tim Baywater and Thomas Sobchak. *An Introduction to Film Criticism.* New York: Longman, 1989.

Kinnard, Roy, and R.J. Vitone. *The American Films of Michael Curtiz.* Metuchen, N.J.: Scarecrow, 1986.

Knight, Stephen. *Robin Hood, A Complete Study of the English Outlaw.* Oxford: Blackwell, 1994.

Magill, Frank, N., ed. *Magill's American Film Guide.* Englewood Cliffs, N.J.: Salem, 1983.

_____, ed. *Magill's Survey of Cinema: English Language Films.* First Series. Englewood Cliffs, N.J.: Salem, 1980.

Morris, George. *Errol Flynn.* New York: Pyramid, 1975.

Nash, Jay Robert, and Stanley Ralph Ross. *The Motion Picture Guide, A–B, 1927–1983.* Chicago: Cinebooks, 1985.

Parish, James Robert, et al. *Errol Flynn.* New York: Cinefax, 1969.

_____, and Don E. Stanke. *The Swashbucklers.* New Rochelle, N.Y.: Arlington House, 1976.

Richards, Jeffrey. *Swordsmen of the Screen from Douglas Fairbanks to Michael York.* London: Routledge and Kegan Paul, 1977.

Robertson, James C. *The Casablanca Man, The Cinema of Michael Curtiz.* New York: Routledge, 1993.

Rosenzweig, Sidney. *Casablanca and Other Major Films of Michael Curtiz.* Ann Arbor, Mich.: UMI Research, 1982.

Thomas, Nicholas, ed. *International Dictionary of Films and Filmmakers— Vol. 1: Films.* 2nd ed. Chicago: St. James, 1990.

_____, ed. *International Dictionary of Films and Filmmakers— Vol. 2: Directors.* 2nd ed. Chicago: St. James, 1991.

Thomas, Tony. *The Films of Olivia de Havilland.* Secaucus, N.J.: Citadel, 1983.

_____. *The Great Adventure Films.* Secaucus, N.J.: Citadel, 1976.

_____, et al. *The Films of Errol Flynn.* Secaucus, N.J.: Citadel, 1969.

Turner, David. *Robin of the Movies.* Kingswinford, Eng.: Yeoman Publishing, 1989.

Valenti, Peter. *Errol Flynn, A Bio-Bibliography.* Westport, Conn.: Greenwood, 1984.

Vermilye, Jerry. *The Films of the Thirties.* Secaucus, N.J.: Citadel, 1982.

5. *The Adventures of Sir Galahad*
(1950)

United States; dir. Spencer G. Bennet; Columbia.

CAST: William Fawcett, Lois Hall, Nelson Leigh, George Reeves.

King Arthur refuses to make Galahad a Knight of the Round Table until he retrieves Excalibur. On his quest, Galahad encounters Merlin, Mordred and the Black Knight. He also discovers and foils a Saxon plot to invade England. Finally, he defeats the Saxons, recovers Excalibur, and is made a Knight of the Round Table.

This 15-part serial starring American television's first Superman, George Reeves, was loosely based on events from the Arthurian legends. The chapterplays (written by George H. Plympton) were comprised of the following episodes:

"The Stolen Sword," "Galahad's Daring," "Prisoners of Ulric," "Attack on Camelot," "Galahad to the Rescue," "Passage of Peril," "Unknown Betrayers," "Perilous Adventure," "Treacherous Magic," "The Sorcerer's Spell," "Valley of No Return," "Castle Perilous," "The Wizard's Vengeance," "Quest for the Queen" and "Galahad's Triumph."

REVIEWS: *Monthly Film Bulletin* 18 (March 1951): 231. *Motion Picture Herald* 14 January 1950: Product Digest Section 155. *To-day's Cinema* 2 February 1951: 10; 9 February 1951: 12.

ADDITIONAL DISCUSSIONS:

Barbour, Alan. *Cliffhanger.* New York: A & W, 1979.

_____. *The Serials of Columbia.* Kew Gardens, N.Y.: Screen Facts, 1967.

Harmon, Jim, and Donald F. Glut. *The Great Movie Serials.* Garden City, N.Y.: Doubleday, 1972.

Weiss, Ken, and Ed Goodgold. *To Be Continued.* New York: Crown, 1972.

Agnes Visconti (1910) see *Agnese Visconti* (1910)

6. *Agnese Visconti* (1910)

Italy; dir. Giovanni Patrone (?); Italia Film (Turin).

ALTERNATE TITLE: *Agnes Visconti*.

CAST: Emilio Ghione.

Francesco I Gonzaga accuses his wife, Agnes of Visconti, of adultery, orders her condemned to death and watches as she is beheaded.

This film is based on a 1873 play of the same title by Felice Cavalotti, and both play and film are in turn based on fact. In 1380, Francesco I Gonzaga (c. 1366–1407), lord of Mantua, entered into a political marriage with Agnes Visconti of Milan. But Agnes's own relatives plotted against her and her husband in an attempt to gain control of all of Italy. Using forged letters, Duke Gian Galeazzo Visconti of Milan, Agnes's cousin, convinced Francesco that she had been unfaithful to him. In anger, Francesco had his wife tried and secretly beheaded in their palace on February 7, 1391.

REVIEW: *Bioscope* 8 September 1910: 45.

ADDITIONAL DISCUSSIONS:

Bernardini, Aldo, and Jean A. Gili, eds. *Le Cinéma italien de La Prise de Rome (1905) à Rome ville ouverte (1945)*. Paris: Centre Georges Pompidou, 1986.

Savada, Elias. *The American Film Institute Catalog of Motion Pictures Produced in the United States: Film Beginnings, 1893–1910*. Metuchen, N.J.: Scarecrow, 1995.

7. *Aimsir Padraig* (1920)

Ireland; dir. Norman Whitten; General Film Supply.

ALTERNATE TITLES: *Days of St. Patrick* and *In the Days of St. Patrick*.

CAST: Ira Allen, Alice Cardinall, Gilbert Green, Alice Keating, Herbert Mayne, Dermot McCarthy, Vernon Whitten.

Brought to Ireland as a prisoner by pirates, Patrick escapes and returns home to France to enter a monastery. Later, he goes to Rome. After Patrick is consecrated a bishop, Pope Celestine sends him back to Ireland as a missionary. After much struggle and persecution, Patrick succeeds in converting Ireland to Christianity.

The original subtitles for this film were in Irish. An epilogue records a 1919 visit by Cardinal Logue to St. Patrick's grave and to the Cathedral of St. Patrick in Armagh.

REVIEWS: *Evening Herald* [Dublin] 13 March 1920: 5; 16 March 1920: 3. *Evening Mail* [Dublin] 16 March 1920: 7. *Irish Times* 16 March 1920: 9. *Moving Picture World* 22 January 1921: 467. *New York Times* 23 May 1921: 6. 2. *Picture Plays* 20 March 1920: 9. *Picture Show* 2 (24 April 1920): 9. *Variety* 14 January 1921: 41.

ADDITIONAL DISCUSSIONS:

Cinema Ireland 1895–1976. [Dublin]: Dublin Arts Festival, 1976.

Connelly, Robert. *The Motion Picture Guide, Silent Film, 1910–1936*. Chicago: Cinebooks, 1986.

McIlroy, Brian. *World Cinema 4: Ireland*. London: Flicks Books, 1988.

O'Leary, Liam. *Cinema Ireland 1896–1950*. [Dublin]: National Library of Ireland, 1990.

Rockett, Kevin, ed. *The Irish Filmography, Fiction Films 1896–1996*. Dublin: Red Mountain Media, 1996.

———, et al. *Cinema and Ireland*. Syracuse: Syracuse University Press, 1988.

Slide, Anthony. *The Cinema and Ireland*. Jefferson, N.C.: McFarland, 1988.

Stevens, Matthew. *Directory of Irish and Irish Related Films*. London: Flicks Books, 1987.

Alberno and Rosamunda (1909) see *Alboino e Rosmunda* (1909)

8. *Alboino e Rosmunda* (1909)

Italy; Pasquali e Tempo.

The barbarian Alboino intends to marry Rosmunda despite her opposition and that of her father, whom he beheads. One of Alboino's officers takes pity on Rosmunda and plots with her to murder Alboino. They succeed and marry.

The same basic plot informs the 1961 film *Sword of the Conqueror*.

DISCUSSIONS:

Bernardini, Aldo, and Jean A. Gili, eds. *Le Cinéma italien de La Prise de Rome (1905) à Rome ville ouverte (1945)*. Paris: Centre Georges Pompidou, 1986.

Savada, Elias. *The American Film Institute Catalog of Motion Pictures Produced in the United States: Film Beginnings, 1893–1910*. Metuchen, N.J.: Scarecrow, 1995.

9. *Alexander Nevsky* (1938)

Soviet Union; dir. S.M. Eisenstein and D.I. Vasiliev; Mosfilm.

ALTERNATE TITLE: *Warrior of Russia*.

CAST: Alexander Abrikosov, Nicholai Arski, Serge Blinikov, Nicholai Cherkasov, Anna Danilova, Vladimir Erschiov, Lev Fenin, Vera Ivasceva, Ivan Lagutin, Varvara Massalitinova, Nicholas Oblopkov, Vassili Novikov, Dmitri Orlov, Naum Rogozhin.

Nikolai Cherkasov in the title role in Sergei Eisenstein's *Alexander Nevsky* (1938).

In the thirteenth century, under the leadership of Prince Alexander Yaroslavich, whose earlier victory over the Swedes on the Neva River gave him the honorary surname Nevsky, the citizens of Novgorod turn back an invasion from the west by the Teutonic-Livonian Knights. The invasion comes on the heels of an assault from the Mongols in the East which was repelled at great cost. The Teutonic Knights capture Paskov and massacre the inhabitants when they refuse to submit to the religious jurisdiction of Rome. The decisive victory against the Teutonic invaders comes in a battle on the ice at Lake Peipus, where the ice breaks under the weight of the heavy armor of the invaders and they drown.

One of the great films of all time, *Alexander Nevsky* is based on real events in the life of the historical title character (c. 1220–1263), who became a Russian national hero and a saint of the Orthodox Church. The famous battle on the ice of Lake Peipus in which Nevsky's army defeated the Teutonic Knights occurred in 1242. In Eisenstein's film, the prince also becomes a hero of Socialism. Events in Europe gave the film contemporary political relevance. Indeed, the film was praised at its opening in 1938 — after which Eisenstein and Cherkasov, who played Nevsky, were given the Order of Lenin — only to be withdrawn in 1939 in light of the Nazi-Soviet Non-aggression Pact. It was rereleased in 1941 after German forces crossed the Soviet border. The score by Sergei Prokofiev gives the film a quality more usually found in grand opera, and the final battle on the ice remains one of the most famous sequences in film history.

REVIEWS: *Boxoffice* 34 (15 April 1939): 61. *Cinema* 29 October 1941: 9–10. *Cinématographie française* 8 July 1950: 18. *Film Daily* 29 May 1939: 9. *Image et son* 125 (November 1959): 16. *Kinematograph Weekly* 21 January 1943: 35; 18 June 1953: 45.

Monthly Film Bulletin 6 (31 May 1939): 101. *Motion Picture Review Digest* 4 (24 April 1939): 1; 4 (26 June 1939): 1–2. *New York Times* 23 March 1939: 27. *Revue du cinéma* [La Saison cinématographique] Hors série 32 (1950–1951): 12–13. *Rob Wagner's Script* 21 (27 May 1939): 22. *Times* [London] 28 October 1941: 6. *To-day's Cinema* 15 January 1943: 4; 15 May 1953: 14. *Variety* 29 March 1939: 16.

ADDITIONAL DISCUSSIONS:

Balter, Leon. "Alexander Nevsky." *Film Culture* 70–71 (1983): 43–87.

Barna, Yon. *Eisenstein.* London: Secker & Warburg, 1973.

Brown, Royal S. *Overtones and Undertones, Reading Film Music.* Berkeley: University of California Press, 1994.

Darby, William, and Jack Du Bois. *American Film Music: Major Composers, Techniques, Trends, 1915–1990.* Jefferson, N.C.: McFarland, 1990.

Eisenstein, Sergei. *Battleship Potemkin, October, and Alexander Nevsky.* Ed. Jay Leyda; trans. Diana Matias. London: Lorimer, 1974. [Screenplay]

_____. *Film Form, Essays in Film Theory.* Ed. and trans. Jay Leyda. New York: Harcourt, 1949.

_____. *The Film Sense.* Ed. and trans. Jay Leyda. London: Faber and Faber, 1948.

_____. *Memories, An Autobiography.* Trans. Herbert Marshall. Boston: Houghton Mifflin, 1983.

_____. *Notes of a Film Director.* Trans. X. Danko. London: Lawrence & Wishart, 1959.

_____. *Selected Works. Volume II: Towards a Theory of Montage.* Ed. Michael Glenny and Richard Taylor; trans. Michael Glenny. London: BFI, 1991.

Gallez, David. "The Prokofiev-Eisenstein Collaboration: *Nevsky* and *Ivan* Revisited." *Cinema Journal* 17 (Spring 1978): 13–35. [See also *Cinema Journal* 18 (Fall 1978): 61.]

Garbicz, Adam, and Jacek Klinowski. *Cinema, the Magic Vehicle.* New York: Schocken, 1983.

Goodwin, James. *Eisenstein, Cinema, and History.* Urbana: University of Illinois Press, 1993.

Hetherington, John, ed. *The Complete Films of Eisenstein.* London: Weidenteld and Nicolson, 1974.

Levaco, Ronald. "The Eisenstein-Prokofiev Correspondence." *Cinema Journal* 13 (Fall 1973): 1–16.

Leyda, Jay. *Kino.* Rev. ed. Princeton: Princeton University Press, 1983.

_____, and Zina Vivnow. *Eisenstein at Work.* New York: Pantheon/Museum of Modern Art, 1982.

Magill, Frank N., ed. *Magill's Survey of Cinema: Foreign Language Films.* Englewood Cliffs, N.J.: Salem, 1985.

Merritt, Russell. "Recharging *Alexander Nevsky:* Tracking the Eisenstein-Prokofiev War Horse." *Film Quarterly* 48 (Winter 1994-95): 34–47.

Nash, Jay Robert, and Stanley Ralph Ross. *The Motion Picture Guide, A–B, 1927–1983.* Chicago: Cinebooks, 1985.

Passek, Jean-Loup, ed. *Le Cinéma russe et soviétique.* Paris: Centre Georges Pompidou, 1981.

Sadoul, George. *Dictionary of Films.* Ed. and trans.

Peter Morris. Berkeley: University of California Press, 1972.

Searles, Baird. *EPIC! History on the Big Screen.* New York: Harry N. Abrams, 1990.

Seton, Marie. *Sergei M. Eisenstein, A Biography.* London: Bodley Head, 1952.

Stoil, Michael Jon. *Cinema Beyond the Danube: The Camera and Politics.* Metuchen, N.J.: Scarecrow, 1974.

Taylor, Richard. *Film Propaganda, Soviet Russia and Nazi Germany.* London: Croom Helm, 1979.

Thomas, Nicholas, ed. *International Dictionary of Films and Filmmakers— Vol. 1: Films.* Chicago: St. James, 1990.

Turner, George. "Alexander Nevsky Comes Back in Style." *American Cinematographer* 68 (November 1987): 90–97.

Tyler, Parker. *Classics of the Foreign Film.* New York: Citadel , 1985.

10. *Alfred the Great* (1969)

Great Britain; dir. Clive Donner; Bernard Smith Films and MGM.

CAST: Colin Blakely, Julian Glover, David Hemmings, Ian McKellen, Prunella Ransome, Vivian Merchant, Michael York.

Young Prince Alfred is intent upon becoming a priest, but the death of his older brother Ethelred makes him an unwilling warrior king as the Danes invade Wessex. His queen, Aelthswith, whom he rejects in a nod toward the vow of chastity he would have taken as priest, is kidnapped and held hostage by Guthrum, the King of Denmark, who beds his not-totally-unwilling hostage. When the tide of battle turns against the West Saxons, Alfred seeks refuge among a band of marshland outlaws. After rallying his forces, Alfred invades Guthrum's camp, rescues the queen and defeats the Danes. The film ends with the promise of a reunion between Alfred and Aelthswith.

The film, which was shot in Ireland, treats only the early days of the reign of King Alfred, called the Great (849–899), ignoring his role as lawgiver and patron of education and culture. The pace of the film drags when there are no battle scenes, and while the dialogue avoids the trap of phony archaisms, the contemporary idiom often seems out of place. The cast brings a mixed bag of talents to their roles, although Ian McKellen is outstanding as Roger, the leader of the outlaws.

REVIEWS: *ABC Film Review* 19 (September 1969): 10–11. *Cinema* 4 (Fall 1968): 26. *Film Daily* 22 October 1969: 4. *Films and Filming* 15 (September 1969): 59–60. *Films in Review* 20 (October 1969):

David Hemmings (center) in the title role in Clive Donner's *Alfred the Great* (1969).

513–14. *Kinematograph Weekly* 19 July 1969: 23. *Monthly Film Bulletin* 36 (September 1969): 187. *Motion Picture Herald* 10 September 1969: Product Digest Section 269–70. *New York Times* 4 December 1969: 70. *Sight and Sound* 36 (Autumn 1969): 220. *Times* [London] 17 July 1969: 9. *To-day's Cinema* 18 July 1969: 9. *Variety* 23 July 1969: 6.

ADDITIONAL DISCUSSIONS:

Elley, Derek. *The Epic Film*. London: Routledge & Kegan Paul, 1984.

Smith, Gary. *Epic Films*. Jefferson, N.C.: McFarland, 1991.

11. *El Aliento del diablo* (1993)

Spain; dir. Paco Lucio; Tesauro S.A.

ALTERNATE TITLE: *The Devil's Breath.*

CAST: Fernando Guillen, Alexander Kaidanovski, Valentina Vargas.

A small family of travelers arrives after a long journey at a village hut, which they claim as home. The family consists of Damian, a mute but skilled hunter, his wife Priscila and their two children, a mute son named Pablo and a beautiful daughter named Agueda. Don Rodrigo, the feudal lord of the village, eyes both the wife and the daughter, whom he kills, only to met a similar fate at the hands of Damian.

Set in the Middle Ages but laden with modern, though never fully explained, symbols and allusions, the film seems in part a commentary on contemporary Spanish-Basque relations.

REVIEWS: *Cineinforme* 641 (September 1993): 12; 644 (December 1993): 67. *Variety* 1 November 1993: 40–41.

ADDITIONAL DISCUSSION:

"Finaliza el rodaje de 'El Aliento del diablo.'" *Cineinforme* 638 (June 1993): 37.

12. *Alisher Navoi* (1947)

Soviet Union; dir. Kamil Yaramatov; Tashkent Studio.

CAST: Asad Ismatov, Razak Khamrayev.

In the fifteenth century, Alisher Navoi is born in Herat. He becomes a noted philosopher, poet, linguist and advisor to the Sultan.

Alisher Navoi (1441–1501), who authored more than 30 books in Persian and Turkish, is generally consider the father of Uzbek literature. This film was awarded the Stalin Prize in 1948.

ADDITIONAL DISCUSSIONS:

Leyda, Jay. *Kino, A History of the Russian and Soviet Film.* New York: Collier, 1973.

Mamatova, L. *Mnogonatsional'noe sovetskoe kino-iskusstvo.* Moscow: Izd-vo, 1982.

Radvanyi, Jean, ed. *Le Cinéma d'asie centrale sovietique.* Paris: Centre Georges Pompidou, 1991.

Vorontsvov, Yuri, and Igor Rachuk. *The Phenomenon of the Soviet Cinema.* Trans. Doris Bradbury. Moscow: Progress Publishers, 1980.

13. *Gli Altri racconti di Canterbury* (1972)

Italy; dir. Mino Guerrini; Transeuropa Film.

ALTERNATE TITLE: *The Other Canterbury Tales.*

CAST: Alida Rossano, Mirella Rossi, Leonora Vivaldi.

A miller lusts after an insatiable widow and calls upon his friends for assistance; they come to his aid but then insist on nightly sexual favors. Crestfallen over the imminent death of his wife, a fisherman seeks consolation from a beautiful maid whom he takes to his bed, only to have his amorous escapades interrupted by his wife's recovery. Seeking escape from a husband who beats her, a woman finds comfort in the arms of a monk whose confreres also decide to give her comfort. A sculptor's wife's lover poses as a statue; he is found out and chased naked from the sculptor's house. Treated with contempt by a couple of newlyweds, an innkeeper has his revenge by staging a robbery and seducing the bride while her husband hides. A husband, discovering his wife sleeping with their lord, shames them both, and gets himself appointed to an important government post.

Despite the reference to Chaucer's best-known literary work in the title, this film has no debt to the English poet in any of the six tales it dramatizes. Instead, it is a poor attempt to emulate Pasolini's 1971 film *The Decameron.* Guerini — who for his 1972 film seemed to think Canterbury was a person rather than a place — also made a sequel, *Decameron n. 2: le altre novelle del Boccaccio* in 1971.

REVIEWS: *Bianco e nero* 35 (March-April 1974): supplement 31. *CinemaTV Today* 14 July 1973: 16–17. *Image et son* 270 (March 1973): 128. *Monthly Film Bulletin* 40 (August 1973): 163.

ADDITIONAL DISCUSSION:

Poppi, Roberto, and Mario Pecorari. *Dizionario del cinema italiano: I Film dal 1970 al 1979.* Rome: Gremese Editore, 1996.

14. *L'An mil* (1985)

France; dir. Jean-Dominique de la Rochefoucald; TFI/Société française de production.

CAST: Gilles Amiot, Benoit Brione, Philippe Celvenot, Simon Choffe, Valerie Dreville, Carol Le Moal, Patrick Raynal, Aurélien Recoing, Della Rochefoucauld, Thierry Vidal.

In the Pyrenees, the people of the village of La Houquette d'Ancizan await the year of the "Great Terror" and the end of the world.

The film, which is set in the eleventh century, was originally shown in three 50-minute episodes on French television. In the National Film Archive in London, there is a copy of a film with the same title released by Gaumont in 1910. This earlier film, which is set in an indefinite but recognizably medieval time, tells of an attempt by Count Martell of Aquitaine to win the hand of Isolde, the daughter of the Duke of Engerrand. Archive files, however, contain no references to or reviews of this earlier film.

REVIEWS: *Film français* 2033 (19 April 1985): 18. *Télérama* 1845 (22 May 1985): 102; 1846 (29 May 1985): 88; 1847 (5 June 1985): 90.

ADDITIONAL DISCUSSIONS:

Renoux, Jacques. "An mil, pas de panique!" *Télérama* 1845 (22 May 1985): 56–57.

_____. "Un Chateau copie conforme." *Télérama* 1847 (5 June 1985): 51–52.

_____. "La Mode de l'an mil expliquée aux enfants de l'an 2000." *Télérama* 1847 (5 June 1985): 52.

15. *Anchoress* (1993)

Great Britain; dir. Chris Newby; British Film Institute.

CAST: Annette Badland, Brenda Bertin, Eugene Bervoets, François Beukelaers, Christopher Eccelston, Natalie Morse, Michael Pas, Pete Postlethwaite, Virginia Quilligan, Judith T. Wallace, Ann Way, Toyah Wilcox.

Christine, a 14-year-old illiterate peasant girl, finds herself increasingly drawn to a statue of the Virgin. At the same time, the village priest and reeve find themselves increasingly drawn to Christine. The reeve proposes marriage to the girl, but Christine refuses his offer, much to the dismay of her mother, Pauline. Instead, at the urging of the priest, who will thereby better be able to watch over and control her, Christine becomes an anchoress so she can live next to the statue to which she is devoted. Christine's decision does not sit well with her mother, who plots against the priest. When Pauline, who is also the village doctor, delivers the priest's lover of a stillborn child, the priest in turn plots against her. The priest accuses Pauline of witchcraft, and she drowns while trying to escape from a howling mob of her fellow villagers. Meanwhile, Christine succeeds in escaping from her cell and flees with her lover to Winchester to seek release from her vows from the bishop. The bishop refuses and orders his men to return Christine to her cell by force, but she escapes and runs away with her lover.

Newby's film is based on the true story of Christine Carpenter, who in the fourteenth century was enclosed as an anchoress in the wall of a village church of Shere in Surrey. The inspiration for the film, according to screenwriter Judith Stanley-Smith, was a letter concerning Christine written by the Bishop of Winchester in 1324. The film, which has an arresting look, was shot in black-and-white.

REVIEWS: *Avant-scène du cinéma* 424 (July 1993): 105. *New York Times* 9 November 1994: C12. *Positif* 389-90 (July-August 1993): 38. *Screen International* 7 May 1993: 40. *Sight and Sound* 3 (October 1993): 38–39. *Times* [London] 9 September 1993: 33. *Variety* 17 May 1993: 96.

ADDITIONAL DISCUSSIONS:
Andrew, Geoff. "Bricks and Martyr." *Time Out* [London] 1 September 1993: 33.
Cameron-Wilson, James, and F. Maurice Speed. *Film Review 1994-95.* London: Virgin Books, 1994.
Levich, Jacob., ed. *The Motion Picture Guide: 1995 Annual (The Films of 1994).* New York: Cine-Books, 1995.
Murphy, Kathleen. "Nativity Scenes." *Film Comment* 31 (January-February 1995): 13–16.

And Trees Grew Out of Stone (1985)
see *Captive of the Dragon* (1985)

And Trees Will Even Grow Out of Rocks (1985) see *Captive of the Dragon* (1985)

Andrei Roublev (1966) see *Andrei Rublev* (1966)

16. Andrei Rublev (1966)
Soviet Union; dir. Andrei Tarkovsky; Mosfilm.

ALTERNATE TITLE: *Andrei Roublev.*
CAST: Nikolai Burlyayev, Roan Bykov, Nikolai Grinko, Mikhail Kononov, Ivan Lapikov, Yuri Narazov, Yuri Nikulin, Irma Rausch, Nikolai Sergeyev, Anatoly Solonitsyn.

In fifteenth-century Russia, icon painter Andrei Rublev takes refuge from the rain in an inn. A jester, who has the temerity to make fun of the local duke, is punished by two of the duke's soldiers. Leaving the inn, Andrei accepts an invitation from Theophanes the Greek to assist him in painting icons for a new church. While assisting the Greek, Andrei argues with his fellow workers about the nature of man and the views of God and sin contained in the Old Testament. One night, Andrei is captured by some revelers upon whom he has been spying. He is freed by a naked woman and escapes just as the revelers are cut down by a troop of horsemen. But his escape is only momentary as the brother of the duke who is Andrei's patron ambushes him and slaughters his assistants. The duke's brother then makes a pact with a roving band of Tartars whom he leads in a raid on the village where Andrei is staying. Andrei himself kills one of the Tartars and escapes with a deaf-mute girl he has been protecting. The Tartars return and kidnap the girl. Meanwhile, the duke gives Boriska, the bell-founder's son, the task of casting a bell for a new church. As the bell is finally cast and rung, the film concludes with a montage of Rublev's religious paintings.

Critics generally regard *Andrei Rublev* as Tarkovsky's finest film. Very little is known about Rublev himself, other than that he was a monk and one of the greatest medieval Russian icon painters. He was born somewhere between 1360 and 1370 and died around 1430. The film is divided into eight episodes with a prologue and an epilogue. Except for the final montage, which was shot in color, the film is in black-and-white. Two different versions of the film exist, one 17 minutes longer than the other. The 17 minutes do not, however, contain any complete scenes. Instead, they add slightly longer running times to a number of scenes.

REVIEWS: *Les Cahiers du cinéma* 218 (March 1970): 67–68; 450 (December 1991): 58–60. *Cineforum* 82 (February 1969): 73. *Cinema nuovo* 240 (March 1976): 131–34. *Cinema Papers* 2 (March-April 1975): 63. *Cinéma* [Paris] 143 (February 1970): 15–17. *CinemaTV Today* 15 September 1973: 13. *Film fran-*

çais 2378 (29 November 1991): 15. *Filmcritica* 261 (January-February 1976): 10–12. *Films and Filming* 20 (November 1973): 47–48. *Hollywood Reporter* 12 October 1973: 20. *Image et son* 236 (February 1970): 112–15. *Independent Film Journal* 73 (4 February 1974): 12. *Iskusstvo kino* 1 (January 1989): 24–33. *Jeune cinéma* 42 (November-December 1969): 1–2. *Los Angeles Times* 1 January 1972: 2. 7; 12 November 1980: 6. 2; 25 October 1983: 6. 3. *Monthly Film Bulletin* 40 (October 1973): 203–04. *New York Times* 10 October 1973: 43; 21 February 1992: C10; 6 August 1992: C20. *Soviet Cinema* 8 (1965): 10–13. *Sunday Times* [London] 19 August 1973: 29. *Time* 102 (22 October 1973): 60. *Times* [London] 21 December 1971: 4; 10 August 1973: 10; 7 September 1973: 10; 12 October 1984: 9; 11 July 1991: 17. *Times* [London] *Literary Supplement* 19 July 1991: 18. *Variety* 4 June 1969: 36.

ADDITIONAL DISCUSSIONS:

"Andrei Tarkovsky on the Film 'Roublev.'" *Young/Jeune Cinema & Theatre* 8 (1965): 16–23.

Belyavsky, Oleg. "The Filming of Andrei Rublyov." *Soviet Cinema* 5 (1966): 18–19, 21.

Dalle Vacche, Angela. *Cinema and Painting.* Austin: University of Texas Press, 1996.

Frezzato, Achille. *Andrej Tarkovskij.* Florence: La Nuova Italia, 1977.

Giavarini, Laurence. "*Andrei Roublev,* un film de Russie." *Cahiers du cinéma* 450 (December 1991): 59–60.

Green, Peter. *Andrei Tarkovsky, The Winding Quest.* Houndsmills, Basingstoke: Macmillan, 1993.

Johnson, Vida. *The Films of Andrei Tarkovsky.* Bloomington: Indiana University Press, 1994.

_____, and Graham Petrie. "Tarkovsky." In Daniel J. Goulding, ed. *Five Filmmakers.* Bloomington: Indiana University Press, 1994.

Le Fanu, Mark. *The Cinema of Andrei Tarkovsky.* London: BFI, 1987.

Leong, Albert. "Stalinist Realism in Tarkovsky's *Andrei Rublev.*" *Studies in Comparative Communism* 17 (Fall-Winter 1984): 227–33.

Liehm, Mira, and Antonín J. Liehm. *The Most Important Art: Eastern European Film After 1945.* Berkeley: University of California Press, 1977.

Magill, Frank N., ed. *Magill's Survey of Cinema: Foreign Language Films.* Englewood Cliffs, N.J.: Salem, 1975.

Montagu, Ivor. "Man and Experience: Tarkovsky's World." *Sight and Sound* 42 (Spring 1973): 89–94.

Nash, Jay Robert, and Stanley Ralph Ross. *The Motion Picture Guide, A–B, 1927–1983.* Chicago: Cinebooks, 1985.

Passek, Jean-Loup, ed. *Le Cinéma russe et sovietique.* Paris: Centre Georges Pompidou, 1981.

Raghavendra, M.K. "The Lost World of Andrei Tarkovsky." *Deep Focus* 1 (January 1989): 32–41.

Rinaldi, Giorgio. "Andrei Tarkovsky — Andrei Roublev." *Cineforum* 151 (January-February 1976): 63–72.

Strick, Philip. "Releasing the Balloon, Raising the Bell." *Monthly Film Bulletin* 58 (February 1991): 34–37.

Tarkovsky, Andrei. *Andrei Roublev.* Ed. Jean Schnitzer and Luda Schnitzer. Paris: Les Éditeurs français réunis, 1970. [Screenplay, interview with Tarkovsky, and commentary.]

_____. *Andrei Rublëv.* Trans. Kitty Hunter-Blair. London: Faber, 1991. [Screenplay.]

_____. *Sculpting in Time.* Trans. Kitty Hunter-Blair. Austin: University of Texas Press, 1989.

_____. *Time Within Time.* Trans. Kitty Hunter-Blair. Calcutta: Seagull, 1991.

_____. *Die Versiegelte Zeit.* Trans. Hans-Joachim Schlegel. Berlin: Ullstein, 1985.

Thomas, Nicholas, ed. *International Dictionary of Films and Filmmakers— Vol. 1: Films.* Chicago: St. James Press, 1990.

Turovskaya, Maya. *Tarkovsky, Cinema as Poetry.* Trans. Natasha Ward. London: Faber, 1989.

Vronskaya, Jeanne. *Young Soviet Film Makers.* London: Allen and Unwin, 1972.

Wierzewski, Wojciech. "The Artist and His Age." *Young/Jeune Cinema* 3 (1973): 26–33.

Zorkaya, Neya. *The Illustrated History of the Soviet Film.* New York: Hippocrene, 1989.

Angelo di Assisi (1960) see *La Tragica notte di Assisi* (1960)

An-Nasr Salah ad-Din (1963) see *Saladin* (1963)

17. *L'Annonce faite a Marie* (1991)

France and Canada; dir. Alain Cuny; Desmichelle Prods., La Sept-Sofica Lumière, and Pax Films.

ALTERNATE TITLE: *The Annunciation of Marie.*

CAST: Roberto Benavente, Christelle Challab, Alain Cuny, Jean des Ligneris, Ulrika Jonsson, Ken Mackenzie, Cecile Potot.

During the Crusades, Vercors betroths his beautiful daughter Violaine to Jacques. She cannot marry Jacques because she has contracted leprosy, so Jacques marries her younger sister Mara. Jacques and Mara's first child dies soon after its birth, and Mara begs Violaine to return from seclusion to restore the child to life.

The screenplay for this film is based on a 1955 play of the same title by Paul Claudel. Cuny, who wrote and directed the film, was Claudel's friend for many years, during which time he gained a reputation as the most important interpreter of the playwright, who himself requested that Cuny adapt this play for the screen.

Anatoly Solonitsyn as the fifteenth century Russian icon painter Andrei Rublev in Andrei Tarkovsky's *Andrei Rublev* (1966). (Still courtesy of the British Film Institute.)

REVIEWS: *Les Cahiers du cinéma* 450 (December 1991): 84–85. *Film français* 29 November 1991: 15. *Le Monde* 18 December 1991: 14. *Positif* 373 (March 1992): 54–55. *Revue du cinéma* 478 (January 1992): 38. *Séquences* 159–60 (September 1992): 51. *Studio* [Paris] 57 (January 1992): 8. *Variety* 16 March 1992: 61. *24 Images* 61 (Summer 1992): 79–80.

ADDITIONAL DISCUSSIONS:
Heymann, Danièle, and Pierre Murat. *L'Année du cinéma 1992*. Barcelona: Calmann-Lévy, 1992.
Repertory of the Long Feature Film Production and French Cinema 91–92. Paris: Unifrance Film, 1992.
Tous les films 1991. Versailles: Éditions Chrétiens-Médias, 1992.

The Annunication of Marie (1991) see
  L'Annonce faite a Marie (1991)

18. *Antonio di Padova* (1949)
  Italy; dir. Pietro Francisci; Oro Film.

CAST: Aldo Fabrizi, Aldo Fiorelli, Silvana Pampanini, Alberto Pomerani.

A World War I veteran has a series of flashbacks in which he finds himself in the Middle Ages where he encounters Saint Antony and a tyrant whom the saint has set out to reform. The tyrant is given to slaughtering infidels and the soldiers of his Christian opponents in the cruelest ways possible.

St. Antony of Padua (1195–1231), one of the earliest and most enthusiastic followers of St. Francis of Assisi, was famous for his skills as a preacher. This film had a wider release than the 1931 silent film made of St. Antony's life, but critics were generally negative in their response to the film.

REVIEWS: *New York Times* 29 March 1952: 19. *Variety* 20 July 1949: 20; 26 March 1952: 6.

ADDITIONAL DISCUSSIONS:
Chiti, Roberto, and Roberto Poppi. *Dizionario del*

cinema italiano. Vol. 2: I Film dal 1945 al 1952.
Rome: Gremese Editore, 1991.

Nash, Jay Robert, and Stanley Ralph Ross. *The Motion Picture Guide, A–B, 1927–1983.* Chicago: Cinebooks, 1985.

19. *Antonio di Padova, il santo dei miracoli* (1931)

Italy; dir. Giulio Antamoro; Società Anonima Cinematographie Religiose Artistiche Sonore.

CAST: Ruggero Barni, Armando Casini, Elio Cosci, Iris D'Alba, Carlo Pinzauti.

Born in Lisbon, the man who would later be known as St. Antony of Padua is consecrated at birth to the Virgin Mary. The devotion and charity of his early life lead him first to enter an Augustinian monastery and then to leave the seclusion of that life to minister to the needy as one of the most famous Franciscan preachers. He travels throughout France and Italy, preaching at one time to the fish when the fishermen refuse to hear him.

Antony was born in 1195 in Lisbon and died in Padua in 1231. Pope Gregory IX canonized him in the following year. The incident of his preaching to fish has become a well-known part of his legend and accounts for his status as patron saint of the lower animals. This film was actually made in 1927, but difficulties with Italian film censors delayed its release for four years. It is, however, far superior to the 1949 film made of the saint's life.

REVIEW: *Bianco e nero* 42 (July-December 1981): 405–06.

ADDITIONAL DISCUSSIONS:

Chiti, Roberto, and Enrico Lancia. *Dizionario del cinema italiano. Vol. 1: I Film dal 1930 al 1944.* Rome: Gremese Editore, 1993.

Savio, Francesco. *Ma l'amore no.* Milan: Sonzogno, 1975.

20. *The Arabian Nights* (1974)

France and Italy; dir. Pier Paolo Pasolini; PEA and Les Productions Artistes Associés.

ALTERNATE TITLES: *Il Fiore delle mille e una notte* and *The Flower of the Arabian Nights.*

CAST: Zeudi Biasolo, Ninetto Davoli, Elisabetta Vito Genovesi, Abadir Ghidei, Francesco Paolo Governale, Franco Merli, Ines Pellegrini, Luigina Rocchi.

The slave Zumurrud selects the inexperienced Nuredin as her new master and initiates him sexually. That evening she tells him a tale designed to show which sex is the weaker. In the morning, she is kidnapped by Bassum, whose master's advances she had previously spurned. Nuredin pursues her, but without luck as Zumurrud is then kidnapped by the Forty Thieves, whose leader she charms. With the Forty Thieves, she arrives at a great city where, disguised as a man, she is crowned king and married to the daughter of the high priest in fulfillment of a prophecy. Zumurrud's wife discovers she is a woman and aids her in luring Nuredin to the city as various stories from the *Arabian Nights* are enacted. In the film's final sequence, Zumurrud and Nuredin are reunited and live happily ever after.

Along with *The Canterbury Tales* and *The Decameron*— both made in 1971—*The Arabian Nights* comprises Pasolini's "trilogy of life." Pasolini turned to medieval texts as sources in an effort to free cinema from contemporary ideological bias. His concern throughout the trilogy was with basic human passions and a purer form of storytelling. In short, he wished to establish a new kind of realistic filmmaking. In the course of making the trilogy, Pasolini gradually stepped further and further back from his films. He appeared on screen as a character in both of the first two parts of the trilogy. Here he established a more neutral narrative stance. The film begins with a title that aptly sums up Pasolini's achievement throughout the whole trilogy: "The complete truth does not lie in one dream but in several."

REVIEWS: *Cinema nuovo* 231 (September-October 1974): 374–75. *CinemaTV Today* 15 March 1975: 14. *Film-echo/Filmwoche* 46 (24 August 1979): 8; 67 (28 November 1979): 8. *Kino* [Germany] 1 (1980): 13. *Monthly Film Bulletin* 42 (April 1975): 79. *New York Times* 27 July 1980: 33. *Rivista del cinematographo* 10–11 (October-November 1979): 34–35. *Sunday Times* [London] 23 March 1975: 37. *Times* [London] 7 March 1975: 13. *Variety* 30 July 1980: 6.

ADDITIONAL DISCUSSIONS:

Bachmann, Gideon. "Pasolini in Persia: The Shooting of *1001 Nights.*" *Film Quarterly* 27 (Winter 1973-74): 25–28.

———. "Pasolini Today." *Take One* 4 (May-June 1973): 18–21.

Friedrich, Pia. *Pier Paolo Pasolini.* Boston: Twayne, 1982.

Pasolini, Pier Paolo. *Trilogia della vita.* Bologna: Cappelli, 1975. [Screenplay.]

Poppi, Roberto, and Mario Pecorari. *Dizionario del cinema italiano: I Film dal 1970 al 1979.* Rome: Gremese Editore, 1996.

Rondolino, Gianni, ed. *Catalogo Bolaffi del cinema italiana 1966/1975.* Turin: Bolaffi Editore, 1975.

Rumble, Patrick. "Stylistic Contamination in the *Trilogia della vita*: The Case of *Il Fiore delle mille e una notte.*" In Patrick Rumble and Bart Testa, eds. *Pier Paolo Pasolini, Contemporary Perspectives*. Toronto: University of Toronto Press, 1994.

Schwartz, David. *Pasolini Requiem*. New York: Pantheon, 1992.

Snyder, Stephen. *Pier Paolo Pasolini*. Boston; Twayne, 1980.

Viano, Maurizio. *A Certain Realism*. Berkeley: University of California Press, 1993.

Willemen, Paul, ed. *Pier Paolo Pasolini*. London: BFI, 1976.

L'Archer de feu (1971) see *L'Arciere di fuoco* (1971)

The Archer of Sherwood Forest (1971)

see *L'Arciere di fuoco* (1971)

21. *L'Arciere di fuoco* (1971)

Italy, France, and Spain; dir. Giorgio Ferroni; Oceanic Produzione.

ALTERNATE TITLES: *The Archer of Sherwood Forest*, *L'Archer de feu*, *L'Arquero de Sherwood* and *The Fiery Archer*.

CAST: Mario Adorf, Lars Bloch, Mark Damon, Luis Davila, Silvia Dionisio, Daniele Dublino, Helga Liné, Manuel Zarzo.

As he returns from the Crusades, England's King Richard is taken prisoner by the German emperor. To raise his ransom, he dispatches his equerry, Sir Henry of Nottingham, to England. To his dismay, Sir Henry discovers that England is being tyrannized by Richard's brother Prince John, who claims that Richard is dead. Taking the name Robin Hood, Sir Henry joins with a group of men still loyal to Richard and leads a revolt against Prince John. Richard is ransomed and returns to England to re-establish peace, reward Sir Henry and exile Prince John.

Ferroni retells the familiar events from the legend of Robin Hood, adding nothing very original to that legend as he does so.

REVIEWS: *Cinefantastique* 1 (Fall 1970): 42. *Intermezzo* 9 (31 May 1971): 11.

ADDITIONAL DISCUSSIONS:

Poppi, Roberto, and Mario Pecorari. *Dizionario del cinema italiano: I Film dal 1970 al 1979*. Rome: Gremese Editore, 1996.

La Produzione italiana 1970/71. Rome: Unitalia Film, 1971.

22. *L'Arciere nero* (1959)

Italy; dir. Piero Pierotti; Diamante Cin.

ALTERNATE TITLE: *The Black Archer*.

CAST: Gérard Landry, Carlo Strober.

When treacherous barons assassinate the gentle lord Corrado, his son, a skilled bowman disguised as the bandit known as "The Black Archer," wages a secret campaign against the usurpers who murdered his father.

This film represents a fairly standard exercise in Italian cinematic swordplay.

DISCUSSIONS:

Chiti, Roberto, and Roberto Poppi. *Dizionario del cinema italiano. Vol. 2: I Film dal 1945 al 1959*. Rome: Gremese Editore, 1991.

Lucanio, Patrick. *With Fire and Sword, Italian Spectacles on American Screens 1958–1968*. Metuchen, N.J.: Scarecrow, 1994.

23. *L'Armata Brancaleone* (1966)

Italy and France; dir. Mario Monicelli; Fair Film S.P.A.

ALTERNATE TITLE: *For Love and Gold*.

CAST: Maria Grazia Buccella, Alfio Caltabianco, Ugo Fangareggi, Vittorio Gassman, Folco Lulli, Carlo Pisacane, Enrico Maria Salerno, Luigi Sangiorgi, Catherine Spaak, Barbara Steel, Gina Maria Volontè.

Around the year 1000, while journeying to take possession of his feudal lands, Arnolfo Manodiferro is set upon by a band of robbers who leave him for dead and take the deed to his lands. The bandits offer the deed to Brancaleone, who sets out on an adventure-filled journey to claim the lands. No sooner does Brancaleone take possession of the lands and castle than the latter is besieged by Saracens who defeat Brancaleone and imprison him and his followers. Just as they are about to be tortured, everyone is rescued by a group of knights led by Arnolfo Manodiferro, who spares the lives of Brancaleone and his followers on the condition that they go to the Holy Land to fight in the Crusades.

The film presents a curious marriage of slapstick with excessive violence, but it represented at the time of its release a new kind of cinematic response to the medieval. Absent here are noble lords and virtuous ladies. Instead, Monicelli's film presents an army of fools and idiots whose speeches fuse Italian, Goliardic verse and "pig" Latin. The film was the inspiration for a 1970 sequel, *Brancaleone alle crociate*.

REVIEWS: *Bianco e nero* 27 (May 1966): 66–68. *Filmblätter* 29–30 (19 July 1968): 651. *Film-echo/*

Bruce Campbell as the reluctant time traveler Ash in Sam Raimi's *Army of Darkness* (1992).

Filmwoche 55–56 (12 July 1968): 12. *Rivista del cine-matografo* 5–6 (May-June 1966): 380–81. *Variety* 1 June 1966: 6.

ADDITIONAL DISCUSSIONS:

Dorigo, Francesco. "L'Armata Brancaleone." *Cineforum* 54 (April 1966): 288–99.

Italian Production 1965. Rome: Unitalia film, 1966.

Poppi, Roberto, and Mario Pecorari. *Dizionario del cinema italiano. Vol. 3: I Film dal 1960 al 1969.* Rome: Gremese Editore, 1992.

Rondolino, Gianni, ed. *Catalogo Bolaffi del cinema italiana 1966/1975.* Turin: Bolaffi Editore, 1975.

24. *Army of Darkness* (1992)

United States; dir. Sam Raimi; Universal/Dino de Laurentiis.

ALTERNATE TITLES: *Evil Dead 3* and *The Medieval Dead.*

CAST: Ian Abercrombie, Bruce Campbell, Embeth Davidtz, Bridget Fonda, Marcus Guilbert, Richard Grove, Michael Earl Reid.

Ash, a twentieth century housewares salesman, finds himself transported back to medieval England where he confronts monsters, attempts to woo a maiden and battles an army of skeletal Deadites.

At one point in this the third film in Raimi's *Evil Dead* series, Ash joins forces with a king identified as Arthur, but there is nothing Arthurian about this film. Instead, in one of the goriest films set in the Middle Ages, Ash loses his arm and, thanks to the chainsaw and shotgun he brings with him from the future, manages to spew more blood and engender more sadistic chaos than he did in the first two *Evil Dead* films. The film's most notable feature is its use of special visual effects.

REVIEWS: *Les Cahiers du cinéma* 463 (January 1993): 44–45; 365 (March 1993): 6; 476 (February 1994): 82. *Cinefantastique* 24 (August 1993): 59. *Entertainment Weekly* 160 (5 March 1993): 40–42. *Los Angeles Times* 19 February 1993: Calendar 8. *New York Times* 19 February 1993: C10. *Sight and Sound* NS 3 (June 1993): 46–47. *Starburst* 176 (April 1993): 42–43. *Sunday Times* [London] 13 June 1993: 9. 12. *Times* [London] 10 June 1993: 33. *Variety* 19 October 1992: 160.

ADDITIONAL DISCUSSIONS:

Biodrowski, Steve. "Army of Darkness." *Cinefantastique* 23 (August 1992): 24–25, 27–28, 30, 35–36, 38, 41, 43–44, 46, 48, 51–52.

_____. "*Evil Dead III*: Introversion Comes of Age." *Cinefantastique* 23 (August 1992): 44–45.

_____. "*Evil Dead III*: KNB's Army of Darkness." *Cinefantastique* 23 (August 1992): 42.

_____. "*Evil Dead III*: The Make-up World of Ash." *Cinefantastique* 23 (August 1992): 32–33.

_____. "*Evil Dead III*: Production Design." *Cinefantastique* 23 (August 1992): 34.

_____. "Sam Raimi's *Evil Dead III*." *Cinefantastique* 23 (February 1993): 14–15.

Brod, Doug. "Don of the Dead." *Entertainment Weekly* 160 (5 March 1993): 40–42.

Cameron-Wilson, James, and F. Maurice Speed. *Film Review 1993-94*. London: Virgin: 1993.

Jankiewicz, Pat. "Graveyard Shift." *Starburst* [Monster Special] 19 (April 1994): 25–29.

_____. "Sam Raimi's *Army of Darkness*." *Starburst* 177 (May 1993): 13–18.

Jonascu, Michael. "Army of Darkness." *Film Threat* 2 (February 1992): 36–41.

Jones, Alan. "Darkman Cometh, An Interview with Sam Raimi." *Starburst* 149 (January 1991): 22–25.

McDonagh, Maitland. *Filmmaking on the Fringe.* New York: Carol Publishing Group, 1995.

Robley, Les Paul. "Mobilizing *Army of Darkness* Via 'Go-Animation.'" *American Cinematographer* 74 (March 1993): 72–80.

Uram, Sue. "Darkman & *Evil Dead III*." *Cinefantastique* 19 (July 1989): 11.

_____. "Dead Hero." *Cinefantastique* 23 (August 1992): 36–37.

_____. "Evil Effects: Tom Sullivan, Gore Auteur." *Cinefantastique* 23 (August 1992): 50.

L'Arquero de Sherwood (1971) see *L'Arciere di fuoco* (1971)

The Arrows of Robin Hood (1977) see *Robin Hood's Arrows* (1977)

Arthur of the Britons (1975) see *King Arthur, the Young Warlord* (1975)

25. *Arthur the King* (1982)

United States and Great Britain; dir. Clive Donner; Martin Poll Productions, Comworld Films and CBS-TV.

ALTERNATE TITLE: *Merlin and the Sword.*

CAST: Candice Bergen, Rupert Everett, Rosalyn Landor, Malcolm McDowell, Liam Neeson, Patrick Ryecart, Philip Sayer, Ann Thornton, Edward Woodward.

Katherine, a tourist wandering around modern-day Stonehenge, stumbles into a hole, where she encounters King Arthur and his knights. Camelot is in chaos. The wine cellar is empty, hundreds of Vikings are expected for dinner, and the Romans have abandoned En-gland. Even worse, the countryside is overrun with dragons and brigands, and the ever-present fog just will not lift. With Katherine's assistance, Merlin and his beloved Niniane restore order to the kingdom by challenging Morgan Le Fay and her ally Mordred, Arthur's illegitimate son.

Donner's film, which was shelved by the studio for several years before being dumped onto television, is one of the silliest films ever made about the Arthurian legend. Everything about the film — acting, dialogue, settings, costumes — is simply dreadful.

REVIEWS: *New York Times* 26 April 1985: 3. 30. *TV Guide* 33 (20–26 April 1985): A-144. *Variety* 8 May 1985: 162.

ADDITIONAL DISCUSSIONS:

Marill, Alvin H. *Movies Made for Television, 1964–1986*. New York: Zoetrope, 1987.

Schobert, Walter, and Horst Shäfer, eds. *Fisher Film Almanach 1987*. Frankfurt am Main: Fisher, 1987.

As in Heaven (1992) see *Svo á Jördu sem á Himni* (1992)

26. *At Sword's Point* (1911)

United States; Reliance.

A boy king's life is threatened by his uncle, who wishes to usurp the throne. His mother is his chief ally. When the uncle succeeds in carrying off the boy, his mother, disguised as a page, rescues him by killing the boy's uncle with her sword.

This early film is noteworthy for the battle scene in which the uncle and his troops are finally defeated.

REVIEW: *Moving Picture World* 1 April 1911: 720.

27. *At the Hour of Dawn* (1914)

Gaumont; France.

CAST: James Breon, Renée Carl, Louis Melchior, Victor Navarre.

When he captures a medieval Italian city, a bandit imprisons and threatens to execute the betrothed of the city's absent ruler, who returns in time to rescue his beloved and save the city.

The opening titles set the film in 1396. Crowd scenes and massive sets lend the production a genuinely medieval atmosphere.

REVIEWS: *Bioscope* 2 April 1914: supplement vii. *Cinema* 26 March 1914: supplement 81. *Kinematograph Monthly Film Record* 24 (April 1914): 132–33. *Moving Picture World* 18 April 1914: 339. *Variety* 8 May 1914: 21.

ADDITIONAL DISCUSSION:
The Film Index: A Bibliography. Vol. 1: The Film as Art. 1941. rpt. White Plains, N.Y.: Kraus International, 1988.

28. *At the Point of the Sword* (1912)

United States; dir. Emmett Campbell Hall; Edison.

CAST: James Gordon, Guy Hedlund, Jessie McAllister, Richard Neil, Charles Ogle, William Randall, Laura Sawyer, Charles Sutton, Benjamin F. Wilson.

Editha, the daughter of a nobleman, is in love with a count despised by her father, who intends her to marry a man as old as he. With the aid of an outlaw, whom she has taken pity upon, and after a series of adventures, Editha marries her true love.

This film offers an elaborately staged and costumed medieval period piece.

REVIEWS: *Bioscope* 6 May 1912: supplement vi. *Edison Kinetogram* 1 May 1912: 6. *Motion Picture Herald* 17 February 1912: 612.

Attack of the Normans (1962) see *Invasion of the Normans* (1962)

Aucassin and Nicolette (1911) see *In the Days of Chivalry* (1911)

29. *The Avaricious Monk* (1912)

Great Britain; dir. Warwick Buckland; Hepworth.

When a monk refuses an old woman's request for charity, Robin Hood takes the monk's purse and gives it to her. The monk then complains to King Richard, who sentences Robin to death. At the last moment, thanks to the pleas of Maid Marian, King Richard grants Robin a pardon.

REVIEW: *Kinematograph Monthly Record* 5 (September 1912): 64.

ADDITIONAL DISCUSSION:
Gifford, Denis. *The British Film Catalogue 1895–1985.* Newton Abbot: David & Charles, 1986.

Ballad of the Valiant Knight Ivanhoe (1983) see *Ballada o doblestnom rystare Aivengo* (1983)

30. *Ballada o doblestnom rystare Aivengo* (1983)

Soviet Union; dir. Sergei Tarasov; Mosfilm.

ALTERNATE TITLE: *Ballad of the Valiant Knight Ivanhoe.*

CAST: Tamara Akulova, Romuald Antsans, Peteris Haudinsh, Boris Khimichev, Leonid Kulagin.

This Soviet screen adaptation of Sir Walter Scott's 1819 novel emphasizes the transcendent values of the story: love, fidelity, duty, honor and commitment to spiritual ideals.

This is the second film in Tarasov's medieval trilogy for Mosfilm, which also includes *Robin Hood's Arrows* (1977) and *Chernaya strela* (1985).

DISCUSSION:
Ballad of the Valiant Knight Ivanhoe. Soviet Film 11 (1983): 20–22.

31. *The Bandit of Sherwood Forest* (1946)

United States; dir. George Sherman and Henry Levin; Columbia.

CAST: Anita Louise, Edgar Buchanan, Henry Daniell, Jill Esmond, Russell Hicks, Cornel Wilde.

Robin Hood, long retired and knighted, returns to public life to oppose William of Pembroke, the tyrannical regent, who is intent upon abolishing the Magna Carta and murdering the boy-king Henry III. Allies new and old, including the queen, rally around Robin's son, Robert of Nottingham, who rescues Henry, kills the regent in a duel, and restores order to England.

This low-budget adventure was based on Paul Castleton's 1941 juvenile novel *The Son of Robin Hood.* It allows Wilde plenty of time to be his swashbuckling best as Robert of Nottingham, but the film's plot and dialogue rely too heavily on clichés to advance the storyline. The Technicolor is, however, excellent.

REVIEWS: *Harrison's Reports* 2 February 1946: 19. *Hollywood Reporter* 18 February 1946: 3. *Kinematograph Weekly* 10 January 1946: 24. *Monthly Film Bulletin* 13 (28 February 1946): 14. *Motion Picture Herald* 23 February 1946: Product Digest Section 2857. *New York Times* 23 March 1946: 8. *Revue du cinéma* [La Saison cinématographique] Hors série 27 (1945–1947): 91. *Times* [London] 3 January 1946: 8. *To-day's Cinema* 4 January 1946: 11; 17 December 1947: 22. *Variety* 20 February 1946: 8.

ADDITIONAL DISCUSSIONS:
Behlmer, Rudy. "Robin Hood on the Screen." *Films in Review* 16 (February 1965): 91–102.

Knight, Stephen. *Robin Hood, A Complete Study of the English Outlaw.* Oxford: Blackwell, 1994.

Nash, Jay Robert, and Stanley Ralph Ross. *The Motion Picture Guide, A–B, 1927–1983.* Chicago: Cinebooks, 1985.

Parish, James Robert, and Don E. Stanke. *The Swashbucklers*. New Rochelle, N.Y.: Arlington House, 1976.

Richards, Jeffrey. *Swordsmen of the Screen from Douglas Fairbanks to Michael York*. London: Routledge & Kegan Paul, 1977.

Turner, David. *Robin of the Movies*. Kingswinford, Eng.: Yeoman Publishing, 1989.

32. *Banovic Strahinja* (1981)

Yugoslavia and West Germany; dir. Vatroslav Mimica; Jadran Film.

CAST: Kole Angelovski, Gert Fröbe, Franco Nero, Dragan Nicolic, Rade Serbedzija, Sanja Vejnovic.

ALTERNATE TITLES: *The Falcon* and *Soko*.

A pillaging band of Turks kidnaps Anda, the wife of nobleman Banovic Strahinja, who sets out to rescue her. After several attempts, he succeeds, but then he faces a dilemma: custom dictates that she must be blinded for infidelity because surely she must have compromised her virtue by having been taken alive as a prisoner. In the end, she is spared this punishment.

Based upon an often-retold Serbian epic, this film is set right before the decisive June 15, 1389, battle of Kosovo Plain, in which invading Turkish armies slaughtered most of the Serbian nobility.

REVIEWS: *Cineforum* 22 (November 1982): 71. *Ekran* [Yugoslavia] 6 (1981): 4–5. *Film a doba* 29 (November 1983): 645–47. *Film-echo/Filmwoche* 28 (15 May 1981): 15; 47–48 (28 August 1981): 19; 10 (18 February 1983): 46. *Jugoslavija Film News* 130 (September 1980): 8; 132 (October 1981): 4. *Variety* 12 August 1981: 20.

ADDITIONAL DISCUSSIONS:

Just, Lothar R., ed. *Das Filmjahr 1984*. Munich: Filmland Presse, 1984.

Tous les films 1983. Paris: Éditions Chrétiens-Médias, 1984.

Barbourossa (1910) see *Federico Barbarossa* (1910)

La Battaglia di Legnano (1910) see *Federico Barbarossa* (1910)

The Beast (1956) see *Ilya Muromets* (1956)

Béatrice (1987) see *La Passion Béatrice* (1987)

33. *Becket* (1910)

United States; dir. Charles Kent; Vitagraph.

ALTERNATE TITLE: *The Martyrdom of Thomas à Becket, Archbishop of Canterbury*.

CAST: Maurice Costello, Charles Kent.

Henry II and Becket, once friends, find themselves opponents in a battle for sovereignty between church and state. The king's henchmen murder the archbishop in his cathedral, but the king's victory is short-lived. In the film's final scenes, a saintly Becket appears before Henry, who has just learned that his sons have seized his possessions in France, that the Scots have crossed the northern border to invade England, and that civil war has broken out in the Midlands.

The source for this film is Tennyson's most important play, *Becket*, begun in 1876 and first published in 1884. In 1892, Henry Irving published an acting edition of the play prefatory to his production of the play, in which he played the title role, at London's Lyceum Theatre. The production opened on February 6, 1893, and ran for 112 nights. Irving toured America in the play in 1893 and 1894 and again in 1895.

REVIEWS: *Bioscope* 6 October 1910: 37. *Moving Picture World* 18 June 1910: 1055; 16 July 1910: 148; 9 July 1910: 103.

ADDITIONAL DISCUSSIONS:

The Film Index: A Bibliography. Vol. 1: The Film as Art. 1941. rpt. White Plains, N.Y.: Kraus International, 1988.

Lindsay, Vachel. *The Art of the Moving Picture*. New York: Macmillan, 1915.

Slide, Anthony. *The Big V: A History of the Vitagraph Company*. Rev. ed. Metuchen, N.J.: Scarecrow, 1987.

Savada, Elias. *The American Film Institute Catalog of Motion Pictures Produced in the United States: Film Beginnings, 1893–1910*. Metuchen, N.J.: Scarecrow, 1995.

Usai, Paolo Cherchi. *Vitagraph Co. of America*. Pordenone: Edizioni Studio Tesi, 1987.

34. *Becket* (1923)

Great Britain; dir. George Ridgewell; Stoll.

CAST: Frank Benson, A.V. Bramble, Bertram Burleigh, Arthur Burne, Mary Clare.

Soldiers of Henry II murder the archbishop for meddling in the king's affairs, especially for his having forced the king's mistress to enter a convent.

Like Vitagraph's 1910 film of the same title, the primary source here is Tennyson's play, though with less critically well-received results.

Becket (Richard Burton) and Henry II (Peter O'Toole) meet for the last time on a note of reconciliation in a scene from Peter Glenville's *Becket* (1964).

REVIEW: *Spectator* 132 (2 February 1924): 171.

ADDITIONAL DISCUSSIONS:

Connelly, Robert. *The Motion Picture Guide, Silent Film, 1910–1936*. Chicago: Cinebooks, 1986.

Gifford, Denis. *The British Film Catalogue, 1895–1985*. Newton Abbot: David & Charles, 1986.

The Film Index: A Bibliography. Vol. 1: The Film as Art. 1941. rpt. White Plains, N.Y.: Kraus International, 1988.

Warren, Patricia. *The British Film Collection, 1896–1984: A History of the British Cinema in Pictures*. London: Elm Tree, 1984.

35. *Becket* (1964)

Great Britain; dir. Peter Glenville; Paramount.

CAST: Pamela Brown, Richard Burton, John Gielgud, Martita Hunt, Peter O'Toole, Sian Phillips, David Weston, Donald Wolfit.

Henry II and Becket share a long friendship during which they drink, wench and beat the clergy at their own games. Becket's sudden elevation to the See of Canterbury as archbishop, however, soon changes everything. A crisis occurs when Henry asserts his right to try members of the clergy for any offenses, and Becket refuses to give ground. Forced to flee, Becket finds refuge — for matters more of politics than of principle — at the courts of Louis VII of France and Pope Alexander III. A reconciliation between the king and archbishop is short-lived, and Becket once again enrages the king. His soldiers murder him on the altar steps of the cathedral.

Based upon Jean Anouilh's 1959 play *Becket, or, The Honor of God*, Glenville's film is excellent in every way, except for its reduction of Eleanor of Aquitaine to a simpering fool. Edward Anhalt's screenplay won an Academy Award, and the film was nominated for Best Picture, Best Director, Best Actor (for both

Burton's Becket and O'Toole's Henry II), and Best Supporting Actor (John Gielgud as Louis VII). In addition, the film was named the best English-language picture by the National Board of Review and the Best Motion Picture Drama by the Golden Globe Awards. O'Toole won the Golden Globe for Best Actor, and the screenplay also won the award for the best-written American drama from the Writers Guild of America.

REVIEWS: *Film Daily* 4 March 1964: 6–7. *Films and Filming* 10 (April 1964): 7–8; 10 (May 1964): 21. *Films in Review* 15 (April 1964): 234, 237–39. *Hollywood Reporter* 4 March 1964: 3. *Kinematograph Weekly* 26 March 1964: 8–9. *Monthly Film Bulletin* 31 (May 1964): 66–67. *Motion Picture Herald* 18 March 1964: 28, 36; 1 April 1964: 20. *New York Times* 12 March 1964: 40. *Times* [London] 24 March 1964: 15. *Variety* 4 March 1964: 6.

ADDITIONAL DISCUSSIONS:

Bragg, Melvyn. *Richard, The Life of Richard Burton.* London: Hodder & Stoughton, 1988.

Comuzlo, Ermanno. "Becket e il suo re." *Cineforum* 34 (April 1964): 319–38.

Magill, Frank N., ed. *Magill's Survey of Cinema: English Language Films.* First Series. Englewood Cliffs, N.J.: Salem, 1980.

Nash, Jay Robert, and Stanley Ralph Ross. *The Motion Picture Guide, A–B, 1927–1983.* Chicago: Cinebooks, 1985.

Searles, Baird. *EPIC! History on the Big Screen.* New York: Harry N. Abrams, 1990.

Sragow, Michael. "*Becket* and *The Lion in Winter.*" *Film Society Review* 5 (December 1969): 36–43.

36. *Beffe, licenzie e amori del Decamerone segreto* (1972)

Italy; dir. Giueseppe Vari; Corinzia.

ALTERNATE TITLE: *Love, Passion, and Pleasure.*

CAST: Claudia Bianchi, Dado Crostarosa, Orchidea De Sanctis, Maliso Lonco, Renato Rinaldi, Giacomo Rizzo.

The poet Cecco Angiolieri arrives with a troupe of actors in a village in Tuscany where he resumes his liaison with a local prostitute, deflowers the abbess of the local convent, attempts unsuccessfully to cuckold the mayor and finally flees town unpunished for his misdeeds.

Based on a conflation of tales from Boccaccio's *Decameron*, Vari's film is one of a series of Italian sexploitation films attempting to capitalize on the popularity and controversy surrounding Pasolini's 1971 film *Decameron*.

REVIEWS: *Bianco e nero* 35 (March-April 1974):

supplement 34. *CinemaTV Today* 4 August 1973: 23. *Monthly Film Bulletin* 41 (March 1974): 43.

ADDITIONAL DISCUSSIONS:

Poppi, Roberto, and Mario Pecorari. *Dizionario del cinema italiano: I Film dal 1970 al 1979.* Rome: Gremese Editore, 1996.

La Produzione italiana. Rome: Unitalia Film, 1972.

Die Befreiung der Schweiz und die Sage von Wilhelm Tell (1913) see *Guillaume Tell* (1913)

37. *La Bella Antonia, prima monaca e poi dimonia* (1972)

Italy; dir. Mariano Laurenti; Flora Film.

ALTERNATE TITLE: *The Naughty Nun.*

CAST: Renato Cecilla, Elio Crovetto, Edwige Fenech, Piero Focaccia, Riccardo Garrone, Umberto D'Orsi, Dada Gallotti, Romano Malaspina, Luciana Turina.

Antonia and Folco intend to marry, but their families have a violent dispute over the amount of her dowry. Claudio, a painter from Perugia, helps the two to marry once Folco succeeds in deflowering Antonia, who has entered a convent.

Although it has no direct debt to Boccaccio's *Decameron*, Laurenti's film is nonetheless another in an Italian series of *Decameron*-like sexploitation films.

REVIEWS: *Bianco e nero* 35 (March-April 1974): supplement 34. *Monthly Film Bulletin* 40 (July 1973): 144.

ADDITIONAL DISCUSSIONS:

Poppi, Roberto, and Mario Pecorari. *Dizionario del cinema italiano: I Film dal 1970 al 1979.* Rome: Gremese Editore, 1996.

La Produzione italiana. Rome: Unitalia Film, 1972.

38. *The Beloved Rogue* (1927)

United States; dir. Alan Crosland; United Artists.

CAST: John Barrymore, Marceline Day, Mack Swain, Conrad Veidt.

The citizens of Paris choose the poet and patriot François Villon to be their king of fools for April Fools' Day, but King Louis XI banishes Villon after the poet makes a joke at the royal expense. Villon steals a cart full of food and distributes it to the poor. He then rescues the king's ward from a forced marriage, becomes a court favorite and uncovers a plot against the king.

While the exploits of the poet and scoundrel François Villon (1431–?) have been a popular source for films, Barrymore eventually disowned this film, and critics almost universally dismissed this enormously expensive production as a slapstick attempt to imitate the swashbuckling films of Douglas Fairbanks.

REVIEWS: *Bioscope* 31 March 1927: 45–46. *Kinematograph Weekly* 24 March 1927: 57. *Moving Picture World* 2 April 1927: 505–06. *New York Times* 14 March 1927: 16. *Photoplay* 32 (June 1927): 139. *Studio* [London] 93 (January 1927): 383–88. *Variety* 16 March 1927: 17.

ADDITIONAL DISCUSSIONS:

Connelly, Robert. *The Motion Picture Guide, Silent Film, 1910–1936.* Chicago: Cinebooks, 1986.

Munden, Kenneth W., ed. *The American Film Institute Catalog, Feature Films 1921–1930.* New York: Bowker, 1971.

Studlar, Gayln. *The Mad Masquerade, Stardom and Masculinity in the Jazz Age.* New York: Columbia University Press, 1996.

The Betrayal of Charles VI of France

(1911) see *A Queen's Treachery* (1911)

39. Bidoni in Medieval Times (1914)

Italy; Cines.

Bidoni, a clown who was a fixture in a number of Italian silent films, falls into a drunken stupor and dreams he has been transported back into medieval Italy, where he has a series of misadventures.

REVIEWS: *Bioscope* 26 February 1914: supplement xiii. *Cinema* 12 February 1914: supplement 86.

40. Black Arrow (1912)

United States; Edison.

CAST: E.L. Davenport, Natalie Jerome, Charles Ogle, Harold Shaw.

Sir Daniel Brackley wants to force his ward Johanna to marry Lord Shoreby. An impending battle interrupts his plans, so he disguises Johanna as a boy and takes her with him to the front. Dick Shelton, Brackley's nephew, rescues Johanna, who in turn warns Dick that his uncle intends to kill him. Dick flees to the woods and joins forces with the enemies of his uncles, led by Will Lawless. In their ensuing adventures, Dick and Will rescue Johanna and the Duke of Gloucester and kill Shoreby and Brackley.

Set during the Wars of the Roses, this well-received film was the first of many screen adaptations of Robert Louis Stevenson's 1888 historical romance *The Black Arrow.*

REVIEWS: *Bioscope* 4 January 1912: 19. *Edison*

Kinetogram 1 January 1912: 6. *Moving Picture World* 4 November 1911: 410.

41. The Black Arrow (1948)

United States; dir. Gordon Douglas; Columbia.

ALTERNATE TITLE: *The Black Arrow Strikes.*

CAST: Janet Blair, Edgar Buchanan, Louis Hayward, George Macready, Rhys Williams.

Richard Shelton thinks that his neighbor, Sir John Sedley, has murdered his (Richard's) father when the real culprit is Richard's uncle, Sir Daniel Brackley. Brackley wishes to secure the Sedley estates and marry the heiress Joanna. Shelton and Johanna outwit Brackley and, with the aid of Will Lawless, foil Brackley's plans. In a trial by combat, Shelton defeats Brackley.

Reviewers of this adaptation of Robert Louis Stevenson's 1888 historical romance commented positively on its "Robin Hood manner." The film is a decent-enough formula swashbuckler that manages to balance romance with derring-do.

REVIEWS: *Kinematograph Weekly* 2 July 1948: 21–22. *Monthly Film Bulletin* 15 (31 August 1948) 110. *Motion Picture Herald* 3 July 1948: Product Digest Section 4225. *New York Times* 4 October 1948: 14. *Today's Cinema* 16 July 1948: 8. *Variety* 30 June 1948: 10.

ADDITIONAL DISCUSSIONS:

Nash, Jay Robert, and Stanley Ralph Ross. *The Motion Picture Guide, A–B, 1927–1983.* Chicago: Cinebooks, 1985.

Richards, Jeffrey. *Swordsmen of the Screen from Douglas Fairbanks to Michael York.* London: Routledge & Kegan Paul, 1977.

The Black Arrow (1959) see *L'Arciere nero* (1959)

42. The Black Arrow (1985)

United States; dir. John Hough; The Disney Channel and Pan-Atlantic Pictures Productions.

CAST: Roy Boyd, Stephan Chase, Donald Pleasence, Fernando Rey, Oliver Reed, Georgina Slowe, Benedict Taylor.

Sir Daniel Brackley, supposed defender of the House of York, is guardian of both Johanna and Richard. The former is the daughter of his enemy, who is known only as "Black Arrow." Banished to France, Black Arrow returns as an outlaw to rescue Richard and Johanna and to lead the Lancastrian forces against the Yorkists.

In this made-for-cable-television adaptation of Robert Louis Stevenson's 1888 historical romance, the villains — Reed as Brackley and Rey as the Earl of Warwick — get top billing and the best lines and scenes.

DISCUSSIONS:
Cine español 1985. Madrid: Ministerio de cultura, 1986.
Marrill, Alvin H. *Movies Made for Television, 1964–1986.* New York: Zoetrope, 1987.

The Black Arrow (1985) see *Chernaya strela* (1985)

The Black Arrow Strikes (1948) see *The Black Arrow* (1948)

43. The Black Cauldron (1985)

United States; dir. Ted Berman and Richard Rich; Disney.

CAST: (the voices of) Grant Bardsley, John Byner, Brandon Call, Nigel Hawthorne, Freddie Jones, Gregory Levinson, Arthur Malet, Adele Malis-Morey, Eda Reiss Merin, Lindsay Rich, Susan Sheridan.

Tarin dreams of becoming a warrior so that he can prevent the Horned King from seizing the black cauldron, a source of supernatural power. To do so, a ragtag group comprised of a psychic pig, a princess and assorted witches and fairies joins forces with Tarin, who eventually triumphs over the villain.

Based on Lloyd Alexander's Newbery Award–winning series of five novels (*The Prydain Chronicles,* originally published in the 1960s), this film took ten years and $25 million to make. It is an example of Disney animation at its best.

REVIEWS: *American Film* 10 (July-August 1985): 8. *Cinefantastique* 13 (June-July 1983): 26–27; 15 (July 1985): 15; 15 (January 1986): 44. *Cinema* [Paris] 331 (27 November–3 December 1985): 5. *Ecran fantastique* 63 (December 1985): 9. *Fantasy and Science Fiction* 69 (October 1985): 109–10. *Films and Filming* 373 (October 1985): 34. *Hollywood Reporter* 22 July 1985: 3, 18. *Los Angeles Times* 24 July 1985: Calendar 1, 3. *Monthly Film Bulletin* 52 (October 1985): 305–06. *New York Times* 26 July 1985: C5. *Revue du cinéma* 411 (December 1985): 30–32. *Screen International* 19–26 October 1985: 416. *Segnocinema* 6 (May 1986): 90. *Séquences* 122 (October 1985): 60–62. *Starburst* 8 (December 1985): 30. *Sunday Times* [London] 13 October 1985: 38. *Times* [London] 11 October 1985: 13. *Variety* 24 July 1985: 16.

ADDITIONAL DISCUSSIONS:
Adamson, Joe. "What's Cooking in the *Black Cauldron.*" *American Cinematographer* 66 (July 1985): 60–68.
Barrier, Mike. *The Black Cauldron. Funnyworld* 20 (Summer 1979): 27–31.
Bouzereau, Laurent. "Taram et le chaudron magique." *Ecran fantastique* 62 (November 1985): 24–29.
Grant, John. *Encyclopedia of Walt Disney's Animated Characters.* New York: Harper & Row, 1987.
Holliss, Richard. *The Black Cauldron. Starburst* 8 (December 1985): 26–30.
Magill, Frank N., ed. *Magill's Cinema Annual, 1986.* Englewood Cliffs, N.J.: Salem, 1986.
Nash, Jay Robert, and Stanley Ralph Ross. *The Motion Picture Guide, 1986 Annual (The Films of 1985).* Chicago: Cinebooks, 1987.

The Black Decameron see *Il Decamerone nero* (1972)

44. Black Knight (1911)

Great Britain; Charles Urban Trading Company.

Two rivals for the hand of Lady Griselle engage in combat, one disguised as the Black Knight.

REVIEW: *Bioscope* 5 January 1911: 41.

45. The Black Knight (1954)

Great Britain; dir. Tay Garnett; Warwick-Columbia.

CAST: Richard Adam, Harry Andrews, Bill Brandon, Anthony Bushnell, Peter Cushing, Alan Ladd, Jean Lodge, Patricia Medina, Andre Morell, Patrick Troughton.

John, a poverty-stricken sword maker, learns that the Viking attacks on England are really the handiwork of Sir Palamides, a knight of the Round Table, and his ally, King Mark. Both intend to overthrow Arthur and supplant Christianity in England with paganism. John becomes a knight and saves the kingdom from Palamides and Mark, while also winning the hand of his lady love, the fair Linet.

Henry and DeSourdis dismiss this film as "so terrible" that it is "fun" (198) — a view generally shared by most critics. More recently, however, Alan Lupack has advanced an alternate reading of the film arguing convincingly that *The Black Knight* needs to be read as a statement against the politics of the 1950s. Against such a backdrop, the film can be "seen as an allegory for the triumph of American values over a Communist threat" (38).

REVIEWS: *Film Daily* 21 October 1954: 6. *Harrison's Reports* 23 October 1954: 120. *Hollywood Re-*

The Princess Eilonwy and Tarin in Ted Berman and Richard Rich's animated *The Black Cauldron* (1985).

porter 9 November 1954: 3. *Kinematograph Weekly* 26 August 1954: 21–22. *Monthly Film Bulletin* 21 (October 1954): 147. *Motion Picture Herald* 23 October 1954: Product Digest Section 185. *New York Times* 29 October 1954: 44. *To-day's Cinema* 25 August 1954: 10. *Variety* 8 September 1954: 6.

ADDITIONAL DISCUSSIONS:
Henry, Marilyn, and Ron De Sourdis. *The Films of Alan Ladd.* Secaucus, N.J.: Citadel, 1981.
Lupack, Alan. "An Enemy in Our Midst: *The Black Knight* and the American Dream." In Kevin J. Harty, ed. *Cinema Arthuriana, Essays on Arthurian Film.* New York: Garland, 1991.
Nash, Jay Robert, and Stanley Ralph Ross. *The Motion Picture Guide, A–B, 1927–1983.* Chicago: Cinebooks, 1985.
Richards, Jeffrey. *Swordsmen of the Screen from Douglas Fairbanks to Michael York.* London: Routledge & Kegan Paul, 1977.
Umland, Rebecca A., and Samuel J. Umland. *The Use of Arthurian Legend in Hollywood Film from Connecticut Yankees to Fisher Kings.* Westport, Conn.: Greenwood, 1996.

46. *The Black Rose* (1950)

United States; dir. Henry Hathaway; 20th Century–Fox.

CAST: Cecile Aubry, Finlay Currie, Jack Hawkins, Henry Oscar, Tyrone Power, Michael Renee, Orson Welles.

In thirteenth-century England, two young Saxons who were still upset about the Norman Conquest join a caravan bound for Persia and the realms of Kublai Khan, whose forces they join in battles against the Chinese. After numerous adventures, they return to England, bringing back with them the wonders of the Orient.

This overly long adaptation of Thomas Costain's 1946 novel *The Black Rose* is impressive enough technically, but the plot drags and the dialogue ranges from the artificial to the downright silly.

Alan Ladd in the title role in Tay Garnett's *The Black Knight* (1954).

REVIEWS: *Film Daily* 8 August 1950: 12. *Hollywood Reporter* 7 August 1950: 3. *Kinematograph Weekly* 13 July 1950: 18–19. *Monthly Film Bulletin* 17 (August 1950): 118. *Motion Picture Herald* 24 June 1950: Product Digest Section 359; 12 August 1950: Product Digest Section 433. *New York Times* 5 September 1950: 11. *Revue du cinéma* [La Saison cinématographique] Hors série 32 (1950–1951): 151–52. *Times* [London] 8 September 1950: 6. *To-day's Cinema* 12 July 1950: 11. *Variety* 9 August 1950: 8.

ADDITIONAL DISCUSSIONS:

Belafonte, David, and Alvin H. Marill. *The Films of Tyrone Power.* Secaucus, N.J.: Citadel, 1979.

Canham, Kingsley. *The Hollywood Professionals: Michael Curtiz, Raoul Walsh, Henry Hathaway.* New York: A.S. Barnes, 1973.

Cardiff, Jack. "Shooting a Medieval Documentary." *American Cinematographer* 31 (November 1950): 378–79, 394.

James, Howard. *The Complete Films of Orson Welles.* New York: Citadel, 1991.

Nash, Jay Robert, and Stanley Ralph Ross. *The Motion Picture Guide, A–B, 1927–1983.* Chicago: Cinebooks, 1985.

Richards, Jeffrey. *Swordsmen of the Screen from Douglas Fairbanks to Michael York.* London: Routledge & Kegan Paul, 1977.

47. *The Black Shield of Falworth* (1954)

United States; dir. Rudolph Maté; Universal-International.

CAST: Tony Curtis, David Farrar, Craig Hill, Ian Keith, Janet Leigh, Herbert Marshall, Daniel O'Herlihy, Patrick O'Neal, Barbara Rush, Torin Thatcher, Rhys Williams.

Because King Henry IV is ailing, real power in England rests with the wicked Earl of Alban. Prince Hal plots with the Earl of Macworth to undermine the wicked earl's influence. Among those who serve at Macworth Castle are two peasants, Myles and Meg Falworth, who are really children of the wrongly dishonored Earl of Falworth. King Henry knights Myles and he defeats Alban, who had defamed and killed Myles and Meg's father.

Based on Howard Pyle's 1892 novel *Men of Iron,* this film is best remembered for Tony Curtis's portrayal of Myles, who combined athletic prowess and determination, but could never quite overcome the actor's New York accent.

REVIEWS: *Film Daily* 3 August 1954: 3. *Films and Filming* 1 (October 1954): 24. *Hollywood Reporter* 3 August 1954: 3. *Kinematograph Weekly* 2 September 1954: 16, 21. *Monthly Film Bulletin* 21 (October 1954): 142–43. *Motion Picture Herald* 7 August 1954: Product Digest Section 97. *New York Times* 7 October 1954: 16. *To-day's Cinema* 30 August 1954: 6. *Variety* 4 August 1954: 6.

DISCUSSIONS:

Hunter, Allan. *Tony Curtis, The Man and His Movies.* New York: St. Martin's, 1985.

Nash, Jay Robert, and Stanley Ralph Ross. *The Motion Picture Guide, A–B, 1927–1983.* Chicago: Cinebooks, 1985.

Parish, James Robert, and Don E. Stanke. *The Swashbucklers.* New Rochelle, N.Y.: Arlington House, 1976.

Richards, Jeffrey. *Swordsmen of the Screen from Douglas Fairbanks to Michael York.* London: Routledge & Kegan Paul, 1977.

48. *Blanche* (1971)

France; dir. Walerian Borowczyk; Abel et Charton/Telepress Films.

CAST: Ligia Brancie, Jacques Perrin, Michel Simon, Lawrence Trimble, Georges Wilson.

In thirteenth century France, the beautiful young Blanche is married to a much older man. Unbeknown to either, her stepson is madly in love with her. The arrival of the king only complicates matters, because both the king and his page also have amorous designs on Blanche. Before matters finally resolve themselves, Blanche commits suicide, and her stepson and the king's page are killed.

An extremely brutal film, *Blanche* (based on the nineteenth century novel *Mazepa* by Juliusz Slowacki) paints a fairly accurate portrait of the Middle Ages, using period castles, costumes and music to underscore the view of the medieval that the film offers.

REVIEWS: *Avant-scène du cinéma* 125 (May 1972): 70–71. *Cinéma* 164 (March 1972): 117–119. *Ecran* 3 (March 1972): 67–68; 5 (May 1972): 58. *Filmcritica* 364 (October 1984): 53, 56. *Films Illustrated* 3 (October 1973): 124–26. *Image et son* 258 (March 1972): 109–11. *Monthly Film Bulletin* 40 (June 1973): 473. *Positif* 138 (May 1972): 70–71. *Sight and Sound* 41 (Winter 1971-72): 33–34; NS 5 (July 1995): 58; NS 6 (April 1996): 61. *Variety* 30 June 1971: 29.

ADDITIONAL DISCUSSIONS:

Bren, Frank. *World Cinema 1: Poland.* London: Flicks Books, 1986.

Nash, Jay Robert, and Stanley Ralph Ross. *The Motion Picture Guide, A–B, 1927–1983.* Chicago: Cinebooks, 1985.

Trémége, Bernard. "Walerian Borwczyck." *Jeune cinéma* 61 (Feburary 1971): 11–12.

Verdi, Emile. "Entretien avec Walerian Borowczyk." *Cinéma* 164 (March 1972): 117–19.

Vialle, Gabriel. "*Blanche.*" *Image et son* 286 (1974): 59–67.

49. *Der Blinde Kreuzritter* (1909)

France; Lux.

A blind crusader returns from the Holy Land, finds his fiancée has married someone else, and has his sight restored.

DISCUSSION:

Birrett, Herbert. *Das Filmangebot in Deutschland.* Munich: Filmbuchverlag Winterberg, 1991.

50. *Boccaccio* (1936)

Germany; dir. Herbert Malsch; UFA.

ALTERNATE TITLES: *Love Tales of Boccaccio* and *Liebesgeschichten von Boccaccio.*

CAST: Fita Benkoff, Tina Eilers, Heli Finkenzeller, Gina Flackenberg, Albert Florath, Willy Fritsch, Paul Kemp, H.H. Schaufuse, Albracht Schonhal, Ernst Waldow, Helmut Weiss.

In operetta form, Malsch tells conflated but clearly bowdlerized tales from *The Decameron,* casting Boccaccio as a poor law clerk who wrote racy tales under a pseudonym only to pay for his wife's extravagant lifestyle.

REVIEWS: *New York Times* 27 February 1937: 9. *Retro* 10 (July-August 1981): 36. *Variety* 16 September 1936: 17; 3 March 1937: 15.

51. *Boccaccio* (1940)

Italy; dir. Marcello Albani; Venus-Scalera.

CAST: Luigi Almirante, Clara Calamai, Osvaldo Genazzani, Silvana Jachino, Osvaldo Valenti.

A young woman disguises herself and pretends to be Boccaccio. Confusion — the plot is liberally drawn from incidents in Boccaccio's *The Decameron*— follows upon the heels of this deception, which is only resolved when the young woman marries the young man of her dreams.

REVIEW: *Cinema* [Rome] 104 (25 October 1940): 313.

DISCUSSIONS:

Chiti, Robert, and Enrico Lancia. *Dizionario del cinema italiano.* Vol. 1: *I Film dal 1930 al 1944.* Rome: Gremese Editore, 1993.

Savio, Francesco. *Ma l'amore no.* Turin: Milan, 1975.

52. *Boccaccio* (1972)

Italy; dir. Bruno Corbucci; Dino de Laurentiis Cinematografica.

ALTERNATE TITLE: *Nights of Boccaccio.*

CAST: Isabella Biagini, Bernard Blier, Sylva Koscina, Alighiero Noschese, Pascale Petit.

Young Buffalmacco wildly pursues wine, women and jest in a series of misadventures loosely based on Boccaccio's *The Decameron.*

Here is yet another unsuccessful and poorly made attempt to imitate Pasolini's 1970 film *Decameron* by turning Boccaccio's works into codpiece comedies.

REVIEWS: *CinemaTV Today* 9 March 1974: 13. *Intermezzo* 5–7 (May-July 1972): 10. *Monthly Film Bulletin* 41 (April 1974): 69.

ADDITIONAL DISCUSSION:

Poppi, Roberto, and Mario Pecorari. *Dizionario del*

cinema italiano: I Film dal 1970 al 1979. Rome: Gremese Editore, 1996.

Boccaccio in Hungary (1981) see *A Zsarnok sziva avagy Boccaccio magyarorszagin* (1981)

Boleslaw smialy (1971) see *King Boleslaus the Bold* (1971)

53. *Le Bon Roi Dagobert* (1911)

France; dir. Georges Monca; Pathé Frères, S.C.A.G.L.

ALTERNATE TITLE: *Good King Dagobert.*

CAST: Gabrielle Chalon, Paul Landrin, Germaine Reuver.

A visual impairment causes Dagobert to see everything askew. But for the help of his prime minister, he would put his crown on crookedly and his clothes on backwards. Finding his equerry at the feet of his beloved Princess Ermintrude, Dagobert attempts to decapitate him, but the fast-thinking equerry suffers no harm by standing on his head. In a dream, the king sees the world upside down and awakens to pardon the princess and the equerry.

Here, as in *Le Bon Roi Dagobert* (1963) and *Dagobert* (1984), the seventh century Merovingian king is reduced to a buffoon.

REVIEW: *Bioscope* 4 May 1911: supplement vii.

ADDITIONAL DISCUSSION:

Bousquet, Henri. *Catalogue Pathé des années 1896 à 1914: 1910–1911.* Paris: Henri Bousquet, 1994.

54. *Le Bon Roi Dagobert* (1963)

France; dir. Pierre Chevalier; Cineurop.

ALTERNATE TITLE: *Dagobert.*

CAST: Gino Cervi, Darry Cowl, Pierre Doris, Jacques Dufilho, Michel Galabru, Marthe Mercadier, Dario Moreno, Pascale Roberts, Jean Tissier.

An eight-year-old schoolboy, who would much rather watch television, tries to write an essay on Dagobert. He imagines a world in which he and his family are figures from Dagobert's life as the king and his minister Saint-Eloi journey to Reims.

This and two other films — the 1911 silent film and the 1984 *Dagobert*—are based on the life of the Merovingian King Dagobert, who was the first to unite the Frankish kingdoms but who then died in 638 after only a decade of rule. All three films reduce him to a buffoon.

REVIEWS: *Cinématographie française* 2041 (30 November 1963): 26. *Film français* 1017 (29 November 1963): 10. *Unifrance Film* [La Production cinématographique française] 42 (October-December 1963): 9–9a.

ADDITIONAL DISCUSSION:
Cinéma français. Paris: Unifrance Film International, 1984.

Le Bon Roi Dagobert (1984) see *Dagobert* (1984)

55. *Boniface VIII* (1911)

France; dir. Geralamo Lo Savio; Pathé Frères and Film d'arte italiana, S.A.P.F.

ALTERNATE TITLE: *Bonifacio VIII*.

CAST: Attilo Fabbri, Dillo Lombardi, Bianca Lorenzoni.

Boniface VIII and Philip of France battle over the king's attempt to tax the clergy. When the king refuses to yield to Boniface, the Pope excommunicates him. The king sends an army against the Pope, who flees Rome. The Pope is captured by William of Nogaret, but at the last minute he is rescued by the citizens of Rome.

Benedetto Caetani (c. 1235–1303) became Pope on December 24, 1294. Controversy surrounded his ascension to the throne and his reign, at the end of which the so-called Babylonian Captivity began and the papacy moved to Avignon. Dante reserved a special place in Hell for Boniface VIII, and for his predecessor Celestine V, among the simoniacs (*Inferno* XIX).

REVIEW: *Bioscope* 27 April 1911: supplement v.

ADDITIONAL DISCUSSIONS:
Abel, Richard. *The Ciné Goes to Town, French Cinema, 1896–1914*. Berkeley: University of California Press, 1994.
Bousquet, Henri. *Catalogue Pathé des années 1896 à 1914: 1910–1911*. Paris: Henri Bousquet, 1994.

Bonifacio VIII (1911) see *Boniface VIII* (1911)

56. *Book of Days* (1988)

United States; dir. Meredith Monk; Alive from Off Center.

CAST: Robert Een, Andrea Goodman, Lenny Harrison, Wayne Hankin, Greger Hansen, Lucas Hoving, Karin Levitas, Rob McBrien, Meredith Monk, Toby Newman.

Twentieth century workers break through a wall to discover a fourteenth century community populated by Christians and Jews living in harmony, though threatened by plague. The film's main character is a young Jewish girl who is a visionary. The screenplay consists of a series of "people-in-the street" interviews with questions posed by contemporary reporters. The arrival of the plague ends any attempt at harmony in the town as the Christians, seeing the Jews as scapegoats, conduct a pogrom.

Monk clearly means to draw parallels here between plagues medieval and modern — the Black Death of 1348-49 and the AIDS pandemic — and the medieval pogrom and modern genocide. Her intriguing and thought-provoking film is part performance art and part experimental cinema.

REVIEWS: *Hollywood Reporter* 15 August 1990: 10, 18; 19 July 1991: 14, 53. *New York Times* 1 October 1989: 61; 19 November 1989: 2.14; 22 January 1990: C14; 19 April 1991: C24. *Variety* 30 November 1988: 13.

ADDITIONAL DISCUSSION:
Lynch, Joan Driscoll. "*Book of Days*, An Anthology of Monkwork." *Millennium Film Journal* 23–24 (Winter 1990-91): 38–47.

57. *Bosco d'amore* (1981)

Italy; dir. Alberto Bevilacqua; Bocca di Leone Cinematografica.

ALTERNATE TITLES: *Forest of Love* and *Wood of Love*.

CAST: Rodolfo Bigotti, Monica Guerritore, Stanko Molnar, Enzo Robutti.

A young couple wishes to marry, but differences in their class status prevent the union. He is a member of the nobility, and she is a peasant. His uncle is, however, sympathetic to their plight, and he sends them away as civil war threatens their hometown in hopes that they will find safety and happiness together.

Set during the turbulent first years of the Avignon Papacy (1309–1377), this film is loosely based on a tale Boccaccio tells in *The Decameron* (Day 5, Tale 3).

REVIEW: *Variety* 17 October 1981: 32.

58. *Le Bouffon* (1909)

France; dir. Victorin Jasset; Eclair.

ALTERNATE TITLE: *The Buffon*.

A jester rears his daughter in secret to protect her from his master, a lecherous prince. One of the prince's soldiers kidnaps the girl and presents her to the prince. In a struggle to

Mel Gibson as William Wallace (center) in his film *Braveheart* (1995).

resist the prince's advances, the girl is accidentally killed. Her father vows revenge, poisons
the prince and throws his body into a lake.

> REVIEW: *Variety* 15 May 1909: 15.
> ADDITIONAL DISCUSSIONS:
> Mitry, Jean. *Filmographie universelle. Tome XXIII:
> France 1910–1925. L'Ecole comique.* Paris: Centre
> national de la cinématographie, 1981.
> Savada, Elias. *The American Film Institute Catalog of
> Motion Pictures Produced in the United States:
> Film Beginnings, 1893–1910.* Metuchen, N.J.:
> Scarecrow, 1995.

Bramy raju (1967) see *Gates to Paradise*
    (1967)

59. *Brancaleone alle crociate* (1970)

Italy; dir. Mario Monicelli; Fair Film S.P.A.
ALTERNATE TITLES: *Brancaleone at the Cru-
sades* and *Brancaleone s'en va-t-aux croisades.*
CAST: Adolfi Celi, Sandro Dori, Vittorio
Gassman, Beba Loncar, Luigi Proietti, Gian-
rico Tedeschi, Lino Toffolo, Paolo Villaggio.
Brancaleone da Norica arrives with his

troops in the Holy Land intent upon freeing
the Holy Sepulcher. Instead, he has a series of
misadventures that find him caught between
the Pope and the anti-pope, who seem more
intent upon fighting each other than the infidel.

A sequel to *L'Armata Brancaleone* (1966),
this film reunites Brancaleone and his ragtag
troop of followers.

> REVIEWS: *Bianco e nero* 32 (January–February
> 1971): 100. *Cinema d'oggi* 11 January 1971: 4. *Ecran*
> 64 (December 1977): 58–59. *Lumière du cinéma* 10
> (December 1977): 26–31. *Positif* 203 (1978): 66–68.
> *Rivista del cinematografo* 1 (January 1971): 38–39.
> *Variety* 4 August 1971: 18.
> ADDITIONAL DISCUSSIONS:
> Poppi, Roberto, and Mario Pecorari. *Dizionario del
> cinema italiano: I Film dal 1970 al 1979.* Rome:
> Gremese Editore, 1996.
> *La Produzione italiana 1970/71.* Rome: Unitalia film,
> 1971.
> Sigal, Pierre André. "*Brancaleone s'en va-t-aux
> croisades:* satire d'un moyen-âge conventionel."
> *Cahiers de la cinémathèque* 42–43 (Summer
> 1985): 152–64.

Brancaleone at the Crusades (1970)
see *Brancaleone alle crociate* (1970)

Brancaleone s'en va-t-aux croisades
(1970) see *Brancaleone alle crociate*
(1970)

60. *Braveheart* (1995)

United States; dir. Mel Gibson; Paramount.
CAST: Mel Gibson, Brendan Gleeson, So-
phie Marceau, Catherine McCormack, Patrick
McGoohan.

At the end of the thirteenth century, with
succession to the Scottish throne in dispute,
Edward I of England lays feudal claim to the
Scottish crown and lands. Scottish patriots
rally around William Wallace against the English king, whose forces he defeats without the
aid of the Scottish nobility. When Wallace
marches south into England, Edward sends his
daughter-in-law Isabelle to negotiate a truce.
Isabelle falls in love with Wallace and warns
him of her father-in-law's treachery. In the battle of Falkirk, the English win because the Scottish nobles betray Wallace. Once again Edward
sends Isabelle as his emissary, and she and Wallace become lovers. Wallace is subsequently betrayed a final time by the Scottish nobility and
brutally executed.

Despite its winning Academy Awards for
Best Picture and Best Direction, *Braveheart* does
little more than mix sentimentality with excessive gore in its depiction of the medieval. *Braveheart* for all its attempts to present a hero for
the 1990s is a pale throwback to earlier epic
films such as *El Cid* and even *Alexander Nevsky*,
films less casual in their handling of the uneasy
mix between history and legend. The film's gra-
tuitously homophobic treatment of Edward II
as a mincing, rouge-cheeked effete is without
basis in history as is its suggestion that the true
father of Edward III was William Wallace (c.
1274–1305). The prince was not born until 1312.
Wallace was indeed the champion of Scottish
independence, whom Edward I had hanged,
drawn, beheaded and quartered. Wallace's exploits were first sung by the poet Henry the
Minstrel (also known as Blind Harry) in *The
Wallace,* a poem composed in about 1460 that
runs 12,000 lines in heroic couplets. The poem
claims as it source an earlier work by John Blair,
who was supposedly Wallace's chaplain.

REVIEWS: *Entertainment Weekly* 276 (26 May
1995): 16–18, 58–60; 318 (15 March 1996): 70–72.
Film & History 25.1–2 (1995): 58–59, 76. *Film Journal* 98 (June 1995): 42. *Film Review* [London] 300
(October 1995): 54–55. *Hollywood Reporter* 19–
21 May 1995: 11, 16. *Los Angeles Times* 24 May 1995:
Calendar 1. *Movieline* 6 (May 1995): 44; 6 (August
1995): 33. *New York Times* 24 May 1995: C15, C19.
Positif 417 (November 1995): 42. *Premiere* 9 (March
1996): 89. *Première* 223 (October 1995): 4, 26. *Sight
and Sound* NS5 (September 1995): 45. *Studio* [Paris]
98 (May 1995): 31; 103 (October 1995): 12. *Sunday
Times* [London] 17 September 1995: 1. 15. *Times*
[London] 7 September 1995: 31. *Variety* 22 May 1995:
91, 96.

ADDITIONAL DISCUSSIONS:

Fhaner, Beth A., and Christopher P. Scanlon, eds.
   Magill's Cinema Annual 1996. Detroit: Gale,
   1996.
Katelan, Jean-Yves. "Mad Mac." *Première* 223 (Oc-
   tober 1995): 58–70.
Lavoignat, Jean-Pierre. "Mel Gibson — l'âme d'un
   guerrier." *Studio* [Paris] 103 (October 1995): 80–
   85.
Levich, Jacob, ed. *The Motion Picture Guide, 1996
   Annual (The Films of 1995)*. New York: Cine-
   Books, 1996.
Probst, Chris. "Cinematic Transcendence." *Ameri-
   can Cinematographer* 77 (June 1996): 74–94.
Shapiro, Marc. "*Braveheart:* A Long Journey into
   Blood." *Film Review* [London] 298 (August 1995)
   51–56.

61. *Brother Sun, Sister Moon* (1972)

Italy; dir. Franco Zeffirelli; Euro Interna-
tional-Vic Films.
ALTERNATE TITLE: *Fratello sole, sorella luna.*
CAST: Judi Bowker, Valentina Cortese,
Kenneth Cranham, Graham Faulkner, Michael
Feast, Alec Guinness, Leigh Lawson, Lee Mon-
tague, Nicholas Willatt.

Francis returns to Assisi from war with Perugia and vows to embrace a religious life.
After some difficulty, he wins papal recogni-
tion of his new order.

This film of the life of St. Francis (1182–
1226) is visually arresting, but fairly placid and
too slow-moving and reverential for its own
good.

REVIEWS: *Amis du film et de la télévision* 209
(October 1973): 10–11. *Cineforum* 112 (March 1972):
90–92. *Cinéma* [Paris] 181 (November 1973):
142–143. *CinemaTV Today* 21 April 1973: 12. *Films
and Filming* 19 (May 1973): 45. *Films in Review* 24
(April 1973): 237. *Hollywood Reporter* 21 March 1973:
3. *Los Angeles Times* 12 April 1973: 4. 1, 20. *Monthly
Film Bulletin* 40 (April 1973): 76. *New York Times* 9
April 1973: 48. *Rivista del cinematografo* 7 (July

Judi Bowker as Clare and Graham Faulkner as Francis in Franco Zeffirelli's *Brother Sun, Sister Moon* (1972).

1972): 365–57. *Séquences* [Canada] 73 (July 1973): 23–26. *Sunday Times* [London] 4 March 1973: 30. *Times* [London] 24 March 1973: 9. *Variety* 21 March 1973: 18.

DISCUSSIONS:

Arnold, James. "St. Francis for the 70s." *St. Anthony Messenger* 80 (May 1973): 32–41.

Demby, Betty Jeffries. "An Interview with Franco Zeffirelli." *Filmmakers Newsletter* 6 (September 1973): 31–34.

Huss, Roy. "The Prodigal Son Theme in Zeffirelli's *Brother Sun, Sister Moon.*" *Film/Pyschology Review* 4 (Winter-Spring 1980): 105–13.

Nash, Jay Robert, and Stanley Ralph Ross. *The Motion Picture Guide, A–B, 1927–1983.* Chicago: Cinebooks, 1985.

Poppi, Roberto, and Mario Pecorari. *Dizionario del cinema italiano: I Film dal 1970 al 1979.* Rome: Gremese Editore, 1996.

La Produzione italiana 1971/72. Rome: Unitalia film, 1972.

The Buffon (1909) see *Le Bouffon* (1909)

62. *El Caballero del dragon* (1985)

Spain; dir. Fernando Colomo; Salamandra Productions.

ALTERNATE TITLES: *The Knight of the Dragon* and *Star Knight.*

CAST: Miguel Bosé, Harvey Keitel, Klaus Kinski, María Lomar, Fernando Rey, Julieta Serrano, José Vivó.

In medieval Spain, an alchemist searching for the fabled philosopher's stone does battle with the small-minded local bishop. Both of them seek the favor of the local count. A spaceship arrives, depositing an extra-terrestrial (whom everyone mistakes for a dragon) in their midst. The extraterrestrial helps the alchemist and ends up marrying the daughter of the count, as the bishop and the count are sent off into outer space.

Things recognizably medieval—the alchemist's name, for instance, is Boethius suggesting a link to Anicius Manlius Severinus

Boethius (c. 475–524), one of the most important figures in medieval thought — regularly pop up in this film whose parts never quite add up to a whole. The models here could have been *E.T. — The Extraterrestrial*, the seriousness of which this film lacks, or anything by Monty Python, whose satiric edge Colomo and his cast seem incapable of even approaching.

REVIEWS: *Cineinforme* 479 (January 1986): 21–22; 480 (February 1986): 35. *Ecran fantastique* 67 (April 1986): 50–51. *Variety* 19 February 1986: 291.

ADDITIONAL DISCUSSIONS:
Cine español 1985. Madrid: Ministerio de Cultura/Instituto de Cine, 1986.
Jordan, Angel. "Fernando Colomo se pasa a la leyenda en 'El Caballero del dragon.'" *Cineinforme* 475 (November 1985): 18–19.
Rège, Philippe. *Klaus Kinski*. Lausanne, Switz.: Pierre-Marcel Favre, 1987.
Schwartz, Ronald. *The Great Spanish Films: 1950–1990*. Metuchen, N.J.: Scarecrow, 1991.

63. *Le Cabinet de Méphistophélès* (1897)

France; dir. Georges Méliès; Star.
ALTERNATE TITLES: *The Devil's Laboratory* and *The Laboratory of Mephistopheles*.
CAST: Georges Méliès.
Mephistopheles the devil appears in several forms before revealing his true self.

Méliès was fascinated by the figure of Mephistopheles, a role he again played in a number of later films.

DISCUSSIONS:
158 scénarios de films disparus de Georges Méliès. Paris: Association les amis de Georges Méliès, 1986.
Savada, Elias. *The American Film Institute Catalog of Motion Pictures Produced in the United States: Film Beginnings, 1893–1910*. Metuchen, N.J.: Scarecrow, 1995.

64. *Cadfael* (1994)

Great Britain; dir. Graham Theakston; Central Films.
CAST: Susan Badel, John Bennett, Mark Charnock, Peter Copley, Michael Culver, Tara Fitzgerald, Susan Fleetwood, Jonathan Firth, Jonathan Hyde, Derek Jacobi, Sean Pertwee.

A former crusader returns home to England to take the monk's cowl under the name of Brother Cadfael. Assigned the position of herbalist, Cadfael uses his powers of detection to help the Undersheriff of Shrewsbury solve an assortment of crimes.

Based on four novels from the popular series of Cadfael mysteries by Ellis Peters (Edith Pargeter), this British import first aired in the United States in January and February 1995 on PBS's *Mystery!* in weekly 90-minute episodes ("The Leper of St. Giles," "One Corpse Too Many," "The Sanctuary Sparrow" and "Monk's Hood").

REVIEWS: *Entertainment Weekly* 258 (20 January 1995): 42. *New York Times* 12 January 1995: C26. *Television Today* 9 June 1994: 23. *Times* [London] 30 May 1994: 31. *TV Guide* 7 January 1995: 45, 203.

ADDITIONAL DISCUSSIONS:
"Act of Faith." *Radio Times* [London] 18 June 1994: 7.
Greaves, William. "This Woman Has Murder on Her Mind." *Radio Times* [London] 28 May 1994: 46–47.

65. *La Calandria* (1973)

Italy; dir. Pasquale Festa Campanile; Filmes Cinematografica.
CAST: Agostina Belli, Barbara Bouchet, Lando Buzzanca, Salvo Randone.

Lidio, a young man with a taste for the finer things in life, is in love with the unhappily married wife of Calandria, a foolish older man. To satisfy his lusts, Lidio disguises himself as a courtesan with whom Calandria promptly falls in love. After a game of mistaken identity, Lidio and the young wife are finally united in the same bed.

This film is based on the 1506 comedy *La Calandria* by Cardinal Bibbiena (Berbardo Diovisi), which combined materials from Boccaccio's *The Decameron* and Plautus's *Menaechmi*.

REVIEW: *Bianco e nero* 35 (March-April 1974): supplement 35.

ADDITIONAL DISCUSSIONS:
Poppi, Roberto, and Mario Pecorari. *Dizionario del cinema italiano: I Film dal 1970 al 1979*. Rome: Gremese Editore, 1996.
La Produzione italiana 1972/73. Rome: Unitalia Film, 1973.

66. *Le Calde notti del Decamerone* (1971)

Italy; dir. Gian Paolo Callegari; Ester Cinematografica.
ALTERNATE TITLE: *The Hot Nights of the Decameron*.
CAST: Don Backy, Femi Benussi, Pupo De Luca, Orchidea De Santis, Carla Mancini,

Krista Nell, Allesandro Perrella, Salvatore Puntillo.

Against the backdrop of an impending crusade, a young boy from a country inn is invited to live in the castle of the local duke, whom he joins in a series of amorous adventures.

While the title here nods in the direction of Boccaccio, this film shares little in common with the poet's collection of tales or Pasolini's oft-imitated 1971 film *The Decameron*. Instead, Callegari presents a series of repetitive and increasingly boring sexual misadventures.

DISCUSSIONS:

Poppi, Roberto, and Mario Pecorari. *Dizionario del cinema italiano: I Film dal 1970 al 1979*. Rome: Gremese Editore, 1996.

La Produzione italiana 1971/72. Rome: Unitalia Film, 1972.

67. *The Call to Arms* (1910)

United States; dir. D.W. Griffith; Biograph.

CAST: Linda Arvidson, Dell Henderson, James Kirkwood, Marion Leonard, Owen Moore, Mary Pickford, Mack Sennett, Henry B. Walthall.

A lord of the manor has in his possession a ruby of great value which a cousin covets. The cousin threatens the mistress of the house, who, in trying to flee from him, falls to her death from a balcony. The lord beheads his cousin.

All that makes *The Call to Arms* an example of medieval film is the simple fact that the actors wear medieval costumes.

REVIEWS: *Bioscope* 8 September 1910: 67. *Moving Picture World* 30 July 1910: 257; 6 August 1910: 296–97.

ADDITIONAL DISCUSSIONS:

Bowser, Eileen, ed. *Biograph Bulletins 1908–1912*. New York: Octagon, 1973.

Griffith, Mrs. D.W. [Linda Arvidson]. *When the Movies Were Young*. 1925. Rpt. New York: Benjamin Blom, 1968.

Niver, Kemp R. *Early Motion Pictures. The Paper Print Collection in the Library of Congress*. Washington, D.C.: Library of Congress, 1985.

Savada, Elias. *The American Film Institute Catalog of Motion Pictures Produced in the United States: Film Beginnings, 1893–1910*. Metuchen, N.J.: Scarecrow, 1995.

68. *Camelot* (1967)

United States; dir. Joshua Logan; Warner Bros.–Seven Arts.

CAST: Richard Harris, David Hemmings, Lionel Jeffries, Laurence Naismith, Franco Nero, Vanessa Redgrave, Estelle Winwood.

Unwilling at first to marry, Arthur by chance encounters his bride-to-be Guinevere in a forest. After the royal wedding, Arthur establishes an order of chivalry whose symbol is the Round Table. The fame of the order spreads and brings the eager Lancelot du Lac from France to join the knights of the Round Table. First resentful of Lancelot, Guinevere soon falls in love with him, and the two become secret lovers. When rumors of their adultery surface, Arthur ignores them and sends those who try to force the issue into exile, where they rally around Mordred, Arthur's illegitimate son. Mordred sets a trap for Lancelot and Guinevere. Lancelot escapes, but Guinevere is found guilty and sentenced to be burned at the stake. Lancelot rescues Guinevere, but the dream of Camelot is doomed.

Based on the successful 1960 Broadway play by Alan Jay Lerner and Frederick Loewe, which was in turn based on T.H. White's *The Once and Future King* (first published as a tetralogy in 1958), this film has had few neutral critics; most of them responded negatively to it. The charges leveled against the film are generally that the lead roles were miscast, that the direction was ponderous and that, at nearly three hours, the film was too long. The film did, nonetheless, win Academy Awards for art and set direction, costume and best musical scoring. It was also nominated for best cinematography and sound.

REVIEWS: *Bianco e nero* 29 (May-June 1968): 161–63. *Daily Cinema* 17 November 1967: 6. *Film Daily* 26 October 1967: 3, 6. *Film Facts* 10 (15 November 1967): 280–81. *Film Quarterly* 21 (Spring 1968): 56. *Films and Filming* 14 (November 1967): 15–17; 14 (January 1968): 22. *Films in Review* 18 (December 1967): 649–50. *Hollywood Reporter* 25 October 1967: 3, 14. *Kinematograph Weekly* 18 November 1967: 10, 18. *Le Monde* 17–18 March 1968: 17. *Monthly Film Bulletin* 35 (January 1968): 3. *Motion Picture Herald* 1 November 1967: Product Digest Section 737. *New York Times* 26 October 1967: 54. *Times* [London] 16 November 1967: 8. *Variety* 25 October 1967: 6.

ADDITIONAL DISCUSSIONS:

Borgzinner, Jon. "The Shining Pageant of Camelot" and "The Limerick Lad in King Arthur's Court." *Life* 63 (22 September 1967): 70–76, 79–80, 84, 86.

Bragg, Melvyn. *Richard, the Life of Richard Burton*. London: Hodder & Stoughton, 1988.

Combs, Carl. Camelot: *The Movie Souvenir Book*. New York: National, 1968.

Elley, Derek. *The Epic Film*. London: Routledge & Kegan Paul, 1984.

Franco Nero (left) as Lancelot, Richard Harris as Arthur, and Vanessa Redgrave as Guinevere in Joshua Logan's *Camelot* (1967).

Grellner, Alice. "Two Films That Sparkle: *The Sword in the Stone* and *Camelot*." In Kevin J. Harty, ed. *Cinema Arthuriana, Essays on Arthurian Film*. New York: Garland, 1981.

Knee, Allan, ed. *Selections from* Idylls of the King *and* Camelot. New York: Dell, 1967.

Krafsur, Richard P., ed. *The American Film Institute Catalog of Motion Pictures: Feature Films 1961– 1970*. New York: Bowker, 1976.

Lightman, Herb A. "Capturing on Film the Mythical Magic of *Camelot*." *American Cinematographer* 49 (January 1968): 30–33.

Logan, Joshua. *Movie Stars, Real People, and Me*. New York: Delacorte, 1978.

Nash, Jay Robert, and Stanley Ralph Ross. *The Motion Picture Guide, C–D, 1927–1983*. Chicago: Cinebooks, 1985.

Parish, James Robert, and Michael R. Pitts. *The Great Hollywood Musical Pictures*. Metuchen, N.J.: Scarecrow, 1992.

Redgrave, Vanessa. *Vanessa Redgrave, An Autobiography*. New York: Random House, 1994.

Schroth, Evelyn. "Camelot: Contemporary Interpretation of Arthur in 'Sens' and 'Matière.'" *Journal of Popular Culture* 17 (Fall 1983): 31–43.

Umland, Rebecca A., and Samuel J. Umland. *The Use of Arthurian Legend in Hollywood Film from Connecticut Yankees to Fisher Kings*. Westport, Conn.: Greenwood, 1996.

69. *Camelot* (1982)

United States; dir. Marty Callner; HBO.

CAST: Richard Backus, Meg Bussert, Richard Harris, Barrie Ingham, Robert Muenz, James Valentine.

HBO's presentation of the Broadway revival of the Lerner and Loewe musical, which first aired on September 26, 1982, received respectable reviews for its production values and for Harris's portrayal of Arthur.

REVIEWS: *Films in Review* 33 (November 1982): 567–69. *Hollywood Reporter* 24 September 1982: 30. *New York Times* 24 September 1982: C27.

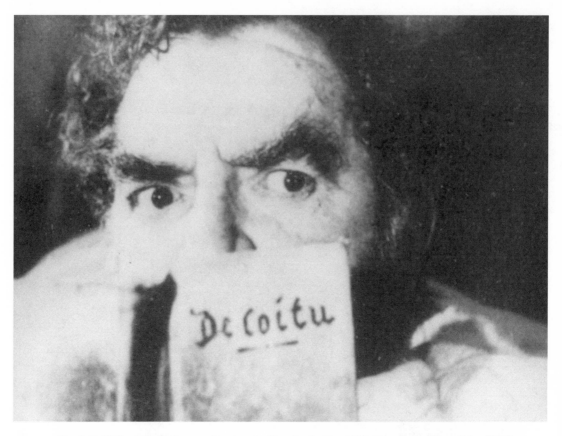

Hugh Griffith as the lecherous January in Pier Paolo Pasolini's _The Canterbury Tales_ (1971).

ADDITIONAL DISCUSSION:
Ashley, Franklin. "They Haven't Heard the Last of Richard Harris." _TV Guide_ 25 September 1982: 27–29.

70. _The Canterbury Tales_ (1971)

Italy; dir. Pier Paolo Pasolini; Cinematografica, Produzioni Europee Associate and Le Productions Artistes Associés.

ALTERNATE TITLE: _I Racconti di Canterbury._

CAST: Laura Betti, George Bethell Datch, Derek Deadman, Hugh Griffith, Pier Paolo Pasolini, J.P. Van Dyne.

This compilation of stories drawn from Chaucer retells in whole or part the tales of the Merchant, the Friar, the Cook, the Miller, the Wife of Bath, the Reeve, the Pardoner and the Summoner.

Pasolini, who plays the role of Chaucer in the film, made this as the second in a trilogy of cinematic retellings of medieval narrative cycles. The first was _The Decameron_ (1971), and

the third was _The Arabian Nights_ (1974). Critical response to the Canterbury film generally finds that it does not even approach the artistry of its source.

REVIEWS: _Cinéma_ [Paris] 164 (March 1972): 56–60; 172 (January 1973): 119–21. _Cinema nuovo_ 220 (November-December 1972): 463. _Films and Filming_ 19 (June 1973): 46–47. _Image et son_ 268 (February 1973): 112–13. _Jeune cinéma_ 68 (February 1973): 30–32. _Los Angeles Times_ 19 March 1980: 6. 10; 31 October 1980: 65. _Monthly Film Bulletin_ 40 (July 1973): 151. _New York Times_ 30 May 1980: C6. _Positif_ 147 (February 1973): 72–73. _Revue du cinéma_ 465 (November 1990): 33. _Rivista del cinematografo_ 3–4 (March-April 1973): 159–60. _Sunday Times_ [London] 17 June 1973: 37. _Téléciné_ 177 (February 1973): 16–17. _Times_ [London] 20 November 1971: 7; 15 June 1973: 9. _Variety_ 12 July 1972: 30.

ADDITIONAL DISCUSSIONS:
Bondanella, Peter. _The Italian Cinema from Neorealism to the Present._ 2nd ed. New York: Ungar, 1990.
Friedrich, Pia. _Pier Paolo Pasolini._ Boston: Twayne, 1982.
Gambetti, Giacomo. "Per una 'trilogia popolare, lib-

era, erotica.'" *Cineforum* 121 (March 1973): 221–29.

Green, Martin. "The Dialectic of Adaptation: *The Canterbury Tales* of Pier Paolo Pasolini." *Literature/Film Quarterly* 4 (Winter 1976): 46–53.

Pasolini, Pier Paolo. *Trilogia della vita.* Bologna: Cappelli, 1975. [Screenplay.]

Poppi, Roberto, and Mario Pecorari. *Dizionario del cinema italiano: I Film dal 1970 al 1979.* Rome: Gremese Editore, 1996.

La Produzione itialana 1971/72. Rome: Unitalia film, 1972.

Rondolino, Gianni, ed. *Catalogo Bolaffi del cinema italiano 1966/1975.* Turin: Bolafi Editore, 1975.

Schwartz, David. *Pasolini Requiem.* New York: Pantheon, 1992.

Snyder, Stephen. *Pier Paolo Pasolini.* Boston: Twayne, 1980.

Viano, Maurizio. *A Certain Realism.* Berkeley: University of California Press, 1993.

Willemen, Paul, ed. *Pier Paolo Pasolini.* London: BFI, 1976.

71. *Capitan Fuoco* (1958)

Italy; dir. Carlo Campogalliani; Transfilm.
ALTERNATE TITLE: *Captain Falcon—Adventurer.*

CAST: Lex Barker, Rossana Rory, Massimo Serato.

Baron Oddo has designs on a neighboring dukedom and hires assassins to kill the reigning duke. The duke's daughter Elena assumes that Captain Falcon—a Robin Hood–like local named Pietro—is responsible for the murder since he had previously championed the cause of the people against her father. When Oddo kidnaps Elena, Falcon rescues her and kills the baron.

Set in thirteenth century Italy, the film represents little more than a spaghetti Western set in the Middle Ages.

REVIEWS: *Cinématographie française* 6 February 1960: 18. *Daily Cinema* 21 April 1961: 9. *Intermezzo* 14 (15 February 1959): 6. *Kinematograph Weekly* 27 April 1961: 42. *Monthly Film Bulletin* 28 (June 1961): 80.

ADDITIONAL DISCUSSION:
Chiti, Roberto, and Robert Poppi. *Dizionario del cinema italiano. Vol. 2: I film dal 1945 al 1959.* Rome: Gremese Editore, 1991.

72. *Il Capitano di Venezia* (1952)

Italy; dir. Gianni Puccini; Italica.
ALTERNATE TITLE: *The Captain of Venice.*

CAST: Andrea Checchi, Leonardo Cortese, Mariella Lotti.

In an incredibly convoluted plot set in the

year 1220, rival noble Italian families hope to use marriage to thwart each other further.

REVIEW: *Intermezzo* 9 (15 March 1954): 5.
ADDITIONAL DISCUSSIONS:
Chiti, Roberto, and Robert Poppi. *Dizionario del cinema italiano. Vol. 2: I Film dal 1945 al 1959.* Rome: Gremese Editore, 1991.

The Italian Production 1952/53. Rome: Unitalia Film, 1953.

Captain Falcon—Adventurer (1958)
see *Capitan Fuoco* (1958)

The Captain of Venice (1952) see *Il Capitano di Venezia* (1952)

73. *The Captive of the Dragon* (1985)

Norway and Soviet Union; dir. Stanislav Rostotsky and Knut Andersen; Gorkij Film.

ALTERNATE TITLES: *And Trees Grew Out of Stone, And Trees Will Even Grow on Rocks, The Captive of the Vikings, Dragens fange, Even on Rocks Trees Grow, I Na kamnjakh rastut derévja* and *Oragens fange.*

CAST: John Andresen, Petronella Barker, Torgeir Fonnlid, Tor Stokke, Sasja Timoskin.

In tenth-century Russia, during a raid on a village in Novgorod, Vikings kidnap a boy whom they take back to Norway, where he falls in love with the daughter of his captor.

The film, which features breathtaking scenery, was originally heralded because it was a joint Russian-Norwegian venture involving a pupil and collaborator of Sergei Eisenstein. Its plot allows for ample intrigue, swordplay and romance.

REVIEWS: *Film og kino* 8 (August 1985): 347; 368–69. *Scandinavian Film News* 3 (December 1983): [5]; 5 (April 1985): [6]; 4 (April 1989): [6–7]. *Soviet Film* 7 (July 1985): 12–14. *Variety* 28 August 1985: 12.

ADDITIONAL DISCUSSION:
Norwegian Films 1986. Oslo: Norwegian Film Institute, 1986.

74. *The Capture of a Vagrant* (1910)

France; Pathé Frères.

In fifteenth-century France during the reign of Louis XI (1423–1483), notorious vagrant Rob Rokers escapes from prison with the aid of a band of brigands whom he joins. He abducts a gypsy girl, whom the chief of police loves. After a series of chases, the chief of police rescues the gypsy girl, and Rokers is executed by hanging.

REVIEW: *Bisocope* 10 March 1910: 53.

Spartaco Santony (left) as Fernán Gonzáles and Cesar Romero as Jeronimo in Javier Seto's *The Castilian* (1963).

75. *Casimir the Great* (1975)

Poland; dir. Ewa and Czeslaw Petelski; Polish Corporation for Film Production.

ALTERNATE TITLE: *Kazimierz Wielki.*

CAST: Krzysztoh Chamiece, Wladyslaw Hanzca, Zofia Saretok.

On his deathbed, Casimir III recalls the events of his reign including the death of his father, his first love, his battles with the Teutonic knights, his several marriages (none of which provided him with an heir), his defeat of the Tartars in a battle on the Vistula, the public madness caused by plague and famine, and his success in establishing order throughout the kingdom.

Casimir III (1310–1370), the only Polish king dubbed "the Great," was the last of the Piast rulers, the first Polish dynasty. In a reign that spanned some 40 years, he developed Poland's economy, codified its laws, strengthened its defenses and, in 1364, founded its first university, the Cracow Academy.

REVIEWS: *Film* [Poland] 4 (19 February 1976): 23; 4 (21 March 1976): 6–7. *Filmowy serwis prasowy* 21 (1–15 March 1976): 2–6. *Kino* [Poland] 6 (1976): 6–9, 10–12. *Polish Film* 2 (1976): 6–9.

ADDITIONAL DISCUSSIONS:

Polish Feature Films, Catalogue. Warsaw: Film Polski, 1975.

Sobanski, Oskar. *Polish Feature Films, A Reference Guide 1945–1985.* West Cornwall, Conn.: Locust Hill, 1987.

76. *The Castilian* (1963)

Spain and United States; dir. Javier Seto; Cinemagic.

ALTERNATE TITLES: *El Valle de las espadas* and *Valley of the Swords.*

CAST: Frankie Avalon, Germán Cobos, Broderick Crawford, Angel Del Pozo, Julio Peña, Fernando Rey, George Rigaud, Cesar Romero, Spartaco Santoni, Alida Valli, Teresa Velázquez.

In tenth century Castile, Fernán Gonzáles returns home from self-imposed exile after the death of his brother to do battle with the Moors and Don Sancho, the King of Navarre. He defeats Dan Sancho but is captured by his son. Freed from prison, Fernán attacks and defeats a vast Moorish army thanks to the heavenly assistance of St. Milan and St. Santiago, who appear to him and offer counsel. Following this victory, the Castilians and Navarrese declare a truce, and Fernán begins a peaceful and prosperous reign as King of Castile.

Based on the anonymous thirteenth century epic *El Poema de Fernán Gonzáles,* this typically adventure-packed film (doubtless meant to cash in on the success of Anthony Mann's 1961 *El Cid*) is notable for its battle scenes and for its rather eclectic cast.

REVIEWS: *Cinématographie française* 30 May 1964: 18. *Daily Cinema* 18 September 1963: 10. *Film Daily* 7 October 1963: 4. *Hollywood Reporter* 4 October 1963: 3. *Monthly Film Bulletin* 30 (November 1963): 157. *Motion Picture Herald* 30 October 1963: Product Digest Section 924. *New York Times* 3 October 1963: 31.

ADDITIONAL DISCUSSIONS:

Krafsur, Richard P., ed. *The American Film Institute Catalog of Motion Pictures: Feature Films 1961–1970.* New York: R.R. Bowker, 1976.

Lucanio, Patrick. *With Fire and Sword, Italian Spectacles on American Screens 1958–1968.* Metuchen, N.J.: Scarecrow, 1994.

Nash, Jay Robert, and Stanley Ralph Ross. *The Motion Picture Guide, C–D, 1927–1983.* Chicago: Cinebooks, 1985.

Richards, Jeffrey. *Swordsmen of the Screen from Douglas Fairbanks to Michael York.* London: Routledge & Kegan Paul, 1977.

The Spanish Cinema. Madrid: Uniespaña, 1964.

Catalan, the Minstrel (1910) see *La Véridique et Doloureuse Histoire de Catelan le ménestrel* (1910)

77. *Il Cavaliere dai cento volti* (1960)

Italy; dir. Pino Mercanti; Titanus-Romana.

CAST: Annie Alberti, Lex Barker, Livio Lorenzon, Liana Orfeo.

A knight, famous for his prowess in tournaments, is falsely accused of murder. To find the real murderer, the Black Knight, he continues to enter tournaments adopting a series of disguises.

REVIEWS: *Cinématographie française* 2 September 1961: 14. *Intermezzo* 15 (15 September 1990): 12.

ADDITIONAL DISCUSSION:

Lucanio, Patrick. *With Fire and Sword, Italian Spectacles on American Screens 1958–1968.* Metuchen, N.J.: Scarecrow, 1994.

78. *Il Cavaliere del castello maledetto* (1959)

Italy; dir. Mario Costa; Romana Film.

ALTERNATE TITLE: *The Knight of the Cursed Castle.*

CAST: Pierre Cressoy, Massimo Serato, Irene Tunc.

At the beginning of the twelfth century, Oliviero, duke of Valgrado, has disappeared, and his nephew Ugone usurps the throne. To solidify his position and to avoid the king's intervention, Ugone seeks to marry his cousin, Isabella, blaming her father's disappearance on a mysterious Black Knight. That knight turns out to be her childhood companion, Duccio, in disguise. Duccio prevents the marriage, exposes Ugone, restores Oliviero and wins the hand of Isabella as his reward.

Costa here directs yet another fairly typical spaghetti Western ostensibly set in the Middle Ages.

REVIEWS: *Cinématographie française* 6 May 1961: 26. *Filmwoche* 16 (18 November 1961): 7. *Guia de filmes* 37 (January-February 1972): 4.

ADDITIONAL DISCUSSIONS:

Chiti, Roberto, and Robert Poppi. *Dizionario del cinema italiano. Vol. 2: I Film dal 1945 al 1959.* Rome: Gremese Editore, 1991.

The Italian Production 1959. Rome: Unitalia Film, 1959.

Il Cavaliere di ferro (1949) see *Il Conte Ugolino* (1949)

79. *Il Cavaliere inesistente* (1970)

Italy; dir. Pino Zac; Instituto Luce Production.

ALTERNATE TITLE: *The Non-Existent Knight.*

CAST: Stefano Oppedisano and Hana Ruziclova.

At the time of Charlemagne, Agilulfo is famous as the knight who never sleeps, who never takes off his armor, and who is invisible. While Charlemagne battles the Turks and a mysterious nun chronicles the king's exploits, Agilulfo sets out to prove that a damsel he has previously rescued is indeed noble. She is not, but this revelation allows her to marry a commoner whom she loves.

This combination animation-live feature,

which has its source in a tale by Italo Calvino, is too much like a second-rate comic strip and not nearly enough a triumph of animation.

REVIEWS: *Bianco et nero* 32 (January-February 1971): 101. *Intermezzo* 26 (31 January 1971): 5. *Variety* 18 November 1970: 40; 1 September 1971: 22.

ADDITIONAL DISCUSSION:
Chiti, Roberto, and Robert Poppi. *Dizionario del cinema italiano. Vol. 3: I Film dal 1960 al 1969.* Rome: Gremese Editore, 1992.

80. *Una Cavalla tutta nuda* (1972)

Italy; Franco Rosetti; Hubris Film.

CAST: Don Backy, Barbara Bouchet, Rita Di Lernia, Renzo Montagnani, Carla Romanelli, Leopoldo Trieste.

In a more than convoluted plot, two impoverished emissaries from a drought-stricken town are sent to a neighboring bishop for assistance. Their journey involves a number of adventures and misadventures. At the palace of the bishop, they can no longer remember why they have come, and they get themselves into further difficulties, find themselves sentenced to death, escape and return home where the drought has seemingly ended.

REVIEW: *Intermezzo* 28 (3 March 1972): 5.
ADDITIONAL DISCUSSIONS:
Poppi, Roberto, and Mario Pecorari. *Dizionario del cinema italiano: I Film dal 1970 al 1979.* Rome: Gremese Editore, 1996.
La Produzione italiana 1971/72. Rome: Unitalia Film, 1972.

81. *I Cento cavalieri* (1964)

Italy and Spain; dir. Vittorio Cottafavi; Domiziana Internazíonale.

ALTERNATE TITLES: *Le Fils du Cid* and *The Hundred Horsemen.*

CAST: Anny Alberti, Lex Barker, Gérard Landry, Livio Lorenzon, Liana Orfei.

In a Spanish village in the year 1000, the peasants find themselves exploited by the nobility when invading Moors arrive and try to impose discipline and order on society. From afar, two groups, one of bandits and one of monks, watch what is going on. Eventually, no one escapes the resulting clashes, which pit Occidental against Oriental, rich against poor and Church against state.

REVIEWS: *Les Cahiers du cinéma* 172 (November 1965): 17; 180 (July 1966): 11–12. *Cinema nuovo* 183 (September-October 1966): 377. *Cinématographie française* 1930 (2 September 1961): 14. *Ecran* 3 (March 1972): 70–72. *Filmcritica* 156-57 (April-May 1965): 317–319. *Image et son* 263-64 (September-Oc-

tober 1972): 110–11. *Intermezzo* 20 (30 April 1965): 4. *Movie* 12 (April 1965): 18–20; 13 (July 1965): 42–43. *Positif* 108 (September 1969): 63–65.

ADDITIONAL DISCUSSIONS:
Gilles, Paul. "Vittorio Cottafavi parle des 'Cent cavaliers.'" *Les Cahiers du cinéma* 207 (December 1968): 75–77.
Poppi, Roberto, and Mario Pecorari. *Dizionario del cinema italiano. Vol. 3: I Film dal 1960 al 1969.* Rome: Gremese Editore, 1992.

82. *A Challenge for Robin Hood* (1967)

Great Britain; dir. C.M. Pennington Richards; Hammer Film Productions.

CAST: John Arnatt, Peter Blythe, Eric Flynn, Leon Green, Gay Hamilton, James Hayter, Barrie Ingham, Jenny Till.

The death of Sir John de Courtenay leaves his lands to be divided between his two sons Henry and Roger. Roger murders his brother and accuses his cousin Robin of the crime. Roger then joins forces with the Sheriff of Nottingham to oppress the Saxon poor while Robin becomes the head of a band of Merry Men who steal from the rich to give to the poor. Robin also manages to thwart the sheriff, kill Roger, succeed to his uncle's title and marry Lady Marian.

Nothing particularly distinguishes this cinematic retelling of a familiar tale, although there is nothing particularly wrong with it either. There are plenty of swordfights and chases and just a little bit of romance.

REVIEWS: *ABC Film Review* 17 (December 1967): 14–15. *Daily Cinema* 29 November 1967: 11. *Film Index* 30 (1974): 100. *Kinematograph Weekly* 2 December 1967: 7. *Monthly Film Bulletin* 35 (January 1968): 8. *New York Times* 18 June 1969: 23. *Variety* 31 July 1968: 6.

ADDITIONAL DISCUSSIONS:
Knight, Stephen. *Robin Hood, A Complete Study of the English Outlaw.* Oxford: Blackwell, 1994.
Johnson, Tom, and Deborah Del Vecchio. *Hammer Films, An Exhaustive Filmography.* Jefferson, N.C.: McFarland, 1996.
Lucanio, Patrick. *With Fire and Sword, Italian Spectacles on American Screens 1958–1968.* Metuchen, N.J.: Scarecrow, 1994.
Nash, Jay Robert, and Stanley Ralph Ross. *The Motion Picture Guide, C–D, 1927–1983.* Chicago: Cinebooks, 1985.
Richards, Jeffrey. *Swordsmen of the Screen from Douglas Fairbanks to Michael York.* London: Routledge & Kegan Paul, 1977.
Turner, David. *Robin Hood of the Movies.* Kingswinford, Eng.: Yeoman Publishing, 1989.

Klaus Kinski (left) as Roland in Frank Cassenti's *La Chanson de Roland* (1978). (Still courtesy of the British Film Institute.)

83. *La Chanson de Roland* (1978)

France; dir. Frank Cassenti; Gaumont.

ALTERNATE TITLE: *The Song of Roland*.

CAST: Pierre Clementi, Alain Cuny, Jean-Pierre Kalfon, Klaus Kinski, Monique Mercure, Dominique Sanda.

To pass the time, a group of twelfth century pilgrims join company with a troupe of actors who dramatize *The Song of Roland*. This dramatization becomes in turn a vehicle to preach against poverty and exploitation throughout the ages.

Cassenti attempts to do too much in his film. There is already a gap of almost 400 years between the time of the pilgrimage and that of Roland — although the earliest surviving manuscript of *The Song of Roland* dates from c. 1100 — a gap exacerbated by an attempt to transcend time by delivering a message that has relevance to the modern world. Kinski shines, however, first as the leader of the troupe of actors, then as Roland, and finally as a disaffected peasant intent on social reform and revolution.

REVIEWS: *Les Cahiers du cinéma* 295 (December 1978): 50–51. *Cinéma* [Paris] 239 (November 1978): 102–03. *Cinéma français* 17 (1977): 12–16; 21 (1978): [27–30]. *Cinématographe* 40 (October 1978): 77. *Continental Film Review* 25 (March 1978): 12–13.

Ecran 72 (September 1978): 65–66. *Film français* 1699 (18 November 1977): 15, 24; 1736 (22 September 1978): 14. *Hollywood Reporter* 25 September 1978: 21. *Jeune cinéma* 112 (July-August 1978): 30–31. *Positif* 212 (November 1978): 75. *Télérama* 1498 (27 November 1978): 107. *Variety* 11 October 1978: 48.

ADDITIONAL DISCUSSIONS:

Cinéma français. Paris: Unifrance Film, 1978.

Martin, Marcel. "Entretien avec Frank Cassenti." *Ecran* 72 (15 September 1978): 66–67.

Rège, Philippe. *Klaus Kinski.* Lausanne, Switz.: Pierre-Marcel Favre, 1987.

The Charge of the Black Lancers

(1961) see *I Lancieri neri* (1961)

84. *The Chastity Belt* (1967)

Italy; dir. Pasquale Festa Campanile; Julia Film.

ALTERNATE TITLES: *La Cintura di castità* and *On the Way to the Crusades, I Met a Woman Who...*

CAST: Nino Castelnuovo, Tony Curtis, Hugh Griffith, John Richardson, Monica Vitti.

The young Guerrando da Montone wins knighthood and the right to claim the land he can cover by horseback within a day. His ride leads him to a peasant hut where a young girl, Boccadoro, tries to seduce him. They marry

Tony Curtis as Guerrando da Montone and Monica Vitti as Boccadoro in Pasquale Festa Campanile's *The Chastity Belt* (1967).

eventually, but when he is called away on crusade, Guerrando locks his new wife in a chastity belt. The furious Boccadoro disguises herself as a man and follows her husband into battle. She has more success than he in defeat-

ing opponents, and after a series of misadventures in which the key to the chastity belt keeps changing hands, husband and wife are finally happily reunited.

In this badly made mishmash, Campanile

cannot quite seem to figure out whether he was directing a fairy tale or a farce.

REVIEWS: *Cinema d'oggi* 13 November 1967: 10. *Films and Filming* 15 (July 1969): 56–57. *Intermezzo* 12 (30 November 1967): 11. *Kinematograph Weekly* 1 March 1969: 27. *Monthly Film Bulletin* 36 (April 1969): 81. *Times* [London] 3 May 1967: 8. *Today's Cinema* 28 February 1969: 6. *Variety* 31 January 1968: 23.

ADDITIONAL DISCUSSIONS:
Hunter, Allan. *Tony Curtis, The Man and His Movies.* New York: St. Martin's, 1985.
Italian Production 1967. Rome: Unitalia Film, 1968.
Nash, Jay Robert, and Stanley Ralph Ross. *The Motion Picture Guide, C–D, 1927–1983.* Chicago: Cinebooks, 1985.
Poppi, Roberto, and Mario Pecorari. *Dizionario del cinema italiano. Vol. 3: I Film dal 1960 al 1969.* Rome: Gremese Editore, 1992.

85. *Chernaya strela* (1985)

Soviet Union; dir. Sergei Tarasov; Mosfilm.
ALTERNATE TITLE: *The Black Arrow.*
CAST: Galina Belayeva, Alexander Filippenko, Leonid Kulagin, Algimantas Masulis, Igor Shaviak, Yuri Smirnov.

Richard Shelton revenges the death of his father using four black arrows to dispatch the killers.

This film, which all but eliminates the political subplots of Robert Louis Stevenson's 1888 historical romance *The Black Arrow*, completes Tarasov's trilogy of medieval films for Mosfilm. The first two films in the trilogy are *Robin Hood's Arrows* (1977) and *Ballada o doblestnom rystare Aivengo* (1983).

REVIEW: *Soviet Film* 9 (1985): 16–18.
ADDITIONAL DISCUSSIONS:
Akchurina, Natalia. "[On Set] The Black Arrow." *Soviet Film* 4 (1985): 28–29.
Carr, Robert E. and R.M. Hayes. *Wide Screen Movies, A History and Filmography of Wide Gauge Filmmaking.* Jefferson, N.C.: McFarland, 1988.

86. *Le Chevalier des neiges* (1912)

France; dir. Georges Méliès; Pathé Frères.
ALTERNATE TITLE: *The Knight of the Snows.*
A princess is engaged to the Knight of the Snows, but a jealous rival makes a pact with the Devil to win her for himself. When the princess is abducted, the Knight of the Snows rescues her with the aid of a good fairy, and the jealous rival is whisked off to Hell.

In this, Méliès's penultimate production, the pioneering director returned to a number of themes that he had used in earlier productions. But this film in some ways marks an end of an era in filmmaking; the same year saw the first production of the elaborate movie spectacle, a genre that would be dominated by D.W. Griffith.

REVIEWS: *Bioscope* 2 January 1913: supplement iii. *Kinematograph Monthly* 9 (January 1913): 90.

ADDITIONAL DISCUSSIONS:
Bousquet, Henri. *Catalogue Pathé des années 1896 à 1914: 1912–1913–1914.* Paris: Henri Bousquet, 1995.
Deslandes, Jacques. *Le Boulevard du cinéma.* Paris: Éditions du Cerf, 1963.
Essai de reconstitution du catalogue français de la Starfilm suivi d'une analyse catalographique des films de Georges Méliès recensés en France. Bois d'Arcy: Publications du Service des Archives du Film du Centre National de la Cinématographie, [1981].
Frazer, John. *Artificially Arranged Scenes: The Films of Georges Méliès.* Boston: G.K. Hall, 1979.

87. *Les Chevaliers de la table ronde* (1990)

France; dir. Denis Llorca; Les Films du Jeudi.
ALTERNATE TITLE: *The Knights of the Round Table.*
CAST: Maria Casarès, Alain Cuny, Mireille Delcroix, Alain Mace, Catherine Rétoré, Michel Vitold.

In its retelling of scenes selected from the thirteenth-century French prose Vulgate cycle, this film presents the stories of Arthur and Guenevere, of Morgan and her jealousy, of Merlin and his enchantment by Vivien, and of Bron, the Fisher King, his daughter and her son, Galahad.

REVIEWS: *Les Cahiers du cinéma* 437 (November 1990): 85. *Film français* 16 October 1990: 13. *Image et son* 465 (November 1990): 29. *Positif* 359 (January 1991): 44–45. *Revue du cinéma* [La Saison cinématographique] Hors série 37 (1990): 27. *Studio* [Paris] 43 (November 1990): 24.

ADDITIONAL DISCUSSIONS:
Les Films français. Paris: Unifrance International Film, 1990.
Heymann, Danièle, and Pierre Murat. *L'Anné du cinéma 1991.* Barcelona: Almann-Lévy, 1991.
Tous les films 1990. Paris: Éditions Chrétiens-Médias, 1991.

The Children of Edward IV (1909) see
Les Enfants d'Édourad (1909)

88. *Christian and Moor* (1911)

United States; Edison.

CAST: James Gordon, Richard Neil, Herbert Prior, Janet Sawyer.

A Christian knight braves numerous perils to rescue his lady love from her Moorish father.

REVIEWS: *Bioscope* 28 September 1911: supplement ix. *Edison Kinetogram* 15 September 1911: 9–10. *Moving Picture World* 29 July 1911: 224; 19 August 1911: 464.

El Cid (1961) see *El Cid* (1961) *under E*

Il Cid (1910) see *Il Cid* (1910) *under I*

La Cintura di castità (1967) see *The Chastity Belt* (1967)

89. *The Cloister's Touch* (1910)

United States; dir. D.W. Griffith; Biograph.

CAST: Linda Arvidson, Verner Clarges, Arthur Johnson, Marion Leonard, Frank Powell, Mack Sennett.

A philandering duke claims the wife of one of his serfs as his bedmate. Grief-stricken over the loss of her husband and child, she dies. Her husband joins a monastery as does the duke, who as an act of penance promises to rear the child as his own.

REVIEWS: *Bioscope* 10 March 1910: 56. *Moving Picture World* 5 February 1910: 179; 12 February 1910: 215. *Variety* 5 February 1910: 35.

ADDITIONAL DISCUSSIONS:

Bowser, Eileen, ed. *Biograph Bulletins 1908–1912.* New York: Octagon, 1973.

"Increase the Beauty of the Pictures." *Moving Picture World* 12 February 1910: 217.

Niver, Kemp R. *Early Motion Pictures. The Paper Print Collection in the Library of Congress.* Washington, D.C.: Library of Congress, 1985.

Savada, Elias.*The American Film Institute Catalog of Motion Pictures Produced in the United States: Film Beginnings, 1893–1910.* Metuchen, N.J.: Scarecrow, 1995.

Cola di Rienze (1910) see *Cola di Rienzi* (1910)

90. *Cola di Rienzi* (1910)

Italy; dir. Mario Caserini; Cines.

ALTERNATE TITLE: *Cola di Rienze, Cola di Rienzo* and *Rienzi.*

Rienzi finds himself chosen tribune of Rome when the barons march off to war. When they return, Rienzi refuses to allow them to enter the city. They lay siege to the city, but are defeated and only spared execution by the pleadings of Rienzi's sister. When plague breaks out in Rome, the barons and citizens turn against Rienzi, who is killed by the mob and the barons.

Rienzi or Rienzo (1313–1354) dominated Italian politics in the first half of the fourteenth century. At one time or another, he was allied with or against several popes, the nobles and the populace of Rome, who revolted against his rule and killed him in a riot on October 8, 1354.

DISCUSSION:

Bernardini, Aldo, and Jean A. Gili, eds. *Le Cinéma italien de La Prise de Rome (1905) à Rome ville ouverte (1945).* Paris: Centre Georges Pompidou, 1986.

91. *Cola di Rienzi* (1911)

France; Pathé Frères and Film d'arte italiana.

CAST: Francesca Bertini, Dillo Lombardi, Giovanni Pezzinga.

Rienzi wants to restore Rome to her former glory and overthrow the nobles, one of whom, Orsini, attempts to kidnap Rienzi's wife. Rienzi, discovering Orsini's plot, imprisons him and all the other nobles. As a reward, the citizens of Rome make Rienzi tribune, but his popularity is short-lived. Orsini leads the barons in an uprising against the tribune and kills Rienzi.

REVIEW: *Bioscope* 7 September 1911: supplement iii.

ADDITIONAL DISCUSSION:

Bousquet, Henri. *Catalogue Pathé des années 1896 à 1914: 1910–1911.* Paris: Henri Bousquet, 1994.

Cola di Rienzo (1910) see *Cola di Rienzi* (1910)

I Coltelli del Vendicatore (1965) see *Knives of the Avenger* (1965)

92. *A Connecticut Yankee* (1931)

United States; dir. David Butler; Fox.

CAST: Frank Albertson, William Farnum, Mitchell Harris, Brandon Hurst, Myrna Loy, Maureen O'Sullivan, Will Rogers.

Hank Martin, a radio repairman, is knocked unconscious by an armored figure while trying to fix a radio for a slightly crazed customer who believes he is listening in on discussions from Arthur's Round Table. In a dream, Martin finds

Will Rogers as the Yankee and Myrna Loy as Morgan in David Butler's *A Connecticut Yankee* (1931).

himself in England in the year 528, where he amazes Arthur's court with his cigarette lighter, motorcycles, automobiles, machine guns, sawed-off shotguns, tanks and airplanes. All these modern additions to life in Camelot only serve to reinforce a plot designed to unite two lovers.

Like the other adaptations of Twain's famous 1889 novel, this film takes some license with details from its source. Rogers's Yankee is wry and unassuming; Loy's Morgan is drawn from the long tradition of the cinematic vamp. In a wonderful would-be seduction scene, Loy forces Rogers to blush bright red — an effect achieved in this black-and-white film by progressively tinting each frame for the scene a darker shade of pink. As with the other adaptations of Twain's novel, the makers of this film eschew any of the misanthropy in the original in favor of comedy.

REVIEWS: *Bioscope* 1 April 1931: 18–19. *Film Daily* 12 April 1931: 32. *Film Spectator* 11 (25 April 1931): 11. *Harrison's Reports* 11 April 1931: 58. *Motion Picture Herald* 21 March 1931: 39. *New York Times* 11 April 1931: 17; 4 May 1936: 16. *Photoplay* 29 (April 1931): 48. *Picturegoer Weekly* NS 13 (22 August 1931): 29. *Retro* 12 (November-December 1981): 20–23. *Rob Wagner's Script* 5 (30 May 1931): 10–11. *Variety* 15 April 1931: 20, 33.

ADDITIONAL DISCUSSIONS:

Fetrow, Alan G. *Sound Films, 1927–1939*. Jefferson, N.C.: McFarland, 1992.

Hanson, Patricia King, ed. *The American Film Institute Catalog of Motion Pictures Produced in the United States: Feature Films, 1931–1940*. Berkeley: University of California Press, 1993.

Harty, Kevin J. "Camelot Twice Removed: *Knightriders* and the Film Versions of *A Connecticut Yankee in King Arthur's Court*." In Kevin J. Harty, ed. *Cinema Arthuriana, Essays on Arthurian Film*. New York: Garland, 1991.

Korsilibas-Davis, James, and Myrna Loy. *Being and*

Becoming. London: Bloomsbury, 1987.

Nash, Jay Robert, and Stanley Ralph Ross. *The Motion Picture Guide, C–D, 1927–1983.* Chicago: Cinebooks, 1985.

Quirk, Lawrence J. *The Films of Myrna Loy.* Secaucus, N.J.: Citadel, 1980.

Rollins, Peter G. *Will Rogers, A Bio-Bibliography.* Westport, Conn.: Greenwood, 1984.

Sterling, Bryan B., ed. *The Will Rogers Scrapbook.* New York: Grosset & Dunlap, 1976.

_____, and Frances N. Sterling. *Will Rogers in Hollywood.* New York: Crown, 1984.

Umland, Rebecca A., and Samuel J. Umland. *The Use of Arthurian Legend in Hollywood Film from Connecticut Yankees to Fisher Kings.* Westport, Conn.: Greenwood, 1996.

"Will Rogers and King Arthur." *New York Times* 29 March 1931: 8. 7.

93. *A Connecticut Yankee* (1954)

United States; dir. Fiedler Cook; Kraft Theatre and ABC-TV.

CAST: Edgar Bergen, Sally Gracie, Victor Jory, Jack Livesey, Carl Reiner, Joey Walsh.

This made-for-television adaptation of Twain's novel emphasizes the farcical, turning Merlin (Victor Jory) into a comical character and shifting the scene with the eclipse to the end of the narrative.

REVIEW: *Variety* 14 June 1954: 30.

94. *A Connecticut Yankee* (1955)

United States; dir. Max Liebman, NBC-TV.

CAST: Eddie Albert, Janet Blair, John Conte, Leonard Elliott, Boris Karloff, Gale Sherwood.

This 90-minute production restages Rodgers and Hart's 1927 musical *A Connecticut Yankee* for television. On the night before he is supposed to marry Fay Morgan, Martin Barrett meets with his former fiancée, Alice Carter. Discovering the two together, the enraged Fay knocks Martin unconscious with a bottle of champagne. While knocked out, he dreams he is in King Arthur's court, where he rescues the Lady Alisande from Queen Morgan Le Fay.

Like its Broadway source, the production takes considerable liberty with Twain's novel and relies upon musical and dance numbers to advance its plot. The musical score and book used for this television production followed those of the 1943 revival rather than those of the original production.

REVIEWS: *Daily Variety* 14 March 1955: 9. *Variety* 16 March 1955: 35.

ADDITIONAL DISCUSSIONS:

Buehrer, Beverley B. *Boris Karloff, A Bio-Bibliography.* Westport, Conn.: Greenwood, 1993.

Hummel, David. *The Collector's Guide to the American Musical Theatre.* Metuchen, N.J.: Scarecrow, 1984.

Nollen, Scott Allen. *Boris Karloff, A Critical Account of His Screen, Stage, Radio, Television and Recording Work.* Jefferson, N.C.: McFarland, 1991.

Richard Rodgers Fact Book (with Supplement). New York: Lynn Farnol Group, 1968.

Terrace, Vincent. *Television Specials.* Jefferson, N.C.: McFarland, 1995.

95. *A Connecticut Yankee at King Arthur's Court* (1920)

United States; dir. Emmett J. Flynn; Fox.

CAST: Charles Clary, Adele Farrington, Carl Formes, Herbert Fortier, Charles Gordon, William MacDonald, Harry C. Meyers, William V. Mong, George Siegmann, Pauline Starke, Rosemary Theby.

Wealthy young Martin Cavendish wants to marry his mother's secretary rather than a snooty titled woman his mother has chosen for his bride. One night while reading a book about chivalry, Cavendish is knocked unconscious by a burglar and, in a dream, he finds himself in sixth century Camelot. Thereafter, the film follows the general outline of the events in Twain's novel with abundant contemporaneous touches added to the screenplay.

Douglas Fairbanks was originally offered the title role in this film, but he turned it down. As with the other screen adaptations of Twain's novel, this film eschews any of the misanthropy in the original in favor of comedy.

REVIEWS: *Exceptional Photoplays* 1 (March 1921): 2, 7. *Exhibitor's Trade Review* 12 February 1921: 1065. *Harrison's Reports* 12 February 1921: 26. *Motion Picture News* 12 February 1921: 1383. *New York Times* 15 March 1921: 14. *Photoplay* 20 (June 1921): 51. *Times* [London] 15 May 1921: 6. *Variety* 28 January 1921: 40. *Wid's Daily* 6 February 1921: 3.

ADDITIONAL DISCUSSIONS:

Connelly, Robert. *The Motion Picture Guide, Silent Film 1910–1936.* Chicago: Cinebooks, 1986.

Hamilton, James Shelley. "Five Pictures." *Exceptional Photoplays* 1 (November 1921): 3, 8, 12.

Hanson, Patricia King, ed. *The American Film Institute Catalog: Feature Films 1911–1920.* Berkeley: University of California Press, 1988.

Harty, Kevin J. "Camelot Twice Removed: *Knightriders* and the Film Versions of *A Connecticut Yankee in King Arthur's Court.*" In Kevin J. Harty, ed. *Cinema Arthuriana, Essays on Arthurian Film.* New York: Garland, 1991.

Munden, Kenneth W., ed. *The American Film Insti-*

Harry Myers as the Yankee and Rosemary Theby as Morgan Le Fay in Emmett J. Flynn's *A Connecticut Yankee at King Arthur's Court* (1920). (Still courtesy of the Film Stills Archive of the Museum of Modern Art.)

tute Catalog, Feature Films 1921–1930. New York: Bowker, 1971.

O'Dell, Scott. *Representative Photoplays Analyzed.* Hollywood, Calif.: Institute of Authorship, 1924.

Patterson, Francis Taylor. *Cinema Craftsmanship.* New York: Harcourt, 1921.

"Special Service Section on *A Connecticut Yankee in* [sic] *King Arthur's Court.*" *Motion Picture News* 26 February 1921: 1673–82.

96. *A Connecticut Yankee in King Arthur's Court* (1949)

United States; dir. Tay Garnett; Paramount.

CAST: William Bendix, Bing Crosby, Virginia Field, Rhonda Fleming, Sir Cedric Hardwicke, Joseph Vitale, Murvyn Vye, Richard Webb, Henry Wilcoxon.

Truer to the details of its source than either the 1920 or the 1931 films, this third screen version of Twain's novel is, nonetheless, in many ways the least successful of the three. The novel has been turned into a musical vehicle (not based on the 1927 Rodgers and Hart Broadway musical) for Bing Crosby. The plot advances by a mix of song and silly dialogue. Twain's novel was an example of comic genius; this film is anything but an example of such genius.

As with the other screen adaptations of Twain's novel, this film also eschews the misanthropy in the original in favor of sometimes-clumsy musical comedy.

REVIEWS: *Film Daily* 24 February 1949: 6. *Harrison's Reports* 26 February 1949: 35. *Hollywood Reporter* 21 February 1949: 3. *Monthly Film Bulletin* 16 (3 March 1949): 48. *Motion Picture Herald* 174 (26 February 1949): Product Digest Section 4513. *New York Times* 8 April 1949: 31. *Photoplay* 35 (April 1949): 22. *Revue du cinéma* [La Saison cinématographique] Hors série 30 (1948/1949): 212. *Times* [London] 21 March 1949: 7. *To-day's Cinema* 4 February 1949: 11. *Variety* 23 February 1949: 10.

ADDITIONAL DISCUSSIONS:

Bookbinder, Robert. *The Films of Bing Crosby.* Secaucus, N.J.: Citadel, 1977.

Harty, Kevin J. "Camelot Twice Removed: *Knight-*

Bing Crosby as the Yankee and Rhonda Fleming as Lady Alisande in Tay Garnett's *A Connecticut Yankee in King Arthur's Court* (1949).

riders and the Film Versions of *A Connecticut Yankee in King Arthur's Court.*" In Kevin J. Harty, ed. *Cinema Arthuriana, Essays on Arthurian Film.* New York: Garland, 1991.

Nash, Jay Robert, and Stanley Ralph Ross. *The Motion Picture Guide, C–D, 1927–1983.* Chicago: Cinebooks, 1985.

Nathan, Paul S. "Books into Films." *Publisher's Weekly* 153 (1 May 1948): 1907.

Umland, Rebecca A., and Samuel J. Umland. *The Use of Arthurian Legend in Hollywood Film from Connecticut Yankees to Fisher Kings.* Westport, Conn.: Greenwood, 1996.

Wachhorst, Wyn. "Time-Travel Romance on Film: Archetypes and Structures." *Extrapolation* 25 (Winter 1984): 340–59.

97. *A Connecticut Yankee in King Arthur's Court* (1952)

United States; dir. Franklin Schaffner; CBS.

CAST: Boris Karloff, Berry Kroeger, Thomas Mitchell.

This live television production compresses Twain's novel into 60 minutes, all but eliminating any hint of the misanthropy of the original. Karloff, who plays Arthur, returned to the role in another 1955 production based on the Rodgers and Hart Broadway musical.

DISCUSSIONS:

Gianakos, Larry James. *Television Drama Series Programming: A Comprehensive Chronicle, 1947–1959.* Metuchen, N.J.: Scarecrow, 1980.

Kim, Erwin. *Franklin J. Schaffner.* Metuchen, N.J.: Scarecrow, 1985.

Klisz, Anjanelle M., ed. *The Video Source Book.* 16th ed. Detroit: Gale Research, 1994.

98. *A Connecticut Yankee in King Arthur's Court* (1970)

Australia; dir. Zoran Janjic; Air Programs International.

CAST: (the voices of) Orson Bean, Ron Haddrick, Barbara Llewellyn, John Llewellyn, L. Ostrich, Brenda Senders.

This animated feature-length version of Twain's novel weaves into the original's basic plot an assortment of more contemporary gadgetry. In the final climactic battle, the Yankee routs an army of 50,000 using compressed air and water cannons.

REVIEW: *Daily News* [New York] 27 November 1970: 63.

ADDITIONAL DISCUSSIONS:

Harty, Kevin J. "Camelot Twice Removed: *Knightriders* and the Film Versions of *A Connecticut Yankee in King Arthur's Court.*" In Kevin J. Harty,

ed. *Cinema Arthuriana, Essays on Arthurian Film.* New York: Garland, 1991.

Wollery, George. *Animated TV Specials.* Metuchen, N.J.: Scarecrow, 1989.

99. *A Connecticut Yankee in King Arthur's Court* (1978)

United States; dir. David Trapper; Once Upon a Classic.

CAST: Richard Basehart, Roscoe Lee Browne, Frederick Coffin, Tovah Feldshuh, Paul Rudd, Dan Shor.

This 60-minute adaptation of Twain's novel is notable only for its attempt in the final scene to nod in the direction of its source's dark conclusion.

REVIEWS: *Christian Science Monitor* 22 May 1978: 23. *New York Post* 23 May 1978: 32.

ADDITIONAL DISCUSSIONS:

Marill, Alvin H. "The Television Scene." *Films in Review* 35 (November 1984): 570–71.

"Recycling Mark Twain." *TV Guide* 20 May 1978: 11.

100. *A Connecticut Yankee in King Arthur's Court* (1989)

United States; dir. Mel Damski; NBC-TV.

CAST: Rene Auberjonois, Hugo E. Blick, Michael Gross, Whip Hubley, Jean Marsh, Keshia Knight Pulliam, Emma Samms.

Karen Jones, a 1980s African American schoolgirl, falls from her horse, is knocked unconscious, and awakens in sixth century Camelot. To the already familiar assortment of items from the modern world, Karen here introduces Arthur and his court to karate, aerobics, Polaroid cameras, Walkmans and tape recorders.

This silly telemovie, primarily a vehicle for two popular television performers, Gross and Pulliam, scrupulously avoids any of the substantive or controversial issues raised by the novel, despite the fact that it originally aired in a year that coincidentally marked the hundredth anniversary of the publication of Twain's novel.

REVIEWS: *New York Times* 3 December 1989: 2. 33; 18 December 1989: 2. 4. *TV Guide* 16 December 1989: 53, 120. *Variety* 20 December 1989: 48.

ADDITIONAL DISCUSSIONS:

Harty, Kevin J. "Camelot Twice Removed: *Knightriders* and the Film Versions of *A Connecticut Yankee in King Arthur's Court.*" In Kevin J. Harty, ed. *Cinema Arthuriana, Essays on Arthurian Film.* New York: Garland, 1991.

Knutzen, Eirik. "Michael Gross in a Royal Role."

Philadelphia Inquirer TV Week 17–23 December 1989: 4–5.

Thompson, Raymond H. "The Ironic Tradition in Arthurian Film Since 1960." In Kevin J. Harty, ed. *Cinema Arthuriana, Essays on Arthurian Film.* New York: Garland, 1991.

Umland, Rebecca A., and Samuel J. Umland. *The Use of Arthurian Legend in Hollywood Film from Connecticut Yankees to Fisher Kings.* Westport, Conn.: Greenwood, 1996.

101. *Connemara* (1989)

France; dir. Louis Grospierre; Lapaca Productions.

CAST: Charley Boorman, Bernard-Oierre Donnadieu, Dierdra Donnelly, Brigitte Marvine, Maurice O'Donoghue, Daragh O'Malley, Steven Rekap, Jean-Pierre Rives, Hervé Schmitz.

An impetuous young man named Loup is sent by his Uncle Mark to fetch his fiancée, Sedrid of the long red tresses. They attempt to remain loyal to Mark, who nonetheless discovers that the two have fallen in love with each other.

The plot of the film is obviously an analogue — though not a very well-made one — to the oft-told medieval tale of Tristan, Isolde and Mark.

DISCUSSIONS:

Les Films français. Paris: Unifrance International Film, 1989.

Tous les films 1990. Paris: Éditions Chrétiens-Médias, 1991.

102. *The Conqueror* (1956)

United States; dir. Dick Powell; RKO.

CAST: Pedro Armendariz, Susan Hayward, Agnes Moorehead, John Wayne.

Intent upon avenging the death of his father, the young Temujin (later to be called Genghis Khan) encounters Bortai, a Tartar princess with whom he falls in love. In his quest for revenge, he also consolidates his power throughout the Gobi region and becomes the unchallenged ruler of the Mongols and Tartars.

Big names, large crowd and battles scenes, and a budget of almost $7 million can do nothing to change the fact that this is simply a very silly film.

REVIEWS: *Daily Film Renter* 1 February 1956: 8. *Film Daily* 21 February 1956: 6. *Films and Filming* 2 (March 1956): 17–18. *Films in Review* 5 (May 1956): 223. *Harrison's Reports* 25 June 1956: 32. *Hollywood Reporter* 21 February 1956: 3. *Kinematograph Weekly* 9 February 1956:8. *Monthly Film Bulletin* 23 (March 1956): 27–28. *Motion Picture Herald* 25 February 1956: Product Digest Section 793. *New York Times* 31 March 1956: 13. *To-day's Cinema* 1 February 1956: 9. *Variety* 22 February 1956: 6.

ADDITIONAL DISCUSSIONS:

"East and West Meet in Wayne." *Life* 40 (7 May 1956): 161–62, 164, 166.

Eyles, Allen. *John Wayne and the Movies.* New York: A.S. Barnes, 1976.

Moreno, Eduardo. *The Films of Susan Hayward.* Secaucus, N.J.: Citadel, 1979.

Nash, Jay Robert, and Stanley Ralph Ross. *The Motion Picture Guide, C–D, 1927–1983.* Chicago: Cinebooks, 1985.

Pfeiffer, Lee. *The John Wayne Scrapbook.* Secaucus, N.J.: Citadel, 1989.

Riggin, Judith. *John Wayne, A Bio-Bibliography.* New York: Greenwood, 1992.

Smith, Gary A. *Epic Films.* Jefferson, N.C.: McFarland, 1991.

Zmijewsky, Steve, Boris Zmijewsky, and Mark Ricci. *The Complete Films of John Wayne.* Secaucus, N.J.: Citadel, 1983.

The Conquest of Albania (1983) see *La Conquista de Albania* (1983)

103. *La Conquista de Albania* (1983)

Spain; dir. Alfonson Ungria; Frontera Films Irun S.A. Production.

ALTERNATE TITLE: *The Conquest of Albania.*

CAST: Miguel Arriba, Klara Badiola, Javier Elorriaga, Chemas Muñoz, Alicia Sánchez, Walter Vidarte.

In the fourteenth century, Carlos II of Navarre decides to send his brother Luis to head a military expedition intent upon conquering Albania, which he has received as part of his wife Jeanne of Anjou's dowry. In a climactic battle, Luis is killed, dying in the arms of his wife, after which his troops return home, abandoning their attempted conquest.

Loosely based on historical fact, this film's claim to fame is that it was (at the time of its release) one of the most expensive Basque films ever made.

REVIEWS: *Cineinforme* 113 (September 1983): 14; 124 (February 1984): 25. *Variety* 12 October 1983: 27.

ADDITIONAL DISCUSSIONS:

Cine para leer 1984. Bilbao: Ediciones Mensajero, 1984.

Hopewell, John. *Out of the Past, Spanish Cinema after Franco.* London: BFI, 1986.

104. *Il Conte Ugolino* (1909)

Italy; dir. Giovanni Pastrone; Itala Film.

John Wayne as Temujin and Susan Hayward as Bortai in Dick Powell's *The Conqueror* (1956).

ALTERNATE TITLES: *Count Ugolini* and *Count Ugolino.*

Ugolino, the Count of Donoratico and a leader of one faction in Pisa in the thirteenth century, forms a secret alliance with Archbishop Ruggieri, the leader of a rival faction. Ugolino betrays his compatriots, only to be betrayed himself by Ruggieri, who has Ugolino sealed up in a prison with his sons and grandsons, all of whom starve to death.

Ugolino's story was told by Dante (*Inferno* XXXIII) and by Chaucer's Monk. Ugolino della

Gherardesca (d. 1289) attempted to seize power in Pisa and was imprisoned for his efforts in 1274. He escaped and joined the Florentines in their war against Pisa, as reward for which he returned to Pisa and assumed power by force. When his supporters turned against him, he was overthrown and, with his two sons and two grandsons, starved to death in prison. His story was again told on film in 1949.

DISCUSSIONS:

Bernardini, Aldo, and Jean A. Gili, eds. *Le Cinéma italien de La Prise de Rome (1905) à Rome ville ouverte (1945)*. Paris: Centre Georges Pompidou, 1986.

Sadoul, Georges. *Histoire générale du cinéma II. Les Pionniers du cinéma (de Méliès à Pathé) 1897–1909*. Paris: Les Éditions Denoël, 1977.

Savada, Elias. *The American Film Institute Catalog of Motion Pictures Produced in the United States: Film Beginnings, 1893–1910*. Metuchen, N.J.: Scarecrow, 1995.

105. *Il Conte Ugolino* (1949)

Italy; dir. Riccardo Freda; Forum.

ALTERNATE TITLE: *Il Cavaliere di ferro*.

CAST: Ciro Berardi, Carla Calò, Gianna Maria Canale, Armando Guarneri, Piero Palermini, Luigi Pavese, Ugo Sasso, Peter Trent.

Ugolino, a man of little patience, plots with his enemies and is eventually betrayed by them. Sentenced to be executed, he is walled up in a prison and starves to death.

Ugolino's story had earlier been told on film in 1909.

REVIEW: *Intermezzo* 5 (30 June 1950): 7.

ADDITIONAL DISCUSSION:

Chiti, Roberto, and Roberto Poppi. *Dizionario del cinema italiano. Vol. 2: I Film dal 1945 al 1959*. Rome: Gremese Editore, 1991.

106. *La Corona di ferro* (1940)

Italy; dir. Alessandro Blasetti; E.N.I.C. Lux.

ALTERNATE TITLE: *The Iron Crown*.

CAST: Primo Carnera, Elisa Cegani, Gino Cervi, Luisa Ferida, Massimo Girotti, Rina Morelli, Paolo Stoppa, Osvaldo Valenti.

Byzantium's emperor sends a sacred iron crown, fashioned around one of the nails from the cross of Christ, to the Pope as a gift. The journey to Rome takes decades as the crown passes through several countries and becomes the focus of wars and battles between rivals.

Based on medieval legend, the plot of this film defies easy synopsis since so much happens on the journey to deliver the crown to the Pope. There is literally a cast of thousands, but the acting style throughout the film is perhaps most kindly described as "operatic." Made at the height of Mussolini's power, the film provides more of a revealing glimpse into the politics of its day than into those of the Middle Ages. The director's 1938 film, *Ettore Fieramosca*, had a similar political subtext.

REVIEWS: *Bianco e nero* 13 (May-June 1952): 85. *Cinéma* 63 (February 1962): 128. *Cinema* [Rome] 129 (10 November 1941): 248–49. *Cinématographie française* 2061 (18 April 1964): 19. *Filmcritica* 37 (February 1986): 118–19. *New York Times* 11 June 1949: 11; 24 June 1994: C27. *Variety* 13 June 1949: 13.

ADDITIONAL DISCUSSIONS:

Bernardini, Aldo, and Jean A. Gili, eds. *Le Cinéma italien de La Prise de Rome (1905) à Rome ville ouverte (1945)*. Paris: Centre Georges Pompidou, 1986.

Buss, Robin. *Italian Films*. New York: Holmes & Meier, 1989.

Chiti, Roberto, and Enrico Lancia. *Dizionario del cinema italiano. Vol. 1: I Film dal 1930 al 1944*. Rome: Gremese Editore, 1993.

Landy, Marcia. *Fascism in Film, The Italian Commercial Cinema, 1931–1943*. Princeton: Princeton University Press, 1986.

Savio, Francesco. *Cinecittà anni trenta*. Rome: Bulzoni, 1979.

_____. *Ma l'amore no*. Milan: Sonzogno, 1975.

Zagarrio, Salizatto, and Vito Zagarrio, eds. *La Corona di ferro, un mododi produzione italiano*. Rome: Di Giacomo Editore, 1986.

107. *Corradino di Svevia* (1909)

Italy; dir. Romolo Bacchini; Vesuvio Film.

ALTERNATE TITLE: *Konrad von Schwaben*.

Conrad, Elizabeth of Bavaria, and Frederick of Austria meet to respond to a plea from an Italian legation that Conrad recapture Sicily from Charles of Anjou. Conrad agrees and sets out with Frederick. Both are betrayed by Pope Clement IV, whose barons hand Conrad over to Charles for beheading.

Conradin of Swabia (1252–1268), also known as Conrad V and Conrad the Younger, was the last surviving Hohenstaufen. In 1268, he lead an army of more than 10,000 troops into Italy to recapture the kingdom of the Two Sicilies from Charles of Anjou. Betrayed, he was taken prisoner in a battle near Tagliacozzo and executed. Historically, his papal antagonist was Urban IV.

DISCUSSIONS:

Aprà, Adriano, and Jean A. Gili. *Naples et le cinéma*. Paris: Centre Georges Pompidou, 1994.

Cecil Parker (left) as King Roderick and Danny Kaye as the jester in Norman Panama and Melvin Frank's *The Court Jester* (1955).

Bernardini, Aldo. "Corradino di Svevia." *Immagine* 4 (April-June 1985): 25–32.
_____, and Jean A. Gili, eds. *Le Cinéma italien de La Prise de Rome (1905) à Rome ville ouverte (1945)*. Paris: Centre Georges Pompidou, 1986.
Savio, Francesco. *Visione Privata*. Rome: Bulzioni Editore, 1972.

Count Ugolini (1909) see *Il Conte Ugolino* (1909)

Count Ugolino (1909) see *Il Conte Uglino* (1909)

108. *The Court Jester* (1956)

United States; dir. Norman Panama and Melvin Frank; Paramount.

CAST: Angela Lansbury, Glynis Johns, Danny Kaye, Robert Middleton, Mildred Natwick, Cecil Parker, Basil Rathbone.

A tyrant rules England in the twelfth century. He thinks he has killed the infant heir to the throne, who in reality is in the care of a band of rebels lead by "The Black Fox." The child is easily distinguished by a posterior birthmark, the Purple Pimpernel. After a long series of intrigues and jests, many unwittingly carried out by the court jester, the rightful heir is restored to the throne.

Kaye is at his farcical best here, and his duel with Rathbone allows the latter to reprise a role and reenact a scene he played in the 1938 film *The Adventures of Robin Hood*.

REVIEWS: *Daily Film Renter* 8 February 1956: 5. *Film Daily* 27 January 1956: 6. *Films and Filming* 2 (March 1956): 17. *Harrison's Reports* 28 January 1956: 14. *Hollywood Reporter* 27 January 1956: 3. *Kinematograph Weekly* 5 April 1956: 16. *Monthly Film Bulletin* 23 (March 1956): 28. *Motion Picture Herald* 28 January 1956: Product Digest Section 761. *New York Times* 2 February 1956: 19; 5 February 1956: 2. 1. *Times* [London] 8 February 1956: 5.

To-day's Cinema 8 February 1956: 14. *Variety* 1 February 1956: 6.

ADDITIONAL DISCUSSIONS:

Bonanno, Margaret Wander. *Angela Lansbury, A Biography.* New York: St. Martin's, 1987.

"Comic Knighthood for Kaye." *Life* 40 (30 January 1956): 93–94, 96.

Druxman, Michael B. *Basil Rathbone, His Life and His Films.* South Brunswick, N.J.: A.S. Barnes, 1975.

Gottfried, Martin. *Nobody's Fool, The Lives of Danny Kaye.* New York: Simon & Shuster, 1994.

Fraser, George MacDonald. *The Hollywood History of the World.* New York: Beech Tree, 1988.

Magill, Frank N., ed. *Magill's American Film Guide.* Englewood Cliffs, N.J.: Salem, 1983.

_____, ed. *Magill's Survey of Cinema: English Language Films.* First Series. Englewood Cliffs, N.J.: Salem, 1980.

Nash, Jay Robert, and Stanley Ralph Ross. *The Motion Picture Guide, C–D, 1927–1983.* Chicago: Cinebooks, 1985.

"Sir Danny Kids Knighthood." *New York Times Magazine* 1 January 1956: 20–21.

Thomas, Tony. *The Great Adventure Films.* Secaucus, N.J.: Citadel, 1976.

La Croisade maudite (1967) see *Gates to Paradise* (1967)

109. *El Cronicón* (1969)

Spain; dir. Antonia Giménenz Ricol; Mota Films.

CAST: Manuel Gómez Bur, Antonio Casal, Cassen, Esperanza Roy, Rossana Yanni.

At the end of the Middle Ages, in a Moslem enclave in Spain known as Alavin, Count Sandro suffers from a rare malady that no one can cure. He sends a famous navigator, Blas Testa de Buey, in search of El Dorado in the hopes that the fabled land will offer a cure for his malady.

REVIEW: *Cinestudio* 94 (February 1971): 26, 56.

ADDITIONAL DISCUSSION:

Spanish Cinema 1970. Madrid: Uniespaña, 1970.

110. *Crossed Swords* (1953)

United States and Italy; dir. Milton Krims; Viva Films and United Artists.

ALTERNATE TITLE: *Il Maestro di Don Giovanni.*

CAST: Cesare Danova, Errol Flynn, Nadia Gray, Gina Lollobrigida, Roldano Lupi, Paola Mori, Alberto Rabagliati.

In the medieval duchy of Sidona, the law requires every man over age 20 to marry. The duke's son, Raniero, and his companion Renzo return from years of wandering abroad but decide to flee the country once again because of the law. When news of a plot to depose the duke reaches them, they return to save the day and to marry.

This rather tepid swashbuckler received little critical attention when released — deservedly so — despite a cast that included Flynn, then long past his swashbuckling prime.

REVIEWS: *Film Daily* 28 July 1954: 6. *Films in Review* 5 (December 1954): 544. *Hollywood Reporter* 28 July 1954: 3. *Kinematograph Weekly* 17 June 1954: 24, 26. *Monthly Film Bulletin* 21 (August 1954): 120. *Motion Picture Herald* 31 July 1954: Product Digest Section 89. *To-day's Cinema* 11 June 1954: 6. *Variety* 28 July 1954: 6.

ADDITIONAL DISCUSSIONS:

Chiti, Roberto, and Roberto Poppi. *Dizionario del cinema italiano. Vol. 2: I Film dal 1945 al 1959.* Rome: Gremese Editore, 1991.

The Italian Production 1952–1953. Rome: Unitalia Film, 1953.

Morris, George. *Errol Flynn.* New York: Pyramid, 1975.

Thomas, Tony, et al. *The Films of Errol Flynn.* New York: Citadel, 1969.

Valenti, Peter. *Errol Flynn, A Bio-Bibliography.* Westport, Conn.: Greenwood, 1984.

111. *The Crown of Richard III* (1914)

France; Pathé Frères.

The Duke of Gloucester calls upon the sorceress Rahel to learn his future. He then proceeds to murder his way to the crown, finally meeting his death at the hands of the Duke of Buckingham.

REVIEW: *Pathé Fortnightly Bulletin* 2. 22 (1914): [10–11].

112. *The Crusade of the Templars* (1911)

France; Gaumont.

When he returns from the Crusades, a prince finds an impostor bearing his title, but he proves his true identity by singing a song to his blind mother.

REVIEWS: *Moving Picture World* 6 May 1911: 1023; 20 May 1911: 1141.

113. *The Crusader* (1911)

United States; Edison.

CAST: James Gordon, Richard Neil, Herbert Prior, Richard Ridgeley, Laura Sawyer, Charles Sutton.

Falsely believing that her lover has been

killed in battle, a grief-stricken woman is about to marry his rival when a message arrives from the Holy Land assuring her of her lover's safety.

REVIEWS: *Edison Kinetogram* 27 June 1911: Film 6817. *Motion Picture World* 8 July 1911: 1586.

114. *The Crusaders* (1911)

Italy; Cines.

ALTERNATE TITLES: *La Gerusalemme liberata* and *Jerusalem Delivered*.

In a vision, Godfrey of Bouillon is told to lead a crusade to rescue the Holy Land. His forces led by Tancred encounter Moslem troops led by Clorinda, a woman warrior, with whom Tancred falls in love. The Crusaders are eventually victorious, but not without a series of setbacks, and Godfrey enters Jerusalem as its king.

Five months in production, this film is based on Torquato Tasso's sixteenth century epic poem *Jerusalem Delivered*.

REVIEWS: *Bioscope* 11 May 1911: 251-53; 29 August 1918: 30–31; 6 March 1919: 66. *Kinematograph Monthly Record* 76 (August 1918): 65–66; 83 (March 1919): 21–22. *Moving Picture World* 11 July 1911: 14–16; 22 July 1911: 128.

ADDITIONAL DISCUSSIONS:

De Lucis, Flavia, ed. *C'era il cinema*. Modena: Edizioni Panini, 1983.

Talbot, Frederick A. *Moving Pictures*. 1912; Rpt. New York: Arno, 1970.

Weinberg, Herman G., ed. *Fifty Years of Italian Cinema*. Rome: Carlo Bestetti-Edizioni d'arte, 1955.

115. *The Crusader's Return* (1908)

France; Gaumont.

A crusader is left for dead on the battlefield, and his companion returns home to tell the crusader's fiancée of his fate. The companion and fiancée marry. When the crusader returns disguised as a monk, he does not interfere with the couple and instead blesses their union.

REVIEWS: *Moving Picture World* 18 April 1908: 353–54; 4 September 1909: 314.

ADDITIONAL DISCUSSION:

Savada, Elias. *The American Film Catalog of Motion Pictures Produced in the United States: Film Beginnings, 1893–1910*. Metuchen, N.J.: Scarecrow, 1995.

116. *The Crusader's Return* (1910)

Italy; Cines.

Isotta wishes to marry Gerald, who is only a page. Her father, a cruel count, tells Gerald he must become a knight to win the hand of his daughter. Gerald rides off to the Crusades to win honor. Meanwhile, Manfred, Isotta's cousin, intent on marrying his cousin himself, tries to convince her that Gerald has died. She agrees to marry Manfred, but Gerald arrives in the nick of time, and the two lovers are reunited.

REVIEW: *Bioscope* 3 March 1910: 52.

117. *The Crusades* (1935)

United States; Cecil B. DeMille; Paramount.

CAST: Katherine DeMille, Ian Keith, C. Aubrey Smith, Henry Wilcoxon, Loretta Young.

Rather than marry the sister of Philip of France, England's Richard I goes on crusade to rescue the Holy Lands from the Saracens. To obtain food and supplies, Richard is forced to marry Berengaria of Navarre, who accompanies him to Palestine. In revenge, Philip plots with Prince John to overthrow Richard. Berengaria, fearing she is the cause of dissension among the ranks of the Christians, allows herself to be wounded by the Saracens. Saladin rescues and nurses her back to health, only to fall in love with his captive. Richard and Saladin negotiate a truce, and Saladin reluctantly returns Berengaria to Richard, who in turn thwarts Prince John's plot against him.

With a cast of nearly 10,000, this film was DeMille's biggest spectacle to date despite the way in which it played fast and loose with history.

REVIEWS: *Daily Film Renter* 22 August 1935: 7. *Film Daily* 5 August 1935: 16. *Film Weekly* 30 August 1935: 27–28. *Harrison's Reports* 31 August 1935: 138. *Hollywood Reporter* 1 August 1935: 3. *Monthly Film Bulletin* 2 (August 1935): 101. *Motion Picture Daily* 2 August 1935: 16. *Motion Picture Herald* 30 March 1935: 50–51; 10 August 1935: 47; 1 May 1948: Product Digest Section 4146. *New York Times* 22 August 1935: 21. *New Yorker* 11 (31 August 1935): 43. *Photoplay* 48 (October 1935): 66. *Rob Wagner's Script* 14 (2 November 1935): 10. *Silver Screen* 5 (October 1935): 56. *Times* [London] 22 August 1935: 10. *Today's Cinema News and Property Gazette* 22 August 1935: 8; 28 August 1935: 10–11. *Variety* 28 August 1935: 12.

ADDITIONAL DISCUSSIONS:

Boone, Andrew R. "Ancient Battles in the Movies." *Scientific American* 153 (August 1935): 61–63.

Fisher, Martin. "Shooting the Days When Knights Were Bold." *Motion Picture Magazine* 50 (September 1935): 34–35, 62.

Fraser, George MacDonald. *The Hollywood History of the World*. New York: Beech Tree, 1988.

Hanson, Patricia King, ed. *The American Film In-*

Loretta Young as Princess Berengaria in Cecil B. DeMille's *The Crusades* (1935).

stitute Catalog of Motion Pictures Produced in the United States: Feature Films, 1931–1940. Berkeley: University of California Press, 1993.

Nash, Jay Robert, and Stanley Ralph Ross. *The Motion Picture Guide, C–D, 1927–1983.* Chicago: Cinebooks, 1985.

Ringgold, Gene, and DeWitt Bodeen. *The Films of Cecil B. DeMille.* New York: Cadillac Publishing, 1969.

Searles, Baird. *EPIC! History on the Big Screen.* New York: Henry N. Abrams, 1990.

Smith, Gary A. *Epic Films.* Jefferson, N.C.: McFarland, 1991.

Thomas, Tony. *The Great Adventure Films*. Secaucus, N.J.: Citadel, 1976.

Wyatt, Euphemia Van Rensselaer. "Richard and Saladin." *Catholic World* 142 (October 1935): 83–88.

118. *Cuando Almanzor tocó el tambor* (1983)

Spain; dir. Luis Maria Delgado; Expomundo.

ALTERNATE TITLE: *When Almanzor Lost His Drum*.

CAST: Quique Camoiras, Alfonso del Real, Juanito Navarro, Vincente Parra.

In tenth century Spain, Almanzor terrifies the Christians under his rule. He demands a monthly tribute of 12 virgins, but his Christian subjects send instead prostitutes from a local brothel who kill the tyrant.

REVIEWS: *Cineinforme* 126 (March 1984): 14; 139 (October 1984): 46–47; 142 (October 1984): 33.

ADDITIONAL DISCUSSION:
Cine español 1984. Madrid: Ministerio de cultura, 1985.

The Curse of the Wandering Minstrel (1910) see *Des Sängers Fluch* (1910)

Dagobert (1963) see *Le Bon Roi Dagobert* (1963)

119. *Dagobert* (1984)

France and Italy; dir. Dino Risi; Opera Film.

ALTERNATE TITLE: *Le Bon Roi Dagobert*.

CAST: Carole Bouquet, Coluche, Isabella Ferrari, Michael Lonsdale, Karin Mi, Francesco Scali, Michel Serrault, Ugo Tognazzi, Antonio Vezza.

Barbarians attack Dagobert while he is traveling through a forest. The king seeks refuge with one of his concubines and the monk Otarus in a tree. Starving wolves surround their shelter, and Dagobert vows to make a pilgrimage to Rome to ask Pope Honorius I for forgiveness if he is spared. His journey to Rome places him in a papal court overrun by plots and counterplots, and the king barely escapes with his life and his pants, which he has on backwards as he flees the city.

This film follows the lead of the 1911 and 1963 films — both entitled *Le Bon Roi Dagobert* — in reducing the seventh-century Merovingian king to a buffoon.

REVIEWS: *Bianco e nero* 45 (October-December 1984): 36. *Les Cahiers du cinéma* 364 (October 1984): 53, 56. *Ciné-revue* 64 (29 March 1984): 6; 64 (6 September 1984): 13. *Cinema d'oggi* 18 (24 October 1984): 26. *Film français* 29 June 1984: 10, 18. *Foreign Sales: Italian Movie Trade* 10 (March 1984): 21. *Positif* 284 (November 1984): 70. *Segnocinema* 4 (November 1984): 40. *Télérama* 1808 (8–14 September 1984): 27. *Variety* 3 October 1984: 20.

ADDITIONAL DISCUSSIONS:
Abet, André. ""Le Bon Roi Dagobert' de Dino Risi." *Cahiers de la cinémathèque* 42–43 (Summer 1985): 155–56.

La Produzione italiana 1984/85. Rome: ANICA, 1985.

Tous les films 1984. Paris: Éditions Chrétiens-Medias, 1985.

La Damnation du Docteur Faust (1904) see *Faust et Marguerite* (1904)

The Damnation of Faust (1903) see *Faust aux enfers* (1903)

Dante e Beatrice (1913) see *The Life of Dante* (1913)

120. *Dante nella vita e nei tempi suoi* (1922)

Italy; dir. Domenico Gaido; V.I.S. Firenze.

CAST: Armando Cresti, Diana Karenne, Guido Maraffi, Amletto Novelli, Celeste Paladini-Ando.

Corso Donati leads the Neri (or Black) faction in Florence in a long and increasingly bloody conflict with the Bianchi (or White) faction. Dante is no passive observer of this continuing civil strife since he is one of the priors of Florence. An attempt to end the strife by a marriage between feuding families only exacerbates the civil unrest in Florence and leads to Dante's exile from the city.

This film interweaves events in the life of Dante (1265–1321) — Corso Donati, who did indeed lead the Neri faction, died in 1308 — with the story of Paolo and Francesca from the *Inferno* (V).

REVIEW: *Bianco e nero* 42 (January–June 1981): 389–93. *Immagine* NS 4 (Winter 1986-1987): 16–19.

ADDITIONAL DISCUSSION:
Weinberg, Herman G., ed. *Fifty Years of Italian Cinema*. Rome: Carlo Bestetti-Edizioni d'arte, 1955.

Dante's Inferno ([Helois] 1910) see *L'Inferno* (1910)

Dante's Inferno ([Milano] 1910) see
L'Inferno (1910)

121. *Dante's Inferno* (1924)

United States; dir. Henry Otto; Fox.

CAST: Lawson Butt, Howard Gaye, Ralph Lewis, Pauline Starke, Joseph Swickard.

Miserly millionaire Mortimer Judd makes a fortune as a slum landlord. When he ignores an appeal for financial aid from his friend Eugene Craig, Craig sends Judd a copy of Dante's *Inferno*. Judd reads the book and dozes off dreaming he is on a tour of Dante's Hell, where a place is reserved for him. He awakens with a start and promises to mend his ways and redress past wrongs.

The sets for this film, which becomes a morality play for the Roaring Twenties, were based on the famous illustrations in Gustave Doré's 1861 edition of *The Inferno*.

REVIEWS: *Exceptional Photoplays* 5 (October-November 1924): 4. *Harrison's Reports* 4 October 1924: 159. *New York Times* 30 September 1924: 27. *Silent Film Newsletter* 2 (September 1994): 113–16. *Variety* 1 October 1924: 22.

ADDITIONAL DISCUSSIONS:

Borst, Ronald V., et al., eds. *Graven Images*. New York: Grove, 1993.

Butler, Ivan. *Silent Magic, Rediscovering the Silent Film Era*. New York: Ungar, 1988.

Connelly, Robert B. *The Motion Picture Guide, Silent Film 1910–1936*. Chicago: Cinebooks, 1986.

Munden, Kenneth E., ed. *The American Film Institute Catalog, Feature Films 1921–1930*. New York: Bowker, 1971.

122. *Dante's Purgatorio* (1913)

Italy; Cinema Productions.

A golden eagle picks Dante up in its talons and takes him to the gates of Purgatory. Dante then journeys through Purgatory, encountering a variety of souls, until Beatrice appears in a cart drawn by a seven-headed beast to take him to Paradise.

This film recounts the stories from the *Purgatorio* of Pia de' Tolomeia (V), the thirteenth century troubadour Sordello (VI), Marco Lombardo (XVI) and the martyrdom of St. Stephen (XV). Again, as with many early films based on Dante, the scenery here was inspired by the famous illustrations in Gustave Doré's 1861 edition of *The Inferno*.

REVIEW: *Bioscope* 20 March 1913: 921.

The Dark Avenger (1955) see *The Warriors* (1955)

123. *The Darling of Paris* (1917)

United States; dir. J. Gordon Edwards; Fox.

CAST: Theda Bara, Louis Dean, John Webb Dillion, Alice Gale, Herbert Heyes, Walter Law, Carey Lee, Glen White.

Claude Frallo, a scientist, first admires and then, with the aid of the hunchbacked Quasimodo, kidnaps Esmeralda, a gypsy girl known by all as the "Darling of Paris." She is rescued by Capt. Phoebus, whose intentions are equally dishonorable. Frallo kills Phoebus but puts the blame for the murder on Esmeralda who confesses under torture. Quasimodo rescues her by denouncing Frallo.

This adaptation of Victor Hugo's famous 1831 novel *Notre Dame de Paris* is notable for Bara's vampy performance and for its attempt not to offend its audience's religious sensibilities by making Frallo a scientist rather than a priest.

REVIEWS: *Bioscope* 12 July 1917: 161, 180. *Exhibitor's Trade Review* 2 February 1917: 635. *Kinematograph and Lantern Weekly* 12 July 1917: 87. *Kinematograph Monthly Record* 64 (August 1917): 54–55. *Moving Picture World* 10 February 1917: 869; 8 February 1919: 808. *Variety* 26 January 1917: 35. *Wid's Independent Review of Feature Films* 15 February 1916: 110–11.

ADDITIONAL DISCUSSIONS:

Connelly, Robert. *The Motion Picture Guide, Silent Film 1910–1936*. Chicago: Cinebooks, 1986.

Genini, Ronald. *Theda Bara*. Jefferson, N.C.: McFarland, 1996.

Golden, Eve. *Vamp: The Rise and Fall of Theda Bara*. Vestal, N.Y.: Empise Books, 1996.

Hanson, Patricia King, ed. *The American Film Institute Catalog of Motion Pictures Produced in the United States: Feature Films, 1911–1920*. Berkeley: University of California Press, 1988.

Days of St. Patrick (1920) see *Aimsir Padraig* (1920)

124. *The Death of King Edward III* (1911)

United States; Vitagraph.

CAST: Helen Gardner, Charles Kent, James Morrison.

England's Edward III finds himself abandoned by everyone except his mistress, Alice Perrers. She awaits his death to secure a prized signet ring. When the king falls unconscious,

Theda Bara as Esmeralda the gypsy girl in J. Gordon Edwards's *The Darling of Paris* (1917).

she steals the ring and also abandons him. Servants rush into the king's bedchamber and steal all his belongings. The king dies, deserted by all except a young priest.

Alice Perrers, or de Windsor (d. 1400), was King Edward III's (1327–1377) long-time mistress. She attempted to use her position to influence public policy and was at times courted for her influence and prosecuted for her interference in the affairs of state. In his last days, she buoyed Edward's spirits, only to abandon him and steal his ring on his deathbed.

REVIEWS: *Moving Picture World* 29 July 1911: 226; 12 August 1911: 358–59. *Vitagraph Life Portrayals* 1 (31 July–13 August 1911): 11–12.

125. *The Decameron* (1971)

Italy; dir. Pier Paolo Pasolini; PEA and Les Productions Artistes Associés.

ALTERNATE TILE: *Il Decamerone.*

CAST: Franco Citti, Ninetto Davoli, Angela Luce, Pier Paolo Pasolini, Silvana Mangano.

Pasolini retells selected tales from Boccaccio, appearing himself in one sequence as an apprentice to the painter Giotto. The film's first part tells the stories of Andreuccio of Perugia (Day 2, Tale 5), the abbess caught in bed with a priest (Day 9, Tale 2), Masetto da Lamporecchio (Day 3, Tale 1), Peronella (Day 7, Tale 2) and Ser Cepparello (Day 1, Tale 1). The film's second part tells the tales of Messer Forese and Giotto (Day 6, Tale 5), Riccardo Manardi (Day 5, Tale 4), Isabetta (Day 4, Tale 5), Compare Pietro and his wife (Day 9, Tale 10) and the two Sienese twins (Day 7, Tale 10).

The first and the best of the three films in Pasolini's "trilogy of life" (the other two films are *The Arabian Nights* [1974] and *The Canterbury Tales* [1971]), *The Decameron* presents an important rereading and deconstruction of its source. One of Italy's highest-grossing films in 1971, Pasolini's *Decameron* inspired an endless series of sexploitative sequels having little to do with Boccaccio.

REVIEWS: *Cineforum* 109 (December 1971): 88–90. *Cinema nuovo* 241 (November-December 1971): 445–47. *Cinema sessanta* 87–88 (1972): 100–01. *Cinema società* 9–10 (March 1972): 36–37. *Cinéma 71* 161 (December 1971): 108–10. *CinemaTV Today* 12 Feb-

Pier Paolo Pasolini (left) as the painter Giotto's assistant in a scene from his **The Decameron** (1971).

ruary 1972: 20. *Cue* 18 December 1971: 72. *Filmcritica* 217 (August 1971): 341–44. *Filmfacts* 14 (1971): 680–83. *Film français* 19 November 1971: 19. *Films and Filming* 18 (March 1972): 49. *Hollywood Reporter* 10 November 1971: 3. *Image et son* 255 (December 1971): 104–08. *Jeune cinéma* 58 (November 1971) 30–32. *Los Angeles Times* 3 April 1972: 4. 8. *Monthly Film Bulletin* 39 (March 1972): 49–50. *New York Times* 5 October 1971: 46. *Positif* 134 (January 1972): 78–79. *Sight and Sound* 41 (Spring 1972): 110–11. *Times* [London] 1 July 1971: 20; 28 February 1972: 11. *Variety* 7 July 1971: 14. *Video Watch Dog* 13 (September-October 1992): 46–47.

ADDITIONAL DISCUSSIONS:

Bergman, Ronald, and Robyn Karney. *Bloomsbury Foreign Film Guide*. London: Bloomsbury, 1992.

Bevan, David G. "Pasolini and Baccaccio [sic]." *Literature/Film Quarterly* 5 (Winter 1977): 23–29.

Bondanella, Peter. *Italian Cinema from Neorealism to the Present*. 2nd ed. New York: Ungar, 1990.

Freixe, Guy. "Approche du *Décameron* de Pier Paolo Pasolini." *Les Cahiers de la cinémathèque* 42–43 (Summer 1985): 143–51.

Friedrich, Pia. *Pier Paolo Pasolini*. Boston: Twayne, 1982.

Galluzzi, Francesco. *Pasolini et la pittura*. Rome: Bulzoni, 1994.

Gambetti, Giacomo. "Per una trilogia popolare, libera, erotica." *Cineforum* 121 (March 1973): 221–29.

Grazzini, Giovanni. "Boccaccio sullo schermo." *Studi sul Boccaccio* 7 (1973): 369–73.

Lawton, Ben. "The Storyteller's Art: Pasolini's *Decameron* (1971)." In Andrew S. Horton and Joan Magretta, eds. *Modern European Filmmakers and the Art of Adaptation*. New York: Ungar, 1981.

_____. "Theory and Praxis in Pasolini's Trilogy of Life: *Decameron*." *Quarterly Review of Film Studies* 2 (November 1977): 395–417.

Marcus, Millicent. "The *Decameron*: Pasolini as a Reader of Boccaccio." *Italian Quarterly* 21 (Fall-Winter 1980): 175–80.

_____. *Filmmaking by the Book, Italian Cinema and Literary Adaptation*. Baltimore: Johns Hopkins, 1993.

Pasolini, Pier Paolo. *Trilogia della vita*. Bologna: Cappelli, 1975. [Screenplay.]

Poppi, Roberto, and Mario Pecorari. *Dizionario del cinema italiano: I Film dal 1970 al 1979*. Rome: Gremese Editore, 1996.

Rondolino, Gianni, ed. *Catalogo Bolaffi del cinema italiano 1966/1975*. Turin: Bolaffi Editore, 1975.

La Produzione italiana 1970/71. Rome: Unitalia Film, 1971.

Schwartz, David. *Pasolini Requiem*. New York: Pantheon, 1992.

Snyder, Stephen. *Pier Paolo Pasolini*. Boston: Twayne, 1980.

Viano, Maurizio. *A Certain Realism*. Berkeley: University of California Press, 1993.

Willemen, Paul., ed. *Pier Paolo Pasolini*. London: BFI, 1976.

Witcombe, R.T. *The New Italian Cinema*. London: Secker & Warburg, 1982.

126. *Decameron Nights* (1924)

Great Britain; dir. Herbert Wilcox; Graham-Wilcox.

CAST: Randel Ayrton, Lionel Barrymore, Xeni Desni, Ivy Duke, Bernard Goetske, Werner Krauss, Hanna Ralph, Albert Steinruke, Hans Sternberg, Jameson Thomas.

Saladin and the King of Algrave wish to conquer the world by first cementing their alliance with a marriage between Saladin's son and the king's daughter. Unfortunately, Saladin's son falls in love with another woman who is killed by his furious father.

This film, which has only the slightest debt to Boccaccio, is in fact based on a successful melodrama by Robert McLaughlin and Boyce Lawrence that enjoyed a long run at London's Drury Lane Theatre.

REVIEWS: *Bioscope* 4 September 1924: 44. *New York Times* 29 May 1928: 17. *Variety* 17 September 1924: 29; 30 June 1928: 30.

ADDITIONAL DISCUSSIONS:

Connelly, Robert. *The Motion Picture Guide, Silent Film 1910–1936*. Chicago: Cinebooks, 1986.

Gifford, Denis. *The British Film Catalogue, 1895–1985*. Newton Abbot: David & Charles, 1986.

Warren, Patricia. *The British Film Collection, 1896–1984: A History of the British Cinema in Pictures*. London: Elm Tree, 1984.

127. *Decameron Nights* (1953)

Great Britain; dir. Hugo Fregonese; Film Locations.

CAST: Binnie Barnes, Bert Bernard, George Bernard, Joan Collins, Joan Fontaine, Louis Jourdan, Meinhart Maur, Hugh Morton, Noel Percell, Godfrey Tearle.

Giovanni Boccaccio, the teller of bawdy tales, learns that virtue triumphs over vice in a story-telling contest between his lady love and himself. The contest consists of a retelling of three tales from Boccaccio, those of Ricciardo di Chinzica (Day 2, Tale 10), Bernabò da Genoa (Day 2, Tale 9) and Giletta of Narbonne (Day 3, Tale 9).

This bowdlerized version of Boccaccio's tale is simply one of a series of films made in the 1950s (both in England and the United States) using medieval settings and plots.

REVIEWS: *Kinematograph Weekly* 8 January 1953: 16, 18a. *Motion Picture Herald* 7 November 1953: Product Digest Section 61. *Monthly Film Bulletin* 20 (February 1953): 18–19. *New York Times* 17 November 1953: 38. *Picturegoer* 14 February 1953: 9. *To-day's Cinema* 1 January 1953: 8. *Variety* 21 January 1953: 6.

ADDITIONAL DISCUSSION:

Nash, Jay Robert, and Stanley Ralph Ross. *The Motion Picture Guide, C–D, 1927–1983*. Chicago: Cinebooks, 1985.

128. *Decameron n. 2: Le Altre novelle del Boccaccio* (1971)

Italy; dir. Mino Guerrini; Compagnia Generale Cinematografica.

CAST: Claudia Bianchi, Mario Brega, Mariangela Giordano, Enzo Pulcrano.

In six stories loosely based on Boccaccio, adultery is the fabric of everyday life in medieval Italy.

Guerrini's film is the first in a series of sexploitative knock-offs of Passolini's 1971 film *The Decameron*.

REVIEWS: *Intermezzo* 5 (May-June 1972): 11. *Monthly Film Bulletin* 40 (February 1973): 26.

ADDITIONAL DISCUSSIONS:

Poppi, Roberto, and Mario Pecorari. *Dizionario del cinema italiano: I Film dal 1970 al 1979*. Rome: Gremese Editore, 1996.

La Produzione italiana 1971/72. Rome: Unitalia Film, 1972.

129. *Decameron n. 3: Le Più belle donne del Boccaccio* (1972)

Italy; dir. Italo Alfaro; Victor Cinematografica.

ALTERNATE TITLE: *Decameron's Jolly Kittens*.

CAST: Femi Benussi, Angela Covello, Beba Loncar, Marina Malfatti.

More sexploitation informs these seven tales loosely indebted to Boccaccio. The film was in turn inspired by Pasolini's 1971 film *The Decameron*, but Alfaro's efforts pale in comparison to its source and inspiration.

REVIEWS: *CinemaTV Today* 25 August 1973: 14–15. *Monthly Film Bulletin* 40 (October 1973): 205.

ADDITIONAL DISCUSSIONS:

Poppi, Roberto, and Mario Pecorari. *Dizionario del*

Lobby card for Hugo Fregonese's *Decameron Nights* (1953).

cinema italiano: I Film dal 1970 al 1979. Rome: Gremese Editore, 1996.

La Produzione italiana 1971/72. Rome: Unitalia Film, 1972.

130. *Decameron proibitissimo* (1972)

Italy; dir. Franco Martinelli [Marino Girolami]; Claudia Cinematografica.

ALTERNATE TITLES: *The Forbidden Decameron* and *Sexy Sinners.*

CAST: Franco Agostini, Gianni De Luca, Laetitia Le Hir, Mariso Longo, Enzo Mandronico, Cristina Perra, Mauro Vestri, Leonora Vivaldi.

A group of aristocrats flees to the countryside to avoid an outbreak of plague. To pass the time, they tell six tales of wives who are unfaithful to their husbands with clergymen, students and servants.

Martinelli's approach is typical of those used by a number of directors in would-be sequels to Pasolini's 1971 film *The Decameron.* It reduces Boccaccio's work to a series of naughty tales in which women are, more times than not, unfaithful to their husbands.

DISCUSSIONS:

Poppi, Roberto, and Mario Pecorari. *Dizionario del cinema italiano: I Film dal 1970 al 1979.* Rome: Gremese Editore, 1996.

La Produzione italiana 1971/72. Rome: Unitalia Film, 1972.

Decameron 3 (1972) see *Novelle galeotte d'amore dal Decamerone* (1972)

131. *Decamerone* (1912)

Italy; Versuvio Films.

This cinematic trilogy retells the stories of Andreuccio of Perugia (Day 2, Tale 5), the Count of Antwerp (Day 2, Tale 8) and the Groom and the Wife of King Agilulf (Day 3, Tale 2) from Boccaccio's *Decameron.*

DISCUSSIONS:

Bernardini, Aldo, ed. *Archivo del cinema italiano. Vol. 1: Il cinema muto 1905–1931.*

Prolo, Maria Adriana. *Storia del cinema muto italiano.* Milan: Poligono Società Editrice, 1951.

Il Decamerone (1971) see *The Decameron* (1971)

132. *Il Decamerone nero* (1972)

Italy; dir. Piero Vivarelli; Finarco Film.

ALTERNATE TITLE: *The Black Decameron.*

CAST: Beryl Cunningham, Djbrill Diop, Serigne N'Diaye Gonzales, Line Senghor.

In a nod toward Boccaccio, a group of African tribespeople gather to tell five stories — the beautiful queen, the cure of the crazy woman, the punished lovers, the prostitute's revenge and Simoa's endless search — all with analogues in *The Decameron.*

REVIEWS: *CinemaTV Today* 26 January 1974: 14. *Monthly Film Bulletin* 41 (February 1974): 26. *Télérama* 1554 (14 November 1979): 151.

ADDITIONAL DISCUSSIONS:

Poppi, Roberto, and Mario Pecorari. *Dizionario del cinema italiano: I Film dal 1970 al 1979.* Rome: Gremese Editore, 1996.

La Produzione italiana 1972/73. Rome: Unitalia Film, 1973.

133. *Il Decamerone proibito* (1972)

Italy; dir. Carlo Infascelli; Roma Film.

ALTERNATE TITLE: *The Forbidden Decameron.*

CAST: Dado Crostarosa, Carlos De Carvalho, Orchidea De Santis, Mario Frera, Gabriella Giorgelli, Margaret Rose Keil, Marisa Longo, Mario Maranzana.

In a small Tuscan town beset by plague, a stranger arrives and, having no fear of the plague, manages to ingratiate himself with the wives of the town. When their husbands discover what he is up to, he flees to a monastery. Grafted onto this central story are two other stories involving wives who stray from their husbands when strange young men come to town.

Misogyny and sexploitation underscore this weak attempt to produce a sequel to Pasolini's 1971 film *The Decameron.*

REVIEWS: *CinemaTV Today* 31 March 1973: 23. *Cinematografia ITA* 39 (15 March–15 April 1972): 145–46. *Films and Filming* 20 (December 1973): 64. *Intermezzo* 28 (May–July 1972): 11. *Monthly Film Bulletin* 40 (May 1973): 95.

ADDITIONAL DISCUSSIONS:

Poppi, Roberto, and Mario Pecorari. *Dizionario del cinema italiano: I Film dal 1970 al 1979.* Rome: Gremese Editore, 1996.

La Produzione italiana 1971/72. Rome: Unitalia Film, 1972.

Decameron's Jolly Kittens (1972) see *Decameron n. 3* (1972)

134. *Decameroticus* (1972)

Italy; dir. Pier Giorgio Ferretti; National Cinematografica.

CAST: Orchidea De Santis, Umberto D'Orsi, Riccardo Garrone, Gabriella Giorgelli, Camille Keaton, Krista Nell, Margareth Rose.

Husbands and wives intent upon trapping each other in adultery set up elaborate schemes, all of which backfire, in yet another sexploitative would-be sequel to Pasolini's 1971 film *The Decameron.*

DISCUSSIONS:

Poppi, Roberto, and Mario Pecorari. *Dizionario del cinema italiano: I Film dal 1970 al 1979.* Rome: Gremese Editore, 1996.

La Produzione italiana 1972/73. Rome: Unitalia Film, 1973.

135. *Le Destin d'un roi* (1913)

France; dir. A.E. Coleby; Pathé Frères.

Scotland's King James I rules tyrannically and meets a fitting end at the hands of kinsmen turned assassins.

James I's rule (1394–1437) was uneasy. His attempted reform of Scotland on the model of the fifteenth century English constitution led to his downfall.

DISCUSSION:

Bousquet, Henri. *Catalogue Pathé des années 1896 à 1914: 1912–1913–1914.* Paris: Henri Bousquet, 1995.

The Devil's Breath (1993) see *El Aliento del diablo* (1993)

The Devil's Envoys (1942) see *Les Visiteurs du soir* (1942)

The Devil's Impostor (1972) see *Pope Joan* (1972)

The Devil's Laboratory (1897) see *Le Cabinet de Méphistophélès* (1897)

136. *Le Diable dans la ville* (1925)

France; dir. Germaine Dulac; Films de France.

CAST: Jacqueline Blanc, Michelle Clairfont, Léon Mathot, Albert Mayer.

The inhabitants of a medieval French village live under the gaze of two statues, one of St. Gabriel and the other that of an evil spirit. When the statue of Gabriel is damaged, evil breaks out. A stranger who suddenly appears in the midst of the townspeople is hard-pressed to quell the hysteria that follows his arrival.

This cinematic study of medieval superstition is most notable because it is the work of an important early woman director, now largely forgotten. The film was based on a scenario by Jean-Louis Bouquet entitled *La Ville des fous,* in which a group of superstitious villagers is duped by a band of robbers hiding underground.

REVIEWS: *Cinéa-ciné pour tous* NS 30 (1 February 1925): 5–6. *Cinémagazine* 5 (26 December 1924): 562–66. *Tirages et restaurations de la cinémathèque française* 2 (1987): 44.

ADDITIONAL DISCUSSIONS:

Abel, Richard. *French Cinema, The First Wave, 1915–1929.* Princeton: Princeton University Press, 1984.

Brunius, Jacques B. *En Marge du cinéma français.* Paris: Arcanes, 1954.

_____. "Experimental Film in France." In Roger Manvell, ed. *Experiment in the Film.* London: Grey Walls, 1949.

Chirat, Raymond. *Catalogue des films français de long métrage. Films de fiction 1919–1929.* Toulouse: Cinémathèque de Toulouse, 1984.

de Munto, J.-A. "Mme Germaine Dulac nous parle du 'Diable dans le ville.'" *Cinémagazine* 4 (9 May 1924): 245–47.

Fescourt, Henri. *Le Foi et les montaignes.* Paris: Montel, 1959.

Flitterman-Lewis, Sandy. *To Desire Differently, Feminism and the French Cinema.* Urbana: University of Illinois Press, 1990.

Ford, Charles. *Dulac.* Paris: Anthologie du cinéma, 1972. [Supplement to *Avant-scène du cinéma* 71 (January 1968).]

_____. *Femmes cinéastes, ou le triomphe de la volonté.* Paris: Denoël, 1972.

Heck-Rabi, Louise. *Women Filmmakers: A Critical Reception.* Metuchen, N.J.: Scarecrow, 1984.

Lejeune, Paule. *Le Cinéma des femmes.* Paris: Éditions Atlas, 1987.

137. *Dimitry Donskoy* (1909)

France; dir. Kai Hansen; Pathé Frères and Le Film russe.

ALTERNATE TITLE: *An Episode from the Life of Dimitri Donskoi* and *Epizod iz zhizni Dmitriya Donskogo.*

CAST: Vladimir Karine, I. Langfeld, Matveieff, Nina Rutkovskaia, Voinoff.

The Tartar hordes overrun Russia. In a small village, they kill the son and kidnap the daughter of an old peasant who appeals to Dimitry Donskoy for assistance. Prince Dimitry mounts a counterattack, defeating the Tartars and rescuing the peasant's daughter.

Prince Dimitri Ivanovich Donskoj or Donskoy (1350–1389) was prince of Moscow, grand prince of Vladimir and one of the great Muscovite military heroes. In his greatest battle, he defeated the Mongolian Golden Horde in 1380 at Kulikovo Field near the River Don.

REVIEWS: *Bioscope* 23 December 1909: 43. *Moving Picture World* 11 June 1910: 1008; 25 June 1910: 1100. *Pathé Frères Weekly Bulletin* 136 (6 June 1910): [7–8].

ADDITIONAL DISCUSSIONS:

Abel, Richard. "Pathé's Stake in Early Russian Cinema." *Griffithiana* 38–39 (October 1990): 242–47.

Bousquet, Henri. *Catalogue Pathé des années 1896 à 1914: 1910–1911.* Paris: Henri Bousquet, 1994.

Savada, Elias. *The American Film Institute Catalog of Motion Pictures Produced in the United States: Film Beginnings, 1893–1910.* Metuchen, N.J.: Scarecrow, 1995.

Usai, Paolo Cherchi, et al., eds. *Silent Witnesses, Russian Films 1908–1919.* London: BFI, 1989.

Vishnevsky, Ven. *Knudozhnestvennye filmy dorevoliutsionnoi rossi.* Moscow: Goskinoizdat, 1945.

138. *Doctor Faustus* (1967)

Great Britain; dir. Richard Burton and Neville Coghill; Oxford University Screen Productions.

CAST: Richard Burton, Elizabeth Taylor.

Faustus, a scholar at Wittenberg, conjures up Mephistopheles and sells him his soul in exchange for 24 years of the devil's servitude. Transformed into a young man, Faustus orders Mephistopheles to help him find beauty and wisdom. He sees the seven deadly sins, taunts the members of a papal synod and raises the spirits of Alexander the Great and Helen of Troy, with whom he falls in love. As his pact with the Devil comes to an end, he follows Helen into Hell.

Based on Marlowe's play *Dr. Faustus*, which was first published in 1604, this film was one of Burton's first efforts as a director. Panned by the critics, Burton nonetheless considered it one of his more successful efforts.

REVIEWS: *Film Daily* 6 February 1968: 6. *Filmfacts* 11 (1 March 1968): 40–42. *Film Quarterly* 21 (Spring 1968): 56. *Films and Filming* 13 (January 1967): 53–55. *Films in Review* 19 (March 1968): 176–77. *Hollywood Reporter* 6 February 1968: 3. *Kinematograph Weekly* 21 October 1967: 21. *Monthly Film Bulletin* 34 (December 1967): 185. *Motion Picture Herald* 28 February 1968: Product Digest Section 777–78. *New York Times* 7 February 1968: 38. *Times* [London] 16 October 1967: 7. *Variety* 25 October 1967: 20.

ADDITIONAL DISCUSSIONS:

Bragg, Melvyn. *Richard, The Life of Richard Burton.* London: Hodder & Stoughton, 1988.

Doria, Luciano. *Burton-Taylor, les magnifiques.* Montréal: Éditions la presse, 1973.

Nash, Jay Robert, and Stanley Ralph Ross. *The Motion Picture Guide, C–D, 1927–1983.* Chicago: Cinebooks, 1985.

Prodolliet, Ernest. *Faust im Kino, Die Geschichte des Faustfilms von den Anfängen bis in die Gegenwart.* Freiburg, Switz.: Universitätsverlag Freiburg, 1978.

Sinyard, Neil. *Filming Literature: The Art of Screen Adaptation.* New York: St. Martin's, 1986.

Steverson, Tyrone. *Richard Burton, A Bio-Bibliography.* Westport, Conn.: Greenwood, 1992.

Vermilye, Jerry, and Mark Ricci. *The Films of Elizabeth Taylor.* Secaucus, N.J.: Citadel, 1976.

139. *Dorotej* (1980)

Yugoslavia; dir. Zdravko Verlimirovic; Avala Film.

CAST: Danco Cevrevski, Darko Damevski, Dragomir Felba, Meto Jovanovski, Gorcia Popovic, Gojko Santic, Velimir Zivojinovic.

In 1308, famine, war and plague ravage the Balkans. The herbalist monk Dorotej wanders the countryside effecting some cures. He cures an abbot, but he must immediately flee the monastery to escape the wrath of a monk who had hoped to succeed the abbot. He next cures a Serbian warlord, but after a chance meeting with the warlord's wife, he and she become lovers. Both are then murdered by yet another warlord who had had designs on the lady.

The film's source is a Serbian epic turned into a popular novel in 1977 by Dobrilo Nenadic. The most impressive things in *Dorotej* are its authentic settings in medieval monasteries and castles then under UNESCO protection as national monuments and treasures.

REVIEWS: *Ekran* [Yugoslavia] 6 (1981): 8–9. *Jugoslavija Film News* 130 (September 1980): 8; 132 (October 1981): 5. *Variety* 12 August 1981: 20.

ADDITIONAL DISCUSSION:

Tasic, Zoran and Jean-Loup Passek, eds. *Le Cinéma yougoslave.* Paris: Centre Georges Pompidou, 1986.

Dragens Fange (1985) see *The Captive of the Dragon* (1985)

140. *Dragonheart* (1996)

United States; dir. Rob Cohen; Universal.

CAST: Julie Christie, Sean Connery (voice of the dragon), Jason Isaacs, Dina Meyer, Lee

Richard Burton in the title role in his *Doctor Faustus* (1967).

Oakes, Pete Postlethwaite, Dennis Quaid, David Thewlis.

In a period after the decline of Arthur's Round Table and the code of justice it upheld, peasants rise up against and kill a tyrannical king, wounding his son Einon at the same time. Queen Aislinn convinces a mighty dragon to share his heart with the prince so that he might be healed. The dragon agrees, but Einon becomes a crueler tyrant than his father. His nemesis eventually becomes Bowen, his former tutor, who madly chases around the country, killing dragons for bounty. Bowen and the last dragon, Draco, join forces at first for their mutual financial benefit and then in order to defeat Einon who can only be killed when Draco is killed since they share the same heart.

The film presents a grab bag of medieval elements that do not add up to any kind of coherent whole. The dragon in *Dragonslayer* is more impressive and fearsome; the talking, facially expressive Draco seems more like an overgrown dog than a mythical beast.

REVIEWS: *Empire* 89 (November 1996): 30–31. *Entertainment Weekly* 328 (24 May 1996): 30; 330 (7 June 1996): 37–38. *EPD Film* 13 (December 1996): 47–48. *Film Journal International* 99 (July 1996): 57–58. *Film Review* [London] November 1996: 24–25. *Hollywood Reporter* 28 May 1996: 11–12. *Los Angeles Times* 31 May 1996: F1. *New York Times* 31 May 1996: C10. *Sight and Sound* NS6 (November 1996): 47–48. *Starburst* 218 (October 1996): 43. *Times* [London] 17 October 1996: 37. *Times* [London] *Educational Supplement* 12 October 1996: 37; 8 November 1996: 7. *Variety* 27 May 1996: 65, 73.

ADDITIONAL DISCUSSIONS:

Chase, Donald. "Years of the Dragon." *Entertainment Weekly* 330 (7 June 1996): 30–33.

Duncan, Jody. "Heart and Soul." *Cinefex* 66 (June 1996): 44–64.

_____. *The Making of* Dragonheart. New York: Boulevard, 1996.

Grant, Edmond, ed. *The Motion Picture Guide: 1997*

Dennis Quaid as the dragonslaying Bowen and Draco, the last dragon, in Rob Cohen's *Dragonheart* (1996).

Annual (*The Films of 1996*). New York: Cine-Books, 1997.

Magid, Ron. "*Dragonheart* Fulfills Filmic Quest." *American Cinematographer* 77 (January 1996): 96–105.

Pogue, Charles Edward. *Dragonheart*. New York: Boulevard Books, 1996. [Novelization.]

Trower, Marcus. "Are You Tolkein to Me?" *Empire* 89 (November 1996): 66–74.

141. *Dragonslayer* (1981)

United States; dir. Matthew Robbins; Disney and Paramount.

CAST: Sydney Bromley, Caitlin Clarke, Peter Eyre, John Hallam, Emrys James, Peter MacNicol, Ralph Richardson, Chloe Salaman, Albert Salmi.

In the sixth century, a fire-breathing dragon (Vermithrax Pejorative) terrorizes Urland, demanding regular sacrifice of a virgin. Galen, a young sorcerer's apprentice, tries to defeat the dragon to save his lady love Valerian from the stake. He succeeds thanks to the help of Ulrich, an aged sorcerer and the last of his kind.

Critics rightly considered this film fairly lame, but the special effects used to create the dragon won both praise and awards.

REVIEWS: *Cinéma* [Paris] 289 (January 1983): 56. *Cinefantastique* 10 (Summer 1980): 33; 11 (September 1981): 46. *Ecran fantastique* 27 (1982): 60. *Films and Filming* 329 (February 1982): 29–30. *Films in Review* 32 (October 1981): 497. *Films on Screen and Video* 2 (July 1982): 41–42. *Jump Cut* 26 (December 1981): 1, 18. *Los Angeles Times* 27 June 1981: 40; 29 June 1981: 6. 2. *Monthly Film Bulletin* 49 (February 1982): 26–27. *Motion Picture Product Digest* 9 (8 July 1981): 10. *New York Times* 26 June 1981: 3. 10. *New Yorker* 57 (13 July 1981): 80–81. *Positif* 262 (December 1982): 71–72. *Screen International* 27 February 1982: 20. *Starburst* 43 (1981): 20–22. *Times* [London] 1 August 1981: 10. *Variety* 24 June 1981: 23.

ADDITIONAL DISCUSSIONS:

Bruzenak, Ken. "Dragonslayer." *Prevue* 2 (February-March 1981): 27–31.

Delcourt, Guy. "Le Dragon du lac." *Ecran fantastique* 27 (October 1982): 38–59.

"*Dragonslayer*: Special Supplement." *Screen International* 16 January 1982: 59–70.

Hutchison, David. "The Flash of the Pencil." *Starlog* 52 (November 1981): 57–61.

———. "The Ultimate Dragon." *Starlog* 53 (December 1981): 57–61.

Lynn, Frances. *Dragonslayer*. *Starburst* 42 (1981): 32–36.

Magill, Frank N., ed. *Magill's Cinema Annual, 1982*. Englewood Cliffs, N.J.: Salem, 1982.

Martin, Bob. *Dragonslayer*. *Fangoria* 13 (June 1981): 46–50.

Nash, Jay Robert, and Stanley Ralph Ross. *The Motion Picture Guide, C–D, 1927–1983*. Chicago: Cinebooks, 1985.

Sutak, Ken. "A *Dragonslayer* Inquiry." *Pro Musica Sana* 9 (Summer 1982): 7–15.

Wilson, S.S. *Dragonslayer*. *Cinefex* 6 (October 1981): 30–61.

142. *Dramma medievale* (1908)

Italy; Cines.

While all copies of this film are apparently lost, two different plot synopses survive. In Bernardini and Gili's synopsis, a prince kidnaps the fiancée of a blacksmith who rescues and marries her and kills the prince. In a synopsis in the records of the British Film Institute, the friend of a pilgrim is murdered by a nobleman. The pilgrim avenges the murder of his friends and marries the nobleman's fiancée.

DISCUSSION:

Bernardini, Aldo, and Jean A. Gili, eds. *Le Cinéma italien de La Prise de Rome (1905) à Rome ville ouverte (1945).* Paris: Centre Georges Pompidou, 1986.

143. *Le Droit de seigneur* (1908)

France; Pathé Frères.

ALTERNATE TITLE: *Nobleman's Right.*

The cruelty of a nobleman towards his serfs leads them to rise up against him. When he is about to be stoned to death, his wife, long known for her kindness to the serfs, intervenes on her husband's behalf. He is saved and mends his ways, promising to outdo his wife in his kindness to the serfs.

REVIEW: *Moving Picture World* 16 May 1908: 446.

ADDITIONAL DISCUSSIONS:

Bousquet, Henri. *Catalogue Pathé des années 1896 à 1914: 1907–1908–1909.* Paris: Henri Bousquet, 1993.

Savada, Elias. *The American Film Institute Catalog of Motion Pictures Produced in the United States: Film Beginnings, 1893–1910.* Metuchen, N.J.: Scarecrow, 1995.

144. *Du Guesclin* (1948)

France; dir. Bernard de Latour; Discina.

CAST: Junie Astor, Gisèle Casadesus, K. Gallian, Fernand Garvey, G. Oury, Noël Roquevert, H. Vernon.

Born into a modestly noble family, Bertrand du Guesclin shows an early flair for warfare. After a wild youth, he becomes the leader of French forces against the English in Brittany and the Spaniards in Navarre. Named Constable of France by Charles V, he vows to rid France of all English occupying armies but dies in battle.

Bertrand du Guesclin (1320–1380) helped turn the tide in the Hundred Years War briefly in favor of the French. He was considered one of the models of chivalry even before his death during the siege of Châteauneuf de Randon on July 13, 1380.

REVIEWS: *Cinématographie française* 1315 (11 June 1949): 20. *Le Monde* 10 June 1949: 9. *Plaisir de France* December 1948: 53–57.

ADDITIONAL DISCUSSIONS:

Bessy, Maurice, and Raymond Chirat. *Histoire de cinéma française: encyclopéde des films 1940–1950.* Paris: Pygmalion, 1986.

Chirat, Raymond. *Catalogue des films français de long métrage: Films de fiction 1940–1950.* Luxembourg: La Cinémathèque municipale de Luxembourg, 1981.

Guibbert, Pierre. "Naivetés et roublardises: Du Guesclin (Bernard de Latour, 1948)." *Cahiers de la cinémathèque* 45 (1986): 51–54.

145. *Il Duca di Atene* (1908)

Italy; Cines.

ALTERNATE TITLE: *The Duke of Athens.*

When a young Florentine nobleman accidentally kills one of the duke's soldiers, his sister goes to plead his case with the tyrannical duke. The duke, Walter of Brienne, agrees to save her brother provided she becomes his lover. When she refuses, the duke signs the brother's death warrant, but a group of noblemen intervene and force the duke to abdicate.

Walter or Gautier VI of Brienne (1312–1356), a Frenchman who held the title of Duke of Athens, was brought to Florence in 1342 by several banking families to save the city from bankruptcy. Never well received, he was expelled from the city after only 11 months of rule.

REVIEW: *Bioscope* 9 February 1911: 42.

146. *I Due crociati* (1968)

Italy; dir. Giuseppe Orlandini; Italian International Film.

ALTERNATE TITLE: *The Two Crusaders.*

CAST: Janeth Ahgren, Franco Borelli, Umberto D'Orsi, Fiorenzo Fiorentini, Franco Franchi, Loris Gizzi, Ciccio Ingrassia.

Franco and Ciccio, two ne'er-do-wells, go on crusade to escape difficulties at home, but life on crusade turns out to be more problematic than life at home. The two fall under the supervision of a fanatic friar, become involved with a Saracen spy, foil a plot to kidnap Godfrey of Bouillon's daughter Clorinda, and somehow manage to defeat Saladin's forces.

DISCUSSIONS:

Italian Production 1968. Rome: Unitalia Film, 1968.

Poppi, Roberto, and Mario Pecorari. *Dizionario del cinema italiano. Vol. 3: I Film dal 1960 al 1969.* Rome: Gremese Editore, 1992.

Steven Waddington as King Edward II (left) and Andrew Tiernan as Gaveston in Derek Jarman's *Edward II* (1991). (Still courtesy of the British Film Institute.)

The Duke of Athens (1908) see *Il Duca di Atene* (1908)

147. *Edward II* (1991)

Great Britain; dir. Derek Jarman; British Screen and BBC Films.

CAST: Kevin Collins, Jerome Flynn, Jody Garber, John Lynch, Dudley Sutton, Tilda Swinton, Nigel Terry, Andrew Tiernan, Steven Waddington.

In a flashback, Edward II recalls his reign. Newly crowned, he summons his lover Gaveston home from exile in France to the scorn of the bishops and peers of England. Edward also incurs the wrath of his queen, Isabella, when he rejects her. The English nobility petition Edward to banish Gaveston, which Edward reluctantly agrees to do out of fear of being deposed. The queen, who has become lovers with Mortimer, has Gaveston recalled so that he can be killed. The king quarrels with the few friends he still has, and Gaveston is killed by Mortimer's troops. Edward tries to rally his forces against Mortimer, but Mortimer imprisons the king and kills his new favorite Spencer. Isabella and Mortimer prepare to rule the kingdom together and dispatch an assassin to murder the king. The assassin refuses to carry out his task, and Isabella and Mortimer are jailed. The young prince assumes the throne as Edward III.

Based on Christopher Marlowe's tragedy *Edward II*, which was first published in 1594, Jarman's film's conclusion departs radically from its source by allowing Edward (1284–1327) to live, thereby following a tradition that suggested the king was not murdered in Berkeley Castle but lived out his life in quiet retreat and exile. Jarman sees Edward as an icon for the 1990s, and he presents the king's story as a gay myth for an age overwhelmed by AIDS and politically sanctioned homophobia. Along with Vincent Ward's 1988 film *The Navigator*, Jarman's film achieves one of the most successful marriages of medieval and modern themes;

Charlton Heston in the title role in Anthony Mann's *El Cid* (1961).

Edward II may just be the most successful cinematic deconstruction of a medieval text.

REVIEWS: *Advocate* 600 (7 April 1992): 79. *Cinema Papers* 89 (August 1992): 32–35. *EPD Film* 9 (May 1992): 31. *Film-dienst* 45 (7 April 1992): 22–23. *Film Faust* 16 (September-October 1991): 42–47. *Film Journal* 95 (April 1992): 38–39. *Film und Fernsehen* 20 (April 1992): 77. *Gay Times* [London] November 1991: 66. *Los Angeles Times* 10 April 1992: Calendar 8; 17 April 1992: Calendar 9. *Mensuel du cinéma* 1 (November-December 1992): 52. *Le Monde* 27 November 1992: 14. *New York Times* 20 March 1992: C16; 24 December 1992: C17. *Positif* 382 (December

1992): 58. *Première* 189 (December 1992): 31. *Segnocinema* 53 (January-February 1992): 46–47. *Séquences* 159-60 (September 1992): 77. *Sight and Sound* NS 1 (November 1991): 41–42. *Studio* [Paris] 68 (December 1992): 20. *Sunday Times* [London] 20 October 1991: 6. 11. *Times* [London] 17 October 1991: 17. *Times* [London] *Higher Education Supplement* 1 December 1991: 19. *Times* [London] *Literary Supplement* 15 November 1991: 19. *Variety* 16 September 1991: 90. *Video Watchdog* 15 (January-February 1993): 13. *24 Images* 62–63 (September-October 1992): 98.

ADDITIONAL DISCUSSIONS:

Chedgzoy, Kate. *Shakespeare's Queer Children.* Manchester: University of Manchester Press, 1995.

Clinch, Minty. "Positive Direction." *Observer Magazine* [London] 13 October 1991: 62–63.

Grundermann, Roy. "History and the Gay Viewfinder." *Cinéaste* 18 (December 1991): 24– 27.

Horger, J. "Derek Jarman's Film Adaptation of Marlowe's *Edward II.*" *Shakespeare Bulletin* 11 (Fall 1993): 37–40.

Jarman, Derek. *At Your Own Risk, A Saint's Testament.* Woodstock, N.Y.: Overlook Press, 1993.

_____. *Queer Edward II.* London: British Film Institute, 1991. [Screenplay.]

Kennedy, Harlan. "The Two Gardens of Derek Jarman." *Film Comment* 29 (November-December 1993): 28–35.

Lippard, Chris, ed. *By Angels Driven: The Films of Derek Jarman.* Westport, Conn.: Praeger, 1996.

McCabe, Colin. "Throne of Blood." *Sight and Sound* NS 1 (October 1991): 12–14.

McGavin, Patrick Z. *Facets Gay & Lesbian Video Guide.* Chicago: Facets Multimedia, 1993.

Miller-Monzon, John, ed. *The Motion Picture Guide: 1993 Annual (The Films of 1992).* New York: Baseline, 1993.

Murray, Raymond. *Images in the Dark, An Encyclopedia of Gay and Lesbian Film and Video.* Rev. ed. New York: Plume, 1996.

O'Pray, Michael. *Derek Jarman: Dreams of England.* London: BFI, 1996.

Raymond, Gerard. "*Edward II* Lives!" *Theatre Week* 247 (4 May 1992): 24–26.

Rich, B. Ruby. "New Queer Cinema." *Sight and Sound* NS 2 (September 1992): 30–34.

Smith, Cheryl. "Queer Questions." *Sight and Sound* NS 2 (September 1992): 34–35.

Stewart, Steve. *Gay Hollywood.* 2nd ed. Laguna Hills, Calif.: Companion Publications, 1994.

Talvacchia, Bette. "Historical Phallicy: Derek Jarman's *Edward II.*" *Oxford Art Journal* 16 (1993): 112–28.

Woods, Chris. "Derek Jarman Breaks the Rules." *Advocate* 593 (31 December 1991): 64–65.

148. *El Cid* (1961)

United States; dir. Anthony Mann; Allied Artists.

CAST: John Fraser, Charlton Heston, Sophia Loren, Genevieve Page, Gary Raymond, Frank Thring, Gerard Tichy, Raf Vallone.

In 1050, Rodrigo Díaz de Vivar rallies Christian forces in Castile, Leon and Aragon to repel the Moorish threat. He routs the Moors, but grants his Moorish captives their freedom, thereby earning the title "El Cid" (the Lord). His mercy is, however, misinterpreted as an act of treason by Count Gormaz, father of his intended Chimene, who challenges Rodrigo to a duel. Rodrigo kills the count in the duel, and Chimene vows to avenge her father's death, although she is obliged by royal decree to marry Rodrigo. When the king dies and his sons quarrel over the succession, Rodrigo is banished by King Alfonso, who must recall him when Moorish troops mass for another attack on Christian Spain. Rodrigo is seriously wounded in battle and dies, but his body is strapped to his horse to lead the final charge against the Moors. They flee in terror, believing Rodrigo to be immortal.

Rodrigo Díaz de Vivar, known as the Cid, died in 1099, after which his life almost immediately became the stuff of legend. His battles against Christians and Moors, his disputes with King Alfonso VI of Castile, his conquest of Valencia in 1094 and his humane treatment of the Moors were first celebrated in the *Poema de mío Cid,* written about 1140. His exploits were subsequently recounted in romances, ballads and plays, the most famous of which was Pierre Corneille's *Le Cid* (1636). Critics who liked the film hailed it as a Spanish *Alexander Nevsky*; those who did not dismissed the film for being more a tedious history lesson than a cinematic entertainment.

REVIEWS: *Les Cahiers du cinéma* 128 (1962): 50–52. *Daily Cinema* 8 December 1961: 9. *Film Daily* 6 December 1961: 6–7. *Filmfacts* 4 (29 December 1961): 307–09. *Film Ideal* 88 (1962): 54–57. *Films and Filming* 8 (February 1962): 30–31; 20 (July 1974): 47–48. *Films in Review* 8 (January 1962): 45–46. *Hollywood Reporter* 4 December 1961: 3. *Kinematograph Weekly* 7 December 1961: 9–10. *Monthly Film Bulletin* 29 (January 1962): 4–5. *Motion Picture Herald* 13 December 1961: Product Digest Section 380. *New York Times* 15 December 1961: 49. *Positif* 45 (1962): 45–49; 368 (October 1991): 100–01. *Times* [London] 22 July 1961: 4; 19 October 1961: 16. *Variety* 6 December 1961: 6.

ADDITIONAL DISCUSSIONS:

Baker, Peter. "And Now—the Greatest Picture Since..." *Films and Filming* 7 (June 1971): 14–15, 36–37.

Basinger, Jeanine. *Anthony Mann*. Boston: Twayne, 1979.

Carr, Robert E., and R.M. Hayes. *Wide Screen Movies*. Jefferson, N.C.: McFarland, 1988.

Crawley, Tony. *The Films of Sophia Loren*. London: LSP Books, 1974.

Darby, William, and Jack Du Bois. *American Film Music*. Jefferson, N.C.: McFarland, 1990.

Elley, Derek. *The Epic Film*. London: Routledge and Kegan Paul, 1984.

Fraser, George MacDonald. *The Hollywood History of the World*. New York: Beech Tree, 1988.

Guber, Peter. *The Making of* El Cid. Madrid: Campadeor, 1962.

Houston, Penelope, and John Gillett. "The Theory and Practice of Blockbusting." *Sight and Sound* 32 (Spring 1963): 68–74.

Hunt, Leon. "What Are Big Boys Made of? *Spartacus, El Cid* and the Male Epic." In Pat Kirkham and Janet Thumin, eds. *You Tarzan: Masculinity, Movies and Men*. New York: St. Martin's, 1993.

Lamb, Harold. *El Cid*. N.p., 1961. [Souvenir booklet.]

Lightman, Herb A. "The Photography of *El Cid* in Technirama-70." *American Cinematographer* 43 (January 1962): 30–41, 44–51.

Lucanio, Patrick. *With Fire and Sword, Italian Spectacles on American Screens 1958–1968*. Metuchen, N.J.: Scarecrow, 1994.

Magill, Frank N., ed. *Magill's Survey of Cinema*. Series II. Clifton Heights, N.J.: Salem, 1981.

Munn, Mike. *The Stories Behind the Scenes of the Great Epic Films*. London: Argus, 1982.

Nash, Jay Robert, and Stanley Ralph Ross. *The Motion Picture Guide, E–G, 1927–1983*. Chicago: Cinebooks, 1986.

Neale, Steve. "Masculinity as Spectacle." *Screen* 24 (November-December 1983): 2–16.

Pickard, Roy. *A Companion to the Movies*. London: Lutterworth, 1972.

Richards, Jeffrey. *Swordsmen of the Screen from Douglas Fairbanks to Michael York*. London: Routledge & Kegan Paul, 1977.

Rovin, Jeff. *The Films of Charlton Heston*. Secaucus, N.J.: Citadel, 1977.

Searles, Baird. *EPIC! History on the Big Screen*. New York: Abrams, 1990.

Smith, Gary A. *Epic Films*. Jefferson, N.C.: McFarland, 1991.

Thomas, Tony. *The Great Adventure Films*. Secaucus, N.J.: Citadel, 1976.

149. *Elckerlijc* (1975)

Netherlands; dir. Jos Stelling; Jos Stelling Film Productions.

ALTERNATE TITLE: *Everyman*.

CAST: George Bruens, Lucie Singeling, Geert Tijssens, Jan vande Steen.

Death comes for Elckerlijc (Everyman), who looks in vain for someone to accompany him on his last journey. Society, Friends and Property all reject his pleas. Knowledge of God, Virtue, Wisdom and Beauty come to his assistance, but only Virtue goes with him to the grave.

A lesser sequel to Stelling's 1974 film *Mariken van Nieumeghen*, *Elckerlijc* is based on the morality play written by Petrus van Diest in the latter half of the fifteenth century. There has been considerable critical discussion about the relationship between the Dutch play and its better-known English counterpart, *Everyman*, in terms of which play was the source for the other. The weight of critical opinion currently favors the idea that the English play is a translation of the Dutch.

REVIEWS: *Amis du film et de la télévision* 245 (October 1976): 33; 252–53 (May-June 1977): 21. *Skoop* 11 (November 1975): 20–21.

ADDITIONAL DISCUSSIONS:

Bertina, B.J., ed. *Dutch Film 1975*. The Hague: Government Printing Office, 1977.

Cowie, Peter. *Dutch Cinema*. London: Tantivy Press, 1979.

The End of a Dynasty (1910) see *La Fin d'une dynastie* (1910)

150. *Les Enfants d'Édouard* (1909)

France; dir. Henri Andréani; Pathé Frères and Film d'Art.

ALTERNATE TITLE: *The Children of Edward IV*.

Young Prince Edward ascends the throne after the death of his father, but his uncle, the Duke of Gloucester, intent upon seizing the crown for himself, has the prince and his brother declared bastards and imprisoned and murdered in the Tower of London. Richard's rule is, however, short-lived, and he dies in battle haunted by visions of his murdered nephews.

This film tells a tale best known through Shakespeare's *Richard III*. Edward V (1470–83) was imprisoned in the Tower of London with his younger brother by their uncle Richard, Duke of Gloucester, in June 1483. They were never heard from again and were presumed murdered on the duke's orders.

REVIEW: *Moving Picture World* 25 June 1910: 1102.

ADDITIONAL DISCUSSION:

Bousquet, Henri. *Catalogue Pathé des années 1896 à 1914: 1907–1908–1909*. Paris: Henri Bousquet, 1993.

Die Entstehung der Eidgenossen-schaft (1924) see *Les Origines de la Confédération* (1924)

The Epic Hero and the Beast (1956) see *Ilya Muromets* (1956)

An Episode from the Life of Dimitri Donskoi (1909) see *Dimitry Donskoy* (1909)

Epizod iz zhizni Dmitriya Donskogo (1909) see *Dimitry Donskoy* (1909)

Erik il vichingo (1964) see *Vengeance of the Vikings* (1964)

151. *Erik the Conqueror* (1961)

Italy and France; dir. Mario Bava; Galatea-Criterion-Société Cinématographique Lyre.

ALTERNATE TITLES: *Fury of the Vikings* and *Gli Invasori.*

CAST: Giorgio Ardisson, Andrea Checchi, Alice Kessler, Ellen Kessler, Folco Lulli, Cameron Mitchell.

When the Viking invaders are defeated, Queen Alice adopts an orphan whom she raises as Erik, Duke of Helfort. Unbeknownst to anyone, he is the brother of Iron, the chief of the Vikings. Years later, Alice is taken prisoner by Gunnar, whom she thought was a trusted counselor. As a reward for his treachery, the Vikings appoint Gunnar governor of Britain. Erik attempts to free Alice and end Viking control of Britain. He meets and recognizes his brother in one-on-one combat, and the two withdraw from the field of battle. Iron contemplates what he should do, but before he can be reconciled with Erik, Iron is murdered by Gunnar. Erik than rallies English and Viking forces to defeat Gunnar and rescue Alice.

This Italian-French co-production is a fairly typical costume piece with little basis in history. It is inferior to the later Viking film *Knives of the Avenger* (1965), in which Mitchell — Iron in *Erik the Conqueror*— also starred.

REVIEWS: *Cinématographie française* 24 August 1963: 2. *Daily Cinema* 26 April 1963: 6. *Film-echo/Filmwoche* 101 (19 December 1962): 7. *Kinematograph Weekly* 25 April 1963: 29. *Monthly Film Bulletin* 30 (June 1963): 86. *Motion Picture Herald* 18 September 1963: Product Digest Section 892. *Nuovo spettatore cinematografico* 30–31 (1962): 253–54.

ADDITIONAL DISCUSSIONS:
Fasoli, Massimiliano, et al., eds. *La Città del cinema.* Rome: Napoleone, 1979.

Italian Production 1961. Rome: Unitalia Film, 1962.

Lucanio, Patrick. *With Fire and Sword, Italian Spectacles on American Screens 1958–1968.* Metuchen, N.J.: Scarecrow, 1994.

Nash, Jay Robert, and Stanley Ralph Ross. *The Motion Picture Guide, E–G, 1927–1983.* Chicago: Cinebooks, 1986.

Poppi, Roberto, and Mario Pecorari. *Dizionario del cinema italiano. Vol. 3: I film dal 1960 al 1969.* Rome: Gremese Editore, 1992.

Smith, Gary A. *Epic Films.* Jefferson, N.C.: McFarland, 1991.

Weldon, Michael. *The Psychotronic Encyclopedia of Film.* New York: Ballantine, 1983.

152. *Erik the Viking* (1989)

Great Britain; dir. Terry Jones; Prominent Features.

CAST: Gary Cady, John Cleese, Terry Jones, Eartha Kitt, Tim McInnerny, Tim Robbins, Mickey Rooney, Antony Sher, Imogen Stubbs.

When a great winter blankets the Viking world, Erik the Viking seeks to end it by awakening the gods who reside at the edge of the world. Erik sets off with a ragtag band of followers, including a blacksmith intent upon sabotaging his mission. The group reaches Hy-Brasil, home to the Horn of Resounding, secure the horn and, after a series of adventures, succeed in awakening the gods.

Terry Jones first developed the character of Erik the Viking in a 1983 collection of short stories for children. Curiously, his attempt to translate the character from page to screen falls flat, despite a good cast (all with respectable comic and acting experience to their credit). Technically, the film is at times interesting, but ultimately, it bores and makes little sense.

REVIEWS: *Cinefantastique* 20 (November 1989): 26; 20 (March 1990): 55. *Films and Filming* 419 (September 1989): 45. *Los Angeles Times* 1 November 1989: Calendar 3. *Monthly Film Bulletin* 56 (October 1989): 299. *New York Times* 28 October 1989: 13. *Positif* 345 (November 1989): 77–78. *Revue du cinéma* 454 (November 1989): 29–30. *Starburst* 134 (October 1989): 22–23. *Sunday Times* [London] 1 October 1989: C8. *Times* [London] 28 September 1989: 22. *Variety* 6 September 1989: 22.

ADDITIONAL DISCUSSIONS:
Jones, Terry. *Eric the Viking.* New York: Applause, 1990. [Screenplay.]

Magill's Cinema Annual 1990, A Survey of the Films of 1989. Pasadena, Calif.: Salem, 1990.

The Motion Picture Guide: 1990 Annual (The Films of 1989). Evanston, Ill.: Cinebooks, 1990.

153. *The Erotic Adventures of Siegfried* (1971)

Germany and the United States; dir. Adrian Hoven; Atlas.

ALTERNATE TITLES: *The Long Swift Sword of Siegfried* and *Siegfried und das Sagenhafte Liebesleben der Nibelungen.*

CAST: Peter Berling, Lance Boyle, Fred Coplan, Sybil Danninger, Katharina Giani, Peter Hard, Heidi Ho.

Siegfried is warmly received at Gunther of Burgundy's court by all but Hagen, where he seeks the hand of Kriemhild, Gunther's sister, in marriage. Gunther agrees if Siegfried will help him defeat the Saxons and Danes and win the hand of Brunhild, Queen of Iceland. Brunhild will marry Gunther only if he can outlast her in a contest of lovemaking. Siegfried, using his gift of invisibility, takes Gunther's place and bests Brunhild in bed. All return to Burgundy where Siegfried marries Kriemhild and Gunther marries Brunhild, who is disappointed in her new husband's sexual prowess.

A hit at the 1971 New York Erotic Film Festival, this film attempts, without much success, to reduce the German epic *Der Nibelungenlied* to a series of soft-core erotic episodes.

REVIEWS: *Filmfacts* 4 (July 1971): 755. *Monthly Film Bulletin* 39 (July 1972): 146.

ADDITIONAL DISCUSSION:

McGillivray, David. "It's All in the Mind." *Films and Filming* 18 (August 1972): 18–23.

154. *Es ist nicht leicht Gott zu sein* (1989)

West Germany and the Soviet Union; dir. Peter Fleischmann; Hallelujah Film.

ALTERNATE TITLES: *It's Hard to Be God* and *Trudno byt bogom.*

CAST: El Gudsha Burduli, Birgit Doll, Aleksandr Filipenko, Anne Gautier, Christine Kaufmann, Hugues Quester, Edward Zentara.

In some unspecified future time, scientists send astronauts to a distant planet that mirrors Earth but whose inhabitants are still living in the Middle Ages. Since Earth has over the centuries become non-violent, the purpose of the mission is to see if the visitors will revert to violence and barbarism. The visitors do indeed have great difficulty staying above the petty squabbles that plague life on the distant planet. In the end, the visitors must be put to sleep and have their memories erased before they can be safely returned to Earth.

As a simple science fiction yarn in which future and past collide in a medieval landscape, this film has possibilities, but clearly the director intends for the film to do more. Based on the 1966 novel *Trudno byt bogum* by Arkadii and Boris Sturgatskii, *Hard to Be a God* seems also to want to take to task a contemporary world consumed by daily violence.

REVIEWS: *EPD Film* 7 (February 1990): 28. *Filmfaust* 76 (March-April 1990): 54–55. *Film français* 2360 (26 July 1991): 13. *Image et son* 474 (September 1991): 40. *Kino* [Germany] 3 (1989): v–vi. *Positif* 345 (November 1989): 55. *Revue du cinéma* 474 (September 1991): 40. *Soviet Film* 6 (June 1990): 4–7. *Variety* 22 September 1989: 41.

ADDITIONAL DISCUSSIONS:

Film-Jahrbuch 1989. Hamburg: Kino Verlag, 1988.

Les Films français production 1990. Paris: Unifrance International Film, 1990.

Mari, Jean-Paul. "Scènes de tournage en Ukraine." *Le Nouvel Observateur* 15 April 1988: 18–19.

Schäfer, Horst, and Walter Schobert, eds. *Fischer Film Almanach 1991.* Frankfurt am Main: Fisher Taschenbuch Verlag, 1991.

155. *The Escape from the Dungeon* (1911)

France; Gaumont.

When a cruel nobleman imprisons her father in his castle, a young woman disguises herself as a minstrel and frees him.

REVIEWS: *Moving Picture World* 18 November 1911: 572; 9 December 1911: 816.

156. *La Esmeralda* (1905)

France; dir. Alice Guy Blaché; Gaumont.

CAST: Denise Becker, Henri Vorins.

The hunchbacked bell-ringer of Notre Dame is condemned to the pillory. Only a young gypsy girl takes pity on him, offering him a cup of water. The hunchback's guardian, the archdeacon, watches the scene with interest, secretly lusting after the girl. The archdeacon commands the hunchback to kidnap the girl, but a captain intervenes and saves her. The girl falls in love with the captain, who returns her affection. When they meet for a secret rendezvous, the archdeacon stabs the captain but places blame for the murder on the girl. The girl is sentenced to death by hanging. The archdeacon views her corpse hanging from the gallows and is filled with remorse. The hunchback flings him to his death from the cathedral towers.

Tim Robbins as the title character in Terry Jones's *Erik the Viking* (1989).

This first film adaptation of Victor Hugo's classic nineteenth century novel *Notre Dame de Paris* is the work of one of the most important and prolific early women directors. Interestingly, it does not change the villain's pro-fession to some secular occupation, as future film adaptations were wont to do for fear of offending the Catholic Church.

REVIEW: *Elge Monthly List* 70 (October 1905): 4–9.

ADDITIONAL DISCUSSIONS:

Druxman, Michael. *Make It Again Sam.* South Brunswick, N.J.: A.S. Barnes, 1975.

Gifford, Denis. *A Pictorial History of Horror Films.* Rev. ed. London: Hamlyn, 1983.

Glut, Donald F. *Classic Movie Monsters.* Metuchen, N.J.: Scarecrow, 1978.

Heck-Rabi, Louise. *Women Filmmakers: A Critical Reception.* Metuchen, N.J.: Scarecrow, 1984.

Lejeune, Paule. *Le Cinéma des femmes.* Paris: Éditions Atlas, 1987.

Leonard, William Torbert. *Theatre: Stage to Screen to Television.* Metuchen, N.J.: Scarecrow, 1981.

Sadoul, Georges. *Histoire générale du cinéma II. Les Pionniers du cinéma (de Méliès à Pathé) 1897–1909.* Paris: Les Éditions Denoël, 1977.

Slide, Anthony, ed. *The Memoirs of Alice Guy Blaché.* Roberta and Simone Blaché, trans. Metuchen, N.J.: Scarecrow, 1986.

Wanamaker, Marc. "Alice Guy Blaché." *Cinema* [Beverly Hills, Calif.] 35 (1976): 10–13.

157. *Ettore Fieramosca* (1938)

Italy; dir. Alessandro Blasetti; Nembo-Film.

CAST: Clara Calamai, Elisa Cegani, Gino Cervi, Mario Ferrari, Lambertto Picasso, Osvaldo Valenti.

Two French knights contemptuously discuss the fate of the Duchy of Monreale; they view the Italians and their culture as inferior. By way of background to their converesation, the populace is being forcibly evacuated from the countryside as a result of the French defeat of the Italians. A counter-insurgency begins under the brash Ettore Fieramosca, who is twice wounded in skirmishes with the French. Fieramosca is motivated by love of his country and of Giovanna, Duchess of Monreale, who is betrothed to another. Both of his devotions give him the strength to be successful when he challenges the French to a combat by tournament that will pit 13 French knights against an equal number of Italian knights. In the tournament, Fieramosca battles Guy de la Motte, the leader of the French forces, and defeats him. In the film's final sequence, Fieramosca prepares to marry Giovanna.

More than a little bit of national pride and propaganda lies behind this Italian film made on the eve of the Second World War. The film is based on the nineteenth century novel *Ettore Fieramosca* by Massimo d'Azeglio (1798–1866). Both the film and the novel commemorate an actual event, the so-called Challenge at Barletta in Apulia in 1503, where in a chivalric tournament 13 Italian mercenaries under the leadership of Fieramosca defeated 13 French knights under the leadership of Pierre Terrail. Terrail (1473–1524) was one of the last great idealized figures of chivalry. He is generally referred to as Le Chevalier Bayard, "le chevalier sans peur et sans reproche." His fame rested on his one-man heroic exploits. He had a low opinion of infantry and firearms, so it was quite fitting that he was killed by a gunshot fired by an infantryman in battle near Sesia. This film, of course, does not celebrate the deeds of Bayard, but rather his defeat at the hands of Fieramosca. The allegory presented in the film is less than subtle. Spain is allied with Italy against France — as it was in the Spanish Civil War — and Italy's national consciousness and identity are assured only when foreigners are expelled from its borders. An even less subtle patriotic agenda underlies the director's 1940 film *La Corona di ferro.*

DISCUSSIONS:

Bernardini, Aldo, and Jean A. Gili, eds. *Le Cinéma italien de La Prise de Rome (1905) à Rome ville ouverte (1945).* Paris: Centre Georges Pompidou, 1986.

Buss, Robin. *Italian Films.* New York: Holmes & Meier, 1989.

Casadia, Gianfranco. *Il Grigio et il nero.* Ravenna: Longu Editore, 1989.

Chiti, Robert, and Enrico Lancia. *Dizionario del cinema italiano. Vol 1: I Film dal 1930 al 1944.* Rome: Gremese Editore, 1993.

"*Ettore Fieramosca.*" *Bianco e nero* 3 (April 1939): 5–131. [Special issue containing screenplay, production details, commentary and reviews.]

"The Italians and Russians Do Films of Armored Knights." *Life* 6 (10 April 1939): 47–49.

Landry, Marcia. *Fascism in Film, The Italian Commercial Cinema, 1931–1943.* Princeton: Princeton University Press, 1986.

Savio, Francesco. *Ma l'amore no.* Milan: Sonzogno, 1975.

Even on Rocks Trees Grow (1985) see *The Captive of the Dragon* (1985)

158. *Everyman* (1913)

United States; Kinemacolor.

Summoned by Death, Everyman finds that Knowledge and Good Deeds offer him advice, but only Confession and Repentance will accompany him into the next life.

REVIEW: *Moving Picture World* 23 August 1913: 823.

Everyman (1961) see *Jedermann* (1961)

Gino Cervi in the title role in Alessandro Blasetti's *Ettore Fieramosca* (1938). (Still courtesy of the British Film Institute.)

Everyman (1975) see *Elckerlijc* (1975)

Evil Dead 3 (1992) see *Army of Darkness* (1992)

159. *Excalibur* (1981)

United States; dir. John Boorman; Orion.

CAST: Robert Addie, Gabriel Byrne, Nicholas Clay, Cherie Lunghi, Helen Mirren, Nigel Terry, Nicol Williamson.

King Uther Pendragon upsets a fragile peace when he lusts after Igrayne, the wife of his former rival. With the aid of Merlin's magic, Uther enters Igrayne's castle disguised as her absent husband and fathers the child Arthur with her. Arthur is then raised by Merlin, and Uther is killed, but not before he thrusts the sword Excalibur into a stone from which it can be withdrawn only by the rightful ruler of the land. Arthur grows up unaware of his lineage and destiny. By accident, he draws Excalibur from the stone and is proclaimed reluctant king. Eventually he establishes peace in the realm that is ensured by the fellowship of the Round Table. He marries Guinevere, but their happiness is shattered when Lancelot arrives. First cool to each other, they are soon involved in an adulterous affair that threatens the realm. Merlin himself is threatened by the wily Morgana, Arthur's half-sister, who has for years been secretly plotting revenge for the murder of her father by Merlin and Uther. When an enraged Arthur breaks Excalibur, the kingdom is plunged into chaos as the knights set forth in search of the elusive Grail, many falling into traps set by Morgana. Only Perceval is successful in his quest for the Grail, which he brings back to Camelot to heal Arthur. The renewed king rides forth to reclaim his land and to defeat Morgana and their son Mordred. In the final battle, Arthur kills Mordred but is himself mortally wounded. As Arthur sets sail in a boat captained by three mysterious women, Perceval returns Excalibur to the Lady of the Lake, its magic denied to future generations for all times.

Loosely based on Sir Thomas Malory's fifteenth-century *Le Morte Darthur*, Boorman's film is a dark, brooding meditation on the Arthurian legend in which Arthur becomes the Grail King. The film has not, however, aged well. It now seems too much a product of its times, dominated by a heavy musical score that is designed to cue audience reactions to scenes, sometimes before they are seen.

REVIEWS: *Les Cahiers du cinéma* 326 (July-August 1981): 61–62. *Ciné revue* 20 (14 May 1981): 5. *Cinefantastique* 11 (Summer 1981): 13; 11(Fall 1981): 47. *Cinéma* [Paris] 270 (June 1981): 112–113. *Cinema Canada* 75 (July 1981): 34. *Cinema nuovo* 31 (February 1982): 49–50. *Cinema Papers* 34 (September-October 1981): 399–401. *Continental Film and Video Review* 28 (July 1981): 6–10. *Ecran fantastique* 19 (1981): 66–67. *Filmcritica* 32 (August 1981): 349–351; 33 (January 1982): 20–24. *Filmfaust* 24 (October-November 1981): 28. *Film Journal* 84 (6 April 1981): 13–14. *Film und Fernsehen* 14 (November 1986): 24. *Films* 1 (June 1981): 26–30; 1 (July 1981): 36–37. *Films in Review* 32 (July 1981): 377. *Hollywood Reporter* 6 April 1981: 2. *Jeune cinéma* 136 (July-August 1981): 41–44. *Los Angeles Times* 27 March 1981: 6. 1–2; 5 April 1981: Calendar 28; 17 June 1981: Calendar 1, 6. *Monthly Film Bulletin* 48 (June 1981): 112. *Motion Picture Product Digest* 15 April 1981: 87. *New York Times* 10 April 1981: 3. 11; 10 May 1981: 2. 13. *Positif* 242 (May 1981): 82. *Prevue* 44 (February-March 1981): 34–37. *Revue du cinéma* [La Saison cinématographique] Hors série 25 (1981): 132–33. *Screen International* 300 (11–18 July 1981): 15. *Segnocinema* 2 (December 1981): 58. *Starburst* 35 (1981): 16–19. *Sunday Times* [London] 5 July 1981: 40. *Sunday Times* [London] *Magazine* 28 June 1981: 36. *Times* [London] 28 June 1981: 36; 3 July 1981: 11. *Times* [London] *Literary Supplement* 17 July 1981: 812. *Variety* 8 April 1981: 18. *24 images* 10 (September 1981): 71–72.

ADDITIONAL DISCUSSIONS:

"The Art of *Excalibur*." *Starburst* 38 (1981): 20–21.

Bartone, Richard C. "Variations on Arthurian Legend in *Lancelot du lac* and *Excalibur*." In Sally Slocum, ed. *Popular Arthurian Traditions*. Bowling Green, Ohio: Bowling Green University Popular Press, 1992.

"Boorman and the Arthurian Legend." *Photoplay* 31 (November 1980): 40–41.

Borie, Bertrand. "Entretien avec John Boorman." *Ecran fantastique* 19 (1981): 6–8.

_____. "Table ronde autour d'*Excalibur*." *Ecran fantastique* 20 (1981): 70–72.

Boyle, Sarah. "From Victim to Avenger: The Women in John Boorman's *Excalibur*." *Avalon to Camelot* 1 (Summer 1984): 42–43.

Brode, Douglas. *The Films of the Eighties*. New York: Citadel, 1990.

Burns, E. Jane. "Nostalgia Isn't What It Used to Be: The Middle Ages in Literature and Film." In George Slusser and Eric S. Rabkin, eds. *Shadows of the Magic Lamp, Fantasy and Science Fiction in Film*. Carbondale: Southern Illinois University Press, 1985.

Chandès, Gérard. "Lancelot dans *Excalibur* de John Boorman." In Ulrich Müller, et al., eds. *Lancelot*. Göppingen: Kümmerle, 1984.

Arthur (Nigel Terry) slays Mordred (Robert Addie) in the final battle in John Boorman's *Excalibur* (1981).

Ciment, Michel. "Deux entretiens avec John Boorman." *Positif* 242 (May 1981): 18–31.

_____. *John Boorman*. Trans. Gilbert Adair. London: Faber, 1986.

Clegg, Cynthia. "The Problem of Realizing Romance in Film: John Boorman's *Excalibur*." In George Slusser and Eric S. Rabkin, eds. *Shadows of the Magic Lamp, Fantasy and Science Fiction in Film*. Carbondale: Southern Illinois University Press, 1985.

Decampo, M., and F. Vega. "John Boorman habla de 'Excalibur.'" *Casablanca* 7–8 (July-August 1981): 52–53, 56–57.

de la Brétèque, François. "L'Épée dans le lac, 'Excalibur' de John Boorman ou les aléas de la puissance." *Les Cahiers de la cinémathèque* 42–43 (Summer 1985): 91–96.

_____. "Une 'Figure obligé' du film de chevalerie: le tournoi." *Les Cahiers de la cinémathèque* 42–43 (Summer 1985): 21–26.

de Weever, Jacqueline. "Morgan and the Problem of Incest." In Kevin J. Harty, ed. *Cinema Arthuriana, Essays on Arthurian Film*. New York: Garland, 1981.

D'Heur, J.M. and J. De Groeve. "Arthur, *Excalibur* and The Enchanter Boorman." *Studia in honorem prof. M. de Riquer, III*. Barcelona: Quaderns Crema, 1988.

"Dossier: *Excalibur*." *Positif* 247 (October 1981): 29–43.

Dubost, Francis. "Merlin et le texte inaugural." *Les Cahiers de la cinémathèque* 42–43 (Summer 1985): 85–89.

Haller, Robert. "*Excalibur* and Innovation." *Field of Vision* 13 (Spring 1985): 2–3.

Holley, Linda Tarte. "Medievalism in Film." *Southeastern Medieval Association Newsletter* 9.2 (1983–1984): 13–17.

"Interview with Alex Thompson." *American Cinematographer* 63 (May 1982): 452, 491–93, 504–06.

"John Boorman Talks About *Excalibur*." *Film Directions* 4. 15 (1981): 16–19.

Kennedy, Harlan. "The World of King Arthur According to John Boorman." *American Film* 6 (March 1981): 30–37.

Lacy, Norris J. "Arthurian Film and the Tyranny of Tradition." *Arthurian Interpretations* 4 (Fall 1989): 75–85.

_____. "Mythopoeia in *Excalibur*." In Kevin J. Harty, ed. *Cinema Arthuriana, Essays on Arthurian Film*. New York: Garland, 1981.

MacCurdy, Marian. "Bitch or Goddess: Polarized Images of Women in Arthurian Films and Literature." *Platte Valley Review* 18 (Winter 1990): 3–24.

Maeder, Edward. *Hollywood and History, Costume Design in Film*. Los Angeles: Los Angeles County Museum of Art, 1987.

Magill, Frank N., ed. *Magill's Cinema Annual 1982, The Films of 1981*. Englewood Cliffs, N.J.: Salem, 1982.

_____. *Magill's Survey of Cinema: English Language Films*. Second Series. Englewood Cliffs, N.J.: Salem, 1981.

Nash, Jay Robert, and Stanley Ralph Ross. *The Motion Picture Guide, E–G, 1927–1983*. Chicago: Cinebooks, 1986.

Nickel, Helmut. "Arms and Armor in Arthurian Film." In Kevin J. Harty, ed. *Cinema Arthuriana, Essays on Arthurian Film*. New York: Garland, 1981.

Piccardi, Adriano. "*Excalibur* di John Boorman." *Cineforum* 21 (October 1981): 39–46.

Rooney, Philip J. "The Quest Elements in the Films of John Boorman." Ph.D. dissertation. University of Nebraska–Lincoln, 1989.

Purdon, Liam O., and Robert Blanch. "Hollywood's Myopic Medievalism: *Ecalibur* [sic] and Malory's *Morte d'Arthur*." In Sally Slocum, ed. *Popular Arthurian Traditions*. Bowling Green, Ohio: Bowling Green University Popular Press, 1992.

Ross, Philippe. "L'heroïc fantasy." *Revue du cinéma* 386 (September 1983): 69–79.

Shictman, Martin B. "Hollywood's New Weston: The Grail Myth in Francis Ford Coppola's *Apocalypse Now* and John Boorman's *Excalibur*." *Post Script* 4 (Autumn 1984): 35–49.

Strick, Philip. "John Boorman's Merlin." *Sight and Sound* 49 (Summer 1980): 168–171.

Umland, Rebecca A., and Samuel J. Umland. *The Use of Arthurian Legend in Hollywood Film from Connecticut Yankees to Fisher Kings*. Westport, Conn.: Greenwood, 1996.

Vaines, Colin. "Magic Moments." *Screen International* 252 (2–9 August 1980): 15.

Verniere, James. "The Technology of Style: An Interview with John Boorman." *Filmmakers Monthly* 14 (June 1981): 22–29.

Whitaker, Muriel. "Fire, Water, Rock: Elements of Setting in *Excalibur*." In Kevin J. Harty, ed. *Cinema Arthuriana, Essays on Arthurian Film*. New York: Garland, 1981.

Yakir, Dan. "The Sorcerer." *Film Comment* 17 (May-June 1981): 49–53.

Les Explorateurs de Louis VI le Gros
(1992) see *Les Visiteurs* (1992)

La Fabuleuse Aventure de Marco Polo (1964) see *Marco the Magnificent* (1964)

The Fabulous Adventures of Marco Polo (1964) see *Marco the Magnificent* (1964)

160. *The Fair Maid of Perth* (1923)

Great Britain; dir. Edwin Greenwood; Anglia Films.

CAST: Sylvia Caine, Lionel D'Aragon, Tristram Rawson, Russell Thorndike.

Harry Gow, a knight without pedigree, seeks the hand of Lady Catherine in marriage, but he fails to obtain it when he loses a tournament. Catherine is also the object of affection of the Duke of Rothesay, who attempts to abduct her but is frustrated by the citizens of Perth led by Gow. The angry duke plots his revenge, but in a climactic scene, Gow defeats the duke and wins the hand of Catherine.

Based on Sir Walter Scott's 1828 novel *St. Valentine's Day; or, The Fair Maid of Perth*, this film's reception was undercut by bad editing and poorly done subtitles.

REVIEW: *Bioscope* 15 October 1925: 37.

ADDITIONAL DISCUSSIONS:

Connelly, Robert. *The Motion Picture Guide, Silent Film, 1910–1936*. Chicago: Cinebooks, 1986.

Warren, Patricia. *The British Film Collection 1896–1984*. London: Elm Tree Books, 1984.

The Falcon (1981) see *Banovic Strahinja* (1981)

The Fall of Novgorod the Great (1910) see *Marfa-Posadnista* (1910)

161. *Faust* (1909)

Italy; dir. Mario Caserini; Cines.

CAST: S. Bazzini, Alfredo Bracci, Fernanda Negri-Pouget.

With the aid of Mephistopheles, the aged Faust regains his youth and wins the hand of the woman he loves, but at the price of his soul.

Shown in two parts, this film version of the Faust legend is based on Goethe's two-part tragedy *Faust*, which the playwright completed in 1808 and 1832.

REVIEWS: *Bioscope* 2 June 1910: 39 and 63.

ADDITIONAL DISCUSSIONS:

Bernardini, Aldo, and Jean A. Gili, eds. *Le Cinéma*

italien de La Prise de Rome (1905) à Rome ville ouverte (1945). Paris: Centre Georges Pompidou, 1986.

Prodolliet, Ernest. *Faust im Kino, Die Geschichte des Faustfilms von den Anfängen bis in die Gegenwart*. Freiburg, Switz.: Universitätsverlag Freiburg, 1978.

Savada, Elias. *The American Film Institute Catalog of Motion Pictures Produced in the United States: Film Beginnings, 1893–1910*. Metuchen, N.J.: Scarecrow, 1995.

162. *Faust* (1909)

United States; Edison.

CAST: Alfred de Manby.

The aged Faust makes a pact with Mephistopheles to win the hand of Marguerite. Faust is transformed into a dashing cavalier and succeeds in winning her affection, though Faust soon betrays and deserts her. Valentine, Marguerite's brother, returns from the wars and seeks to defend his sister's honor, but he is killed by Faust in a duel. Marguerite in despair kills the child she has borne Faust and is thrown into prison, where in her dying breath she confesses her love for Faust. Mephistopheles declares her damned, but angels appear to take her to Heaven, as Faust sinks into the depths of Hell.

This well-received film version of the Faust legend uses Charles Gounod's 1859 opera as source. Selections from the opera were used as musical accompaniment.

REVIEWS: *Bioscope* 10 February 1910: 51; 29 August 1912: 614. *Moving Picture World* 25 December 1909: 927; 15 January 1910: 58. *New York Clipper* 18 December 1909: 1131. *New York Dramatic Mirror* 1 January 1910: 17.

ADDITIONAL DISCUSSIONS:

Prodolliet, Ernest. *Faust im Kino, Die Geschichte des Faustfilms von den Anfängen bis in die Gegenwart*. Freiburg, Switz.: Universitätsverlag Freiburg, 1978.

Savada, Elias. *The American Film Institute Catalog of Motion Pictures Produced in the United States: Film Beginnings, 1893–1910*. Metuchen, N.J.: Scarecrow, 1995.

163. *Faust* (1910)

France; Eclair.

An exhausted Faust, weary from years of frustrating work in his laboratory, contemplates suicide, but instead calls upon the powers of darkness for assistance. Mephistopheles offers him youth and endless pleasure in exchange for his soul. Faust agrees, and Mephis-topheles arranges for him to fall in love with Marguerite, who bears him a child. When her brother is killed by Faust in a duel meant to reclaim her honor, Marguerite sinks into despair and is thrown into prison. Mephistopheles tries to make Faust forget about the girl, but to no avail. Faust rushes to the prison, arriving in time to hear her dying words of forgiveness.

Once again, the source for this film version of the legend of Faust was Goethe's two-part tragedy, *Faust*.

REVIEW: *Moving Picture World* 2 July 1910: 47.

164. *Faust* (1910)

France; dir. Henri Andréani and Georges Fagot; Pathé Frères, Production S.A.P.F.

Faust is rescued from a moment of despair by a demon who promises him youth and pleasure in exchange for his soul. Faust immediately falls in love with the innocent Marguerite, whom he seduces and abandons. Wracked by grief, Marguerite kills their child and is thrown into prison. Faust rushes to her side just in time for her to die in his arms.

This film version of the legend of Faust uses selected incidents from Goethe's *Faust* along with original touches supplied by Andréani.

REVIEWS: *Bioscope* 3 November 1910: 39. *Bulletin of the Museum of Modern Art: The Film Library* 3 (November 1935): N.p. [*Film Notes* 1939, Series I, Program I]. *Moving Picture World* 24 June 1911: 1439; 1 July 1911: 1520; 17 July 1911: 1390.

ADDITIONAL DISCUSSIONS:

Bousquet, Henri. *Catalogue Pathé des années 1896 à 1914: 1910–1911*. Paris: Henri Bousquet, 1994.

Prodolliet, Ernest. *Faust im Kino, Die Geschichte des Faustfilms von den Anfängen bis in die Gegenwart*. Freiburg, Switz.: Universitätsverlag Freiburg, 1978.

165. *Faust* (1926)

Germany; dir. F.W. Murnau; UFA.

CAST: Wilhelm Dieterle, Gösta Ekman, Yvette Guilbert, Camilla Horn, Emil Jannings.

Mephisto and an archangel strike a bargain: If the devil can gain the allegiance of Faust, then evil can triumph. Mephisto then ravages an entire town with plague, and the citizens run for help to Faust, their most learned and devout compatriot. When Faust cannot save the life of a dying mother, he rages against God and in despair conjures up Mephisto. Faust agrees to give up his soul for a day if Mephisto will help him save the townspeople from the plague. Mephisto agrees, but the people turn against Faust, accusing him of being in league with the Devil when Faust shrinks from the sight of a crucifix. Faust once again sinks into despair and is on the verge of suicide when Mephisto reappears and offers to restore his youth in exchange for an extension of their pact. Faust agrees and finds himself in Italy, where he seduces the Duchess of Parma on her wedding night. This initial seduction is followed by a string of debaucheries which Faust finds wearisome until he espies the innocent Marguerite, with whom he falls immediately in love. Faust gains entry to Marguerite's bedroom, but the shock of finding him there kills her mother. When Marguerite's brother attempts to save her honor, Mephisto kills him. At the funeral, Marguerite is barred from the cathedral, and then abandoned by Faust. When their child dies from the harshness of the winter, Marguerite is accused of murder and sentenced to die at the stake. When Faust learns of her fate, he rages at Mephisto and curses his own decision to become young again. Mephisto transforms Faust back into an old man, in which form he joins Marguerite at the stake. The two embrace, are engulfed with flames, and die proving that love conquers evil.

One of the great silent films, Murnau's *Faust* is a masterpiece of technical achievement and characterization. Jannings's Mephisto is a figure of great depth and emotion. Lillian Gish was originally offered the part of Marguerite, but declined the role, which went to newcomer Horn, whose creation of pathos is spellbinding. Murnau drew from several sources, including Goethe's *Faust*, Christopher Marlowe's seventeenth century play *Doctor Faustus,* the folk tradition of the legend codified in the anonymous sixteenth century *Faustbuch* and an earlier screenplay by Ludwig Berger, *Das verlorene Paradies.* A recent Spanish film documents the painstaking efforts required to restore Murnau's *Faust.* See Luciano Berriatúa's *Los Cinco Faustos de F. W. Murnau* (Filmoteca española, 1994).

REVIEWS: *Bioscope* 6 January 1927: 74. *Film Daily* 12 December 1926: 12. *Harrison's Reports* 18 December 1926: 202. *Kinematograph Weekly* 6 January 1927: 59–60. *Moving Picture World* 11 December 1926: 440. *National Board of Review Magazine* 1 (November 1926): 9–10. *New York Times* 7 December 1926: 21. *Pathéscope Monthly* (November 1933): 8–10. *Photoplay* 31 (January 1927): 52. *Picturegoer* 13 (February 1927): 8–9. *Variety* 17 November 1926: 16; 8 December 1926: 16.

ADDITIONAL DISCUSSIONS:

Arecco, S. "La 'Heimat' di Faust." *Filmcritica* 44 (April 1993): 179–84.

Brennicke, Ilona, and Joe Hembus. *Klassiker des deutschen Stummfilms 1910–1930.* Munich: Goldmann Verlag, 1983.

Connelly, Robert B. *The Motion Picture Guide, Silent Film, 1910–1936.* Chicago: Cinebooks, 1986.

Dahlke, Günther, and Günter Karl, eds. *Deutsche Spielfilme von Anfängen bis 1933.* Berlin: Henschelverlag, 1988.

Disher, M. Willson. "Classics Into Films." *Fortnightly Review* 130 (1 December 1928): 784–92.

Eisner, Lotte H. *The Haunted Screen.* Berkeley: University of California Press, 1973.

_____. *Murnau.* Berkeley: University of California Press, 1973.

Elliott, C.K. "*Faust,* An Appreciation of the Film and the Director." *Flickers* 36 (January 1978): 13–18.

"*Faust.*" *Avant-scène du cinéma* 190–91 (July–September 1977): 7–41. [Screenplay.]

Huff, Theodore. *An Index to the Films of F.W. Murnau.* London: BFI, 1948. [Special supplement to *Sight and Sound* 15 (August 1948).]

Körte, Peter. "Die Kraft des Lichts, Der Regisseur Friedrich Wilhelm Murnau." In Hans-Michael Bock and Michael Töteberg, eds. *Das Ufa-Buch.* Frankfurt am Main: Zweitausendeins, 1992.

Kracauer, Siegfried. *From Caligari to Hitler: A Psychological History of German Film.* Princeton: Princeton University Press, 1947.

Kriegk, Otto. *Des deutsche Film im Spiegel der UFA.* Berlin: UFA Buchverlag, 1943.

Le Moal–Piltzing, Pia. "Le 'Faust' de Goethe, tentation du théâtre et du cinéma." In *Théâtre et cinéma annés vingt, une quête de la modernité.* Lausanne: L'Age d'homme, 1990.

Magill, Frank N., ed. *Magill's Survey of Cinema: Silent Films.* Englewood Cliffs, N.J.: Salem, 1982.

Ott, Frederick W. *The Great German Films.* Secaucus, N.J.: Citadel, 1986.

Pedler, Garth. "Murnau's *Faust.*" *Classic Images* 139 (January 1987): 13–15.

Prodolliet, Ernest. *Faust im Kino, Die Geschichte des Faustfilms von den Anfängen bis in die Gegenwart.* Freiburg, Switz.: Universitätsverlag Freiburg, 1978.

Rohmer, Eric. *L'Organisation de l'espace dans le 'Faust' de Murnau.* Paris: Union générale d'editions, 1977.

_____. "Les Trois Faust." *Avant-scène du cinéma* 190–91 (July-September 1977): 6.

166. *Faust* (1960)

Germany; dir. Peter Gorski; Gloria Films.

CAST: Ella Büchi, Elisabeth Flickenschildt, Uwe Friedrichsen, Gustaf Gründgens, Eduard Marks, Herman Schomberg.

Emil Jannings (left) as Mephisto and Gösta Ekman as Faust in F.W. Murnau's *Faust* (1926). (Still courtesy of the British Film Institute.)

This film offers an impressionistic cinematic record of a production of the first part of Goethe's *Faust* as staged by the Deutschen Schauspielhaus in Hamburg. Gründgens starred in his signature role as Mephisto.

REVIEWS: *Filmkritik* 11 (November 1960): 315–16. *Filmwoche* 15 (15 October 1960): 5. *Variety* 23 November 1960: 6; 15 July 1964: 6.

ADDITIONAL DISCUSSION:
Prodolliet, Ernest. *Faust im Kino, Die Geschichte des Faustfilms von den Anfängen bis in die Gegenwart.* Freiburg, Switz.: Universitätsverlag Freiburg, 1978.

167. *Faust and Marguerite* (1900)

United States; dir. Edwin S. Porter; Edison.
The Devil and Marguerite marry in this film version of the legend.

DISCUSSIONS:
Niver, Kemp R. *Early Motion Pictures. The Paper Print Collection in the Library of Congress.* Washington: Library of Congress, 1985.
Prodolliet, Ernest. *Faust im Kino, Die Geschichte des Faustfilms von den Anfängen bis in die Gegenwart.* Freiburg, Switz.: Universitätsverlag Freiburg, 1978.

Faust and Marguerite (1904) see *Faust et Marguerite* (1904)

168. *Faust and Marguerite* (1910)

France; Gaumont.
Marguerite is at first greatly in love with Faust, but she soon tires of his constant attention. Summoned by angels to Heaven, she leaves a despairing Faust alone on Earth.

REVIEW: *Bioscope* 30 June 1910: 31.

169. *Faust and the Devil* (1949)

Italy; dir. Carmine Gallone; Cineopera.

ALTERNATE TITLE: *La Leggenda di Faust.*

CAST: Nelly Corradi, Therese Dorny, Gino Mattera, Gilles Queant, Italo Tajo.

Faust sells his soul to the Devil in exchange for youth and the love of Marguerite. She gives in to his entreaties, but he soon abandons her after killing her brother in a duel meant to protect her honor. Driven mad by grief and guilt, she kills their child and is sentenced to die at the stake. As the flames lap at her, angels appear to lead her to Heaven. Faust is damned to Hell at the same time.

For its sources, this filmed operatic version of the legend of Faust combines scenes from Goethe's play with scenes from two operas, Gounod's *Faust* (1859) and Arrigo Boito's *Mefistofele* (1868).

REVIEWS: *Cinématographie française* 1489 (25 October 1952): 10. *Harrison's Reports* 6 May 1950: 72. Monthly *Film Bulletin* 17 (December 1950): 187. *New York Times* 1 May 1950: 18. *Times* [London] 1 March 1951: 8. *To-day's Cinema* 1 November 1950: 13–14. *Variety* 26 April 1950: 8.

ADDITIONAL DISCUSSIONS:

Chiti, Roberto, and Roberto Poppi. *Dizionario del cinema italiano. Vol. 2: I Film dal 1945 al 1959.* Rome: Gremese Editore, 1991.

Prodolliet, Ernest. *Faust im Kino, Die Geschichte des Faustfilms von den Anfängen bis in die Gegenwart.* Freiburg, Switz.: Universitätsverlag Freiburg, 1978.

170. *Faust aux enfers* (1903)

France; dir. Georges Méliès; Star.

ALTERNATE TITLE:*The Damnation of Faust.*

CAST: Georges Méliès.

Mephistopheles and Faust journey into the depths of Hell, where Faust is thrown into a fiery pit.

Méliès was fascinated by the legend of Faust, which he used as the basis for five films; his chief source for this 1903 film was Hector Berlioz's 1848 cantata *La Damnation de Faust.*

REVIEW: *Moving Picture World* 24 April 1909: 530.

ADDITIONAL DISCUSSIONS:

Abel, Richard. *The Ciné Goes to Town, French Cinema, 1896–1914.* Berkeley: University of California Press, 1994.

The Complete Catalogue of Genuine and Original "Star" Films Manufactured by Geo. Méliès. New York: Star Films, [1907?].

Essai de reconstruction du catalogue français de la Star-film suivi d'une analyse catalographique des

films de Georges Méliès recensés en France. Bois d'Arcy: Publications du Service des Archives du Film du Centre National de la Cinématographie, [1981].

Frazer, John. *Artificially Arranged Scenes, The Films of Georges Méliès.* Boston: G.K. Hall, 1979.

Gaudreault, André, ed. *Cinema 1900–1906.* Brussels: FIAF, 1982.

Niver, Kemp R. *Early Motion Pictures. The Paper Print Collection in the Library of Congress.* Washington: Library of Congress, 1985.

Prodolliet, Ernest. *Faust im Kino, Die Geschichte des Faustfilms von den Anfängen bis in die Gegenwart.* Freiburg, Switz.: Universitätsverlag Freiburg, 1978.

Savada, Elias. *The American Film Institute Catalog of Motion Pictures Produced in the United States: Film Beginnings, 1893–1910.* Metuchen, N.J.: Scarecrow, 1995.

171. *Faust et Marguerite* (1900)

France; dir. Georges Méliès; Star.

Marguerite sits before a fireplace as Mephistopheles orders Faust to behead her. When he refuses to do so, Mephistopheles draws a sword across her throat as she suddenly disappears.

DISCUSSION:

Savada, Elias. *The American Film Institute Catalog of Motion Pictures Produced in the United States: Film Beginnings, 1893–1910.* Metuchen, N.J.: Scarecrow, 1995.

172. *Faust et Marguerite* (1904)

France; dir. Georges Méliès; Star.

ALTERNATE TITLES: *La Damnation du Docteur Faust* and *Faust and Marguerite.*

Faust, having sold his soul to the Devil, becomes infatuated with Marguerite, whom he seduces and then abandons. When her brother challenges Faust to a duel to restore his sister's honor, Faust kills him. Marguerite, driven mad by shame and sorrow, kills her child. She is arrested and sentenced to be burned at the stake. As she nears death from the flames, angels appear to escort her to Heaven, leaving Faust to his infernal destiny.

Méliès here uses Gounod's opera as the basis for this film of the Faust legend.

REVIEWS: *Avant-scène du cinéma* 360 (May 1987): 55–56. *Moving Picture World* 20 April 1909: 530.

ADDITIONAL DISCUSSIONS:

Abel, Richard. *The Ciné Goes to Town, French Cinema, 1896–1914.* Berkeley: University of California Press, 1994.

Catalogue of Films. London: Charles Urban Trading Company, 1904. [Supplement 1 January 1904].

Les Cinématographes de la Saint Romain de Rouen 1896–1907. Rouen: Académie de Rouen, 1981.

The Complete Catalogue of Genuine and Original "Star" Films Manufactured by Geo. Méliès. New York: Star Films, [1907?].

Essai de reconstruction du catalogue français de la Star-film suivi d'une analyse catalographique des films de Georges Méliès recensés en France. Bois d'Arcy: Publications du Service des Archives du Film du Centre National de la Cinématographie, [1981].

Frazer, John. *Artificially Arranged Scenes, The Films of Georges Méliès.* Boston: G.K. Hall, 1979.

Gaudreault, André, ed. *Cinema 1900–1906.* Brussels: FIAF, 1982.

Niver, Kemp R. *Early Motion Pictures. The Paper Print Collection in the Library of Congress.* Washington: Library of Congress, 1985.

Savada, Elias. *The American Film Institute Catalog of Motion Pictures Produced in the United States: Film Beginnings, 1893–1910.* Metuchen, N.J.: Scarecrow, 1995.

173. *Faust sauvé des enfers* (1911)

France; Pathé Frères.

Faust is spared the flames of Hell after he performs a good deed in Paris.

DISCUSSION:

Bousquet, Henri. *Catalogue Pathé des années 1896 à 1914: 1910–1911.* Paris: Henri Bousquet, 1994.

174. *La Favorita* (1952)

Italy; dir. Cesare Barlacchi; M.A.S. Film.

CAST: Sofia Lazzaro, Paolo Silveri, Gino Sininbeghi.

In fourteenth century Spain, Fernando, a commoner, falls in love with a noble lady who happens to be the king's favorite. Fernando goes off to fight in the king's wars and becomes a great hero. The king agrees to grant him anything he wishes, and he asks for the lady's hand in marriage. But when Fernando learns who the lady really is, he declines to marry her.

This film presents a slavishly faithful screen version of Donizetti's 1840 opera *La Favorita.*

REVIEWS: *Eco del cinema* 4 (15 June 1953): 270. *Motion Picture Herald* 31 October 1953: Product Digest Section 2047. *New York Times* 30 October 1953: 27.

ADDITIONAL DISCUSSION:

Chiti, Roberto, and Roberto Poppi. *Dizionario del cinema italiano. Vol. 2: I Film dal 1945 al 1959.* Rome: Gremese Editore, 1991.

175. *Federico Barbarossa* (1910)

Italy; dir. Mario Caserini; Cines.

ALTERNATE TITLES: *Barbourossa* and *La Battaglia di Legnano.*

CAST: Amleto Novelli, Etorre Pesci, Orlando Ricci.

Having defeated the Milanese and destroyed their city, Frederick Barbarossa now faces a new challenge: Troops from Lombardy under the command of Albert of Guissanio have joined forces with the remnants of the Milanese army. The combined army routes the emperor at Legnano, where the emperor and many of his troops die.

This historical drama mixes up some of its history. The Holy Roman Emperor Frederick Barbarossa (c. 1123–90) died while on the Third Crusade. He did indeed, however, suffer a great defeat in the 1176 Battle of Legnano at the hands of troops from Lombardy who were in revolt against his attempt to establish a united kingdom in the north of Italy.

REVIEW: *Bioscope* 21 April 1910: 35. *Moving Picture World* 25 June 1910: 1123.

ADDITIONAL DISCUSSION:

Savada, Elias. *The American Film Institute Catalog of Motion Pictures Produced in the United States: Film Beginnings, 1893–1910.* Metuchen, N.J.: Scarecrow, 1995.

176. *La Fée carabosse* (1906)

France; dir. Georges Méliès; Star Films.

ALTERNATE TITLES: *Le Poignard fatal* and *The Witch.*

Lothaire, a young knight who is the last surviving member of his family, consults a witch about what the future holds for him. She shows him a portrait of the woman he will marry and tells him that he must overcome a thousand obstacles to rescue his future wife from a dungeon deep in her father's castle. She offers him a magical four-leaf clover that will make him virtually invincible, but he has nothing with which to pay her for the charm. Ever resourceful, he tricks the witch into thinking that a purse filled with sand is really filled with gold. He then sets off to rescue his bride-to-be. When the witch finds that she has been tricked, she follows Lothaire, making his journey doubly difficult. Kindly Druids and the spirits of his ancestors come to his aid time and again. Lothaire defeats all foes, including the witch, and marries his promised bride.

Méliès here tells a complicated story — based on a Breton folktale — in a film filled with trick effects and the most fascinating array of monsters, witches, gnomes, and other creatures of horror.

The young knight Lothaire is granted a vision of the woman he will marry in Georges Méliès's fantasy *La Fée carabosse* (1906).

DISCUSSIONS:
Abel, Richard. *The Ciné Goes to Town.* Berkeley: University of California Press, 1994.
The Complete Catalogue of Genuine and Original "Star" Films Manufacted by Geo. Méliès of Paris. New York: Geo. Méliès, [1907?].
Essai de reconstruction du catalogue français de la Star-film suivi d'une analyse catalographique des films de Georges Méliès recensés en France. Bois d'Arcy: Publications du Service des Archives du Film du Centre National de la Cinématographie, [1981].
Gaudreault, André, ed. *Cinema 1900–1906.* Brussels: FIAF, 1982.
Jenn, Pierre. *Georges Méliès Cinéaste.* Paris: Editions Albatros, 1984.
Malthête, Jacques. "Il était une fois … la fée carabosse." *1895* 7 (1900): 73–83.
Savada, Elias. *The American Film Institute Catalog of Motion Pictures Produced in the United States: Film Beginnings, 1893–1910.* Metuchen, N.J.: Scarecrow, 1995.

177. *Feudal Right* (1910)
Italy; Cines.

A cruel duke lusts after the daughter of one of his serfs. He disguises himself as a pilgrim and abducts the girl, intending to force his affections upon her. Her father and lover follow and gain entry to the duke's chambers, free the girl and burn his castle to the ground.
REVIEW: *Bioscope* 8 December 1910: 35–36.

Feuer und Schwert (1981) see *Fire and Sword* (1981)

The Fiery Archer (1971) see *L'Arciere di fuoco* (1971)

178. *Les Filles de La Rochelle* (1961)
France; dir. Bernard Deflandre; Guepard Production.
CAST: Raymond Bussières, Geneviéve Cluny, Guy Decomble, Max Desrau, Philippe Lemarie, Paul Mercey, Pierre Parel, Annette Poivre.
During the Hundred Years War, the English fleet unsuccessfully attempts to capture the

French port at La Rochelle, which is protected by a great chain that stretches across the harbor entrance. English spies land in the port and attempt to lower the chain, but their efforts are foiled by the women of the city who rise to defend the honor of France.

The English loss at La Rochelle in 1372 temporarily ended their control of the sea lanes and threatened their possessions in the Aquitaine. History lies behind this film, which is a slapstick comedy that seems to want to be a spoof on the order of future Monty Python escapades, but the Gallic humor here cannot rise to that level.

REVIEWS: *Film français* 7 September 1962: 13. *Unifrance film—la production cinématographique française* 36 (April 1962); 9.

Le Fils du Cid (1964) see *I Cento cavalieri* (1964)

179. La Fin de Louis XI (1912)

France; Pathé Frères, Production il film d'arte italiani and Milanese Film.

When King Louis XI has the Duke of Nemours arrested and executed, the duke's son vows revenge. The young duke's plans are discovered, and he too is arrested. Friends at court arrange his escape, and he vows anew to kill the king, who suddenly dies of a seizure.

An earlier Italian film, *Luigi XI, re di Francia* (1909), tells a similar story about Louis XI (1461–1483), who was known as a harsh ruler. A second Pathé film made in 1912, *La Vengeance du Prince Visconti*, borrows the plot device of having the royal villain die of a seizure as the hero is about to kill him.

DISCUSSION:
Bousquet, Henri. *Catalogue Pathé des annés 1896 à 1914: 1912–1913–1914*. Paris: Henri Bousquet, 1995.

180. La Fin d'une dynastie (1910)

France; Pathé Frères.

ALTERNATE TITLE: *The End of a Dynasty*.

When Frederick I is nominated Margrave of Brandenberg, the ducal brothers Conrad and Dietrich raise an army to prevent his assuming the position. Dietrich imprisons the mayor of Strasbourg for supporting Frederick's claim; when the mayor escapes, Conrad prevents his brother from killing the man. The two brothers end up in a duel, with Conrad killing Dietrich. One of Dietrich's vassals then rushes forward to kill Conrad.

This film takes a page from medieval German history but garbles the facts. The Hohenstaufen dynasty began with Henry IV's enfeoffment of Frederick I (1079–1105) with the duchy of Swabia as reward for Frederick's support of Henry against the rebellious dukes of Bavaria, Carinthia and Swabia. Frederick also married Henry's daughter Agnes, and his brother Otto was bishop of Strasbourg from 1083 to 1100.

REVIEW: *Bioscope* 7 July 1910: 31, 33.

ADDITIONAL DISCUSSIONS:
Bousquet, Henri. *Catalogue Pathé des années 1896 à 1914: 1910–1911*. Paris: Henri Bousquet, 1994.
Savada, Elias. *The American Film Institute Catalog of Motion Pictures Produced in the United States: Film Beginnings, 1893–1910*. Metuchen, N.J.: Scarecrow, 1995.

Il Fiore delle mille e una notte (1974) see *The Arabian Nights* (1974)

181. Fire and Sword (1981)

Germany; dir. Veith von Fürstenberg; Genée and von Fürstenberg Filmproduktion.

ALTERNATE TITLES: *Feuer und Schwert* and *Die Legende von Tristan und Isolde*.

CAST: Peter Firth, Leigh Lawson, Walo Lüönd, Antonia Presser, Christoph Waltz

Tristan, a knight of Cornwall, is locked in mortal combat with Morholt of Ireland, who is supposedly invincible. Tristan wins, but at a price: He is seriously wounded. Set adrift in a boat, he washes up on the shores of Ireland where he is found by Princess Isolde, who nurses him back to health and with whom he falls in love. He returns home to Cornwall only to be sent back to Ireland by his uncle, King Mark, to fetch home an Irish bride (the union is meant to cement a Cornish-Irish peace) for Mark. When the princess turns out to be Isolde, she and Tristan return to Cornwall and carry on an adulterous love affair. Discovered by Mark, Tristan is exiled, but Isolde follows him and bears his child. Cornwall and Ireland are in an uproar over what has happened, and Isolde agrees to return to Mark in order to prevent further bloodshed. Tristan meanwhile becomes an outlaw. Wounded in a skirmish, he calls out for Isolde. Isolde realizes that lasting peace between Cornwall and Ireland is impossible and runs away, reaching Tristan's side just before he dies.

Fire and Sword presents probably the most

Sean Connery (left) as King Arthur and Richard Gere (right) as Lancelot in Jerry Zucker's *First Knight* (1995).

faithful film version of the medieval legend of Tristan and Isolde.

REVIEWS: *Continental Film and Video* 29 (November 1981): 18. *Das Fernsehspiel im ZDF* 44 (March-May 1984): 43–46. *Film-dienst* 35 (26 January 1982): 16–17. *Film-echo/Filmwoche* 47–48 (28 August 1981): 18. *Film und Fernsehen* 12. 7 (1984): 35. *Kino* 4 (August 1981): 33. *Variety* 10 June 1981: 18.

ADDITIONAL DISCUSSIONS:
Kerdelhue, Alain. "'Feuer und Schwert,' lecture materielle du mythe." In Ulrich Müller, et al., eds. *Tristan et Iseut, mythe européen et mondial*. Göppingen: Kümmerle, 1987.
McMunn, Meradith T. "Filming the Tristan Myth: From Text to Icon." In Kevin J. Harty, ed. *Cinema Arthuriana, Essays on Arthurian Film*. New York: Garland, 1991.

182. *First Knight* (1995)

United States; dir. Jerry Zucker; Columbia Pictures.

CAST: Sean Connery, Ben Cross, Liam Cunningham, Richard Gere, Julia Ormond, Christopher Villiers.

The aging Arthur decides to marry the much-younger Guinevere, in part to protect her kingdom. But the peace of Camelot is shattered when Malagant tries to kidnap Guinevere, who is rescued by Lancelot, an itinerant knight and ne'er-do-well. Lancelot joins the knights of the Round Table and conducts a passionate, though chaste, affair with Guinevere. Arthur discovers them in an embrace and orders them tried for adultery. The trial is interrupted when Malagant's forces attack Camelot. In the ensuing battle, Arthur and Malagant are killed, and Camelot and Guinevere pass into Lancelot's hands for safe keeping.

Given that there is no one version of the tale of Arthur, Lancelot and Guinevere, filmmakers can be granted some license in their interpretation of that legend. But nothing here quite works. Clearly, Zucker intends his film to be an Arthuriad for the 1990s, but it fails to capture the spirit of the original legend or to make a case for its contemporary translation of an oft-told story.

REVIEWS: *Arthuriana* 5 (Fall 1995): 137–40. *Empire* 74 (August 1995): 30. *Entertainment Weekly* 276 (26 May 1995): 36; 283 (14 July 1995): 34–35. *EPD Film* 12 (September 1995): 49–50. *Film Journal* 98 (August-September 1995): 30. *Film Review* 297 (August 1995): 64. *Films in Review* 46 (September-October 1995): 56–57. *Los Angeles Times* 7 July 1995: Calendar 1. *Movieline* 6 (May 1995): 46–47; 7 (Sep-

tember 1995): 37. *New York Times* 7 July 1995: C10. *Positif* 416 (October 1995): 38. *Sight and Sound* NS 5 (August 1995): 49–50. *Soundtrack* 14 (September 1955): 19. *Studio* [Paris] 101 (July-August 1995): 18. *Sunday Times* [London] 9 July 1995: 10.6. *Times* [London] 6 July 1995: 33. *Times* [London] *Educational Supplement* 14 July 1995: SS16. *Variety* 26 June 1995: 78, 85.

ADDITIONAL DISCUSSIONS:
Brett, Anwar. "*First Knight* No Nerves." *Film Review* 298 [Special Issue 12] (1995): 62–65.
Fhaner, Beth A., and Christopher P. Scanlon, eds. *Magill's Cinema Annual 1996*. Detroit: Gale, 1996.
Fisher, Bob. "Camelot in Shadows." *American Cinematographer* 76 (July 1995): 56–58, 60, 62, 64.
Levich, Jacob, ed. *The Motion Picture Guide, 1996 Annual (The Films of 1995)*. New York: Cinebooks, 1996.
Tirard, Laurent. "Richard Gere sans peur et sans reproche." *Studio* [Paris] 101 (July-August 1995): 71–77.
Umland, Rebecca A., and Samuel J. Umland. *The Use of Arthurian Legend in Hollywood Film from Connecticut Yankees to Fisher Kings*. Westport, Conn.: Greenwood, 1996.

183. *The Flame and the Arrow* (1950)

United States; dir. Jacques Tourneur; Warner Bros.

CAST: Frank Allenby, Lynne Baggett, Nick Cravat, Robert Douglas, Gordon Gebert, Burt Lancaster, Aline MacMahon, Virginia Mayo.

In medieval Lombardy, Dardo's wife leaves him to become the mistress of Ulrich, commander of the Hessian mercenaries who occupy the region. When his wife attempts to kidnap their son, Dardo fights back, killing several Hessians and sustaining a serious wound himself. After he recovers, he kidnaps Ulrich's niece Anne, who soon falls in love with him. Captured by Ulrich's men, Dardo is sentenced to be hanged, and he only escapes death by wearing a special harness that prevents his being strangled by the hangman's noose. He escapes and joins forces with a group of acrobats who storm Ulrich's castle and drive the Hessians from Lombardy.

Based on Waldo Salt's 1949 novel *The Hawk and the Arrow*, this typical example of cinematic swashbuckling borrows a page or two from the legend of Robin Hood — which is appropriate since the production used sets left over from Michael Curtiz's 1938 film *The Adventures of Robin Hood*. As Dardo, Lancaster did all his own acrobatic stunts.

Burt Lancaster as Dardo in Jacques Tourneur's *The Flame and the Arrow* (1950).

Jennifer Jason Leigh as Agnes and Rutger Hauer as Martin in Paul Verhoeven's *Flesh and Blood* (1985).

REVIEWS: *Film Daily* 20 June 1950: 8. *Harrison's Reports* 24 June 1950: 98. *Hollywood Reporter* 20 June 1950: 3. *Monthly Film Bulletin* 17 (December 1950): 187–88. *Motion Picture Herald* 24 June 1950: Product Digest Section 353; 12 August 1950: 45. *New York Times* 8 July 1950: 7. *Revue du cinéma* [La Saison cinémathographique.] Hors série 32 (1950–1951): 77. *Times* [London] 23 December 1950: 9. *Today's Cinema* 3 November 1950: 10. *Variety* 21 June 1950: 8.

ADDITIONAL DISCUSSIONS:
Clinch, Minty. *Burt Lancaster*. London: Barker, 1984.
Crowther, Bruce. *Burt Lancaster, A Life in Films*. London: Robert Hale, 1991.
Fury, David. *The Cinema of Burt Lancaster*. Minneapolis: Artist's Press, 1989.
Hunter, Allan. *Burt Lancaster: The Man and His Movies*. New York: St. Martin's, 1984.
Lacourbe, Roland. *Burt Lancaster*. Paris: Edilig, 1987.
Nash, Jay Robert, and Stanley Ralph Ross. *The Motion Picture Guide, E–G, 1927–1983*. Chicago: Cinebooks, 1986.
Richards, Jeffrey. *Swordsmen of the Screen from Douglas Fairbanks to Michael York*. London: Routledge and Kegan Paul, 1977.
Thomas, Tony. *Burt Lancaster*. New York: Pyramid, 1975.
_____. *The Great Adventure Films*. Secaucus, N.J.: Citadel, 1977.
Vermilye, Jerry. *Burt Lancaster: A Pictorial Treasury of His Films*. New York: Falcon, 1971.
Windeler, Robert. *Burt Lancaster*. New York: St. Martin's, 1984.

184. *Flesh and Blood* (1985)

Netherlands and United States; dir. Paul Verhoeven; Orion Pictures.

CAST: Tom Burlinson, Rutger Hauer, Fernando Hillbeck, Ronald Lacey, Jennifer Jason Leigh, Susan Tyrrell, Jack Thompson.

In 1501, Lord Arnolfini hires mercenaries to help him recapture his city, whose citizens have expelled him. He promises them that they may loot the city for 24 hours when it falls, but he reneges on his promise once his victory is assured. The mercenaries leave, vowing to have their pay from Arnolfini one way or another, and rally around Martin, who kidnaps and rapes Arnolfini's daughter-in-law Agnes. The mercenaries then terrorize the countryside, slaughtering all the inhabitants of a nearby castle, which they claim as their residence. Arnolfini lays siege to the castle, which is ravaged by plague, and rescues his daughter-in-law. Everyone thinks Martin dies in the attack, but the final frames of the film show him escaping from the flames as Arnolfini's troops burn the castle to the ground.

Released straight to video in the United States, this film left more than one critic at a loss for words when it came to reviewing it. It may be the bloodiest and least romanticized film ever set in the Middle Ages. The blood flows freely; the violence and carnage are everywhere. Several critics suggested that a better title for the film would have been "Mad Max Meets the Middle Ages."

REVIEWS: *Les Cahiers du cinéma* 377 (November 1985): 58. *Cinéma* [Belgium] 92 (December 1985): 532. *Cinema, Films & Video* 86 (January 1985): 60–62. *Ecran fantastique* 61 (October 1985): 8–9; 62 (November 1985): 9. *Film News* [Australia] 15 (December 1985): 13–14. *Films and Filming* 380 (May 1986): 30–31. *Hollywood Reporter* 12 June 1985: 3, 11. *Los Angeles Times* 30 August 1985: 6. 6. *Monthly Film Bulletin* 53 (May 1986): 145–46. *Photoplay* 37 (May 1986): 30. *Positif* 296 (October 1985): 74–75. *Revue du cinéma* [La Saison cinématographique] Hors série 33 (1986): 32–33. *Starburst* 8 (May 1986): 10–11. *Times* [London] 2 May 1986: 15. *Variety* 19 June 1985: 24, 26.

ADDITIONAL DISCUSSIONS:
Borie, Bertrand. "'La Chair et le sang': entretien avec Paul Verhoeven." *Ecran fantastique* 61 (October 1985): 26–29.
den Drijver, Ruud. "Interview: Rutger Hauer." *Cinéma* [Belgium] 92 (December 1985): 566–75.
Dutch Film 84/85. The Hague: Government Publishing Office, 1985.
Magill, Frank N., ed. *Magill's Cinema Annual, 1989 (A Survey of the Films of 1985)*. Englewood Cliffs, N.J.: Salem, 1986.
Nash, Jay Robert, and Stanley Ralph Ross. *The Motion Picture Guide, 1986 Annual (The Films of 1985)*. Chicago: Cinebooks, 1987.
Het Nederlands Jaarboek Film 1986. Houten: Unieboek, 1986.

Seberechts, Karin. "Flesh and Blood: Mad Max in de Middeleeuwen." *Film en televisie* 342 (November 1985): 9–11.

Flight of the Raven (1984) see *When the Raven Flies* (1984)

The Flower of the Arabian Nights (1974) see *The Arabian Nights* (1974)

185. *The Flowers of St. Francis* (1950)
Italy; dir. Roberto Rossellini; Rizzoli.
ALTERNATE TITLES: *Francesco, giullare di Dio; Francis, God's Fool* and *Francis, God's Jester.*
CAST: Aldo Fabrizi, Arabella Lemaître, Fra' Nazario.

Francis of Assisi returns with his fellow friars from Rome. Brother Ginepro gives his habit to a beggar and returns naked. Francis meets and kisses a leper. Others flock to join Francis's order, and the monks are visited by Sister Clare. Ginepro goes off to preach and encounters Nicolaio of Viterbo, a tyrant who tortures him. When Ginepro bears his sufferings in silence, Nicolaio (almost in terror) releases him. Francis then tells his brethren to go forth in all directions to preach the gospel.

An anthology film presenting 11 episodes from *I Fioretti di San Francesco* and the *Vita de frate Ginepro*, two collections of legends about St. Francis of Assisi (1181?–1226), *The Flowers of St. Francis*, with screenplay by Rossellini and Federico Fellini, succeeds in rendering the simplicity, fervor and charity of Francis and his early followers. Most of the actors in the film were non-professionals drawn from the ranks of the Franciscan friars at Nocere Inferiore Monastery.

REVIEWS: *Les Cahiers du cinéma* 1 (April 1951): 51–53. *Cinema* [Rome] 35 (30 March 1950): 175–77. *Filmcritica* 147–48 (July-August 1964): 369–72. *Film Daily* 16 October 1952: 6. *Hollywood Quarterly* 5 (Summer 1951): 389–400. *Le Monde* 8 March 1951: 8. *Motion Picture Herald* 11 October 1952: Product Digest Section 1559. *New York Times* 7 October 1952: 26. *Positif* 400 (June 1994): 89–90. *Revue du cinéma* [La Saison cinématographique] Hors série 32 (1950-1951): 131. *Theatre Arts* 36 (September 1952): 76–77. *Variety* 27 September 1950: 20.

ADDITIONAL DISCUSSIONS:
Aristarco, Guido. "Alla ricerca di dio." *Cinema* [Rome] 46 (15 September 1950): 134–38, 161.

Fra' Nazario as St. Francis surrounded by his followers in Roberto Rossellini's *The Flowers of St. Francis* (1950).

Thomas Guiry as Chris Millard transformed into the valiant knight, Sir Millard, in The Disney Channel's made-for-television film *The Four Diamonds* (1995). (Still courtesy of The Disney Channel.)

Baldelli, Pio. "Dibattito per 'Francesco' di Rossellini." *Rivista del cinema italiano* 3 (December 1954): 55–69.

_____. "Falsificazione umana di un guillare di dio." *Cinema* [Rome] 55 (1 February 1951): 37–39, 57.

Bondanella, Peter. *The Films of Roberto Rossellini.* New York: Cambridge University Press, 1993.

Brunette, Peter. *Roberto Rossellini.* New York: Oxford University Press, 1987.

Chiti, Roberto, and Roberto Poppi. *Dizionario del cinema italiano. Vol. 2: I Film dal 1945 al 1959.* Rome: Gremese Editore, 1991.

Falconi, Carlo. "Il cinema cattolico." *Cinema nuovo* 4 (January 1955): 26–28.

"Films about St. Francis of Assisi." *Times* [London] 1 June 1950: 8.

Garbicz, Adam, and Jacek Klinowski. *Cinema, The Magic Vehicle.* New York: Schocken, 1983.

Guarner, José Luis. *Roberto Rossellini.* Trans. Elisabeth Cameron. London: Studio Vista, 1970.

Leprohon, Pierre. *The Italian Cinema.* Trans. Roger Greaves and Oliver Stallybrass. New York: Praeger, 1966.

Liehm, Maria. *Passion and Defiance: Films in Italy from 1942 to the Present.* Berkeley: University of California Press, 1984.

Masi, Stephano. *I Film di Roberto Rossellini.* Rome: Gremese Editore, 1987.

Mauriac, François. "Pèlerinage a Assise." *France il-lustration* 6 (30 September 1950): 326–29.

Phelps, Donald. "Rossellini and *The Flowers of Saint Francis*." *Moviegoer* 1 (Winter 1964): 19–25.

Rondi, Brunello. *Cinema a realtà.* Rome: Edizioni cinque lune, 1957.

Rondolino, Gianni. *Catalogo Bolaffi del cinema italiano 1945/1965.* 2nd ed. Turin: Giulio Bolaffi Editore, 1977.

_____. *Roberto Rosellini.* Turin: UTET, 1989.

Rossellini, Roberto. *My Method, Writings and Interviews.* Ed. Adriano Aprà. New York: Marsilio, 1992.

Rossi, Patrizio. *Roberto Rossellini, A Guide to References and Resources.* Boston: Hall, 1988.

Schutz, Victoria. "Interview with Roberto Rossellini." *Film Culture* 52 (Spring 1971): 1–43.

Visentini, Gino. "Rossellini o della trascendenza." *Bianco e nero* 13 (February 1952): 17–19.

Weinberg, Herman G., ed. *Fifty Years of Italian Cinema.* Rome: Carlo Bestetti–Edizioni d'arte, 1955.

For Love and Gold (1966) see *L'Armata Brancaleone* (1966)

The Forbidden Decameron (1972) see *Il Decamerone proibitissimo* (1972) and *Il Decamerone proibito* (1972)

Forest of Love (1981) see *Bosco d'amore* (1981)

186. *The Four Diamonds* (1995)

United States; dir. Peter Werner; The Disney Channel.

CAST: Jayne Brook, Kevin Dunn, Thomas Guiry, Sarah Rose Karr, Christine Lahti.

Fourteen-year-old Chris Millard is dying from a rare form of nasal cancer. To distract himself as well as to find some courage to deal with what he faces, he imagines an Arthurian world in which he is a squire in search of four diamonds — courage, wisdom, honesty and strength — which he must find in order to become a knight of the Round Table.

A contemporary examination of the theme of the return to Camelot, this made-for-television movie is one of the better cinematic uses of the Arthurian legend. The film is based on a short story written by the real Chris Millard, who died in 1972.

REVIEWS: *Arthuriana* 6 (Summer 1996): 115–18. *Daily Variety* 8 August 1995: 16. *Hollywood Reporter* 11 August 1995: 35. *New York Times* 11 August 1995: B14. *TV Guide* 12 August 1995: 69, 74.

187. *Francesca da Rimini, or The Two Brothers* (1907)

United States; dir. William V. Ranous; Vitagraph.

CAST: Hector Dean, William Raymond, Florence Turner.

Francesca receives a letter from the hunchbacked Lanciotto of Rimini asking for her hand in marriage. The letter is delivered by Lanciotto's handsome brother Paolo. Francesca and Lanciotto do marry, but when Lanciotto is called away to war, Paolo and Francesca begin an affair. The court jester discovers and reports their adultery to Lanciotto, who kills the jester, his wife, his brother and then himself.

The Vitagraph film draws upon George Henry Boker's 1855 verse tragedy *Francesca da Rimini* as a source, but ultimately the story of Francesca and Paolo can be traced to real events recounted by Dante in his *Inferno* (Canto V). Dante places the lovers among the carnal. In 1275, Giovanni Malatesta of Rimini, the brave but lame warrior, proposed a marriage of political convenience to Francesca, the daughter of the Duke of Ravenna. She soon fell in love with her brother-in-law Paolo, with whom she carried on an adulterous affair for at least a decade. Giovanni caught them in an embrace and killed them both.

REVIEWS: *Bioscope* 23 February 1911: 31. *Kinematograph and Lantern Weekly* 2 (17 February 1908): 289–90. *Moving Picture World* 8 February 1908: 103; 21 March 1908: 233; 26 November 1910: 1248. *New York Dramatic Mirror* 23 November 1910: 3. *Variety* 22 February 1908: 11. *Vitagraph Bulletin* 224 (15 November–1 December 1910): 9–11.

ADDITIONAL DISCUSSIONS:

Blum, Daniel. *A Pictorial History of the Silent Screen.* New York: Grosset & Dunlap, 1953.

Connelly, D.H. "*Francesca da Rimini* Truly Magnificent." *Vitagraph Bulletin* 226 (15 December 1910–1 January 1911): 31.

"The Costume Play." *Moving Picture World* 8 December 1910: 1279.

Savada, Elias. *The American Film Institute Catalog of Motion Pictures Produced in the United States: Film Beginnings, 1893–1910.* Metuchen, N.J.: Scarecrow, 1995.

Uricchio, William, and Roberta E. Pearson. *Reframing Culture, The Case of the Vitagraph Quality Films.* Princeton: Princteon University Press, 1993.

_____. "Who Is Francesca da Rimini? Problems of Historical Reception." *Cinémas* [Canada] 2 (Spring 1992): 32–55.

188. *Francesca da Rimini* (1910)

France; dir. Ugo Falena; Pathé Frères and Il Film d'arte italiana, S.A.P.F.

ALTERNATE TITLES: *Françoise de Rimini* and *Paul and Francesca*.

CAST: Francesca Bertini, Stanislas Ciarli, Gustavo Conforti, Francesco di Gennaro, Guilio Grassi.

Sent by his brother to fetch his new bride, Paolo falls in love with his future sister-in-law. Their ardor only grows when Francesca discovers her new husband is a hunchback. Paul asks to be sent away, but he is recalled, and he and Francesca begin a torrid affair that is discovered by the court jester. The jester informs on them, and Francesca's enraged husband kills her and Paolo.

As with the 1907 film of the story of Francesca da Rimini, this film recounts historical events found in Dante's *Inferno*.

REVIEWS: *Bioscope* 1 September 1910: 27. *Moving Picture World* 20 May 1911: 1144; 2 June 1911: 1258.

ADDITIONAL DISCUSSIONS:

Bousquet, Henri. *Catalogue Pathé des années 1896 à 1914: 1910–1911*. Paris: Henri Bousquet, 1994.

Savada, Elias. *The American Film Institute Catalog of Motion Pictures Produced in the United States: Film Beginnings, 1893–1910*. Metuchen, N.J.: Scarecrow, 1995.

189. *Francesca da Rimini* (1922)

Italy; dir. Mario Volpe; Floreal-Film.

CAST: Mary Bayma-Riva, Dante Capelli, Bepo A. Corradi, Filippo Ricci, Carlos A. Troisi.

Francesca tragically falls in love with her brother-in-law Paolo after she marries the crippled Gianciotto Malatesta, who kills them both when he discovers their adulterous relationship.

REVIEW: *Bianco e nero* 42 (January–June 1981): 423–24.

190. *Francesco* (1989)

Italy and West Germany; dir. Liliana Cavani; Karol Film.

ALTERNATE TITLE: *Franziskus*.

CAST: Helena Bonham Carter, Paolo Bonacelli, Andrea Ferreol, Mickey Rourke, Hans Zischler.

After seeing Perugia defeat his native Assisi, Francis spends a year in contemplation. To the amazement of his friends and family, he sheds his former arrogance and his worldly possessions. Soon others flock to Francis's side to follow his example. With his followers, he journeys to Rome, where he receives papal approval to found a religious order for simple brothers. Pressed by his followers to write a rule, Francis escapes into the mountains to live a life of solitude. There he dies, bearing the marks of the stigmata.

The screenplay by Cavani, who also directed the 1966 made-for-Italian-television film *Francesco di Assisi*, is based on Hermann Hesse's 1902 monograph *Francis of Assisi*. Released theatrically at 155 minutes in Europe, this film was dumped straight to video in the United States, with 40 minutes of footage edited out. The film is impressive to look at, but the text is marred by anachronisms, bad and uneven accents, and even worse acting. Of the several films about St. Francis of Assisi (1181?–1226), this is among the least impressive.

REVIEWS: *Cinema nuovo* 38 (November-December 1989): 55. *Entertainment Weekly* 231 (15 July 1994): 74. *EPD Film* 7 (December 1989): 29. *Film-critica* 40 (May 1989): 323–26. *Film-echo/Filmwoche* 43 (24 November 1989): 23. *Film français* 2244–45 (5–12 May 1989): 29. *Hollywood Reporter* 26 May 1989: 16. *Movieline* 6 (November 1994): 82. *Variety* 12 April 1989: 20.

ADDITIONAL DISCUSSIONS:

Levich, Jacob, ed. *The Motion Picture Guide, 1995 Annual (The Films of 1994)*. New York: Cinebooks, 1994.

Mickey Rourke in Francesco. Rome: Istituto Luce, 1989. [Press book.]

The Motion Picture Guide, 1990 Annual (The Films of 1989). Evanston, Ill.: Cinebooks, 1990.

Padovani, Marcel. "La Solitude de Mickey." *Le Nouvel Observateur* 11 May 1989: 70.

191. *Francesco di Assisi* (1966)

Italy; dir. Liliana Cavani; Radiotelevisione Italiana.

CAST: Ken Belton, Lou Castel, Riccardo Cucciola, Ludmilla Lvova, Grazia Marescalchi, Giancarlo Sbragia.

This made-for-Italian-television film rejects the standard pious interpretation of the life of St. Francis, seeing him instead as a simple subversive who rejected the Church establishment and revolutionized ideas about the poor.

REVIEW: *Bianco e nero* 29 (July–August 1966): 186–88.

ADDITIONAL DISCUSSIONS:

Bondanella, Peter. *Italian Cinema from Neorealism to the Present*. 2nd ed. New York: Ungar, 1990.

Buache, Freddy. *Le Cinéma italien d'Antonioni a Rosi*. Yverdon, Switz.: La Thièle, 1969.

Bradford Dillman in the title role in Michael Curtiz's *Francis of Assisi* (1961).

Francesco, guillare di Dio (1950) see *The Flowers of St. Francis* (1950)

Francis, God's Fool (1950) see *The Flowers of St. Francis* (1950)

Francis, God's Jester (1950) see *The Flowers of St. Francis* (1950)

192. *Francis of Assisi* (1961)

United States; dir. Michael Curtiz; 20th Century–Fox.

CAST: Pedro Armendariz, Finlay Currie, Bradford Dillman, Dolores Hart, Cecil Kellaway, Stuart Whitman.

The hedonistic Francis joins the army of Innocent II to fight for the liberation of Sicily. In the middle of a major battle, an inner voice prompts him to return home, where he is branded a coward and jailed. Once released, he again hears the voice, which instructs him to rebuild a ruined church. He gathers around him a group of followers who petition the Pope to establish them as a religious order. The Pope then sends Francis off to the Holy Lands to help the Crusaders fight the armies of the Sultan, who is impressed with Francis's faith but refuses to renounce Islam. Returning home, he finds that some of his followers have abandoned their vow of poverty, so he retreats to a cave. He soon dies blind, but clearly seeing God.

Based on Louis De Wohl's 1958 novel *The Joyful Beggar*, this is a surprisingly dull film, given Curtiz's impressive credits as a director.

REVIEWS: *Daily Cinema* 18 October 1961: 14. *Film Daily* 12 July 1961: 6. *Films in Review* 12 (August-September 1961): 433. *Harrison's Reports* 22 July 1961: 114. *Hollywood Reporter* 12 July 1961: 3. *Kinematograph Weekly* 19 October 1961: 10. *Monthly Film Bulletin* 28 (September 1961): 128. *Motion Picture Herald* 15 July 1961: Product Digest Section 203. *New York Times* 29 July 1961: 8. *Variety* 12 July 1961: 6.

ADDITIONAL DISCUSSIONS:

Guidorizzi, Mario. *Michael Curtiz, Un Europeo a Hollywood.* Verona: Mazziana, 1981.

Nash, Jay Robert, and Stanley Ralph Ross. *The Motion Picture Guide, E–G, 1927–1983.* Chicago: Cinebooks, 1986.

Robertson, James C. *The Casablanca Man, The Cinema of Michael Curtiz.* New York: Routledge, 1993.

193. *François Villon* (1945)

France; dir. M. Zwobada; Corona.

CAST: Jacques-Henri Duval, Renée Faure, Serge Reggiani.

The rascal François Villon earns the enmity of Catherine de Vauxcelles by murdering a money lender with whom she is in love. Arrested and tried for murder, Villon is exiled to Orleans, where he becomes an assistant to the crown prosecutor. Lured back to Paris with the promise of Catherine's affections, Villon is killed by a gang of robbers.

In recounting its version of the life of the French poet and thief François Villon (1431–?), this film manages to leave out all the poetry.

REVIEWS: *Le Monde* 19 September 1945: 7. *New York Times* 3 July 1950: 9. *Revue du cinéma* [La Saison cinématographique] Hors série 27 (1945–1947): 93. *Variety* 19 October 1949: 18.

Françoise de Rimini (1910) see *Francesca da Rimini* (1910)

Franziskus (1989) see *Francesco* (1989)

194. *Frate Francesco* (1927)

Italy; dir. Guilio Antamoro; I.C.S.A., Firenze.

ALTERNATE TITLE: *The Passion of St. Francis.*

CAST: Romouald Joube, Alberto Pasquali, Alfredo Rober, Franz Salla.

The young Francis abandons his career as a soldier and his life as a libertine to follow a simple life of poverty. With the blessing of the Pope, he establishes a religious order of men. He devotes the rest of his life to the service of the poor, and he dies surrounded by those whom he has served.

Reverential in its treatment of Francis, the film is badly edited, so that its narrative is dis-jointed. To the expected scenes, the film adds one of a Greek slave girl whom Francis rescues from a cruel nobleman.

REVIEWS: *Bianco et nero* 42 (July–December 1981): 305–08. *New York Times* 17 December 1932: 22. *Variety* 20 December 1932: 16; 20 July 1949: 20.

DISCUSSIONS:

Bernardini, Aldo, and Jean A. Gili, eds. *Le Cinéma italien de La Prise de Rome (1905) à Rome ville ouverte (1945).* Paris: Centre Georges Pompidou, 1986.

Buss, Robin. *Italian Films.* New York: Holmes & Meier, 1989.

Camerini, Claudio. "Tre film francescani." *Immagine* 2 (June–September 1982): 25–28.

"Frate Francesco." *Cinematografo* Supplemento No. 2 (1 April 1927): [1–8].

Martinelli, Vittorio. "Filmographie de Francesco d'Assisi." *Les Cahiers de la cinémathèque* 42–43 (Summer 1985): 36–37.

Frate Julianus (1991) see *Julianus* (1991)

195. *Frate Sole* (1918)

Italy; dir. Mario Corsi; Tespi Films.

ALTERNATE TITLE: *San Francesco d'Assisi.*

CAST: Rina Calabria, Silvia Malinverni, Lucienne Myosa, Uberto Palmarini, Bruno Emanuel Palmi, Filippo Ricci.

Francis visits a leper colony, comforts the poor of Assisi, undergoes temptation and dies in peace displaying the stigmata.

DISCUSSIONS:

Bernardini, Aldo, and Jean A. Gili, eds. *Le Cinéma italien de La Prise de Rome (1905) à Rome ville ouverte (1945).* Paris: Centre Georges Pompidou, 1986.

Camerini, Claudio. "Tre film francescani." *Immagine* 2 (June–September 1982): 25–28.

Corsi, Mario. "Une Grande film del 1918." *Cinema* [Rome] 3 (10 April 1938): 226–27.

Martinelli, Vittorio. "Filmographie de Francesco d'Assisi." *Les Cahiers de la cinémathèque* 42–43 (Summer 1985): 36–37.

Weinberg, Herman G., ed. *Fifty Years of Italian Cinema.* Rome: Carlo Bestetti–Edizioni d'Arte, 1955.

196. *Fratello homo, sorella bona— nel Boccaccio superproibito* (1973)

Italy; dir. Mario Sequi; Capitolina Produzioni Cinematografica.

ALTERNATE TITLES: *Get Thee to a Nunnery, Love Games in the Convent* and *Roman Scandals '73.*

CAST: Sergio Leonardi, Nazzareno Natale, Krista Nell, Antonia Santillo, Luciano Timoncini.

To escape the plague that is rampant in Florence, four prostitutes join a convent while four of their patrons join a monastery. To save the mayor's daughter from an arranged marriage, they stage a miracle.

The only thing more rampant than the plague in this codpiece farce are the sex lives of the four men and four women after they enter religious life.

REVIEW: *Monthly Film Bulletin* 40 (December 1973): 227, 258.

ADDITIONAL DISCUSSION:
Poppi, Roberto, and Mario Pecorari. *Dizionario del cinema italiano: I Film dal 1970 al 1979*. Rome: Gremese Editore, 1996.

Fratello solo, sorella luna (1972) see *Brother Sun, Sister Moon* (1972)

197. *Das Frauenhaus von Brescia* (1920)

Germany; dir. Hubert Moest; Segal Film.

Henry VII invades Lombardy and lays siege to Brescia. He sends for his queen, but she is taken prisoner by the king's enemy, Francesco de Barbiano, who wants her confined to a bordello. Henry renews his attacks upon the city and rescues his queen.

In 1311, Henry VII (1269–1313) invaded Italy, where he laid siege to Florence and was hailed by Dante as the restorer of peace and order. He died of a sudden illness near Sienna, having failed to end civil strife in Italy.

DISCUSSION:
Lamprecht, Gerhard. *Deutsche Stummfilme 1920*. Berlin: Deutsche Kinemathek, 1968.

Fury of the Vikings (1961) see *Erik the Conqueror* (1961)

198. *Galgameth* (1996)

United States; dir. Sean McNamara; Simon Sheen Productions.

CAST: Tom Dugan, Stephen Macht, Sean McNamara, Devin Oatway, Johna Stewart, Time Winters.

The young Prince Davin accidentally wounds his father the king in a joust. While the king is recovering, his chief knight El El poisons him and has himself declared regent. Unaware of what El El has done, Davin, believing he has killed his father, retreats into the solitude of his grief. El El then inaugurates a reign of terror and plots to do away with Davin, whose only defense is a magical statue called Galgameth that comes to life when it is watered by tears. Galgameth grows to an enormous size and helps Davin to rally the kingdom to defeat El El and to return Davin to his rightful place on the throne.

Shot on location in Romania, this film has a genuinely medieval look to it. It is, however, simply a well-made and entertaining fairy tale about a boy and his pet monster set in what the producers and director imagine is the Middle Ages.

REVIEW: *Variety* 10 June 1996: 45.

199. *A Game Old Knight* (1915)

United States; dir. Mack Sennett; Triangle-Keystone.

CAST: Louise Fazenda, Charles Murray.

A king orders a knight to marry his extremely unattractive daughter. The knight would rather marry her sister, a noted beauty, who is unfortunately betrothed to a handsome prince. Those loyal to the knight's cause kidnap the prince, but to no avail, as the knight is thrown in jail and threatened with torture. The prince escapes from his kidnappers and marries the fairer princess. The knight in turns marries her less attractive sister.

This film offered an example of Sennett's comic burlesque at its best. The scenes in the torture chamber manage to be the funniest in a film that is genuinely funny from beginning to end.

REVIEW: *Variety* 29 October 1915: 23.

200. *Gates to Paradise* (1967)

Great Britain; dir. Andrzej Wajda; Jointex Films.

ALTERNATE TITLES: *Bramy raju* and *La Croisade maudite*.

CAST: Jenny Agutter, Matthieu Carrière, Pauline Challoner, John Fordyce, Ferdy Mayne, Lionel Stander.

As thousands of young people are caught up in the fervor of a march to Jerusalem to win the Holy Land back peacefully from the Saracens, a monk accompanying the would-be crusaders as spiritual guide and confessor begins to see that what motivates many of the young people is not religious fervor. Rather, many on the march seem simply mesmerized by the physical attractiveness of the two leaders of the crusade, who are also the object of the lustful attentions of a mysterious Count Ludovic. The monk tries in vain to halt the pilgrimage, but ends up being trampled underfoot by the frenzied marchers.

Based on the 1960 novel *Bramy raju* by Jerzy Andrejewski, Wajda's film uses the so-called Children's Crusades of the early thirteenth century to make a statement about the ways in which idealism in any age can be cleverly exploited by the unscrupulous. In 1212, independent of each other, two groups of young people, rather than children, set out from France and Germany to convert the Saracens and recapture the Holy Land. United by a common bond of poverty and misplaced religious fervor, both groups followed self-styled prophets who predicted that the waters would part before them and that they would cross to the Holy Land without getting even their feet wet. Once there, the marchers would accomplish what the rich and powerful armies of Europe had not been able to do: recapture the Holy Land from the infidel. Their separate marches were disastrous, producing great suffering; many fell by the wayside. Once the young people arrived in Genoa and the seas declined to part, many boarded ships whose captains offered to take them to the Holy Land free of charge. Unfortunately, many of these captains then sold their young charges into slavery in North Africa. The so-called Children's Crusade is also the subject of Franklin Schaffner's 1987 film *Lionheart*.

REVIEWS: *Action* [Austria] 5 (August 1968): 15. *Films and Filming* 19 (February 1973): 20–21. *Filmwoche* 51 (27 June 1968): vii. *Jeune cinéma* 123 (December 1979-January 1980): 39–41. *Image et son* 345 (December 1979): 127–28. *Positif* 226 (January 1980): 56–58. *Rivista del cinematografo* 8 August 1968: 469. *Spielfilm im ZDF* 1 (January 1976): 10–11. *Télérama* 1555 (31 October 1979): 111. *Variety* 3 July 1968: 28.

ADDITIONAL DISCUSSIONS:

Douin, Jean-Luc. *Wajda*. Paris: Éditions Cana, 1981.
Eder, Klaus, et al. *Andrzej Wayda*. Nantes: L'Atalante, 1982.
Michalek, Bolestaw. *The Cinema of Andrzej Wajda*. trans. Edward Rothert. London: Tantivy, 1973.
_____, and Frank Turaj. *Le Cinéma polonais*. Paris: Centre Georges Pompidou, 1992.
Nash, Jay Robert, and Stanley Ralph Ross. *The Motion Picture Guide, E–G, 1927–1983*. Chicago: Cinebooks, 1986.

201. *Gawain and the Green Knight* (1973)

Great Britain; dir. Stephen Weeks; United Artists and Sancrest.

CAST: Nigel Green, Robert Hardy, Murray Head, Ronald Lacey, David Leland, Ciaran Madden, Anthony Sharp.

A knight clad wholly in green arrives at King Arthur's court, challenging all present to enter into an exchange of ax blows with him. Only Gawain, a young squire, accepts the challenge. He chops off the head of the stranger, but the corpse magically regains its severed head. The Green Knight tells him he has a year in which to discover his home and defeat him, or else Gawain must submit to a blow from the Green Knight's ax. Gawain sets out in the company of his squire to find the Green Knight. He first stumbles upon a shrine of stone on which he pours water. By doing so, he angers the Black Knight, who guards the shrine and challenges Gawain to a joust. Gawain kills the Black Knight and journeys on to his castle where Linet, a young maiden, gives him a ring which will render him invisible. At the castle, the widow of the Black Knight decides to make Gawain her new consort, but Gawain is in love with Linet, and the two try to flee. Gawain escapes, but Linet is captured by an evil seneschal named Oswald. The two lovers are finally reunited with the aid of Sir Bertilak. An exhausted Gawain prepares to face the Green Knight, only to have him crumble to dust in front of him. Gawain and Linet ride happily off together.

Ostensibly indebted to the anonymous fourteenth century romance *Sir Gawain and the Green Knight*, this film also borrows heavily from Chrétien de Troyes's twelfth century romance, *Yvain*. But it is one thing to borrow, and another thing to know how to use what has been borrowed. Weeks manages here to reduce great literature to silly cinema. Not content to leave bad enough alone, Weeks remade the film in 1983 under the title *Sword of the Valiant*, a film that is even sillier than its original.

REVIEW: *Monthly Film Bulletin* 40 (April 1973): 168–69.

ADDITIONAL DISCUSSIONS:

Berry, Dave. "Stephen Weeks." *Film* 37 (May 1976): 6–7.
Berry, David. *Wales and Cinema, The First Hundred Years*. Cardiff: University of Wales Press, 1994.
Blanch, Robert J., and Julian N. Wasserman. "Gawain on Film." In Kevin J. Harty, ed. *Cinema Arthuriana, Essays on Arthurian Film*. New York: Garland, 1991.

Elley, Derek. *The Epic Film*. London: Routledge & Kegan Paul, 1984.

Nash, Jay Robert, and Stanley Ralph Ross. *The Motion Picture Guide, E–G, 1927–1983*. Chicago: Cinebooks, 1986.

Genevieve (1932) see *Genoveffa* (1932).

202. *Geneviève de Brabant* (1907)

France; Pathé Frères.

When a knight goes off to war, he leaves his wife Geneviève and their children behind in the care of his steward Golo. Golo attempts to make love to Geneviève, but she refuses his advances and he has her and the children thrown out of the castle. Left to wander the forest in the dead of winter, they almost perish until a deer offers its milk to the children. Years later, the knight returns and discovers what has happened in his absence. He punishes Golo and sets out to find his missing wife and children. He stumbles on the trail of a deer which leads him to a cave where he discovers his wife and now-grown children safe.

This is one of a series of films to treat the curious legend of Geneviève of Brabant. The legend, which survives in several medieval versions, was probably first written down by the Carmelite Matthew Emich in 1472. The legend is based distantly on events in the life of Maria of Brabant, sometimes called Blessed but never Saint, who was beheaded in 1266 by her enraged husband, Louis II of Bavaria (called the Severe), who wrongly believed she had been unfaithful to him. Despite its lack of authenticity, the story of Geneviève, supposed daughter of the Duke of Brabant and Countess Palatine of Treves (Trier), who lived around the year 1100, has proven popular in literary and cinematic history. It was the subject of plays by Ludwig Teck (*Das Leben und Tod der heiligen Genoveva* [1799]), and Friedrich Hebbel (*Genoveva* [1843]), as well as operas by Franz Joseph Haydn (1777), Robert Schumann (1847) and Jacques Offenbach (1859). Offenbach's *opéra-bouffe*, *Geneviève de Brabant*, is generally the immediate source for the film versions of the legend, which set the action in the time of Charles Martel (c. 688–741) and reenact his attempts to prevent the Moors from invading France from their strongholds in Spain. Geneviève's husband, Count Siegfried, joins Charles's crusade against the Spanish Moors

when Golo attempts to make her his lover and then abandons her in the wilderness.

REVIEW: *Kinematograph and Lantern Weekly* 11 July 1907: 140.

ADDITIONAL DISCUSSIONS:

Bousquet, Henri. *Catalogue Pathé des années 1896 à 1914: 1907–1908–1909*. Paris: Henri Bousquet, 1993.

Savada, Elias. *The American Film Institute Catalog of Motion Pictures Produced in the United States: Film Beginnings, 1893–1910*. Metuchen, N.J.: Scarecrow, 1995.

203. *Genghis Khan* (1952)

Phillipines; dir. Lou Salvador, Manuel Conde Films.

CAST: Dramo Agosta, Manuel Conde, Africa De La Rosa, Inday Jalandroni, Elvira Reyes, Lou Salvador, José Villafrance.

In 1206, Temujin, a little-known Mongolian chieftain, enters what is the equivalent of the decathlon to prove his tribe's rights to a well and his worthiness to be leader of all the tribes. Taking the name Genghis Khan, he then conquers half of the known world.

This film has some novelty value as the rare Philippine production to tackle a medieval story, but the emphasis here is on bloody violence rather than on historical accuracy. In the United States and Great Britain, the film was screened with dialogue in Tagalog accompanied by a superimposed English narrative read by James Agee.

REVIEWS: *Bianco e nero* 9–10 (September-October 1952): 89. *Cinématographie française* 30 August 1952: 22; 5 September 1953: 16. *Daily Film Renter* 27 August 1952: 7. *Eco del cinema* 4 (31 January 1953): 231. *Film Daily* 20 July 1953: 11. *Film français* 11 September 1953: 15. *Harrison's Reports* 4 July 1953: 108. *Hollywood Reporter* 18 June 1953: 3. *Kinematography Weekly* 11 February 1954: 19. *Monthly Film Bulletin* 21 (March 1954): 36. *Saturday Review* 36 (13 June 1953): 29. *Theatre Arts* 37 (July 1953): 88. *Time* 61 (22 June 1953): 84, 86. *To-day's Cinema* 8 February 1954: 6. *Variety* 17 September 1952: 22; 8 July 1953: 16.

204. *Genghis Khan* (1965)

United States; dir. Henry Levin; BLC/Columbia Pictures.

CAST: Stephen Boyd, Françoise Dorleac, Michael Hordern, James Mason, Robert Morley, Telly Savalas, Omar Sharif, Eli Wallach.

Temujin, the young son of a murdered Mongol chieftain, is reared as a slave by his fa-

Omar Sharif (right) in the title role in Henry Levin's *Genghis Khan* (1965).

ther's murderer, Jamuga, chief of the Merkits. When he reaches maturity, Temujin escapes to the mountains, where Mongol tribesmen rally around him. He abducts Bortei, Jamuga's intended bride, and marries her himself. Temujin's forces then ride eastward to China where they are at first well received for protecting the empire from the Merkits. This initial welcome soon, however, sours when the Chinese emperor who has renamed Temujin Genghis Khan begins to fear that the powerful Mongol will turn against him. The emperor enlists Jamuga's help to assassinate Temujin, but the plot fails. Eventually, the Khan defeats the Merkits, but he suffers a fatal wound in the final battle against them. He dies knowing his son will realize his dream of world conquest.

Plagued by miscasting (Mason's bucktoothed Chinese prime minister is an offensive and inept stereotyping) and a poor script, this film cost a fortune to make—a fortune that, except for financing several decent battle scenes, was wasted. The story of Genghis Khan would seem to lend itself to an epic cinematic retelling, but this film disappoints.

REVIEWS: *Cinématographie française* 2117 (5 June 1965): 14. *Daily Cinema* 21 June 1965: 10. *Film Daily* 15 April 1965: 5. *Film français* 21 May 1965: 15. *Films and Filming* 11 (August 1965): 30. *Hollywood Reporter* 15 April 1965: 3. *Kinematograph Weekly* 17 June 1965: 121, 127. *Monthly Film Bulletin* 32 (August 1965): 123–24. *Motion Picture Herald* 28 April 1965: Product Digest Section 274. *New York Times* 24 June 1965: 28. *Times* [London] 17 June 1965: 17. *Variety* 21 April 1965: 6.

ADDITIONAL DISCUSSIONS:
Hirschhorn, Clive. *The Films of James Mason*. London: LSP Books, 1975.
Lucanio, Patrick. *With Fire and Sword, Italian Spectacles on American Screen, 1958–1968*. Metuchen, N.J.: Scarecrow, 1994.
Fraser, George MacDonald. *The Hollywood History of the World*. New York: Beech Tree Books, 1988.
Nash, Jay Robert, and Stanley Ralph Ross. *The Motion Picture Guide, E–G, 1927–1983*. Chicago: Cinebooks, 1986.
Smith, Gary A. *Epic Films*. Jefferson, N.C.: McFarland, 1991.

205. *Genghis Khan* (1986)

China; dir. Zhan Xiangchi; Inner Mongolia Film Studios.

CAST: Siqin Gaowa, Deli Gel.

Overcoming personal hardship and political rivalries, Genghis Khan succeeds in uniting the various factions among the Mongolian tribes into a powerful kingdom. He also founds China's Yuan Dynasty.

A cooperative effort on the part of the Chinese and Mongolian film industries, this film presents the biography of Genghis Khan (1162-1227), the man it considers the founder of the nation of Mongolia.

DISCUSSION:
"Genghis Khan." *China Screen* 1 (1986): 18–21.

206. *Genoveffa* (1932)

Italy and the United States; dir. Giulio Amauli; Italian-American Photofilm Company.

ALTERNATE TITLE: *Genevieve.*

CAST: Giulio Amauli, Dina Lanza.

Count Siegfried and his wife Genevieve discuss the mounting Moslem threat to France and all of Christendom. The king's messenger arrives to summon Siegfried to join the king's army. Reluctantly, the count leaves his wife (who faints when he departs) in the care of Golo. The lustful Golo carries Genevieve to her chambers and attempts to molest her. Genevieve writes a letter to her husband explaining what has happened, but Golo intercepts the message, kills the messenger and accuses Genevieve of committing adultery with the messenger. Golo imprisons her, and an enraged Siegfried, believing Golo's accusation, orders the death of his wife and son. Golo offers to spare them if Genevieve will consent to be his lover, but again she refuses. Executioners take Genevieve and the boy to the forest, but they balk at killing a mother and her child. When Genevieve promises never to leave the forest, the executioners depart, leaving her to die from exposure. Years pass, and Siegfried returns home to learn the truth of what has happened. He punishes Golo. One day while out hunting, Siegfried stumbles upon his wife and son asleep in a cave, and they are all happily reunited.

This film is yet another retelling of the apocryphal legend of St. Geneviève of Brabant, although it omits the famous episode where the starving child is fed by the deer, which became the standard for iconographic representations of that legend. This film is itself a remake of a silent film probably released in 1925 for which no records seem to have survived. The 1932 film, which had both English and Italian titles and dialogue, was based on the opera by Offenbach.

DISCUSSIONS:

Hanson, Patricia King, ed. *The American Film Institute Catalog of Motion Pictures Produced in the United States: Feature Films, 1931–1940.* Berkeley: University of California Press, 1993.

"Italian Costume Talker." *Film Daily* 22 August 1932: 2.

207. *Genoveffa di Brabante* (1965)

Italy and Spain; dir. José Luis Monter; Imprecine and Hispamer Films.

CAST: Maria José Alfonso, Beni Deus, Stephen Forsyth, Alberto Lupo, Angela Rhu.

When Count Siegfried goes off to fight the invading Moslems, his wife Genevieve must face the amorous advances of his deputy, Golo. When she spurns him, Golo orders her and her son into the forest to die from starvation and exposure. When Siegfried finally returns from the wars, he punishes Golo and rescues his wife and son.

This film version of the life of St. Geneviève of Brabant is based on the medieval legend which was first written down at the end of the fifteenth century.

REVIEW: *Segnocinema* 64 (November-December 1993): 64.

ADDITIONAL DISCUSSION:

Poppi, Roberto, and Mario Pecorari. *Dizionario del cinema italiano. Vol. 3: I Film dal 1960 al 1969.* Rome: Gremese Editore, 1992.

La Gerusalemme liberata (1911) see *The Crusaders* (1911)

208. *Gerusalemme liberata* (1918)

Italy; dir. Enrico Guazzoni; Guazzoni Film.

CAST: Olga Benetti, Edy Darclea, Amleto Novelli, Elena Sangro.

This film adaptation of Tasso's sixteenth century epic poem about the Crusades, *Gerusalemme liberata*, relocates the action to Rome. Full of pomp and circumstance, the production constantly deviates from its source for no discernible reason. Tasso's poem, with its theme of the 1099 reconquest of Jerusalem and much of Palestine from the Saracens by Godfrey of Bouillon, proved a favorite source for filmmakers.

DISCUSSIONS:

Bernardini, Aldo, and Jean A. Gili, eds. *Le Cinéma italien de La Prise de Rome (1905) à Rome ville ouverte (1945).* Paris: Centre Georges Pompidou, 1986.

Buss, Robin. *Italian Films.* New York: Holmes & Meier, 1989.

Gerusalemme liberata (1957) see *The Mighty Crusaders* (1957)

Get Thee to a Nunnery (1973) see *Fratello homo, sorella bona—nel Boccaccio superproibito* (1973)

209. *Giovanna I d'Angiò, regine di Napoli* (1920)

Italy; dir. Gemma Bellincioni; Bellincioni Film.

CAST: Gemma Bellincioni, Lea Campioni, Bepo A. Corradi, Giuseppe Majone Diaz, Ignazio Mascalchi, Augusto Mastripietri.

Only 17 when she succeeds her grandfather Robert to the throne of Naples, Joanna quickly becomes a nuptial pawn among warring factions. When Naples is invaded, only the intervention of Pope Urban VI (1318–1389) saves Joanna's throne. The victory is short-lived when Urban concludes she is sympathetic to the anti-pope Clement VI in Avignon, withdraws his protection and excommunicates her. She is then arrested and executed by Charles III of Durazzo.

Internecine battling between the Neapolitan and Hungarian branches of the Angevins contributed to political chaos throughout Italy in the fourteenth and fifteenth centuries. Joanna I of Naples (1343–1382) succeeded her grandfather Robert to the throne, but she was murdered by her relative, Charles III of Durazzo, who was in turn murdered by his Hungarian relatives in 1386. This film, while fairly accurate, tends to reduce Joanna (no passive player in the political intrigues of her day) to a pawn in the hands of her male relatives. Gemma Bellincioni wrote, directed and played the title role in this film.

REVIEW: *Bianco e nero* 41 (July–December 1980): 162–63.

210. *Giovanna d'Arco al rogo* (1954)

Italy and France; dir. Roberto Rossellini; Produzione Cinematografiche.

ALTERNATE TITLE: *Joan at the Stake.*

CAST: Ingrid Bergman, Tullio Carminati, Giacinto Prantelli, Augusto Romani.

Gemma Bellincioni in the title role in the film which she also wrote and directed, *Giovanna I d'Angiò, regine di Napoli* (1920).

Surrounded by the flames of the stake, Joan of Arc hears the voice of her confessor, Friar Dominic, telling her she will soon be free. The priest shows her a book written by the angels that tells her true story. With him, she reviews the events of her life that led her to this horrible moment.

Rossellini here directed Bergman in her second film about Joan of Arc. She had previously starred in the 1948 film *Joan of Arc*, which was a success (unlike this second film). For a source, Rossellini used Paul Claudel and Arthur Honneger's 1939 oratorio *Jeanne d'Arc au bûcher*, which presented the director with problems not easily overcome on film. The text of the oratorio called for Joan to be stationary; chained to a stake, she could not obviously move about in front of the camera. Rossellini did present some visually arresting scenes, but on the whole the film just does not work. It was so badly received critically that it was never given a general release, and copies remain difficult to find.

REVIEWS: *Les Cahiers du cinéma* 44 (February 1955): 41; 48 (June 1955): 38. *Cineforum* 270 (December 1987): 53–56. *Cinema nuovo* 54 (10 March 1955): 191. *New York Times* 6 October 1987: C14. *Variety* 11 November 1954: 11.

ADDITIONAL DISCUSSIONS:
Beylie, Claude. "Défense de *Jeanne au bûcher* ou la sérénité des abîmes." *Études cinématographiques* 18-19 (Autumn 1962): 72–78.
Blaetz, Robin J. "Strategies of Containment: Joan of Arc in Film." Ph.D. dissertation. New York University, 1989.
Bondanella, Peter, *The Films of Roberto Rossellini*. New York: Cambridge University Press, 1993.
Brunette, Peter. *Roberto Rossellini*. New York: Oxford University Press, 1987.
Chiti, Roberto, and Roberto Poppi. *Dizionario del cinema italiano. Vol. 2: I Film dal 1945 al 1959*. Rome; Gremese Editore, 1991.
Esteve, Michel. "*Jeanne au bûcher*, de Roberto Rossellini: les seductions de l'oratorio filmé ou le merveilleux contre le surnaturel." *Études cinématographiques* 18-19 (Autumn 1962): 65–71.
Falconi, Carlo. "Il Cinema cattolico." *Cinema nuovo* 50 (October 1955): 26–28.
Guarner, José Luis. *Roberto Rosselini*. Trans. Elisabeth Cameron. London: Studio Vista, 1970.
Harty, Kevin J. "Jeanne au cinéma." In Bonnie Wheeler and Charles T. Wood, eds. *Fresh Verdicts on Joan of Arc*. New York: Garland, 1996.
Italian Film Production 1954–1955. Rome: Unitalia Film, 1955.
Margolis, Nadia. *Joan of Arc in History, Literature, and Film*. New York: Garland, 1990.
Masi, Stephano. *I Film di Roberto Rossellini*. Rome: Editore Gremese, 1987.

Nash, Jay Robert, and Stanley Ralph Ross. *The Motion Picture Guide, H–K, 1927–1983*. Chicago: Cinebooks, 1986.
Rondolino, Gianni. *Roberto Rossellini*. Turin: UTET, 1989.
Rossi, Patrizio. *Roberto Rossellini, A Guide to References and Resources*. Boston: Hall, 1988.

211. *Giovanni de Medici* (1910)
Italy; Cines.
ALTERNATE TITLE: *Giovanni of Medici*.

Giovanni de Medici meets and falls in love with Emma, the sister of the painter Caravaggio. After they have an assignation, the painter attempts to restore the family honor by challenging Giovanni to a duel. Giovanni escapes, but within a few years, he lays siege to the town where the Caravaggio family lives. In the ensuing battle, Emma barely escapes with her life, and her mother is cruelly slain. Embittered, Emma refuses to marry Giovanni, who is mortally wounded in a subsequent battle. Despite her grief, Emma rushes to Giovanni's side arriving just before he dies.

Giovanni de Medici (1498–1526), called Giovanni of the Black Band when he had his troops change their white insignia to black after the death of Pope Leo X, was a noted warrior in the service of the Papal States. He was father of Cosimo, who as Cosimo I founded the Medici ducal dynasty.

REVIEWS: *Bioscope* 30 June 1910: 41. *Motion Picture News* 8 October 1910: 11. *Moving Picture World* 1 October 1910: 770; 15 October 1910: 878.

ADDITIONAL DISCUSSION:
Savada, Elias. *The American Film Institute Catalog of Motion Pictures Produced in the United States: Film Beginnings, 1893–1910*. Metuchen, N.J.: Scarecrow, 1995.

Giovanni of Medici (1910) see *Giovanni de Medici* (1910)

212. *Giulia Colonna* (1910)
Italy; Cines.
ALTERNATE TITLE: *Julie Colonna*.

Prince Filippo Orsini is madly in love with Giulia Colonna, who refuses his proposal of marriage. Enraged, Orsini kidnaps Giulia and confines her in a prison, threatening never to release her unless she marries him. Giulia's brother mounts a rescue of his sister. The Pope sends a legate to intercede between the two families, but Giulia's brother seizes the legate as a hostage, kills Orsini and frees his sister.

From the earliest times, the Colonnas and the Orsinis were rivals for influence in Rome with both families having ecclesiastical authority (through family members who were cardinals and bishops) and civil authority (through family members who were captains in the armies of Italy).

REVIEW: *Bioscope* 12 May 1910: 33. *Moving Picture World* 24 September 1910: 711.

ADDITIONAL DISCUSSION:

Savada, Elias. *The American Film Institute Catalog of Motion Pictures Produced in the United States: Film Beginnings, 1893–1910.* Metuchen, N.J.: Scarecrow, 1995.

213. *The Golden Horde* (1951)

United States; dir. George Sherman; Universal-International.

ALTERNATE TITLE: *The Golden Horde of Genghis Khan.*

CAST: Ann Blyth, Peggie Castle, Richard Egan, David Farrar, George Macready, Marvin Miller, Howard Petrie, Donald Randolph.

In 1220, Princess Shalimar finds her city Samarkand threatened by the forces of Genghis Khan. A group of Crusaders offer to come to her aid, but she schemes to turn the Khan's sons against each other and thus divert the Mongols. In a climactic scene, troops from Samarkand join with the Crusaders to defeat the hordes of Genghis Khan.

This film consistently sacrifices coherence and historical accuracy for pure pageantry. At best a spoof of history, it is one of a series of costume epics released by Universal-International in the 1950s.

REVIEWS: *Harrison's Reports* 15 September 1951: 147. *Monthly Film Bulletin* 18 (September 1951): 330. *Motion Picture Herald* 15 September 1951: Product Digest Section 1014. *Revue du cinéma* [La Saison cinématographique] 32 (1950–1951): 143. *To-day's Cinema* 13 August 1951: 13. *Variety* 29 September 1951: 6.

ADDITIONAL DISCUSSIONS:

Nash, Jay Robert, and Stanley Ralph Ross. *The Motion Picture Guide, E–G, 1927–1983.* Chicago: Cinebooks, 1986.

Richards, Jeffrey. *Swordsmen of the Screen from Douglas Fairbanks to Michael York.* London: Routledge & Kegan Paul, 1977.

Smith, Gary A. *Epic Films.* Jefferson, N.C.: McFarland, 1991.

The Golden Horde of Genghis Khan

(1951) see *The Golden Horde* (1951)

214. *The Golden Supper* (1910)

United States; dir. D.W. Griffith; Biograph.

CAST: Claire McDowell, Alfred Paget, Dorothy West.

Julian greatly loves his cousin and foster sister Camilla, but she marries his friend and rival Lionel. The newlyweds' bliss is shattered when Camilla develops a fever and appears to die. She is buried in the family vault while a distraught Lionel becomes a recluse and an equally distraught Julian keeps a vigil by her tomb. Julian soon discovers that Camilla is still alive, and he hosts a supper, during which he will according to custom bestow his most prized possession on a friend. At the supper, he presents Camilla to Lionel, and the two live happily ever after.

This film's medieval pedigree is impressive. Its immediate source is Tennyson's poem "The Lover's Tale" (1879), which was in turn based on Boccaccio's tale of Messer Gentil de' Carisendi (*Decameron* Day 10, Story 4).

REVIEWS: *Bioscope* 2 February 1911: 39; 10 May 1917: 538. *Moving Picture World* 17 December 1910: 1426; 24 December 1910: 1478.

ADDITIONAL DISCUSSIONS:

Bowser, Eileen, ed. *Biograph Bulletins 1908–1912.* New York: Octagon, 1973.

Savada, Elias. *The American Film Institute Catalog of Motion Pictures Produced in the United States: Film Beginnings, 1893–1910.* Metuchen, N.J.: Scarecrow, 1995.

Good King Dagobert (1911) see *Le Bon Roi Dagobert* (1911)

Good King Dagobert (1963) see *Le Bon Roi Dagobert* (1963)

215. *Good King Wenceslas* (1994)

United States; Michael Tuchner; Griffin and Family Productions.

CAST: Jonathan Brandis, Charlotte Chatton, Joan Fontaine, Perry King, Leo McKern, Stefanie Powers.

In the tenth century, young Wenceslas is heir to the throne of Bohemia and affianced to the daughter of a neighboring duke who is rich in gold and land. His stepmother has other ideas, wishing instead to place her own son

Stefanie Powers as the villainous Queen Ludmilla in The Family Channel's made-for-television's *Good King Wenceslas* (1994). (Still courtesy of The Family Channel.)

Boleslaw on the throne. The dynastic squabbling takes on added significance because Wenceslas is Christian and his stepmother and her son are not. Through her would-be consort Lord Tunna, the queen plots to turn the people against Wenceslas. Initially they are successful, but Wenceslas succeeds in securing the throne and the Christian faith of his people.

This tame bit of family fare, which aired in the United States in 1994 as a Thanksgiving special on The Family Channel, has some historical basis. St. Wenceslas (c. 903–935) — the "Good King Wenceslas" of Christmas carol fame — was duke of Bohemia. He clashed with his mother over matters of religion. To ensure the continuation of Christianity in his realm, he put his duchy under the protection of the Saxon King Henry I, for which action he was murdered by his brother Boleslaw. Wenceslas was venerated as patron saint of Bohemia shortly after his death. His legend was first told in the early eleventh century by Laurentius, Bishop of Monte Cassino, in his *Passio sancti Venceslai*.

REVIEWS: *Chicago Tribune* 23 November 1994: Tempo 3. *Variety* 21 November 1994: 32.

216. *Grendel Grendel Grendel* (1981)

Australia; dir. Alexander Stitt; Victorian Film Corporation and Animation Australia.

CAST: (the voices of) Allison Bird, Ernie Bourne, Bobby Bright, Arthur Dingham, Barry Hill, Julie McKenna, Keith Mitchell, Ric Stone, Peter Ustinov.

King Hrothgar's attempts to subdue his neighbors and establish harmony within his kingdom are interrupted by the arrival of Grendel, a monster who favors solitude but who must feed off of Hrothgar's retainers so that he and his mother can survive. Hrothgar fears Grendel will only further destabilize his rule, so the king summons Beowulf from across the seas to rid his kingdom of the monster and his mother.

Based on John Gardner's 1971 novel *Grendel*, this animated musical retells the Anglo-Saxon epic poem *Beowulf* from the point of view of Grendel, arguing that man, not monster, is the truly destructive and frightening creature.

REVIEWS: *Cinefantastique* 12 (July–August 1982): 91. *Cinema Papers* 33 (July–August 1981): 286–87. *Hollywood Reporter* 14 April 1982: 9. *Metro*

56 (Winter 1981): 64–65. *New York Times* 11 April 1982: 46 and 2A. 15. *Variety* 4 November 1981: 26.

ADDITIONAL DISCUSSIONS:
"An Animated Progress Report on: *Grendel Grendel Grendel.*" *Cinema Papers* 21 (May–June 1979): 99–101; 12 (April–May 1980): 41–43.
Nash, Jay Robert, and Stanley Ralph Ross. *The Motion Picture Guide, E–G, 1927–1983*. Chicago: Cinebooks, 1986.

Griselda (1912) see *Griséldis* (1912)

217. *Griséldis* (1912)

France; Production Série d'Art Pathé Frères.
CAST: Berthe Bovy.

The lowly shepherdess Griselda finds herself unexpectedly the object of the Prince of Saluces's affections. The prince takes her to his palace and marries her, to the dismay of the jealous Countess Bertrande, who convinces the prince that Griselda has been unfaithful to him. Griselda is dismissed from court, but when the truth of her innocence comes out, she and the prince are reunited.

The story of the ever-patient Griselda was extremely popular in the Middle Ages, though more modern sensibilities may see it as a misogynic nightmare. Boccaccio, Petrarch and Chaucer each chronicle Griselda's meekness in the face of the increasing cruelty of her monstrous husband. This cinematic version of her tale, which is based on a late seventeenth century retelling of the Griselda story by Charles Perrault, tones down the husband's cruelty considerably.

REVIEWS: *Bisoscope* 29 February 1912: supplement iii; 11 December 1913: supplement xi.
ADDITIONAL DISCUSSION:
Bousquet, Henri. *Catalogue Pathé des années 1896 à 1914: 1912–1913–1914*. Paris: Henri Bousquet, 1995.

218. *Guglielmo Tell* (1949)

Italy; dir. Giorgio Pastina; Fauno Film.
ALTERNATE TITLE: *William Tell.*
CAST: Gino Cervi, Paul Muller, Aldo Nicodemi, Monique Orban, Raf Pindi.

Schiller's play is the putative source here, but the film focuses on a love affair between two minor characters with which Gessler interferes, instead of on Tell's exploits to free the Swiss from Austrian tyranny.

The story of William Tell is the stuff of legend based on events that supposedly happened early in the fourteenth century when Switzerland suffered under oppressive Austrian rule. Tell's name appears in a ballad dated around 1470, and his story was first told fully in Aegidius Tsudi's *Chronicon helveticum* (1572).

REVIEW: *Variety* 10 August 1949: 8.

ADDITIONAL DISCUSSIONS:

Chiti, Roberto, and Roberto Poppi. *Dizionario del cinema italiano. Vol. 2: I Film dal 1945 al 1959.* Rome: Gremese Editore, 1991.

"Lincoln et Guillaume Tell sur l'autel de la patrie." *Les Cahiers de la cinémathèque* 45 (1986): 55–59.

219. *Guillaume le conquérant* (1987)

France; dir. Jean-Claude Rivière; Les Films Normands.

CAST: François Dyrek, Serge Gaborieau, Christine Lemaitre, Philippe Marie, Carole Rouland.

Combining fiction and documentary and using the Bayeux Tapestry as its source, this film presents the life of William the Conqueror in Normandy and in England after the Conquest in 1066.

Earlier, in 1982, French television had presented a six-hour mini-series on the life of William the Conqueror, directed by Gilles Grangier.

DISCUSSION:

Les Films français. Paris: Unifrance Film International, 1987.

220. *Guillaume Tell* (1903)

France; dir. Lucien Nonguet; Pathé Frères.

ALTERNATE TITLE: *William Tell.*

CAST: Edmond Boutillon.

Five tableaux depict how Swiss peasants led by William Tell defeated the tyrant Gessler. The scenes—"Tell's Heroism," "The Plot," "The Apple," "The Death of Gessler" and "The Swiss Cheer Their Leader"— were shot against striking background scenery.

DISCUSSIONS:

Bousquet, Henri, and Riccardo Redi. *Pathé Frères. Les films del al production Pathé (1896–1914).* Florence: Quarderni di cinema, 1988; rpt. and updated as *Catalogue Pathé des annés 1896 à 1914: 1896 à 1906.* Paris: Henri Bousquet, 1996. [Originally published as issue 37 of *Quarderni di cinema* (January–March 1988).]

Dumont, Hervé. *Histoire du cinéma suisse.* Lausanne: Cinémathèque suisse, 1987.

Films et cinémathographiques Pathé. Paris: Pathé Frères, 1907.

Pathé Frères Cinematograph and Phonograph Catalog [Supplement for] September-October 1903: 11–12.

Sadoul, Georges. *Histoire générale du cinéma II. Les Pionniers du cinéma (de Méliès à Pathé) 1897–1909.* Paris: Les Éditions Denoël, 1977.

Savada, Elias. *The American Film Institute Catalog of Motion Pictures Produced in the United States: Film Beginnings, 1893–1910.* Metuchen, N.J.: Scarecrow, 1995.

The "Walturdaw" Animated Pictures Catalogue. London: Walturdaw, 1904.

221. *Guillaume Tell* (1911)

France; dir. Guiseppe Kaschmann; Pathé Frères and Il Film d'arte italiana.

ALTERNATE TITLE: *William Tell.*

Because he refuses to bow his head to the tyrant Gessler's hat, Tell is condemned to death, though he is granted a reprieve if he can shoot an apple off of his son's head. Tell succeeds, but the seeds of rebellion have been sown. In the ensuing struggle, Gessler is killed and the Austrians are driven from Switzerland.

This second film about William Tell from Pathé Frères is based on Schiller's play.

REVIEWS: *Bioscope* 6 July 1911: supplement v; 9 October 1913: supplement xi.

ADDITIONAL DISCUSSION:

Bousquet, Henri. *Catalogue Pathé des années 1896 à 1914. 1910–1911.* Paris: Henri Bousquet, 1994.

222. *Guillaume Tell* (1912)

Switzerland; dir. George Wäckerlin; Dramatischer Verein Interlacken.

ALTERNATE TITLES: *Wilhelm Tell* and *William Tell.*

CAST: Hans Aerni, Carl Barbier, Hans Brunner, August Flückiger, Franz Nelkel, Jakob Wäckerlin.

According to publicity for this film version of Schiller's play, the hundreds of peasants who form the staged crowds are "the lineal descendants of the patriots who fought under the great Swiss liberator."

REVIEW: *Bioscope* 19 March 1914: 1311.

ADDITIONAL DISCUSSION:

Dumont, Hervé. *Historie du cinéma suisse.* Lausanne: Cinémathèque suisse, 1987.

223. *Guillaume Tell* (1913)

Germany; dir. Friedrich Fehér; Deutsche Mutoscop- & Biograph-Gesellschaft.

ALTERNATE TITLE: *Die Befreiung der Schweiz und die Sage von Wilhelm Tell* and *William Tell.*

CAST: Rudolph Benzinger, Hans Bilrose, Friedrich Fehér, Karl Kienlechner, Emil Lind, Fritz Orlop, Ilse von Tasso, Margarete Wilkens.

William Tell gives shelter to Baumgarten, who has just killed a servant of the Austrian tyrant Gessler. Tell also refuses to bow to Gessler's hat as it sits atop a pole in the village square. For these offenses, Tell is ordered to shoot an apple from off his son's head. Tell succeeds, but a second arrow meant for Gessler's heart drops from his sleeve. When Tell is imprisoned, the Swiss rise in revolt, and Tell escapes from prison to lead them in the uprising. Tell kills Gessler, and the Swiss ransack his castle and repel the Austrian occupying forces.

REVIEWS: *Cinema* 7 May 1914: supplement 78. *Moving Picture World* 2 May 1914: 652. *Variety* 12 June 1914: 21.

ADDITIONAL DISCUSSION:

Dumont, Hervé. *Histoire du cinéma suisse.* Lausanne: Cinémathèque suisse, 1987.

224. *Guillaume Tell* (1914)

Switzerland; dir. M. Maistre; Lémania Film.

This filmed production of Schiller's play employed an army of Swiss actors and herds of livestock.

REVIEW: *Bioscope* 14 May 1914: supplement vii.

ADDITIONAL DISCUSSION.

Dumont, Hervé. *Histoire du cinéma suisse.* Lausanne: Cinémathèque suisse, 1987.

Guillaume Tell (1960) see *Wilhelm Tell-Burgen in Flammen* (1960)

225. *Guinevere* (1994)

United States; dir. Jud Taylor; Lifetime Productions.

CAST: Brid Brennan, Sheryl Lee, Donald Pleasence, Noah Wyle.

The young Guinevere has had the kind of education usually reserved for a man. She can fight with a sword and negotiate skillfully. When her father meets an untimely death, she is thrust into the role of ruler, which requires her to abandon her affection for Lancelot.

This made-for-cable-television retelling of the legend of Arthur as "her"-story is very loosely based on the series of popular novels written during the 1980s by Persia Woolley.

REVIEWS: *Times-Picayune* [New Orleans] 1 May 1994: TV4. *TV Guide* 7 May 1994: 67, 76.

Gypsy Fury (1950) see *The Mask and the Sword* (1950)

Hagbard and Signe (1967) see *The Red Mantle* (1967)

226. *Häxan* (1921)

Sweden; dir. Benjamin Christensen; Svensk Filmindustri.

ALTERNATE TITLE: *Witchcraft Through the Ages.*

CAST: Benjamin Christensen, Mara Pederson, Clara Pontoppidan, Oscar Stirbolt, Tora Teje.

After a brief prologue which describes earlier views on devils and witches, this film examines medieval reactions to witches and witchcraft. An epilogue suggests that people who once would have been considered possessed are now in hospitals and mental institutions receiving the care they need.

The style here is that of the quasi-documentary. The medieval portion of the film unflinchingly presents the squalor, cruelty and superstitions of the Middle Ages. We see nude flagellants and the excesses of the Inquisition. A witch-craze leads to the destruction of an entire family and mass hysteria. This sometimes-surreal gem was ahead of its time in technical achievement and in its treatment of the macabre.

REVIEWS: *Cinéma* [Paris] 130 (November 1968): 122–23; 241 (January 1979): 101–02. *Cinématographe* 42 (December 1978): 69. *Daily Cinema* 11 November 1968: 6. *Dossiers art et essai* 46 (2 May 1968): 33–34. *Films and Filming* 15 (February 1969): 48. *Image et son* 221 (November 1968): 115–16; 233 (1969): 175–77. *Kinematograph Weekly* 2 November 1968: 17. *Monthly Film Bulletin* 35 (December 1968): 193; 45 (May 1978): 107. *Revue du cinéma* 468 (February 1991): 35.

ADDITIONAL DISCUSSIONS:

Ernst, John. *Benjamin Christensen.* Copenhagen: Danske Filmmuseum, 1967.

Garbicz, Adam, and Jacek Klinowski. *Cinema, the Magic Vehicle.* Metuchen, N.J.: Scarecrow, 1975.

Hardy, Forsyth. *Scandinavian Film.* London: Falcon, 1952.

Magill, Frank N., ed. *Magill's Survey of Cinema: Silent Films.* Englewood Cliffs, N.J.: Salem, 1982.

Routt, William D. "Buried Directors." *Focus!* 7 (Spring 1972): 9–12, 38.

Sadoul, Georges. *Histoire générale du cinéma 5. L'Art muet 1919–1929. Premier volume: L'Après-guerre en Europe.* Paris: Denoël, 1975.

Thomas, Nicholas, ed. *International Directory of Films and Filmmakers—1. Films.* 2nd ed. Chicago: St. James, 1990.

227. *Heart Beats of Long Ago* (1911)

United States; Biograph.

A feud between two noble Italian families separates a young man and woman who are madly in love with each other. The young

Advocate Richard Coutrois (Colin Firth) and Filette d'Auferre (Lysette Anthony) in a scene from Leslie Megahey's *L'Heure du cochon* (1994). (Still courtesy of the British Film Museum.)

woman attempts a liaison with her beloved during a feast called to announce her engagement to someone else. The attempted assignation fails, and the young lover is killed.

This costume piece is set in the fourteenth century.

REVIEWS: *Bioscope* 23 March 1911: 32. *Moving Picture World* 11 February 1911: 320.

ADDITIONAL DISCUSSION:
Bowser, Eileen, ed. *Biograph Bulletins 1908–1912.* New York: Octagon Books, 1973.

Heart of a Tyrant (1981) see *A Zsarnok sziva avaby Boccaccio magyarorszagin* (1981)

228. *The Heir of Clavancourt Castle* (1909)

France; dir. Victorin Jasset; Eclair.

An aging baron receives an ambassador from abroad at his castle. The ambassador is really a brigand who kills the baron's granddaughter in an attempt to extort treasure from his host. Angels descend from on high to punish the brigand, and the baron reconciles himself to what has happened.

This film is clearly set in the Middle Ages, though its purpose is more religious than historical, suggesting as it does that the baron needs to reconcile himself unquestioningly to the will of God.

REVIEWS: *Bioscope* 25 February 1915: supplement i. *Variety* 18 December 1909: 15.

ADDITIONAL DISCUSSION:
Savada, Elias. *The American Film Institute Catalog of Motion Pictures Produced in the United States: Film Beginnings, 1893–1910.* Metuchen, N.J.: Scarecrow, 1995.

A Hercegnö és a kobold (1992) see *The Princess and the Goblin* (1992)

229. *L'Heure du cochon* (1994)

France and Great Britain; dir. Leslie Megahey; BBC Films.

ALTERNATE TITLES: *The Advocate* and *The Hour of the Pig.*

CAST: Amina Annabi, Lysette Anthony, Jim Carter, Colin Firth, Ian Holm, Donald Pleasence, Nicol Williamson.

A Parisian lawyer moves to a rural village to better serve the people. His first client is a pig accused of murdering a Jewish boy. The pig's owner is a beautiful gypsy girl with whom the lawyer falls in love. In his attempt to defend the pig, the lawyer exposes the superstition and intolerance that is so imbedded in rural fourteenth century France.

Surviving records suggest that, in medieval times, animals were actually tried for crimes — and punished if convicted — because it was believed that animals were subject to human laws. In this film's chilling opening sequence, a man and a donkey are accused of having had carnal knowledge of each other. As they are about to be hanged for their crime, a last minute reprieve arrives — and the donkey is spared. But in this fascinating film, Megahey's interest is not in bestiality but in the intolerance and superstition of the period and the ways that those in power used that intolerance and superstition to exploit the poor and the defenseless.

REVIEWS: *Audience* 180 (December 1994-January 1995): 44–45. *Empire* 56 (February 1994): 30. *Film Review* [London] February 1994: 19. *Los Angeles Times* 24 August 1994: Calendar 8. *New York Times* 24 August 1994: C11. *Sight and Sound* NS 4 (February 1994): 53; NS 4 (September 1994): 56. *Studio* [France] 68 (December 1992): 44. *Sunday Times* [London] 23 January 1994: 9. 54. *Times* [London] 18 January 1994: 32. *Variety* 25 October 1993: 82.

ADDITIONAL DISCUSSIONS:

Brennan, Shawn, ed. *Magill's Cinema Annual 1995.* New York: Gale Research, 1996.

Cameron-Wilson, James, and F. Maurice Speed. *Film Review 1994–95.* London: Virgin Books, 1994.

Levich, Jacob, ed. *The Motion Picture Guide, 1995 Annual (The Films of 1994).* New York: CineBooks, 1994.

230. *The High Crusade* (1994)

Germany; dir. Holger Neuhaüser; Overseas Film Group.

CAST: Patrick Brymer, Rick Overton, John Rhys-Davies.

A group of Crusaders hijack an alien spaceship to take them to the Holy Land, only to be spirited away to the planet Tharixan in the distant future.

This film, based on Poul Anderson's 1960 novel *The High Crusade*, was released straight to video for good reason — it is terrible in every way possible.

REVIEWS: *Film-Echo/Filmwoche* 20 May 1994: 22; 10 June 1994: 12. *Time Out* [London] 31 May 1995: 164.

Las Hijas del Cid (1962) see *Sword of El Cid* (1962)

231. *Hildegard* (1994)

Great Britain; James Runcie; BBC.

CAST: Michael Byrne, Robert Gwilym, Edward Jewesbury, Amanda Root, Patricia Routledge, Janet Suzman, Peter Vaughan.

Inspired by visions she claims are heavenly, Hildegard of Bingen rebels against church law that puts her under the authority of a man. Together with some fellow nuns, she founds her own community for religious women who devote themselves to praising God through song.

Hildegard (now St. Hildegard) of Bingen (1098–1179) was probably the most important woman of her time. She was known for her prophetic visions, for her skills as a physician and for her talents as a musician. Chants attributed to her have been rediscovered in the 1990s as part of a revival of interest in medieval music and of a reassessment of the works of medieval women writers.

REVIEWS: *Radio Times* [London] 26 March–1 April 1994: 74. *Television Today* 7 April 1994: 23. *Time Out* [London] 23–30 March 1994: 159.

ADDITIONAL DISCUSSION:

Duncan, Andrew. "'I'm a Cynical Realist. I Can't Stand All the Luvie Stuff.'" *Radio Times* [London] 26 March–1 April 1994: 26–28.

232. *L'Histoire très bonne et très joyeuse de Colinot trousse-chemise* (1973)

France; dir. Nina Companeez; Parc Film.

ALTERNATE TITLE: *The Edifying and Joyous Story of Colinot the Skirt Puller-Upper.*

CAST: Brigitte Bardot, Nathalie Delon, Francis Huster, Bernadette Lafont, Ottavia Piccoli, Alice Sapritch.

In the mid–fifteenth century, Colinot is in pursuit of his beloved and the kidnappers who have spirited her away. He meets all kinds of women, but remains faithful to his missing beloved until he finds out that she has married a nobleman.

This film is a farce from beginning to end — more a codpiece comedy typical of Italian cinema at the time than the Rabelaisian picaresque tale it wants to be. Its only notable feature is Bardot's too-brief appearance as Arabelle, a noblewoman who finally teaches Colinot the true meaning of love.

REVIEWS: *Cinéma* [Paris] 182 (December 1973): 126–28. *Écran* 20 (December 1973): 75. *Variety* 21 November 1973: 6.

ADDITIONAL DISCUSSION:
Guibbert, Pierre, and Marcel Oms. *L'Histoire de France au cinéma*. Paris: CinémAction, 1993.

The Hot Nights of the Decameron
(1971) see *Le Calde notti del Decamerone* (1971)

The Hour of the Pig (1994) see *L'Heure du cochon* (1994)

Hrafninn Flygur (1984) see *When the Raven Flies* (1984)

233. *The Hunchback* (1909)
United States; Vitagraph.

Gertrude, a young woman known for her kindness, comes upon a hunchback confined to the stocks for having assaulted a noble. She takes pity on him and gives him a drink of water. She secures his release and brings him home with her to work as her gardener. When she is kidnapped by two libertines, the hunchback comes to her aid, killing her assailants but dying in the effort.

With its nod in the direction of the plot of Victor Hugo's classic nineteenth century novel *Notre Dame de Paris*, this film continues the tradition of adapting that novel for the screen.

REVIEWS: *Bioscope* 21 October 1909: 38. *New York Dramatic Mirror* 11 September 1909: 14. *Moving Picture World* 4 September 1909: 355; 11 September 1909: 35. *Variety* 4 September 1909: 13.

ADDITIONAL DISCUSSION:
Savada, Elias. *The American Film Institute Catalog of Motion Pictures Produced in the United States: Film Beginnings, 1893–1910*. Metuchen, N.J.: Scarecrow, 1995.

The Hunchback (1982) see *The Hunchback of Notre Dame* (1982)

234. *The Hunchback of Notre Dame* (1922)
Great Britain; dir. Edwin J. Collins; Master Films.

ALTERNATE TITLE: *Esmeralda*.

CAST: Booth Conway, Annesley Hely, Arthur Kingsley, Sybil Thorndike.

The gypsy Esmeralda first befriends and then is rescued by a hunchback.

This one-reeler is part of an anthology film in which Thorndike played the lead in six "tense moments from great plays." Another of the one-reelers was *Jane Shore*, which featured Thorndike as the doomed mistress of England's Edward IV.

REVIEW: *Kinematograph Weekly* 13 July 1922: 45.

ADDITIONAL DISCUSSION:
Gifford, Denis. *The British Film Catalogue 1895–1985*. Newton Abbot: David & Charles, 1986.

235. *The Hunchback of Notre Dame* (1923)
United States; dir. Wallace Worsley; Universal.

CAST: Winifred Bryson, Lon Chaney, Nigel Du Brulier, Brandon Hurst, Norman Kerry, Kate Lester, Patsy Ruth Miller, Ernest Torrence.

Jehan, the evil brother of the Archdeacon of Notre Dame, convinces the deformed bell-ringer Quasimodo to kidnap the beautiful gypsy girl Esmeralda. Phoebus, captain of the royal guard, rescues her, and Quasimodo is sentenced to be whipped in the square in front of the cathedral. As Quasimodo suffers, Esmeralda offers him some water, and he is from then on her devoted servant. When Phoebus announces he plans to marry Esmeralda, Jehan stabs him and places the blame for the attack on the gypsy girl, who is promptly sentenced to death. With Quasimodo's help, she manages to escape to the cathedral and claim the right of sanctuary, but the crowds urged on by Jehan storm Notre Dame. Quasimodo single-handedly defends Esmeralda until Phoebus (who, it turns out, was only wounded in the attack) comes to their aid. Esmeralda is rescued, but Quasimodo dies.

The release of this film was a major box office event; it was at the time the most expensive film ever made. The sets took a year to build (it was shot entirely on the Universal lot) and the cast numbered more than 3,500. Because the plot of Victor Hugo's nineteenth century novel *Notre Dame de Paris* was altered to make the villain the Archdeacon's brother rather than the cleric himself (a similar change was made in *Esmeralda*, a 1905 film version of

Patsy Ruth Miller as Esmeralda and Lon Chaney as Quasimodo in Wallace Worsley's *The Hunchback of Notre Dame* (1923).

the novel), the film even had the blessing of the Catholic Church, a development that would doubtless have amused the anticlerical Hugo. Chaney's Quasimodo, whose heavy hump made it impossible for the actor to stand erect, steals the film; his performance remains one of the all-time great pieces of film acting.

REVIEWS: *Bioscope* 19 August 1931: 26; 29 November 1923: 57–58. *Exceptional Photoplays* 4 (October-November 1923): 4. *Film Daily* 16 September

Charles Laughton as Quasimodo in William Dieterle's *The Hunchback of Notre Dame* (1939).

1923: 4. *Film User* 15 (November 1961): 589. *Harrison's Reports* 22 September 1923: 151. *Kinematograph Weekly* 22 November 1923: 59. *Monthly Film Bulletin* 42 (April 1975): 91–92. *New York Times* 3 September 1923: 9. *Photoplay* 24 (November 1923): 74. *Rob Wagner's Script* 14 (23 December 1923): 17–18. *Variety* 6 September 1923: 22.

ADDITIONAL DISCUSSIONS:

Brosnan, John. *The Horror People.* New York: St. Martin's, 1976.

Clarens, Carlos. *An Illustrated History of the Horror Film.* New York: Capricorn, 1967.

Connelly, Robert. *The Motion Picture Guide, Silent Film, 1910–1936.* Chicago: Cinebooks, 1986.

Glut, Donald F. *Classic Movie Monsters*. Metuchen, N.J.: Scarecrow, 1978.

Magill, Frank N., ed. *Magill's Survey of Cinema: Silent Films*. Englewood Cliffs, N.J.: Salem, 1982.

Manago, James V. "Comparison: The 1923–1939 Versions *Hunchback of Notre Dame*." *Classic Images* 102 (December 1983): 57–59.

Miller, Patsy Ruth. *My Hollywood—When Both of Us Were Young*. Absecon, N.J.: MagicImage Film Books, 1988.

Norden, Martin F. *The Cinema of Isolation*. New Brunswick: Rutgers University Press, 1994.

Riley, Philip J. *The Hunchback of Notre Dame*. Absecon, N.J.: MagicImage Film Books, 1988. [Reconstructed screenplay.]

Senn, Bryan, and John Johnson. *Fantastic Cinema Subject Guide*. Jefferson, N.C.: McFarland, 1992.

Sheehan, Perly Poore. *The Hunchback of Notre Dame*. New York: George D. Swartz, [1923]. [Screenplay.]

Studlar, Gaylin. *This Mad Masquerade, Stardom and Masculinity in the Jazz Age*. New York: Columbia University Press, 1996.

Turner, George E. "A Silent Giant: *The Hunchback of Notre Dame*." *American Cinematographer* 66 (June 1985): 34–43.

_____. "*The Hunchback of Notre Dame*." In George E. Turner, ed. *The Cinema of Adventure, Romance & Terror*. Hollywood, Calif.: ASC, 1989.

236. *The Hunchback of Notre Dame*
(1939)

United States; dir. William Dieterle; RKO.

CAST: Walter Hampden, Cedric Hardwicke, Charles Laughton, Alan Marshal, Thomas Mitchell, Edmond O'Brien, Maureen O'Hara.

The King's Justice, Frollo, tyrannizes the citizens of Paris, especially the gypsies. Frollo's lecherous eye falls on the gypsy girl Esmeralda, whom he orders his crippled servant Quasimodo to kidnap. She escapes and announces her intention to marry Phoebus, a captain of the king's guard. The jealous Frollo kills Phoebus and has Esmeralda blamed for the crime. Arrested and dragged before Frollo, Esmeralda is condemned to death. She is rescued by Quasimodo, who flees with her into the Cathedral of Notre Dame claiming the right of sanctuary. Frollo incites the crowds to storm the cathedral. In the resulting chaos, Frollo dies, but Esmeralda is saved.

Chaney's Quasimodo was a difficult act to follow, but Laughton succeeded in putting his own stamp on the role, giving what many say is his finest performance. The film, which remains one of the finest screen adaptations of a literary text, ran the risk of being ignored when it was released in 1939, the same year *as Gone with the Wind, Ninotchka, Mr. Smith Goes to Washington, Wuthering Heights, The Wizard of Oz* and many other screen classics.

REVIEWS: *Film Daily* 15 December 1939: 4. *Harrison's Reports* 23 December 1939: 202. *Hollywood Reporter* 15 December 1939: 3. *Hollywood Spectator* 23 December 1939: 15. *Kinematograph Weekly* 1 February 1940: 16; 7 March 1957: 19. *Monthly Film Bulletin* 7 (January 1940): 21. *Motion Picture Daily* 15 December 1939: 1, 4. *Motion Picture Herald* 23 December 1939: 37, 40. *New York Times* 1 January 1940: 29. *Studio* 119 (May 1940): 179. *Télérama* 1839 (13–19 April 1985): 94–95. *Times* [London] 12 February 1940: 4. *To-day's Cinema* 31 January 1940; 20 November 1950: 6. *Variety* 20 December 1939: 14.

ADDITIONAL DISCUSSIONS:

Brown, William. *Charles Laughton*. New York: Falcon, 1970.

Fetrow, Alan G. *Sound Films, 1927–1939*. Jefferson, N.C.: McFarland, 1992.

Flannery, Tom. *1939, The Year in Movies*. Jefferson, N.C.: McFarland, 1990.

Glut, Donald F. *Classic Movie Monsters*. Metuchen, N.J.: Scarecrow, 1978.

Halliwell, Leslie. *Halliwell's Harvest*. New York: Scribner's, 1986.

Hanson, Patricia King, ed. *The American Film Institute Catalog of Motion Pictures Produced in the United States: Feature Films, 1931–1940*. Berkeley: University of California Press, 1993.

Magill, Frank N., ed. *Magill's American Film Guide*. Englewood Cliffs, N.J.: Salem, 1983.

_____, ed. *Magill's Survey of Cinema: English Language Films*. First Series. Englewood Cliffs, N.J.: Salem, 1980.

Manago, James V. "Comparison: The 1923–1939 Versions *Hunchback of Notre Dame*." *Classic Images* 102 (December 1983): 57–59.

Nash, Jay Robert, and Stanley Ralph Ross. *The Motion Picture Guide, H–K, 1927–1983*. Chicago: Cinebooks, 1986.

Norden, Martin F. *The Cinema of Isolation*. New Brunswick: Rutgers University Press, 1994.

Senn, Bryan, and John Johnson. *Fantastic Cinema Subject Guide*. Jefferson, N.C.: McFarland, 1992.

Vermilye, Jerry. *More Films of the Thirties*. New York: Citadel, 1989.

237. *The Hunchback of Notre Dame*
(1956)

France and Italy; dir. Jean Delannoy; Paris Films.

CAST: Alain Cuny, Jean Danet, Gina Lollobrigida, Anthony Quinn.

The hunchback Quasimodo is chosen as the king of the fools. His mentor, the sinister alchemist Frollo, orders him to kidnap the gypsy girl Esmeralda. She is rescued by the dashing

Gina Lollobrigida as Esmeralda and Anthony Quinn as Quasimodo in Jean Delannoy's *The Hunchback of Notre Dame* (1956).

captain Phoebus. When Quasimodo is lashed for his crime, Esmeralda takes pity on him and offers him some water. Frollo then attempts to kill Phoebus and arranges for Esmeralda to be blamed. Quasimodo rescues her from the scaffold and flees with her into the nearby cathedral, claiming the right of sanctuary. Frollo convinces the king to lift the right of sanctuary for a day, and crowds storm into the cathedral. In the carnage and mayhem that follow, most of the principals are killed.

While this was the first film version of Victor Hugo's nineteenth century novel *Notre Dame de Paris* to be filmed on location in France, everything about it, especially Quinn's hunchback, pales in comparison with the 1923 and the 1939 versions.

REVIEWS: *Les Cahiers du cinéma* 67 (January 1957): 55. *Cinéma* 15 (February 1957): 68–71. *Cinématographie française* 29 December 1956: 14. *Daily Film Renter* 21 February 57: 3. *Film Daily* 4 November 1957: 10. *Film français* 28 December 1956: 9. *Films and Filming* 3 (April 1957): 30. *Harrison's Reports* 9 November 1957: 179. *Hollywood Reporter* 31 October 1957: 3. *Kinematograph Weekly* 28 February 1957: 21. *Monthly Film Bulletin* 24 (April 1957): 48. *New York Times* 11 November 1956: 4. 22; 21 December 1957: 35. *To-day's Cinema* 21 February 1957: 3; 1 March 1957: 8. *Variety* 6 November 1957: 6.

ADDITIONAL DISCUSSIONS:

Falvius, F. Louis. *Great Horror Movies*. New York: Scholastic Book Services, 1974.

Glut, Donald F. *Classic Movie Monsters*. Metuchen, N.J.: Scarecrow, 1978.

Marill, Alvin H. *The Films of Anthony Quinn*. Secaucus, N.J.: Citadel, 1975.

Nash, Jay Robert, and Stanley Ralph Ross. *The Motion Picture Guide, H–K, 1927–1983*. Chicago: Cinebooks, 1986.

Ponzi, Maurizio. *The Films of Gina Lollobrigida*. Trans. Sheila Atil Curto. Secaucus, N.J.: Citadel, 1982.

Senn, Bryan, and John Johnson. *Fantastic Cinema Subject Guide*. Jefferson, N.C.: McFarland, 1992.

238. *The Hunchback of Notre Dame* (1976)

Great Britain; dir. Alan Cooke; BBC.

CAST: Warren Clarke, Christopher Gable, Kenneth Haigh, Richard Morant, Michelle Newell, David Rintoul.

The Archdeacon Frollo lusts after the gypsy girl Esmeralda. As his passion consumes him, he sets in motion a series of events that lead to his death and that of Quasimodo and the girl.

This made-for-television version of Hugo's novel follows the plot of its source faithfully, emphasizing the clerical corruption and economic imbalances of medieval Paris. The acting throughout is competent, but doesn't equal that in the 1923 and 1939 screen versions.

REVIEWS: *Daily News* [New York] 31 May 1977: 64. *New York Times* 18 July 1977: 50. *Radio Times* [London]18 December 1976–1 January 1977: 89. *Variety* 27 July 1977: 46.

ADDITIONAL DISCUSSIONS:

Glut, Donald F. *Classic Movie Monsters*. Metuchen, N.J.: Scarecrow, 1978.

Marill, Alvin H. *Movies Made for Television 1964–1986*. New York: Zoetrope, 1987.

239. *The Hunchback of Notre Dame*
(1982)

United States; dir. Michael Tuchner; Norman Rosemont/Columbia Pictures TV.

ALTERNATE TITLE: *The Hunchback*.

CAST: Lesley-Anne Down, John Gielgud, Anthony Hopkins, Derek Jacobi, Robert Powell.

The familiar events of Hugo's novel are reprised here, but with a new interpretation. The film examines the complex motivations that underlie Archdeacon Frollo and Quasimodo's actions in a telefilm that highlights what television at its best can do to provide challenging yet enjoyable entertainment.

REVIEWS: *Cinefantastique* 12 (April 1982): 87. *Hollywood Reporter* 5 February 1982: 39. *New York Times* 31 January 1982: 2A. 3; 4 February 1982: C22. *TV Guide* 30 January 1982: A-5, A-109. *Variety* 10 February 1982: 102.

ADDITIONAL DISCUSSIONS:

Falk, Quentin. *Anthony Hopkins, Too Good to Waste*. London: Columbus Books, 1989.

Marill, Alvin H. *Movies Made for Television 1964–1986*. New York: Zoetrope, 1987.

240. *The Hunchback of Notre Dame*
(1996)

United States; dir. Gary Trousdale; Walt Disney Pictures.

CAST: (the voices of) Jason Alexander, Mary Kay Bergman, Corey Burton, Jim Cummings, Bill Fagerbakke, Tom Hulce, Tony Jay, Paul Kandel, Charles Kimbrough, Kevin Kline, Heidi Mollenhauer, Demi Moore, Patrick Penny, David Ogden Stiers, Gary Trousdale, Mary Wickes.

A gypsy couple smuggle their deformed infant into Paris, where Judge Frollo arrests the father and the mother is run down by a horse. Frollo's first instinct is to kill the child, but a priest threatens to excommunicate him if he does. As a penance, Frollo must raise the child as his own. Twenty years pass, and the child called Quasimodo has remained hidden in the bell tower of the Cathedral of Notre Dame. As the Feast of Fools approaches, Quasimodo is encouraged by three gargoyle friends to join the celebrations. Quasimodo is crowned king by the crowd, which recoils in fright when they discover he is not wearing a mask. Esmeralda, a gypsy girl, offers him comfort, and Quasimodo becomes her devoted companion. When Frollo lusts after her, Quasimodo assists Capt. Phoebus in frustrating the judge's plans. But the judge returns with a vengeance, imprisoning Phoebus, Esmeralda and Quasimodo. In a final struggle, Quasimodo and Frollo fight over Esmeralda, and the judge falls from the bell tower of the cathedral. Quasimodo, Phoebus and Esmeralda are proclaimed heroes by the people of Paris.

This Disney animated musical adds a redemptive happy ending to Hugo's novel. Its sanitized message has nothing to do with the anticlericalism of the original. Rather, the film offers the more modern, politically correct idea that it is acceptable to be different.

REVIEWS: *Empire* 86 (August 1996): 24. *Entertainment Weekly* 328 (24 June 1996): 34–35; 332 (21 June 1996): 43–44. *Film Journal International* 99 (July 1996): 51–52. *Film Review* [London] August 1996: 18. *Films in Review* 47 (September–October 1996): 59–60. *Hollywood Reporter* 17 June 1996: 6, 22. *Los Angeles Times* 21 June 1996: Calendar 1, 10. *New York Times* 21 June 1996: C14. *Positif* 432 (February 1997): 42–43. *Premiere* [England] 4 (August 1996): 15. *Sight and Sound* NS6 (August 1996): 51–52. *Starburst* 216 (August 1996): 46. *Times* [London] *Educational Supplement* 30 August 1996: 21. *Variety* 17 June 1996: 51.

ADDITIONAL DISCUSSIONS:

Grant, Edmond, ed. *The Motion Picture Guide: 1997 Annual (The Films of 1996)*. New York: CineBooks, 1997.

Jeffries, Neil. "King of the Swingers." *Empire* 86 (August 1996): 66–72.

The Gargoyles Victor, Hugo, and Laverne and Esmeralda and Quasimodo in the Disney animated version of *The Hunchback of Notre Dame* (1996).

Rebello, Stephen. *The Art of* The Hunchback of Notre Dame. New York: Hyperion, 1996.

Ross, Pippin, and Lisa Stiepock. *"The Hunchback of Notre Dame." Disney Magazine* 1 (Summer 1996): 48–57.

Rynning, Roald. "Ring My Bell." *Film Review* [London] August 1996: 39–42.

Saenger, Diana. "Writing for Animation on *The Hunchback of Notre Dame." scr(i)pt* 2 (July-August 1996): 28–33.

Thompson, Anne. "Playing a Hunch." *Entertainment Weekly* 332 (21 June 1996): 28–33.

Williamson, Kim. "Playing a Hunch." *Boxoffice* 132 (June 1996): 12–16.

The Hundred Horsemen (1964) see *I Cento cavalieri* (1964)

The Huns (1960) see *La Regina dei tartari* (1960)

Den Hvite Viking (1991) see *The White Viking* (1991)

I na Kamnjahk Rastut Derévja (1988) see *Captive of the Dragon* (1988)

I Skugga Hrafnsina (1988) see *In the Shadow of the Raven* (1988)

241. If I Were King (1910)
Italy; Ambrosio.

A poor woodcutter bemoaning his sorry state gazes upon a portrait of the king. He dozes off, and in a dream he is visited by a fairy who dresses him in royal robes and has him brought to the palace. There his every whim is satisfied, until a neighboring king invades, drives him from the palace and has him executed. The woodcutter awakens from his dream, terrified but safe.

REVIEWS: *Bioscope* 29 December 1910: 25. *Moving Picture World* 29 June 1912: 1228.

242. If I Were King (1915)
Great Britain; Gaumont.

The rabble of Paris in the reign of Louis XI see poet François Villon as their leader. Villon gets caught up in a plot to kill the king, which ends with the poet being made Grand Constable of France for eight days, after which time he is to be executed if no one agrees to die in his place. At the last minute, Villon is spared and allowed by the king to marry a noble-woman with whom he has been in love.

The story of François Villon (1431–?), the poet and rascal, has proven immensely popu-lar for filmmakers who have turned to a mod-ern, rather than a medieval, source for their screenplays: *If I Were King,* a 1901 novel (then stage play) by Justin Huntly McCarthy.

REVIEWS: *Kinematograph Monthly Record* 38 (June 1915): 95. *Variety* 6 August 1915: 20.

243. *If I Were King* (1920)

United States; dir. J. Gordon Edwards; Fox.

CAST: Betty Ross Clarke, William Farnum, Renita Johnston, Walter Law, Fritz Leiber.

François Villon is on his way to steal the plate from the royal chapel when he encoun-ters Katherine, the ward of Louis XI. Smitten with the lady, he writes her a poem instead of robbing the chapel. Katherine returns Villon's affection and uses her influence with the king to aid the people of Paris. Villon is then made Constable of Paris and charged with rallying the populace to defend the city against the Bur-gundians. He escapes death and saves Paris when Katherine again comes to his aid.

Reviewers hailed this film for its skill in adapting its source (*If I Were King,* the 1901 novel and then stage play by Justin Huntly Mc-Carthy) and for the all-around excellence of the actors, especially Farnum (as Villon).

REVIEWS: *Bioscope* 1 April 1920: 63–64. *Ex-hibitor's Herald* 17 July 1920: 63. *Exhibitor's Trade Review* 10 July 1920: 627. *Harrison's Reports* 21 Au-gust 1920: 101. *Kinematograph Monthly Record* 97 (May 1920): 17; 106 (February 1921): 36. *Kinemato-graph Weekly* 1 April 1920: 96. *Motion Picture News* 10 July 1920: 511. *Moving Picture World* 10 July 1920: 193. *New York Times* 10 August 1920: 10. *Picturegoer* 1 (March 1921): 32–33. *Times* [London] 5 April 1920: 6. *Variety* 2 July 1920: 28. *Wid's Daily* 4 June 1920: 3.

ADDITIONAL DISCUSSIONS:

Connelly, Robert. *The Motion Picture Guide, Silent Film, 1910–1936.* Chicago: Cinebooks, 1986.

Hanson, Patricia King, ed. *The American Film In-stitute Catalog of Motion Pictures Produced in the United States: Feature Films, 1911–1920.* Berkeley: University of California Press, 1988.

244. *If I Were King* (1938)

United States; dir. Frank Lloyd; Paramount.

CAST: Ronald Colman, Frances Dee, Ellen Drew, C.V. France, Basil Rathbone.

The court of Louis XI is a center for intrigue as the Burgundians lay siege to the city. The king continues to live well, but the siege means the poor are starving. François Villon boasts how he could relieve their misery if only he were king. Arrested for treason, he is given eight days to act as Grand Constable, dispens-ing justice throughout the city. His actions meet with the approval of the king and his fel-low citizens, whom he rallies to defeat the Bur-gundians.

Critics were divided in their appraisals of this film version of *If I Were King,* the 1901 novel (then stage play) by Justin Huntly Mc-Carthy. Some found Dennis King's Villon in the 1930 musical *The Vagabond King* more fiery than Colman's here. The original screenplay, much revised as the film was being shot, was the work of Preston Sturges.

REVIEWS: *Boxoffice* 24 September 1938: 35. *Cue* 1 October 1938: 10. *Daily Variety* 14 September 1938: 3. *Film Curb* 8 October 1938: 9. *Film Daily* 19 Sep-tember 1938: 8. *Film Weekly* 29 October 1938: 21. *Harrison's Reports* 8 October 1938: 162. *Hollywood Reporter* 14 September 1938: 3. *Hollywood Spectator* 1 October 1938: 9–10. *Monthly Film Bulletin* 5 (30 November 1938): 259. *Motion Picture Daily* 15 Sep-tember 1938: 16. *Motion Picture Herald* 17 Septem-ber 1938: 37, 40. *Motion Picture Review Digest* 3 (26 December 1938): 39–40. *New York Times* 29 Sep-tember 1938: 31. *Photoplay* 52 (December 1938): 52. *Variety* 21 September 1938: 12.

ADDITIONAL DISCUSSIONS:

Druxman, Michael B. *Basil Rathbone, His Life and His Films.* South Brunswick, N.J.: A.S. Barnes, 1975.

Hanson, Patricia King, ed. *The American Film In-stitute Catalog of Motion Pictures Produced in the United States: Feature Films, 1931–1940.* Berkeley: University of California Press, 1993.

Herzberg, Max J. "A Guide to the Discussion and Appreciation of *If I Were King.*" *Photoplay Stud-ies* 4.8 (1938): 1–14.

Magill, Frank N., ed. *Magill's Survey of Cinema, Eng-lish Language Films.* Second Series. Englewood Cliffs, N.J.: Salem, 1981.

Nash, Jay Robert, and Stanley Ralph Ross. *The Mo-tion Picture Guide, H–K, 1927–1983.* Chicago: Cinebooks, 1986.

Parish, James Robert, and Don E. Stanke. *The Swashbucklers.* New Rochelle, N.Y. Arlington House, 1976.

Quirk, Lawrence J. *The Films of Ronald Colman.* Se-caucus, N.J.: Citadel, 1977.

Richards, Jeffrey. *Swordsmen of the Screen from Douglas Fairbanks to Michael York.* London: Routledge & Kegan Paul, 1977.

Smith, R. Dixon. *Ronald Colman, Gentleman of the Cinema.* Jefferson, N.C.: McFarland, 1991.

Ronald Colman as François Villon with Frances Dee in a scene from Frank Lloyd's *If I Were King* (1938).

245. *Il Cid* (1910)

Italy; dir. Mario Caserini; Cines.

ALTERNATE TITLE: *The Triumphant Hero.*

CAST: Amleto Novelli.

Don Rodriguez falls in love with Climene. When their fathers quarrel, they are separated and forbidden to see each other, as family honor takes precedence over love. When Don Rodriguez's father is given royal preferment, Climene's father is furious and insults his rival. Don Rodriguez defends his family's honor by challenging Climene's father to a duel and killing him. He then must flee and joins royal troops fighting the Moors. Soon made commander in chief, he handily defeats the Moors, earning the title "El Cid." He returns to court honored, and the king and queen effect a reconciliation between the two lovers.

This film, unlike the better-known 1961 film starring Charlton Heston and Sophia Loren, is based solely on Pierre Corneille's 1636 tragedy *Le Cid.*

REVIEW: *Bioscope* 10 February 1910: 65.

ADDITIONAL DISCUSSION:

Bernardini, Aldo, and Jean A. Gili, eds. *Le Cinéma italien de La Prise de Rome (1905) à Rome ville ouverte (1945)*. Paris: Centre Georges Pompidou, 1986.

246. *Ilya Muromets* (1956)

Soviet Union; dir. Alexander Ptushko; Mosfilm.

ALTERNATE TITLES: *The Beast, The Epic Hero and the Beast* and *The Sword and the Dragon.*

CAST: Andrei Abrikosov, Boris Andreyev, Shukur Burkhanov, Sol Martinson, Nina Medvedeva, Ninel Myshkova, Alexei Shvorin.

In the thirteenth century, Tugar tribesmen sack a small village and kidnap the wife of Ilya Muromets, who is himself wounded and left for dead. Nursed back to health by pilgrims who also give him the "Magical Sword of Invinsor," Ilya pursues the Tugars and almost defeats them until traitors in the court of Prince Vanda convince the monarch that Ilya wants to usurp the throne. Ilya is imprisoned briefly until Vanda learns the truth. Sent back once again at the head of the prince's army to defeat the Tugars, Ilya enters into one-on-one combat with the leader of the Tugars, who turns out to be his own son, kidnapped years ago and reared as a Tugar. Together they defeat the Tugars, rescue Ilya's wife, destroy a three-headed dragon and reestablish peace.

Based on medieval Russian folktales, this film is impressive in its use of special effects to portray the dragon and the other mythical beasts that Ilya encounters.

REVIEWS: *Daily Cinema* 4 November 1959: 9; 15 March 1963: 10–11. *Filmblätter* 13 (1959): 274. *Filmfacts* 3 (9 December 1960): 284. *Kinematograph Weekly* 12 November 1959: 10; 14 March 1963: 22. *Monthly Film Bulletin* 26 (December 1959): 155. *New York Times* 17 November 1960: 46. *Times* [London] 2 November 1959: 3. *Variety* 5 August 1959: 20.

ADDITIONAL DISCUSSIONS:
Birkos, Alexander S. *Soviet Cinema.* Hamden, Conn.: Archon Books, 1976.
"Ilya Muromets." *Soviet Film* 8 (1958): 7–12.
Lucanio, Patrick. *With Fire and Sword, Italian Spectacles on American Screens 1958–1968.* Metuchen, N.J.: Scarecrow Press, 1994.
Nash, Jay Robert, and Stanley Ralph Ross. *The Motion Picture Guide, S, 1927–1983.* Chicago: Cinebooks, 1987.
Rovin, Jeff. *The Fabulous Fantasy Films.* South Brunswick, N.J.: A.S. Barnes, 1977.

247. *In the Days of Chivalry* (1911)

United States; Edison.

ALTERNATE TITLE: *Aucassin and Nicolette.*

A duke's son rescues a peasant girl from his own father's soldiers and immediately falls in love with her. When he asks permission to marry the girl, his father becomes enraged and throws the girl into prison. The son agrees to lead his father's armies if he is given permission to marry the girl when he returns. He goes off to war and is successful, but his father still refuses to sanction his marriage to the peasant. The two then run off, but the young girl is kidnapped by pirates who take her to Carthage where she is recognized as a long-lost princess. Reunited with her own family, she leaves home and marries her former love.

This film was an ambitious undertaking translating to the screen the thirteenth century anonymous French romance *Aucassin et Nicolette.* In the original romance, the marriage of the two lovers is not sanctioned because, as

princess of Carthage, Nicolette would have been a Moslem.

REVIEWS: *Bioscope* 23 February 1911: 41. *Edison Kinetogram* 15 February 1911: 4–5. *Moving Picture World* 14 January 1911: 90; 21 January 1911: 149–150.

ADDITIONAL DISCUSSION:
Spottiswoode, Raymond. *A Grammar of Film.* 1935. Rpt. Berkeley: University of California Press, 1969.

248. *In the Days of Robin Hood* (1913)

Great Britain; dir. F. Martin Thornton; Natural Colour Kinematograph.

CAST: Harry Agar Lyons.

Robin Hood disguises himself as a monk to rescue one of his men from the Sheriff of Nottingham.

This film version of the exploits of Robin Hood, which is based on a nineteenth century short story by Howard Pyle, was actually shot in Sherwood Forest.

REVIEWS: *Bioscope* 4 December 1913: supplement vii. *Kinematograph Monthly Record* 19 (November 1913): 69–70.

ADDITIONAL DISCUSSIONS:
Behlmer, Rudy. "Robin Hood on the Screen." *Films in Review* 16 (February 1965): 91–102.
Knight, Stephen. *Robin Hood, A Complete Study of the English Outlaw.* Oxford: Blackwell, 1994.
Richards, Jeffrey. *Swordsmen of the Screen from Douglas Fairbanks to Michael York.* London: Routledge & Kegan Paul, 1977.
Turner, David. *Robin of the Movies.* Kingswinford, Eng.: Yeoman Publishing, 1989.

In the Days of St. Patrick (1920) see *Aimsir Padraig* (1920)

249. *In the Shadow of the Raven* (1988)

Iceland; dir. Hrafn Gunnlaugsson; Sandrews.

ALTERNATE TITLES: *I Skugga Hrafnsina* and *The Shadow of the Raven.*

CAST: Reine Brynolfsson, Tinna Gunnlaugsdottir, Egill Ólafsson, Sune Maangs, Helgi Skúlason.

In medieval Iceland, two rival tribes continue their long-standing family feud. Trausti, a young warrior, kills the leader of the rival tribe, whose daughter Isold vows revenge. A powerful bishop tries to arrange a marriage between Trausti and Isold, but the two are not united before their familial feud plays itself out further in death and bloodshed.

This is a sequel to Gunnlaugsson's 1985 film *When the Raven Flies.* The director here resets the story of Tristan and Isolde in his native Iceland.

REVIEWS: *Chaplin* 219 (December 1988): 308–09. *Filmrutan* 31.4 (1988): 35–36. *Hollywood Reporter* 9 October 1990: 11, 151. *New York Times* 13 July 1991: 12. *Variety* 19 October 1988: 249, 255.

ADDITIONAL DISCUSSIONS:

Cowie, Peter, ed. *Le Cinéma des pays nordiques.* Paris: Centre Georges Pompidou, 1990.

_____, ed. *Variety International Film Guide 1990.* Hollywood, Calif.: Samuel French, 1989.

Fridgeirsson, Asgeir. "The Bishop and the Actor." *Iceland Review* 29.3 (191): 37–40.

Icelandic Films 1979–1988. Reykjavík: Icelandic Film Fund, 1988.

Jónsdóttir, Solveig K. "Once Upon a Time in the North." *Iceland Review* 25.4 (1987): 4–11.

The Motion Picture Guide, 1989 Annual (The Films of 1988). Evanston, Ill.: Cinebooks, 1989.

Swedish Film Institute Film Catalogue. Stockholm: Swedish Film Institute, 1989.

250. *L'Inferno* (1910)

Italy; Helios.

Dante journeys through the circles of Hell encountering (among others) Paolo, Francesca, Count Ugolino and Satan chained in the deepest of pits.

This film version of Dante's *Inferno* was a critical disaster. The film suffers in comparison to the well-received Milano version that was released the same year. It also inspired a lawsuit by the American distributors of the Milano film, who charged Helios with copyright infringement.

REVIEW: *Moving Picture World* 6 January 1912: 23.

ADDITIONAL DISCUSSIONS:

Bernardini, Aldo. "Industrializzazione e classi sociali." In Renzo Renzi, ed. *Sperduto nel buio.* Bologna: Cappelli Editore, 1991.

_____. "*L'Inferno* della Milano-Films." *Bianco et nero* 46 (October–December 1985): 91–111.

Brunetta, Gian Piero. *Storia del cinema muto italiano 1895–1945.* Rome: Editori Riunti, 1979.

Paolella, Roberto. *Storia del cinema muto.* Naples: Giannini, 1956.

251. *L'Inferno* (1910)

Italy; dir. Francesco Bertolini, Adolfo Padovan and Giuseppe De Liguoro; Milano.

ALTERNATE TITLE: *Dante's Inferno.*

Dante encounters Virgil and together they journey through Hell encountering, among others, Francesca da Rimini and Count Ugolino.

The film consists of more than a hundred scenes and runs two hours — a remarkable accomplishment for its time. Its American distributors filed a lawsuit charging violation of copyright against the artistically inferior Helios film of Dante's *Inferno* that was also released in 1910. The Milano film was well-reviewed as it played in movie houses across Europe and the United States. (See the clippings file in the New York Public Library Performing Arts Division at Lincoln Center for reviews from newspapers throughout the American South singing the praises of the Milano film.)

REVIEWS: *Bioscope* 31 October 1912: 319; 7 November 1912: 385. *Moving Picture World* 22 July 1911: 101. *New York Dramatic Mirror* 2 August 1911: 25–26.

ADDITIONAL DISCUSSIONS:

"Alleged Infringing Dante Film Seized." *New York Dramatic Mirror* 2 August 1911: 21.

Bernardini, Aldo. *Cinema muto italianao: arte, divismo e mercato 1910/1914.* Rome: Editori Laterza, 1982.

_____. "*L'Inferno* della Milano-Films." *Bianco e nero* 46 (April–July 1985): 91–111.

_____, and Jean A. Gili, eds. *Le Cinema italien de La Prise de Rome (1905) à Rome ville ouverte (1945).* Paris: Centre Georges Pompidou, 1986.

Brunetta, Gian Piero. *Storia del cinema muto italiano 1895–1945.* Rome: Editori Riunti, 1945.

Bush, W. Stephen. "Dante's *Divina Commedia* in Moving Pictures." *Moving Picture World* 8 July 1911: 1572–73.

_____. "Dante's *L'Inferno.*" *Moving Picture World* 29 July 1911: 188–89.

Cher, John. "Parisian Notes." *Bioscope* 7 March 1912: 671; 14 March 1912: 747.

Costa, Antonio. "Dante, D'Annunzio, Pirandello." In Renzo Renzi, ed. *Sperduto nel buio.* Bologna: Cappelli Editore, 1991.

De Lucis, Flavia, ed. *C'era il cinema.* Modena: Edizioni Panini, 1983.

"La Divine comédie à Paris." *Ciné-Journal* 18 March 1911: 5–6.

The Film Index: A Bibliography. Vol. 1: The Film as Art. 1941. Rpt. White Plains, N.Y.: Kraus International, 1988.

Leprohon, Pierre. *The Italian Cinema.* Trans. Roger Greaves and Oliver Stallybrass. New York: Praeger, 1972.

Paolella, Roberto. *Storia del cinema muto.* Naples: Giannini, 1956.

Schenk, Imbert. *Der Italienische Historienfilm von 1905 bis 1914.* Bremen: Uni, 1991.

Sinn, Charles E. "Music for the Picture." *Moving Picture World* 22 July 1911: 116.

252. *Invasion of the Normans* (1962)

France and Italy; dir. Giuseppe Vari; Galatea-Lyre Société Cinématographique.

ALTERNATE TITLES: *The Attack of the Normans* and *I Normanni.*

CAST: Genevieve Grad, Philippe Hersent, Ettore Manni, Cameron Mitchell.

At the end of the tenth century, Vilfred usurps the English throne, imprisoning King Dagobert and placing the blame on Normans led by Olaf. Vilfred then seeks to suppress the Normans, whose champion, Oliver, rallies his people against Vilfred. After a bloody battle, Vilfred is killed, Dagobert is rescued and restored to his throne, and Oliver is married to the king's daughter.

A screen version of a comic book at best, this film has nothing going for it: It plays fast and loose with historical fact, it has an impossibly convoluted plot, and it is so badly directed that the actors all seem to be in different films.

REVIEWS: *Cinématographie française* 2010 (6 April 1963): 10. *Daily Cinema* 8 November 1963: 7. *Film-Echo/Filmwoche* 90 (10 November 1962): 11. *Kinematograph Weekly* 557 (31 October 1963): 18. *Monthly Film Bulletin* 30 (December 1963): 173.

ADDITIONAL DISCUSSIONS:

Italian Production 1962. Rome: Unitalia Film, 1963.

Lucanio, Patrick. *With Fire and Sword, Italian Spectacles on American Screens 1958–1968.* Metuchen, N.J.: Scarecrow, 1994.

Poppi, Roberto, and Mario Pecorari. *Dizionario del cinema italiano. Vol. 3: I Film dal 1960 al 1969.* Rome: Gremese Editore, 1992.

Gli Invasori (1961) see *Erik the Conqueror* (1961)

253. *The Invincible Sword* (1910)

France; Gaumont.

ALTERNATE TITLE: *The Knight Roland.*

Roland has been told that he will remain invincible as long as he never falls in love. Roland falls in love, and while he handily defeats a rival for his ladylove's hand, he is mortally wounded in a great battle. He blows his horn for assistance which arrives too late.

This film, loosely based on the medieval epic *The Song of Roland,* subordinates a political story to a romantic one.

REVIEWS: *Bioscope* 9 June 1910: 33. *Moving Picture World* 9 July 1910: 99; 23 July 1910: 192.

ADDITIONAL DISCUSSION:

Savada, Elias. *The American Film Institute Catalog of*

Motion Pictures Produced in the United States: Film Beginnings, 1893–1910. Metuchen, N.J.: Scarecrow, 1995.

Iolanta (1963) see *Iolanthe* (1963)

254. *Iolanthe* (1963)

Soviet Union; dir. Vladimir Gorikker; Riga Film Studio.

ALTERNATE TITLES: *Iolanta, Yolande* and *Yolanta.*

CAST: Alexandre Beliavsky, Ian Filipson, Pyotr Glebov, Fédor Nikitine, Valentina Ouchakova, Youri Perov, Natalia Rudnaya, Valdis Zanberg.

King René of Provence conceals from his daughter the fact that she is blind. When Duke Robert of Burgundy arrives to claim Iolanthe as his bride, he tells her of her blindness, from which she is cured by a Moorish doctor.

This film presents a competent screen version of Tchaikovsky's 1893 opera *Iolanta*—itself based on the 1843 Danish play *King René's Daughter* by Henrik Hertz—as performed by the Bolshoi Opera Company.

REVIEWS: *Kinematograph Weekly* 22 April 1967: 16. *Monthly Film Bulletin* 34 (August 1967): 125. *New York Times* 23 December 1964: 22. *Soviet Film* 7 (July 1963): 13. *Variety* 30 December 1964: 6.

ADDITIONAL DISCUSSIONS:

Nash, Jay Robert, and Stanley Ralph Ross. *The Motion Picture Guide, W–Z, 1927–1984.* Chicago: Cinebooks, 1987.

Quinn, Christie. *The British National Film Catalogue.* London: British Industrial and Scientific Film Association, 1972.

Tous les films 1984. Paris: Éditions Chrétiens-Médias, 1985.

Iron Crown (1940) see *La Corona di ferro* (1940)

255. *Istvan, a Kiraly* (1984)

Hungary; dir. Gabor Koltay; Budapest Studio and Mafilm.

ALTERNATE TITLES: *Istvan, the King; King Stephen* and *Stephen, the King.*

CAST: Kati Berek, Jácint Juhász, László Pelőczy, Bernadett Sára, Máté Victor.

In 996, the heir to the throne of Hungary, Prince Stephen, marries Gisela, daughter of Henry II, Duke of Burgundy. A faction in Hungary views this development with alarm since the princess is accompanied to Hungary by Christian missionaries. The king's death only heightens tensions as civil war threatens. Stephen is able to defeat all his opponents. On Christmas Day 1000, he is crowned King of Hungary as the country freely embraces Christianity.

Based on Miklós Boldizsár's rock opera *Turn of the Millennium*, which was inspired by an opera that Beethoven abandoned in 1811, this film presents a popularized version of the life of King Stephen I of Hungary (c. 975–1038), who was canonized in 1087. Koltay directed another film about medieval Hungary, *Julianus*, in 1991.

REVIEWS: *Cinéma* [Paris] 306 (June 1984): 26. *Film a doba* 31 (February 1985): 112–13. *Filmowy serwis prasowy* 32 (1–15 January 1986): 17–21. *Hungarofilm Bulletin* 2 (1984): 4–5. *Kino* [Poland] 18 (December 1984): 48–49. *Revue du cinéma* 396 (July-August 1984): 46. *Variety* 7 March 1984: 216.

Istvan, the King (1984) see *Istvan, a Kiraly* (1984)

It's Hard to Be God (1989) see *Es ist nicht leicht Gott zu sein* (1989)

Ivanhoe (1913) see *Rebecca the Jewess* (1913)

256. *Ivanhoe* (1913)

United States; dir. Herbert Brenon; Imp Company.

CAST: King Baggot, Leah Baird, Herbert Brenon, W. Scott Craven, Evelyn Hope, W. Thomas.

In the late twelfth century, Sir Cedric's son Ivanhoe returns from the Crusades. He comes to the rescue of Isaac of York and his daughter Rebecca when they are kidnapped by knights loyal to Prince John, who is attempting to seize the throne from the absent King Richard. Prince John's forces kidnap Rebecca again, charge her with sorcery and prepare to burn her at the stake. Ivanhoe again saves her, assisted by a mysterious Black Knight who reveals himself to be the absent Richard. The king reclaims his throne and punishes Prince John and his followers.

This screen version of Sir Walter Scott's 1819 novel *Ivanhoe* was filmed in England at Chepstow Castle. Reviewers were unanimous in their praise for every aspect of this film.

REVIEWS: *Bioscope* 24 July 1913: 290–93. *Kinematograph Monthly Film Record* 17 (September 1913): 150–52. *Moving Picture World* 6 September 1913: 1051; 20 September 1913: 1286, 1318. *Photoplay* 4 (October 1913) 27–34. *Universal Weekly* 20 September 1913: 13, 16.

ADDITIONAL DISCUSSIONS:

Connelly, Robert. *The Motion Picture Guide, Silent Film, 1910–1936.* Chicago: Cinebooks, 1986.

Hanson, Patricia, ed. *The American Film Institute Catalog of Motion Pictures: Feature Films, 1911–1920.* Berkeley: University of California Press, 1988.

"Ivanhoe." *Illustrated Films Monthly* 1 (September 1913–February 1914): 23–33.

"Making *Ivanhoe* in England." *Moving Picture World* 2 August 1913: 517–18.

McDonald, Gerald. "US Filmmaking Abroad." *Films in Review* 5 (June-July 1954): 257–62.

"Producing *Ivanhoe* at Chepstow." *Bioscope* 3 July 1913: 8–11.

"The Story of Ivanhoe." *Photoplay Magazine* 4 (October 1913): 27–34.

257. *Ivanhoe* (1952)

Great Britain; dir. Richard Thorpe; MGM.

CAST: Joan Fontaine, Guy Rolfe, George Sanders, Elizabeth Taylor, Robert Taylor, Norman Wooland.

The Saxon Sir Wilfred of Ivanhoe secretly returns from the Crusades to raise money to ransom King Richard, who is being held prisoner in Austria. Ivanhoe discovers a plot to deprive Richard of his throne and attempts to thwart the efforts of Prince John and his followers to rule England. Ivanhoe fights a series of jousts defending his honor and the lives of his father, his fiancée and Rebecca, a Jewish woman. In the end, Ivanhoe is successful. Richard returns to claims his throne and punish those who plotted against him.

Based on Sir Walter Scott's 1819 novel *Ivanhoe*, this film remains one of the most lavish costume pieces made in the 1950s. In playing down the issues of religion so prominent in the novel, this film can also be seen as providing a commentary on the climate of McCarthyism in America in the early 1950s.

REVIEWS: *American Cinematographer* 33 (July 1952): 284. *Cinématographie française* 30 August 1952: 20. *Cue* 2 August 1952: 25. *Daily Film Renter* 5 June 1952: 22. *Film Daily* 16 June 1952: 4. *Films in Review* 3 (August-September 1952): 355–56. *Grand angle* 168-69 (February-March 1994): n.p. *Harrison's Reports* 21 June 1952: 100. *Kinematograph Weekly* 12 June 1952: 22. *Monthly Film Bulletin* 19 (August 1952): 106. *Motion Picture Herald* 21 June 1952: Prod-

Leah Baird as Rebecca and King Baggott as Ivanhoe disguised as a pilgrim in Herbert Brenon's *Ivanhoe* (1913).

uct Digest Section 1417. *New York Times* 1 August 1952: 8. *To-day's Cinema* 5 June 1952: 6. *Variety* 11 June 1952: 6.

ADDITIONAL DISCUSSIONS:

Eckman, Sam. "Preview of *Ivanhoe*." *Kinematograph Weekly* 12 June 1952: i–xiv [between 22 and 23].

"Knighthood Never Had It So Good." *Life* 33 (11 August 1952): 53–54, 56, 58.

Leniham, John H. "English Classics for Cold War America." *Journal of Popular Film & Television* 20 (Fall 1992): 42–51.

Magill, Frank N., ed. *Magill's American Film Guide.* Englewood Cliffs, N.J.: Salem, 1983.

_____, ed. *Magill's Survey of Cinema: English Language Films.* Second Series. Englewood Cliffs, N.J.: Salem, 1981.

Nash, Jay Robert, and Stanley Ralph Ross. *The Motion Picture Guide, H–K, 1927–1983.* Chicago: Cinebooks, 1986.

Quirk, Lawrence J. *The Films of Robert Taylor.* Secaucus, N.J.: Citadel, 1975.

Richards, Jeffrey. *Swordsmen of the Screen from Douglas Fairbanks to Michael York.* London: Routledge & Kegan Paul, 1977.

Rozsa, Miklos. "More Music for Historical Films." *Film Music* 12 (November-December 1952): 13–17.

Thomas, Tony. *The Great Adventure Films.* Secaucus, N.J.: Citadel, 1976.

Vermilye, Jerry, and Mark Ricci. *The Films of Elizabeth Taylor.* Secaucus, N.J.: Citadel, 1976.

Wayne, Jane Ellen. *Robert Taylor.* New York: St. Martin's, 1987.

258. *Ivanhoe* (1982)

United States; dir. Douglas Camfield; Columbia Pictures TV.

CAST: Anthony Andrews, Lysette Anthony, Julian Glover, Michael Hordern, Olivia Hussey, James Mason, Sam Neill.

Ivanhoe returns from the Crusades to find England under the tyrannical rule of Prince John. He raises money to ransom King Richard and repeatedly comes to the aid of his fiancée, Lady Rowena, and of Rebecca, the daughter of Isaac of York, a Jewish moneylender. In the end, Richard and peace and harmony are restored to England.

This made-for-television version of Sir Walter Scott's 1819 novel shifts its emphasis away from the possible political subtext of the 1952

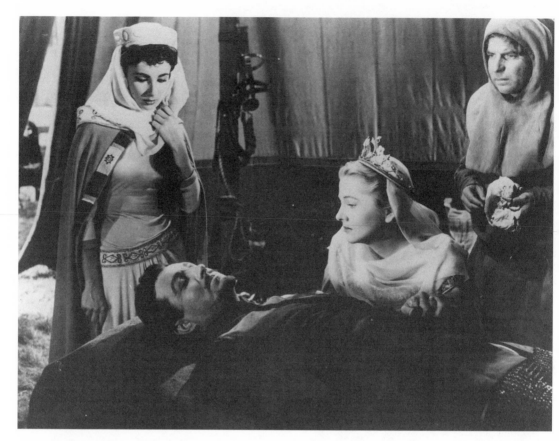

Elizabeth Taylor (left) as Rebecca, Robert Taylor as Ivanhoe, and Joan Fontaine as Rowena in Richard Thorpe's *Ivanhoe* (1952).

MGM film. Performances are serviceable, but pale in comparison with those in Richard Thorpe's epic MGM production.

REVIEWS: *Hollywood Reporter* 23 February 1982: 6. *New York Times* 21 February 1982: 2A. 3; 23 February 1982: C14. *TV Guide* 20 February 1982: A-6. *TV Times* [London] *Magazine* 25 September 1982: 31. *Variety* 10 March 1982: 46.

ADDITONAL DISCUSSION:
Marill, Alvin R. *Movies Made for Television 1964–1985.* New York: Zoetrope, 1987.

259. *Ivanhood* (1992)

Holland, dir. Paul Ruven; Ariel Film Produkties B.V.

CAST: Maike Meyer, Christo van Klaveren, Odette van der Molen.

The knight Ivanhood must solve the riddle of his own birth and ancestry or die. He sets forth to find the country of his birth, Atlantis. Once there, he finds a land ravaged by drought, war and famine — and inhabited by bearded women, who look upon him as their savior.

Despite similarities in title, this minimalist film bears no relationship to Sir Walter Scott's novel *Ivanhoe*.

REVIEW: *Skrien* 186 (October-November 1992): 32–33.

ADDITIONAL DISCUSSION:
Dutch Films. Amsterdam: Holland Film Promotion, 1992.

260. *Jabberwocky* (1977)

Great Britain; dir. Terry Gilliam; Umbrella Entertainment Productions.

CAST: Annette Badland, Rodney Bewes, Bernard Bresslaw, Harry H. Corbett, Brenda Cowling, Deborah Fallender, John LeMesurier, Warren Mitchell, Michael Palin, Max Wall.

The Jabberwock, a fierce dragon, is wreaking havoc throughout the kingdom of King Bruno the Questionable. The king summons all of his knights to his castle for the tourna-

Christo van Klaveren as the title character in Paul Ruven's *Ivanhood* (1992). (Still courtesy of the Nederlands Filmmuseum.)

Michael Palin as Dennis Cooper in Terry Gilliam's *Jabberwocky* (1977).

ment. The winner will be given the hand of the king's daughter in marriage, and the opportunity to slay the Jabberwock. After a long series of misadventures, Dennis Cooper, a failed cooper and unlikely hero, slays the dragon and wins the princess.

This film, created by a splinter group from the Monty Python troupe, certainly debunks the pristine and bowdlerized portraits of the medieval that are so common in film. The film's inspiration is Lewis Carroll's poem "Jabberwocky"; critics were fairly divided about its merits. Clearly a spoof, though of what is not always clear, *Jabberwocky* is at times funny, crude, violent, gory — perhaps even disgusting — all of which the Middle Ages would in reality prove to be to modern sensibilities.

REVIEWS: *Cinéma* [Paris] 224-25 (August-September 1977): 186–87. *Cinefantastique* 6 (Winter 1977): 24. *Cue* 30 April 1977: 34. *Filmfacts* 20 (1977): 208–11. *Films & Filming* 23 (June 1977): 38–39. *Hollywood Reporter* 27 April 1977: 2. *Image et son* 319 (September 1977): 105–06. *Los Angeles Times* 29 July 1977: 4. 10. *Montage* 38-39 (1977): 9, 26. *Monthly Film Bulletin* 44 (April 1977): 72–73. *New York Times* 16 April 1977: 14. *Radio Times* 14–20 March 1987: 19. *Sunday Times* [London] 27 March 1977: Magazine 62; 3 April 1977: 37. *Times* [London] 1 April 1977: 17. *Variety* 6 April 1977: 26.

ADDITIONAL DISCUSSIONS:

Nash, Jay Robert., and Stanley Ralph Ross. *The Motion Picture Guide, H–K, 1927–1983*. Chicago: Cinebooks, 1986.

Palin, Michael, and David Castell. "The Making of Jabberwocky." *Films Illustrated* 6 (May 1977): 342–44

Perry, George. *The Life of Python*. London: Pavillion, 1983.

Sigoloff, Marc. *The Films of the Seventies*. Jefferson, N.C.: McFarland, 1984.

261. *Jane Shore* (1908)

Great Britain; Gaumont.

Jane Shore, the wife of a goldsmith, becomes King Edward IV's mistress. Jealous of Jane, the queen and the Duke of Gloucester, himself infatuated with Jane, plot against her. When Edward is suddenly taken ill and dies in his mistress' arms, the queen and duke seek their revenge by accusing Jane of witchcraft. Jane is delivered up to the Church, which excommunicates her as a witch and then turns her over to a crowd which stones her to death.

This was the first of several silent film treatments of the story of Jane Shore and Edward IV (1442–1483). The source is Nicholas Rowe's 1714 tragedy *Jane Shore.*

ADDITIONAL DISCUSSION:

Savada, Elias. *The American Film Institute Catalog of Motion Pictures Produced in the United States: Film Beginnings, 1893–1910.* Metuchen, N.J.: Scarecrow, 1995.

262. *Jane Shore* (1912)

Great Britain; dir. Frank Powell; Brittania/Pathé Frères.

CAST: Florence Barker.

Jane Shore, the wife of a goldsmith, catches the eye of King Edward IV. The king first brings her to court as lady-in-waiting to the queen but soon makes her his mistress. The king's brother, the Duke of Gloucester, is also in love with Jane, but she rejects him — and her husband — to stay at Edward's side. When Edward is suddenly taken ill and dies in his mistress' arms, the duke and the queen (who feels she has been humiliated by Jane and the king) take their revenge and accuse Jane of witchcraft. The Church excommunicates Jane and turns her over to a crowd which then stones her to death.

This second film version of Rowe's play develops further details from the play's plot than the earlier 1908 version does.

REVIEWS: *Bioscope* 4 January 1912: supplement vi. *Moving Picture World* 20 April 1912: 262. *Talbot Tatler* 1 (January 1912): 74.

ADDITIONAL DISCUSSION:

Bousquet, Henri. *Catalogue Pathé des annés 1896 à 1914: 1912-1913-1914.* Paris: Henri Bousquet, 1995.

263. *Jane Shore* (1915)

Great Britain; dir. F. Martin Thornton and Bert Haldane; Barker.

ALTERNATE TITLE: *The Strife Eternal.*

CAST: Blanche Forsyth, Tom MacDonald, Nelson Phillips, Robert Purdie, Roy Travers.

Matthew Shore leads a plot against King Edward. When the plot fails, Jane Shore saves her husband's life by agreeing to be the king's mistress. When the king is poisoned, Richard, Duke of Gloucester, accuses Jane of witchcraft and regicide. Church authorities agree, and they condemn Jane to walk barefoot through the snowy streets of London. Matthew arrives to rescue her, but he is too late: He finds his wife lying dead in the street.

This third film version of the story of Jane Shore expands on the plots of its two predecessors. The film was considered a great spectacle in its day; the scene in which Edward lands back in England after a brief period of exile attracted especially favorable critical comment.

REVIEWS: *Bioscope* 25 March 1915: 1117. *Kinematograph Monthly Record* 37 (May 1915): 49–50. *Motion Picture News* 12 (4 December 1915): 90. *Variety* 4 June 1915: 18.

ADDITIONAL DISCUSSIONS:

Barker, Will. "Making a Great Historical Picture." *Kinematograph Year Book, Film Diary and Directory* (1916): 453–54.

Connelly, Robert. *The Motion Picture Guide, Silent Film, 1910–1936.* Chicago: Cinebooks, 1986.

[Promotional Stills and Excerpts from Reviews.] *Bioscope* 29 April 1915: 411–18.

"Trade Topics." *Bioscope* 20 May 1915: 716.

264. *Jane Shore* (1922)

Great Britain; dir. Edwin J. Collins; Master Films.

CAST: Booth Conway, Lewis Gilbert, Gordon Hopkirk, Sybil Thorndike.

Jane Shore becomes the mistress of King Edward IV. When the king suddenly dies, she is accused of witchcraft and executed.

This one-reeler is part of an anthology film in which Thorndike played the lead female character in six "tense moments from great plays." Another of the one-reelers was a much-abridged version of *The Hunchback of Notre Dame,* which featured Thorndike as Esmeralda.

REVIEW: *Kinematograph Weekly* 13 July 1922: 45.

265. *Jeanne d'Arc* (1897)

France; dir. Georges Méliès; Star Films.

CAST: Mlle. Calvière, Georges Méliès, Madame Méliès.

Joan follows the lead of her voices in appealing to the Dauphin to drive English troops from French soil. She is successful, and Charles is crowned in Reims. Joan's fortunes change, when she is captured by the Burgundians, tried by the English and burned at the stake as a heretic.

Possibly the first film to treat a medieval theme, the 1897 version of *Jeanne d'Arc* was remade and expanded upon by Méliès several times. In each version, Méliès first emphasizes Joan's role as national hero and (in the film's final tableau) her role as a potential saint of the Church.

DISCUSSIONS:

Blaetz, Robin J. "Strategies of Containment: Joan of Arc in Film." Ph.D. dissertation. New York University, 1989.

Complete Catalogue of Genuine and Original "Star" Films Manufactured by Geo. Méliès of Paris. New York: Star Films, [1907?].

Harty, Kevin J. "Jeanne au cinéma." In Bonnie Wheeler and Charles T. Wood, eds. *Fresh Verdicts on Joan of Arc.* New York: Garland, 1996.

Jenn, Pierre. *Georges Méliès Cinéaste.* Paris: Éditions Albatros, 1984.

Jacobs, Lewis. *The Emergence of Film Art.* 2nd ed. New York: Norton, 1979.

Margolis, Nada. *Joan of Arc in History, Literature, and Film.* New York: Garland, 1990.

"Le Premier 'Jeanne d'Arc' fut tourne en 1897." *Ecran française* 159 (13 July 1948): 3, 14.

Sadoul, Georges. *Histoire générale du cinéma 2. Les Pionniers du cinéma 1897–1909.* Paris: Denoël, 1948.

_____. *Lumière et Méliès.* rev. ed. Paris: Lherminier, 1985.

Savada, Elias. *The American Film Institute Catalog of Motion Pictures Produced in the United States: Film Beginnings, 1893–1910.* Metuchen, N.J.: Scarecrow, 1995.

The "Walturdaw" Animated Pictures Catalogue. London: Walturdaw, 1904.

Warwick Film Catalogue. London: Warwick Trading Company, 1901.

266. *Jeanne d'Arc* (1909)

France; dir. Albert Capellani; Pathé Frères.

ALTERNATE TITLES: *Joan of Arc* and *La Vie de Jeanne d'Arc.*

CAST: Léontine Massart.

Joan hears voices and describes them to her family. She persuades Capt. Baudricourt to help her get an audience with the Dauphin. With the Dauphin's blessing, she lifts the siege of Orleans. After several more victories, Charles is crowned in Reims, but Joan is soon taken prisoner by the Burgundians and English. Interrogated by ecclesiastical authorities, she refuses to recant. After having yet another vision, she kisses the cross and is burned at the stake in Rouen.

Capellani's film was released to coincide with the beatification of Joan on April 18, 1909. The film takes both a republican view of Joan as national hero and a more royalist view of her as potential saint of the Church.

REVIEWS: *Bioscope* 2 October 1913: supplement xlv. *Kinematograph & Lantern Weekly* 17 June 1909: 295. *Moving Picture World* 19 June 1909: 847; 3 July 1909: 14. *New York Dramatic Mirror* 3 July 1909: 16. *Pathé Frères Weekly Bulletin* 86 (21 June 1909): [6–7].

ADDITIONAL DISCUSSIONS:

Abel, Richard. *The Ciné Goes to Town, French Cinema, 1896–1914.* Berkeley: University of California Press, 1994.

Blaetz, Robin J. "Strategies of Containment: Joan of Arc in Film." Ph.D. dissertation. New York University, 1989.

Bousquet, Henri. *Catalogue Pathé années 1896 à 1914: 1907–1908–1909.* Paris: Henri Bousquet, 1993.

Ford, Charles. *Albert Capellani.* Bois d'Arcy: Centre national de la cinématographie, 1984.

Harty, Kevin J. "Jeanne au cinéma." In Bonnie Wheeler and Charles T. Wood, eds. *Fresh Verdicts on Joan of Arc.* New York: Garland, 1996.

Margolis, Nada. *Joan of Arc in History, Literature, and Film.* New York: Garland, 1990.

Savada, Elias. *The American Film Institute Catalog of Motion Pictures Produced in the United States: Film Beginnings, 1893–1910.* Metuchen, N.J.: Scarecrow, 1995.

267. *Jeanne la pucelle* (1994)

France; dir. Jacques Rivette; Pierre Grise Productions.

CAST: Sandrine Bonnaire, Marcel Bozonnet, André Marcon, Jean-Louis Richard, Didier Sauvergrain.

Having won a decisive victory for the French against the English at Orleans, Jean persuades a reluctant Dauphin to travel to Reims and then to attack Troyes, claiming that she is only obeying her voices. Once Charles is crowned, she urges him to march on Paris, but during that campaign she is wounded and Charles makes peace with the Burgundians. Joan, however, keeps fighting until she is taken prisoner at Compiègne and eventually sold to the English. After a trial that lasts five months, she is excommunicated and burned at the stake.

Really two films, each running almost three hours, *Jeanne la pucelle* features spare sets and relies upon an equally spare narrative with references to precise dates and times of day. Witnesses appear at strategic moments in the film to fill in narrative gaps by explaining the po-

Sandrine Bonnaire as Joan in Jacques Rivette's *Jeanne la pucelle* (1994).

litical and religious forces at work in the events portrayed on the screen. Rivette seems to have had no hidden agenda in making the film. Joan's last cry of "Jesus" seems one both of anger and of pain. Respectfully received at a number of film festivals, the film could nonetheless benefit from additional cutting and editing.

REVIEWS: *Les Cahiers du cinéma* 476 (February 1994): 24–26. *Cinébulles* 14 (Winter-Spring 1995): 53–54. *Le Figaro magazine* 14 May 1994: 105. *Film-echo/Filmwoche* 7 (18 February 1994): 22. *Film français* 4 February 1994: 4–5, 28. *Grand angle* 168–169 (February-March 1994): n.p. *Le Monde* 10 February 1994: Arts & Spectacles I–III. *New York Times* 29 November 1996: C14. *Positif* 396 (February 1994): 26–27. *Premiére* 203 (February 1994): 45. *Studio* [Paris] 83 (February 1994): 13. *Times* [London] 31 August 1995: 29. *Variety* 21 February 1994: 46.

ADDITIONAL DISCUSSIONS:
Bonnaire, Sandrine. *Jeanne la pucelle.* Paris: Éditions Jean-Claude Lattès, 1994.
———. "Sur les traces de Jeanne d'Arc." *Studio* [Paris] 83 (February 1994): 70–73.
Harty, Kevin J. "Jeanne au cinéma." In Bonnie Wheeler and Charles T. Wood, eds. *Fresh Verdicts on Joan of Arc.* New York: Garland, 1996.

Kennedy, Harlan. "Sam & Jim's Excellent Adventure and Other Side Trips at the 44th Berlin Filmfestspiele." *Film Comment* 30 (March–June 1994): 72–75.
Laurent, Christine, and Paschal Bonitzer. "Jeanne la pucelle." *Cahiers du cinéma* 464 (February 1993): 18–25.
Pascaud, Fabienne. "'Jeanne d'Arc est un peu tête à claques.'" *Télérama* 9 February 1994: 32–40.
Pernoud, Régine. "Jeanne d'arc, le coup de coeur." *Le Figaro magazine* 691 (22 January 1994): 51–56.
Strauss, Fréderic, and Vincent Vatrican. "Entretien avec Sandrine Bonnaire." *Cahiers du cinéma* 476 (February 1994): 27–32.

268. *Jedermann* (1961)

Austria; dir. Gottfried Reinhardt; Bavaria Film.

ALTERNATE TITLE: *Everyman.*

CAST: Ewald Balser, Viktor Braun, Edward Cossovel, Paul Dahlke, Wolfgang Gasser, Walter Reyer, Ellen Schwers, Sonja Sutter.

Everyman, fearing death, repents his life's sins once he learns what will really stand him in good stead in the next life.

This work presents a film record of a staged

Maria Jacobini as Joan confronts her accusers in Nino Oxilias's *Joan of Arc* (1913).

production of Hugo von Hoffmannstahl's 1912 play *Jedermann* as performed at the 1961 Salzburg Music and Theatre Festival.

REVIEW: *Variety* 17 January 1962: 7.

Jerusalem Delivered (1911) see *The Crusaders* (1911)

Joan at the Stake (1954) see *Giovanna d'Arco al rogo* (1954)

Joan of Arc (1897) see *Jeanne d'Arc* (1897)

Joan of Arc (1908) see *Jeanne d'Arc* (1908)

269. *Joan of Arc* (1913)

Italy; dir. Nino Oxilia; Savoia.

CAST: Arturo Garzes, Maria Jacobini, Alberto Nepoti.

To the familiar tale of Joan of Arc (from her days as a simple peasant girl to her death at the stake in Rouen), director Oxilia adds two spe-cial touches. Throughout her ordeals, Joan is accompanied by Bertrand, simply identified as her "companion." And in her final captivity, the Earl of Stafford attempts to stab Joan, and her confessor tries to trick her into declaring her guilt. His last appearance in the film shows him groveling in the dirt, begging for Joan's pardon.

Oxilia, whose brilliant career as a director was cut short when he was killed in the trenches during the First World War, presents a balanced portrait of Joan as both saint of the Church and mother of the nation. His film was praised by reviewers on both sides of the Atlantic.

REVIEWS: *Bioscope* 9 October 1913: 105; 18 December 1913: 1203. *Kinematograph Monthly Film Record* 22 (February 1914): 42–43. *Moving Picture World*: 12 February 14: 790; 7 March 1914: 1215. *Picturegoer* 17 January 1914: 460–65. *Variety* 17 July 1914: 17.

ADDITIONAL DISCUSSIONS:

Blaetz, Robin J. "Strategies of Containment: Joan of Arc in Film." Ph.D. dissertation. New York University, 1989.

Harty, Kevin J. "Jeanne au cinéma." In Bonnie

Ingrid Bergman as Joan in Victor Fleming's *Joan of Arc* (1948).

Wheeler and Charles T. Wood, eds. *Fresh Verdicts on Joan of Arc*. New York: Garland, 1996.

Margolis, Nada. *Joan of Arc in History, Literature, and Film*. New York: Garland, 1990.

Prolo, Maria Adriana. *Storia del cinema muto italiano*. Milan: Poligono Società Editrice, 1951.

270. *Joan of Arc* (1948)

United States; dir. Victor Fleming; RKO.

CAST: Ingrid Bergman, Ward Bond, Jose Ferrer, J. Carrol Naish, Francis L. Sullivan.

Joan, a young girl living in Domremy, hears voices telling her to drive the English from her country. She convinces the Dauphin of the righteousness of her cause and, at the head of the French army, she lifts the siege at Orleans, turning the tide of the war in France's favor. She then leads the Dauphin to Reims to be crowned king. But the now-king, Charles VII, jealous of her popularity, dismisses her. Soon captured by the English, she is tried before civil and ecclesiastical courts and burned at the stake as a heretic.

Fans and Bergman herself long identified the actress with the role of Joan — she had already played the role on Broadway and would return to the screen in 1954 as Joan in *Giovanna d'Arco al rogo*. Her performance here is at times riveting, though not well enough supported by those of her fellow actors or the script. The source for this film is Maxwell Anderson's 1946 play *Joan of Lorraine*, which the playwright himself helped adapt for the screen.

REVIEWS: *Cue* 13 November 1948: 20. *Daily News* [New York] 12 November 1948: 74. *Harrison's Reports* 23 October 1948: 170. *Le Monde* 25 October 1949: 8; 3 November 1949: 8. *Monthly Film Bulletin* 16 (31 August 1949): 142. *Motion Picture* January 1949: 43. *Motion Picture Herald* 30 October 1948: Product Digest Section 4366. *New York Times* 12 November 1948: 30. *Revue du cinéma* [La Saison cinématographique] Hors série 30 (1948–1949): 111. *Times* [London] 7 April 1949: 8. *Today's Cinema* 6 April 1949: 12. *Variety* 20 October 1948: 11.

ADDITIONAL DISCUSSIONS:

Aachen, George. *Memorable Films of the Forties.* Sydney: Rastar Press, 1987.

Anderson, Maxwell, and Andrew Solt. *Joan of Arc.* New York: Sloane, 1948. [Screenplay.]

Bell-Metereau, Rebecca. *Hollywood Androgyny.* New York: Columbia University Press, 1985.

Bergman, Ingrid, and Alan Burgess. *Ingrid Bergman, My Story.* London: Michael Joseph, 1980.

Berstein, Matthew. "Hollywood Martyrdoms: *Joan of Arc* and Independent Production in the Late 1940s." In Bruce A. Austin, ed. *Current Research in Film: Audiences, Economics and Law, Vol. 4.* Norwood, N.J.: Ablex, 1988.

Blaetz, Robin J. "Strategies of Containment: Joan of Arc in Film." Ph.D. dissertation. New York University, 1989.

Damico, James. "Ingrid from Lorraine to Stromboli: Analyzing the Public's Perception of a Film Star." In Jeremy G. Butler, ed. *Star Texts, Image and Performance in Film and Television.* Detroit: Wayne State University Press, 1991.

de Saint-Pierre, Michel. "Humanisme du cinéma." *Études* [Paris] 263 (December 1949): 370–378.

Doncoeur, Paul. "Ingrid Bergman and Joan of Arc." *America* 80 (13 November 1948): 158–159.

_____. "Joan of Arc." *Sign* 28 (November 1948): 26–28.

_____. "Joan of Arc in Fact and Fiction." *Month* NS 1 (May 1949): 313–21.

"*Joan of Arc*: Ingrid Bergman Plays the Saint Who Saved France." *Life* 25 (15 November 1948): 78–87.

Harty, Kevin J. "Jeanne au cinéma." In Bonnie Wheeler and Charles T. Wood, eds. *Fresh Verdicts on Joan of Arc.* New York: Garland, 1996.

Lallou, William J. "St. Joan on the Screen." *American Ecclesiastical Review* 119 (December 1948): 401–06; Rpt. in *Catholic Digest* 13 (December 1948): 113–17.

Margolis, Nada. *Joan of Arc in History, Literature, and Film.* New York: Garland, 1990.

Mico, Ted, et al., eds. *Past Imperfect, History According to the Movies.* New York: Henry Holt, 1995.

Nash, Jay Robert, and Stanley Ralph Ross. *The Motion Picture Guide, H–K, 1927–1983.* Chicago: Cinebooks, 1986.

Pithon, Rémy. "*Joan of Arc* de Victor Fleming: de la résistance à la nuée." *Cahiers de la cinémathèque* 42–43 (Summer 1985): 50–58.

Quirk, Lawrence J. *The Films of Ingrid Bergman.* New York: Citadel, 1970.

271. *Joan the Woman* (1917)

United States; dir. Cecil B. DeMille; Paramount.

CAST: Hobart Bosworth, Charles Clary, Geraldine Farrar, Raymond Hatton, Tully Marshall, James Neil, Larry Peyton, Wallace Reid, Theodore Roberts.

On the night before he is to undertake a suicide mission, Eric Trent, a British soldier in the French trenches during the First World War, discovers a fragment of a sword he imagines to be Joan of Arc's. Trent is a reincarnation of an English soldier who was rescued by and subsequently fell in love with Joan. Caught up in the familiar events of Joan's life, the medieval Trent unwittingly aids in her undoing. As he sees Joan burn at the stake, Trent feels his life is over, and in the film's final sequence the modern-day Trent does indeed die on his suicide mission.

The first cinematic spectacle devoted to the life of Joan, DeMille's film is nothing less than a plea for America to become involved in the First World War and come to the aid of France. Joan here is a woman who mothers a nation, not a saint of the Church.

REVIEWS: *Bioscope* 22 January 1920: 47–48. *Exhibitor's Trade Review* 6 January 1917: 349. *Kinematograph Monthly Record* 94 (February 1920): 63; 98 (June 1920): 32–33. *Kinematograph Weekly* 22 January 1920: 121. *Motion Picture News* 6 January 1917: 111. *Motography* 13 January 1917: 96. *Moving Picture World* 30 December 1916: 1944; 13 January 1917: 239. *New York Dramatic Mirror* 30 December 1916: 28. *New York Times* 25 December 1916: 7. *Photoplay* 11 (March 1917): 113–16. *Variety* 29 December 1916: 22. *Wid's* 4 January 1917: 9

ADDITIONAL DISCUSSIONS:
Blaetz, Robin J. "Cecil B. DeMille's *Joan the*

Geraldine Farrar as Joan follows Raymond Hatton as the Dauphin in the coronation procession into Reims Cathedral in Cecil B. DeMille's *Joan the Woman* (1917).

Woman." In Kathleen Verduin ed. *Medievalism in North America*. Studies in Medievalism 6. Cambridge, Eng.: D.S. Brewer, 1994.

_____. "Strategies of Containment: Joan of Arc in Film." Ph.D. dissertation. New York University, 1989.

DeBauche, Leslie Midkiffe. *Reel Patriotism, The Movies and World War I*. Madison: University of Wisconsin Press, 1997.

Donnell, Dorothy. "Joan of Arc, A Short Story Written from the DeMille Photo-spectacle." *Motion Picture Magazine* 12 (December 1916): 102–10.

Farrar, Geraldine. "The Story of My Life." *Photoplay* 15 (February 1919): 24–26, 90, 92–94; (March 1919): 70–71, 102–04; (April 1919): 52–54, 106.

_____. *Such Sweet Compulsion, The Autobiog-*

raphy of Geraldine Farrar. New York: Greystone, 1938.

Hanson, Patricia King, ed. *The American Film Institute Catalog: Feature Films, 1911–1920*. Berkeley: University of California Press, 1988.

Harty, Kevin J. "Jeanne au cinéma." In Bonnie Wheeler and Charles T. Wood, eds. *Fresh Verdicts on Joan of Arc*. New York: Garland, 1996.

Higashi, Sumiko. *Cecil B. DeMille and American Culture: The Silent Era*. Berkeley: University of California Press, 1994.

Lescarboura, Austin C. "Generals of Shadowland Warfare." *Scientific American* 16 (5 May 1917): 446–47, 456–57, 459–60.

Magill, Frank N., ed. *Magill's Survey of Cinema: Silent Films*. Englewood Cliffs, N.J.: Salem, 1982.

Margolis, Nada. *Joan of Arc in History, Literature, and Film.* New York: Garland, 1990.

Ringgold, Gene, and DeWitt Bodeen. *The Films of Cecil B. DeMille.* New York: Cadillac Publishing, 1969.

Slide, Anthony, and Edward Wagenknecht. *Fifty Great American Silent Films 1912–1920.* New York: Dover, 1980.

The Judgment of God (1950) see *Le Jugement de Dieu* (1950)

272. Le Jugement de Dieu (1950)

France; dir. Raymond Bernard; B.U.P Métrage.

ALTERNATE TITLE: *The Judgment of God.*

CAST: Andrée Debar, Gabrielle Dorziat, Jean-Claude Pascal, Pierre Renoir.

In the fifteenth century, Bavarian Crown Prince Albert causes civil war to break out in his country when he falls in love with a commoner's daughter, Agnès Bernauer, instead of marrying the heir to the throne of a nearby duchy. Agnès is condemned as a sorceress by the Inquisition and thrown into the Danube with a great stone tied around her neck. Albert jumps into the river after her, and the lovers are finally united in death.

Inspired by a fifteenth century legend from the Rhineland, this film received highly favorable reviews for its pageantry and the poignancy of the scene in which Agnès and Albert meet their deaths.

REVIEWS: *Cinématographie française* 6 September 1952: 10. *Le Technique cinématographique* 23 (September 1952): 221.

ADDITIONAL DISCUSSION:
Chirat, Raymond. *Catalogue des films français de long métrage. Films de fiction 1919–1929.* Toulouse: Cinémathèque de Toulouse, 1984.

273. The Juggler of Our Lady (1957)

United States; dir. Al Kousel; 20th Century–Fox.

CAST: (the voice of) Boris Karloff.

Candlebert, intent upon making the world a better place, joins a monastery where he tries to follow the example of his new confreres, who do work in honor of the Virgin. Candlebert soon finds that he has no skills other than juggling, so he dedicates his juggling to the Virgin.

This animated cartoon, based on a twelfth century folktale, is unusual not only for its theme but also for its being a CinemaScope animated feature.

REVIEWS: *Film News* 34 (June 1959): 26. *Kinematograph Weekly* 19 December 1957: 14. *Monthly Film Bulletin* 25 (November 1958): 147. *Motion Picture Herald* 14 December 1957: Product Digest Section 642.

ADDITIONAL DISCUSSION:
Buehrer, Beverley Bare. *Boris Karloff, A Bio-Bibliography.* Westport, Conn.: Greenwood, 1993.

274. Julianus (1991)

Hungary; dir. Gabor Koltay; Inter-Cine.

CAST: Hirtling Istvan, Nino Manfredi, Franco Nero, Raf Vallone.

ALTERNATE TITLES: *Frate Julianus* and *Friar Julianus.*

Julianus, a young Hungarian peasant, joins a monastery, but he soon flees his new home in disgust once he discovers that the monks live in luxury. He petitions the king to undertake a pilgrimage in search of the origins of the Magyar people, but is denied royal sanction for his journey. He then travels to Italy before finally receiving the king's permission for his journey. Julianus and a group of monks set sail and encounter persecution at the hands of the Saracens.

The Magyars were originally a nomadic people who lived in parts of what was to become the Ottoman Empire. In 1984, Koltay directed another film about medieval Hungary, *Istvan, a Kiraly.*

DISCUSSION:
The Italian Production 1991/1992. Rome: ANICA, 1992.

Julie Colonna (1910) see *Giulia Colonna* (1910)

Jungfrukällan (1959) see *The Virgin Spring* (1959)

Kazimierz Wielki (1975) see *Casimir the Great* (1975)

275. A Kid in King Arthur's Court (1995)

United States; dir. Michael Gottlieb; Walt Disney Pictures.

CAST: Joss Ackland, Paloma Baeza, Daniel Craig, Art Malik, Ron Moody, Thomas Ian Nicholas, David Tysall, Kate Winslet.

Sir Calvin of Reseda, formerly Calvin Fuller (Thomas Ian Nicholas), confers with King Arthur (Joss Ackland) in a scene from Michael Gottlieb's *A Kid in King Arthur's Court* (1995). (Still courtesy of Walt Disney Pictures.)

Calvin Fuller, a California little leaguer with low self-esteem, finds himself transported back to Camelot and King Arthur's Court where he meets a disembodied and befuddled Merlin. The magician has confused a spell that was supposed to bring a great warrior to Camelot to help the aging King Arthur defeat Lord Belasco, who wants to secure the throne by any means, including marriage to Arthur's older daughter, Princess Sarah. Calvin becomes smitten by Sarah's younger sister, Princess Katey, to whom he introduces a variety of modern gadgets. Eventually, Calvin, now known as Sir Calvin of Reseda, defeats Belasco and helps Arthur restore order to Camelot. A now self-assured Calvin returns to the twentieth century and hits a home run.

The latest film adaptation of Twain's famous novel to recast the Yankee as a teenager, this film relies on the predictable to advance its plot. Ackland's Arthur is a doddering fool; Moody plays Merlin a second time, having performed the role with a more sinister twist in 1979 in *Unidentified Flying Oddball*. The film's only bright spot is its countering of the largely misogynic Arthurian tradition in having Princess Sarah (disguised as the Black Knight) help Calvin save the day.

REVIEWS: *Arthuriana* 6 (Summer 1996): 115–18. *Daily Variety* 11 August 1995: 4. *Film Journal* 98 (October-November 1995): 33. *Hollywood Reporter* 11 August 1995: 10, 35. *Los Angeles Times* 11 August 1995: F4. *New York Times* 11 August 1995: C16. *Variety* 14 August 1995: 55, 59.

ADDITIONAL DISCUSSIONS:

Fhaner, Beth A., and Christopher P. Scanlon, eds. *Magill's Cinema Annual 1996*. Detroit: Gale, 1996.

Levich, Jacob, ed. *The Motion Picture Guide, 1996 Annual (The Films of 1995)*. New York: Cine-Books, 1996.

Umland, Rebecca A., and Samuel J. Umland. *The Use of Arthurian Legend in Hollywood Film from Connecticut Yankees to Fisher Kings*. Westport, Conn.: Greenwood, 1996.

276. *Kilian's Chronicle* (1994)

United States; dir. Pamela Berger; Lara Classics Productions.

Ignacy Gogolewski in the title role in Witold Lesiewicz's *King Boleslaus the Bold* (1971). (Still courtesy of the British Film Institute.)

CAST: Christopher Johnson, Eva Kim, Jonah Ming Lee, Robert McDonough.

Kidnapped by Vikings, Kilian, a young Irishman, escapes from his captors with the aid of a tribe of Passamaquoddies when they all land in Vinland. The tribesmen are peaceful people who only go to war when attacked. While among the tribe, Kilian serves as mentor for a young boy and falls in love with a girl named Turtle.

Kilian's Chronicle is at best a low-budget, would-be movie epic built around the premise that Viking mariners discovered the New World almost 500 years before Columbus. The film's dialogue is in English and Passamoquoddy with English subtitles.

REVIEWS: *Boston Globe* 5 October 1994: 36. *Boston Phoenix* 14 October 1994: 3. 10. *New York Times* 6 October 1995: C12. *Variety* 10 October 1994: 85.

ADDITIONAL DISCUSSIONS:

Levich, Jacob, ed. *The Motion Picture Guide, 1996 Annual (The Films of 1995)*. New York: CineBooks, 1996.

Wanat, Thomas. "Film Maker Focuses on America Before Columbus." *Chronicle of Higher Education* 19 October 1994: A8.

King Arthur and the Siege of the Saxons (1963) see *The Siege of the Saxons* (1963)

King Arthur; or, The Knights of the Round Table (1910) see *Il Re Artù e i cavalieri della tavola rotonda* (1910)

277. *King Arthur, the Young Warlord* (1975)

Great Britain; dir. Sidney Hayers, Patrick Jackson, Patrick Sasdy; Heritage Enterprises.

ALTERNATE TITLE: *Arthur of the Britons*.

CAST: Brian Blessed, Peter Firth, Michael Gothard, Oliver Tobias, Jack Watson.

The Celtic warrior Arthur fights Saxons, Picts and Jutes, as well as King Mark of Cornwall, to protect his people and the integrity of his homeland.

Never commercially released, this film is really just a cobbled-together videotape version of three episodes of *Arthur of the Britons,* a British television series that aired on the Harlech Television Channel in 1972 and 1973. The series consisted of 24 half-hour episodes.

ADDITIONAL DISCUSSIONS:
Vahimagi, Tise. *An Illustrated Guide to British Television.* London: Oxford University Press, 1994.
The Video Sourcebook 1997. 18th ed. Detroit: Gale, 1996.

278. *King Boleslaus the Bold* (1971)

Poland; dir. Witold Lesiewicz; Kraj Film Unit.

ALTERNATE TITLE: *Boleslaw smialy.*

CAST: Maria Ciesielska, Ignacy Gogolewski, Jerzy Kaliszewski, Zdzislaw Mrozewski.

In 1079, the battle between Church and state that has been raging across Europe comes to a head in Poland. Boleslaus II, known as the Bold, both wins and loses this battle. The king executes Stanislaus Szczepanowski, the Bishop of Krakow, but the outraged Polish nobility soon force Boleslaus into exile in Hungary, where he dies two years later.

When the teenage Boleslaus II ascended the throne, the Polish state was at best a weak confederacy. The new king immediately set out on a policy of aggressive expansion both within and outside of Poland's borders. A supporter of Pope Gregory VII in his conflict with Emperor Henry IV, Boleslaus was crowned king on Christmas Day 1076 with Gregory's blessing. Almost immediately, his battles with the nobility, both lay and clerical, escalated. In 1079, the king executed the Bishop of Krakow, now St. Stanislaus Martyr and Patron Saint of Poland, for reasons that are not entirely clear. An outraged Polish nobility then forced the king into exile.

REVIEW: *Polish Film* 2 (1971): 4–7.

ADDITIONAL DISCUSSIONS:
Polish Feature Films '71. Warsaw: Film Polski, [1971?].
Sobanski, Oskar. *Polish Feature Films, A Reference Guide 1945–1985.* West Cornwall, Conn.: Locust Hill Press, 1987.
Trémége, Bernard. "Walerian Borwczwck." *Jeune cinéma* 61 (February 1972): 11–12.

King Philip the Fair and the Templars (1910) see *Le Roi Philippe le Bel et les templiers* (1910)

279. *King Richard and the Crusaders* (1954)

United States; dir. David Butler; Warner Bros.

CAST: Nick Cravat, Robert Douglas, Rex Harrison, Laurence Harvey, Virginia Mayo, Michael Pate, Paula Raymond, George Sanders.

England's Richard I barely survives an assassination attempt by disloyal Crusaders. Emir Ilderim, the leader of the Saracens, rides into the Crusader camp posing as a doctor to aid in Richard's recovery, only to fall in love with the king's ward, Lady Edith. Ilderim then helps Richard's only trustworthy knight, Sir Kenneth (who is engaged to marry Edith), to expose the conspirators. The traitors are punished, and Kenneth and Edith go home to the knight's native Scotland despite the king's protest that he needs Kenneth in his army for future battles.

Based on Sir Walter Scott's 1825 novel *The Talisman,* this perfectly terrible film is memorable for two reasons: the overly tanned Rex Harrison's portrayal of the Saracen leader, and the last lines that Mayo as Lady Edith delivers when King Richard wants Kenneth to stay and fight with him: "War! War! That's all you think of, Dick Plantagenet! You burner! You pillager!"

REVIEWS: *Film Daily* 8 July 1954: 6. *Films and Filming* 1 (October 1954): 25. *Harrison's Reports* 10 July 1954: 110. *Hollywood Reporter* 7 July 1954: 3. *Kinematograph Weekly* 14 October 1954: 24. *Monthly Film Bulletin* 21 (November 1954): 157. *Motion Picture Herald* 10 July 1954: Product Digest Section 57. *New York Times* 23 August 1954: 20. *Times* [London] 13 October 1954: 9; 18 October 1954: 2. *To-day's Cinema* 7 October 1954: 8. *Variety* 7 July 1954: 6.

ADDITIONAL DISCUSSIONS:
Nash, Jay Robert, and Stanley Ralph Ross. *The Motion Picture Guide, H–K, 1927–1983.* Chicago: Cinebooks, 1986.
Richards, Jeffrey. *Swordsmen of the Screen from Douglas Fairbanks to Michael York.* London: Routledge & Kegan Paul, 1977.
Smith, Gary A. *Epic Films.* Jefferson, N.C.: McFarland, 1991.

280. *King Robert of Sicily* (1912)

Great Britain; dir. Hay Plumb; Hepworth.

CAST: Alma Taylor, Alec Worcester.

The proud King Robert is self-consumed, rude to his people — especially members of the clergy — and irreverent. Announcing that no one on earth or in heaven has power over him,

Laurence Harvey (left) as Sir Kenneth and Rex Harrison as Emir Ilderim in David Butler's *King Richard and the Crusaders* (1954).

Robert soon finds himself transformed into a jester and his jester into the king. Finally repentant, he reclaims his throne now the model of a Christian ruler, as the jester reveals himself to be an angel.

Robert of Anjou (1278–1343) was king of Naples and nominal king of Sicily. He was a noted patron of literature and the arts. His friend Petrarch said Robert was "the only monarch of the age who was the friend of both learning and virtue." His story has been variously told since Dante (*Paradiso* V). This film uses the version of the story found in Longfellow's poem "King Robert of Sicily" from the first part of the poet's *Tales of a Wayside Inn* (1863). Longfellow's source was probably the *Gesta Romanorum,* a fourteenth century compilation of tales.

REVIEWS: *Bioscope* 14 November 1912: 523, 525; 12 December 1912: supplement vii, ix.

King Stephen (1984) see *Istvan, a Kiraly* (1984)

Kingdom of Violence (1963) see *Sfida al re di castiglia* (1963)

281. *The Knight and the Friar* (1912)
Great Britain; Majestic.

Sir Tristram serenades his beloved Lady Alice against the will of her father. Friar Tuck interrupts the two and summons Alice's father. Tristram flees vowing revenge on the friar. The knight ambushes the friar and steals his robe. When Lady Alice comes for confession, she finds her beloved Tristram disguised as her confessor. Tristram then forces the friar to marry them.

This film simply borrows names from several medieval traditions without recounting any of the stories usually associated with those names.

REVIEWS: *Bioscope* 19 September 1912: supplement xxvi. *Moving Picture World* 6 July 1912: 44.

282. *A Knight Errant* (1907)

Great Britain; dir. J.H. Martin; Robert W. Paul Animatograph Works.

CAST: Langford Reed.

A knight rescues a damsel in distress from a giant and a witch and returns her to her father, who gives the knight the hand of his daughter in marriage.

This film reworks the plot of the Paul company's 1901 film *The Magic Sword*.

REVIEW: *Optical Lantern and Cinematograph Journal* 3 (November 1906): 151.

ADDITIONAL DISCUSSION:

Savada, Elias. *The American Film Institute Catalog of Motion Pictures Produced in the United States: Film Beginnings, 1893–1910.* Metuchen, N.J.: Scarecrow, 1995.

283. *The Knight Errant* (1911)

United States; Selig Polyscope.

Lady Ettarre, tiring of her young daughter Yoetta, abandons her. Reared by peasants, the girl leads a hard life until she is rescued by a knight who disguises her as his page. Together they travel the countryside seeking adventure. They chance upon Lady Ettarre, who is in danger, and come to her aid. The knight is wounded but later cared for by Lady Ettarre in her castle. Eventually, the three are reunited as one family.

REVIEWS: *Bioscope* 28 September 1911: supplement xix. *Moving Picture World* 29 June 1911: 223.

The Knight of the Black Art (1905) see *Le Tambourin fantastique* (1905)

284. *The Knight of the Cross* (1911)

United States; Edison.

ALTERNATE TITLE: *The Crusaders.*

CAST: James Gordon, Richard Neil, Herbert Prior, Richard Ridgeley, Laura Sawyer, Charles Sutton.

Two rival suitors for the hand of Lady Eleanor, Sir Roderick and Norman the Strong, set out for the Crusades. Roderick carries with him a love token from Eleanor. When Roderick is wounded, he sends a message along with the token back to England. Norman intercepts the message. Returning to England, he spreads the rumor that Roderick is dead. Lady Eleanor reluctantly agrees to marry Norman, but on their wedding day, Roderick returns. Norman is punished, and true love prevails.

This film was well received critically, with reviewers singling out for praise the scenes in the Holy Land, which were shot in Cuba.

REVIEWS: *Bioscope* 24 August 1911: 16. *Edison Kinetogram* 1 August 1911: 9. *Moving Picture World* 8 July 1911: 1586.

The Knight of the Cursed Castle (1957) see *Il Cavaliere del castello maladetto* (1957)

The Knight of the Dragon (1985) see *El Caballero del dragon* (1985)

The Knight of the Snows (1912) see *Le Chevalier des neiges* (1912)

The Knight Roland (1910) see *The Invincible Sword* (1910)

285. *The Knights of Rhodes* (1912)

Italy; Ambrosio.

The Knights of the Hospital of St. John of Jerusalem unsuccessfully defend the fortress on Rhodes against the Ottoman army.

The Knights first captured Rhodes in 1309; they defended the island for more than 300 years until their fortress fell to the Ottomans in 1522.

REVIEW: *Moving Picture World* 8 March 1913: 977.

286. *Knights of the Round Table* (1953)

United States and Great Britain; dir. Richard Thorpe; MGM.

CAST: Felix Aylmer, Stanley Baker, Anne Crawford, Mel Ferrer, Ava Gardner, Maureen Swanson, Robert Taylor.

The friendship of Arthur and Lancelot grows until Arthur refuses to banish the troublemaker Modred from Camelot. When Arthur and Guinevere marry, Lancelot reappears and falls in love with the queen. Guinevere in turn falls in love with Lancelot, but their affair is limited to a kiss. Modred, eager for revenge against Lancelot, tries to discredit him. To allay any suspicion, Lancelot marries Elaine, who

Ava Gardner and Robert Taylor as Guinevere and Lancelot in Richard Thorpe's *Knights of the Round Table* (1953).

dies in childbirth, leaving him only his son Galahad as consolation. Modred continues to scheme, and Lancelot and the queen are accused of treachery. Lancelot is banished, and she is shut up in a convent. Modred next plots

the overthrow of Arthur, who on his deathbed forgives Lancelot. Lancelot finally defeats Modred.

Those responsible for *Knights* claimed Sir Thomas Malory's fifteenth century *Le Morte*

Darthur as their source, but the film's real debt is to the American movie Western and the *Classics Illustrated* series. The film's significance lies in its being MGM's first CinemaScope production, not in any new light it sheds on the legend of Arthur and the Knights of the Round Table.

REVIEWS: *Film Daily* 23 December 1953: 6. *Films and Filming* 5 (June 1963): 37. *Films in Review* 5 (February 1954): 90–91. *Harrison's Reports* 26 December 1953: 208. *Kinematograph Weekly* 446 (20 May 1954): 19–20. *Monthly Film Bulletin* 21 (July 1954): 100–01. *Motion Picture Herald* 193 (26 December 1953): Product Digest Section 2117. *New York Times* 8 January 1954: 17. *Picturegoer* 12 June 1954: 20. *Times* [London] 14 May 1954: 8; 15 May 1954: 12. *To-day's Cinema* 13 May 1954: 7–8. *Variety* 23 December 1953: 6.

ADDITIONAL DISCUSSIONS:
Carr, Robert E., and R.M. Hayes. *Wide Screen Movies*. Jefferson, N.C.: McFarland, 1988.
de la Bretèque, François. "Le Table ronde au farwest: 'Les Chevaliers de la table ronde' de Richard Thorpe (1953)." *Les Cahiers de la cinémathèque* 42–43 (Summer 1985): 97–102.
Fraser, George MacDonald. *The Hollywood History of the World*. New York: Morrow, 1988.
Fowler, Karin J. *Ava Gardner, A Bio-Bibliography*. New York: Greenwood Press, 1990.
Knights of the Round Table: A Souvenir Booktlet. New York: Al Greenstone, 1954.
Nash, Jay Robert, and Stanley Ralph Ross. *The Motion Picture Guide, H–K, 1927–1983*. Chicago: Cinebooks, 1986.
Quirk, Lawrence J. *The Films of Robert Taylor*. Secaucus, N.J.: Citadel, 1975.
Richards, Jeffrey. *Swordsmen of the Screen from Douglas Fairbanks to Michael York*. London: Routledge & Kegan Paul, 1977.
Smith, Gary A. *Epic Films*. Jefferson, N.C.: McFarland, 1991.
Umland, Rebecca A., and Samuel J. Umland. *The Use of Arthurian Legend in Hollywood Film from Connecticut Yankees to Fisher Kings*. Westport, Conn.: Greenwood, 1996.
Wayne, Jane Ellen. *Robert Taylor*. New York: St. Martin's, 1987.

The Knights of the Round Table

(1990) see *Les Chevaliers de la table ronde* (1990)

287. Knights of the Teutonic Order

(1960)
Poland; dir. Alexsander Ford; Studio Unit.
ALTERNATE TITLE: *Krzyzacy*.
CAST: Henryk Borowski, Stanislaw Jasiukiewicz, Urszula Modrzynska, Grazyna Staniszewska, Andrzej Szalawski.

In the early fifteenth century, Zbyszko falls in love with Danusia, whose mother has been killed by Teutonic Knights. Swearing to avenge his beloved's mother's death, Zbyszko attacks the envoy of the Teutonic Knights to Poland and is himself condemned to death. He is saved by royal intervention but soon finds that Danusia has been kidnapped by the Teutonic Knights, in whose prison she goes mad before returning home where she dies. In a great battle, Polish forces rally and decisively defeat the invading army of Teutonic Knights.

At the end of the fourteenth and the beginning of the fifteenth centuries, the Teutonic Knights were intent upon expanding their territories and pursuing their activities as crusaders. In 1385, the heir to the Polish throne, Jadwiga, married a pagan Lithuanian prince who converted to Christianity and took the name Jagiello Wladyslaw II. When his wife died in 1399, Jagiello became the undisputed ruler of Poland. The Teutonic Knights were suspicious of his conversion, and they used their suspicions as the justification for a holy war against Poland. In 1409, the Knights attacked Poland and Lithuania, but were decisively beaten back the following year at the Battle of Grunwald. Some critics have compared this film, which is based on Henryk Sienkiewicz's 1900 novel *Krzyzacy*, to Eisenstein's 1938 classic *Alexander Nevsky* because of its depiction of an epic clash between Germanic and Slavic cultures.

REVIEWS: *Cinema 61* (July 1961): 111–12. *Cinématographie française* 10 September 1960: 5; 17 June 1961: 15. *Daily Cinema* 4 December 1963: 8. *Film* [Poland] 27 (1 July 1984): 8–9. *Film français* 16 June 1961: 24. *Hollywood Reporter* 26 June 1961: 3. *Image et son* 144 (October 1961): 24–25. *Monthly Film Bulletin* 31 (January 1964): 5–6. *Times* [London] 12 September 1960: 3. *Variety* 7 September 1960: 15.

ADDITIONAL DISCUSSIONS:
Bren, Frank. *World Cinema 1: Poland*. London: Flick Books, 1986.
Film Polski 1960. Warsaw: Polish Film State Company, [1960?].
Grzelecki, Stanislaw. *Twenty Years of Polish Cinema Film 1947–1967*. Warsaw: Art and Film Publishers, 1969.
Haudiquet, Philippe. *Nouveaux cinéastes polonais*. Lyon: Serdoc, 1963.
Hine, Daryl. *Polish Subtitles*. London: Abelard-Schuman, 1962.
Liehm, Mira, and Antonin J. Liehm. *The Most Important Art*. Berkeley: University of California Press, 1977.

Stanislaw Jasiukiewicz as Grand Master Ulrich in Alexsander Ford's *Knights of the Teutonic Order* (1960). (Still courtesy of the British Film Institute.)

Lucanio, Patrick. *With Fire and Sword, Italian Spectacles on American Screens 1958–1968.* Metuchen, N.J.: Scarecrow, 1994.

Michalek, Boleslaw, and Frank Turaj. *Le Cinéma polonais.* Paris: Centre Georges Pompidou, 1992.

Nash, Jay Robert, and Stanley Ralph Ross. *The Motion Picture Guide, H–K, 1927–1983.* Chicago: Cinebooks, 1986.

Sobanski, Oskar. *Polish Feature Films, A Reference Guide 1945–1985.* West Cornwall, Conn.: Locust Hill, 1987.

Stoil, Michael Jon. *Cinema Beyond the Danube.* Metuchen, N.J.: Scarecrow, 1974.

288. *Knives of the Avenger* (1965)

Italy; dir. John Hold (Mario Bava); World Entertainment/Sider Films.

ALTERNATE TITLES: *I Coltelli del vendicatore* and *Raffica di cotelli.*

CAST: Cameron Mitchell, Elissa Mitchell, Giacomo Rossi Stuart, Fausto Tozzi.

During King Harald's absence, renegade Vikings led by Aghen plunder his land and attempt to kidnap his wife Karen, who is saved by a mysterious stranger. Years before, Aghen had murdered the stranger's son and wife and, in a fit of rage, the stranger had attacked Harald's camp and raped Karen. Still intent on revenging himself against Aghen, the stranger nonetheless wishes to atone for his wrongs to Karen and Harald. When Harald returns, he recognizes the stranger as the man who raped his queen, and the king challenges the stranger to a duel. The duel is interrupted when Aghen kidnaps Harald's son. The stranger and the king unite to defeat Aghen and rescue the prince.

The plot of this film, which is little more than a spaghetti Western set in the Middle Ages, obviously has little to do with anything genuinely medieval.

REVIEWS: *Film-echo/Filmwoche* 49 (21 June 1967): 10. *Variety* 20 December 1967: 14.

ADDITONAL DISCUSSIONS:
Italian Production 1965. Rome: Unitalia Film, 1966.
Lucanio, Patrick. *With Fire and Sword, Italian Spectacles on American Screens 1958–1968*. Metuchen, N.J.: Scarecrow, 1994.
Nash, Jay Robert, and Stanley Ralph Ross. *The Motion Picture Guide, H–K, 1927–1983*. Chicago: Cinebooks, 1986.
Poppi, Roberto, and Mario Pecorari. *Dizionario del cinema italiano. Vol. 3: I Film dal 1960 al 1969*. Rome: Gremese Editore, 1992.
Weldon, Michael. *The Psychotronic Encyclopedia of Film*. New York: Ballantine, 1983.

289. *Knyaz Igor* (1970)

Soviet Union; dir. Roman Tikhomirov; Lenfilm.

ALTERNATE TITLE: *Prince Igor*.

CAST: Boris Khmelnitsky, Invetta Margoyeva, Nelly Pshennaya, Boris Tokarev, Bimbulat Vatayev.

The Russian Prince Igor leaves his wife and village to fight invaders from the East. His army suffers a great defeat, and the prince is taken prisoner. He escapes, returns home to raise a new army and finally defeats the invaders, saving his homeland from foreign domination.

This film presents a screen version of Aleksandr Porfirevich Borodin's 1869 opera *Prince Igor*. Borodin in turn based his opera on the epic poem *The Lay of Igor's Host*, which was supposedly composed around 1187.

REVIEWS: *Cue* 13 January 1973: 10. *Monthly Film Bulletin* 38 (October 1971): 199. *New York Times* 22 December 1972: 21. *Soviet Film* 9 (September 1970): 22–23.

ADDITIONAL DISCUSSIONS:
Carr, Robert E., and R.M. Hayes. *Wide Screen Movies*. Jefferson, N.C.: McFarland, 1988.
Tous les films 1984. Paris: Éditions Chrétiens-Médias, 1985.

Konrad von Schwaben (1909) see *Corradino di Svevia* (1909)

Korpen Flyger (1984) see *When the Raven Flies* (1984)

Kriemhild's Revenge (1924) see *Die Nibelungen* (1924)

Kriemhilds Rache (1924) see *Die Nibelungen* (1924)

290. *Kristin Lavransdatter* (1995)

Sweden; dir. Liv Ullmann; Norsk Film AS.

CAST: Elisabeth Matheson, Sverre Anker Ousdal, Bjøn Skagestad, Rut Tellefsen.

The young Kristin is betrothed to the son of a wealthy landowner. Almost raped by a neighbor, she persuades her family to send her to a convent until she can marry. While there, she falls madly in love with a knight who, unbeknownst to her, has a reputation for seducing and abandoning women. The two run off, and only after great difficulty are they united in marriage.

Based on Sigrid Unset's Nobel Prize–winning trilogy — *The Bridal Wreath* (1920), *The Mistress of Husaby* (1921) and *The Cross* (1922) — this film, like its source, paints a full picture of the life of a woman in medieval Norway from her childhood to her death some 50 years later as the Black Death marched across Europe. A labor of love for director Ullmann, the film runs more than three hours, from which Ullmann has been adamant about not cutting any material. This decision has kept the film from having a wider circulation.

REVIEWS: *Catholic New Times* [Toronto] 24 September 1995: 8. *Variety* 11 September 1995: 11.

ADDITIONAL DISCUSSIONS:
"A Dream Comes True." *Scandinavian Film News* 1 (February 1994): 12.
Funke, Phyllis Ellen. "From the Icy North, A Tale of Love and Rebellion." *New York Times* 7 April 1996: 2. 22.
Kraakenes, Sidsel. "Major Nordic Project." *Scandinavian Film News* 3 (August 1993): 1–2.
Løchen, Kalle. "Kristins speilbilde." *Film og kino* 5 (1995): 24–25, 40–41.

Krzyzacy (1960) see *Knights of the Teutonic Order* (1960)

Kublai Khan (1964) see *Marco the Magnificent* (1964)

The Laboratory of Mephistopheles (1897) see *Le Cabinet de Méphistophélès* (1897)

Elisabeth Matheson as the title character in Liv Ullmann's *Kristin Lavransdatter* (1995). (Still courtesy of Norsk Film AS.)

291. *Lady Godiva* (1911)

United States; dir.Charles Kent; Vitagraph.

CAST: Stanley Dunn, Robert Gaillord, Alfred Hollingsworth, Kate Price, Julia Swayne, Harold Wilson.

Leofric, the Earl of Coventry, imposes yet another heavy tax upon the townspeople who are already on the verge of starvation. His wife pleads with him to repeal the tax and, in jest, he tells her he will do so if she will ride naked through the town. She agrees, and at noon on the appointed day, Lady Godiva rides through the town covered only by her long flowing tresses. All of the townspeople avert their eyes except for one man, who is struck blind and henceforth known as "peeping Tom." His wife's ride completed, Leofric repeals the tax.

Leofric was Earl of Mercia during the reign of Edward the Confessor (c. 1003–66). The legend of his wife's sacrifice to relieve the citizens of Coventry has been retold by, among others, Michael Drayton and William Dugdale in the seventeenth century and Leigh Hunt and Tennyson in the nineteenth. The source for this treatment of the legend is Tennyson's 1842 poem "Godiva," which was based on Dugdale's account in *Antiquities of Warwickshire* (1656).

REVIEWS: *Bioscope* 11 January 1912: supplement vii. *Moving Picture World* 14 October 1911: 148; 21 October 1911: 214; 4 November 1911: 379. *Vitagraph Life Portrayals* 1 (17 October–1 November 1911): 9.

ADDITIONAL DISCUSSION:
Bush, W. Stephen. "The Added Attraction." *Moving Picture World* 25 November 1911: 617.

292. *Lady Godiva* (1922)

United States; Wistaria Productions.

Lady Godiva is married to an unscrupulous earl who will destroy the town of Coventry unless his wife's lover surrenders to him. Her husband agrees to spare the town if she will ride naked through the streets of Coventry. She agrees, and all avert their eyes, except her husband. The lover returns to shield Lady Godiva with his cloak, and the earl flees into his castle which collapses around him.

There is nothing to recommend this second silent version of the legend of Lady Godiva, which takes substantial liberties with the details of that legend despite its claim to follow its source (Tennyson's 1842 poem "Godiva") faithfully.

REVIEWS: *Harrison's Reports* 20 May 1922: 78. *Variety* 12 May 1922: 32.

293. *Lady Godiva* (1955)

United States; dir. Arthur Lubin; Universal-International.

ALTERNATE TITLE: *Lady Godiva of Coventry.*

CAST: Leslie Bradley, Eduard Franz, Alec Harford, Victor McLaglen, George Nader, Maureen O'Hara, Torin Thatcher.

Against a backdrop of escalating conflict between Saxons and Normans about who will succeed Edward the Confessor to the throne, Lady Godiva rides through the streets of Coventry to prove she and her husband are not traitors to the Saxon cause. All of the citizens avert their eyes as she passes except for a tailor who promptly has his eyes plucked out.

This film version of the legend of Lady Godiva is a costume period piece that presents O'Hara as a thoroughly modern Lady Godiva insisting on being her husband's equal in political matters. Leofric here is recast as a Saxon patriot rather than a heartless exploiter of the poor. Clint Eastwood, who was just beginning his acting career, has a small role in the film as "First Saxon."

REVIEWS: *Film Daily* 17 October 1955: 6. *Harrison's Reports* 8 October 1955: 163. *Hollywood Reporter* 7 October 1955: 3. *Kinematograph Weekly* 5 May 1955: 25. *Monthly Film Bulletin* 22 (June 1955): 90–91. *Motion Picture Herald* 15 October 1955: Product Digest Section 634. *New York Times* 3 December 1955: 13. *To-day's Cinema* 28 April 1955: 7. *Variety* 28 September 1955: 8.

ADDITIONAL DISCUSSION:
Nash, Jay Robert, and Stanley Ralph Ross. *The Motion Picture Guide, L–M, 1927–1983.* Chicago: Cinebooks, 1986.

Lady Godiva of Coventry (1955) see
Lady Godiva (1955)

294. *The Lady of Shallot* (1912)

Great Britain; dir. Elwin Neame; Hepworth.

CAST: Ivy Close.

In this film version of Tennyson's famous poem, Neame uses a mirror to create several trick illusions. This film was more faithful to its source ("The Lady of Shallot," first published in 1833 and subsequently extensively revised) than the 1915 cinematic version.

REVIEWS: *Bioscope* 17 October 1912: 171. *Kinematograph Monthly* October 1912: 65.

ADDITIONAL DISCUSSION:
Low, Rachel. *The History of the British Film 1906–1914.* London: George Allen & Unwin, 1949.

Rutger Hauer as Etienne of Navarre (left) and Matthew Broderick as the pickpocket Philippe Gaston in Richard Donner's *Ladyhawke* (1985).

295. *The Lady of Shallot* (1915)

United States; dir. C.J. Williams; Vitagraph.

CAST: Jay Dwiggins, Flora Finch, Kate Price, William Shea.

This film, loosely based on Tennyson's 1833 poem, was a comic vehicle for Finch in which she portrays a "romantic spinster."

REVIEW: *Moving Picture World* 10 April 1915: 233.

296. *Ladyhawke* (1985)

United States; dir. Richard Donner; 20th Century–Fox.

CAST: Matthew Broderick, Rutger Hauer, Ken Hutchison, Leo McKern, Michelle Pfeiffer, John Wood.

Prompted by jealousy and lust, the Bishop of Aquila curses Etienne of Navarre and the Lady Isabeau, who have fallen deeply in love. At night, he becomes a wolf; by day, she becomes a hawk. Etienne seeks a way back into the fortress of Aquila to kill the bishop and break the curse. He is aided in his attempt by a young pickpocket.

Set in thirteenth-century France, this medieval fairy tale is a visual treat, though architecturally the sets are more modern–faux medieval than genuinely Gothic or Romanesque.

REVIEWS: *Cinefantastique* 15 (July 1985): 49–50. *Cinéma* [Paris] 316 (April 1985): 46. *Cinema Papers* 52 (July 1985): 69–70. *Ecran fantastique* 55 (April 1985): 5. *Films and Filming* 370 (July 1985): 38. *Jeune cinéma* 167 (June 1985): 36–37. *Los Angeles Times* 12 April 1985: Calendar 1. *Monthly Film Bulletin* 52 (July 1985): 217. *New York Times* 12 April 1985: C5. *Positif* 293–94 (July-August 1986): 119. *Retro* 27 (June–November 1985): 4. *Séquences* 121 (July 1985): 33–35. *Segnocinema* 5 (May 1985): 62. *Sunday Times* [London] 11 August 1985: 39. *Times* [London] 9 August 1985: 13. *Variety* 3 April 1985: 14.

ADDITIONAL DISCUSSIONS:

Burns, James. "Ladyhawke." *Starburst* 81 (May 1985): 11–15.

Goldberg, Lee. "Ladyhawke: Entretien avec Richard Donner." *Ecran fantastique* 55 (April 1985): 30–35.

_____. "Richard Donner: Directing Is Believing."
    Starlog 93 (April 1985): 18–22.
_____. "Rutger Hauer, Knight Wolf to a *Lady-
    hawke.*" *Starlog* 95 (June 1985): 65–67.
Magill, Frank N., ed. *Magill's Cinema Annual 1986:
    A Survey of the Films of 1985.* Englewood Cliffs,
    N.J.: Salem, 1986.
Nash, Jay Robert, and Stanley Ralph Ross. *The Mo-
    tion Picture Guide, 1986 Annual (The Films of
    1985).* Chicago: Cinebooks, 1987.
Rabkin, William. "Lauren Schuler: Producing *La-
    dyhawke.*" *Starlog* 94 (May 1985): 36–40.
Strasser, Brendan. "Michelle Pfeiffer and Rutger
    Hauer: The Lovers of *Ladyhawke.*" *Prevue* 59
    (April-May 1985): 18–23
Thompson, Douglas. *Pfeiffer, Beyond the Age of In-
    nocence.* London: Smith Gryphon, 1993.
Weinberg, Marc. "Matthew Broderick: Tough Times
    with *Ladyhawke.*" *Starlog* 95 (June 1985): 68–69.

Lancelot and Elaine (1909) see *Laun-
celot and Elaine* (1909)

Lancelot and Guinevere (1963) see
The Sword of Lancelot (1963)

297. *Lancelot du lac* (1974)

France; dir. Robert Bresson; Mara Films.
ALTERNATE TITLE: *Lancelot of the Lake.*
CAST: Vladimir Antolek-Oresek, Humbert
Balsan, Laura Duke Condominas, Luc Simon.

Led by Lancelot, the Knights of the Round
Table return from their unsuccessful quest for
the Holy Grail. Lancelot swears to continue the
quest on his own and tells Guinevere that they
can no longer be lovers. Lancelot attempts one
final assignation with the Queen but changes
his mind at the last minute, thus foiling a plot
by Mordred to catch the two in the act of adultery. Instead, Lancelot attends a tournament in
disguise, but nonetheless distinguishes himself
by his skill. Lancelot is, however, wounded in
the last joust and rides off into the forest where
an old woman tends his wounds. Meanwhile,
Mordred has accused the Queen of adultery,
and Lancelot returns just in time to rescue her,
accidentally killing Gawain's brother Agravain.
Gawain swears revenge and is killed by Lancelot in battle. Guinevere insists on returning to
Arthur, and Lancelot returns her soon thereafter, riding at Arthur's side to put down a rebellion led by Mordred. Lancelot is killed in
that rebellion, the last word from his lips being
"Guinevere."

This moody film — generally either loved or
loathed by the critics — is Bresson's personal

meditation on the downfall of the Middle Ages.
The Grail itself is consciously absent from the
film, a symbol of the era's apocalyptic loss of a
sense of the spiritual. For the general outlines
of its plot, the film borrows extensively from
the *Mort Artu,* the final section of the thirteenth century prose Arthurian Vulgate Cycle.

REVIEWS: *Avant-scène du cinéma* 408–09 (January-February 1992): 102–08. *Cinefantastique* 4 (Summer 1975): 37. *Cinéma* [Paris] 190–91 (September-
October 1974): 273–75. *Cinema nuovo* 33
(September-October 1974): 366–68. *Ecran* 29 (October 1974): 57–59. *Empire* 65 (November 1994): 40.
Études [Paris] 341 (November 1974): 593–95. [Brit-
ish] *Federation* [of Film Societies] *News* 33 (December 1975): 5. *Film* 22 (January 1975): 3; 32 (December 1975): 4. *Film français* 1546 (6 September 1974):
14. *Film Review* [London] November 1994: 22. *Hollywood Reporter* 7 October 1974: 17. *Image et son* 285
(June-July 1974): 29; 291 (December 1974): 98–102;
292 (January 1975): 2–3. *Independent Film Journal*
75 (14 May 1975): 10. *Los Angeles Times* 26 August
1975: 4. 12. *Monthly Film Bulletin* 42 (September
1975): 199–200. *New York Times* 1 October 1974: 33;
5 June 1975: 50. *Positif* 162 (October 1974): 55–57;
163 (November 1974): 71–74. *Revue du cinéma* 291
(December 1974): 98–102. *Sight and Sound* 43 (Summer 1974): 128–30; NS4 (November 1994): 62. *Sunday Times* [London] 23 October 1994: 10. 54; 17 November 1974: 35; 4 January 1976: 36; 31 August 1975:
24; 7 September 1975: 36. *Thousand Eyes* 2 (March
1977): 7. *Times* [London] 20 October 1994: 37; 14 November 1974: 14; 5 September 1975: 7. *Variety* 12 June
1974: 24.

ADDITIONAL DISCUSSIONS:

Baby, Yvonne. "Metal Makes Sounds: An Interview
    with Robert Bresson." (Trans. Nora Jacobson.)
    Field of Vision 13 (Spring 1985): 4–5.
Bartone, Richard C. "Variations on Arthurian Leg-
    end in *Lancelot du lac* and *Excalibur.*" In Sally K.
    Slocum, ed. *Popular Arthurian Traditions.* Bowl-
    ing Green, Ohio: Bowling Green State University
    Popular Press, 1992.
Bertin-Maghit, Jean-Pierre. "De L'ecran à la classe:
    Lancelot du lac de Robert Bresson." *Pédagogie* 31
    (February 1976): 53–64.
Codell, Julie F. "Decapitation and Deconstruction:
    The Body of the Hero in Robert Bresson's
    Lancelot du lac." In Debra Mancoff, ed. *The
    Arthurian Revival, Essays on Form, Tradition, and
    Transformation.* New York: Garland, 1992.
Comuzio, Ermanno. "Robert Bresson, 'Lancillotto e
    Ginevra.'" *Cineforum* 134 (July 1974): 537–53.
Crotta, Bruno. "*Lancelot du lac:* La guerre, le simul-
    care de la vertu." *Camera/Stylo* 5 (January 1985):
    83–86.
Cugier, Alphonse. "'Lancelot du lac' de Robert Bres-
    son: Le Moyen Âge revisité ou la dimension trag-
    ique de xxᵉ siècle." *Les Cahiers de la cinémathèque*
    42–43 (Summer 1985): 119–24.

Laura Duke Condominas as Guinevere in Robert Bresson's *Lancelot du lac* (1974).

de la Bretèque, François. "Une 'Figure oblige' du film de chevalrie: le tournoi." *Cahiers de la cinémathèque* 42–43 (Summer 1985): 91–96.

Delmas, J. "*Lancelot du lac*: Robert Bresson et ses armures." *Jeune cinéma* 82 (November 1974): 19–24.

Dempsey, Michael. "Despair Abounding: The Recent Films of Robert Bresson." *Film Quarterly* 34 (Fall 1980): 2–15.

Estève, Michel. *Cinéma et condition humaine.* Paris: Albatros, 1978.

_____. *Robert Bresson.* Rev. ed. Paris: Seghers, 1974.

Hanlon, Lindley. *Fragments: Robert Bresson's Film Style.* Rutherford, N.J.: Fairleigh Dickinson University Press, 1986.

"*Lancelot du lac*, un film de Robert Bresson." *Avant-scène du cinéma* 155 (February 1975): 46–50.

Le Dantec, Mireille Latil. "Lancelot." *Cinématographe* 10 (November-December 1974): 38–42.

Margetts, John. "Robert Bressons 'Lancelot du lac': Monotonie und Depression." In Jürgen Kühnel at al., eds. *Mittelalter-Rezeption II.* Göppingen: Kümmerle, 1982.

Nash, Jay Robert, and Stanley Ralph Ross. *The Motion Picture Guide, L–M, 1927–1983.* Chicago: Cinebooks, 1986.

Paquette, Jean-Marcel. "La Dernière métamorphose de Lancelot." *Cahiers de la cinémathèque* 42–43 (Summer 1985): 113–18.

_____. "La Dernière métamorphose de Lancelot: Robert Bresson." In Ulrich Müller, et al., eds. *Lancelot.* Göppingen: Kümmerle, 1984.

Prédal, René. "Poétique de Robert Bresson: expression plastique et approche de l'indicible dans *Lancelot du lac.*" *Recherches et travaux* [Université Stendhal] 37 (1989): 103–16.

_____, et al. "Dossier: Robert Bresson." *Cinéma* [Paris] 294 (June 1983): 3–32.

Pruitt, John. "Robert Bresson's *Lancelot du lac.*" *Field of Vision* 13 (Spring 1985): 5–9.

Rider, Jeff, et al. "The Arthurian Legend in French Cinema: *Lancelot du Lac* and *Perceval le Gallois.*" In Kevin J. Harty, ed. *Cinema Arthuriana, Essays on Arthurian Film.* New York: Garland, 1981.

Sloan, Jane. *Robert Bresson, A Guide to References and Resources.* Boston: Hall, 1983.

Thomas, Nicholas, ed. *International Dictionary of Films and Filmmakers— Vol. 2: Directors.* 2nd ed. Chicago: St. James, 1991.

Tinazzi, Giorgio. "'Lancelot du lac': a proposito di Bresson." *Cinema e cinema* 2 (April–July 1975): 83–92.

Williams, Alan. "On the Absence of the Grail." *Movietone News* 47 (January 1976): 10–13.

Lancelot of the Lake (1974) see *Lancelot du lac* (1974)

298. *I Lancieri neri* (1961)

Italy and France; dir. Giacomo Gentilomo; Royal Films and France Cinéma.

ALTERNATE TITLES: *The Charge of the Black Lanciers* and *Les Lanciers noirs.*

CAST: Jean Claudio, Mel Ferrer, Yvonne Furneaux, Leticia Roman.

To celebrate his victory over the Kirghiz tribes, King Stephen holds a great tournament, planning to reward the victor with the hand of Princess Mascia. The favored victor is Duke Serghej, who wants not only the hand of the princess but Stephen's crown as well. When Mascia is kidnapped by the Kirghiz, Serghej rides to her rescue until he meets Yassa, the Queen of the Kirghiz. Smitten by Yassa and promised Stephen's crown as a reward, Serghej leads the Kirghiz troops against his homeland. Serghej is defeated by Stephen's forces under the command of his own brother Andrej, to whom Stephen now gives Mascia's hand in marriage.

This fairly standard CinemaScope costume epic relies more on action-packed adventure than on historical fact to inform its plot. The Turkic Moslem Kirghiz were a dominant power in Central Asia during the ninth and tenth centuries. In the early thirteenth century, they were conquered by Genghis Khan and his Mongolian hordes, who obliterated their ethnic identity. Stephen III of Moldavia (1457–1504)— variously known as the Great and the Athlete of Christ—defended his country and those of his neighbors against the encroachments of the Ottoman Turks.

REVIEWS: *Cinématographie française* 22 September 1962: 19. *La Fiera del cinema* 4 (March 1962): 58–59. *Daily Cinema* 27 November 1963: 8. *Kinematograph Weekly* 28 November 1963: 16. *Monthly Film Bulletin* 31 (January 1964): 9–10.

ADDITIONAL DISCUSSIONS:
Italian Film Production 1961. Rome: Unitalia Film, 1962.
Lucanio, Patrick. *With Fire and Sword, Italian Spectacles on American Screens 1958–1968.* Metuchen, N.J.: Scarecrow, 1994.

Poppi, Roberto, and Mario Pecorari. *Dizionario del cinema italiano. Vol. 3: I Film dal 1960 al 1969.* Rome: Gremese Editore, 1992.

Les Lanciers noirs (1961) see *I Lancieri neri* (1961)

299. *Landamann Stauffacher* (1941)

Switzerland; dir. Leopold Lindtberg; Praesens Film.

CAST: Cesar Alemanni, Anne-Marie Blanc, Heinrich Gretler, Fred Tanner, Robert Troesch, Ellen Widmann.

Thanks to Habsburg protection and patronage, the Abbey of Einsiedeln has grown rich and prosperous at the expense of the Swiss peasantry. Under the leadership of Heinrich von Stauffacher, the Swiss invade the abbey, pillage its riches and imprison its monks. In retaliation, the Habsburg Duke Leopold attacks the Swiss, who ambush his army at Morgarten Pass. Leopold manages to escape with his life, but his defeat ensures Swiss independence from the Habsburgs.

Presenting a historical parallel to the legend of the quasi-historical William Tell and his role in establishing Swiss independence from Austria, this film could not avoid having yet another political subtext in 1941 with Nazi troops massed along neutral Switzerland's borders. At the beginning of the fourteenth century, Habsburg plans to expand the family's empire suffered a major setback thanks to the defeat of Duke Leopold by the Swiss at Morgarten Pass. According to *Das weisse Buch von Sarnen* (c. 1470), one of the oldest Swiss historical documents, among the leaders of the Swiss in battle at Morgarten Pass was Rudolf or Werner von Stauffacher, one of the canton representatives or Landamänner.

ADDITIONAL DISCUSSIONS:
Dumont, Hervé. *Histoire du cinéma suisse.* Lausanne: Cinémathèque suisse, 1987.
_____. "Leopold Lindtberg et le cinéma suisse 1935–1953." *Travelling* 44–46 (Autumn 1975): 110–27.

300. *The Last King of Wales* (1922)

Great Britain; dir. George Ridgwell; Universal Films.

CAST: Charles Ashton, Malvine Longfellow, Cynthia Murtaugh.

After long battling the English under Edward I, Llywelyn ap Gruffydd concludes a truce that allows him to marry his fiancée, Eleanor de Montfort, with the king's blessing.

Llywelyn ap Gruffydd was the last Welsh noble to hold the title of Prince of Wales. His death in a minor skirmish in 1282 ended the Welsh rebellion against English rule and cemented Edward's control of the kingdom.

ADDITIONAL DISCUSSION:

Gifford, Denis. *The British Film Catalogue 1895–1985.* Newton Abbot: David & Charles, 1986.

301. *The Last of the Saxons* (1910)

United States; dir. J. Stuart Blackton; Vitagraph.

CAST: William Humphries, Clara K. Young, James Young.

Harold of Wessex is betrothed to Lady Edith and takes her to meet his mother when news arrives of the death of King Edward. Even though William of Normandy was promised right of succession, Harold seizes the throne. To strengthen his claim, he decides to break his engagement to Edith and marry Princess Ealdgyth. Edith never stops loving Harold, and when he is killed during the Battle of Senlac near Hastings, she joins the search for his body. Spying the corpse of her beloved, she dies of a broken heart.

Critics reacted favorably to the pageantry of this film, which seems more interested in telling a love story than in rehearsing English history. Edith Swan-neck, the mother of Harold's five children, did, however, discover Harold's body among the dead at Senlac.

REVIEWS: *Bioscope* 12 January 1911: 36. *Motion Picture News* 15 October 1910: 8–9; 5 November 1910: 16. *Moving Picture World* 8 October 1910: 824.

ADDITIONAL DISCUSSIONS:

Savada, Elias. *The American Film Institute Catalog of Motion Pictures Produced in the United States: Film Beginnings, 1893–1910.* Metuchen, N.J.: Scarecrow, 1995.

Usai, Paolo Cherchi, ed. *Vitagraph Co. of America.* Pordenone: Edizioni Studio Tesi, 1987.

302. *The Last of the Vikings* (1960)

Italy and France; dir. Giacomo Gentilomo; Tiberius-Galatea-Cyclope-Criterion Films.

ALTERNATE TITLE: *L'Ultimo dei vikinghi.*

CAST: Isabelle Corey, Cameron Mitchell, Edmond Purdom, Helen Remy.

Prince Harold returns to his home at Viken to discover that King Sven of Norway has murdered his father. Sven is also intent upon forcing Hilde, Harold's half-sister, to marry the King of Denmark to allow him to control all of Scandinavia. Harold and a band of loyal Vikings slip into the Danish palace, but they are discovered. Barely escaping with their lives, they return with a Viking army which defeats Sven's forces, rescues Hilde and restores peace to Viken.

Critics rightly agreed that this costume melodrama was simply boring.

REVIEWS: *Daily Cinema* 19 March 1962: 5. *Film Daily* 8 May 1962: 6. *Filmfacts* 5 (21 September 1962): 205. *Film française* 18 (22 September 1961): 31. *Kinematograph Weekly* 22 March 1962: 10. *Monthly Film Bulletin* 29 (May 1962): 70. *New York Times* 27 September 1962: 33. *Video Watchdog* 23 (May–June 1994): 22–23.

ADDITIONAL DISCUSSIONS:

Italian Production 1960. Rome: Unitalia Film, 1961.

Lucanio, Patrick. *With Fire and Sword, Italian Spectacles on American Screens 1958–1968.* Metuchen, N.J.: Scarecrow, 1994.

Nash, Jay Robert, and Stanley Ralph Ross. *The Motion Picture Guide, L–M, 1927–1983.* Chicago: Cinebooks, 1986.

Poppi, Roberto, and Mario Pecorari. *Dizionario del cinema italiano. Vol. 3: I Film dal 1960 al 1969.* Rome: Gremese Editore, 1992.

Smith, Gary A. *Epic Films.* Jefferson, N.C.: McFarland, 1991.

303. *Launcelot and Elaine* (1909)

United States; dir. Charles Kent; Vitagraph.

ALTERNATE TITLE: *Lancelot and Elaine.*

CAST: W. Blackton, Leo Delaney, Charles Kent, Paul Panzer, Florence Turner.

King Arthur declares a tournament, but the queen feigns illness. Launcelot then announces he will not compete, hoping that he can meet secretly with the queen during the tournament. However, the queen orders him to compete incognito, so he borrows a shield from the castle of Astolot, agreeing also to wear the sleeve of Lady Elaine in the tournament. When Launcelot is seriously wounded in the tournament and carried from the field to a hermit's cave for healing, Elaine arrives to nurse him back to health. Launcelot declares his love for the queen, and Elaine dies of a broken heart after penning the story of her unrequited love for Launcelot. When news of her death and its cause reach Arthur's court, Elaine is given a solemn burial. The queen places flowers on her bier, and Launcelot keeps nightly vigil by her body to atone for his sins.

Based on Tennyson's poem "Elaine," which was first published in *Idylls of the King* (1859), this film was critically well received because of its pageantry and the skill with which it told a love story.

REVIEWS: *Bioscope* 27 January 1910: 53; 15 January 1914: supplement xxxi. *Moving Picture World* 23 October 1909: 565; 27 November 1909: 759; 27 November 1909: 773. *New York Dramatic Mirror* 20 November 1909: 16.

ADDITIONAL DISCUSSIONS:
"Launcelot and Elaine." *Vitagraph Bulletin* 1–15 November 1909: n.p. [film 949].
"Notes of the Trade." *Moving Picture World* 25 September 1909: 409.
Savada, Elias. *The American Film Institute Catalog of Motion Pictures Produced in the United States: Film Beginnings, 1893–1910.* Metuchen, N.J.: Scarecrow, 1995.

304. *Layla, ma raison* (1989)

Tunisia and Algeria; dir. Taieb Louchichi; Productions Tanit.

ALTERNATE TITLES: *Mágnún and Layla* and *Mágnún et Layla.*

In the seventh century, the young poet Qays and Layla fall in love. Contrary to custom, and to the consternation of Layla's family, Qays openly declares their love in his poetry. Forbidden further contact with Layla, Qays at first declares his love even more often, but soon he is driven to insanity by his grief and flees to the desert where he becomes a mágnún, a madman. An attempted reconciliation between the two fails and Layla is forcibly married off to another. Qays remains a madman in the desert. Both eventually die, unable to live without each other.

Based on the 1984 novel *Layla, ma raison* by André Miquel, this film tells a familiar story of star-crossed lovers separated by their families.

REVIEW: *Variety* 27 September 1989: 36.

The Legend of Gawain and the Green Knight (1983) see *Sword of the Valiant* (1983)

The Legend of Genoveffa (1951) see *La Leggenda di Genoveffa* (1951)

305. *The Legend of Robin Hood* (1968)

United States; dir. Alan Handley; NBC.

CAST: Lee Berry, Victor Buono, Douglas Fairbanks, Jr., Steve Forrest, Noel Harrison, Roddy McDowall, Walter Slezak, David Watson, Bruce Yarnell.

In this television special, the adventures of Robin and his Merry Men are set to music with disastrous results.

REVIEWS: *New York Times* 19 February 1968: 79. *Variety* 21 February 1968: 42.

ADDITIONAL DISCUSSIONS:
Messina, Matt. "Schooling Rang Bell for *Robin Hood.*" *Sunday News* [New York] 18 February 1968: S28.
Windeler, Robert. "Noel Harrison Knows He Can't Go Home Again." *New York Times* 18 February 1968: D21.

306. *The Legend of Robin Hood* (1971)

Australia: Zoran Janjic; Air Programs International.

CAST: (the voices of) Tim Elliott, Peter Guest, Ron Haddrick, John Kingley, John Llewellyn, Helen Morse, Brenda Senders.

This fairly pedestrian animated retelling of the standard incidents in the legend of Robin Hood, which aired in the United States on CBS, is surprisingly thin on action.

REVIEW: *Variety* 17 November 1971: 70.

307. *The Legend of Suram Fortress* (1984)

Soviet Union; dir. Sergei Paradzhanov and Dodo Abashidze; Georgianfilm Studio.

ALTERNATE TITLE: *Legenda suramskoi kreposti.*

CAST: Dodo Abashidze, Lela Alibegashvili, Sofiko Chiarureli, Zurab Kipshidze, Levan Uchaneishvili.

To defend their native Georgia from foreign invaders, the people of Suram build a great fortress, but each time it is nearly completed the walls collapse under their own weight. A fortune-teller predicts that the fortress will only stand when the "most handsome of young men" is bricked up inside. A young man arrives and agrees to have the fortress become his tomb. The fortress is erected and the motherland, inspired by his selfless sacrifice, is protected.

Paradzhanov was ever a thorn in the side of the Soviet authorities, and this film, like his others, did nothing to endear him to the Communist Party. Based on a medieval Georgian legend, the film's implications are clearly modern.

REVIEWS: *Les Cahiers du cinéma* 390 (December 1986): 10–15. *Cinéma* [Paris] 379 (3 December

Zurab Kipshidze as the unnamed king in Sergei Paradzhanov's *The Legend of Suram Fortress* (1984). (Still courtesy of the British Film Institute.)

1986): 5. *Cinématographe* 124 (November 1986): 60.
EPD Film 4 (August 1987): 39. *Films and Filming* 386
(November 1986): 38. *Iskusstvo kino* 5 (May 1987):
54–67. *Listener* 18 October 1990: 37. *Los Angeles
Times* 12 March 1987: Calendar 1. *Monthly Film Bulletin* 53 (November 1986): 337–39, 356. *New York
Times* 18 February 1987: C18. *Positif* 310 (December
1986): 47–48. *Soviet Film* 11 (1986): 12–15. *Variety* 24
July 1985: 17.

ADDITIONAL DISCUSSIONS:
Alekseychuk, Leonid. "A Warrior in the Field." *Sight
and Sound* 60 (Winter 1990-1991): 20–26.
Galichenko, Nicholas. *Glasnost— Soviet Cinema Responds.* Austin: University of Texas Press, 1991.
Nash, Jay Robert, and Stanley Ralph Ross. *The Motion Picture Guide, 1986 Annual (The Films of
1985).* Chicago: Cinebooks, 1987.
Payne, Robert. "The Storm of the Eye: Culture, Spectacle, Paradzhanov." *Spectator* [University of
Southern California] 10 (Fall 1989): 32–45.
Radvanyi, Jean. *Le Cinéma georgien.* Paris: Centre
Georges Pompidou, 1988.
Stanbrook, Alan. "The Return of Paradjanov." *Sight
and Sound* 55 (Autumn 1986): 257–60.
Thomas, Nicholas. *International Directory of Films
and Filmakers— Vol. 2. Directors.* 2nd ed. Chicago: St. James, 1991.
Tous les films 1986. Paris: Éditions Chrétiens-Médias,
1987.
Vartanov, Michael. "Les Cîmes du monde: entretien
avec Serguei Paradjanov." *Cahiers du cinéma* 381
(March 1986): 43–47.

The Legend of the Golden Prince
(1970) see *Ruslan i Lyudmila* (1970)

The Legend of the Good Knight (1909)
see *La Legende du bon chevalier* (1909)

Legend of William Tell (1933) see *Wilhelm Tell* (1933)

Legenda suramskoi kreposti (1984)
see *The Legend of Suram Fortress* (1984)

308. La Legende du bon chevalier
(1909)
France; Eclair.
ALTERNATE TITLE: *The Legend of the Good
Knight.*
CAST: Harry Baur.
A knight comes to the rescue of a young
queen after she is kidnapped by two evil lords
who plan to kill her and seize her kingdom.
This film garnered praise for the quality of
its photography, especially in interior scenes.

REVIEW: *Moving Picture World* 11 December
1909: 842.
ADDITIONAL DISCUSSION:
Savada, Elias. *The American Film Institute Catalog of
Motion Pictures Produced in the United States:
Film Beginnings, 1893–1910.* Metuchen, N.J.:
Scarecrow, 1995.

La Leggenda di Faust (1949) see *Faust
and the Devil* (1949)

309. La Leggenda di Genoveffa (1951)
Italy; dir. Arthur Maria Rabenalt; Produzione Venturini.
ALTERNATE TITLE: *The Legend of Genoveffa*
and *The Mistress of Treves.*
CAST: Rossano Brazzi, Gianni Santucci,
Ann Vernon.
Count Siegfried goes off to the Crusades
leaving his estates and his wife Genevieve in
the care of his servant Golo. Golo, long in love
with his mistress, intercepts letters between his
master and mistress and tricks Siegfried into
ordering Genevieve's execution for adultery.
Genevieve is led into the forest for execution,
but a sudden storm frightens her would-be executioners, who leave her to die exposed to the
elements. Years pass, and Siegfried returns to
find his kingdom in ruin because of Golo's idleness and debauchery. Golo commits suicide
rather than face his master's wrath and Siegfried goes in search of his wife, with whom he
is finally reunited.
This film is yet another retelling of the apocryphal legend of Geneviève de Brabant. The
immediate source here is Jacques Offenbach's
opéra-bouffe, *Geneviève de Brabant* (1859).

REVIEWS: *Kinematograph Weekly* 26 February
1953: 28. *Monthly Film Bulletin* 20 (April 1953): 55.
To-day's Cinema 19 February 1953: 12.
ADDITIONAL DISCUSSIONS:
Chiti, Roberto, and Roberto Poppi. *Dizionario del
cinema italiano. Vol. 2: I Film dal 1945 al 1959.*
Rome: Gremese Editore, 1991.
Italian Production 1951–52. Rome: Unitalia Film,
1952.

Licentious Tales of Lusting Virgins
(1972) see *Novelle licenziose di vergini
vogliose* (1972)

The Life of a Nun (1911) see *Nonnen fra
Asminderød* (1911)

Katharine Hepburn as Queen Eleanor and Peter O'Toole as King Henry in Anthony Harvey's *The Lion in Winter* (1968).

310. *The Life of Dante* (1913)

Italy; dir. Mario Caserini; Ambrosio.

ALTERNATE TITLE: *Dante e Beatrice.*

The poet Dante finds himself caught up in the politics of his day. Exiled from his native Florence, he finds a friend in the painter Giotto. Citizen, statesman, soldier and writer, he leaves his mark on his own time and a legacy for ours.

This biography of the poet presents a wealth of information about his literary endeavors as well as about his life.

REVIEW: *Moving Picture World* 22 March 1913: 1202.

ADDITIONAL DISCUSSION:
Prolo, Maria Adriana. *Storia del cinema muto italiano.* Milan: Poligono Società Editrice, 1951.

311. *The Life of St. Patrick* (1912)

United States; dir. J. Theobald Walsh; Photo-Historic Film Company.

Patrick arrives back in Ireland (where he had previously been a slave) and banishes all the reptiles from the island kingdom. He then converts the Irish to Christianity and dies surrounded by angels.

This example of cinematic hagiography was advertised as having the blessing of the Catholic Church and as being suitable for all, regardless of their religion, because of the inspirational story it told.

REVIEWS: *Bioscope* 11 July 1912: 91. *Moving Picture World* 25 October 1913: 390.

312. *The Lion in Winter* (1968)

Great Britain; dir. Anthony Harvey; Avco Embassy.

CAST: John Castle, Timothy Dalton, Katharine Hepburn, Anthony Hopkins, Jane Merrow, Peter O'Toole, Nigel Stock, Nigel Terry.

Henry II summons Queen Eleanor, their three sons, his mistress and her brother, the King of France, to a Christmas gathering to settle the question of who will succeed Henry to the throne. What follows is a battle royal among all those present as each tries to out-scheme the other.

From James Goldman's 1966 play *The Lion in Winter,* this film allowed Hepburn and O'Toole, who had played a younger Henry in the 1964 film *Becket,* the opportunity to deliver bravura performances (Hepburn earned her third Oscar as Best Actress). While the film takes liberties with historical fact, it is a feast for the eyes — and ears.

REVIEWS: *Cinema* [United States] 4 (Fall 1968): 27; 4 (December 1968): 34–35. *Film Daily* 18 October 1968: 3. *Filmfacts* 11 (15 November 1968): 315–17. *Films and Filming* 15 (March 1969): 52–54. *Films in Reviews* 19 (November 1968): 579–80. *Hollywood Reporter* 18 October 1968: 3. *Kinematograph Weekly* 4 January 1969: 12, 20. *Monthly Film Bulletin* 36 (March 1969): 49–50. *Motion Picture Herald* 23 October 1968: Product Digest Section 43. *New York Times* 31 October 1968: 54. *Sight and Sound* 38 (Winter 1968-1969): 44. *Take One* 1 (July-August 1968): 22–24. *Times* [London] 1 January 1969: 13. *To-day's Cinema* 3 January 1969: 6. *Variety* 23 October 1968: 6.

ADDITIONAL DISCUSSIONS:
Dickens, Homer. *The Films of Katharine Hepburn.* New York: Citadel, 1971.
Falk, Quentin. *Anthony Hopkins, Too Good to Waste.* London: Columbus, 1989.
Goldman, James. *The Lion in Winter.* In Sam Thomas, ed. *Best American Screenplays 2.* New York: Crown, 1990.
Magill, Frank N., ed. *Magill's Survey of Cinema: English Language Films.* Second Series. Englewood Cliffs, N.J.: Salem, 1981.
Nash, Jay Robert, and Stanley Ralph Ross. *The Motion Picture Guide, L–M, 1927–1983.* Chicago: Cinebooks, 1986.
Sragow, Michael. "*Becket* and *The Lion in Winter.*" *Film Society Review* 5 (December 1969): 36–43.

313. *Lionheart* (1987)

United States; dir. Franklin Schaffner; Taliafilm II.

CAST: Gabriel Byrne, Nicholas Clay, Nicola Cowper, Neil Dickson, Dexter Fletcher, Eric Stoltz.

Rather than join King Richard the Lion-hearted on Crusade, young nobleman Robert Nerra chooses to do battle with one of his neighbors over property rights. During the fray, Robert panics and runs away. Wandering the countryside in disgrace, he is mistaken for a brave Crusader by a ragtag group of children who seek his protection from the Black Prince, a rogue Crusader who sells Christian children to the Saracens as slaves. The Black Prince vows to kill Robert and sets a trap which Robert and his children fall into. Robert and the Black Prince fight, and Robert wins as King Richard appears. Robert now joins the King on Crusade.

The first of a projected Crusade trilogy cut short by Schaffner's death, this film readily sacrifices historical accuracy. The so-called

Eric Stolz as Robert Nerra rallies a troop of children to join him on crusade in Franklin Schaffner's *Lionheart* (1987).

Children's Crusade of 1212 hardly ended on the happy note that the crusade in this film does. Schaffner's directing credits also include the 1965 film *The War Lord*, another medieval epic that is pleasant enough to watch but which also plays fast and loose with fact, and the 1952 telefilm of Twain's *Connecticut Yankee*.

REVIEWS: *Soundtrack* 7 (March 1988): 14–15. *Variety* 26 August 1987: 15.

ADDITONAL DISCUSSIONS:

The Motion Picture Guide: 1991 Annual (The Films of 1990). New York: Baseline, 1991.

Nash, Jay Robert, and Stanley Ralph Ross. *The Motion Picture Guide, 1988 Annual (The Films of 1987)*. Chicago: Cinebooks, 1988.

314. *The Little Princes in the Tower* (1909)

France; Pathé.

Richard, Duke of Gloucester, will stop at nothing, including the murder of his two nephews, to secure the throne of England for himself.

The tale here presented is best known through Shakespeare's *Richard III*. The film itself is impressive in every detail except the cos-tumes. The two princes look more like pau-pers.

REVIEW: *Bioscope* 18 November 1909: 43.

315. *The Little Princess's Christmas Gift* (1911)

Great Britain; Urban Trading Company.

On his deathbed, King Othberg appoints his infant son his heir and his brother, Count Otto, regent. Otto poisons his nephew. The boy's sister prays that, as a Christmas gift, her brother may be restored to life. An angel appears and leads the boy from his tomb to Otto's corona-tion. The uncle's treachery is exposed, and the boy is proclaimed king.

REVIEWS: *Bioscope* 23 November 1911: 587–88; 21 December 1911: supplement v.

316. *Lochinvar* (1909)

United States; Edison.

Lochinvar falls in love with Ellen, who is betrothed against her will to Douglas. Lochin-var attends the wedding festivities and is granted a last dance with Ellen. He seizes a sword and takes Ellen in his arms. The two ride off and are married.

Sidney Poitier (left) as El Mansuh and Richard Widmark as Rolfe in Jack Cardiff's *The Long Ships* (1963).

The film's source is Sir Walter Scott's poem "Lochinvar," which was first published as part of *Marmion* in 1808.

REVIEWS: *Bioscope* 30 September 1909: 33. *Edison Kinetogram* 6 August 1909: Film 6495. *Moving Picture World* 31 July 1909: 173; 7 August 1909: 203; 21 August 1909: 254. *New York Dramatic Mirror* 14 August 1909: 15.

ADDITIONAL DISCUSSION:
Savada, Elias. *The American Film Institute Catalog of Motion Pictures Produced in the United States: Film Beginnings, 1893–1910.* Metuchen, N.J.: Scarecrow, 1995.

317. *Lochinvar* (1911)
United States; Thanhouser.

The fair Ellen is forced into a marriage with a man known only as "the laggard in war and dastard in love." Lochinvar rescues her, and the two are married.

From the 1808 poem "Lochinvar" by Sir

Walter Scott, this film version's twist is to follow Scott's lead and deny the would-be husband a name, since he is so despicable.

REVIEWS: *Moving Picture World* 23 September 1911: 908; 7 October 1911: 43.

318. *Lochinvar* (1915)
Great Britain; dir. Leslie Seldon-Truss; Gaumont.

CAST: Peggy Hyland, Godfrey Tearle.

Lochinvar saves the fair Ellen from a forced marriage to a cruel lord. The source here again is the 1808 poem "Lochinvar" by Sir Walter Scott.

REVIEW: *Kinematograph Monthly Record* 42 (October 1915): 97–98.

319. *The Long Ships* (1963)
Great Britain; dir. Jack Cardiff; Avala Films–Warwick Film Productions.

CAST: Oscar Homolka, Lionel Jeffries, Sidney Poitier, Rosanna Schiaffino, Russ Tamblyn, Richard Widmark.

Rolfe, a Viking warlord and shipbuilder, sails forth to find the Golden Bell of St. James, but his ship is wrecked in a vortex, and he and his crew are taken prisoners by El Mansuh, a leader of the Moors who also seeks the bell. El Mansuh forces Rolfe to lead him through the vortex to retrieve the bell. Rolfe's father King Harald and his army intercept the Moors. The Vikings take the bell and kill El Mansuh, as Rolfe sails off to seek yet another treasure.

After the fact, everyone associated with this film, based on the 1941 novel *Rode Orm* by Frans Bengtsson, rightly agreed that it was a disaster and an embarrassment.

REVIEWS: *Daily Cinema* 26 June 1963: 14–15. *Film Daily* 11 June 1964: 4. *Hollywood Reporter* 29 May 1964: 3. *Kinematograph Weekly* 27 February 1964: 10–11. *Monthly Film Bulletin* 31 (April 1964): 57–58. *Motion Picture Herald* 24 June 1964: 73. *Movieline* 7 (April 1991): 76. *New York Times* 25 June 1964: 25. *Variety* 11 March 1964: 6.

ADDITIONAL DISCUSSIONS:

Carr, Robert E., and R.M. Hayes. *Wide Screen Movies*. Jefferson, N.C.: McFarland, 1988.

Guez, Gilbert. "Héros sauvages." *Cinémonde* 4 June 1963: 7–9.

Holston, Kim. *Richard Widmark, A Bio-Bibliography*. New York: Greenwood, 1990.

Keyser, Lester J., and André H. Ruszkowski. *The Cinema of Sidney Poitier*. San Diego: A.S. Barnes, 1980.

Klotman, Phyllis Rauch. *Frame by Frame—A Black Filmography*. Bloomington: Indiana University Press, 1979.

Lucanio, Patrick. *With Fire and Sword, Italian Spectacles on American Screens 1958–1968*. Metuchen, N.J.: Scarecrow, 1994.

Marill, Alvin H. *The Films of Sidney Poitier*. Secaucus, N.J.: Citadel, 1978.

Nash, Jay Robert, and Stanley Ralph Ross. *The Motion Picture Guide, L–M, 1927–1983*. Chicago: Cinebooks, 1986.

The Long Swift Sword of Siegfried (1971) see The Erotic Adventures of Siegfried (1971)

Louis XI (1909) see Luigi XI, re di Francia (1909)

320. Love Boccaccio Style (1977)

United States; dir. Sam Phillips; Sophisticated Films.

CAST: Lindis Guinness, Vincent Hall, Patti Lee, Eastman Price.

To pass the time as they flee the plague, a group of Florentines entertain each other by telling stories, each relentlessly phallic.

This codpiece comedy is typical of the Italian sequels to Passolini's 1971 film *The Decameron*, only it was made in America, proving bad taste knows no national boundaries.

REVIEW: *Monthly Film Bulletin* 48 (December 1981): 250.

Love Games in the Convent (1973) see Fratello homo, sorella bona— nel Boccaccio superproibito (1973)

Love, Passion, and Pleasure (1972) see Beffe, licenzie e amori del Decamerone segreto (1972)

321. Love's Crucible (1922)

Sweden; dir. Victor Sjöström; Svensk Filmindustri.

ALTERNATE TITLES: *Mortal Clay* and *Vem Dömer?*

CAST: Gösta Ekman, Jenny Hasselqvist, Ivan Hedqvist, Tore Svennberg.

In medieval Florence, the sculptor Anton marries a young woman, Ursula, who does not love him and wishes him dead. Ursula purchases some poison to put into her husband's drink, but a wandering monk substitutes a harmless powder for the potion. When Anton dies of a heart attack, his widow is accused of murder, but she is acquitted after a trial by fire.

Unfairly overlooked or ignored, this film is one of Sjöström's masterpieces. When he moved to Hollywood in 1923, the director changed his surname to Seastrom.

REVIEWS: *Monthly Film Bulletin* 46 (January 1978): 15. *Variety* 30 June 1922: 33.

ADDITIONAL DISCUSSIONS:

Cowie, Peter. *Swedish Cinema*. London: A. Zwemmer, 1966.

Forslund, Bengt. *Victor Sjöström*. Trans. Peter Cowie. New York: Zoetrope, 1988.

Hardy, Forsyth. *Scandinavian Film*. London: Falcon, 1952.

Patterson, Frances Taylor. "The Swedish Photoplays." *Exceptional Photoplays* 3 (December 1922): 3–4.

Pensel, Hans. *Seastrom and Stiller in Hollywood*. New York: Vantage, 1969.

Petrie, Graham. *Hollywood Destinies*. London: Routledge & Kegan Paul, 1985.

Svensk Filmografi 2: 1920–1929. Stockholm: Svenska Filminstitutet, 1982.

Lovespell (1979) see *Tristan and Isolt* (1979)

Ludwig XI (1909) see *Luigi XI, re di Francia* (1909)

322. *Luigi XI, re di Francia* (1909)

Italy; dir. Luigi Maggi; Ambrosio.

ALTERNATE TITLES: *Louis XI* and *Ludwig XI.*

CAST: Mario Voller Buzzi, Albert Capozzi, Lydia de Roberti, Luigi Maggi, Mirra Principi, Maria Cleo Tarlarini.

Displeased with the actions of the Duke of Nemours, Louis orders his arrest and execution. The son of the duke tries unsuccessfully to protect his father, going so far as to challenge the king to a duel. The king escapes but soon has a seizure and dies.

Louis XI, who reigned from 1461 until 1483, is remembered as a harsh and unloved ruler, but he left France a much more powerful nation at his death than it had been when he ascended to the throne. For a later film telling the same story about Louis XI, see *La Fin de Louis XI* (1912). The same storyline also appears in *La Vengeance du Prince Visconti* (1912), although the monarch in that film is Ludovico the Moor, Duke of Milan, not Louis XI.

ADDITIONAL DISCUSSIONS:

Bernardini, Aldo, and Jean A. Gili, eds. *Le Cinéma italien de La Prise de Rome (1905) à Rome ville ouverte (1945).* Paris: Centre Georges Pompidou, 1986.

Prolo, Maria Adriana. *Storia del cinema muto italiano.* Milan: Poligono Società Editrice, 1951.

Savada, Elias. *The American Film Institute Catalog of Motion Pictures Produced in the United States: Film Beginnings, 1893–1910.* Metuchen, N.J.: Scarecrow, 1995.

Weinberg, Herman G., ed. *Fifty Years of Italian Cinema.* Rome: Carlo Bestetti-Edizioni d'arte, 1955.

323. *Lusty Wives of Canterbury* (1972)

Italy; dir. Lucio Dandolo; C.G./Cinecenta.

ALTERNATE TITLE: *I Racconti di Canterbury Nr. 2.*

CAST: Mario Brega, Claudia Bianchi, Fortunato Cecilia, Dada Gallotti, Riki Marie Odile.

In a brothel, the young ladies interrupt their love-making to tell six tales of even more amorous activities.

In this, yet another codpiece comedy with just the right amount of nudity to escape being labeled hard-core, husbands are cuckolded and clerics are baited.

REVIEW: *CinemaTV Today* 7 January 1974: 9. *Monthly Film Bulletin* 41 (February 1974): 33.

324. *Das Mädchen Johanna* (1935)

Germany; dir. Gustav Ucicky; UFA.

CAST: Willy Birgel, René Detlgen, Heinrich George, Gustaf Gründgens, Veit Harlan, Theodor Loos, Erich Ponto, Angela Salloker, Aribert Wäscher.

English forces under Lord Talbot, allied with those of the Duke of Burgundy, are about to take the city of Orléans, which has endured a long siege. A young woman named Joan appears before the Dauphin, who is shut up in the city. She rallies the French forces and defeats the English. The Dauphin is crowned in Reims, and the Duke of Burgundy rallies to the French cause. The newly crowned king realizes that Joan is of more value to him as a martyr than a military commander, and he allows her to be tried and executed by the English. Years later, she is vindicated, and the king claims Joan as his and the nation's own.

This slick piece of Nazi propaganda, whose screenplay may or may not have been partially the work of Goebbels, plays fast and loose with the legend of Joan of Arc. The film's hero is the Dauphin, a wily politician intent on reclaiming lands that have been lost to a traditional enemy in a recent war — read Hitler and Lorraine here. The film's closing scene shows dirndl-clad young women with braided blonde hair laying flowers at the site of Joan's death as they also lay claim to her legacy. While the French press ignored the film, the Nazi press — not surprisingly — gushed over it. Astonishingly, the American and British press seemed to find no political subtext to the film, which they generally reviewed positively.

REVIEWS: *Der Angriff* 27 April 1935: 5. *Berliner Morgen Post* 27 April 1935: n.p.; 28 April 1935: n.p. *Berliner Tageblatt* 27 April 1935: n.p. *Deutsche Allgemeine Zeitung* 25 April 1935: n.p. *Der Film* 27 April 1935: n.p. *Film Weekly* 18 October 1935: 33. *Filmwelt* 11 (17 March 1935): 3–5; 14 (7 April 1935): 3–5; 17 (28 April 1935): 5–7. *Kinematograph Weekly* 10 October 1935: 34. *Kreuz-Zeitung* 28 April 1935: 15. *Life and Letters To-day* 13 (December 1935): 185–86. *Monthly Film Bulletin* 2 (October 1935): 147. *New York Times* 9 October 1935: 27. *Sight and Sound* 4

Angela Salloker as Joan of Arc in *Das Mädchen Johanna* (1935).

(Winter 1935-1936): 176. *Spectator* 115 (25 October 1935): 663.

ADDITIONAL DISCUSSIONS:

Blaetz, Robin J. "Strategies of Containment: Joan of Arc on Film." Ph.D. dissertation. New York University, 1989.

Harty, Kevin J. "Jeanne au cinéma." In Bonnie Wheeler and Charles T. Wood, eds. *Fresh Verdicts of Joan of Arc*. New York: Garland, 1996.

_____. "The Nazis, Joan of Arc, and Medievalism Gone Awry: Gustav Ucicky's 1935 Film *Das Mädchen Johanna*." In [the Centenary College Department of English, ed.] *Rationality and the Liberal Spirit, A Festschrift Honoring Ira Lee Morgan*. Shreveport: Centenary Publications, 1997.

Kanzog, Klaus. *Staatspolitsch Besonders Wertvoll: Ein Handbuch zu 30 Deutschen Spielfilmen der Jahre 1934 bis 1945*. Munich: Münchner Beträge zur Filmphilologie, 1994.

Margolis, Nadia. *Joan of Arc in History, Literature, and Film*. New York: Garland, 1990.

"A New Saint Joan." *The Sphere* [London] 25 May 1935: 350.

Steinberg, Heniz. "*Das Mädchen Johanna*, de Gustav Uciky [sic] ou Joanne et Goebbels." *Études cinématographiques* 18–19 (Autumn 1962): 53–57.

Il Maestro di Don Giovanni (1953) see *Crossed Swords* (1953)

325. *The Magic Sword; or, A Mediaeval Mystery* (1901)

Great Britain; dir. W.R. Booth; Robert W. Paul Animatograph Works.

ALTERNATE TITLE: *The Magical Sword*.

A knight and his lady meet at midnight on the battlements of a castle. A ghost and a witch appear, and both of them elude the knight when he tries to grab them. An ogre, at least 15 feet tall, reaches over the battlements and seizes the lady. The knight sinks into the depths of despair but a good fairy comes to his aid, giving him a flaming sword with which to search for the lady. The battlements fade into a cavern where the knight encounters the ogre and the witch, defeats them and reclaims his beloved.

For its time, this short film is a marvel of trick photography in which the Robert Paul Company was a pioneer. The company later reworked the plot of this film and rereleased it in 1907 as *A Knight Errant*.

DISCUSSIONS:

Catalogue of Paul's Animatographs & Films. London: Robert W. Paul, 1901.

Savada, Elias. *The American Film Institute Catalog of Motion Pictures Produced in the United States: Film Beginnings, 1893–1910*. Metuchen, N.J.: Scarecrow, 1995.

Talbot, Frederick A. *Moving Pictures*. Philadelphia: Lippincott, 1912.

The Magical Sword (1901) see *The Magic Sword; or, A Mediaeval Mystery* (1901)

326. *Magnificat* (1993)

Italy; dir. Pupi Avati; Duea Film.

CAST: Eleonora Alessandrelli, Massimo Bellinzoni, David Celli, Marcello Cesena, Luigi Diberti, Consuelo Ferrara, Dalia Lahav, Brizio Montinaro, Lorella Morlotti, Arnaldo Ninchi, Massimo Sarchielli, Andrea Scorzoni.

In 926, a group of pilgrims sets off during Holy Week for the monastery of the Visitation at Malfole. Each pilgrim has a different reason for being on the journey to a shrine that houses the tunic which the Virgin Mary supposedly wore when she visited her cousin Elisabeth, and each learns a lesson about the efficacy of faith.

Avati here offers a portrait of life in tenth century Italy as he explores the power of faith, offering medieval and modern perspectives on the issue of belief. Avati's literary ancestor is Chaucer; his cinematic ancestor is Pasolini, though without the latter's sustained interest in political subtext.

REVIEWS: *Avant-scène du cinéma* 424 (July 1993): 103. *Film Français* 7–14 May 1993: 50. *Foreign Sales, Italian Movie Trade* 18 (March 1993): 12, 35–36. *Le Monde* 19 May 1993: 1. *Première* 195 (June 1993): 108. *Segno cinema* 61 (May-June 1993): 41. *Studio* [Paris] 74 Hors série [Special Cannes] (1993): 28. *Variety* 24 May 1993: 46.

ADDITIONAL DISCUSSIONS:
Cowie, Peter, ed. *Variety International Film Guide 1994.* Hollywood, Calif.: Samuel French, 1993.
Kennedy, Harlan. "The Past Recapsuled." *Film Comment* 29 (July-August 1993): 74–77.

327. *El Magnifico Robin Hood* (1970)

Italy and Spain; dir. Roberto Bianchi Montero; Marco Claudio Cinematografica and R.M. Films.

CAST: Frank Braña, Jim Clay, Max Dean, Chris Huerta, George Martin, Sheyla Rosin.

Lord Linton has managed to raise money from loyal Saxons and Normans to ransom King Richard, who is in prison in Austria. Prince John demands the ransom, which Linton has had the foresight to hide, for himself. When he will not comply with Prince John's wishes, Linton is murdered. Prince John then kidnaps Linton's daughter Rovena and threatens to torture her if she will not reveal where the treasure is hidden. Robin Hood rescues her and takes the treasure to Austria. Richard returns, punishes his brother and offers Robin and his followers rewards which they decline, opting instead to return to their simple lives in the forest. Back in the forest, Rovena joins Robin, and the two are married.

This innocuous cinematic retelling of the legend of Robin Hood has little to recommend it. It borrows its heroine's name from the related legend of Ivanhoe.

REVIEW: *Bianco e nero* 32 (May-June 1971): 139.
ADDITIONAL DISCUSSIONS:
Poppi, Roberto, and Mario Pecorari. *Dizionario del cinema italiano: I Film dal 1970 al 1979.* Rome: Gremese Editore, 1996.
The Spanish Cinema. Madrid: Uniespaña, 1971.

Mágnún and Layla (1989) see *Layla, ma raison* (1989)

Mágnún et Layla (1989) see *Layla, ma raison* (1989)

Ma-Ko Po-Lo (1975) see *Marco Polo* (1975)

The Man on the Golden Horse (1982) see *Vsadnik na Zolotam Krone* (1982)

328. *Marco* (1973)

United States; dir. Seymour Robbie; Tomorrow Entertainment Productions.

CAST: Desi Arnaz, Jr., Van Christie, Aimee Eccles, Zero Mostel, Tetsu Nakamura, Fred Sadoff, Mafumi Sakamoto, Jack Weston, Cie Cie Win.

In the thirteenth century, the young Marco Polo accompanies his father and brother on a journey from Venice to the court of Kublai Khan, who secretly admires Western ways. The Khan treats Marco like a son and intends Marco to wed one of the princesses of his court, a troublesome niece, Princess Aigiarm. However, Marco falls in love with Princess Kuklatoi, the Khan's youngest daughter. Marco then becomes the Khan's special envoy, traveling in his service as far as Madagascar. In the end, Marco marries neither princess. He returns home to Venice, now a man rich in wealth and in experience.

This musical version of the thirteenth century travels of Marco Polo freely mixes fact with fiction. Arnaz is a hippie-like Marco, and Mostel steals the film as Kublai Khan. Noteworthy for its lavish sets and its location scenes filmed throughout the Far East, the film includes a musical sequence with Arnaz and some

Zero Mostel (left) as Kublai Khan and Desi Arnaz, Jr., as Marco Polo in Seymour Robbie's *Marco* (1973).

clay puppets featuring "animagic," a process that combines animation and live action.

REVIEWS: *Films in Review* 25 (March 1974): 183–84. *Hollywood Reporter* 18 December 1973: 3. *Variety* 26 December 1973: 14.

ADDITIONAL DISCUSSION:
Nash, Jay Robert, and Stanley Ralph Ross. *The Motion Picture Guide, L–M, 1927–1983*. Chicago: Cinebooks, 1986.

329. *Marco Polo* (1961)

Italy; dir. Hugo Fregonese; Panda Film-Transfilmorsa.

CAST: Rory Calhoun, Michael Chow, Pierre

Cressoy, Robert Hundar, Camillo Pilotto, Yoko Tani.

In the thirteenth century, Marco Polo, known as much for his amorous adventures as for his legendary travels, rescues the Princess Amuroy, daughter of Kublai Khan, from bandits. He conveys her safely to Peking, where he is imprisoned by Prime Minister Mongka by mistake. The Khan finally summons Marco to the palace to ask him to serve as a peace envoy to the rebel leader Cuday. Mongka tries to interfere with efforts to establish peace and imprisons the Khan and his daughter, assuming the throne himself. Marco rallies Cuday's forces, defeats Mongka in the first battle to use gunpowder as a weapon, and rescues the Khan and his daughter.

Calhoun's Marco is a swashbuckling adventurer — and ladies' man — in a characterization more indebted to modern views of medieval derring-do than to the memoirs Marco Polo himself dictated while he was in prison in Genoa from 1296 to 1299.

REVIEWS: *Cinématographie française* 8 June 1963: 2. *Daily Cinema* 7 November 1962: 7. *Film-echo/ Filmwoche* 26 September 1962: 8. *Filmfacts* 5 (30 November 1962): 281–82. *Monthly Film Bulletin* 29 (December 1962): 172–73. *Motion Picture Herald* 3 October 1962: Product Digest Section 666. *New York Times* 20 September 1962: 29.

ADDITIONAL DISCUSSIONS:
Italian Production 1961. Rome: Unitalia Film, 1962.
Krafsur, Richard A., ed. *The American Film Institute Catalog of Motion Pictures, Feature Films 1961–1970.* New York: Bowker, 1976.
Lucanio, Patrick. *With Fire and Sword, Italian Spectacles on American Screens 1958–1968.* Metuchen, N.J.: Scarecrow, 1994.
Nash, Jay Robert, and Stanley Ralph Ross. *The Motion Picture Guide, L–M, 1927–1983.* Chicago: Cinebooks, 1986.
Poppi, Roberto, and Mario Pecorari. *Dizionario del cinema italiano. Vol. 3: I Film dal 1960 al 1969.* Rome: Gremese Editore, 1992.

330. *Marco Polo* (1975)

Hong Kong; dir. Chang Cheh; Shaw Brothers Productions.

ALTERNATE TITLE: *Ma-Ko Po-Lo.*

CAST: Richard Harrison, Chi Kuan-chun, Alexander Fu Sheng, Shih Szu.

Marco Polo so impresses Kublai Khan that the Venetian is soon made governor of Yangchow. When the Khan is attacked, Marco saves his life and sets out to track down the would-be assassins. In a distant palace, he discovers a cabal against the Khan. Almost single-handedly, he defeats all those who plot against the Khan.

The travels of Marco Polo here become the excuse for a kung fu action-adventure film that keeps distancing itself further and further from fact the longer it runs.

REVIEWS: *Revue du cinéma* 407 (July-August 1985): 57. *Variety* 4 February 1976: 16.

331. *Marco Polo* (1981)

Italy; dir. Giuliano Montaldo; RAI TV Channel 1.

CAST: Anne Bancroft, Denholm Elliott, John Gielgud, John Houseman, Burt Lancaster, Tony LoBianco, Ken Marshall, Ian McShane, Leonard Nimoy, Ying Ruocheng, Sada Thompson, David Warner.

In Venice, the young Marco Polo finds life boring until he accompanies his father and older brother on a return journey to the Orient. En route, they journey through the Holy Land and witness Christians and Saracens slaughtering each other. Moving on, the explorers cross the Gobi Desert, where they almost die of thirst, survive an outbreak of plague, and narrowly escape an avalanche in the mountains of Afghanistan. Finally arriving at the court of Kublai Khan, they are well received, and Marco is appointed to the unpopular position of tax collector. To fulfill the duties of his new office, Marco sets out for the southern provinces, where he foils a plot to overthrow the Khan.

Originally a mini-series for Italian and American television, this film boasted an international cast and was filmed in Italy, Morocco and the People's Republic of China (the first western production filmed there since the late 1940s). The story is told in flashback as the imprisoned Marco dictates his adventures to Rusticello of Pisa, as the real Marco Polo did while in prison in the city of Genoa from 1296 to 1299.

REVIEWS: *Film français* 9 December 1983: 21. *Filmrutan* 1 (1982): 20–21. *Hollywood Reporter* 14 May 1982: 11. *New York Times* 14 May 1982: C30; 16 May 1982: 35. *Prevue* 47 (April-May 1982): 40–43. *TV Guide* 15 May 1982: 27, A45. *Variety* 26 May 1982: 54.

Additional discussions:
Fury, David. *The Cinema History of Burt Lancaster.* Minneapolis: Artist's Press, 1989.

Ken Marshall (left) as Marco Polo accompanies Ying Ruocheng as Kublai Khan (center) in Giuliano Montaldo's *Marco Polo* (1981).

Marill, Alvin H. *Movies Made for Television 1964–1986.* New York: Zoetrope, 1987.
Patterson, Richard. "The Filming of *Marco Polo*." *American Cinematographer* 63 (May 1982): 465–71.

332. *Marco the Magnificent* (1964)
Italy; dir. Denys de la Patelliere and Noel Howard; Ittac/Avala.

ALTERNATE TITLES: *The Fabulous Adventures of Marco Polo, La Fabuleuse aventure de Marco Polo* and *Kublai Khan.*

CAST: Horst Buchholz, Elsa Martinelli, Anthony Quinn, Omar Sharif, Orson Welles.

Pope Gregory X sends Marco Polo and a party of adventurers to the East to bring Christianity to the Mongols. Their journey is not easy. They arrive in Jerusalem during a great battle, they cross the Himalayas and they almost die in the Gobi Desert. Set upon on all sides by Mongolian bandits, Marco and his traveling companions suffer great losses and endure the cruelest of tortures. Finally arriving at the court of Kublai Khan, they aid the Khan in fighting a rebellion led by his son. Marco is the first to use gunpowder in battle and saves the Khan's throne.

From start to finish, this production was overwhelmed by problems, mainly financial. Originally, Alain Delon was to play the title role, and Denys de la Patelliere was the film's fourth director. The producers' intention was to produce a lavish spectacle unlike any other previously seen on the screen. The result was an overproduced film, long on spectacle and short on plot.

REVIEWS: *Cinématographie française* 2126 (4 September 1965): 14–15. *Daily Cinema* 29 December 1967: 9. *Film Daily* 20 July 1966: 6. *Filmfacts* 9 (15 January 1967): 335–36. *Film français* 27 August 1965: 10. *Hollywood Reporter* 12 July 1966: 3. *Kinematograph Weekly* 6 January 1968: 12, 16. *Le Monde* 10 August 1965: 8. *Monthly Film Bulletin* 35 (September 1968): 139. *Motion Picture Herald* 20 July 1966: Production Digest Section 561. *New York Times* 15 December 1966: 60. *Variety* 1 September 1956: 6.

ADDITIONAL DISCUSSIONS:
Bessy, Maurice, et al. *Histoire du cinéma français, encyclopédie des films 1961–1965.* Paris: Pygmalion, 1991.
Krafsur, Richard P., ed. *The American Film Institute Catalog of Motion Pictures, Feature Films 1961–1970.* New York: Bowker, 1976.
"Marco Polo." *Unifrance Film* 37 (July 1962): 8A–8B.
Marill, Alvin H. *The Films of Anthony Quinn.* Secaucus, N.J.: Citadel, 1975.
Lucanio, Patrick. *With Fire and Sword, Italian Spectacles on American Screens 1958–1968.* Metuchen, N.J.: Scarecrow, 1994.
Nash, Jay Robert, and Stanley Ralph Ross. *The Motion Picture Guide, L–M, 1927–1983.* Chicago: Cinebooks, 1986.
Poppi, Roberto, and Mario Pecorari. *Dizionario del cinema italiano. Vol. 3: I Film dal 1960 al 1969.* Rome: Gremese Editore, 1992.

333. *Marco Visconti* (1909)

France; Ugo Falena; Pathé Frères.
CAST: Francesca Bertini, Gemma De Sanctis, Dillo Lombardi.

Marco Visconti seeks to marry Ermelinde, but her father opposes the union and convinces his daughter that Marco is dead, when he is not. Sixteen years later, Ermelinde, now Countess del Balzo, wants to marry her daughter to Otterino Visconti, Marco's cousin, but Marco falls in love with the girl and kidnaps her. Ermelinde goes to plead for her daughter's release. Once Marco and Ermelinde recognize each other, the daughter is allowed to marry Otterino.

Historical figures inform this piece of cinematic romantic fiction, based, as are the subsequent films about Marco Visconti, on Tommaso Grossi's 1834 novel of the same title. Marco Visconti (d. 1329) was a distinguished Milanese soldier; the family fortune was founded by Otto, sometimes Ottone, Visconti (1207–1295), who was named archbishop of Milan in 1257. According to a listing in *Bioscope* (18 February 1909: 19), there was also a 1909 Italian film from Cines that had the same title.

REVIEWS: *Bioscope* 7 December 1911: v.
ADDITIONAL DISCUSSION:
Bousquet, Henri. *Catalogue Pathé des années 1896 à 1914: 1910–1911.* Paris: Henri Bousquet, 1994.

334. *Marco Visconti* (1925)

Italy; dir. Aldo De Benedotti; V.I.S. (Florence).
CAST: Ruggero Barni, Bruto Castellani, Adolfo Geri, Toto Lo Bue, Amleto Novelli, Gino Soldarelli, Cecyl Tryan, Perla Yves.

Marco Visconti loves a woman but her family will not allow him to marry her. Twenty years pass, and Marco meets the woman's daughter and promptly falls in love with the young girl. She, however, loves the younger brother of Marco. Marco blesses their union and devotes the rest of his life to his career as a soldier.

The source here is Tommaso Grossi's 1834 historical romance *Marco Visconti*.

REVIEW: *Bianco e nero* 42 (July–December 1981): 231–33.

335. *Marco Visconti* (1941)

Italy; dir. Mario Bonnard; Lux Films.
CAST: Ernesto Almirante, Alberto Capozai, Augusto di Giovanni, Mario Gallina, Mariella Lotti, Carlo Ninchi, Roberto Villa.

Marco Visconti is caught up in familial strife with one cousin over affairs of the heart and with another over affairs of state.

This film combines two threads, one more

historical than the other, in retelling the story of Marco Visconti's love for the daughter of a woman who spurned him. Politics in Milan in the thirteenth and fourteenth centuries reflected not only the general turmoil throughout Italy caused by factions loyal to the popes battling factions loyal to the emperors, but also the constant squabbles and power plays among members of the ruling Visconti family who were forever plotting against, exiling and murdering each other. The source here is Tommaso Grossi's 1834 historical romance *Marco Visconti*.

REVIEW: *Variety* 24 September 1947: 11.

336. *Marfa-Posadnista* (1910)

Russia; dir. André Maître; Pathé Frères (Moscow)-Film d'art russe.

ALTERNATE TITLES: *The Fall of Novgorod the Great, Marfa the City Governor,* and *Padenie novgoroda velikogo.*

CAST: S. Lazarev, A. Lesnogorskii, Z. Mamonova, Arkad'eva Rostanova, Nikolai Vekov.

In the late fifteenth century, the free city state of Novgorod faces a choice. It can bow to the will of the Grand Princes of Muscovy or form an alliance with Lithuania. The head of the pro–Lithuanian faction is Marfa Boretskaya, better known as Marfa-Posadnitsa. When Grand Prince Ivan III captures the city, Marfa is captured and executed.

Ivan III moved against Novgorod in 1471 to keep the city from falling into Lithuanian hands and under Polish control, since Lithuania was Poland's ally against Russia. In a bloody battle near the river Shelon, the carnage was so great the dead could not be numbered. Once Ivan secured control of the city, he abolished the *veche,* the city's autonomous parliament, and Novgorod lost all hope of future independence.

DISCUSSION:
Usai, Paolo Cherchi, et al., eds. *Silent Witnesses, Russian Films 1908–1919.* London: BFI, 1989.

Marfa the City Governor (1910) see *Marfa-Posadnista* (1910)

337. *The Margrave's Daughter* (1912)

France; Gaumont.

ALTERNATE TITLE: *La Fille du Margrave.*

Genevieve, daughter of the Margrave of Hesse, falls in love with Christian, the captain of her father's guard. Attempting a secret rendezvous, they are discovered, and the Margrave sentences Christian to death for treason. The hooded young captain approaches the executioner's block with his father confessor, whose face is also obscured by his cowl. Both drop their hoods to reveal their true identities. The prisoner is really Genevieve, and the confessor is Christian. When both lay their heads on the executioner's block, the Margrave relents, pardons them and blesses their marriage.

Reviewers reacted favorably to the use here of pageantry in the battle and crowd scenes.

REVIEWS: *Bioscope* 18 January 1912: 191; 15 February 1912: supplement ix. *Moving Picture World* 9 March 1912: 875–76; 20 April 1912: 231.

ADDITIONAL DISCUSSION:
Abel, Richard. *The Ciné Goes to Town, French Cinema 1896–1914.* Berkeley: University of California Press, 1994.

Mariken (1974) see *Mariken van Nieumeghen* (1974)

338. *Mariken van Nieumeghen* (1974)

Netherlands; dir. Jos Stelling; Tuschinski Films/Joseph Green Pictures.

ALTERNATE TITLE: *Mariken.*

CAST: Sander Bais, Wil Hildebrand, Leo Koenen, Ronnie Montagne, Alida Sonnega, Diet van de Hulst, William Van de Kooy.

The village of Anvers blames the arrival of the plague on Mariken and her one-eyed companion Moenen, either because he is the Devil incarnate or because they have lived lives devoted to sin. When they are confronted, Moenen flees, and Mariken is left to her own devices. Pretending herself to be a victim of the plague, she escapes the stake.

Mariken van Nieumeghen, the source for this film, is the best of the medieval Dutch miracle plays. Written around the year 1500, it tells the story of a young woman who follows the Devil for seven years until she is moved to repent for her sins by seeing a performance of a play about a struggle between the Devil and Christ for a Christian's soul. Stelling's film is indebted to both Brueghel and Roger Corman in its depiction of Dutch life on the threshold of the Renaissance. The director followed *Mariken van Nieumeghen* with a film of the morality play *Everyman (Elckerlijc)* in 1975.

REVIEWS: *Amis du film et de la télévision* 232

(September 1976): 38; 252–53 (May-June 1977): 21. *Hollywood Reporter* 16 December 1975: 18. *Independent Film Journal* 77 (10 December 1975): [9]. *Variety* 14 May 1975: 30.

ADDITIONAL DISCUSSIONS:

Cowie, Peter. *Dutch Cinema*. London: Tantivy, 1979.

Wallagh, Constant. *Dutch Film 1974*. The Hague, Government Printing Office, 1975.

339. *Marin Faliero, Doge di Venezia* (1909)

Italy; dir. Giuseppe De Liguoro; SAFFI-Luca Comerio (Milan).

CAST: Giuseppe De Liguoro, Salvatore Papa, Arturo Pirovano.

Marin Faliero, the Doge of Venice, marries the much younger Annunziata despite the fact that she really loves Steno Contarini. When the two former lovers continue to meet, Faliero attempts to have Steno condemned by the Council of Ten. The council, citing Steno's youth, sentences him to two months in prison and a year's exile from Venice. Faliero is furious, and he conspires to overthrow the council. His plot discovered, Faliero is arrested, condemned to death and beheaded.

This film mixes fact and fiction in its depiction of events from the history of Venice. Marino Falieri or Faliero (c. 1278–1355) was a member of one of the oldest noble families of Venice. A hero of the great 1346 Venetian victory in Dalmatia, he was subsequently elected doge in 1354. But Venice's defeat shortly thereafter at the hands of Genoa turned the Venetian nobility against Falieri and his family. Falieri then conspired with the common people against his fellow noblemen in the hopes of overthrowing the Council of Ten. His plot discovered, Falieri was convicted of treason and executed. In the Palace of the Doges, the place for his portrait in the Hall of the Grand Council is today still covered by an empty plaque.

DISCUSSION:

Bernardini, Aldo, and Jean A. Gill, eds. *Le Cinéma italien de La Prise de Rome (1905) à Rome ville ouverte (1945)*. Paris: Centre Georges Pompidou, 1986.

Martyrdom of Thomas à Becket, Archbishop of Canterbury (1910)

see *Becket* (1910)

The Marvelous Life of Joan of Arc (1929) see *Le Merveilleuse Vie de Jeanne d'Arc* (1929)

340. *The Mask and the Sword* (1950)

Sweden; dir. Christian Jaque, Terrafilm.

ALTERNATE TITLES: *Gypsy Fury*, *Saga of Singoalia*, *Singolia* and *Wind Is My Lover*.

CAST: Michel Auclair, Romney Brent, Johnny Chambot, Marie-Helene Daste, Viveca Lindfors, Henri Nassiet, Louis Seignier.

In fourteenth century Sweden, Erland, the lord of a castle, goes out hunting and meets a troop of gypsies. He soon falls in love with a gypsy girl, Singoalia, and she returns his love. The two secretly marry but, on their wedding night, the gypsies drug Erland and steal the castle's treasure. Ten years later, Singoalia returns to the castle with her son, who reveals the location of the treasure to Erland, and Erland recognizes the boy as his own son. The gypsies attack the castle and succeed in razing it, but Erland and Singoalia finally find happiness at the film's end.

There are three versions of this film, Swedish, French, and English. Reviews were mixed, although critics found the photography noteworthy. Generically, the film is a hybrid, part fairy tale and part swashbuckling adventure yarn.

REVIEWS: *Daily Film Renter* 25 (7 February 1951): 6. *Kinematograph Weekly* 15 February 1951: 20. *Monthly Film Bulletin* 19 (March 1951): 234. *To-day's Cinema* 7 February 1951: 13.

ADDITIONAL DISCUSSION:

Nash, Jay Robert, and Stanley Ralph Ross. *The Motion Picture Guide, E–G, 1927–1983*. Chicago: Cinebooks, 1986.

341. *The Mask of the Red Death* (1911)

Italy; Ambrosio.

Plague ravages Naples, and the king and his court flee to a distant castle, taking with them a poor peasant woman and her two children. Inside the court, the king and his retainers defy death and give themselves up to the pleasures of the flesh. Only the peasant prays that she and her children may be spared. A ghost carrying a scythe stalks the halls of the castle, killing all except the peasant woman and her children.

This Italian film, noteworthy for its chilling special effects, never directly acknowledges its debt to Edgar Allan Poe's short story.

REVIEW: *Moving Picture World* 30 September 1911: 994.

Vincent Price (right) as Prince Prospero encounters Death in Roger Corman's *The Masque of the Red Death* (1964).

ADDITIONAL DISCUSSION:
The Film Index: A Bibliography. Vol. 1: The Film as Art. 1941. Rpt. White Plains, N.Y.: Kraus International, 1988.

342. *The Masque of the Red Death* (1964)

United States; dir. Roger Corman; Alta Vista and American International Films.

CAST: Jane Asher, Hazel Court, Nigel Green, Patrick Magee, Skip Martin, Vincent Price, John Westbrook.

In the twelfth century, Prince Prospero rules over Esteban with a cruel and heavy hand. The approaching plague forces him to withdraw into his castle, where he surrounds himself with friends and every delight, and where it is revealed that Prospero is in league with the Devil. The plague ravages the village and appears in the castle in the form of a figure in a red masque during a costume ball. The masqued figure kills everyone who crosses his path, including Prospero, who is the last to die.

The set for this English-made film was a series of corridors extending over two miles. In the early 1960s, Corman made a career out of adapting the stories of Edgar Allan Poe for the screen — he made eight such adaptations altogether. Not his most successful attempt, this film, which also nods in the directions of Ingmar Bergman's 1957 film *The Seventh Seal*, does manage to examine in detail the psychological states of the main characters.

REVIEWS: *ABC Film Review* 14 (July 1964): 19. *American Film* 15 (June 1990): 53. *Daily Cinema* 24 June 1964: 7. *Film Daily* 25 May 1964: 10. *Films and Filming* 10 (August 1964): 24. *Hollywood Reporter* 24 June 1964. *Kinematograph Weekly* 25 June 1964: 8. *Monthly Film Bulletin* 31 (August 1964): 116–17. *Motion Picture Herald* 10 June 1964: Product Digest Section 67. *New York Times* 17 September 1964: 52.

Times [London] 25 June 1964: 14. *Variety* 24 June 1964: 7.

ADDITIONAL DISCUSSIONS:

Bourgoin, Stéphane. *Roger Corman*. Paris: Edilig, 1983.

Corman, Roger. "*La Masque de la mort rouge.*" *Avant-scène du cinéma* 248 (15 May 1980): 9–71. [Screenplay.]

DiFranco, J. Philip. *The Movie World of Roger Corman*. London: Chelsea House, 1979.

French, Lawrence. "Price on Poe." *Cinefantastique* 19 (January 1989): 63–66, 119.

Friedman, L. Favius. *Great Horror Movies*. New York: Scholastic Book Services, 1974.

Hilier, Jim, and Aaron Lipstadt. *Roger Corman's New Worlds*. London: British Film Institute, 1981.

McAsh, Ian F. *The Films of Vincent Price*. London: Barden Castell Williams, 1984.

McGee, Mark Thomas. *Roger Corman: The Best of the Cheap Acts*. Jefferson, N.C.: McFarland, 1988.

———. *Fast and Furious, The Story of American International Pictures*. Jefferson, N.C.: McFarland, 1984.

Morris, Gary. *Roger Corman*. Boston: Twayne, 1985.

Naha, Ed. *The Films of Roger Corman: Brillance on a Budget*. New York: ARCO, 1982.

Nash, Jay Robert, and Stanley Ralph Ross. *The Motion Picture Guide, L–M, 1927–1983*. Chicago: Cinebooks, 1986.

Pirie, David. "Roger Corman's Descent into the Maelstrom." In Paul Willemen, et al. *Roger Corman, The Millenic Visions*. Edinburgh: Edinburgh Film Festival, 1970.

Roger Corman. [Special issue.] *Cinema nuovo* 33 (January-February 1984): 1–55.

Thomas, Nicholas, ed. *International Dictionary of Films and Filmmakers–1 Films*. 2nd ed. Chicago: St. James, 1990.

343. *The Masque of the Red Death* (1989)

United States; dir. Larry Brand; Concorde Films.

CAST: Clare Hoak, Patrick Magee, Jeff Osterhage, Adrian Paul, Tracy Reiner.

Prince Prospero marries his sister and tortures anyone, even his best friends, who disobeys him. As news of plague spreads throughout the countryside, Prospero determines to escape death by sealing up his castle, inviting his friends and many of the young women from the nearby village to join him. A mysterious stranger dressed in red appears in the village as the inhabitants fall dead from the plague. The stranger gains entry into Prospero's castle, and when ordered by the Prince to doff his red masque, the stranger reveals himself to be Prospero's former tutor. The tutor also re-

moves his gloves, and anyone whom he touches soon drops dead from the plague. Terrified, Prospero flees to the dungeons where he had tortured so many people. Offered a choice of death by suicide or from the plague, Prospero kills himself.

This film was produced by Roger Corman, who directed the 1964 screen version of Poe's short story — a film to which this remake cannot hold a candle. The plot is hopelessly convoluted, and the sets, which were borrowed from another Concorde exercise in medieval filmmaking, *Time Trackers* (1989), accent the cheapness of the film's production values.

REVIEWS: *Cinefantastique* 20 (March 1990): 55–56. *Variety* 13 September 1989: 19.

ADDITIONAL DISCUSSIONS:

Magill, Frank N., ed. *Magill's Cinema Annual 1990, A Survey of the Films of 1989*. Pasadena, Calif.: Salem, 1990.

The Motion Picture Guide: 1991 Annual (The Films of 1990). New York: Baseline, 1991.

Master of Love (1973) see *Racconti proibiti di nulla vestiti* (1973)

Matthias the Just (1986) see *Matys az igazsagos* (1986)

344. *Matys az igazsagos* (1986)

Hungary; dir. Laszlo Ujvary; Pannonia Film Studios.

ALTERNATE TITLE: *Matthias the Just*.

In order to assess the state of his kingdom, King Matthias of Hungary leaves the court at Buda and travels incognito throughout his country. While on his travels, the king encounters intrigues and injustices, all of which he sets about to foil or to remedy. He returns to the court a better ruler only to discover a plot to overthrow him. A gypsy woman warns him, the king escapes with his life, and he rewards the gypsy who saved his life.

This animated film relies more on fiction than fact in its account of the life of King Matthias (c. 1443–1490), popularly surnamed Corvinus because of the eagle on his coat of arms, who expanded the borders of Hungary, defeated the Turks and instituted a literary and artistic renaissance during his reign. Despite his accomplishments, history renders a mixed judgment on Matthias, who taxed his country heavily and who ruled as much by whim as by a strict sense of justice.

REVIEW: *Hungarofilm Bulletin* 2 (1986): 8–9.

The Medieval Dead (1992) see *Army of Darkness* (1992)

345. *Men of Sherwood Forest* (1954)

Great Britain; dir. Val Guest; Hammer Films.

CAST: Reginald Beckwith, Patrick Holt, David King-Wood, Eileen Moore, Don Taylor, John Van Eyssen.

Two traitors in the employ of Prince John, pretending to be supporters of King Richard, send Robin Hood on a suicide mission to free the imprisoned king. Disguised as a troubadour, Robin is captured and imprisoned in a German castle. His band of merry men follow him to Germany and free him and the king.

This harmless Hammer film features all the familiar Sherwood Forest characters though in an unfamiliar series of adventures.

REVIEWS: *Kinematograph Weekly* 4 November 1954: 18. *Monthly Film Bulletin* 21 (December 1954): 179. *To-day's Cinema* 28 October 1954: 6.

ADDITIONAL DISCUSSIONS:

Behlmer, Rudy. "Robin Hood on the Screen." *Films in Review* 16 (February 1965): 91–102.

Johnson, Tom, and Deborah Del Vecchio. *Hammer Films, An Exhaustive Filmography.* Jefferson, N.C.: McFarland, 1996.

Knight, Stephen. *Robin Hood, A Complete Study of the English Outlaw.* Oxford: Blackwell, 1994.

Nash, Jay Robert, and Stanley Ralph Ross. *The Motion Picture Guide, L–M, 1927–1983.* Chicago: Cinebooks, 1986.

Richard, Jeffrey. *Swordsmen of the Screen from Douglas Fairbanks to Michael York.* London: Routledge & Kegan Paul, 1977.

Turner, David. *Robin of the Movies.* Kingswinford, Eng.: Yeoman Publishing, 1989.

346. *Mephisto and the Maiden* (1909)

United States; dir. Frank Boggs; Selig Polyscope.

CAST: James L. McGee, Tom Santschi, Harry Todd, Jean Ward.

In a dream, Friar Hugo pledges his soul to the Devil in exchange for an hour of youth and enjoyment.

This film is loosely based on Goethe's great tragedy *Faust.*

REVIEWS: *Moving Picture World* 24 April 1909: 528; 8 May 1909: 596–96. *New York Dramatic Mirror* 8 May 1909: 16. *Nickelodeon* 1 (May 1909): 146.

ADDITIONAL DISCUSSIONS:

Prodolliet, Ernest. *Faust im Kino, Die Geschichte des Faustfilms von den Anfängen bis in die Gegenwart.* Freiburg, Switz.: Universitätsverlag Freiburg, 1978.

Savada, Elias. *The American Film Institute Catalog of Motion Pictures Produced in the United States: Film Beginnings, 1893–1910.* Metuchen, N.J.: Scarecrow, 1995.

347. *Le Meravigliose avventure di Guerrin Meschino* (1951)

Italy; dir. Piero Francisci; Oro Films.

ALTERNATE TITLE: *The Wonderful Adventures of Guerrin Meschino.*

CAST: Anna Di Leo, Aldo Fiorelli, Tamara Lees, Gino Leurini, Leonora Ruffino.

The young Guerrin has to overcome numerous obstacles to be reunited with his beloved Elisenda, daughter of the King of Constantinople. Those adventures include a battle with the son of the Sultan for the hand of Elisenda. Guerrin is himself a prince, but he was kidnapped by pirates while still an infant. No one knows his true identity until he defeats his adversary, also saving Constantinople from being overrun by Saracens. Guerrin then sets out to find his parents and reclaim his patrimony.

The Tuscan Andrea da Barberino (c. 1370–after 1431) first wrote about the adventures of Guerrin Meschino. His *Guerrin Meschino* is part of a cycle of long prose romances that traces the history of France from its origins to the descendants of Charlemagne. This film is loosely based on materials from that prose romance.

REVIEWS: *Cinémathographie française* 15 November 1952: 18. *Eco del cinema* 22 (15 April 1952): 136. *Unitalia Film* 3 (March 1952): [92].

ADDITIONAL DISCUSSIONS:

Chiti, Roberto, and Roberto Poppi. *Dizionario del cinema italiano. Vol. 2: I Film dal 1945 al 1959.* Rome: Gremese Editore, 1991.

The Italian Production 1951–52. Rome: Unitalia Film, 1952.

348. *The Mercenary* (1912)

France; Pathé Frères.

A mercenary, injured in a fall from his horse, repays the kindness of a nobleman who cares for him by kidnapping the nobleman's daughter. The mercenary's compatriots help the nobleman rescue his daughter.

Simone Genevois as Joan rallies her troops in Marco de Gastyne's *La Merveilleuse Vie de Jeanne d'Arc* (1928). (Still courtesy of the British Film Institute.)

REVIEWS: *Bioscope* 11 April 1912: 143; 9 May 1912: supplement iii; 29 April 1915: supplement v.

Gifford, Denis. *The British Film Catalogue 1895–1985.* Newton Abbot: David & Charles, 1986.

Merlin and the Sword (1982) see *Arthur the King* (1982)

349. The Merry Men of Sherwood (1932)

Great Britain; dir. Widgey R. Newman; Delta Pictures.

CAST: Eric Adeney, Patrick Barr, Terence de Marney, Aileen Marson, John Milton, John Thompson.

Robin Hood comes to the rescue of Maid Marian and restores King Richard to his throne.

This little known film apparently tells a fairly standard version of events from the legend of Robin Hood — the first talking film to do so.

DISCUSSION:

350. La Merveilleuse Vie de Jeanne d'Arc (1928)

France; dir. Marco de Gastyne; Production Natan.

ALTERNATE TITLES: *The Marvelous Life of Joan of Arc* and *Saint Joan the Maid.*

CAST: Cabrier, Jean Debucourt, Pierre Douvan, Simone Genevois, Philippe Hériat, Mailly, Choura Milena, Paulais.

Convinced she is divinely inspired, Joan persuades the Dauphin to place her at the head of the French army to drive the English from France. Initially victorious, she is eventually captured by the English. Abandoned by the king, Joan is tricked into confessing that she is a heretic. As she is burned at the stake, the French mob realizes it has delivered a saint into the hands of their enemies.

This film version of the life of Joan is an

overlooked gem. It concentrates on her military exploits and emphasizes her unique role in French history as national hero.

REVIEWS: *Cinéa-ciné-pour tous* 132 (1 May 1929): 5. *Kinematograph Weekly* 19 February 1931: 45. *Pathéscope Monthly* March 1934: 8–10. *Picturegoer Weekly* 1 (25 July 1931): 30. *Restaurations de la cinémathèque française* 1 (1986): 77. *Times* [London] 13 February 1931: 12; 14 February 1931: 10. *Variety* 1 October 1986: 36.

ADDITIONAL DISCUSSIONS:
Blaetz, Robin J. "Strategies of Containment: Joan of Arc on Film." Ph.D. dissertation. New York University, 1989.
Harty, Kevin J. "Jeanne au cinéma." In Bonnie Wheeler and Charles T. Wood, eds. *Fresh Verdicts on Joan of Arc*. New York: Garland, 1996.
"Jeanne d'arc à l'ecran." *La Petite illustration* 408 (24 November 1928): 10–14.
Margolis, Nadia. *Joan of Arc in History, Literature, and Film*. New York: Garland, 1990.
Oms, Marcel. "Histoire et géographie d'une France imaginaire." *Cahiers de la cinémathèque* 33–34 (Autumn 1981): 77–88.

351. *Metti lo diavolo tuo ne lo mio inferno* (1972)

Italy; dir. Bitto [Adalberto] Albertini; Esteban Cinematografica-Cinemar.

ALTERNATE TITLE: *Put Your Devil in My Hell.*

CAST: Antonio Cantafora, Mario Frera, Margareth Rose Keil, Alessandra Moravia, Melinda Pillion.

When the pope decrees a holy year that will bring streams of pilgrims to Rome, the mayor of Monte Lepone schemes to attract pilgrims to his town as they journey toward the Eternal City. He persuades his fellow citizens — male and female — to become prostitutes so that they may meet the non-spiritual needs of all the pilgrims who pass through Monte Lepone. Their customers include a lecherous cardinal, a troop of homosexual German soldiers and a young noblewoman who claims to be the world's greatest sinner and who teaches the citizens a few things about the fine art of seduction. This silly example of cinematic anticlericalism and soft-core pornography (the film's title is a slang phrase for coitus) plagiarizes bits and pieces from Chaucer and Boccaccio, when it is not indulging in an endless series of anachronisms.

REVIEWS: *Bianco e nero* 35 (March-April 1974): 51. *Monthly Film Bulletin* 40 (May 1973): 104.

ADDITIONAL DISCUSSIONS:
Poppi, Roberto, and Mario Pecorari. *Dizionario del cinema italiano: I Film dal 1970 al 1979*. Rome: Gremese Editore, 1996.
La Produzione italiana 1972/73. Rome: Unitalia Film, 1973.

352. *The Midwife's Tale* (1996)

United States; dir. Megan Siler; Heresy Pictures.

CAST: Anthony Abate, Mitchell Anderson, Gayle Cohen, Stacey Havener, Antonio Kitto, Carla Milford, Ben Prager, Delbert Spain.

Lady Eleanor is a headstrong young woman married to Lord William, a man intent upon reining her in. When Eleanor becomes pregnant, she fears for her life, since her own mother died in childbirth. She seeks an abortion from the local midwife, only to find that the old woman has been condemned to death as a witch. A second, much younger midwife, Gwenyth, appears, and she and Eleanor become inseparable. A jealous William imprisons his wife and seeks to have Gwenyth also condemned as a witch. Separately, the two manage to escape (Eleanor becomes a "lady knight"), rendezvous and live happily ever after as lovers.

This feminist fairy tale is told as a bedtime story to a contemporary young girl by her mother and her mother's lover.

REVIEWS: *Philadelphia Inquirer* 19 July 1996: Weekend 14. *Variety* 20 November 1995: 51.

353. *The Mighty Crusaders* (1957)

Italy; dir. Carlo Ludovico Bragaglia; Max Productions.

ALTERNATE TITLES: *Gerusalemme Liberata* and *La Muraille de feu.*

CAST: Rik Battaglia, Gianna Maria Canale, Philippe Hersent, Sylva Koscina, Francisco Rabal.

During the siege of Jerusalem, Tancrid, a Crusader, falls in love with Clorinda, the daughter of the Saracen king of Persia. She in turn dons armor and leads a charge against the Christian forces, during which Tancrid unknowingly wounds her mortally. In her dying breath, Clorinda asks to be baptized a Christian by Tancrid.

Nominally indebted to Tasso's sixteenth century epic *Jerusalem Delivered,* this film presents yet another opportunity for scantily clad actors to parade across the screen. The dubbing in the version released in the United States is especially noteworthy — for its poor quality.

REVIEWS: *Cinématographie française* 18 July 1959: 15. *Daily Cinema* 15 November 1961: 8. *Kinematograph Weekly* 16 November 1961: 23. *Monthly Film Bulletin* 28 (December 1961): 169. *New York Times* 23 September 1961: 17. *Variety* 27 September 1961: 6.

ADDITIONAL DISCUSSIONS:
Chiti, Roberto, and Roberto Poppi. *Dizionario del cinema Italiano. Vol. 2: I Film dal 1945 at 1959.* Rome: Gremese Editore, 1991.
The Italian Production 1957. Rome: Unitalia Film, 1958.
Lucanio, Patrick. *With Fire and Sword, Italian Spectacles on American Screens 1958–1968.* Metuchen, N.J.: Scarecrow, 1994.
Nash, Jay Robert, and Stanley Ralph Ross. *The Motion Picture Guide, L–M, 1927–1983.* Chicago: Cinebooks, 1986.
Smith, Gary. *Epic Films.* Jefferson, N.C.: McFarland, 1991.

The Minstrel (1910) see *La Véridique et Douloureuse Histoire de Catelan le ménestrel* (1910)

354. La Mirabile Visione (1921)

Italy; dir. Fausto Salvatore; Tespi-Film.

CAST: Ettore Berti, Alfredo Boccolini, Carmen di San Giusto, Ciro Galvani, Lamberto Picasso, Gustavo Salvini, Giovanna Scotto, Luigi Servanti, Camillo Talamo.

The poet Dante finds himself caught up in the political turmoil that engulfs not only his native Florence but also all of Italy. While remaining fully engaged in the political life of his time, he begins writing parts of the *Divine Comedy.*

Released in honor of the six hundredth anniversary of Dante's death, this film interweaves details of Dante's life with scenes from the *Divine Comedy,* telling (among other tales) those of Francesca da Rimini (*Inferno* V) and Count Ugolino (*Inferno* XXXIII).

REVIEW: *Bianco e nero* 42 (January–June 1981): 194–98. *Times* [London] 27 September 1921: 8.

ADDITIONAL DISCUSSION:
"Dante on the Film." *Times* [London] 30 December 1920: 9.

355. Le Miracle des loups (1924)

France; dir. Raymond Bernard; Les Films historiques.

ALTERNATE TITLE: *The Miracle of the Wolves.*

CAST: Armand Bernard, Charles Dullin, Philippe Hériat, Roumouald Joube, Vannie Marcoux, Ernest Maupain, Gaston Modot, Yvonne Sergyl.

In the war between King Louis XI and Charles the Bold, Duke of Burgundy, the king is saved by his ward Jeanne Fouquet, who is miraculously aided by a pack of hungry wolves. Jeanne leads citizens loyal to Louis as Charles's army advances on Beauvais. Louis and his allies win the day, and Jeanne is reunited with her Burgundian lover, Robert Cottereau.

From the 1924 novel *Le Miracle des loups* by Henri Dupuy-Mazoul, this film was the first to be screened at the Paris Opera. Its premiere with full orchestral accompaniment on November 13, 1924, was a national event presided over by the President of the Republic. The film interweaves the love story between Jeanne and Robert with its recapitulation of events in French history.

REVIEWS: *Bioscope* 26 February 1923: 46–47. *Cinémagazine* 4 (21 November 1924): 315–16. *Exceptional Photoplays* 5 (February-March 1925): 2. *Kinematograph Weekly* 26 February 1925: 56–57. *New York Times* 24 February 1925: 17; 28 July 1930: 22. *Photoplay* 27 (May 1925): 46. *Télérama* 1528 (25 April 1979): 56–57. *Variety* 2 February 1925: 30; 30 July 1930: 28.

ADDITIONAL DISCUSSIONS:
Abel, Richard. *French Cinema, The First Wave, 1915–1929.* Princeton: Princeton University Press, 1984.
Barsacq, Léon. *Calagari's Cabinet and Other Grand Illusions.* Rev. ed. Elliott Stein, ed. Boston: New York Graphic Society, 1976.
Beylie, C. "Le Vrai miracle des loups." *Ecran* 81 (15 June 1979): 6–7.
Borger, Lenny. "Le Décade prodigieuse." *Positif* 384 (February 1993): 79–82.
Borger, Raymond. "Spectacular Stories." *Sight and Sound* NS 2 (June 1992): 20–25.
Chirat, Raymond. *Catalogue des films français de long métrage. Films de fiction 1919–1929.* Toulouse: Cinémathèque de Toulouse, 1984.
Flammard, Gilbert. "Le Miracle des loups." *Cinémagazine* 4 (24 February 1924): 346–48.
Magill, Frank N., ed. *Magill's Survey of Cinema: Silent Films.* Englewood Cliffs, N.J.: Salem, 1982.
Oms, Marcel. "Histoire et géographie d'une France imaginaire." *Cahiers de la cinémathèque* 33–34 (Autumn 1981): 77–88.
Salles, Jacques. "Raymond Bernard." *Avant-scène du cinéma* 256 [Anth. cin. 106] (15 November 1980): 177–208.
Stein, Elliott. "Homo Homini Lupus." *Film Comment* 14 (September-October 1978): 57–58.

Battle scene from Raymond Bernard's *Le Miracle des loups* (1924). (Still courtesy of the British Film Institute.)

356. *Le Miracle des loups* (1961)

France; dir. Andre Hunebelle; Pathé Cinéma.

ALTERNATE TITLE: *The Miracle of the Wolves*.

CAST: Jean-Louis Barrault, Guy Delorme, Roger Hanin, Jean Marais, Rosanna Schiaffino.

Charles, Duke of Burgundy, invites his cousin and rival, Louis XI, to a banquet in the duke's honor. Charles asks for the hand of the king's ward Jeanne in marriage, but Louis refuses. Charles responds by having Jeanne kidnapped, but she is rescued by Robert of Neuville, the king's champion. In anger, Charles accuses Louis of turning the citizens of Liège against him when a message sent with Jeanne fails to arrive. Jeanne has been followed by Charles's agents who throw her to the wolves, but she miraculously survives. An ecclesiastical court clears Louis of charges of conspiring against Charles, and Robert and Jeanne are married.

This remake of the 1924 film suffers in comparison to its predecessor, which remains one of the great French films of the silent era.

REVIEWS: *Cinématographie française* 23 September 1961: 19. *Kinematograph Weekly* 21 March 1963: 23. *Variety* 27 September 1961: 6.

357. *Mr. Magoo in Sherwood Forest* (1964)

United States; dir. Abe Levitow; Paramount.

CAST: (the voice of) Jim Backus.

Mr. Magoo, in the role of Friar Tuck, helps Robin Hood and his men in their fight against Prince John and the Sheriff of Nottingham.

DISCUSSIONS:
Bowker's Complete Video Directory. New Providence, N.J.: R.R. Bowker, 1996.
Erickson, Hal. *Television Cartoon Shows, An Illustrated Encyclopedia, 1949 through 1993*. Jefferson, N.C.: McFarland, 1995.

The Mistress of Treves (1951) see *La Leggenda di Genoveffa* (1951)

358. *Le Moine et la sorcière* (1987)

France; dir. Suzanne Schiffman; Bleu Productions.

ALTERNATE TITLE: *The Sorceress*.

CAST: Christine Boisson, Jean Carmet, Tcheky Karyo.

Etienne de Bourbon, a Dominican friar, arrives in a small village to hunt for heretics. Elda, a faith healer living in the woods, immediately attracts his attention. While following her into the woods one day, he discovers that she and her fellow villagers worship a dog saint, Guinefort, which sacrificed its own life to save that of a young child. When Elda takes a sick child to Guinefort's grave to be healed, Etienne accuses her of sorcery and condemns her to death. But Etienne soon learns that he too must confront demons from his own past when a mute girl appears in the village; she turns out to be his daughter, conceived when (in an attempt to prove his virility) he raped a young woman years earlier. In the end, Elda is set free, and Etienne learns a lesson about humility, human frailty and forgiveness.

The film is based on the writings of the thirteenth century friar Etienne de Bourbon (1190–1261), which describe a mysterious cult led by a woman which venerated a greyhound as a saint. The friar first achieved fame in 1226 when he preached against the Albergensians; in 1235, he was named inquisitor for all France.

REVIEWS: *Les Cahiers du cinéma* 399 (September 1987): 45–46. *Cinéaste* 16 (1988): 44–46. *Cinéma* 409 (23–29 September 1987)· 1–3. *Film français* 28 August 1987: 16; 18 September 1987: 4–5. *Films in Review* 39 (August 1988): 423–24. *Los Angeles Times* 26 August 1988: Calendar 1. *New York Times* 1 April 1988: 3. 23. *Positif* 319 (September 1987): 75–76. *Première* 126 (September 1987): 21; 127 (October 1987): 41. *Revue du cinéma* 431 (October 1987): 60. *Variety* 23 September 1987: 28.

ADDITIONAL DISCUSSIONS:
Les Films français. Paris: Unifrance Film International, 1987.
Jackson, Lynne. "*Sorceress*, An Interview with Pamela Berger." *Cinéaste* 16 (1988): 45.
Tous les films 1987. Paris: Éditions Chrétien-Médias, 1988.

I Mongoli (1960) see *The Mongols* (1960)

359. *The Mongols* (1960)

Italy and France; dir. André De Toth and Leopoldo Savona; Royal Films and France Cinema Productions.

ALTERNATE TITLE: *I Mongoli*.

CAST: Anita Ekberg, Gianni Garko, Roldano Lupi, Jack Palance, Gabriella Pallota, Franco Silva, Tuen Wang.

In 1240, as Mongol hordes threaten to overrun Europe, Henry of Valois and Stephen of Krakow set out to negotiate a truce with Genghis Khan. The two emissaries are ambushed by Ogotai, the Khan's son, who wishes to continue the war. They escape and finally arrive at the court of the Khan, where they convince him of their peaceful intentions. But the assassination of the Khan brings an end to any hope of peace, as Mongol hordes march against Europe. Stephen defeats Ogotai's armies by forcing them into quicksand; he then marries a Mongol princess and thereby ensures future peace between the Mongols and all of Europe.

This action-packed costume spectacle freely reinvents history. Mongol invasions of Poland started in 1241 and continued for more than a century. Genghis Khan died in 1227, and his kingdom was divided among his several sons, including Ögadai Khan.

REVIEWS: *Cinématographie française* 7 October 1961: 16. *Film français* 6 June 1961: 19–20. *Daily Cinema* 28 June 1963: 9. *Kinematograph Weekly* 4 July 1963: 27. *Monthly Film Bulletin* 30 (August 1963): 119.

ADDITIONAL DISCUSSIONS:
The Italian Production 1960. Rome: Unitalia Film, 1961.

Lucanio, Patrick. *With Fire and Sword, Italian Spectacles on American Screens 1958–1968.* Metuchen, N.J.: Scarecrow, 1994.

Nash, Jay Robert, and Stanley Ralph Ross. *The Motion Picture Guide, L–M, 1927–1983.* Chicago: Cinebooks, 1986.

Poppi, Roberto, and Mario Pecorari. *Dizionario del cinema italiano. Vol. 3: I Film dal 1960 al 1969.* Rome: Gremese Editore, 1992.

Smith, Gary. *Epic Films.* Jefferson, N.C.: McFarland, 1991.

360. *Monna Vanna* (1922)

Germany; dir. Richard Eichberg; Münchener Lichtspiel-Kunst.

CAST: Lee Parry, Lydia Salmonova, Paul Wegener.

When her native Pisa is besieged by Florence, Monna Vanna, wife of the city's commander, agrees to give herself to the Florentine commander for one night in order to save the city. The Florentine is so moved by her innocence and beauty that he returns her unharmed and untouched to her husband in the morning. But her husband refuses to believe that she has spent an innocent night with the Florentine, who then decides to flee with Monna.

From the 1902 play *Monna Vanna* by Maurice Maeterlinck, this film (like its source) argues that sexual fidelity may be sacrificed for some greater good, first to save thousands of lives and then when one of the partners in a marriage proves unworthy of the other.

REVIEWS: *Exceptional Photoplays* 3 (Fall 1923):

4. *New York Times* 25 September 1923: 8.2. *Variety* 8 February 1923: 42; 27 September 1923: 24.

ADDITIONAL DISCUSSIONS:
Eisner, Lotte H. *The Haunted Screen.* London: Thames and Hudson, 1969.

Kobal, John, ed. *Great Film Stills of the German Silent Era.* New York: Dover, 1981.

Lamprecht, Gerhard. *Deutsche Stummfilme 1921–1922.* Berlin: Deutsche Kinemathek, 1968.

Möller, Kai. *Paul Wegener, Sein Leben und Seine Rollen.* Hamburg: Rowohlt, 1954.

361. *Monty Python and the Holy Grail* (1975)

Great Britain; dir. Terry Gilliam and Terry Jones; Python Pictures.

CAST: Graham Chapman, John Cleese, Terry Gilliam, Eric Idle, Terry Jones, Michael Palin.

Arthur, King of the Britons, rules uneasily. As he journeys throughout his kingdom on his trusty steed Patsy, he encounters peasants who yell Marxist socio-economic theory at him, the Black Knight, whom he defeats (eventually), and the Knights Who Say "Ni," whom he placates with shrubbery. Meanwhile, Arthur's knights are having their own difficulties. Lancelot cannot seem to find anyone genuinely in need of rescue, and Sir Robin and Sir Galahad seem a bit reluctant to join Arthur in the quest for the Grail.

Perhaps the funniest movie set in medieval times, *Monty Python and the Holy Grail* gives free rein to the comic talents of the six actors who comprise the Monty Python troupe. What is being skewered here is not so much the legend of Arthur as previous cinematic treatments of that legend.

REVIEWS: *Cinéaste* 7 (Fall 1975): 15–18. *Cinefantastique* 4 (Fall 1975): 39. *Cinéma* 205 (January 1976): 143. *Cineforum* 159 (November 1976): 717–18. *Film Review* 25 (June 1975): 8–9. *Films and Filming* 21 (May 1975): 40. *Films Illustrated* 4 (May 1975): 326. *Hollywood Reporter* 13 March 1975: 18. *Image et son* 301 (December 1975): 117. *Independent Film Journal* 75 (30 April 1975): 13–14. *Jeune cinéma* 93 (March 1976): 29–30. *Los Angeles Times* 23 July 1974: 4. 1. *Monthly Film Bulletin* 42 (April 1975): 84–85. *New York Times* 28 April 1975: 34. *Positif* 171–72 (July-August 1975): 68. *Revue du cinéma* 301 (December 1975): 117; 309–10 (October 1976): 247–48. *Times* [London] 10 May 1975: 9. *Variety* 19 March 1975: 32. *Video Watchdog* 17 (May-June 1993): 61–64.

ADDITIONAL DISCUSSIONS:
Abel, Christian, et al. "Entretien: Monty Python." *Revue du cinéma* 351 (June 1980): 74–81.

Graham Chapman as Arthur and Terry Gilliam as Patsy, Arthur's trusty steed, in Gilliam and Terry Jones's *Monty Python and the Holy Grail* (1975).

Bishop, Ellen. "Bakhtin, Carnival and Comedy: The New Grotesque in *Monty Python and the Holy Grail*." *Film Criticism* 15 (Fall 1990): 49–64.

Blanch, Robert J., and Julian N. Wasserman. "Gawain on Film." In Kevin J. Harty, ed. *Cinema Arthuriana, Essays on Arthurian Film*. New York: Garland, 1991.

Burde, Mark. "Monty Python's Medieval Masterpiece." In Keith Busby, ed. *The Arthurian Yearbook III*. New York: Garland, 1993.

Burns, E. Jane. "Nostalgia Isn't What It Used to Be: The Middle Ages in Literature and Film." In George Slusser and Eric S. Rabkin, eds. *Shadows of the Magic Lamp, Fantasy and Science Fiction in Film*. Carbondale: Southern University of Illinois Press, 1985.

Byron, Stuart, and Elisabeth Weiss, eds. *The National Society of Film Critics on Film Comedy*. New York: Grossman, 1977.

Day, David D. "Monty Python and the Medieval Other." In Kevin J. Harty, ed. *Cinema Arthuriana, Essays on Arthurian Film*. New York: Garland, 1991.

Magill, Frank N., ed. *Magill's Survey of Cinema: English Language Films*. Second Series. Englewood Cliffs, N.J.: Salem, 1981.

McCall, Douglas L. *Monty Python: A Chronological Listing of the Troupe's Creative Output, and Articles and Reviews about Them, 1969–1989*. Jefferson, N.C.: McFarland, 1991.

Monty Python and the Holy Grail (Book). New York: Methuen, 1977 [Screenplay and related documents.]

Nash, Jay Robert, and Stanley Ralph Ross. *The Motion Picture Guide, L–M, 1927–1983*. Chicago: Cinebooks, 1986.

Nickel, Helmut. "Arms and Armor in Arthurian Film." In Kevin J. Harty, ed. *Cinema Arthuriana, Essays on Arthurian Film*. New York: Garland, 1991.

Perry, George. *Life of Python*. London: Pavillion, 1983.

Sigoloff, Marc. *The Films of the Seventies*. Jefferson, N.C.: McFarland, 1984.

Thompson, Raymond H. "The Ironic Tradition in Arthurian Film Since 1960." In Kevin J. Harty, ed. *Cinema Arthuriana, Essays on Arthurian Film*. New York: Garland, 1991.

Umland, Rebecca A., and Samuel J. Umland. *The Use of Arthurian Legend in Hollywood Film from Connecticut Yankees to Fisher Kings*. Westport, Conn.: Greenwood, 1996.

362. *Moorish Bride* (1911)

Italy; Cines.

As the Moors rally to the cause of John of Austria (seeking relief from the oppression of other, less sympathetic Christian princes), two lovers are separated but eventually reunited.

This film is clearly set in the Middle Ages, but the plot presents a confused version of historical fact. John of Austria (1547–1578) defeated the Moorish armies at Grenada in 1570 and the Turks in the next year at the great sea battle at Lepanto. Subsequently, as duke in Milan and Spanish viceroy in the Netherlands, he was known as a just ruler.

REVIEWS: *Bioscope* 20 July 1911: supplement vi. *Moving Picture World* 23 March 1912: 1063.

Mortal Clay (1922) see *Love's Crucible* (1922)

363. *The Morte d'Arthur* (1984)

Great Britain; dir. Gillian Lynne; BBC2.

CAST: John Barton, Jeremy Brett, Nickolas Grace, Barbara Keller, David Robb.

Arthur sees his kingdom dissolve in squabbles among his knights over the innocence or guilt of Guinevere.

This made-for-television film of the last two books of Sir Thomas Malory's fifteenth century *Le Morte Darthur* is part dance piece, part staged reading, part mime show and part teledrama.

REVIEWS: *Sunday Times* [London] 13 May 1984: 54. *Television Today* 21 April 1984: 19. *Times* [London] 7 May 1984: 15. *Times* [London] *Educational Supplement* 11 May 1984: 25. *Times* [London] *Literary Supplement* 18 May 1984: 551.

ADDITIONAL DISCUSSION:
Totten, Eileen. "The Knight's Tale." *Radio Times* [London] 5–11 May 1984: 8–9.

364. *A Moura encantada* (1985)

Portugal; dir. Manuel Costa e Silva; Costa e Silva Production Company.

CAST: António Assunção, Teresa Goucho, Adelaide João, Vitorino Salomé, Luís Varela.

This film presents a view of the Arabic culture of Portugal based on Arabic literature from the eleventh, twelfth and thirteenth centuries and on António Borges Coelho's 1989 study of that literature, *Portugal na espanha arabe*.

REVIEW: *Film français* 19 September 1986: 15.

ADDITIONAL DISCUSSIONS:
Nash, Jay Robert, and Stanley Ralph Ross. *The Motion Picture Guide, 1986 Annual (The Films of 1985).* Chicago: Cinebooks, 1987.
Portugal filme. Lisbon: Instituto português de cinema, 1986.

La Muraille de feu (1957) see *The Mighty Crusaders* (1957)

365. *Murder in the Cathedral* (1951)

Great Britain; dir. George Hoellering; Classic Pictures.

CAST: T.S. Eliot, John Groser, Alexander Gauge, Leo McKern, Paul Rogers, David Ward.

Thomas Becket, long a friend of Henry II, is first Chancellor of England and then Archbishop of Canterbury — all part of Henry's plan to further his control over England. But Becket remains first and foremost a man of principle who has no time for political expediency. His inflexibility on matters of principle eventually leads to his martyrdom.

This film version of Eliot's 1935 verse play *Murder in the Cathedral*, which garnered rave reviews in the religious and less enthusiastic ones in the secular press, featured Eliot himself speaking the part of the Fourth Tempter.

REVIEWS: *Film Music* 11 (May-June 1952): 8. *Films in Review* 3 (February 1952): 84–88. *Monthly Film Bulletin* 19 (April 1952): 47. *Motion Picture Herald* 5 April 1952: Product Digest Section 1307. *New York Times* 26 March 1952: 35. *Picturegoer* 29 March 1952: 13. *Sight and Sound* 21 (April–June 1952): 172; 22 (July–September 1952): 43–44. *Theatre Arts* 36 (February 1952): 33, 90. *Times* [London] 29 February 1952: 6; 1 March 1952: 10. *To-day's Cinema* 26 February 1952: 27. *Variety* 2 April 1952: 22. *Vision: Church and Film* 2 (May-June 1952): 28.

ADDITIONAL DISCUSSIONS:
Eliot, T.S. "Preface to the Film Version of *Murder in the Cathedral*." *Authors on Screenwriting.* Ed. Harry M. Geduld. Bloomington: Indiana University Press, 1972.
_____, and George Hoellering. *The Film of Murder in the Cathedral.* New York: Harcourt, Brace, 1952. [Screenplay.]
Nash, Jay Robert, and Stanley Ralph Ross. *The Motion Picture Guide, L–M, 1927–1983.* Chicago: Cinebooks, 1986.
Walker, Roy. "The Film of the Play." *Theatre* 6 (24 May 1962): 10–16.

366. *The Name of the Rose* (1986)

Germany; dir. Jean-Jacques Annaud; Neue Constantin Films and 20th Century–Fox.

Sean Connery (left) as William of Baskerville and F. Murray Abraham as the Papal Inquisitor in Jean-Jacques Annaud's *The Name of the Rose* (1986).

CAST: F. Murray Abraham, Elya Baskin, Feodor Chaliapin, Sean Connery, William Hickey, Michael Lonsdale, Ron Perlman, Volker Prechtel, Helmut Qualtinger, Christian Slater, Valentina Vargas.

In 1327, a synod is to be held at a Benedictine abbey to discuss what the poverty of Christ means to the everyday life of the Catholic Church. Debating the issue will be Franciscan friars noted for strict adherence to their vow of poverty and representatives of the pope at Avignon. The abbey is also the scene of a series of murders, and the abbot asks William of Baskerville, a visiting Franciscan friar, to investigate. Friar William uncovers a plot to conceal a unique manuscript copy of Aristotle's treatise on comedy and also encounters an old nemesis, the papal inquisitor, who sees the murders as the work of the Devil. Friar William eventually solves the mystery of who is guilty of the murders and why (the librarian, who believes laughter is sinful, has been poisoning his confreres to keep them from reading Aristotle's treatise), but not before the scriptorium goes up in flames that consume all its priceless manuscripts. The film never resolves the debate over what implications, if any, the poverty of Christ may have. Friar William and the papal representatives simply leave the monastery, which has been reduced to a charred ruin.

This screen version of Umberto Eco's 1980 novel *The Name of the Rose* faced a daunting task in trying to translate the multi-layered and convoluted plot of its source to the screen. Critics are divided as to the film's success, and it remains one of the most widely discussed recent cinematic depictions of the medieval. The film is visually stunning, and it certainly does focus on the darker elements of the so-called Dark Ages.

REVIEWS: *Bianco e nero* 1 (January-March 1987): 81–85. *Les Cahiers du cinéma* 391 (January 1987): 51–52. *Cineform* 26 (December 1986): 19–22. *Cinéma* [Paris] 381 (17 December 1986–6 January 1987): 2. *Cinema nuovo* 36 (January-February 1987): 41–42. *Cinema Papers* 62 (March 1987): 52–53. *Cinématographe* 126 (January 1987): 56. *EPD Film* 11 (November 1986): 29. *Film-echo/Filmwoche* 55 (3 October 1986): 14; 61 (31 October 1986): 12. *Films and*

Filming 388 (January 1987): 38. *Films in Review* 37 (December 1986): 620. *Hollywood Reporter* 19 September 1986: 3, 38. *Jeune cinéma* 180 (April-May 1987): 27–30. *Los Angeles Times* 24 September 1986: Calendar 1. *Millimeter* 14 (August 1986): 206–08. *Monthly Film Bulletin* 54 (February 1987): 53. *New York Times* 24 September 1986: C21. *Positif* 311 (January 1987): 68–69. *Sight and Sound* 55 (Spring 1986): 129–31. *Starburst* 102 (February 1987): 12–13. *Sunday Times* [London] 25 June 1987: 51. *Times* [London] 17 January 1987: 18; 23 January 1987: 17. *Times* [London] *Literary Supplement* 23 January 1987: 87. *Variety* 24 September 1986: 324. *Video* April 1987: 72. *Video Review* March 1987: 66. *24 Images* 31–32 (Winter 1987): 61–63.

ADDITIONAL DISCUSSIONS:

Chase, Donald. "Abraham after Amadeus." *Horizon* 29 (October 1986): 57–58.

Gross, Anna, and Jean Turner. "*The Name of the Rose*, A Medieval Mystery." *American Cinematographer* 67 (October 1986): 51–54.

Katz, Robert. "*Name of the Rose.*"*American Film* 11 (September 1986): 26–31.

Lamm, Robert. "Can We Laugh at God?" *Journal of Popular Film & Television* 19 (Summer 1991): 81–90.

Magill, Frank N., ed. *Magill's Cinema Annual 1987: A Survey of the Films of 1986.* Pasadena, Calif.: Salem, 1987.

Nash, Jay Robert, and Stanley Ralph Ross. *The Motion Picture Guide, 1987 Annual (The Films of 1986).* Chicago: Cinebooks, 1987.

Parker, John. *Sean Connery.* London: Gollancz, 1993.

Pfeiffer, Lee, and Philip Lisa. *The Films of Sean Connery.* New York: Citadel, 1993.

Sellers, Robert. *The Films of Sean Connery.* New York: St. Martin's, 1990.

Tantitch, Robert. *Sean Connery.* London: Chapmans, 1992.

The Naughty Nun (1972) see *La Bella Antonia, prima monaca e poi dimonia* (1972)

367. The Navigator: An Odyssey Across Time (1988)

New Zealand; dir. Vincent Ward; Arenafilm and Film Investment Corporation of New Zealand.

CAST: Noel Appleby, Chris Haywood, Paul Livingston, Bruce Lyons, Hamish McFarlane, Marshall Napier, Sarah Pierse.

The inhabitants of an isolated mining village in Cumbria live in fear of the advancing plague. The time is 1348, the year in which the Black Death will sweep across Europe. A miner named Connor returns from the outside world in despair until his younger brother Griffin tells of a vision he has had to ensure the village's survival. They must place a cross atop the spire of a cathedral in a distant town. Four villagers set out to find the cathedral. Their journey takes them down a mine shaft from whose black and white depths they emerge into the full color of present day New Zealand. After a series of adventures, the medieval visitors manage to achieve their goal and return to their village, which is spared the plague but at the price of Griffin's life.

One of several recent films to link medieval and modern concerns, *The Navigator* finds stark parallels between a world threatened with destruction by the Black Death and a world threatened with destruction by AIDS and nuclear holocaust. The film is a fascinating exercise in the visual and a tribute to the power of faith.

REVIEWS: *Cinéma* 443 (25 May 1988): 11. *Empire* 58 (April 1994): 98. *EPD Film* 6 (June 1989): 35. *Films and Filming* 413 (March 1989): 34–35. *Hollywood Reporter* 30 March 1989: 4, 23. *Los Angeles Times* 5 April 1989: Calendar 5. *Metro* 78 (Summer 1988-1989): 53–54. *Monthly Film Bulletin* 56 (May 1989): 144–45. *New York Times* 28 June 1989: C7. *Positif* 329–330 (July-August 1988): 86–87. *Séquences* 141–42 (September 1989): 101–02. *Sunday Times* [London] 14 May 1989: C9. *Times* [London] 11 May 1989: 19. *Times Literary Supplement* [London] 12 May 1989: 515. *Variety* 11 May 1989: 28.

ADDITIONAL DISCUSSIONS:

Hughes, Peter. "The Two Ages of the Navigator." *Cinema Papers* 72 (March 1989): 26–27.

Jones, Alan. "The Navigator." *Cinefantastique* 19 (May 1989): 38–39, 61.

Lewis, Brent. "*The Navigator.*" *Films and Filming* 413 (March 1989): 10–11.

Magill, Frank N., ed. *Magill's Cinema Annual 1990: A Survey of the Films of 1989.* Englewood Cliffs, N.J.: Salem, 1990.

The Motion Picture Guide: 1989 Annual (The Films of 1988). Evanston, Ill.: Cinebooks, 1989.

Murray, Scott, ed. *Australian Cinema.* St. Leonards, N.S.W. [Aus.]: Allen & Ulwin, 1994.

Nayman, Michaele. "*The Navigator.*" *Cinema Papers* 69 (May 1988): 30–31.

"*The Navigator*— Not Just a New Zealand Film." *Encore* 6 (27 October–9 November 1988): 18–22.

Wilmington, Michael. "Firestorm and Dry Ice." *Film Comment* 20 (May-June 1993): 51–54.

The New Adventures of a Connecticut Yankee in King Arthur's Court (1987) see *Novye prikluchenia janke pri dvore Korola Artura* (1987)

(From left to right) Paul Livingston as Martin, Hamish McFarlane as Griffin, and Bruce Lyons as Connor in Vincent Ward's *The Navigator* (1988). (Still courtesy of the British Film Institute.)

368. *Die Nibelungen* (1924)

Germany; dir. Fritz Lang; UFA.

ALTERNATE TITLES: *Kriemhilds Rache, Kriemhild's Revenge, The Nibelungs* and *Siegfried.*

CAST: Bernhard Goetzke, Rudolph Klein-Rogge, Theodor Loos, Paul Richter, Margarete Schön, Hans Adalbert von Schlettow.

The young Siegfried, inspired by a song in praise of the beauty of the Burgundian princess Kriemhild, sets out to win her hand. En route, he encounters and slays a dragon, bathing in its blood to ensure his invincibility in all future combat. Set upon by the Nibelung dwarfs, Siegfried defeats their leader Alberich and claims his magic net (which allows its owner to assume any shape) and the treasure of the Nibelungs. He finally reaches Kriemhild's castle, where news of his exploits has preceded him. Kriemhild's brother, King Gunther, promises Siegfried his sister's hand in marriage if Siegfried will help him win Brunhilda, the Queen of Iceland, as his bride. Using the magic net, Siegfried disguises himself as Gunther and wins Brunhilda as the king's bride. They all then return to Burgundy, but rivalry soon develops between Kriemhild and Brunhilda, and Siegfried is slain by Gunther's vassal Hagen. A furious Kriemhild is then sent off to the East to be bride to Attila the Hun. Several years pass, and Kriemhild invites Gunther and his court to visit her. They do so, and Kriemhild springs a long-nurtured trap that results in the destruction of the Burgundians and the Huns.

By any measure, this is one of the great films of all times. Lang's production from a script by his wife Thea von Harbou is one of the most successful translations of medieval texts to the screen. The film's source is the anonymous thirteenth century German epic *The Nibelungenlied,* and, like its source, the film celebrates the most popular of Teutonic myths. The film's sets and use of space are especially noteworthy.

REVIEWS: *Berliner Tageblatt* 15 February 1924; 2 May 1924. *Bioscope* 8 May 1924: 47. *Exceptional Photoplays* 6 (October 1925): 1. *Film* [Germany] 5 (May 1986): 6–7. *Film Daily* 30 August 1925: 4. *Harrison's Reports* 2 January 1926: 2. *Kinematograph Weekly* 10 April 1924: 25; 8 May 1924: 60. *Literary*

Digest 86 (26 September 1925): 27–29. *Monthly Film Bulletin* 43 (June 1976): 134–35. *New York Times* 24 August 1925: 17. *Photoplay* 28 (August 1925): 50. *Stoll Herald* 24 November 1924: 3–5. *Variety* 16 April 1924: 26; 12 April 1967: 6.

ADDITIONAL DISCUSSIONS:

Armour, Robert A. *Fritz Lang.* Boston: Twayne, 1977.

Barr, Alfred H., Jr. "Nationalism in German Films." *Hound and Horn* 7 (January–March 1934): 278–83.

Beyfuss, E., and A. Kossowsky. *Das Kulturfilmbuch.* Berlin: Chryselius & Schulz, 1924.

Bock, Michael, and Michael Töteberg, eds. *Das Ufa-Buch.* Frankfurt am Main: Zweitausendeins, 1992.

Brennicke, Ilona, and John Hembus. *Klassiker des deutschen Stummfilms 1910–1930.* Munich: Goldman Verlag, 1983.

Bulleid, H.A.V. "*Siegfried,* a Critical Commentary." *Amateur Cine World* 1 (December 1941): 155–60.

Coates, Paul. *The Gorgon's Gaze.* New York: Cambridge University Press, 1991.

"Colossal German Film Enterprise." *Bioscope* 21 February 1924: 36–37.

Connelly, Robert B. *The Motion Picture Guide, Silent Film, 1910–1936.* Chicago: Cinebooks, 1986.

Dahlke, Günther, and Günter Karl, eds. *Deutsche Spielfilme von dem Anfänger bis 1933.* Berlin: Henschekverlag Kunst und Gesellschaft, 1988.

De Laet, Danny. *Fritz Lang.* Rotterdam: Film International, 1975.

Düsel, Friedrich. "Dramatische Rundschau." *Westermanns Monatshefte* 136 (March-April 1924): 300–06.

Eder, Klaus. "Der Nibelungen Nöthigung." *Film* [Germany] 2 (February 1967): 26–27.

Eibel, Alfred, ed. *Fritz Lang.* Paris: Présence du cinéma, 1964.

Eisner, Lotte H. *Fritz Lang.* New York: Oxford University Press, 1977.

_____. *The Haunted Screen.* Berkeley: University of California Press, 1973.

_____. "Notes sur le style de Fritz Lang." *Revue du cinéma* 5 (1 February 1947): 3–26.

Fliesler, Joseph R., ed. *Siegfried; A Music-Photo Drama with Wagner's Immortal Score.* New York: Patrick McNerney, 1925.

Garbicz, Adam, and Janel Klinowski. *Cinema, The Magic Vehicle.* Metuchen, N.J.: Scarecrow, 1975.

Hake, Sabine. "Architectural Hi/stories: Fritz Lang and *The Nibelungs.*" *Wide Angle* 12 (July 1990): 38–57.

Harbou, Thea von. *Das Nibelungenbuch.* Munich: Drei Masken Verlag, 1923. [Screenplay.]

_____. *Das Nibelungenbuch.* Munich: Drei Masken Verlag, 1924. [Screenplay and introduction.]

Hauer, Stanley R. "The Sources of Fritz Lang's *Die Nibelungen.*" *Literature/Film Quarterly* 18 (1990): 103–10.

Jacobs, Lewis. *The Emergence of Film.* New York: Hopkinson and Blake, 1982.

Jenkins, Stephen. *Fritz Lang, The Image and the Look.* London: BFI, 1981.

Jouvet, Pierre. "Les Images de Kriemhilde." *Cinématographe* 23 (January 1977): 5–8.

Kaplan, E. Ann. *Fritz Lang, A Guide to References and Resources.* Boston: Hall, 1981.

Kracauer, Siegfried. *From Caligari to Hitler.* 1947. Rpt. Princeton: Princeton University Press, 1974.

Lang, Fritz. "Arbeitsgemeinschaft im Film." *Der Kinematograph* 887 (2 February 1924): 7–9.

_____. "Nous essayons déja de photographier des idées, quatre textes, 1924–1929." *Positif* 365–66 (July-August 1991): 151–56.

_____. "La Nuit viennoise." *Cahiers du cinéma* 169 (August 1965): 42–58; 179 (June 1966): 51–63.

Lennig, Arthur. "The Nibelungen Saga (Parts I and II)." *Film Notes of the Wisconsin Film Society.* ed. Arthur Lenning. Madison: Wisconsin Film Society, 1960.

_____. *The Silent Voice.* Albany: Faculty-Student Association of the State University of New York, 1966.

Lorenzen, Dagnar. "Les Nibelungen de Fritz Lang à Harald Reinl." *Cahiers de la cinémathèque* 42–43 (Summer 1985): 106–12.

Maibohm, Ludwig von. *Fritz Lang.* Munich: Wilhelm Heyne Verlag, 1981.

Magill, Frank N., ed. *Magill's Survey of Cinema: Silent Films.* Englewood Cliffs, N.J.: Salem, 1982.

Manvell, Roger. "Revaluations—1: *Siegfried.*" *Sight and Sound* 19 (April 1950): 83–85.

Ott, Frederick W. *The Films of Fritz Lang.* Secaucus, N.J.: Citadel, 1979.

Phillips, Gene D. "Fritz Lang Remembers." *Focus on Film* 20 (Spring 1975): 43–51.

"Pure Cinema." *Independent* [New York] 118 (19 March 1927): 311–14.

The She-Devil. London: Granger's Exclusives, 1925. [Souvenir program.]

Simsolo, Noël. *Fritz Lang.* Paris: Edilig, 1982.

Stiles, Victoria. "Fritz Lang's Definitive *Siegfried* and Its Versions." *Literature/Film Quarterly* 13 (1985): 258–74.

_____. "The Siegfried Legend and the Silent Screen … Fritz Lang's Interpretation of a Hero Saga." *Literature/Film Quarterly* 8 (1980): 232–36.

Thomas, Nicholas, ed. *International Dictionary of Films and Filmmakers—1. Films.* Chicago: St. James, 1990.

369. *Die Nibelungen* (1966)

Germany; dir. Harald Reinl; CCC Filmkunst.

ALTERNATE TITLE: *Whom the Gods Wish to Destroy.*

CAST: Uwe Beyer, Karin Dor, Mario Girotti, Rolf Henninger, Herbert Lom, Maria Marlow, Skip Martin, Hans von Borsody, Fred Williams, Siegfried Wischnewski.

Paul Richter as Siegfried in Fritz Lang's *Die Nibelungen* (1924). (Still courtesy of the British Film Institute.)

After slaying the dragon and securing the Nibelung treasure, Siegfried arrives in the Burgundian court at Worms to ask for the hand of Kriemhild in marriage. Her brother, King Gunther, agrees to the marriage if Siegfried will help him win the hand of Brunhilda of Iceland.

Siegfried is successful, but the double marriage only brings discord to Worms, as Brunhilda is really in love with Siegfried. Gunther's vassal Hagen slays Siegfried, and a grief-stricken Brunhilda kills herself. Kriemhild decides to leave the court with her son and her husband's treasure, but she is ambushed by Hagen, who kills the child and sinks the treasure in the waters of the Rhine. Kriemhild, now doubly embittered, agrees to marry Attila, the King of the Huns. Years later, she invites the Burgundians to celebrate the birth of her sec-

ond son. The invitation masks a plot for revenge, which destroys both the Burgundians and the Huns.

Any attempt to make a new film of *The Nibelungenlied* has to be made in the shadow of Fritz Lang's 1924 masterpiece. Interestingly, when this film was first proposed, it was hoped that Lang would direct — and that Marlon Brando would play Siegfried. What was produced, a film clearly fascinated with gore and bloodshed, is not all that memorable.

REVIEWS: *Film* [Germany] 7 (July 1966): 34; 4 (April 1967): 42. *Filmblätter* 1 (6 January 1967): 5; 8 (24 February 1967): 152; 13 (31 March 1967): 20. *Film-echo/Filmwoche* 101–02 (23 December 1966): 29; 19 (8 March 1967): 9. *Films and Filming* 16 (1 October 1969): 50. *Monthly Film Bulletin* 36 (September 1969): 197. *Kinematograph Weekly* 26 April 1969: 10. *To-day's Cinema* 25 April 1969: 8. *Variety* 12 April 1967: 6.

Karin Dor as Brunhilda in Harald Reinl's *Die Nibelungen* (1966).

ADDITIONAL DISCUSSIONS:
Eder, Klaus. "Der Nibelungen Nöthigung." *Film* [Germany] 2 (February 1967): 26–27.
Joseph, Bob. "The Ring." *Films and Filming* 13 (October 1966): 56–57.
Lorenzen, Dagnar. "*Les Nibelungen* de Fritz Lang à Harald Reinl." *Les Cahiers de la cinémathèque* 42–43 (Summer 1985): 106–12.

370. *I Nibelunghi* (1910)

Italy; dir. M. Bernacchi; Milano Films.

Siegfried kills the dragon and steals the treasure it protected. He boasts of his feat to Hagen and Gunther and gives the treasure to Kriemhild. Brunhild orders Hagen to kill Siegfried. Invading Huns approach Worms, and Kriemhild marries Attila, presumably to spare the city. In reality, she needs Attila for the revenge she plans. Attila's armies kill Gunther and Hagen, and Kriemhild stabs Attila to death.

This abridged version of *The Nibelungenlied* is not one of the better films made by Milano, one of the premier Italian silent film companies.

DISCUSSION:

Prolo, Maria Andriana. *Storia del cinema muto italiano.* Milan: Poligono Società Editrice, 1951.

The Nibelungs (1924) see *Die Nibelungen* (1924)

Nights of Boccaccio (1972) see *Boccaccio* (1972)

Nobleman's Rights (1908) see *Le Droit de seigneur* (1908)

The Non-Existent Knight (1970) see *Il Cavaliere inesistente* (1970)

371. *Nonnen fra Asminderød* (1911)

Denmark; Nordisk and Great Northern Films.

ALTERNATE TITLES: *The Life of a Nun* and *The Nun.*

A monk secretly lusts after a young girl. When her lover visits her, the monk convinces the girl's father to force her to enter a convent. On the night before she is to take the veil, she and her lover meet, but they are discovered. The lover is thrown into jail, and the young girl is attacked by the monk, whom she fends off with a crucifix. In anger, the monk then accuses the young girl of blasphemy, and she is ordered to be walled up alive in a tomb. The lover tells a sympathetic prince of their predicament, and the girl is released just before the last stone in her tomb is about to be put in place. The two marry, and the monk is led off for punishment.

The scene in which the young girl uses the crucifix as a weapon to defend herself from the monk's lecherous advances proved controversial. Audiences objected to such handling of the crucifix without proper reverence.

REVIEWS: *Bioscope* 16 February 1911: 36. *Moving Picture World* 13 May 1911: 1089; 27 May 1911: 1202.

ADDITIONAL DISCUSSIONS:

Engberg, Marguerite. *Registrant over danske film 1896–1914. Bind II: 1910–1912.* Copenhagen: Institut for Filmvidenskab, 1977.

"Facts and Comments." *Moving Picture World* 22 July 1911: 101.

I Normani (1961) see *Invasion of the Normans* (1961)

The Normans (1961) see *Invasion of the Normans* (1961)

372. *The Norseman* (1978)

United States; dir. Charles B. Pierce; Fawcett-Majors Productions.

CAST: Susie Coelho, Christopher Connelly, Jack Elam, Mel Ferrer, Kathleen Freeman, Lee Majors, Denny Miller, Cornel Wilde.

Thorvald Helge sets out to find his father, who has been missing for a year. A long sea journey takes him to the shores of a land that he calls Vinland, where he finds that the native peoples have blinded his father and enslaved him and his fellow Vikings. With the assistance of a sympathetic native woman, Thorvald rescues his father, destroys the native settlement and sails back home.

The opening credits announce that "this story is based on fact." Where the facts come from is not entirely clear. Any connections between this Viking film — more properly a very bad grade B Western — and the travels of Leif Erickson or his followers (c. 1000), who may have indeed landed somewhere on the North American continent — is coincidental.

REVIEWS: *Film Bulletin* October-November 1978: Reviews G. *Hollywood Reporter* 3 July 1978: 2. *Monthly Film Bulletin* 46 (March 1979): 48–49. *Variety* 5 July 1978: 16.

ADDITIONAL DISCUSSION:

Nash, Jay Robert, and Stanley Ralph Ross. *The Motion Picture Guide, N–R, 1927–1983.* Chicago: Cinebooks, 1986.

373. *Notre Dame de Paris* (1911)

France; dir. Albert Capellani; Pathé Frères, S.C.A.G.L.

CAST: René Alexandre, Claude Garry, Henry Krauss, Stacia Napierkowska.

The gypsy Esmeralda is elected queen of the rabble and catches the attention of Archdeacon Frollo. He instructs his servant, the hunchbacked bell-ringer Quasimodo, to kidnap the girl, but Quasimodo's attempt to do so is frustrated by Capt. Phoebus of the King's Archers. Quasimodo is whipped; only Esmeralda takes pity on him, offering him a cup of water. The growing affection between Phoebus and Esmeralda enrages Frollo, who stabs Phoebus and fixes the blame on Esmeralda. She is condemned to death, but Frollo promises to help her escape if she will become his lover. She refuses. As Esmeralda is led to her execution, Quasimodo rescues her and, claiming the right of sanctuary, houses her in the great Cathedral of Notre Dame. Frollo, again rebuffed by Esmeralda, delivers her to her execution. Quasimodo, grief-stricken, hurls the archdeacon from the bell tower to his death.

Unlike later cinematic versions of Victor Hugo's nineteenth century novel *Notre Dame de Paris,* Frollo remains a cleric in this film. Out of fear of offending Catholic sensibilities, it became popular in later films to turn him into a lawyer, a move which undercuts the intended anticlericalism central to the original novel.

REVIEWS: *Bioscope* 21 September 1911: 635–636; 16 October 1913: supplement v. *Moving Picture World* 16 December 1911: 884–85.

ADDITIONAL DISCUSSIONS:
Abel, Richard. *The Ciné Goes to Town, French Cinema 1896–1914.* Berkeley: University of California Press, 1994.
Bousquet, Henri. *Catalogue Pathé des années 1896 à 1914: 1910–1911.* Paris: Henri Bousquet, 1993.
Glut, Donald F. *Classic Movie Monsters.* Metuchen, N.J.: Scarecrow, 1978.

Notre Dame de Paris (1956) see *The Hunchback of Notre Dame* (1956)

374. *Novelle galeotte d'amore dal Decamerone* (1972)

Italy; dir. Antonio Margheriti; Seven Films.

ALTERNATE TITLE: *Decameron 3.*

CAST: Alessandro Alessandroni, Alberto Atenari, Pupo De Luca, Eva Maria Grubmuller, Ray O'Connor, Martina Orlop, Gastone Pescucci, Marlene Rahn.

A man lusts after the wife of a moneylender, but she demands a huge sum in return for her favors. The man borrows the money from her husband and then tells him he has repaid the money to his wife. A nobleman returns from the Holy Land to find himself the father of a red-haired son who bears a striking resemblance to his court painter. His attempt to punish his wife and the painter backfires on himself. The wife of a baker tricks her husband, to whom she has been unfaithful, and escapes his wrath by sending her servant in her place for a rendezvous with her lover. A jealous knight returns home from the Crusades to his wife, whom he locked into a chastity belt designed to emasculate intruders. He finds that most of the men in his village have been castrated and that his wife has run off with the blacksmith.

In yet another attempt to capitalize on the success of Pasolini's 1971 film *Decameron,* Margheriti directs a film whose first and third tales are indeed taken from Boccaccio (Day 8, Tale 1 and Day 7, Tale 8). On the whole, though, the film is at best silly, content (as are all the other attempts) to mirror Pasolini, while offering little more than cheap titillation.

REVIEWS: *CinemaTV Today* 3 March 1973: 31. *Intermezzo* 2 (October-November 1973): 12. *Monthly Film Bulletin* 40 (April 1973): 74; 40 (October 1973): 219.

ADDITIONAL DISCUSSIONS:
Poppi, Roberto, and Mario Pecorari. *Dizionario del cinema italiano: I Film dal 1970 al 1979.* Rome: Gremese Editore, 1996.
La Produzione italiana 1972/73. Rome: Unitalia Film, 1973.

375. *Novelle licenziose di vergini vogliose* (1972)

Italy; dir. Michael Wotruba [Aristide Massaccesi]; Elektra Films.

ALTERNATE TITLE: *Licentious Tales of Lusting Virgins.*

CAST: Gabriella Giorgelli, Margaret Rose Keil, Enza Sbordone, Antonio Spaccatini.

As he composes the tales of *The Decameron,* Boccaccio falls asleep and finds himself in Hell where Geoffrey Chaucer is his guide. As they travel through the circles of Hell, Chaucer tells Boccaccio the stories of the people they met. When Boccaccio awakens, he fears he himself will go to Hell because of his writings. He vows to burn all his works, but Petrarch prevails upon him not to do so.

Yet another attempt to exploit the popularity of Pasolini's 1971 film *The Decameron*, this film manages to conflate and confuse a number of medieval literary works.

DISCUSSIONS:
Poppi, Roberto, and Mario Pecorari. *Dizionario del cinema italiano: I Film dal 1970 al 1979*. Rome: Gremese Editore, 1996.
La Produzione italiana 1972/73. Rome: Unitalia Film, 1973.

376. *Novye prikluchenia janke pri dvore Korola Artura* (1987)

Soviet Union; dir. Viktor Gres; Dovzhenko Studios.

ALTERNATE TITLE: *The New Adventures of a Connecticut Yankee in King Arthur's Court.*

CAST: Albert Filozov, Evdokia Ghermanova, Mark Gres, Alexander Kaidanovsky, Sergei Koltakov, Anastasia Vertinskaya.

Hank Morgan, an American military pilot, crashes in the desert and awakens in the world of King Arthur, where he sets out to introduce the age of chivalry to the wonders of modern technology. Arthur's world is none too keen to accept what Hank has to offer, so Hank challenges them to trial by combat. In the final battle, Lancelot defeats Hank, chivalric values are protected and Hank returns to the twentieth century.

The hero in this cinematic musical version of Twain's novel is Lancelot, who defeats Hank by discovering a great bell which, when rung, establishes harmony among all who hear its tolling.

REVIEWS: *Iskusstvo kino* 3 (March 1989): 87–91. *Soviet Film* 4 (April 1989): 18–19.

ADDITIONAL DISCUSSIONS:
Cowie, Peter, ed. *Variety International Film Guide 1990*. Hollywood, Calif.: Samuel French, 1989.
The Motion Picture Guide: 1989 Annual (The Films of 1988). Evanston, Ill.: Cinebooks, 1989.
"On the Spot Report." *Soviet Film* 6 (1987): 18–19.

The Nun (1911) see *Nonnen fra Asminderød* (1911)

377. *The Oath of A Viking* (1914)

United States; dir. J. Searle Dawley; Picture Playhouse Films.

Olaf, a young Viking fleeing his own people after having been found guilty of an unspecified crime, is befriended by a rival tribe. He soon falls in love with Lydia, the daughter of the rival tribe's leader. Lydia is, however, bethrothed to another, and Olaf tries several times to win her hand by deceit and treachery before he is returned to his own tribe for punishment.

REVIEWS: *Motion Picture World* 15 August 1914: 942. *Variety* 18 August 1915: 18.

378. *L'Œuvre au noir* (1988)

Belgium; dir. André Delvaux; Philippe Dussart Productions.

ALTERNATE TITLE: *The Abyss.*

CAST: Jean Bouise, Pierre Dherte, Sami Frey, Anna Karina, Johan Leysen, Jacques Lippe, Gina Maria Volonté.

After spending 20 years hiding from the Inquisition, the alchemist Zénon returns to his native Bruges secure in the thought that he will have been forgotten. Now a doctor of medicine, Zénon, who uses the name Sébastien Théus, is soon recognized and summoned before the authorities. The courts are at first inclined to be merciful given his good work as a physician, but religion wins out. After a lengthy trial, Zénon is condemned to die at the stake.

From Marguerite Yourcenar's 1968 award-winning novel *L'Œuvre au noir*, Delvaux fashions a tale set in the dark final days of the Middle Ages when superstition and ignorance prevailed over reason and enlightenment. The film's real strength lies in its success in invoking the mood of the frenzied madness afoot in Flanders at the dawn of the Renaissance.

REVIEWS: *Cinéma* [Paris] 441 (11–17 May 1988): 8–9. *Jeune cinéma* 189 (July-August 1988): 29–30. *Première* 134 (May 1988): 21 and 108–10. *Screen International* 9 July 1988: 14. *Segnocinema* 38 (May 1989): 41–42. *Séquences* 137 (November 1988): 76. *Variety* 18 May 1988: 38.

ADDITIONAL DISCUSSIONS:
Bavelier, Ariane. "Un Héros ... entretien avec Gina Maria Volonté." *Avant-scène du cinéma* 371 (May 1988): 20–23.
Beylie, Claude. "Moins noir que vous ne pensez: note sur Marguerite Yourcenar." *Avant-scène du cinéma* 371 (May 1988): 18–19.
Blampain, Daniel. "D'André Delvaux à Marguerite Yourcenar: un dialogue avant le film." *Avant-scène du cinéma* 371 (May 1988): 24–27.
Camy, Gérard. "Entretien avec André Delvaux." *Jeune cinéma* 189 (July-August 1988): 30–32.
Chevassu, F. "Le Cinéma en partie double." *Revue du cinéma* 439 (June 1988): 54–72.
Delvaux, André. "L'Œuvre au noir." *Avant-scène du cinéma* 371 (May 1988): 28–107. [Screenplay.]

Les Films français. Paris: Unifrance International, 1988.

Jost, François. "Entretien — André Delvaux." *Avant-scène du cinéma* 371 (May 1988): 4–17.

Nysenholc, Adolphe. "Themes et sitiations dans *L'Œuvre au noir* d'André Delvaux." *Cahiers du scenario* [Belgium] 4–5 (Winter 1988-1989): 115–18.

Ofelas (1987) see *Pathfinder* (1987)

On the Way to the Crusades, I Met a Woman Who (1967) see *The Chastity Belt* (1967)

Oragens Fange (1985) see *The Captive of the Dragon* (1985)

379. Les Origines de la Confédération (1924)

Switzerland; dir. Emil Harder; Sunshine Films and Turicia-Film AG.

ALTERNATE TITLES: *Die Entstehung der Eidgenossenschaft, Wilhelm Tell,* and *William Tell.*

CAST: Robert Kleinert, Felix Orell, George Roberts.

William Tell refuses to bow to Gessler's hat and thereby accept Austrian sovereignty over Switzerland. As punishment, he is ordered to shoot an apple off of his son's head with an arrow. He succeeds and subsequently leads an army that drives the Austrian oppressors from his native land.

This film, a Swiss-American co-production shot on location in Switzerland, presents a rather plodding rehearsal of familiar events in the life of William Tell. It is undercut by subtitles punctuated with contemporary American colloquialisms that have an unintentionally comic effect.

REVIEWS: *Harrison's Reports* 6 June 1925: 91. *New York Times* 20 May 1925: 26. *Variety* 20 May 1925: 47.

ADDITIONAL DISCUSSIONS:

Dumont, Hervé. *Histoire du cinéma suisse.* Lausanne: Cinémathèque suisse, 1987.

Guttinger, Fritz. "Lets [sic] Get This William Tell Thing Straight." *Classic Images* 113 (November 1984): [Center] 3–4.

380. Orlando e i paladini di Francia (1956)

Italy; dir. Piero Francisci; Italgamma Film.

ALTERNATE TITLES: *Roland and the Knights of France* and *Roland the Mighty.*

CAST: Rik Battaglia, Lorella De Luca, Clelia Mantania, Fabrizio Mioni, Vittorio Sanipoli, Rosanna Schiaffino.

The Moorish king of Spain, Agramante, sends the beautiful Angelica into Charlemagne's camp to stir up discord. Both Rinaldo and Orlando fall in love with her, and the traitorous Gano di Maganza hopes to use their rivalry in a plan to betray Charlemagne and hand the king over to the Moors. Rinaldo and Orlando save the day, and Gano flees to the Moorish camp where he is killed by Agramante.

Borrowing freely from the Old French *Song of Roland* (c. 1100) and Ludovico Aristo's sixteenth century poem *Orlando furioso,* Francisci's film is little more than a predictable adventure tale built around a lame love story.

REVIEWS: *Cinématographie française* 1751 (4 January 1958): 15. *Film français* 17 January 1958: 26.

ADDITIONAL DISCUSSIONS:

Chiti, Roberto, and Roberto Poppi. *Dizionario del cinema italiano. Vol 2: I Film dal 1945 al 1959.* Rome: Gremese Editore, 1991.

The Italian Production 1955–56. Rome: Unitalia Film, 1956.

Lucanio, Patrick. *With Fire and Sword, Italian Spectacles on American Screens 1958–1968.* Metuchen, N.J.: Scarecrow, 1994.

381. Orlando furioso (1974)

Italy; dir. Luca Ronconi; R.A.I–TV.

CAST: Edmonda Aldini, Peter Chatel, Silvia Dionisio, Massimo Foschi, Claudia Giannotti, Hiram Keller, Ettore Manni, Sergio Nicolai.

Against a backdrop of Charlemagne's war with the Moors, Orlando falls into madness when the woman he loves, a pagan princess, marries another. Cured by a sympathetic sorcerer, Orlando rejoins Charlemagne's forces and kills the Moorish king.

This version of the epic poem *Orlando furioso* by Ludovico Aristo (1474–1533) was made for Italian television.

REVIEWS: *Cineforum* 144 (May 1975): 333–39. *Cinema nuovo* 234 (May-April 1975): 136–37. *Jeune cinéma* 84 (February 1975): 19–21. *Rivista del cinematografo* 7 (July 1975): 322–23.

ADDITIONAL DISCUSSIONS:

Poppi, Roberto, and Mario Pecorari. *Dizionario del cinema italiano: I Film dal 1970 al 1979.* Rome: Gremese Editore, 1996.

La Produzione italiana 1971/72. Rome: Unitalia Film, 1972.

The Other Canterbury Tales (1972) see *Gli Altri racconti di Canterbury* (1972)

The hall of the Grail King in Edwin S. Porter's *Parsifal* (1904). (Still courtesy of the Library of Congress.)

Outlaw (1981) see *Utlaginn* (1981)

Padenie novgoroda velikogo (1910)
see *Marfa-Posadnista* (1910)

382. *I Paladini* (1983)

Italy; dir. Giacomo Battiato; Vides Cinematografica.

ALTERNATE TITLES: *Le Armi e gli amori, Hearts in Armour* and *Storia d'armi e d'amori.*

CAST: Barbara De Rossi, Rick Edwards, Leigh McCloskey, Ron Moss, Tania Roberts.

Saracen and Christian knights battle over affairs of religion — and of the heart. Bradamante, a woman knight, pines for Ruggero, the Saracen leader, who loves her in return. In each other's arms, the two easily forget that a war rages around them. Similarly, the Christian champion Rolando pines for Ruggero's sister Isabella, and, once in her arms, he too forgets about fighting. The four unite to defeat three Saracen champions, abandon warfare and live happily ever after.

Battiato here directs a comic book version of the medieval, with a minor nod in the direction of events from *The Song of Roland* (c. 1100). The film's aim is simply to provide action-packed adventure, and it succeeds in doing so in a minor way. Tania Roberts, who played Isabella, is better know to television audiences as one of the title characters from *Charlie's Angels.*

REVIEWS: *Ecran fantastique* 37 (September 1983): 57; 41 (January 1984): 43–44. *Positif* 275 (January 1984): 63–65. *Segnocinema* 4 (September 1984): 33. *Variety* 2 November 1983: 20.

ADDITIONAL DISCUSSION:
La Produzione italiana 1982/83. Rome: Unitalia Film, 1983.

383. *Parsifal* (1904)

United States; dir. Edwin S. Porter; Edison.
CAST: Adelaide Fitz-Allen, Robert Whittier.

Using a highly exaggerated style of acting, interspersed with trick camera effects, a group of actors presents the following scenes from Wagner's opera: "Parsifal Ascends the Throne," "Ruins of A Magic Garden," "Exterior of Klingson's Castle," "Magic Garden," "Interior of the Temple," "Scene Outside the Temple," "Return of Parsifal" and "In the Woods."

With this film, Edison hoped to capitalize on the success of the 1903 stage production of the opera in New York, but the film's run had to be shortened when the owner of the copyright successfully sued Edison for using the script without permission.

REVIEW: *Optical Lantern and Cinematograph Journal* 1 (1905): 52.

ADDITIONAL DISCUSSIONS:

Bush, W. Stephen. "The Possibilities of Synchronization." *Motion Picture World* 2 September 1911: 607–608.

Catalogue of Educational Motion Picture Films. Chicago: George Kleine, 1910.

Musser, Charles. *Before the Nickelodeon.* Berkeley: University of California Press, 1991.

Niver, Kemp R. *The First Twenty Years, A Segment of Film History.* Los Angeles: Locare Research Group, 1968.

_____. *Motion Pictures from the Library of Congress Paper Print Collection, 1894–1912.* Berkeley: University of California Press, 1967.

"Parsifal." *Edison Films* July 1906: 50–53.

Savada, Elias. *The American Film Institute Catalog of Motion Pictures Produced in the United States: Film Beginnings, 1893–1910.* Metuchen, N.J.: Scarecrow Press, 1995.

Spears, Jack. "Edwin S. Porter." *Films in Review* 21 (June-July 1970): 327–54.

384. *Parsifal* (1912)

Italy; dir. Mario Caserini; Ambrosio Films.

Parsifal, having overcome a number of opponents and various temptations, assumes his rightful place as the guardian of the Holy Grail, curing the wounded King Amfortas in the process.

More detailed than Porter's 1904 film, Caserini's *Parsifal* still suffers from a problem common to many early filmed operas, the inability to synchronize the film itself with the musical accompaniment.

REVIEWS: *Bioscope* 30 October 1913: 427; 27 November 1913: 811–13. *Kinematograph Monthly Record* 20 (December 1913): 59–60. *Moving Picture World* 28 December 1912: 1307–08.

ADDITIONAL DISCUSSIONS:

Jarratt, Vernon. *The Italian Cinema.* London: Falcon, 1951.

Lephrohon, Pierre. *The Italian Cinema.* Trans. Roger Greaves and Oliver Stallybrass. New York: Praeger, 1972.

Weinberg, Herman G., ed. *Fifty Years of Italian Cinema.* Rome: Carlo Bestetti-Edizioni d'Arte, 1955.

385. *Parsifal* (1953)

Spain; dir. Daniel Mangrane; Cine-Español.

CAST: Gustavo Rojo, Ludmilla Tcherina.

In fifth-century Spain as the barbarians invade, Parsifal seeks and eventually finds the Holy Grail, bringing peace to his troubled homeland.

This film version blends elements from Wagner's opera with elements from medieval legend and literature concerning the Grail.

REVIEW: *Film français* 448 (13 November 1953): 20.

386. *Parsifal* (1982)

Germany; dir. Hans-Jürgen Syberberg; Gaumont–TMS Films.

CAST: Edith Clever, Aage Haugland, Armin Jordan, Karin Krick, Michael Kutter, Robert Lloyd, Martin Speer.

The wounded King Amfortas awaits the arrival of a chaste fool who can cure him. A young man who has just killed a swan — a heinous act — is brought before him, and the court suspects that this simple boy may be the one to cure Amfortas. The boy accompanies Amfortas and his retinue to the Grail Castle and witnesses many wonders which so overwhelm him that he says nothing and is dismissed. The young man later appears at the castle of Klingsor, Amfortas's enemy, and learns his name (Parsifal) and the meaning of everything he earlier witnessed. He defeats Klingsor and goes off into the forest. Years later, Parsifal returns and initiates the Grail ceremony, healing Amfortas. The Grail itself spreads its benediction to all who salute Christ the Redeemer.

Undoubtedly one of the most complex and possibly the greatest opera film ever made, Syberberg's film, which runs for more than four hours, presents Wagner's opera in a claustrophobic labyrinth that is constructed out of the cracks and crevices of an enormous model of the composer's death mask. The film succeeds by using elaborate sets, puppets, expert dubbing and the daring conceit of having the

Parsifal as both a woman (Karin Krick) and a man (Michael Kutter) arriving at the Chapel of the Grail in Hans-Jürgen Syberberg's *Parsifal* (1982).

title character played by both a man and a woman.

REVIEWS: *Avant-scène du cinéma* 338 (July-August 1982): 51–55. *Cinéma* [Paris] 283–284 (July-August 1982): 95. *Cinema nuovo* 32 (August–October 1983): 8–9. *Cinématographe* 79 (June 1982): 71–72. *Ciné revue* 21 (20 May 1982): 44. *Continental Film and Video Review* 29 (August 1982): 44–45; 30 (May 1983): 10–11. *Ecran fantastique* 25 (1982): 19–20. *Études* [Paris] 357 (August-September 1982): 235–37. *Film Journal* 86 (18 February 1983): 41. *Films* 3

(June 1983): 34. *High Fidelity and Musical America* 33 (June 1983): [between] 80 and 83 [18–20]. *Hollywood Reporter* 11 March 1983: 34. *Image et son* 374 (July-August 1982): 78–80. *Los Angeles Times* 20 July 1983: 6. 3. *Monthly Film Bulletin* 50 (May 1983): 137–38. *New York Times* 23 January 1983: 1. 46; 11 February 1984: 3. 8. *Opera* [England] 34 (June 1983): 686–88. *Opera News* 47 (12 March 1983): 42–43. *Positif* 259 (September 1982): 65–66. *Revue du cinéma* (La Saison cinématographique) Hors serie 26 (1982): 251–52. *Séquences* 115 (January 1984): 40–42. *Sunday Times* [London] 3 April 1983: 39. *Times* [London] 26 March 1983: 11; 31 March 1983: 10. *Times* [London] *Literary Supplement* 8 April 1983: 352. *Variety* 26 May 1982: 16; 9 February 1983: 18. *Video Review* 11 (September 1990): 11. *24 Images* 19 (Winter 1983-1984): 13–14. *Wagner News* 22 (April-May 1983): 11–15.

ADDITIONAL DISCUSSIONS:

Bianciotti, Hector. "Le Sourire de Parsifal." *Le Nouvel Observateur* 26 December 1981: 70–72.

Bonnet, Jean-Claude, and Michel Celemski. "Entretien avec Hans-Jürgen Syberberg." *Cinématographe* 78 (May 1982): 12–19.

Borie, Bertrand. "Entretien avec Hans-Jürgen Syberberg." *Ecran fantastique* 25 (1982): 20–21.

Ellero, Robert, et al. "Conversazione con Hans-Jürgen Syberberg." *Cinema e cinema* 10 (January–March 1983): 66–69.

Just, Lothar R., ed. *Das Filmjahr '82/83.* Munich: Filmland Presse, 1983.

Lévi-Strauss, Claude. "Od Chrétiena de Troyesa do Richarda Wagnerja." *Ekran* 8. 6 (1983): 9–13.

Magill, Frank N., ed. *Magill's Cinema Annual, 1983.* Englewood Cliffs, N.J.: Salem, 1984.

Müller, Ulrich. "Blank, Syberberg, and the German Arthurian Tradition." In Kevin J. Harty, ed. *Cinema Arthuriana, Essays on Arthurian Film.* New York: Garland, 1991.

Nash, Jay Robert, and Stanley Ralph Ross. *The Motion Picture Guide, N–R, 1927–1983.* Chicago: Cinebooks, 1986.

Nattiez, Jacques. *Wagner Androgyne.* Princeton: Princeton University Press, 1993.

Porter, Andrew. "Musical Events: By Comparison Made Wise." *New Yorker* 59 (21 February 1983): 112–16, 119.

Socci, Stefano. "*Parsifal*, film-opera dell'avvenire." *Filmcritica* 381–83 (January-February 1988): 7–13.

Stanbrook, Alan. "The Sight of Music." *Sight and Sound* 56 (Spring 1987): 132–35.

Syberberg, Hans-Jürgen. "Filmisches bei Richard Wagner." In Gerhard Heldt, ed. *Richard Wagner: Mittler zwischen Zeiten.* Anif, Austria: Müller-Speiser, 1990.

_____. "'nur der Kranke hält es aus.'" *Medium* 12 (April 1982): 27–29.

_____. "'ohne Neugier und Lust und Informationsredlichkeit.'" *Medium* 12 (September-October 1982): 78–80.

_____. *Parsifal, ein Filmessay.* Munich: Heyne, 1982.

_____. "'Vorführen braucht soviel Energie und Phantasie wie Machen.'" *Medium* 12 (December 1982): 31–33.

_____. "'wir sollen den anderen ins Gesicht spuken.'" *Medium* 12 (July 1982): 40–41.

387. *Parisina, un amore alla corte di Ferrara nel XV secolo* (1909)

Italy; dir. Giuseppe De Liguoro; SAFFI-Luca Comerio (Milan).

Parisina, the second wife of Nicolò III, the Duke of Ferrara, falls in love with her husband's son. When their adultery is discovered, the duke has them both executed.

The film, which won a prize for cinematography, was shot in Ferrara using the city's castle and cathedral for sets. Nicolò III d'Este (1393–1441), the Duke of Ferrara, was a notorious libertine, proudly claiming to have fathered more than 20 illegitimate children in addition to his children by his several wives. His second wife Parisina Malatesta, a woman much younger than he, fell in love with the duke's second son, Ugo. When the duke discovered their affair, he had them both beheaded on May 23, 1425.

DISCUSSION:

Bernardini, Aldo, and Jean A. Gili, eds. *Le Cinéma italien de La Prise de Rome (1905) à Rome ville ouverte (1945).* Paris: Centre Georges Pompidou, 1986.

388. *Parzival* (1980)

West Germany; dir. Richard Blank; West Deutsche Rundfunk.

CAST: Wolfram Kinkel, Eva Schuchardt.

In a windowless attic, using puppets and toy props, a group of actors stage a much-abridged version of Wolfram von Eschenbach's epic poem *Parzival*.

Made for German television, this film is unusual in its use of von Eschenbach rather than Wagner as a source.

DISCUSSIONS:

Harty, Kevin J. "The Arthurian Legends on Film: An Overview." In Kevin J. Harty, ed. *Cinema Arthuriana, Essays on Arthurian Film.* New York: Garland, 1991.

Müller, Ulrich. "Blank, Syberberg, and the German Arthurian Tradition." In Kevin J. Harty, ed. *Cinema Arthuriana, Essays on Arthurian Film.* New York: Garland, 1991.

_____. "Parzival 1980—auf der Bühne, im Fernsehem und im Film." In Jürgen Kühnel, et al, eds.

Mittelalter-Rezeption II. Göppingen: Kümmerle, 1982.

389. *La Passion Béatrice* (1987)

France; dir. Bertrand Tavernier, Cléa Productions.

ALTERNATE TITLES: *Béatrice* and *The Passion of Beatrice.*

CAST: Monique Chaumette, Julie Delpy, Robert Dhéry, Bernard-Pierre Donnadieu, Nils Tavernier.

In 1360, the Lord of Contremare prepares to go off to the Crusades. As a final gesture, he takes his young son François into his arms, hugging him, giving him his dagger and commending his mother to his care. The boy runs to show his mother the dagger only to find her in the arms of another man, whom he kills with the dagger. Twenty-five years later, François, having succeeded to his father's title, returns from the French defeat at Crécy after his daughter, Béatrice, mortgages the family lands to obtain his release and that of her brother Arnaud from the English. François comes home a changed and violent man who rapes his daughter and insists they live openly as husband and wife. Béatrice, a match for her father in terms of willfulness, plots her revenge and kills him with the same dagger that he used to dispatch his mother's lover almost three decades earlier.

Tavernier's film is an unflinching examination of human frailty and cruelty in a time in France where frailty had no place and cruelty was the order of the day. The precedent here in terms of an examination of the dark primal forces at work within people is ancient Greek tragedy.

REVIEWS: *American Film* 13 (March 1988): 9. *Les Cahiers du cinéma* 402 (December 1987): 52. *Cineforum* 6 (June 1989): 27. *Cinéma* [Paris] 415 (11–18 November 1987): 3–4. *Cinema nuovo* 37 (May-June 1988): 55. *EPD Film* 6 (June 1989): 27. *Études* [Paris] 367 (December 1987): 675–76. *Film français* 2165 (30 October 1987): 19. *Film Journal* 91 (February-March 1988): 65. *Hollywood Reporter* 19 April 1988: 3, 78. *Jeune cinéma* 185 (January-February 1988): 35–36. *Los Angeles Times* 13 April 1988: Calendar 1. *New York Times* 18 March 1988: C25. *Positif* 322 (December 1987): 69–71. *Première* 128 (November 1987): 12–13. *Revue du cinéma* 432 (November 1987): 28–30. *Séquences* 134 (June 1988): 50–51. *Variety* 9 December 1987: 16. *24 Images* 37 (Spring 1988): 65.

ADDITIONAL DISCUSSIONS:
Douin, Jean-Luc. *Tavernier.* Paris: Edilig, 1988.

Les Films français. Paris: Unifrance Film International. 1987.
Loiseau, Jean-Claude. "Le Sang maudit." *Première* 128 (November 1987): 75–85, 160.
Mosca, Bertrand. "Bernard-Pierre Donnadieu." *Première* 123 (June 1987): 128, 176–77.
_____. "La Passion Béatrice." *Première* 123 (June 1987): 124–33.
The Motion Picture Guide, 1989 Annual (The Films of 1988). Evanston, Ill.: Cinebooks, 1989.
Rabinovici, Jean. "Entretien avec Bertrand Tavernier." *Cinéma* [Paris] 415 (11–18 November 1987): 5–6.
Toumarkine, Doris. "'Tavernier's *Béatrice* Presents Dark Vision of the Middle Ages." *Film Journal* 91 (February-March 1988): 41, 119.
Tous les films 1987. Paris: Éditions Chrétien-Médias, 1988.

La Passion de Jeanne d'Arc (1928) see *The Passion of Joan of Arc* (1928)

The Passion of Beatrice (1987) see *La Passion Béatrice* (1987)

390. *The Passion of Joan of Arc* (1928)

France; dir. Carl Theodor Dreyer; Société Générale des Films.

ALTERNATE TITLE: *La Passion de Jeanne d'Arc.*

CAST: Antonin Artaud, André Berley, Jean d'Yd, Mlle. Falconetti, Louis Ravet, Maurice Schultz, Eugene Silvain, Michel Simon.

The 19-year-old Joan is brought before a tribunal on charges of heresy and witchcraft, though her real crimes were her successes against the English in battle. She is denounced for wearing men's clothes and for claiming to her the voices of the saints. She refuses to renounce her voices and, shown the instruments of her torture, she faints. Denied the Eucharist and shown the pyre, she relents. Seeing a pile of straw that resembles Christ's crown of thorns, she demands that she be taken to the pyre for execution. As she burns, the crowds turn against her executioners

Dreyer's *Passion* is without a doubt the finest film on the legend of Joan of Arc and one of the most important films ever made. Shot in closeup with the camera held at obtuse angles, Falconetti (whose previous work had been in comedies) is provided with a vehicle to deliver one of *the* great screen performances.

REVIEWS: *Bioscope* 9 April 1930: 38. *Close Up* 2 (June 1928): 72–73; 3 (July 1928): 15–23. *Educational Screen* 8 (April 1929): 107, 121. *Experimental Cinema*

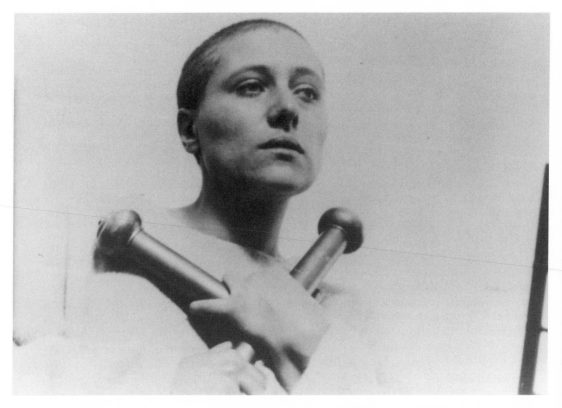

Mlle. Falconetti as Joan in Carl Theodor Dreyer's *The Passion of Joan of Arc* (1928). (Still courtesy of the British Film Museum.)

1 (February 1930): 7–10. *Film Daily* 9 September 1933: 6. *Film Mercury* 9 (12 April 1929): 6. *Moving Picture Herald* 16 September 1933: 39. *National Board of Review Magazine* 4 (January 1929): 7–9. *New York Times* 12 August 1928: 7. 3; 20 January 1929: 7; 29 March 1929: 21; and 31 March 1929: 8. 7. *Photoplay* 35 (February 1929): 52. *La Petite illustration* 408 (24 November 1928): 15–16. *Revue du cinéma* 2 (February 1929): 66–67. *Times* [London] 12 November 1930: 12. *Variety* 10 April 1929: 25.

ADDITIONAL DISCUSSIONS:

Amengual, Barthélemy. "Les Pouvoirs de l'abstraction." *Positif* 430 (December 1996): 79–84.

Blaetz, Robin J. "Strategies of Containment: Joan of Arc in Film." Ph.D. dissertation. New York University, 1989.

Blakeston, Oswell. *Through a Yellow Glass.* London: Pool, 1928.

Bond, Kirk. "Notes on the Modern Cinema." *Europa* 1 (October 1933): 32–36.

Breitbart, Eric. "A Classic Film Rises from the Ashes." *Sightlines* 20 (Fall 1986): 26–28.

"Carl Th. Dreyer: *La Passion de Jeanne d'Arc.*" *Avant-scène du cinéma* 367–68 (January-February 1988): 1–179. [Special issue.]

Connelly, Robert. *The Motion Picture Guide: Silent Film 1910–1936.* Chicago: Cinebooks, 1986.

D., H. "*The Passion of Joan of Arc*: An Appreciation." *Close Up* 4 (March 1929): 56–68.

Delteil, Joseph. "*The Passion of Joan of Arc.*" *Literature/Film Quarterly* 13 (Fall 1975): 292–98.

Dreyer, Carl Theodor. *Four Screenplays.* Trans. Oliver Stallybrass. London: Thames and Hudson, 1970.

_____. *Œuvres cinématographiques 1926–1934.* Ed. Maurice Drouzy and Charles Tesson. Paris: Cinémathèque française, 1983. [Screenplay.]

_____. *La Passione di Giovanna D'Arco.* Milan: Domus, 1945. [Screenplay.]

Drouzy, Maurice. *Carl Th. Dreyer né Nilsson.* Paris: Les Éditions du Cerf, 1982.

_____. "Jeanne d'Arc livré aux bourreaux." *Cinématographe* 3 (June 1985): 62–67.

_____. "Jeanne d'Arcs mange angister." *Kosmorama* 176 (Summer 1986): 50.

Engberg, Marguerite. "Historien om den genfundne 'Jeanne d'Arc.'" *Kosmorama* 171 (May 1985): 39–42.

_____. "Il Ritrovamento della 'Passione di Giovanna d'Arco.'" *Immagine* NS 1 (Winter 1986): 18–23.

Falconetti, Hélène. *Falconetti.* Paris: Les Éditions du Cerf, 1987.

Fescourt, Henri. *La Foi et les montagnes.* Paris: Montel, 1959.

The Film Society Programme [London] 16 November 1930: n.p.

Garbicz, Adam, and Jacek Klinowski. *Cinema, The Magic Vehicle.* Metuchen, N.J.: Scarecrow, 1975.

Harty, Kevin J. "Jeanne au cinéma." In Bonnie Wheeler and Charles T. Wood, eds. *Fresh Verdicts on Joan of Arc.* New York: Garland Publishing, 1996.

Jacobs, Lewis. *The Emergence of the Cinema.* 2nd ed. New York: Norton, 1979.

Jeancolas, Jean-Pierre. "Jeanne sauvée du bûcher." *Positif* 289 (March 1985): 58–59.

"Jeanne d'arc à l'ecran." *La Petite illustration* 408 (24 November 1928): 15–16.

Jehanne: la passion et la mort d'une sainte. Paris: Maison du Danemark, 1989.

Kelman, Ken. "Film as Poetry." *Film Culture* 29 (Summer 1963): 22–27.

Kinder, Marsha, and Beverle Houston. *Close-Up, A Critical Perspective on Film.* New York: Harcourt, 1972.

Landy, Marcia. "Woman, Iconograpy, and Transcendence in Dreyer's *The Passion of Joan of Arc.*" *Field of Vision* 9–10 (Winter-Spring 1980): 12–18.

Leff, Leonard J. *Film Plots, Vol. I.* Ann Arbor, Mich.: Pierian, 1983.

Linderman, Deborah. "Uncoded Images in the Heterogeneous Text." *Wide Angle* 3 (1979): 34–41.

Luft, Herbert G. "Dreyer — An Interview." *Films and Filming* 7 (June 1961): 11.

MacPherson, Kenneth. "As Is." *Close Up* 3 (July 1928): 5–10; 5 (December 1929): 446–54.

Magill, Frank N., ed. *Magill's Survey of Cinema: Silent Films.* Englewood Cliffs, N.J.: Salem, 1982.

Manvell, Roger. *The Film and the Public.* Baltimore: Penguin, 1955.

Margolis, Nadia. *Joan of Arc in History, Literature, and Film.* New York: Garland, 1990.

_____. "Trail by Passion: Philology, Film and Ideology in the Portrayal of Joan of Arc (1900–1930)." *Journal of Medieval and Early Modern Studies* 27 (Fall 1997): 445–93.

Milne, Tom. *The Cinema of Carl Dreyer.* New York: A.S. Barnes, 1971.

Nash, Mark. *Dreyer.* London: BFI, 1977.

_____. "Joan Complete." *Sight and Sound* 54 (Summer 1985): 157–58.

Neergaard, Ebbe. *Carl Dreyer, A Film Director's Work.* Trans. Marianne Helweg. London: BFI, 1950.

O'Brien, Charles. "Rethinking National Cinema: Dreyer's *La Passion de Jeanne d'Arc* and the Academic Aesthetic." *Cinema Journal* 35 (Summer 1996): 3–30.

"*La Passion de Jeanne d'Arc* [Special section]." *Skrien* 144 (November-December 1985): 27–42.

"*La Passione de Jeanne d'Arc.*" *Universal and International Exhibition of Brussels 1958: Presentation of the Best Films of All Time.* Brussels: Belgian Film Library, 1958.

Petley, Julian. "*The Passion of Joan of Arc.*" *Movies of the Silent Years.* Ed. Ann Lloyd. London: Orbis, 1984.

Pipolo, Tony. "Metaphorical Structures in *La Passion de Jeanne d'Arc.*" *Millenium Film Journal* 19 (1987–1988): 52–84.

_____. "The Spectre of Joan of Arc." *Film History* 2 (1988): 301–24.

Potamkin, Harry Alan. "Pabst and the Social Film." *Hound and Horn* 6 (January–March 1933): 293–305.

_____. "Phases of Cinematic Unity." *Close Up* 4 (May 1929): 27–38; 5 (September 1929): 171–84; 6 (June 1930): 463–74.

Potter, Nicole. "*The Passion of Joan of Arc*/Voice of Light." *Films in Review* 47 (March-April 1996): 28–30.

Rowland, Richard. "Carl Dreyer's World." *Hollywood Quarterly* 5 (Fall 1950): 53–60.

Schaub, Martin. "*La Passion de Jeanne d'Arc.*" *Film* [Germany] 2 (February 1968): 41–52.

Sémolué, Jean. "'Douleur, noblesse unique' or la passion chez Carl Dreyer." *Études cinématographiques* 10–11 (Autumn 1961): 150–61.

_____. *Dreyer.* Paris: Éditions universitaires, 1962.

_____. "Dreyer: De Jeanne d'Arc a dies irae." *Avant-scène du cinéma* 100 (February 1970): 8–9.

Slide, Anthony. *Fifty Classic French Films 1912–1982.* New York: Dover, 1987.

Solomon, Stanley J., ed. *The Classic Cinema, Essays in Criticism.* New York: Harcourt, 1973.

Stanbrook, Alan. "*The Passion of Joan of Arc.*" *Films and Filming* 7 (June 1961): 11–13, 40.

Thomas, Nicholas, ed. *International Directory of Films and Filmmakers—1. Films.* Chicago: St. James, 1990.

Tyler, Parker. *Classics of the Foreign Film.* New York: Citadel, 1962.

Vaughan, Dai. "Carl Dreyer and the Theme of Choice." *Sight and Sound* 43 (Summer 1974): 156–62.

Weinberg, Herman. "Composing Each View." *Movie Makers* 9 (June 1934): 235, 250.

_____. "Lubitsch Views the Movies." 4 (September 1929): 570–71.

The Passion of St. Francis (1927) see
Frate Francesco (1927)

391. *Pathfinder* (1987)

Norway; dir. Nils Gaup; Filmkameratene A/S.

ALTERNATE TITLES: *Ofelas* and *Veiviseren.*

CAST: Ellen Anne Buljo, Mikkel Gaup, Ingvald Gottorm, John S. Kristensen, Svein Scharpfenberg, Helgi Skúlason, Inger Utsi, Nils Utsi, Nils-Aslak Valkeapää, Knut Walle.

Aigin, a 16-year-old boy, returns from a hunting trip on the frozen plains of Lapland to find that a band of Tchude warriors has killed his family. Wounded when the Tchudes discover him spying on them, he flees to a nearby village, where he receives a hostile welcome because the villagers fear that the Tchudes will follow Aigin and massacre them. The villagers flee to yet another village, but Aigin stays behind to seek revenge. In a dream, he is visited by a Lapp noiadi (shaman) who cautions him against allowing the thirst for revenge to consume his life. Trapped and forced to lead the Tchudes to the larger village, Aigin tricks them and leads them off a cliff to their death.

Nominated for an Academy Award as best foreign language film and based on a twelfth-century tale called "The Pathfinder and the Torch," *Pathfinder* has the distinction of being one of the few films with dialogue in Lapp, a language incomprehensible even to most Norwegians. All the Lapp roles are played by actors from a theater troupe in Kautokeino, high above the Arctic circle. The parts of the Tchudes were played by Norwegian and Icelandic actors. The Tchudes, nomads from northern Russia and Finland, terrorized the Lapps in the Middle Ages. Basically a peaceful people, the Lapps relied upon the harshness of the terrain and the smallness of their communities for protection. The only way they were vulnerable to the Tchudes was when one of their numbers was forced to be a pathfinder and betray his or her fellow Lapps.

REVIEWS: *Les Cahiers du cinéma* 415 (January 1989): 57. *EPD Film* 5 (September 1988): 35. *Film Journal* 93 (June 1990): 45. *Film og kino* 1 (1988): 30–31, 52. *Filmrutan* 31.3 (1988): 380–39. *Films and Filming* 408 (September 1988): 36–37. *Grand angle* 114 (March 1989): [35–36]. *Kosmorama* 186 (Winter 1988): 49. *Los Angeles Times* 22 June 1990: Calendar 8. *Levende billeder* 4 (November 1988): 30–32. *Monthly Film Bulletin* 55 (September 1988): 278. *New York Times* 11 May 1990: C10. *Positif* 337 (March 1989): 78–79. *Revue du cinéma* 445 (January 1989): 32. *Revue du cinéma* (Saison cinématographique) Hors série 36 (1989): 81. *Scandinavian Film News* 6 (November 1986): [8]. *Sunday Times* [London] 25 September 1988: C8. *Times* [London] 22 September 1988: 18. *Times* [London] *Higher Education Supplement* 7 October 1988: 16. *Variety* 14 October 1987: 9.

ADDITIONAL DISCUSSIONS:

Cardullo, Bert. "Rites of Passage." *Hudson Review* 44 (Spring 1991): 96–104.

Cowie, Peter, ed. *International Film Guide 1989*. New York: Zoetrope, 1989.

Magill, Frank N., ed. *Magill's Cinema Annual 1991, A Survey of the Films of 1990*. Pasadena, Calif.: Salem, 1991.

Mikkel Gaup as Aigin the Pathfinder in Nils Gaup's *Pathfinder* (1987). (Still courtesy of the British Film Institute.)

The Motion Picture Guide: 1991 Annual (The Films of 1990). New York: Baseline, 1991.

Norwegian Films 88. Oslo: Norwegian Film Institute, [1988].

Pathfinder. London: Guild Film Distribution, [1988]. [Press book.]

Paul and Francesca (1910) see *Francesca da Rimini* (1910)

392. *A Penitent of Florence* (1910)

France; Gaumont.

Two brothers, each a gifted vocalist, fall in love with the same woman. When she makes clear her preference for the younger brother, the older stabs him. Thinking he has killed his brother, the older brother then goes into exile for 20 years. Finally returning home, he goes to hear Mass at the cathedral, only to find his brother singing the service for Good Friday. The brothers are then reunited, and all is forgiven.

This film, which according to the titles takes place in Florence during the eleventh century, was given a critically acclaimed screening with an elaborate musical accompaniment when it was shown at Chicago's Orpheum Theater in 1910.

(From left to right) Fabrice Luchini as Perceval, André Dussolier as Gauvain, Marie-Christine Barrault as Guinevere, and Marc Eyraud as Arthur in Eric Rohmer's *Perceval le gallois* (1978).

REVIEWS: *Moving Picture World* 9 April 1910: 551; 16 April 1910: 591; 23 April 1910: 655.

ADDITIONAL DISCUSSIONS:

Bradlet, John M. "A Film That Stirs the Audience." *Moving Picture World* 7 May 1910: 743.

"Feature Films for Feature Music." *Moving Picture World* 16 April 1910: 591.

"Remarkable Demonstration of Moving Pictures." *Moving Picture World* 7 May 1910: 728–29.

Ruth, T. "Quality vs. Quantity." *Moving Picture World* 9 April 1910: 551–52.

Savada, Elias. *The American Film Institute Catalog of Motion Pictures Produced in the United States: Film Beginnings, 1893–1910*. Metuchen, N.J.: Scarecrow, 1995.

Perceval (1978) see *Perceval le gallois* (1978)

393. *Perceval le gallois* (1978)

France; dir. Eric Rohmer; Gaumont-Films du Losange.

ALTERNATE TITLE: *Perceval*.

CAST: Marie-Christine Barrault, Arielle Dombrasie, André Dussolier, Marc Eyraud, Fabrice Luchini.

After a series of adventures which bring him knighthood at King Arthur's court, the young Perceval has a vision of the Holy Grail but fails to realize what he has seen. He then sets off in a quest to find the Grail again, a quest that takes him on yet another series of adventures. Finally, assuming the central role in a Passion play, Perceval is granted a second vision of the Grail.

Unique among films dealing with Perceval and the Quest for the Grail, this movie's source is Chrétien de Troyes's unfinished twelfth century romance. The dialogue retains the verse form of the original romance in a modern French translation. Rohmer uses stylized painted sets (reminiscent of manuscript illustrations) that give the film a genuinely medieval look to provide a commentary on the necessity for the quest for the spiritual, in a medieval or a modern world.

REVIEWS: *Amis du film et de la télévision* 272 (January 1979): 18; 275 (April 1979): 33. *Les Cahiers du cinéma* 299 (April 1979): 41–46. *Cinema nuovo* 290–91 (August–October 1984): 61–62. *Cinemateca revista* 39 (November 1983): 79. *Cinématographe* 44 (February 1979): 11–15. *Continental Film Review* 25 (August 1978): 16–17. *Ecran* 76 (15 January 1979): 71–72. *Études* [Paris] 350 (April 1979): 541–45. *Film Quarterly* 33 (Winter 1979-1980): 49–52. *Films in Review* 76 (January 1979): 53–54. *Hollywood Reporter* 12 October 1978: 1. *Image et son* 334 (December 1978): 109–12. *Jeune cinéma* 116 (December 1978): 28–31. *New York Times* 6 October 1978: n.p. *Positif* 216 (March 1979): 74. *Segnocinema* 13 (May 1984): 68. *Take One* 7 (January 1979): 9–10. *Télérama* 1517 (10–16 February 1979): 86–89. *Times* [London] 14 November 1979: 10. *Time Out* [London] 8–15 January 1992: 143. *Variety* 13 September 1978: 36.

ADDITIONAL DISCUSSIONS:

Adair, Gilbert. "Rohmer's *Perceval*." *Sight and Sound* 47 (Autumn 1978): 230–34.

Angeli, Giovanna. "*Perceval le gallois* d'Eric Rohmer et ses sources." *Cahiers de l'Association Internationale des Études Françaises* 47 (1995): 33–48.

Beatie, Bruce. "The Broken Quest: The 'Perceval' Romances of Chrétien de Troyes and Eric Rohmer." In Debra Mancoff, ed. *The Arthurian Revival, Essays on Form, Tradition, and Transformation.* New York: Garland, 1992.

Burns, E. Jane. "Nostalgia Isn't What It Used to Be: The Middle Ages in Literature and Film." In George Slusser and Eric S. Rabkin, eds. *Shadows of the Magic Lamp, Fantasy and Science Fiction in Film.* Carbondale: Southern Illinois University Press, 1985.

Cinéma français. Paris: Unifrance Film, 1978.

Cormier, Raymond J. "Rohmer's Grail Story: Anatomy of a French Flop." *Yale French Review* 5 (Winter 1981): 391–96.

Crisp, C.H. *Eric Rohmer: Realist and Moralist.* Bloomington: Indiana University Press, 1988.

Douin, Jean-Luc. "Entretien avec Eric Rohmer; *Perceval*, C'est Buster Keaton au moyen âge." *Télérama* 1517 (10–16 February 1979): 90–91.

"Eric Rohmer Talks about the Concept of *Perceval*." *Continental Film Review* 26 (June 1979): 16–17.

"Eric Rohmer's *Perceval le gallois*." *Avant-scène du cinéma* 221 (1 February 1979): 9–64. [Screenplay.]

Fieschi, Jacques. "Un Innocence mortelle." *Avant-scène du cinéma* 221 (1 February 1979): 4–6.

Fisher, Lucy. "Roots: The Medieval Tale as Modernist Cinema." *Field of Vision* 9–10 (Winter-Spring 1980): 21–25, 33.

Grimbert, Joan Tasker. "Aesthetic Distance in Rohmer's *Perceval le gallois*." In Maud S. Walther, ed. *Proceedings of the Purdue University Fifth Annual Conference on Film October 30–November 1, 1980.* West Lafayette, Ind.: Purdue University, 1980.

Huchet, Jean-Charles. "Mereceval." *Litterature* 40 (1980): 69–84.

Jourdat, Alain. "L'Espace comme support d'un récit romanesque." *Le Technicien du film* 272 (15 July–15 September 1979): 8–11.

Magill, Frank N., ed. *Magill's Survey of Cinema: Foreign Language Films.* Englewood Cliffs, N.J.: Salem, 1985.

Magny, Joël, and Dominique Rabourdin. "Entretien avec Eric Rohmer." *Cinéma* [Paris] 242 (February 1979): 11–19.

_____. *Eric Rohmer.* Paris: Rivages, 1986.

_____. "Eric Rohmer ou la quête du graal." *Cinéma* [Paris] 242 (February 1979): 20–23.

Marty, Joseph. "*Perceval le gallois* d'Eric Rohmer, un itinéraire roman." *Les Cahiers de la cinémathèque* 42–43 (Summer 1985): 125–32.

_____. "*Perceval le gallois*: un symbolisme de l'alliance chrétienne." In Michael Estève, ed. *Eric Rohmer 2.* Paris: Minard, 1986.

Milne, Tom. "Rohmer's Seige Perilous." *Sight and Sound* 50 (Summer 1981): 192–95.

Movshovitz, Howard P. "Rohmer's *Perceval*: Narrative Time and Space in Medieval Literature and Film." In Maud S. Walther, ed. *Proceedings of the Purdue University Fifth Annual Conference on Film October 30–November 1, 1980.* West Lafayette, Ind.: Purdue University, 1980.

Rider, Jeff, et al. "The Arthurian Legend in French Cinema: *Lancelot du lac* and *Perceval le Gallois*." In Kevin J. Harty, ed. *Cinema Arthuriana, Essays on Arthurian Film.* New York: Garland, 1991.

Rohmer, Eric. "Note sur la traduction et sur le mise en scène de *Perceval*." *L'Avant-scène du cinéma* 221 (1 February 1979): 6–7.

Smith, Sarah W.R. "Rohmer's *Perceval* as Literary Criticism." In Maud S. Walther, ed. *Proceedings of the Purdue University Fifth Annual Conference on Film October 30–November 1, 1980.* West Lafayette, Ind.: Purdue University, 1980.

Tesich-Savage, Nadja. "Rehearsing the Middle Ages." *Film Comment* 14 (September-October 1978): 50–56.

Williams, Linda. "Eric Rohmer and the Holy Grail." *Literature/Film Quarterly* 11 (April 1983): 71–82.

394. *Die Pest in Florenz* (1919)

Germany, dir. Otto Rippert; Decla Film Gesellschaft.

CAST: Erich Bartels, Theodor Becker, Juliette Brandt, Erner Hübsch, Marga Kierska, Otto Mannstaedt.

In medieval Florence, a courtesan seduces a devout monk who is a follower of Savanarola. Both die as plague devastates the city.

The great film director Fritz Lang wrote the screenplay for this film.

DISCUSSIONS:

Brennicke, Ilona, and Joe Hembus. *Klassiker des deutschen Stummfilms 1910–1930.* Munich: Goldmann Verlag, 1983.

Kaplan, E. Ann. *Fritz Lang, A Guide to References and Resources.* Boston: Hall, 1981.

Lamprecht, Gerhard. *Deutsche Stummfilme 1919*. Berlin: Deutsche Kinemathek, 1968.

Weinberg, Herman G. *An Index to the Creative Work of Fritz Lang*. London: British Film Institute, 1946. [Special supplement to *Sight and Sound* Index Series 5 (February 1946).]

395. *Petri Tarar* (1995)

Sweden; dir. Erich Hortnagl; Svensk Filminductri Productions.

ALTERNATE TITLES: *Petris Tarrar* and *The Tears of Saint Peter*.

CAST: Leif Andre, Enrico Bonavera, Carl-Einar Hackner, Rolf Lassgard, Lasse Poysti, Izabella Scorupco.

In the 1480s, Carla, a young woman who travels disguised as a man, attempts to cheat a prosperous mayor out of some of his wealth. Carla's scheme involves using a magic elixir made from the tears of St. Peter to bring back to life a girl from the mayor's village who has been dead for ten years. Carla's scheme goes awry when she falls in love with the dead girl's former fiancé.

It is difficult to tell whether this rather confused and confusing film is or is not intended to be a farce.

REVIEW: *Variety* 30 November 1995: 83.

Petris Tarar (1995) see *Petri Tarar* (1995)

396. *Pia de' Tolomei* (1908)

Italy; dir. Mario Caserini; Cines.

The noble Pia de' Tolomei is charged with adultery and put to death by her husband Nello dei Pannocchieschi.

This is the first of a series of films to tell Pia's story. She was the daughter of a wealthy Siennese family who married her off to Nello or Paganello dei Pannocchieschi, a Guelf leader who was lord of Maremma Castle. Either out of jealousy or because of a desire to marry a richer heiress, Nello murdered her in 1295 under circumstances that are not clear. Pia appears in Dante's *Purgatorio* (V) among those who died without a chance to repent.

DISCUSSION:

Bernardini, Aldo, and Jean A. Gili, eds. *Le Cinéma italien de La Prise de Rome (1905) à Rome ville ouverte (1945)*. Paris: Centre Georges Pompidou, 1986.

397. *Pia de' Tolomei* (1910)

France; dir. Gerolamo lo Savio; Pathé Frères, Film d'arte italiana.

CAST: Francesco di Dennaro, Guilio Grassi, Gastone Monaldi, Attila Ricci, Tina Sansoldo.

Pia finds her husband and father on opposite sides during the Guelf and the Ghibelline conflict. Rinaldo, her husband, entrusts his wife to the care of Hugo, whom he thinks a friend. Hugo tries to seduce Pia. When she spurns him, he accuses her of adultery. Rinaldo imprisons Pia, who dies of the plague in her husband's arms after Hugo confesses his treachery.

REVIEW: *Bioscope* 1 September 1910: 25.

ADDITIONAL DISCUSSIONS:

Bernardini, Aldo, and Jean A. Gili, eds. *Le Cinéma italien de La Prise de Rome (1905) à Rome ville ouverte (1945)*. Paris: Centre Georges Pompidou, 1986.

Bousquet, Henri. *Catalogues Pathé des années 1896 à 1914: 1910–1911*. Paris: Henri Bousquet, 1994.

398. *Pia de' Tolomei* (1922)

Italy; dir. Giovanni Zannini; Zannini-Film.

CAST: Alfredo Mazotti, Vittorio Simbolotti, Roberto Villani.

Unjustly accused of adultery, Pia dies of malaria in prison before proven innocent.

REVIEW: *Bianco e nero* 42 (January–June 1981): 243–44.

399. *Pia de' Tolomei* (1941)

Italy; dir. Luigi Giacosi; Manderfilm.

CAST: Antonio Baldanello, Nino Crisman, Germana Paolieri, Carlo Tamberlani.

Falsely accused of adultery, Pia dies in prison before her overly possessive and jealous husband learns she is innocent of the charges brought against her.

REVIEW: *Cinema* [Rome] 128 (25 October 1941): 267.

ADDITIONAL DISCUSSIONS:

Chiti, Roberto, and Enrico Lancia. *Dizionario del cinema italiano*. Vol. 1: *I Film dal 1930 al 1944*. Rome: Gremese Editore, 1993.

Savio, Francesco. *Ma l'amore no*. Milan: Sonzogno, 1975.

400. *Pia de' Tolomei* (1958)

Italy; dir. Sergio Grieco; Do.Re.Mi.–Procenix.

CAST: Bella Darvi, Arnoldo Foà, Illaria Occhini, Jacques Sernas.

The Guelf tyrant Nello della Pietra holds Pia, the daughter of the exiled Ghibelline leader, as hostage. Nello tries to seduce her, but Pia rebuffs him. Her father seeks revenge on Nello, but is convinced to urge his daughter to marry Nello when the latter promises to end hostilities against the Ghibellines. Pia marries Nello only because she thinks her true love, Duccio, has been killed. A jealous servant denounces Pia for adultery, and Nello exiles her to a marshland where an attempted rescue by Duccio fails. Nello stabs Pia, and she dies in Duccio's arms. Nello is swallowed up by the marshlands near the castle.

REVIEWS: *Film français* 843 (15 July 1960): 11. *Film italiano* 25 (December 1958): 25.

ADDITIONAL DISCUSSIONS:
Chiti, Roberto, and Roberto Poppi. *Dizionario del cinema italiano. Vol. 2: I Film dal 1945 al 1959*. Rome: Gremese Editore, 1991.
The Italian Production 1958. Rome: Unitalia Film, 1959.

401. *The Pied Piper* (1971)

Great Britain; dir. Jacques Demy; Sagittarius Productions/Goodtimes Enterprises.

CAST: Donovan, Michael Hordern, John Hurt, Roy Kinnear, Donald Pleasence, Jack Wild.

In the fourteenth century, the corrupt town of Hamelin, already caught up in a conflict between the Pope and the emperor, finds itself overrun with rats. As the citizens of the town and the local nobility battle over how to raise money for and whom to support in the battle between church and state, the rats threaten the city with plague. A piper offers to rid the town of the rodents, but for a price. Afterwards, when the citizens refuse to pay him what he is owed, he takes their children instead.

The sources here are the versions of the legend found in the fairy tale by the Brothers Grimm and the poem by Robert Browning. In this particular cinematic version — which is definitely not intended for young audiences — plague looms large everywhere as a metaphor for a society corrupt from top to bottom. The piper's final act, leading the children from the city, does not so much punish their parents as spare them from the plague which rages throughout the city in the film's final scenes.

REVIEWS: *Cinefantastique* 1 (Fall 1971): 46; 2 (Winter 1973): 37. *Cinéma* [Paris] 206 (February 1976): 162–64. *CinemaTV Today* 5 August 1972: 19. *Cue* 3 June 1972: 7. *Filmfacts* 15 (1972): 234–36. *Films and Filming* 19 (March 1973): 48–49. *Hollywood Reporter* 28 April 1972: 3, 23. *Jump Cut* 10–11 (June 1976): 16–17. *Monthly Film Bulletin* 39 (September 1972): 193. *New York Times* 26 May 1972: 16. *Positif* 180 (April 1976): 66–68. *Take One* 3 (July 1972): 23–24. *Variety* 10 May 1972: 20.

ADDITIONAL DISCUSSIONS:
Nash, Jay Robert, and Stanley Ralph Ross. *The Motion Picture Guide, N–R, 1927–1983*. Chicago: Cinebooks, 1986.
Washington, Irving. "Hot Rats." *Time Out* [London] 6–12 August 1971: 53–54.
Weldon, Michael. *The Psychotronic Encyclopedia of Film*. New York: Ballantine, 1983.

402. *The Pied Piper of Hamelin* (1911)

United States; Thanhouser Films.

Promised a fee of a thousand guilders, the piper rids Hamelin of the rats that have infested the city. When he seeks payment, the citizens balk and give him only 15 guilders. The piper then leads all the children except one crippled young boy out of the city. Faced with the prospect of allowing this one boy to grow up alone without any children around him, the piper relents and returns the children. The grateful citizens, having learned a lesson about the value of honesty, pay him his full fee.

From Browning's poem, this silent film adds a happy ending to the legend of the Pied Piper.

REVIEW: *Moving Picture World* 29 July 1911: 226–28.

403. *The Pied Piper of Hamelin* (1912)

France; Pathé Frères.

Having reneged on their agreement to pay the piper for his services when he rids Hamelin of rats, the citizens see him turn his skills to leading their children from the city. Having second thoughts about what they have done, they pay him the agreed-upon amount, and he returns the children to them.

This film follows the lead of the 1911 Thanhouser film and changes the conclusion of the tale to allow for a happy ending.

REVIEW: *Bioscope* 28 March 1912: supplement v.

404. *The Pied Piper of Hamelin* (1913)

United States; dir. George Lessley; Edison.

CAST: Robert Bower, Herbert Prior.

The greedy citizens of Hamelin come to regret not paying the piper his fee when he rids their town of a rat infestation. The angry piper leads their children away. Later, rather than leaving them buried deep inside of a mountain as the legend suggests, he restores them to their parents, who agree finally to pay the piper.

The Edison Company constructed an elaborate set, which follows the lead of earlier films in providing a happy ending to the tale.

REVIEWS: *Bioscope* 16 October 1913: supplement iii. *Edison Kinetogram* 16 August 1913: Film 7397. *Moving Picture World* 9 August 1913: 664.

ADDITIONAL DISCUSSIONS:

Horwitz, Rita, and Harriet Harrison. *The George Kleine Collection of Early Motion Pictures in the Library of Congress, A Catalog.* Washington, D.C.: Library of Congress, 1980.

"'The Pied Piper of Hamelin' Is an Edison Film." *Moving Picture World* 19 February 1910: 261.

405. *The Pied Piper of Hamelin* (1957)

United States; dir. Bretaigne Windust; NBC Television.

CAST: Stanley Adams, Jim Backus, Van Johnson, Rene Kroper, Lori Nelson, Claude Rains, Kay Starr, Doodles Weaver.

The familiar tale of the piper, the children, and the rats is here told in song without much distinction despite a score based on Edvard Grieg's *Peer Gynt Suite.*

REVIEWS: *Daily Cinema* 18 August 1961: 6. *Kine Weekly* 24 August 1961: 21. *Monthly Film Bulletin* 28 (October 1961): 144. *New York Times* 27 November 1957: 55. *Variety* 4 December 1957: 23.

406. *Pimple's Ivanhoe* (1913)

Great Britain; Phoenix Films.

In this farce, the popular film clown Pimple rescues the fair Rebecca from the evil Sir Briarwood Gilbert.

REVIEWS: *Bioscope* 27 November 1913: supplement xi; 16 November 1916: supplement iii. *Kinematograph Monthly Film Record* 20 (December 1913): 74–75.

Le Più Belle Donne del Boccaccio
(1972) see *Decameron n. 3: Le Più Belle Donne del Boccaccio* (1972)

The Plague in Florence (1919) see *Die Pest in Florenz* (1919)

407. *The Plague-Stricken City* (1912)

France; Gaumont.

When plague threatens a town, the prince of a nearby castle gathers revelers around him and refuses to help the townspeople. Among the revelers are a captain and his beautiful wife and two daughters. Lusting for the three women, the prince kills the captain. The women escape and go into the village to tend the sick and dying. Exposed to the plague, they return to the castle to infect all the revelers.

This film presents an analogue to Poe's short story "The Masque of the Red Death."

REVIEWS: *Bisocope* 11 April 1912: 143; 16 May 1912: supplement vi.

408. *Poet of the People* (1911)

United States; Thanhouser Films.

The poet Grengoire appears before King Louis IX of France to read a poem critical of the monarchy. Louis is not amused and orders the poet to be hanged. The King's ward, Annette, is secretly in love with Grengoire and pleads for his life. At the last minute, Louis relents, frees Grengoire and allows his ward to marry the poet.

Despite a change in the main character's name, this film was among the first to tell the story of the poet and rascal François Villon (1431–?).

REVIEWS: *Moving Picture World* 29 April 1911: 968; 6 May 1911: 1021.

Le Poignard fatal (1906) see *La Fée carabosse* (1906)

409. *A Poor Knight and the Duke's Daughter* (1908)

France; Gaumont.

When his lack of fortune and fame prevents a knight from marrying his lady love, the knight sets forth on a quest to achieve both. In his absence, a second knight wishes to marry the lady, but she refuses, vowing fidelity to her true love. With the aid of a witch, the second knight conjures up an illusion that shows the first knight being unfaithful to the lady. In anger, she agrees to marry the deceiving knight. As the wedding party proceeds down the aisle of the cathedral, the first knight returns. Broken-hearted at seeing his beloved about to be married to another, the first knight falls dead. The lady rushes to his side, but she too falls dead of a broken heart. Finally united in death, the two are buried together in the crypt of the cathedral.

REVIEW: *Moving Picture World* 27 June 1908: 548–49.

ADDITIONAL DISCUSSION:

Savada, Elias. *The American Film Institute Catalog of Motion Pictures Produced in the United States: Film Beginnings, 1893–1910.* Metuchen, N.J.: Scarecrow, 1995.

Liv Ullmann (left) as the young Joan and Olivia de Havilland as the Mother Superior in Michael Anderson's *Pope Joan* (1972).

410. *Pope Joan* (1972)

Great Britain; dir. Michael Anderson; Big City Productions.

ALTERNATE TITLE: *The Devil's Impostor.*

CAST: Olivia de Havilland, Lesley-Anne Down, Keir Dullea, Trevor Howard, Jeremy Kemp, Patrick Magee, Franco Nero, Maximilian Schell, Liv Ullmann.

Joan is a small-town midwestern preacher who decries modern moral degradation and identifies herself with the supposed woman pope from the ninth century. Taken to see a psychiatrist, she regresses to a former self and wakes up in the ninth century as Joan, a young well-educated woman who flees to a convent to avoid raping and pillaging marauders. The convent offers only temporary refuge as massive civil disorder erupts with the death of Charlemagne. Joan flees (disguised as a man) to Greece, where she continues her education

and attracts papal notice. Leo IV, thinking her a man, appoints her his private secretary and makes her a cardinal. Upon Leo's death, Joan becomes Pope John VI, but Nero the emperor protests. Nero, it turns out, had earlier slept with Joan when she was in the convent. He now recognizes her and sleeps with her again, promising that they will validate each other's claims to their respective thrones. War calls Nero away, and he returns nine months later to find a very pregnant pope about to give birth to his child. Both mother and child are stoned to death, and Joan awakens in the present-day psychiatrist's office also trying to hide a pregnancy. She and the child die in childbirth.

Legend has it that a woman reigned as Pope John VI from 855 until 858 and was stoned to death, when, on a procession from St. Peter's Basilica to the Lateran Palace, she gave birth to a child. (Supposedly, the same route has never since been followed by papal processions.) The Middle Ages knew of Joan from various sources, including Boccaccio's *De claris mulieribus*, completed sometime around 1362. In modern times, the legend of a woman pope has had intermittent interest. The Greek writer Emmanuel Rhoïdes (or Royidis) published a long novel about Pope Joan in 1866, which Lawrence Durrell translated and adapted into English in 1960. More recently, Joan appears as one of the characters in Caryl Churchill's 1982 play *Top Girls*. This film, however, adds nothing to the legend. It is badly directed and just plain boring. Worst of all, it misappropriates the talents of an international cast of stars.

REVIEWS: *Cinefantastique* 1 (Fall 1971): 46. *CinemaTV Today* 11 November 1972: 20. *Cue* 19 August 1972: 7. *Filmfacts* 15 (1972): 592–95. *Films and Filming* 19 January 1973: 51–52. *Hollywood Reporter* 24 August 1972: 3, 13. *Monthly Film Bulletin* 39 (December 1972): 256–57. *New York Times* 17 August 1972: 29. *Sunday Times* [London] 29 October 1972: 36. *Times* [London] 27 October 1972: 9. *Variety* 23 August 1972: 6. *Village Voice* 17 August 1972: 9.

ADDITIONAL DISCUSSIONS:
Clarke, Sue. "A Pope at Bray." *To-day's Cinema* 25 March 1971: 8–9.
Munn, Michael. *Trevor Howard: The Man and His Films*. London: Robson, 1989.
Nash, Jay Robert, and Stanley Ralph Ross. *The Motion Picture Guide, N–R, 1927–1983*. Chicago: Cinebooks, 1986.
Thomas, Tony. *The Films of Olivia de Havilland*. Secaucus, N.J.: Citadel, 1983.

411. *Il Poverello di Assisi* (1911)

Italy; dir. Enrico Guazzoni; Cines.
ALTERNATE TITLE: *Saint Francis*.
CAST: Emilio Ghione, Italia Manzini.
In a dream, Francis has a vision of poverty personified. He breaks with his rich family and founds an order of friars. He visits the Sultan of Damietta, who respects him but refuses to convert to Christianity. The Pope accepts his order, and a scene follows in which Francis dictates his celebrated "Canticle to the Sun." The film closes with Francis blessing Assisi right before his death surrounded by his beloved monks, his longtime friend Clare and her order of nuns.

The film was shot on location in Assisi and shows a level of sophistication in filmmaking that had not previously been achieved by Italian filmmakers.

REVIEWS: *Bioscope* 23 November 1911: supplement xiii. *Kinematograph and Lantern Weekly* 23 November 1911: supplement xv.

ADDITIONAL DISCUSSIONS:
Bernardini, Aldo, and Jean A. Gili, eds. *Le Cinéma italien de La Prise de Rome (1905) à Rome ville ouverte (1945)*. Paris: Centre Georges Pompidou, 1986.
Camerini, Claudio. "Tre film francescani." *Immagine* 2 (June–September 1982): 25–28.
De Lucis, Flavia, ed. *C'era il cinema*. Modena: Edizioni Panini, 1983.
"Il Poverello di Assisi." *Immagine* 2 (June–September 1982): 29–33.
Savio, Francesco. *Visione privata*. Rome: Bulzoni Editore, 1972.

412. *La Prigioniera della torre di fuoco* (1951)

Italy; dir. G.W. Chili; Lia Film.
ALTERNATE TITLE: *The Prisoner in the Fuoco Tower*.
CAST: Rossano Brazzi, Elisa Cegani, Carlo Giustani, Milly Vitale.
In the year 1400, the wars between two rival Italian families threaten their ability to defend the Holy Land against the Saracens. They strike a truce that is short-lived. Plans for a marriage between members of the two households only lead to more bloodshed. At the film's conclusion, with almost all their relatives dead, the two newlyweds find happiness in each other's arms.

Convoluted and burdened with inane dialogue punctuated with the names of famous Italian families, this film makes little sense. It is little more than a silly costume drama, set for no particular reason in the Middle Ages.

REVIEWS: *Cinématographie française* 1 August 1953: 20. *Eco del cinema* 4 (15 June 1953): 269. *Film français* 21 August 1953: 48.

ADDITIONAL DISCUSSIONS:
Chiti, Roberto, and Roberto Poppi. *Dizionario del cinema italiano. Vol. 2: I Film dal 1945 al 1959*. Rome: Gremese Editore, 1991.
The Italian Production 1952–53. Rome: Unitalia Film, 1953.

413. *Prima Veras Saga om Olav den Hellige* (1983)

Norway; dir. Herodes Falsk; Iste Klasses Film & Video.
ALTERNATE TITLE: *The Saga of the Viking Saint Olav*.
CAST: Ølivind Blunck, Herodes Falsk, Tom Mathiesen, Jahn Teigen.
Under the rule of Olaf II, later St. Olaf, the

Fenge (Gabriel Byrne) and Gerruth (Helen Mirren) embrace in a scene from Gabriel Axel's *The Prince of Jutland* (1994). (Still courtesy of Vine International Pictures Ltd.)

Viking peoples of Norway are united and converted to Christianity.

The comedians who make up Prima Vera are Norway's answer to Britain's Monty Python troupe. Their version of the life of the only Norwegian king canonized by the Catholic Church is, to say the least, a bit irreverent.

REVIEWS: *Film og kino* 8 (1983): 287–88, 296. *Scandinavian Film News* 3 (May 1983): 3; 3 (December 1983): [5].

ADDITIONAL DISCUSSION:
Norwegian Films/Films Norvégiens 83. Oslo: Norwegian Film Institute, 1983.

Prince Igor (1970) see *Knyaz Igor* (1970)

414. *The Prince of Jutland* (1994)

Denmark; dir. Gabriel Axel; Les Films Ariane.

CAST: Christian Bale, Kate Beckinsale, Gabriel Byrne, Brian Cox, Brian Glover, Tony Haygarth, Freddie Jones, Helen Mirren, Steven Waddington, Saskia Wickham.

In sixth-century Jutland, Prince Fenge murders the king and his son and beds the queen, taking her as his wife. Fenge's nephew Amled

pretends to be mad after he witnesses the killings, but secretly plans his revenge. Fenge in turn suspects his nephew is not really mad and plots to have him murdered, too. Amled foils his uncle's plans and returns to Jutland to slay Fenge.

Axel does more than justice here to his source, the twelfth century *Gesta Danorum* by the author known only as Saxo Grammaticus (*fl.* 1185–1208) and its original version of the story of Hamlet.

From this same source, Axel also directed *The Red Mantle* (1967).

REVIEWS: *Film-echo/Filmwoche* 24 (18 June 1993): 10. *Le Film français* 4 February 1994: 30. *Le Monde* 24 February 1994: Arts & Spectacles VII. *Positif* 398 (April 1994): 58–59. *Première* 204 (March 1994): 41. *Sight and Sound* NS 6 (February 1996): 60. *Studio* [Paris] 84 (March 1994): 22. *Télérama* 2302 (23 February 1994): 41. *Time Out* [London] 6 December 1995: 188. *Variety* 28 February 1994: 71.

ADDITIONAL DISCUSSIONS:
Danish Films 1994/95. Copenhagen: Danish Film Institute, 1995.
Roddick, Nick, and Jo Roddick. *The Berlin Catalogue 1994*. Trans. Dagmar Heuer. Brighton: Split Screen Publication, 1994.

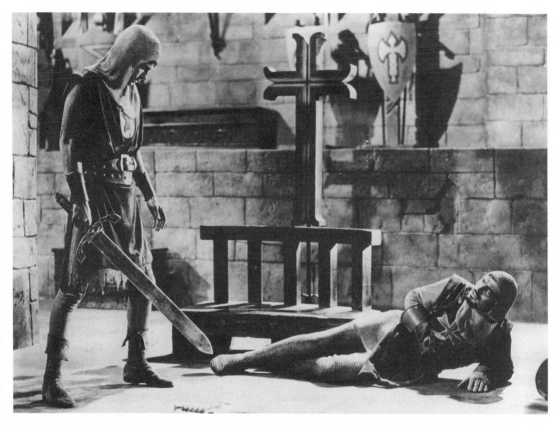

Prince Valiant (Robert Wagner) defeats Sir Brack (James Mason) in Henry Hathaway's *Prince Valiant* (1954).

415. *The Prince of Thieves* (1948)

United States; dir. Howard Bretherton; Columbia Pictures.

CAST: Michael Duane, Jon Hall, Adele Jergens, Patricia Morison, Alan Mowbray, H.B. Warner.

Robin Hood helps Sir Allan Claire and Lady Christabel overcome their families' opposition to their marriage.

Loosely based on an 1872 novel (*Robin Hood, le prince des voleurs*) that is attributed to Alexander Dumas the Elder, and with a plot much like that in the American Standard Film's 1913 *Robin Hood*, this film is meant for younger audiences, who may nonetheless find it as forgettable as their parents would.

REVIEWS: *Harrison's Reports* 10 January 1948: 6. *Kinematograph Weekly* 27 July 1948: 21. *Monthly Film Bulletin* 15 (31 August 1948): 117. *Motion Picture Herald* 17 January 1948: Product Digest Section 4018. *Revue du cinéma* [La Saison cinématographique] Hors série 30 (1948–49): 166. *To-day's Cinema* 16 July 1948: 7–8. *Variety* 14 January 1948: 10.

ADDITIONAL DISCUSSIONS:

Behlmer, Rudy. "Robin Hood on the Screen." *Films in Review* 16 (February 1965): 91–102.

Knight, Stephen. *Robin Hood, A Complete Study of the English Outlaw.* Oxford: Blackwell, 1994.

Nash, Jay Robert, and Stanley Ralph Ross. *The Motion Picture Guide, N–R, 1927–1983.* Chicago: Cinebooks, 1986.

Richards, Jeffrey. *Swordsmen of the Screen from Douglas Fairbanks to Michael York.* London: Routledge & Kegan Paul, 1977.

Turner, David. *Robin of the Movies.* Kingswinford, Eng.: Yeoman Publishing, 1989.

416. *Prince Valiant* (1954)

United States; dir. Henry Hathaway; 20th Century–Fox.

CAST: Brian Aherne, Donald Crisp, Sterling Hayden, Janet Leigh, James Mason, Victor McLaglen, Robert Wagner.

Exiled for crimes he did not commit, Prince Valiant travels to King Arthur's court to plead his cause. En route, he overhears a plot by an unidentified Black Knight to murder Arthur and alerts the king, who makes him a squire of the Round Table as reward. Valiant soon becomes one of the most accomplished swordsmen of Arthur's court. Word from home reaches him that his father is in trouble, and he returns to free his family from prison and, in a spectacular scene, burn down the castle of his enemies. Returning to Camelot, he exposes the Black Knight, who turns out to be a disloyal knight of the Round Table. Again he is rewarded by Arthur, who makes him a knight. Valiant then marries his lady love with the king's blessing.

Based on the long-running syndicated comic strip by Harold Foster, this film is a CinemaScope epic most notable for the climactic burning of the evil Vikings' castle.

REVIEWS: *Film Daily* 2 April 1954: 6. *Films in Review* 5 (May 1954): 241–42. *Harrison's Reports* 3 April 1954: 55. *Hollywood Reporter* 2 March 1954: 3. *Kinematograph Weekly* 6 May 1954: 16. *Monthly Film Bulletin* 21 (July 1954): 85–86. *Motion Picture Herald* 3 April 1954: 30; 10 April 1954: Product Digest Section 2254–55. *New York Times* 7 April 1954: 40. *New Yorker* 30 (April 1954): 93–94. *Times* [London] 3 May 1954: 9. *To-day's Cinema* 29 April 1954: 6. *Variety* 7 April 1954: 6.

ADDITIONAL DISCUSSIONS:
Fuchs, Wolfgang J. "Prinz Eisenherz." *Jugend, Film, Fersehen* 19.3 (1975): 183–84.
Hirschhorn, Clive. *The Films of James Mason.* London: LSP, 1975.
Hofstede, David. *Hollywood and the Comics.* N.p.: Zanne-3, 1991.
Nash, Jay Robert, and Stanley Ralph Ross. *The Motion Picture Guide, N–R, 1927–1983.* Chicago: Cinebooks, 1986.
Richards, Jeffrey. *Swordmen of the Silver Screen from Douglas Fairbanks to Michael York.* London: Routledge & Kegan Paul, 1977.
Smith, Gary A. *Epic Films.* Jefferson, N.C.: McFarland, 1991.

417. *The Princess and the Goblin* (1992)

Hungary; dir. Jósef Gémes; Siriol Productions and Pannonia Films.

ALTERNATE TITLE: *A Hercegnö és a kobold.*

CAST: (the voices of) Joss Ackland, Claire Bloom, Sally Ann Marsh, Rik Mayall, Peggy Mount, Peter Murray.

Princess Irene joins forces with the son of a poor miner, Curdie, to defeat evil goblins who threaten to leave the underworld and overrun her kingdom.

This adaptation of George MacDonald's 1872 classic children's novel *The Princess and the Goblin* is a masterpiece of animation.

REVIEWS: *Empire* 43 (January 1993): 28. *Film und Fernsehen* 21.5 (1993): 68. *Film-dienst* 46 (14 September 1993): 22. *Filmkultura* 28.1 (1992): 57–62. *Los Angeles Times* 3 June 1994: Calendar 6; 5 June 1994: Calendar 23. *New York Times* 3 June 1994: C15. *Sight and Sound* NS 3 (January 1993): 50–51. *Times* [London] 17 December 1992: 27. *Variety* 11 January 1993: 64–65.

ADDITIONAL DISCUSSIONS:
Brennan, Shawn, ed. *Magill's Cinema Annual 1995.* New York: Gale Research, 1996.
Cameron-Wilson, James, and F. Maurice Speed. *Film Review 1993–1994.* London: Virgin, 1993.
Levich, Jacob, ed. *The Motion Picture Guide: 1995 Annual (The Films of 1994).* New York: CineBooks, 1994.

418. *Princess of the Nile* (1954)

United States; dir. Harmon Jones; 20th Century–Fox.

CAST: Michael Ansara, Jeffrey Hunter, Debra Paget, Michael Rennie.

Prince Haidi, the son of the Caliph, returns home after winning a decisive battle in the Crusades to discover that a tyrant has imprisoned the rightful ruler of a nearby city and threatened to kill the ruler's daughter if she will not marry him. Haidi defeats the tyrant, restores the rightful ruler to his throne and brings the princess home with him as his bride.

The plot here has no basis in fact, but the film drew favorable notices for its exotic sets and colorful costumes.

REVIEWS: *Film Daily* 23 June 1954: 10. *Harrison's Reports* 19 June 1954: 100. *Hollywood Reporter* 11 June 1954: 3. *Kinematograph Weekly* 9 September 1954: 18. *Monthly Film Bulletin* 21 (October 1954): 148–49. *Motion Picture Herald* 19 June 1954: Product Digest Section 33. *New York Times* 12 June 1954: 13. *To-day's Cinema* 9 September 1954: 6. *Variety* 16 June 1954: 6.

ADDITIONAL DISCUSSIONS:
Nash, Jay Robert, and Stanley Ralph Ross. *The Motion Picture Guide, N–R, 1927–1983.* Chicago: Cinebooks, 1986.
Richards, Jeffrey. *Swordsmen of the Screen from Douglas Fairbanks to Michael York.* London: Routledge & Kegan Paul, 1977.
Smith, Gary A. *Epic Films.* Jefferson, N.C.: McFarland, 1991.

The Prisoner in the Fuoco Tower

(1951) see *La Prigioniera della torre di fuoco* (1951)

Le Procès de Jeanne d'Arc (1962) see
The Trial of Joan of Arc (1962)

419. *Il Prode Anselmo e il suo scud-iero* (1973)

Italy; dir. Bruno Corbucci; Dino de Laurentiis Cinematografica.

CAST: Mario Carotenuto, Enrico Montesano, Alighiero Noschese, Marie Sophie.

Anselmo and a German soldier fight a duel. Anselmo wins unfairly and must flee a troop of angry German soldiers. He heads for Rome entrusted with a relic for the Pope. The relic proves a fake, and Anselmo only barely escapes the Pope's wrath with the assistance of the German soldiers who have been pursuing him.

A farce from beginning to end, this film seems little more than a cinematic exercise designed to prove that Italians are funny and Germans are not — at least in medieval times.

REVIEW: *Cinematografia ITA* 40 (January-February 1973): 75–76.

ADDITIONAL DISCUSSIONS:
Poppi, Roberto, and Mario Pecorari. *Dizionario del cinema italiano: I Film dal 1970 al 1979.* Rome: Gremese Editore, 1996.
La Produzione italiana 1971/72. Rome: Unitalia Film, 1972.

Purgatorio (1974) see *Skärseld* (1974)

420. *Purgatory and Paradise* (1911)

Italy; Helios.

Dante and Virgil journey first through Purgatory and then through Paradise, where the Italian poet is united with Beatrice.

This film is a sequel to the Helois *Inferno,* made a year earlier.

REVIEW: *Moving Picture World* 6 April 1912: 30.

Put Your Devil in My Hell (1972) see
  Metti lo diavolo tuo ne lo mio inferno (1972)

Queen of the Tartars (1960) see *La Regina dei tartari* (1960)

The Queen's Pity (1911) see *Le Siège de Calais* (1911)

421. *A Queen's Treachery* (1911)

France; Gaumont.

ALTERNATE TITLE: *The Betrayal of Charles VI of France.*

Queen Isabel and her admirer, the Duke of Orleans, plot to overthrow King Charles. When an assassination attempt fails but leaves Charles mentally debilitated, those loyal to Charles kill the duke. In desperation, Isabel persuades her weak-minded husband to name King Henry of England his heir, but Charles's followers foil her plan and preserve France's independence.

Charles VI went insane in 1392, 12 years after he ascended the throne. The Treaty of Troyes, which Charles signed in 1420, named England's Henry V heir to the French throne.

REVIEW: *Moving Picture World* 9 December 1911: 827.

422. *Quentin Durward* (1912)

France; dir. Adrien Caillard; Pathé Frères, S.C.A.G.L.

CAST: René Alexandre, Henri Etiévant, Claude Garry, Marie Ventura.

While in France, Quentin Durward rescues Isabelle de Croye (who is seeking the protection of Louis XI) from the powerful Duke of Burgundy and from William de la Marck, to whom she is betrothed.

Louis Mauzin's scenario for this film retains the outline of events from its source, Sir Walter Scott's 1823 novel *Quentin Durward.*

REVIEWS: *Bioscope* 15 February 1912: supplement iii; 10 September 1914: supplement vii.

ADDITIONAL DISCUSSION:
Bousquet, Henri. *Catalogue Pathé des années 1896 à 1914: 1912–1913–1914.* Paris: Henri Bousquet, 1995.

423. *Quentin Durward* (1955)

United States and Great Britain; Richard Thorpe; MGM.

ALTERNATE TITLE: *The Adventures of Quentin Durward.*

CAST: George Cole, Alex Clunes, Kay Kendall, Duncan Lamont, Robert Morley, Robert Taylor, Harcourt Williams.

Sent from Scotland to France to bring back a bride for his aging uncle, Quentin Durward falls in love with his uncle's intended, Isabelle, Countess of Macroy. Caught up in the intrigues of the French court, Durward saves Isabelle from a series of traps. Eventually, his uncle having conveniently died, the two marry.

Again, the source for this film is Sir Walter

Kay Kendall as Isabelle, Countess of Macroy, and Robert Taylor as Quentin Durward in Richard Thorpe's *Quentin Durward* (1955).

Scott's 1823 novel *Quentin Durward*. Taylor, who played the title role, had a career playing swashbuckling heroes; he played Lancelot in the 1952 film *Knights of the Round Table* and the title role in the 1952 film version of *Ivanhoe*. Here he is dashing enough performing one deed of derring-do after another as dictated by a plot that does not always make sense. The film's climactic battle scene has Taylor and his foe dueling while hanging by ropes from a belfry.

REVIEWS: *Cue* 26 November 1955: 20. *Daily Film Renter* 12 January 1956: 4. *Films and Filming* 2 (March 1956): 17. *Harrison's Reports* 15 October 1955: 166. *Kinematograph Weekly* 19 January 1956: 21. *Monthly Film Bulletin* 23 (March 1956): 30–31. *Motion Picture Herald* 15 October 1955: Product Digest Section 633. *New York Times* 24 November 1955: 41. *Times* [London] 5 March 1956: 12. *To-day's Cinema* 12 January 1956: 6, 8. *Variety* 19 October 1955: 6.

ADDITIONAL DISCUSSIONS:
"Battle in a Belfry." *Life* 39 (21 November 1955): 157–58, 161.

Fraser, George MacDonald. *The Hollywood History of the World*. New York: Beech Tree, 1988.
Nash, Jay Robert, and Stanley Ralph Ross. *The Motion Picture Guide, N–R, 1927–1983*. Chicago: Cinebooks, 1986.
Quirk, Lawrence J. *The Films of Robert Taylor*. Secaucus, N.J.: Citadel, 1975.
Richards, Jeffrey. *Swordsmen of the Screen from Douglas Fairbanks to Michael York*. London: Routledge & Kegan Paul, 1977.
Wayne, Jane Ellen. *Robert Taylor*. New York: St. Martin's, 1987.

424. *The Quest of the Holy Grail* (1915)

United States; D.W. Griffith; Triangle Productions.

Griffith had hoped to make a film based on the famous series of Grail murals by Edwin Austin Abbey in the Boston Public Library. The project was temporarily shelved in 1915. An attempt to revive it after the First World War also failed, and the project remained unrealized.

DISCUSSIONS:

"Film Flashes." *Variety* 28 May 1915: 16.

"Griffith to Make Holy Grail Picture." *Moving Picture World* 1 May 1915: 769.

Stern, Seymour. *An Index to the Creative Work of David Wark Griffith. Part II: The Art Triumphant. (b) Triangle Productions: 1915–1916.* Special Supplement to *Sight and Sound.* London: British Film Institute, 1946.

I Racconti di Canterbury (1971) see *The Canterbury Tales* (1971)

I Racconti di Canterbury Nr. 2 (1972) see *Lusty Wives of Canterbury* (1972)

425. *Racconti proibiti di nulla vestiti* (1973)

Italy; dir. Brunello Rondi; Chiara Films.

ALTERNATE TITLE: *Master of Love.*

CAST: Janet Agren, Tina Aumont, Norberto Botti, Barbara Bouchet, Rossano Brazzi, Mario Carotenuto, Enzo Cerusico, Ben Ekland, Antonio Falsi, Silvia Monti, Magali Noël, Karin Schubert, Venantino Venantini.

Sir Lorenzo, widely known as the irresistible "Master of Love," takes the son of a friend, a young scholar too interested in his studies to pursue women, under his tutelage. The two set out across medieval Tuscany to provide the scholar with a taste of what life is really about — women. A quick study, the student soon replaces his teacher as the master.

There is not much to recommend this silly medieval sex comedy — a staple of the Italian cinema in the 1970s — which suggests that all women are either whores or saints eager to be deflowered.

REVIEWS: *CinemaTV Today* 13 July 1974: 12. *Monthly Film Bulletin* 41 (August 1974): 183–84.

ADDITIONAL DISCUSSIONS:

Poppi, Roberto, and Mario Pecorari. *Dizionario del cinema italiano: I Film dal 1970 al 1979.* Rome: Gremese Editore, 1996.

La Produzione italiana 1972/73. Rome: Unitalia Film, 1973.

Raffica di Coltelli (1965) see *Knives of the Avenger* (1965)

426. *The Raven* (1963)

United States; dir. Roger Corman; American International Pictures.

CAST: Hazel Court, Boris Karloff, Peter Lorre, Jack Nicholson, Vincent Price.

Erasmus Craven, a sorcerer depressed over the supposed death of his wife, frees Bedlo, a fellow sorcerer, from a curse that has turned him into a raven. Craven learns from Bedlo that the wife has left him — rather than died — so that she can be the lover of an even more powerful sorcerer, Scarabus. A battle among sorcerers ensues in which Craven and Bedlo finally defeat Scarabus, destroying him and his castle.

Obliquely indebted to Edgar Allan Poe's famous poem "The Raven," this film is — depending upon one's view of Corman as a filmmaker — either a lame or a clever parody of horror films. The film's most notable feature is its cast, which brings together three masters of the genre — Lorre, Karloff, and Price — as well as a then-unknown Nicholson.

REVIEWS: *American Film* 15 (June 1990): 53. *Commonweal* 77 (15 February 1963): 542. *Daily Cinema* 19 August 1961: 3. *Film Daily* 30 January 1963: 3. *Monthly Film Bulletin* 30 (October 1963): 142. *Motion Picture Herald* 20 February 1963: Product Digest Section 755. *Movie Club* 3 (May 1994): 38–39. *New York Times* 26 January 1963: 5. *Sight and Sound* 32 (Autumn 1963): 198. *Variety* 6 February 1963: 6.

ADDITIONAL DISCUSSIONS:

Buehrer, Beverley Bare. *Boris Karloff, A Bio-Bibliography.* Westport, Conn.: Greenwood, 1993.

Nash, Jay Robert, and Stanley Ralph Ross. *The Motion Picture Guide, N–R, 1927–1983.* Chicago: Cinebooks, 1986.

Nollen, Scott Allen. *Boris Karloff.* Jefferson, N.C.: McFarland, 1991.

The Raven Flies (1984) see *When the Raven Flies* (1984)

427. *Il Re Artù e i cavalieri della tavola rotonda* (1910)

Italy; dir. Giuseppe De Liguoro; Milano Films.

ALTERNATE TITLE: *King Arthur; or, The Knights of the Round Table.*

This early King Arthur film, about which few details survive, featured a cast of almost 100 actors. It was distributed in Great Britain by New Agency Films.

REVIEW: *Bioscope* 15 September 1910: 39.

ADDITIONAL DISCUSSIONS:

Bernardini, Aldo. *Archivo del cinema italiano. Volume 1: Il cinema muto 1905–1931.* Rome: ANICA, 1991.

Prolo, Maria Adriana. *Storia del cinema muto italiano.* Milan: Poligono Società Editrice, 1951.

428. *I Reali di Francia* (1959)

Italy; dir. Mario Costa; Schermi Distibuzione.

ALTERNATE TITLE: *The Royalty of France.*

CAST: Chelo Alonso, Rik Battaglia, Gérard Landry, Livio Lorenzo.

Roland, Count of Besançon, accompanies the grandchildren of France's Louis VII to see their grandfather. While en route, they encounter a raiding party of Moors from across the Spanish border. Roland captures Suliema, the daughter of the Moorish leader Achirro, whom he hopes to hold hostage, but she escapes with the aid of a traitor in Roland's camp. Roland does battle with the Moors and is wounded, but he is finally victorious when the king comes to his aid. In reward for his valor, King Louis allows Roland to marry Suliema.

Despite the hero's name and his battles for France against the Moors, this film, a fairly standard Italian adventure film, bears little relationship to *The Song of Roland*, the earliest extant poem of any substantial length in Old French and the best known *chanson de geste* (c. 1100).

REVIEW: *Film français* 24 February 1961.

ADDITIONAL DISCUSSIONS:

Chiti, Roberto, and Roberto Poppi. *Dizionario del cinema italiano. Vol. 2: I Film dal 1945 al 1959.* Rome: Gremese Editore, 1991.

The Italian Production 1959. Rome: Unitalia Film, 1960.

429. *Rebecca the Jewess* (1913)

Great Britain; dir. Leedham Bantock; Zenith Films.

ALTERNATE TITLE: *Ivanhoe.*

CAST: Nancy Bevington, Edith Brachwell, Hubert Carter, Henry Lonsdale, Lauderdale Maitland, Austin Milroy.

Ivanhoe, a discredited knight, rescues Rebecca, a young Jewish woman, after she is accused of sorcery.

A selective retelling of events from Sir Walter Scott's 1819 novel *Ivanhoe*, this British film suffers in comparision to the American film version of *Ivanhoe* which was released in the same year.

REVIEW: *Moving Picture World* 17 January 1914: 291.

ADDITIONAL DISCUSSION:

Connelly, Robert. *The Motion Picture Guide, Silent Film, 1910–1936.* Chicago: Cinebooks, 1986.

430. *The Red Mantle* (1967)

Denmark; dir. Gabriel Axel; ASA Film.

ALTERNATE TITLES: *Den Røde kappe* and *Hagbard and Signe.*

CAST: Gunnar Bjornstrand, Eva Dahlbeck, Gitte Haenning, Hakan Jahnberg, Johannes Meyer, Lisben Movin, Henning Palmer, Oleg Vidov.

In medieval Iceland, Hagbard and his brothers seek to avenge the death of their father, King Hamund, by entering into a blood feud with the family of his killer, King Sigvor. Hagbard and his brothers meet Sigvor's three sons in a day-long battle. Because the opponents are so evenly matched, their battle ends in a draw, and Sigvor offers Hagbard and his brothers a truce and an alliance. At Sigvor's castle, Hagbard falls in love with his host's daughter Signe, but a rival suitor stirs up dissension that leads to a resumption of the blood feud. Dressed in a red mantle to cloak his identity, Hagbard revisits Signe, but the two are discovered. Hagbard is hanged and Signe sets fire to her room, killing herself.

Filming on location in Iceland, Axel does more than justice here to his source, the twelfth century *Gesta Danorum* by the anonymous author known as Saxo Grammaticus (*fl.* 1185–1208). From this same source, Axel also directed *The Prince of Jutland* (1994), based on the *Gesta*'s original telling of the story of Hamlet.

REVIEWS: *Cinema* 4 (Fall 1968): 42–43. *Filmfacts* 11 (1 August 1968): 203–04. *Film og kino* 9 (November 1967): 330. *Films and Filming* 15 (April 1969): 50–51. *Films in Review* 19 (June-July 1968): 377. *Hollywood Reporter* 15 August 1968: 3. *Kinematograph Weekly* 15 February 1969: 18. *Monthly Film Bulletin* 36 (March 1969): 60. *New York Times* 17 May 1968: 56. *To-day's Cinema* 7 February 1969: 9. *Variety* 25 January 1967: 21.

ADDITIONAL DISCUSSIONS:

Krafsur, Richard P., ed. *The American Film Institute Catalog of Motion Pictures, Feature Films 1961–1970.* New York: Bowker, 1976.

Nash, Jay Robert, and Stanley Ralph Ross. *The Motion Picture Guide, H–K, 1927–1983.* Chicago: Cinebooks, 1986.

Svensk Filmografi 6: 1960–1969. Uppsala: Svenska Filminstitutet, 1977.

431. *La Regina dei tartari* (1960)

Italy; dir. Sergio Grieco, Film Columbus.

ALTERNATE TITLES: *The Huns, The Queen of the Tartars* and *La Reine des barbares.*

CAST: Chelo Alonso, Folco Lulli, Jacques Sernas.

Two warring tribes, the Barlas and the Black Tartars, battle over territory in medieval Europe that each wishes to conquer. Forces loyal to Tanya, the Barlas queen, capture the Black Tartar chieftain, Malok. Malok and Tanya fall in love, and their warring factions form an alliance and ride off together against their common enemy, a rich neighboring kingdom ripe for plundering.

This film is yet another action-packed Italian costume spectacle with more similarities to an American Western than anything even remotely medieval.

REVIEWS: *Cinématographie française* 15 April 1961: 31. *Daily Cinema* 4 August 1961: 9. *Film français* 14 April 1961: 44. *Intermezzo* 15 (15 November 1960): 10. *Kinematograph Weekly* 10 August 1961: 19. *Monthly Film Bulletin* 28 (September 1961): 132.

ADDITIONAL DISCUSSIONS:
Italian Production 1960. Rome: Unitalia Film, 1961.
Poppi, Roberto, and Mario Pecorari. *Dizionario del cinema italiano. Vol. 3: I Film dal 1960 al 1969.* Rome: Gremese Editore, 1992.

La Reine des barbares (1960) see *La Regina dei tartari* (1960)

Le Retour de Martin Guerre (1982)
see *The Return of Martin Guerre* (1982)

432. *The Return of Martin Guerre* (1982)

France; dir. Daniel Vigne; SFPC, SPFMD and FR3.

ALTERNATE TITLE: *Le Retour de Martin Guerre.*

CAST: Maurice Barrier, Nathalie Baye, André Chaumeau, Gerard Depardieu, Pierre Depardieu, Bernard-Pierre Donnadieu, Sylvie Méda, Roger Planchon.

An immature Martin Guerre goes off to fight in the king's wars. Years later, someone claiming to be Martin returns to his village. Martin's wife Bertrande loves the new man because her real husband had been so cruel, but the couple's happiness is short-lived when a financial dispute divides the village about whether the returned man is really Martin or an impostor. A trial is held to decide the matter when the real Guerre returns and the impostor is hanged.

Based on accounts published in Lyons in 1561, this film (which takes place in a region of France still firmly grounded in the medieval) is most interesting for its examination of the wife's perspective on the deception that is central to the plot. A mediocre American remake, Jon Amiel's *Sommersby* (1993), was set right after the Civil War.

REVIEWS: *Les Cahiers du cinéma* 338 (July-August 1982): 66. *Ciné revue* 18 (29 April 1982): 18–21. *Cinéaste* 13 (1984): 47. *Cineinforme* 139 (October 1984): 49–50. *Cinéma 82* (June 1982): 94. *Cinéma de France* 64 (April 1982): 14. *Cinématographe* 80 (July-August 1982): 56. *Continental Film and Video Review* 29 (September 1982): 16. *Empire* 49 (July 1993): 101. *Film Quarterly* 38 (Fall 1984): 34–37. *Films and Filming* 357 (June 1984): 18. *Hollywood Reporter* 21 June 1983: 16. *Image et son* 373 (June 1982): 30–31. *Jeune cinéma* 143 (June 1982): 39–41. *Los Angeles Times* 22 July 1983: Calendar 1. *Monthly Film Bulletin* 51 (May 1984): 158–59. *New York Times* 10 June 1983: 3. 12. *Positif* 259 (September 1982): 74. *Séquences* 112 (April 1983): 36–37. *Sunday Times* [London] 24 June 1984: 51. *Times* [London] 22 June 1984: 8. *24 Images* 16 (March 1983): 46–47. *Variety* 9 June 1982: 16.

ADDITIONAL DISCUSSIONS:
Benson, Ed. "Martin Guerre, The Historian and the Filmmakers: An Interview with Natalie Zemon Davis." *Film and History* 13 (September 1983): 49–65.
Biggs, Melissa E. *French Films, 1945–1993.* Jefferson, N.C.: McFarland, 1996.
Davis, Natalie Zemon. "'On the Lame.'" *American Historical Review* 93 (June 1988): 572–603.
Finlay, Robert. "The Refashioning of Martin Guerre." *American Historical Review* 93 (June 1988): 553–71.
Guneratne, Anthony. "Cinehistory and the Puzzling Case of Martin Guerre." *Film and History* 21 (February 1991): 2–19.
Magill, Frank N., ed. *Magill's Cinema Annual 1984 (A Survey of 1983 Films).* Englewood Cliffs, N.J.: Salem, 1984.
Nash, Jay Robert, and Stanley Ralph Ross. *The Motion Picture Guide, N–R, 1927–1983.* Chicago: Cinebooks, 1986.
Pauly, Rebecca M. *The Transparent Illusion: Image and Ideology in French Text and Film.* New York: Peter Lang, 1993.
Staiger, Janet. "Securing the Fictional Narrative as a Tale of the Historical Real." *South Atlantic Quarterly* 88 (Spring 1989): 393–413.
Toplin, Robert Brent. "The Filmmaker as Historian." *American Historical Review* 93 (December 1988): 1210–27.

433. *The Revenge of Ivanhoe* (1965)
Italy; dir. Amerigo Anton; Tevere Films.
ALTERNATE TITLE: *La Rivincita di Ivanhoe.*
CAST: Andrea Aureli, Gilda Lousek, Duilio

Nathalie Baye as Bertrande de Rois and Gerard Depardieu as the impostor Martin Guerre in Daniel Vigne's *The Return of Martin Guerre* (1982).

Marzio, Furio Meniconi, Glauco Onorato, Clyde Rogers.

Ivanhoe returns from the Crusades to find England tyrannized by King John and his ally, Bernard d'Hastings. With the aid of the peasants, he leads an uprising, saves his beloved Rovena from charges of treason and forces King John to reign justly and fairly.

With only incidental connections to Sir Walter Scott's 1819 novel *Ivanhoe*, this film is yet another standard Italian costume picture set in the Middle Ages.

REVIEWS: *Cinématographie française* 2137 (20 November 1965): 18. *Film-echo/Filmwoche* 99 (4 December 1965): 9.

ADDITIONAL DISCUSSIONS:
Italian Production 1964. Rome: Unitalia Film, 1965.
Poppi, Roberto, and Mario Pecorari. *Dizionario del cinema italiano.* Vol. 3: *I Film dal 1960 al 1969.* Rome: Gremese Editore, 1992.

Revenge of the Barbarians (1984) see
When the Raven Flies (1984)

434. *The Ribald Tales of Robin Hood* (1969)

United States; dir. Richard Kanter; Mondo Films.

CAST: Lawrence Adams, Danielle Carver, Ralph Jenkins, Dee Lockwood, C.S. Poole.

Maid Marian visits her former lover Robin Hood to convince him to surrender to Prince John.

The popularity of the legend of Robin Hood perhaps accounts for the decision to make this soft-core pornographic film in which what goes on in Sherwood Forest has little to do with robbing the rich and giving to the poor. "Fly jabbing" is the primary activity here for both merry men — and merry women.

REVIEWS: *Daily Variety* 19 August 1969: 8. *Hollywood Reporter* 19 August 1969: 3. *Variety* 27 August 1969: 18, 34.

ADDITIONAL DISCUSSION:
McGillivray, David. "It's All in the Mind." *Films and Filming* 18 (August 1972): 18–23.

435. *Richard the Lion-Hearted* (1923)

United States; dir. Chet Withey; Associated Authors.

CAST: Wallace Beery, Kathleen Clifford, Marguerite De La Motte, Charles Gerrard.

During the Crusades, the brother of the King of Scotland, disguised as a lowly knight, saves King Richard's life. He is rewarded with a dagger, which through a series of misunderstandings passes from the hands of his lady love Edith into those of the Queen. King Richard, suspecting the worst, banishes the knight. Renegade Christian knights led by Sir Conrade try to poison Richard, but he is saved by Saladin, who arrives in the Christian camp disguised as a physician. The Scottish knight returns to Richard's camp also disguised, defeats Conrade, helps Richard establish a truce with Saladin and marries Edith, his true identity finally revealed.

Despite its somewhat convoluted plot, this film, based on Sir Walter Scott's 1825 novel *The Talisman; A Tale of the Crusaders*, received good notices because of its production values.

REVIEWS: *Exceptional Photoplays* 3 (Fall-Summer 1923): 6. *Kinematograph Weekly* 27 March 1924: 41–42. *New York Times* 23 October 1923: 17. *Variety* 25 October 1923: 22.

ADDITIONAL DISCUSSION:
Connelly, Robert. *The Motion Picture Guide, Silent Film, 1910–1936.* Chicago: Cinebooks, 1986.

Rienzi (1910) see *Cola di Rienzi* (1910)

La Rivincita di Ivanhoe (1965) see *The Revenge of Ivanhoe* (1965)

436. *Robert Bruce, épisodes des guerres de l'indépendance écossaise* (1911)

France; dir. Paul Capellani; Pathé Frères, S.C.A.G.L.

ALTERNATE TITLE: *Robert the Bruce.*

With the death of Wallace, Robert Bruce is declared King of Scotland. All the Scottish nobles swear fealty to him except Red Comyn, who thinks he should succeed to the throne. In a rage, Bruce kills Comyn, and Comyn's followers ally themselves with the English against the Scots. An invading English army almost manages to capture Bruce and defeat his forces, but Comyn's ghost appears to Bruce in a dream and encourages him to turn back the English invaders and secure the freedom of Scotland, which he does.

After murdering John Comyn, who was at the time the leading Scottish patriot, Robert Bruce (1274–1329) was crowned King of Scotland in 1306. Until his death, Bruce continued to fight or intrigue against the English to ensure that he and his successors would not be their vassals.

REVIEW: *Bioscope* 2 November 1911: supplement iii.

ADDITIONAL DISCUSSION:

Bousquet, Henri. *Catalogue Pathé des années 1896 à 1914: 1910–1911*. Paris: Henri Bousquet, 1994.

Robert the Bruce (1911) see *Robert Bruce, épisodes des guerres de l'indépendance écossaise* (1911)

437. *Robin and His Merry Men* (1908)

Great Britain; dir.Percy Stow; Clarendon Films.

ALTERNATE TITLE: *Robin Hood and His Merry Men*.

The Earl of Huntington flees to Sherwood Forest, joins forces with Friar Tuck and Maid Marian, and saves a condemned man from the sheriff's gallows.

This film inaugurates a rich tradition of Robin Hood films, borrowing the gallows scene from a long dramatic tradition about Robin .

REVIEW: *Moving Picture World* 24 April 1909: 530.

ADDITIONAL DISCUSSIONS:

Behlmer, Rudy. "Robin Hood on the Screen." *Films in Review* 16 (February 1965): 91–102.

Knight, Stephen. *Robin Hood, A Complete Study of the English Outlaw*. Oxford: Blackwell, 1994.

Richards, Jeffrey. *Swordsmen of the Screen from Douglas Fairbanks to Michael York*. London: Routlege & Kegan Paul, 1977.

Savada, Elias. *The American Film Institute Catalog of Motion Pictures Produced in the United States: Film Beginnings, 1893–1910*. Metuchen, N.J.: Scarecrow, 1995.

Turner, David. *Robin of the Movies*. Kingswinford, Eng.: Yeoman Publishing, 1989.

438. *Robin and Marian* (1976)

United States; dir. Richard Lester; Columbia Pictures.

CAST: Ronnie Barker, Sean Connery, Denholm Elliott, Kenneth Haigh, Richard Harris, Audrey Hepburn, Ian Holm, Robert Shaw, Nicol Williamson.

After almost 20 years of fighting with King Richard, Robin Hood and Little John disobey his order to slaughter the women and children hiding in a defenseless castle. Richard is killed by an arrow, and Robin and John return to an England suffering under the tyranny of King John. Like Robin, the remnants of his band of men and the Sheriff of Nottingham have all

aged. Marian has become a nun and is now Abbess of Kirkly. When the Sheriff and Sir Ranulf of Pudsey arrive to arrest Marian, Robin rescues her against her will. Sir Ranulf imprisons several nuns from the abbey in hopes of setting a trap for Robin. Robin rescues the nuns, escapes the trap and returns to the forest with Sir Ranulf in hot pursuit. Robin easily defeats Sir Ranulf, and the Sheriff and King John raise an army against Robin. The army encamps outside the forest, and Robin and the Sheriff agree to single combat. After Robin wins, Sir Ranulf, breaking the truce, cuts down Robin's men, seriously wounding Robin. Marian and Little John carry Robin back to Kirkly Abbey, where Marian and Robin drink from a poisoned cup after instructing Little John to bury them together.

Lester's film is a marked departure from other Robin Hood screen efforts. Legendary characters are generally ageless, and the typical depiction of Robin Hood (regardless of the actor playing the role's real age) is that of a young man. Here Robin and his compatriots are clearly middle-aged; the film's genius lies in its reexamination of a more-than-familiar legend that celebrates the swashbuckling through the lens of maturity.

REVIEWS: *American Film* 15 (May 1990): 56. *Entertainment Weekly* 75 (19 July 1991): 65. *Film Bulletin* 45 (March 1976): 34–35. *Film Heritage* 11 (1976): 42–43. *Filmfacts* 19 (1976): 25–29. *Films and Filming* 22 (April 1976): 25–28; 22 (June 1976): 28–29. *Films Illustrated* 5 (June 1976): 366. *Films in Review* 27 (April 1976): 241; 27 (May 1976): 308–10. *Hollywood Reporter* 11 March 1976: 6. *Independent Film Bulletin* 77 (17 March 1976): 9. *Los Angeles Times* 28 March 1976: Calendar 1, 37–38. *Millimeter* 4 (May 1976): 28–30. *Monthly Film Bulletin* 43 (May 1976): 105. *Motion Picture Product Digest* 24 March 1976: 82. *Movietone News* 49 (April 1976): 13–17; 50 (June 1976): 46–47. *New York Times* 12 March: 1976: 28; 14 March 1976: 2. 1, 13. *Sunday Times* [London] 30 May 1976: 37. *Times* [London] 28 May 1976: 11. *Variety* 10 March 1976: 22.

ADDITIONAL DISCUSSIONS:

Callan, Michael Feeney. *Sean Connery*. New York: Stein and Day, 1983.

Goldman, James. *Robin and Marian*. New York: Bantam, 1976. [Screenplay.]

Harris, Warren G. *Audrey Hepburn, A Biography*. New York: Simon and Schuster, 1994.

Karney, Robyn. *A Star Danced, The Life of Audrey Hepburn*. London: Bloomsbury, 1993.

Knight, Stephen. *Robin Hood, A Complete Study of the English Outlaw*. Oxford: Blackwell, 1994.

Sean Connery as Robin and Audrey Hepburn as Marian in Richard Lester's *Robin and Marian* (1976).

Magill, Frank N., ed. *Magill's Survey of Cinema: English Language Films.* Second Series. Englewood Cliffs, N.J.: Salem, 1981.

Maychick, Diana. *Audrey Hepburn, An Intimate Portrait.* New York: Birch Lane, 1993.

Morley, Sheridan. *Audrey Hepburn, A Celebration.* London: Pavillon Books, 1993.

Nash, Jay Robert, and Stanley Ralph Ross. *The Motion Picture Guide, N–R, 1927–1983.* Chicago: Cinebooks, 1986.

Parker, John. *Sean Connery.* London: Gollancz, 1993.

Passingham, Kenneth. *Sean Connery.* London: Sidgwick and Jackson, 1983.

Pfeiffer, Lee, and Philip Lisa. *The Films of Sean Connery.* New York: Citadel, 1993.

Richards, Jeffrey. *Swordsmen of the Screen from Douglas Fairbanks to Michael York.* London: Routledge & Kegan Paul, 1977.

Rosenfeldt, Diane. *Richard Lester: A Guide to References and Resources.* Boston: Hall, 1979.

Sellers, Robert. *The Films of Sean Connery.* New York: St. Martin's, 1990.

Sinyard, Neil. *The Films of Richard Lester.* Totowa, N.J.: Barnes & Noble, 1985.

Sigoloff, Marc. *The Films of the Seventies.* Jefferson, N.C.: McFarland, 1984.

Stapleford, Richard. "Robin Hood and the Contemporary Idea of the Hero." *Literature/Film Quarterly* 8 (1980): 182–87.

Tanitch, Robert. *Sean Connery.* London: Chapmans, 1992.

Turner, David. *Robin of the Movies.* Kingswinford, Eng.: Yeoman Publishing, 1989.

Yule, Andrew. *The Man Who "Framed" the Beatles.* New York: Donald I. Fine, 1994.

439. *Robin Hood* (1908)

Great Britain; Kalem.

This film, set in a natural forest and, according to the *Bioscope* review, correctly costumed, presents several humorous episodes involving Robin and his band of merry men.

REVIEW: *Bioscope* 11 August 1910: 33.

ADDITIONAL DISCUSSION:

Savada, Elias. *The American Film Institute Catalog of Motion Pictures Produced in the United States:*

Film Beginnings, 1893–1910. Metuchen, N.J.: Scarecrow, 1995.

440. *Robin Hood* (1912)

United States; dir. Étienne Arnaud; American Eclair Company.

CAST: Alex B. Francis, Robert Frazer, M. Hannafly, Lamar Johnstone, Barbara Tennant.

Marian's father intends that she marry Guy de Gisbourne, but, with Friar Tuck's help, she escapes to Sherwood Forest to join her true love, Robin. Guy's men follow and capture Robin, tying him to a tree. Robin's men free him and turn the tables, binding Guy and his soldiers to trees in Sherwood. Marian's father, the Sheriff, and Guy then hatch an elaborate conspiracy that inadvertently threatens the safety of King Richard, who has returned to England in disguise. Richard joins forces with Robin, defeats his enemies and sanctions Robin's marriage to Marian.

This film's unique spin on the legend of Robin is to have Marian's father in league with Robin's traditional enemies.

REVIEWS: *Moving Picture World* 3 August 1912: 435–37. *New York Dramatic Mirror* 31 July 1912: 31.

ADDITIONAL DISCUSSIONS:

Higgins, Steven. "American Eclair, 1911–1915." *Griffithiana* 44–45 (May–September 1992): 89–129.

Turner, David. *Robin of the Movies.* Kingswinford, Eng.: Yeoman Publishing, 1989.

441. *Robin Hood* (1913)

United States; dir. Theodore Marston; Thanhouser Films.

ALTERNATE TITLE: *Robin Hood and Maid Marian.*

CAST: Harry Benham, John Dillon, Walter Gibbs, Gerda Holmes, William Russell, David Thompson.

Ignoring an edict forbidding hunting in Sherwood Forest, Robin kills a deer. The Sheriff of Nottingham arrives to arrest Robin, who escapes, but not before the Sheriff's men kill Maid Marian's father. Robin rallies his men to defend the poor against the oppressed. King Richard (disguised as a beggar) arrives in the forest and, impressed with their patriotism of Robin and his followers, pardons them when he returns to his throne.

In addition to using the episode of Richard's appearance in disguise, this film includes the even more familiar episode of Robin entering and winning an archery contest.

REVIEWS: *Bioscope* 7 May 1914: 659. *Kinematograph Monthly Record* 26 (June 1914): 47–48. *Moving Picture World* 29 November 1913: 1054. *Reel Life* 3 (8 November 1913): 4–6.

ADDITIONAL DISCUSSIONS:

Behlmer, Rudy. "Robin Hood on the Screen." *Films in Review* 16 (February 1965): 91–102.

Hanson, Patricia King, ed. *The American Film Institute Catalog of Motion Pictures Produced in the United States: Feature Films, 1911–1920.* Berkeley: University of California Press, 1988.

Knight, Stephen. *Robin Hood, A Complete Study of the English Outlaw.* Oxford: Blackwell, 1994.

"Thanhouser Makes Robin Hood." *Moving Picture Notes* 14 October 1913: 24.

"The Thanhouser Production of *Robin Hood.*" *Reel Life* 3 (4 October 1913): 12.

Turner, David. *Robin of the Movies.* Kingswinford, Eng.: Yeoman Publishing, 1989.

442. *Robin Hood* (1913)

United States; American Standard Films.

Will Scarlet unsuccessfully tries to woo Lady Christabel, the daughter of Baron Fitz Akvine, the Sheriff of Nottingham. In a rage, the Sheriff has him banished under threat of death. He joins with Robin Hood and his followers, who attempt to aid him in his romantic endeavors. The Sheriff discovers Will's attempt to kidnap his daughter and orders him hanged. In the nick of time, Robin and his men arrive and save Will, who marries Christabel.

The focus here shifts from Robin to one of the regular members of his band, but Robin's appearances allow him to perform the expected deeds of derring-do. Both he and Will are expert archers. The original source here is a two-volume novel, *Robin Hood, le proscrit* and *Robin Hood, le prince des voleurs,* attributed to Alexandre Dumas the Elder, published in 1872 and 1873 and first translated into English in 1903.

REVIEWS: *Bioscope* 21 August 1913: supplement xlvi. *Variety* 22 August 1913: 14.

443. *Robin Hood* (1922)

United States; dir. Allan Dwan; United Artists.

CAST: Wallace Beery, Enid Bennett, Sam De Grasse, Paul Dickey, Douglas Fairbanks, William Lowery.

The Earl of Huntingdon prepares to join King Richard in the Holy Land as his second in command. After a magnificent tournament,

Douglas Fairbanks in the title role in Allan Dwan's *Robin Hood* (1922). (Still courtesy of the British Film Institute.)

they march off to the Crusades, although the Earl leaves with some reluctance since his love, Lady Marian, stays behind. The Earl returns when he learns from Marian that Prince John is trying to secure the throne for himself. Under the name of Robin Hood, he leads a group of followers intent upon stealing from the rich and giving to the poor. He manages to rescue Marian from Prince John's prison, only to be taken prisoner himself. Richard returns to rescue Robin and thwart Prince John's plans.

Dwan's film defined the swashbuckler for the silent screen, much as Michael Curtiz's 1938 *The Adventures of Robin Hood* would do for the talkies. The film also presented Fairbanks with the role of his career. In the film's first part, he is confined — as is his character — within the castle walls. In the film's second half, he breaks free, just as Robin Hood roams freely throughout Sherwood Forest, and gives a bravura performance.

REVIEWS: *Exceptional Photoplays* 3 (January 1923): 1. *Film Daily* 5 November 1922: 2. *Harrison's Reports* 11 November 1922: 178. *Kinematograph Weekly* 21 November 1922: 39–40. *Literary Digest* 75 (18 November 1922): 32–33. *New York Times* 31 October 1922: 15. *Photoplay* 23 (January 1923): 64. *Variety* 20 October 1922: 40.

ADDITIONAL DISCUSSIONS:

Behlmer, Rudy. "Robin Hood on the Screen." *Films in Review* 16 (February 1965): 91–102.

Bogdanovich, Peter. *Allan Dwan, The Last Pioneer.* New York: Praeger, 1971.

Bowser, Eileen, ed. *Film Notes.* New York: Museum of Modern Art, 1969.

Brownlow, Kevin. *The Parade's Gone By.* Berkeley: University of California Press, 1968.

Carey, Gary. *Doug & Mary.* New York: Dutton, 1977.

Connelly, Robert. *The Motion Picture Guide: Silent Film, 1910–1936.* Chicago: Cinebooks, 1986.

Fleming, John. "Douglas Fairbanks in *Robin Hood.*" *Pictures and Picturegoer* 6 (December 1923): 45–48.

Hancock, Ralph, and Letitia Fairbanks. *Douglas Fairbanks: The Fourth Musketeer.* New York: Henry Holt and Company, 1953.

Knight, Stephen. *Robin Hood, A Complete Study of the English Outlaw.* Oxford: Blackwell, 1994.

Magill, Frank N., ed. *Magill's Survey of Cinema: Silent Films.* Englewood Cliffs, N.J.: Salem, 1982.

Munden, Kenneth W., ed. *The American Film Institute Catalog, Feature Films 1921–1930.* New York: Bowker, 1971.

O'Dell, Scott. *Representative Photoplays Analyzed.* Hollywood, Calif.: Palmer Institute of Authorship, 1924.

Parish, James Robert, and Don E. Stanke. *The Swashbucklers.* New Rochelle, N.Y.: Arlington House, 1976.

Richards, Jeffrey. *Swordsmen of the Screen from Douglas Fairbanks to Michael York.* London: Routledge & Kegan Paul, 1977.

Schickel, Richard. *The Fairbanks Album.* London: Secker & Warburg, 1975.

_____. *His Picture in the Papers.* New York: Charterhouse, 1973.

Sherwood, Robert. *The Best Moving Pictures of 1922–23.* New York: Revisionist, 1974.

Tibbetts, John C., and James M. Welsh. *His Majesty the American: The Cinema of Douglas Fairbanks, Sr.* New York: A.S. Barnes, 1977.

Turner, David. *Robin of the Movies.* Kingswinford, Eng.: Yeoman Publishing, 1989.

Woods, Lotta. *Douglas Fairbanks in Robin Hood.* [Los Angeles]: Douglas Fairbanks Picture Corporation, 1922.

444. *Robin Hood* (1973)

United States; dir. Wolfgang Reitherman; Walt Disney Productions.

CAST: (the voices of) Brian Bedford, Andy Devine, Monica Evans, Phil Harris, Roger Miller, Terry Thomas, Peter Ustinov.

With Richard away in the Holy Land, Prince John usurps the throne with the aid of the Sheriff of Nottingham. Robin and Little John, disguised as female fortune-tellers, rob the Prince of his ill-gotten gains and flee to the forest. The Sheriff sets out to extort even more money from the poor, and Prince John announces an archery contest in the hopes of trapping Robin. The Sheriff competes against Robin and despite the Sheriff's efforts to cheat, Robin wins. Prince John springs his trap and Robin is imprisoned, but he soon escapes and rejoins Marian in Sherwood Forest. Prince John increases his efforts to bleed the country dry, imprisoning everyone who cannot pay their taxes. The Prince decides to hang Friar Tuck in the hopes of flushing Robin out of hiding. Robin arrives in disguise and again thwarts Prince John's plans. King Richard returns, and Robin and Marian marry as Prince John and the Sheriff are confined in a penal rock-breaking quarry.

Disney here presents an animated version of the legend in which animals take on the roles of the familiar legendary characters. The film is enjoyable enough, although it is not one of the premier examples of Disney animation.

REVIEWS: *Cinefantastique* 1 (Fall 1970): 45. *CinemaTV Today* 7 January 1974: 8. *Cinema, Video & Cable Digest* 1 (9 August 1991): 56–57. *Entertainment Weekly* 75 (19 July 1991): 65. *Films and Filming* 20 (January 1974): 44–45. *Hollywood Reporter* 2 November 1973: 3, 11. *Los Angeles Times* 21 December

Robin Hood steals the tax money Prince John has extorted from the poor in Wolfgang Reitherman's animated *Robin Hood* (1973).

1973: 4. 31. *Monthly Film Bulletin* 41 (January 1974): 13. *New York Times* 9 November 1973: 29. *Variety* 7 November 1973: 9.

ADDITIONAL DISCUSSIONS:

Finch, Christopher. *The Art of Walt Disney*. New York: Harry N. Abrams, 1973.

Grant, John. *Encyclopedia of Walt Disney's Animated Characters*. New York: Harper & Row, 1987.

Johnston, Ollie, and Frank Thomas. *The Disney Villain*. New York: Hyperion, 1993.

Knight, Stephen. *Robin Hood, A Complete Study of the English Outlaw*. Oxford: Blackwell, 1994.

Nash, Jay Robert, and Stanley Ralph Ross. *The Motion Picture Guide, N–R, 1927–1983*. Chicago: Cinebooks, 1986.

445. *Robin Hood* (1991)

United States; dir. John Irvin; 20th Century–Fox.

CAST: Patrick Bergin, Edward Fox, Jeroen Krabbe, Jürgen Prochnow, Uma Thurman.

The Saxon Sir Robert Hode angers two Norman noblemen, Sir Miles Folcanet and Sir Roger Daguerre, who strip him of his title and confiscate his lands. Robert, now Robin, joins a band of thieves who steal from the rich and give to the poor; because the bounty on Robin and his men's heads is so high and the people are so poor, bribery is the only way to win the affection of the masses. Robin kidnaps Maid Marian from Folcanet, and her abduction inaugurates a series of adventures in which Robin finally defeats his Norman foes and marries Marian.

Irvin's film, which had the misfortune of being released (in the United States on television only) at the same time as Kevin Reynolds's *Robin Hood, Prince of Thieves*, presents a curiously modern portrait of the principals. Thurman's Marian is no shy, demure medieval lady-in-waiting, and Bergin's Robin seems motivated more by a delight in getting into trouble than by some form of principled opposition to Norman tyranny.

REVIEWS: *Encore* 9 (2–15 August 1991): 10. *Entertainment Weekly* 75 (19 July 1991): 65. *EPD Film* 8 (June 1991): 39. *Film Review* [London] June 1991: 14. *Los Angeles Times* 13 May 1991: Calendar 12. *Le*

Patrick Bergin in the title role in John Irvin's *Robin Hood* (1991).

Monde 22 June 1991: 13. *New York Times* 13 May 1991: C14. *Positif* 365-66 (July-August 1991): 47. *Revue du cinéma* [La Saison cinématographique] Hors série 39 (1991): 92–93. *Sight and Sound* NS 1 (June 1991): 57. *Studio* 52 (July-August 1991): 22. *Sunday Times* [London] 19 May 1991: 6. 11. *Times* [London] 16 May 1991: 17. *Variety* 20 May 1991: 41.

ADDITIONAL DISCUSSIONS:
Bishop, Peter. "Muddy Realism—and No Green Tights." *Film Review* [London] June 1991: 28–29.

Gensler, Howard. "The Sharpshooter of Sherwood Has Stayed on Target with Audiences Through the Ages." *TV Guide* 39 (11 May 1991): 24–26.

Knight, Stephen. *Robin Hood, A Complete Study of the English Outlaw.* Oxford: Blackwell, 1994.

Speed, F. Maurice, and James Cameron-Wilson. *Film Review 1991–1992.* New York: St. Martin's, 1991.

Robin Hood and His Merry Men

(1908) see *Robin and His Merry Men* (1908)

Robin Hood and Maid Marian (1913)

see *Robin Hood* (1913)

Robin Hood and the Pirates (1960)

see *Robin Hood e i pirati* (1960)

446. Robin Hood and the Sorcerer

(1984)

Great Britain; dir. Ian Sharp; Harlech TV and Goldcrest Films.

CAST: Robert Addie, Nickolas Grace, Philip Jackson, Clive Mantle, Michael Praed, Judi Trott, Anthony Valentine, Ray Winstone.

When Norman soldiers plunder a Saxon village, only a small boy escapes unharmed. Fifteen years later, the boy has become Robin Hood who, with a band of followers, is intent upon avenging Norman wrongs against his fellow Saxons. His nemesis is Baron de Belleme, an evil sorcerer intent upon sacrificing Maid Marian to the Devil.

This made-for-television film served as the pilot for two British television series about Robin and his men. Jason Connery eventually replaced Praed as Robin in the series.

REVIEWS: *Hollywood Reporter* 26 January 1984: 22. *Starburst* 92 (April 1986): 25–29; 96 (August 1986): 38–39.

ADDITIONAL DISCUSSIONS:

Airey, Jean. "The Man Who Killed Robin Hood." *Starlog* 175 (February 1992): 82, 91–93.

Knight, Stephen. *Robin Hood, A Complete Study of the English Outlaw.* Oxford: Blackwell, 1994.

Marill, Alvin H. *Movies Made for Television 1964–1986.* New York: Zoetrope, 1987.

Turner, David. *Robin of the Movies.* Kingswinford, Eng.: Yeoman Publishing, 1989.

447. Robin Hood e i pirati (1960)

Italy; dir. Giorgio Simonelli; F. Ci-T.

ALTERNATE TITLE: *Robin Hood and the Pirates.*

CAST: Lex Barker, Jackie Lane, Rossana Rory, Mario Scaccia.

While he is held captive aboard a pirate ship off the coast of Scotland, Robin learns that the evil Brooks has killed his father and stolen his lands. Brooks also intends to marry Kareen, Robin's childhood sweetheart. Robin escapes from the pirates but returns to enlist their help against Brooks. Together, they defeat Brooks and save Kareen, whom Robin marries.

This Lex Barker vehicle simply provides the actor with another swordsman's role. The film's plot owes nothing to the standard legend of Robin Hood.

REVIEWS: *Cinématographie française* 6 May 1961: 27. *Film français* 14 April 1961: 50. *Intermezzo* 16 (15 May 1961): 4.

ADDITIONAL DISCUSSIONS:

Italian Production 1960. Rome: Unitalia Film, 1961.

Lucanio, Patrick. *With Fire and Sword, Italian Spectacles on American Screens 1958–1968.* Metuchen, N.J.: Scarecrow, 1994.

Poppi, Roberto, and Mario Pecorari. *Dizionario del cinema italiano. Vol. 3: I Film dal 1960 al 1969.* Rome: Gremese Editore, 1992.

Turner, David. *Robin of the Movies.* Kingswinford, Eng.: Yeoman Publishing, 1989.

448. Robin Hood, el arquero invencible (1971)

Spain and Italy; dir. José Luis Merino; Hispamer Films.

ALTERNATE TITLE: *Robin Hood, l'arciere invincible.*

CAST: Pascale Basile, Alfredo Calles, Mariano Vidal Molina, Carina Monti, Franca Polesello, Charles Quiney, Paola Senatore.

Sir Allan Clare returns to England after fighting alongside King Richard in the Holy Lands to find that Baron Fritz-Alvise of Nottingham has seized his lands and given them to Sir Tristan, to whom he has also promised the hand of Isabel, Sir Allan's niece, in marriage. Robin Hood lends Sir Allan sufficient funds to recover his possessions and together they try to rescue Isabel, whom Sir Tristan and the Baron have imprisoned. A last-minute ruse saves Isabel from marrying Sir Tristan, and everyone flees back to Sherwood Forest to continue the fight on King Richard's behalf against the tyranny of the Baron and his allies.

Much like Italian films made in the 1970s, this film (co-produced with an Italian film studio) simply uses stray details from the legend of Robin Hood to tell a tale that is little more than a series of swashbuckling scenes.

REVIEW: *Cinestudio* 94 (February 1971): 57.

ADDITIONAL DISCUSSIONS:

Poppi, Roberto, and Mario Pecorari. *Dizionario del cinema italiano: I Film dal 1970 al 1979.* Rome: Gremese Editore, 1996.

The Spanish Cinema. Madrid: Uniespaña, 1971.

449. *Robin Hood, frecce, fagioli e karatè* (1975)

Italy; dir. Tonino Ricci; Scale Film–Panorama Arco Film.

CAST: Victoria Abril, Ria De Simone, Pino Ferrara, Chris Huerta, Alan Steel.

In Sherwood Forest, Robin Hood and his men have established a camp — and a series of traffic lights. If anyone crosses against the red light, he or she must pay a tax. Robin already counts the Baron of Nottingham his archenemy when the Baron imprisons Sir Allan in the hopes of forcing his sister to marry him. Robin comes to Sir Allan's aid, winning an archery contest and fooling the Baron — and marrying Sir Allan's sister to boot.

Italian filmmakers, long attracted to medieval (or pseudo-medieval) plot lines, continue to make some very silly films.

DISCUSSIONS:

Tous les films 1982. Paris: Éditions Chrétiens-Médias, 1983.

La Produzione italiana 1975/76. Rome: Unitalia Film, 1976.

450. *Robin Hood, Junior* (1923)

United States; dir. Clarence Bricker; East Coast Productions.

CAST: Stanley Bingham, Peggy Cartwright, Ashley Cooper, Phillip Dunham, Harry La Mont, Frankie Lee.

A young boy and girl create an imaginary kingdom in which they, their friends and family members act out the legend of Robin Hood. The staging here is elaborate, but the acting is inconsistent since only the roles of Robin and Marian are played by children. The film was dedicated to Douglas Fairbanks in appreciation for his work in Allan Dwan's *Robin Hood,* which had been released the previous year.

REVIEWS: *Bioscope* 8 November 1923: 69. *Harrison's Reports* 21 April 1923: 63.

ADDITIONAL DISCUSSION:

Munden, Kenneth W., ed. *The American Film Institute Catalog, Feature Films 1921–1930.* New York: Bowker, 1971.

451. *Robin Hood, Junior* (1975)

Great Britain; dir. Matt McCarthy and John Black; Children's Film Foundation.

An acrobatic group of boys and girls — Saxons all — foil the plans of their oppressive Norman overlords.

REVIEW: *Sunday Times* [London] 20 April 1975: 39.

Robin Hood, l'arciere invincible (1971)

see *Robin Hood, el arquero invencible* (1971)

452. *Robin Hood: Men in Tights* (1993)

United States; dir. Mel Brooks; 20th Century–Fox.

CAST: Mark Blankfield, Mel Brooks, David Chappelle, Cary Elwes, Eric Allan Kramer, Richard Lewis, Roger Rees, Patrick Stewart, Tracey Ullman, Amy Yasbeck.

In Jerusalem, Robin escapes from his Saracen jailers and swims home. Arriving at Dover, he finds England tyrannized by Prince John and the Sheriff of Rottingham who have confiscated his lands. Robin flees to Sherwood and surrounds himself with a band of followers, including Will Scarlet O'Hara, Little John and Rabbi Tuckman. Maid Marian is back at court alternately bored and busy resisting the Sheriff's romantic overtures. Having caught a quick glimpse of Robin, she falls madly in love with him. Prince John, worried about Robin, consults the court sorcerer Latrine and Don Giovanni, the local Mafia boss. At the latter's suggestion, he holds an archery contest. Robin attends and is imprisoned and sentenced to be hanged. A last-minute rescue by his band of men frees Robin, who then kills the Sheriff in a duel. Robin marries Marian; halfway through the ceremony, King Richard arrives, knights him and punishes Prince John.

This film presents Mel Brooks at his most irreverent — which can be good or bad, depending upon one's reaction to Brooks's brand of humor. The parody here is both of the genre of Robin Hood films in general and of Kevin Reynolds's *Robin Hood, Prince of Thieves* starring Kevin Costner in particular.

REVIEWS: *Entertainment Weekly* 172 (28 May 1993): 30–31; 182 (6 August 1993): 34–35, 71. *EPD Film* 10 (December 1993): 32–33. *Empire* 55 (January 1994): 28. *Film français* 26 November 1993: 30.

David Chappelle (left) as Ahchoo and Cary Elwes as Robin Hood in Mel Brooks's *Robin Hood: Men in Tights* (1993).

Film Review [London] January 1994: 15. *Films in Review* 44 (September-October 1993): 338–39. *Grand angle* 166 (December 1993): n.p. *Los Angeles Times* 28 July 1993: Calendar 5. *Le Monde* 17 December 1993: 16. *New York Times* 28 July 1993: C13, C18. *Positif* 396 (February 1994): 35. *Première* 202 (January 1994): 16. *Sight and Sound* NS 4 (January 1994): 51–52. *Times* [London] 16 December 1993: 31. *Variety* 9 August 1993: 35.

ADDITIONAL DISCUSSIONS:
Cameron-Wilson, James, and F. Maurice Speed. *Film Review 1994–1995*. London: Virgin Books, 1994.
Knight, Stephen. *Robin Hood, A Complete Study of the English Outlaw*. Oxford: Blackwell, 1994.
_____. "*Robin Hood: Men in Tights*: Fitting the Tradition Snugly." In Deborah Cartmell et al., eds. *Pulping Fictions, Consuming Culture Across the Literature/Media Divide*. London: Pluto, 1996.

453. *Robin Hood nunca muere* (1975)

Spain; dir. Francisco Bellmunt; Profilmes.
CAST: Charly Bravo, Emma Cohen, Luis Induni, Manía Reniu, Fernando Rubio.
News of Robin Hood's death at the hands

of the Sheriff of Nottingham rapidly spreads throughout England, and the Sheriff decides to increase his efforts at extorting money from the poor. A magician resurrects Robin from what proves to be a faked death, and Robin's band of followers gather to steal the Sheriff's treasure. Robin and his men catch the Sheriff by surprise, imprison him and his soldiers and celebrate their triumph over tyranny.

The only addition to the legend in this modest, if not mediocre, film is the false report of Robin's death.

REVIEWS: *Cineinforme* 234 (November 1975): 21. *Cinema* [Spain] 2202 (April 1975): 12–13.
ADDITIONAL DISCUSSION:
Cine español. Madrid: Uniespaña, 1975.

454. *Robin Hood Outlawed* (1912)

Great Britain; dir. Charles Raymond; British and Colonial Films.
CAST: Edward Durrant, George Foley, Jack Houghton, J. Leonard, Harry Lorraine, Ivy Martinek, A. Brian Plant.

Robin forms his band of men and rescues Maid Marian from an evil knight in a film indebted to Victorian melodrama and not to the 1872 novel of the same title attributed to Alexandre Dumas the Elder.

DISCUSSIONS:

Behlmer, Rudy. "Robin Hood on the Screen." *Films in Review* 16 (February 1965): 91–102.

Gifford, Denis. *The British Film Catalogue 1895–1985.* Newton Abbot: David and Charles, 1986.

Knight, Stephen. *Robin Hood, A Complete Study of the English Outlaw.* Oxford: Blackwell, 1994.

Richards, Jeffrey. *Swordsmen of the Screen from Douglas Fairbanks to Michael York.* London: Routledge & Kegan Paul, 1977.

455. *Robin Hood, Prince of Thieves*
(1991)

United States; dir. Kevin Reynolds; Warner Bros. and Morgan Creek.

CAST: Brian Blessed, Sean Connery, Kevin Costner, Morgan Freeman, Mary Elizabeth Mastrantonio, Geraldine McEwan, Alan Rickman, Christian Slater.

Robin and a cultured Moor, Azeem, escape from a Jerusalem prison and return from the Crusades to England. Robin finds that his father has been murdered and his lands confiscated. Robin soon encounters and does battle with the Sheriff of Nottingham, who is overtaxing the poor and plotting to overthrow King Richard. Robin and Azeem seek shelter in Sherwood Forest, where they join company with a band of outlaws. Robin, Azeem, and the outlaws bedevil the Sheriff, who lusts after Maid Marian (Robin's love and Richard's ward). Marian helps Robin defeat the Sheriff, and, in a final scene, the two are married as Richard arrives back in England.

Intended as a remake of Errol Flynn's 1938 classic *The Adventures of Robin Hood*, Reynolds's film constantly falls short, though audiences found it enjoyable. The presence of a Moor in medieval England as one of Robin Hood's companions does, however, stretch credulity. Connery's uncredited appearance as King Richard provides a link with his earlier appearance as Robin in *Robin and Marian* (1976).

REVIEWS: *American Film* 16 (June 1991): 56–57. *Les Cahiers du cinéma* 447 (September 1991): 75. *Cinema, Video & Cable Movie Digest* 1 (July 1991): 16. *Encore* 9 (2–15 August 1991): 10. *Entertainment Weekly* 71 (21 June 1991): 38–40. *EPD Film* 8 (September 1991): 36. *Film français* 26 July 1991: 12. *Film Journal* 94 (July 1991): 19–20. *Film Review* [London]

August 1991: 29. *Films in Review* 42 (July-August): 252–53. *Hollywood Reporter* 12 June 1991: 6, 12; 18 June 1991: 12. *Los Angeles Times* 14 June 1991: Calendar 1. *Le Monde* 23 June 1991: 13; 9 August 1991: 7. *New York Times* 14 June 1991: C1, C3. *Positif* 367 (October 1991): 49–50. *Premiere* 4 (June 1991): 55–57. *Première* 173 (August 1971): 12–13. *Revue du cinéma* [La Saison cinémathographique] Hors série 39 (1991): 94. *Sight and Sound* NS 1 (June 1991): 4–5; NS 1 (August 1991): 52–53. *Starburst* 156 (August 1991): 31. *Studio* [Paris] 52 (July-August 1991): 19. *Sunday Times* [London] 14 July 1991: 5. 1–2; 21 July 1991: 5. 11. *Times* [London] 18 July 1991: 15. *Times* [London] *Literary Supplement* 2 August 1991: 16. *Variety* 17 June 1991: 65.

ADDITIONAL DISCUSSIONS:

Calhoun, John. "*Robin Hood, Prince of Thieves*: Designing a Postmodern Middle Ages." *Theatre Crafts* 25 (August-September 1991): 48.

d'Yvoire, Christophe. "La Bataille de Robin des Bois." *Studio* [Paris] 52 (July-August 1991): 98–103.

Falk, Quentin. "Kevin's a Legend in Lincoln Green." *Flicks* 4 (July 1991): 18–19.

Gensler, Howard. "The Sharpshooter of Sherwood Has Stayed on Target with Audiences Through the Ages." *TV Guide* 39 (11 May 1991): 24–26.

Green, Simon. *Robin Hood, Prince of Thieves.* New York: Berkley, 1991. [Novelization.]

Jones, Alan. "Costner Makes Merrie." *Film Review* [London] April 1991: 8–10.

_____. "*Robin Hood, Prince of Thieves*." *Cinefantastique* 21 (June 1991): 8–9, 62.

_____. "*Robin Hood, Prince of Thieves*." *Starburst* 156 (August 1991): 40–43.

Keith, Todd. *Kevin Costner.* London: Ikonprint, 1991.

Kilday, Gregg, and Garth Pearce. "The Battle of Sherwood Forest." *Entertainment Weekly* 71 (21 June 1991): 16–22.

Knight, Stephen. *Robin Hood, A Complete Study of the English Outlaw.* Oxford: Blackwell, 1994.

Magill, Frank N., ed. *Magill's Cinema Annual 1992, A Survey of the Films of 1991.* Pasadena, Calif.: Salem, 1992.

McFerran, Ann. "Tough Act to Follow." *Entertainment Weekly* 78 (9 August 1991): 28–31.

Miller-Monzon, John. *The Motion Picture Guide, 1992 Annual (The Films of 1991).* New York: Baseline, 1992.

Parker, Jean. *Sean Connery.* London: Gollancz, 1993.

Pearce, Garth. "*Robin Hood, Prince of Thieves*." *Empire* 26 (August 1991): 72–80.

_____. *Robin Hood, Prince of Thieves: The Official Movie Book.* New York: Mallard, 1991.

Pfeiffer, Lee, and Philip Lisa. *The Films of Sean Connery.* New York: Citadel, 1993.

Pirani, Adam. "Prince of Stuntmen." *Action Heroes* 4 [Overall Series 5] (1991): 43–49.

_____. "Robin Hood." *Action Heroes* 4 [Overall Series 5] (1991): 22–26

Rose, Cynthia. "Maid in Heaven." *Entertainment Weekly* 76 (26 July 1991): 26–27.

Mary Elizabeth Mastrantonio as Maid Marian and Kevin Costner as Robin Hood in Kevin Reynolds's *Robin Hood, Prince of Thieves* (1991).

Williams, John. "*Robin Hood, Prince of Thieves.*" *Mediascene Prevue* 84 (May-August 1991): 20–29.

456. *Robin Hood's Arrows* (1977)

Soviet Union; dir. Sergei Tarasov; Riga Studios.

ALTERNATE TITLES: *The Arrows of Robin Hood* and *Striely Robin Guda.*

CAST: Int Buran, Yuri Kamory, Boris Khmelnitsky, Algis Masyulis, Ragina Razuma.

Frustrated by Robin Hood's constant harassment, the Bishop of Nottingham and Sir Guy Gisbourne plot to capture Maid Marian and set a trap for Robin.

This is the first in a trilogy of medieval films that Tarasov made. It was followed by *Ballada o doblestnom rystare Aivengo* (*Ballad of the Valiant Knight Ivanhoe*, 1983) and *Chernaya strela* (*Black Arrow*, 1985).

REVIEW: *Film* [Poland] 23 (27 February 1977): 6.
ADDITIONAL DISCUSSIONS:
"[Shooting in Progress] Robin Hood's Arrows." *Soviet Film* 11 (1975): 38–39.
Turner, David. *Robin of the Movies.* Kingswinford, Eng.: Yeoman Publishing, 1989.

Den Røde kappe (1967) see *The Red Mantle* (1967)

457. *Rogues of Sherwood Forest* (1950)

United States; dir. Gordon Douglas; Columbia Pictures.

CAST: John Derek, Alan Hale, Diana Lynn, George Macready.

Robin, Earl of Huntington and son of the great Robin Hood, battles King John, who is pressed for money and taxing the poor to raise it. Robin is captured by the King, but freed by his ward Marianne, whom John has promised in marriage to the Earl of Flanders. Robin rallies his father's band of men, rescues Marianne, forces John to sign the Magna Carta and marries Marianne.

This swashbuckler garbles history considerably, but Derek makes an appealing hero. The film also afforded Alan Hale a third opportunity to play Little John; he had played the role opposite both Douglas Fairbanks in the 1922 *Robin Hood* and Errol Flynn in the 1938 *The Adventures of Robin Hood.*

REVIEWS: *Kinematograph Weekly* 17 August 1950: 30; 19 March 1959: 27. *Monthly Film Bulletin* 17 (September 1950): 142. *Motion Picture Herald* 17 June 1950: Product Digest Section 347. *Revue du cinéma* [La Saison cinématographique] Hors série 32 (1950-1951): 149. *To-day's Cinema* 10 August 1950: 6. *Variety* 21 June 1950: 8.

ADDITIONAL DISCUSSIONS:
Knight, Stephen. *Robin Hood, A Complete Study of the English Outlaw.* Oxford: Blackwell, 1994.
Nash, Jay Robert, and Stanley Ralph Ross. *The Motion Picture Guide, N–R, 1927–1983.* Chicago: Cinebooks, 1986.
Richards, Jeffrey. *Swordsmen of the Screen from Douglas Fairbanks to Michael York.* London: Routledge & Kegan Paul, 1977.
Turner, David. *Robin of the Movies.* Kingswinford, Eng.: Yeoman Publishing, 1989.

458. *Le Roi Philippe le Bel et les templiers* (1910)

France; dir. Victorin Jasset; Eclair Films.

ALTERNATE TITLE: *King Philip the Fair and the Templars.*

King Philip, in an attempt to gain control over the Knights Templar and their vast wealth, convinces the Pope that their leader, Jacques Molay, is guilty of heresy. Molay is tortured and confesses to crimes he did not commit. On his deathbed, he tells the King that the two will meet again before the year is out. Molay's last words haunt the King, who goes out hunting, falls from his horse and dies as the ghost of Molay appears to him, summoning Philip to Hell.

Philip IV first moved against the Templars in 1307 and, on his orders, their Grand Master de Molay was burned at the stake in 1314 on a false charge of heresy. In his last breath, Molay summoned Philip to God's quick judgment.

REVIEWS: *Bioscope* 29 December 1910: 35. *Moving Picture World* 25 February 1911: 438.

Roland and the Knights of France (1956) see *Orlando e i paladini di Francia* (1956)

Roland the Mighty (1956) see *Orlando e i paladini di Francia* (1956)

Roman Scandals '73 (1973) see *Fratello homo, sorella bona—nel Boccaccio superproibito* (1973)

459. *Ronja rövardotter* (1984)

Sweden; dir. Tage Danielsson; Svensk Filmindustri.

John Derek as Robin, Earl of Huntington (and son of the legendary outlaw), in Gordon Douglas's *Rogues of Sherwood Forest* (1950).

ALTERNATE TITLE: *Ronya, The Robber's Daughter.*

CAST: Börje Ahstedt, Allan Edwall, Dan Häfström, Lena Nyman, Per Oscarsson, Med Reventberg, Hanna Zetterberg.

Two tribes of bandits live as rivals in the forest under the leadership of Mattis and Borka. One night, during a violent thunderstorm, Mattis's wife bears him a daughter, Ronja, while Borka's wife bears her husband a son,

Jean Seberg as Joan in Otto Preminger's *Saint Joan* (1957).

Birk. Years later, the two children meet, and to the consternation of their families, Ronja and Birk fall in love. At first, the lovers flee to the forest to be together, but eventually their love overcomes family enmity.

From the 1981 novel of the same title by Astrid Lindgren, this film presents a plot that combines folklore with fairy tale. While in the forest, Birk and Ronja encounter an assortment of dwarfs, gnomes and witches.

REVIEWS: *Chaplin* 196 (February 1985): 50–51. *Film og kino* 1 (1985): 12–13; 2 (1985): 75. *Filmrutan* 28.1 (1985): 5. *Levende billeder* 11 (January 1985): 57–58. *New York Times* 23 May 1986: C4. *Scandinavian Film News* 3 (Autumn 1983): 8; 4 (December 1984): 4. *Variety* 19 December 1984: 88.

ADDITIONAL DISCUSSIONS:
Cowie, Peter, ed. *International Film Guide 1986.* London: Tantivy Press, 1986.
Norwegian Films 1985. Oslo: Norwegian Film Institute, 1985.
Swedish Films 85. Stockholm: Swedish Film Institute, 1985.

Ronya, the Robber's Daughter (1984)
see *Ronya rövardotter* (1984)

Rosmunda e Albino (1961) see *Sword of the Conqueror* (1961)

The Royalty of France (1959) see *Reali di Francia* (1959)

Ruslan and Liudmila (1970) see *Ruslan i Lyudmila* (1970)

460. Ruslan i Lyudmila (1970)
Soviet Union; dir. Alexander L. Ptushko; Mosfilm.

ALTERNATE TITLES: *Legend of the Golden Prince* and *Ruslan and Liudmila.*

CAST: Vladimir Fyodorov, Valeri Kozinets, Natalya Petrova, Igor Yasulovich.

Ruslan, a knight errant, saves Lyudmila, the daughter of the Duke of Kiev, from Tchernomor, the evil dwarf, who had kidnapped her under the cover of darkness. As a reward, the Duke gives Ruslan Lyudmila's hand in marriage.

This film's source is "Ruslan i Lyudmila," an epic poem written by Alexander Pushkin and first published in 1820.

REVIEWS: *Ecran fantastique* 3 (1973): 80–81. *Positif* 160 (June 1974): 35. *Image et son* 288–89 (October 1974): 321–22. *Los Angeles Times* 16 October 1976: 2. 9. *Soviet Film* 7 (1970): 14–15; 2 (1973): 38–39. *Variety* 17 April 1974: 20.

Rypa i justeddal (1994) see *Trollsyn* (1994)

The Saga of Gisli (1981) see *Utlaginn* (1981)

Saga of Singoalia (1950) see *The Mask and the Sword* (1950)

The Saga of the Viking Saint Olav (1983) see *Prima Veras Saga om Olav den Hellige* (1983)

The Saga of the Viking Women and Their Voyage to the Waters of the Great Sea Serpent (1957) see *The Viking Women and the Sea Serpent* (1957)

Saint Francis (1911) see *Il Poverello di Assisi* (1911)

Saint Francis of Assisi (1943) see *San Francisco de Asís* (1943)

461. Saint Joan (1957)
Great Britain and United States; dir. Otto Preminger; United Artists.

CAST: Felix Aylmer, Finlay Currie, John Gielgud, Kenneth Haigh, Barry Jones, Jean Seberg, Richard Todd, Richard Widmark.

In a flashback, a peasant girl named Joan arrives at Vaucoleurs Castle in 1429 saying she has been sent by God to relieve Orléans, drive the English from France and install the Dauphin as king. Joan does indeed lead the French armies in defeating the English, but the fickle Dauphin neglects her. When she is captured by the Burgundians and sold to the Earl of Warwick, the king does nothing to rescue her. Warwick in turn delivers Joan to the Church, which tries her for heresy and witchcraft and has her burned at the stake. In an epilogue, the principal characters return to discuss the main events of the film.

With a script by Graham Greene from the play by Shaw, this film should be much better than it is, but both Seberg and Widmark are miscast.

REVIEWS: *Les Cahiers du cinéma* 73 (July 1954): 38–40. *Daily Film Renter* 20 June 1957: 5. *Film Daily* 8 May 1957: 11. *Films and Filming* 3 (July 1957): 21. *Films in Review* 8 (June-July 1957): 280–81. *Harrison's Reports* 11 May 1957: 76. *Hollywood Reporter* 8 May 1957: 3. *Kinematograph Weekly* 20 June 1957: 20. *Monthly Film Bulletin* 24 (July 1957): 98. *Motion Picture Herald* 11 May 1957: Product Digest Section 369. *New York Times* 27 June 1957: 21; 30 June 1957: 2. 1. *Sight and Sound* 27 (Summer 1957): 38. *Times* [London] 13 May 1957: 14; 20 June 1957: 3. *To-day's Cinema* 20 June 1957: 8. *Variety* 8 May 1957: 6.

ADDITIONAL DISCUSSIONS:

Blaetz, Robin J. "Strategies of Containment: Joan of Arc in Film." Ph.D. dissertation. New York University, 1989.

"Dramatic Scenes from *St. Joan*, Otto Preminger's New Film Based on the Play by Bernard Shaw." *Illustrated London News* 1 June 1957: 908–09.

Garbicz, Adam, and Jacek Klinowski. *Cinema, The Magic Vehicle.* New York: Schocken, 1983.

Harty, Kevin J. "Jeanne au cinéma." In Bonnie Wheeler and Charles T. Wood, eds. *Fresh Verdicts on Joan of Arc.* New York: Garland, 1996.

Holston, Kim. *Richard Widmark, A Bio-Bibliography.* New York: Greenwood, 1990.

Mattern, Marjorie. *Saint Joan.* New York: Feature Book, 1957. [Novelization.]

Mico, Ted., et al., eds. *Past Imperfect, History According to the Movies.* New York: Henry Holt, 1995.

Nash, Jay Robert, and Stanley Ralph Ross. *The Motion Picture Guide, S, 1927–1983.* Chicago: Cinebooks, 1987.

Pratley, Gerald. *The Cinema of Otto Preminger.* New York: A.S. Barnes, 1971.

Saint Joan the Maid (1929) see *La Merveilleuse Vie de Jeanne d'Arc* (1929)

462. *Saladin* (1963)

Egypt; dir. Youssef Chahine; Lotus Films.
ALTERNATE TITLE: *An-Nasr Salah ad-Din.*
CAST: Nadia Loutfi, Ahmed Mazhar, Salah Zulfikar.

During the Third Crusade, Saladin leads an uprising against the occupying French forces led by Prince Renaud. In a pitched battle, Saladin kills Renaud, whose widow Virginia summons aid from Kings Richard and Philip Augustus. Their combined armies invade the Holy Land and meet with initial success. Richard wants to seek an accommodation with Saladin, but Philip and Virginia, secretly aided by Prince John, insist on continuing the war. When Richard's armies advance on Jerusalem, he is badly wounded, but Saladin has him nursed back to health. The English sue for peace and depart from the Holy Land, now firmly under Saladin's control.

In its time the most expensive Arabic film production ever made (an Egyptian blockbuster), *Saladin* is unique among Crusader films in presenting familiar events from the unfamiliar Arabic point of view.

REVIEWS: *Monthly Film Bulletin* 46 (August 1979): 167. *Variety* 24 July 1963: 6.

ADDITIONAL DISCUSSIONS:

Ibrahim, Mounir Mohamed. *Directory of Egyptian Films 1927–1982.* Cairo: Cinema Development Fund, 1983.

Khan, Mohamed. *An Introduction to the Egyptian Cinema.* London: Informatics, 1969.

Lucanio, Patrick. *With Fire and Sword, Italian Spectacles on American Screens 1958–1968.* Metuchen, N.J.: Scarecrow, 1994.

San Francesco d'Assisi (1918) see *Frate Sole* (1918)

463. *San Francisco de Asís* (1943)

Mexico; dir. Alberto Gout; Azteca Films.
ALTERNATE TITLE: *Saint Francis of Assisi.*
CAST: Crox Alvarado, Antonio Bravo, Alicia de Phillips, Elene D'Orgaz, José Luis Jiménez, Carmen Molina, Ella Ortiz.

As the birth of her son nears, a wealthy woman leaves her lavish Assisi home, so that the child can be born in a stable. The child is christened Francis and grows up leading a life that wants for nothing that wealth and power can provide. Francis gains a reputation as someone who enjoys wine, women, song and dueling, until he rejects all worldly pleasure and comfort and embraces a strict life of denial. He founds an order of friars, cures the sick, and dies having received the stigmata.

The fairly well-known events of the saint's life are here presented in a static but reverential treatment. A subplot develops a love story between two of Francis's closest friends.

REVIEWS: *Motion Picture Herald* 1 April 1944:

Ahmed Mazhar (center) as the title character in Youssef Chahine's *Saladin* (1963). (Still courtesy of the British Film Institute.)

Product Digest Section 1826. *New York Times* 5 April 1947: 12.

ADDITIONAL DISCUSSIONS:

Butler, Ian. *Religion in the Cinema*. New York: A.S. Barnes, 1969.

Garciá Riera, Emilio. *El Cine mexicano*. [Mexico City]: Ediciones Era, 1963.

———. *Historia documental del cine mexicano. Época sonora. Tomo II: 1941–1944*. [Mexico City]: Ediciones Era, 1970.

———, and Fernando Macotela.*La Guía del cine mexicano de la pantalla grande a la televisión 1919–1984*. [Mexico City]: Editorial Patria, 1984.

464. *Des Sängers Fluch* (1910)

Germany; Messter-Film.

ALTERNATE TITLES: *The Curse of the Wandering Minstrel* and *The Singer's Curse*.

Two minstrels arrive at a castle to entertain a feudal lord and his lady. When the lady begins to flirt with one of the minstrels, her en-

raged husband stabs him to death. Horrified, the other minstrel curses the lord and predicts that catastrophe will befall him and his castle. The prophecy quickly comes true as the castle comes under siege, and the lord is captured and dies under the rubble as the castle is leveled.

The film is based upon an 1814 ballad by Ludwig Uhland, itself based on a Scottish ballad that Johann Gottfried Herder had published in a German translation at the end of the eighteenth century.

REVIEW: *Bioscope* 10 February 1910: 58.

ADDITIONAL DISCUSSION:

Birett, Herbert. *Das Filmangebot in Deutschland 1895–1911*. Munich: Filmbuchverlag Winterberg, 1991.

465. *Sans peur et sans reproche* (1988)

France; dir. Gérard Jugnot; CPFI.

ALTERNATE TITLE: *Without Fear or Blame*.

CAST: Victoria Abril, Ann Gisel-Glass, Gérard Jugnot, Martin Lamotte, Remi Martin.

At the end of the fifteenth century, French armies cross Italy intent upon recapturing the Kingdom of Naples. Among their number is a low-born squire who achieves military prowess and wins the hand of his lady love.

Those responsible, both behind and in front of the camera, for this farce, whose sense of humor and timing is vaguely reminiscent of that of the Monty Python troupe, lack the inspired mayhem of their English counterparts. The French knight Pierre Terrail (1473–1524) was one of the last idealized figures of chivalry. He was generally referred to as Le Chevalier Bayard, "le chevalier sans peur et sans reproche." This film reduces his reputation and his exploits to the farcical. Terrail receives better treatment in the 1938 Italian film *Ettore Fieramosca*.

REVIEWS: *Positif* 336 (February 1989): 75. *Première* 141 (December 1988): 17. *Revue du cinéma* 445 (January 1989): 32. *Variety* 28 December 1988: 12.

ADDITIONAL DISCUSSIONS:
Boulat, Antoinette. "Messire Jougnot." *Première* 141 (December 1988): 118–21.
_____. "Sans peur et sans reproche." *Première* 137 (August 1988): 78–85.
Les Films français. Paris: Unifrance International Film, 1988.
The Motion Picture Guide: 1989 Annual (The Films of 1988). Evanston, Ill.: Cinebooks, 1989.
Tous les films 1988. Paris: Éditions Chrétiens-Médias, 1989.

466. *The Saracen Blade* (1954)

United States; dir. William Castle; Columbia Pictures.

CAST: Michael Ansara, Edgar Barrier, Whitfield Connor, Rick Jason, Carolyn Jones, Ricardo Montalban, Betta St. John.

In thirteenth-century Italy, Pietro seeks revenge when a local baron murders his blacksmith father. By chance, Pietro and Iolanthe, the daughter-in-law of the baron, meet and fall in love. With the help of the Holy Roman Emperor, Pietro becomes a knight and carries out an elaborate plan to avenge his father's death, killing the baron and his son and marrying Iolanthe.

This fairly typical and predictable swashbuckler is adapted from Frank Yerby's best-selling 1952 novel *The Saracen Blade.*

REVIEWS: *Film Daily* 20 May 1954: 10. *Harrison's Reports* 22 May 1954: 83. *Hollywood Reporter* 14 May 1954: 3. *Kinematograph Weekly* 8 July 1954: 19. *Monthly Film Bulletin* 21 (August 1954): 122. *Motion Picture Herald* 22 May 1954: Product Digest Section 2. *New York Times* 15 May 1954: 13. *To-day's Cinema* 2 July 1954: 12. *Variety* 19 May 1954: 6.

ADDITIONAL DISCUSSIONS:
Nash, Jay Robert, and Stanley Ralph Ross. *The Motion Picture Guide, S, 1927–1983.* Chicago: Cinebooks, 1987.
Smith, Gary A. *Epic Films.* Jefferson, N.C.: McFarland, 1991.

Scanderbeg (1953) see *Skanderbeg* (1953)

467. *Sea Dragon* (1990)

Great Britain; dir. Agust Gudmundsson; Thames Television.

CAST: Bernard Latham, Janek Lesniak, Graham McGrath, Baard Owe, Pat Roach, Øystein Wiik.

In the tenth century, Thormod and his slave, Jestyn the Briton, sail for England to find those responsible for the murder of Thormod's father.

Originally a four-part television series, *Sea Dragon*, based on Rosemary Sutcliff's 1977 novel *Blood Feud*, was subsequently released as a film.

REVIEWS: *Screen International* 11 August 1990: 25. *Television Today* 29 November 1990: 24.

Second Sight (1994) see *Trollsyn* (1994)

Le Seigneur de la guerre (1965) see *The War Lord* (1965)

468. *The Servant* (1953)

Great Britain; dir. Douglas Allen; BBC.

CAST: Pamela Alan, Peter Copley, John Glen, Marjorie Manning, Jonathan Meddings, Philip Ray, Arthur Young.

A young girl named Joan finds herself torn between the call of the quiet country life she has enjoyed and inner voices summoning her to a role as France's savior against the English invaders. In private, she meets with the Dauphin at Chinon, convincing him of the validity of her cause. She then sets forth to rally the French armies to victory. At Reims, she battles the Archbishop, jealous of her prominence, and then she once again returns to her troops. Betrayed to her enemies, she defies the ecclesiastical courts that would condemn her, but is tricked by Bishop Cauchon into signing a confession and is burned at the stake.

Death (Bengst Ekerot) and the Knight Antonius Block (Max von Sydow) play chess in Ingmar Bergman's *The Seventh Seal* (1957).

The familiar story of Joan of Arc is retold here in a BBC television production adapted by Juliet Mansel from the 1945 play *The Servant* by Marcelle-Maurette. The treatment of Joan focuses on her inner thoughts and private moments and celebrates her as France's national hero rather than as a saint of the Church that would first condemn and than canonize her.

REVIEW: *Radio Times* [London] 26 June 1953: 14.

469. *The Seventh Seal* (1957)

Sweden; dir. Ingmar Bergman; Svensk Film-industri.

ALTERNATE TITLE: *Det Sjunde Inseglet.*

CAST: Bibi Andersson, Gunnar Björnstrand, Bengst Ekerot, Max von Sydow.

A disillusioned knight returns from the Crusades unmoved by the turmoil in his now plague-infested homeland. To determine if God really exists, he plays a game of chess with Death to extend his life. Traveling across the Swedish countryside, he meets a company of actors. He next encounters a group of flagellants who beat and torture themselves to save their souls, and he witnesses the torture and burning of a witch. Nowhere does he find the answers he seeks. Forfeiting his game of chess to Death, he and many of his companions die.

Bergman here directs one of the great cinematic depictions of the medieval. In this case, he presents a morality play that exposes the brutality, ignorance and superstition of medieval times while also drawing parallels between these medieval horrors and the horror of a modern nuclear disaster.

REVIEWS: *Biografägaren* 4–5 (1957): 47. *Les Cahiers du cinéma* 83 (May 1958): 43–46. *Cinéma* [Paris] 28 (June 1958): 115–16. *Cinéma 57* May 1957: 30–32. *Daily Cinema* 10 March 1958: 9. *Film* 14 (November-December 1957): 20–21. *Film français* 675–676 (Spring 1957): 26. *Film Quarterly* 12 (Spring 1959): 42–44. *Filmfacts* 1 (19 November 1958): 194–95. *Films and Filming* 9 (January 1963): 25–29. *Films in Review* 11 (November 1958): 515–17. *Kine-matograph Weekly* 13 March 1958: 16. *Le Monde* 26 April 1953: 13. *Monthly Film Bulletin* 25 (May 1958): 59–60. *New York Times* 14 October 1958: 44; 19 October 1958: 2.1. *Sight and Sound* 27 (Spring 1958): 199–200. *Times* [London] 20 May 1957: 3; 10 March 1958: 5. *Variety* 5 June 1957: 22.

ADDITIONAL DISCUSSIONS:

Archer, Eugene. "The Rack of Life." *Film Quarterly* 12 (Summer 1959): 3–16.

Bergman, Ingmar. *The Seventh Seal.* Trans. Lars Malmström and David Kushner. London: Lorrimer, 1960. [Screenplay.]

_____. *Das siebente Siegel.* Trans. Tabitha von Bonin. Hamburg: Marion von Schröder, 1963. [Screenplay.]

Björkman, Stig, et al. *Bergman on Bergman.* Trans. Paul Britten Austin. London: Secker & Warburg, 1973.

Blackwell, Marilyn Johns. *Gender and Representation in the Films of Ingmar Bergman.* Columbia, S.C.: Camden House, 1997.

Blackwood, Caroline. "The Mystic of Ingmar Bergman." *Encounter* 16 (April 1961): 54–57.

Blake, Richard A. "Quest for Understanding in *The Seventh Seal.*" *Drama Critique* 10 (Winter 1967): 16–24.

Boyum, Joy Gould, and Adrienne Scott, eds. *Film as Film.* Boston: Allyn and Bacon, 1971.

Colledge, Eric. "A Penitential Pilgrimage." *Month* NS 20 (July 1958): 5–11.

Cowie, Peter. *Antonini, Bergman, Resnais.* New York: A.S. Barnes, 1963.

_____. *Ingmar Bergman.* Loughton, Essex: Motion Monographs, 1961.

_____. *Ingmar Bergman, A Critical Biography.* London: Secker & Warburg, 1982.

_____. *Max von Sydow from* The Seventh Seal *to* Pelle the Conqueror. Stockholm: Chaplin/Swedish Film Institute, 1989.

_____. "Milieu and Texture in *The Seventh Seal.*" In Stanley J. Solomon, ed. *The Classic Cinema.* New York: Harcourt, 1973.

_____. *World Cinema 2: Sweden 2.* New York: A.S. Barnes, 1970.

Donner, Jörn. *The Films of Ingmar Bergman.* New York: Dover, 1972.

Fovez, Élie. "Le Septième Sceau." *Téléciné* 77 (August-September 1958): 1–8.

Gado, Frank. *The Passion of Ingmar Bergman.* Durham, N.C.: Duke University Press, 1986.

Garbicz, Adam, and Jacek Klinowski. *Cinema, The Magic Vehicle.* New York: Schocken, 1983.

Gibson, Arthur. *The Silence of God.* New York: Harper & Row, 1969.

Gill, Jerry H. *Ingmar Bergman and the Search for Meaning.* Grand Rapids, Mich.: Eerdmans, 1969.

Hill, Geoffrey. *Illuminating Shadows, The Mythic Power of Film.* Boston: Shambhala, 1992.

Holland, Norman H. "The Puzzling Movies: Three Analyses and a Guess at Their Appeal." *Journal of Social Issues* 20 (January 1964): 71–96.

_____. "*The Seventh Seal*: Film as Iconography." *Hudson Review* 12 (Summer 1959): 266–70.

Ingemanson, Birgitta. "Bergman's Endings: Glimmeries of Hope." *Lamar Journal of the Humanities* 8 (Spring 1982): 29–38.

Ketcham, Charles B. *The Influence of Existentialism on Ingmar Bergman.* Lewiston, N.Y.: Mellen, 1986.

Kwiatkowski, Aleksander. *Swedish Film Classics.* New York: Dover, 1983.

Lauder, Robert E. *God, Death, Art and Love.* New York: Paulist, 1989.

Lauritzen, Einar. *Swedish Films.* New York: MOMA, 1962.

Lefevre, Raymond. *Ingmar Bergman.* Paris: Edilig, 1983.

Leff, Leonard J. *Film Plots, Vol. I.* Ann Arbor, Mich.: Pierian, 1983.

Lennig, Arthur, ed. *Film Notes of the Wisconsin Film Society.* Madison: Wisconsin Film Society, 1960.

Lloyd, Ann, ed. *Movies of the Fifties.* London: Orbis, 1982.

Long, Robert Emmet. *Ingmar Bergman, Film and Stage.* New York: Harry N. Abrams, 1994.

Magill, Frank N., ed. *Magill's Survey of Cinema: Foreign Language Films.* Englewood Cliffs, N.J.: Salem, 1985.

Marty, Joseph. *Ingmar Bergman, un poétique du désir.* Paris: Les Éditions du Cerf, 1991.

McIlroy, Brian. *World Cinema 2: Sweden.* London: Flick Books, 1986.

Mellen, Joan. *Women and Their Sexuality in the New Film.* New York: Horizon, 1973.

Mishler, William. "*The Virgin Spring* and *The Seventh Seal*: A Girardian Reading." *Comparative Drama* 30 (Spring 1996): 106–34.

Mosley, Philip. *Ingmar Bergman: The Cinema as Mistress.* London: Marion Boyars, 1981.

Phillips, Gene. "Through a Glass Darkly: The Films of Ingmar Bergman." *Clergy Review* 52 (October 1967): 801–09.

Pressler, Michael. "The Idea Fused in the Fact: Bergman and *The Seventh Seal.*" *Literature/Film Quarterly* 13 (1985): 96–101.

Sarris, Andrew. "*The Seventh Seal.*" *Film Culture* 19 (April 1959): 51–61.

Scott, James F. "The Achievement of Ingmar Bergman." *Journal of Aesthetics and Art Criticism* 24 (Winter 1965): 263–72.

"Le Septieme Sceau." *Avant-scène du cinéma* 410 (March 1992): 1–94. [Special issue devoted to the film; includes screenplay.]

Siclier, Jacques. *Ingmar Bergman.* Rev. ed. Paris: Classiques du cinéma, 1966.

Slayton, Ralph Emil. "Ingmar Bergman's *The Seventh Seal*: A Criticism." Ph.D. diss. Columbia University, 1972.

Steene, Birgitta. *Ingmar Bergman*. New York: Twayne, 1968.

_____. *Ingmar Bergman: A Guide to References and Resources*. Boston: Hall, 1982.

_____. "The Milk and Strawberry Sequence in *The Seventh Seal*." *Film Heritage* 8 (Summer 1973): 10–18.

_____, ed. *Focus on* The Seventh Seal. Englewood Cliffs, N.J.: Prentice-Hall, 1972.

Svensk Filmografi: 5, 1950–1959. Stockholm: Svenska Filminstitutet, 1983.

Wood, Robin. *Ingmar Bergman*. London: Studio Vista, 1969.

Young, Vernon. *Cinema Borealis*. New York: David Lewis, 1971.

Sexy Sinners (1972) see *Decameron proibitissimo* (1972)

470. *Sfida al re di castiglia* (1963)

Italy; dir. Ferdinando Baldi; Alexandra Cinematografica.

ALTERNATE TITLE: *Kingdom of Violence*.

CAST: Mark Damon, Carlos Estrada, Paolo Gozlino, Maria Orsini, Rada Rassimov, Anna Maria Surdo.

Outraged when he discovers his three half-brothers and his wife are plotting against him, Pedro I of Castile has two of his half-brothers executed and sends his wife Blanche back to France. Enrico, the remaining half-brother and now sole heir to the throne, openly courts Blanche while Pedro, once known as a kind and generous ruler, becomes a cruel tyrant. A final battle between Pedro's and Enrico's armies leaves both dead.

History confers two verdicts on Pedro I, who reigned from 1350 until 1369, calling him both Pedro the Cruel and Pedro the Just. His deeds were alternately praised and condemned in Spanish literature from the fourteenth century on. This film takes a middle ground, trying to explain his sudden change in character by attributing it to the treachery which increasingly surrounded him.

REVIEWS: *Daily Cinema* 3 November 1965: 8. *Kinematograph Weekly* 4 November 1965: 17. *Monthly Film Bulletin* 32 (December 1965): 185.

ADDITIONAL DISCUSSIONS:
Italian Production 1963. Rome: Unitalia Film, 1964.
Poppi, Roberto, and Mario Pecorari. *Dizionario del cinema italiano*. Vol. 3: *I Film dal 1960 al 1969*. Rome: Gremese Editore, 1992.

The Shadow of the Raven (1988) see
In the Shadow of the Raven (1988)

471. *Le Siège de Calais* (1911)

France; dir. Henry Andréani; Pathé Frères.

ALTERNATE TITLES: *The Queen's Pity* and *The Siege of Calais*.

CAST: Georges Dorival, Henri Etiévant, Léontine Massart.

On August 31, 1346, fresh from their victory at Crécy, the army of England's Edward III lays siege to and captures the French city of Calais despite attempts by the King of France to rescue the city. Edward's terms are at first unconditional surrender, but he settles for the lives of six of the city's leading citizens. The French reluctantly agree. As the men are being surrendered to the English for execution, Edward's queen Phillipa, moved by pity, persuades her husband to spare their lives.

Siège is one of the first French historical films to stage crowd scenes successfully.

REVIEWS: *Bioscope* 12 October 1911: 117; 26 October 1911: 261. *Moving Picture World* 23 March 1912: 1063; 17 August 1912: 660. *Talbot Tatler* 1 (25 November 1911): 3.

ADDITIONAL DISCUSSIONS:
Abel, Richard. *The Ciné Goes to Town, French Cinema 1896–1914*. Berkeley: University of California Press, 1994.
Bousquet, Henri. *Catalogue Pathé des années 1896 à 1914: 1910–1911*. Paris: Henri Bousquet, 1994.

The Siege of Calais (1911) see *Le Siège de Calais* (1911)

472. *Siege of the Saxons* (1963)

Great Britain; dir. Nathan Juran; Columbia Pictures.

ALTERNATE TITLE: *King Arthur and the Siege of the Saxons*.

CAST: Mark Dignam, Ronald Howard, John Laurie, Ronald Lewis, Janette Scott.

After assassinating King Arthur, Edmund of Cornwall seizes the throne and kidnaps Arthur's daughter Katherine in hopes of forcing her to marry him to legitimize his claim to the throne. The outlaw Robert Marshall intervenes, rescues Katherine and, with the aid of Merlin, overthrows Edmund and the Saxons. Katherine is crowned queen and takes Robert as her consort.

This unorthodox film version of the legend of Arthur incorporates elements of the legend of Robin Hood into its plot, but the end result is still a flatly-directed and only moderately interesting adventure film.

REVIEWS: *Daily Cinema* 24 July 1963: 10. *Film Daily* 8 August 1963: 4. *Films and Filming* 9 (September 1963): 24. *Kinematograph Weekly* 25 July 1963: 31–32. *Hollywood Reporter* 22 August 1963: 3. *Monthly Film Bulletin* 30 (September 1963): 133. *Motion Picture Herald* 230 (4 September 1963): Product Digest Section 884. *Variety* 21 August 1963: 17.

ADDITIONAL DISCUSSIONS:

Nash, Jay Robert, and Stanley Ralph Ross. *The Motion Picture Guide, S, 1927–1983.* Chicago: Cinebooks, 1987.

Umland, Rebecca A., and Samuel J. Umland. *The Use of Arthurian Legend in Hollywood Film from Connecticut Yankees to Fisher Kings.* Westport, Conn.: Greenwood, 1996.

473. *Siegfried* (1912)

Italy; dir. Mario Caserini; Ambrosio.

Siegfried sets out to win Krimhild, but her brother requires that he first help him win the hand of Brunhild. They are successful, but Brunhild's jealousy of her sister-in-law leads her to conspire with Hagen to kill Siegfried. Siegfried is slain, and Krimhild leads his army in pursuit of Brunhild and Hagen (who have fled to Burgundy). The conspirators are killed and their castle is burned to the ground.

Critics praised this version of Wagner's opera for its excellent sets, costumes and cast.

REVIEWS: *Kinematograph Monthly Film Record* 7 (November 1912): 115–16. *Moving Picture World* 9 November 1912: 545. *Variety* 9 April 1915: 20.

ADDITIONAL DISCUSSION:

Bernardini, Aldo. *Archivo del cinema italiano. Volume I: Il cinema muto 1905–1931.* Rome: ANICA, 1991.

Siegfried (1957) see *Sigfrido* (1957)

Siegfried und das Sagenhafte Liebesleben der Nibelungen (1971) see *The Erotic Adventures of Siegfried* (1971)

Siegfried's Death (1924) see *Die Nibelungen* (1924)

Siegfrieds Tod (1924) see *Die Nibelungen* (1924)

474. *Sigfrido* (1957)

Italy; dir. Giacomo Gentilomo; Aeffe Cin. ca.

CAST: Sebastian Fischer, Katharina Mayberg, Ilaria Occhini, Rolf Tasna.

Young Siegfried kills the dragon and lays claim to the treasure of the Nibelungs. He falls in love with Krimhild, the sister of Gunther of Burgundy, whom he helps win the hand of Brunhilda. Brunhilda is, however, in love with Siegfried and asks Gunther to have him killed. The king's vassal Hagen kills Siegfried, and Krimhild plots her revenge. As Hagen goes to claim the treasure of the Nibelungs, the mountains collapse, burying him alive.

Although this film uses Wagner's music as background, its plot follows more closely that of *The Nibelungenlied.*

DISCUSSIONS:

Chiti, Roberto, and Roberto Poppi. *Dizionario del cinema italiano. Vol. 2: I Film dal 1945 al 1959.* Rome: Gremese Editore, 1991.

"Les Dragons à l'ecran." *Ecran fantastique* 27 (October 1982): 45–46.

The Italian Production 1957. Rome: Unitalia Film, 1958.

"Siegfried's Death." *Opera News* 26 (22 January 1962): 74–75.

475. *Sigurd drakedreper* (1990)

Norway; dir. Lars Rasmussen; Mediagjölgerne.

ALTERNATE TITLE: *Sigurd the Dragon Slayer.*

Sigurd, the 11-year-old son of a Viking chieftain, must prove himself worthy to be his father's heir. He prefers peace to warfare, but his people depend upon battles abroad for their livelihood and are constantly under threat from a neighboring tribe of warriors. Sigurd, who has been named after a mythical dragon slayer, finally lives up to the reputation his name promises and becomes a wise and just ruler.

Intended for a young audience and based on the 1982 novel *Sigurd Drakedreperen* by Torill Thorstad Hauger, this film balances scenes of swordplay fought against picturesque Norwegian backdrops with a discussion of the struggle between good and evil that the young title character encounters.

REVIEW: *Variety* 18 April 1990: 24.

ADDITIONAL DISCUSSION:

Norwegian Films 1990. Oslo: Norwegian Film Institute, 1990.

Sigurd the Dragon Slayer (1990) see *Sigurd drakedreper* (1990)

476. *Silvestre* (1981)

Portugal; dir. Joao César Montiero; V. O. Films.

ALTERNATE TITLE: *Sylvestre.*

CAST: Luis Miguel Cintra, Maria de Medieros, Jorge Silva Melo, Xosé Maria Sanchez.

Dom Rodrigo has two daughters: Silvia is legitimate, Susanna is not. Growing old and still without a male heir, he decides to marry Silvia off to Dom Paio, a rich neighbor. His journey to invite the king to the nuptials precipitates a bizarre series of murderous events.

Based on two fifteenth-century Portuguese folk tales — the Judeo-Iberian "The Maiden Who Went to War" and "The Dead One's Hand" from the Bluebeard cycle — this film's plot defies easy synopsis once Dom Rodrigo begins his journey to find the king. While he is gone, Susanna is raped by a pilgrim, a dragon appears out of nowhere and is slain by a mysterious knight, and Silvia disguises herself as a knight named Silvestre.

REVIEWS: *Les Cahiers du cinéma* 460 (October 1992): 52–54. *Celulóide* 334 (April 1982): 96–97; 336 (July 1982): 186–87. *Cineinforme* 71 (December 1981): 26. *Positif* 381: (November 1992): 42–43. *Variety* 16 September 1981: 22.

ADDITIONAL DISCUSSIONS:

Portugal filme: A mais recente produção cinematográfica portuguesa em longas metragens. Lisbon: Instituto português de cinema, 1982.

Seabra, Augusto M., et al., eds. *Cinema novo portoghese e oltre.* Pesaro: XXIV Mostra internazionale del nuovo cinema, 1988.

Passek, Jean-Loup. *Le Cinéma portugais.* Paris: Centre Georges Pompidou, 1982.

The Singer's Curse (1910) see *Des Sängers Fluch* (1910)

Singoalia (1950) see *The Mask and the Sword* (1950)

Det Sjunde Inseglet (1957) see *The Seventh Seal* (1957)

477. *Skanderbeg* (1953)

Soviet Union; dir. Mary Antjaparidze, Mikhail Gomorov and Victor Stratoberdha; Mosfilm and New-Albania Productions.

ALTERNATE TITLES: *Scanderbeg* and *Veliky Voine Albany, Scanderbeg.*

CAST: Adivie Alibali, Veriko Anjaparidze, G. Chernovolenko, Naim Frasheri, Besa Imani, Saymon Sokolovsky.

In the fifteenth century, the young Skanderbeg, the sole survivor of a Turkish massacre of his village, returns to his native Albania to organize resistance to the Turkish oppressors. After a long struggle, Skanderbeg's forces are victorious and Albania is freed from Turkish domination.

This film, which won a grand prize at the 1954 Cannes Film Festival, is a ponderous and overly reverential account of the life of George Kastriotis, popularly known as Skanderbeg, who in 1444 organized a League of Albanian Princes against their Turkish overlords. With assistance from the Pope and from Venice and Naples, he held the Turks at bay until his death in 1468. In the following century, the Turks prevailed, and the majority of Albanians were forcibly converted to Islam.

REVIEWS: *Bianco e nero* 18 (August 1957): 50. *Deutsche Film Kunst* 1 (1955): 20–24. *Film français* 508–509 (Spring 1954): 42. *Film User* 9 (June 1955): 305. *Kinematograph Weekly* 2622 (14 November 1957): 22. *New York Times* 5 July 1954: 6. *Variety* 7 July 1954: 22.

478. *Skärseld* (1975)

Sweden; dir. Michael Meschke; Bengt Forslund.

ALTERNATE TITLE: *Purgatorio.*

CAST: Jan Blomberg, Michaela Meschke, Inger Jalmert Moritz, Ake Nygren, Carin Rosén, Ing-Mari Tirén.

After an attempted suicide, a famous middle-aged Swedish author suffers a complete breakdown. In the hospital, he hallucinates that he is in Hell where he encounters many of the people Dante enshrined there. With help and guidance from Virgil, he examines his own sufferings in light of those whom he encounters and finally returns completely recovered to the present.

This fascinating film is one of the more successful attempts to juxtapose the medieval and the modern.

REVIEWS: *Swedish Films/Films suédois* 1 (1975): 1–2. *Variety* 4 December 1974: 22.

Soko (1981) see *Banovic Strahinja* (1981)

479. *Son of Robin Hood* (1958)

Great Britain; dir. George Sherman; Argo Film Productions.

CAST: David Farrar, Marius Goring, David Hedison, June Laverick.

Accompanied by an army of mercenaries, Des Roches, known as the Black Duke, storms

Chester Castle in preparation for seizing the throne of England. The Earl of Chester flees to Sherwood Forest to seek the aid of Robin Hood. Robin has been dead for ten years, but his followers eagerly await the arrival of his son Deering, who turns out to be a woman. Because the Earl fears that the band of outlaws will be reluctant to follow a woman into battle, he persuades Jamie, his brother, to impersonate Deering and Robin's daughter to pretend to be his page. When Des Roches imprisons the Earl, Jamie and Robin's daughter rescue him and lead their band of outlaws to kill Des Roches and his mercenaries. The throne of England saved, Jamie marries Robin Hood's daughter.

Intended for a younger audience, this film exploits the swashbuckling elements usually associated with screen versions of the legend of Robin Hood and his followers.

REVIEWS: *Daily Cinema* 31 October 1958: 5. *Film Daily* 23 June 1959: 6. *Harrison's Reports* 20 June 1959: 99. *Hollywood Reporter* 18 June 1959: 3. *Kinematograph Weekly* 30 October 1958: 17. *Monthly Film Bulletin* 25 (December 1958): 158. *Motion Picture Herald* 27 June 1959: 316. *Variety* 24 June 1959: 6.

ADDITIONAL DISCUSSIONS:

Behlmer, Rudy. "Robin Hood on the Screen." *Films in Review* 16 (February 1965): 91–102.

Knight, Stephen. *Robin Hood, A Complete Study of the English Outlaw.* Oxford; Blackwell, 1994.

Lucanio, Patrick. *With Fire and Sword, Italian Spectacles on American Screens 1958–1968.* Metuchen, N.J.: Scarecrow, 1994.

Nash, Jay Robert, and Stanley Ralph Ross. *The Motion Picture Guide, S, 1927–1983.* Chicago: Cinebooks, 1987.

Richards, Jeffrey. *Swordsmen of the Screen from Douglas Fairbanks to Michael York.* London: Routledge & Kegan Paul, 1977.

Turner, David. *Robin of the Movies.* Kingswinford, Eng.: Yeoman Press, 1989.

480. *Son of the Guardsman* (1946)

United States; dir. Derwin Abrahams; Columbia Pictures.

CAST: Jim Diehl, Robert Henry, Daun Kennedy, Charles King, Leonard Penn, Hugh Prosser, Robert Shaw.

In medieval England, David Trent breaks with his robber-baron uncle and joins a group of free men known as "the outlaws." Together, they battle a succession of villains and ensure that Prince Richard is crowned king.

This 15-part serial is obviously indebted to the legend of Robin Hood, although (with the exception of King Richard) none of the characters have names associated with that legend.

REVIEWS: *Monthly Film Bulletin* 19 (January 1952): 12. *Motion Picture Herald* 28 December 1946: Product Digest Section 3387. *Today's Cinema* 31 October 1951: 14.

ADDITIONAL DISCUSSIONS.

Barbour, Alan G. *Cliffhanger.* New York: A&W, 1979.

———. *The Serials of Columbia.* Kew Gardens, N.Y.: Screen Facts, 1967.

Cline, William C. *In the Nick of Time.* Jefferson, N.C.: McFarland, 1984.

Harmon, Jim, and Donald F. Glut. *The Great Movie Serials.* Garden City, N.Y.: Doubleday, 1972.

Kinnard, Roy. *Fifty Years of Serial Thrills.* Metuchen, N.J.: Scarecrow, 1983.

Weiss, Ken, and Ed Goodgold. *To Be Continued.* New York: Crown, 1972.

The Song of Roland (1978) see *Le Chanson de Roland* (1978)

Sorceress (1987) see *Le Moine et la sorcière* (1987)

The Spaceman and King Arthur (1979) see *The Unidentified Flying Oddball* (1979)

La Spada del Cid (1962) see *Sword of El Cid* (1962)

481. *La Spada normanna* (1974)

Italy; dir. Roberto Mauri; Oceania Produzioni Internazionali.

CAST: Mark Damon, Luis Davila, Kristanel Doris, Aveline Jolande, Manuel Zarzo.

On his deathbed, England's Henry I delivers the Norman sword, a symbol of the crown, into safe hands fearing that the Duke of Wilford will usurp the throne. Wilford imprisons the king's daughter and heir, as the sword mysteriously disappears. Returning from the Crusades, Ivanhoe comes to the princess' rescue, retrieves the sword and defeats Wilford.

This film offers a fairly typical example of medieval cinematic swordplay and little else.

DISCUSSIONS:

Poppi, Roberto, and Mario Pecorari. *Dizionario del cinema italiano: I Film dal 1970 al 1979.* Rome: Gremese Editore, 1996.

La Produzione italiana 1970/71. Rome: Unitalia Film, 1971.

482. *Spade senza bandiera* (1960)

Italy; dir. Carlo Veo; A. D. Cinematografica.

CAST: Mara Berni, Claudio Gora, Folco Lulli, Leonora Ruffo, Renato Speziali.

In 1350, an unknown outlaw terrorizes the population of an Italian town. The outlaw's identity is revealed, as is a long-simmering feud between warring Italian nobles.

An improbably complicated plot does nothing to redeem this tepid swashbuckler.

DISCUSSIONS:

Italian Production 1960. Rome: Unitalia Film, 1961.

Poppi, Roberto, and Mario Pecorari. *Dizionario del cinema italiano. Vol. 3: I Film dal 1960 al 1969.* Rome: Gremese Editore, 1992.

483. *The Spanish Sword* (1962)

Great Britain; dir. Ernest Morris; United Artists.

CAST: Trader Faulkner, Nigel Green, Ronald Howard, Robin Hunter, Derrick Sherwin, Barry Shawzin, June Thorburn, Sheila Whittingham.

In 1264, learning of a plot to overthrow Henry III, Sir Richard Clovell rushes to the king's aid and foils those who would usurp the throne.

A colorless plot and one-dimensional characterization make this film little more than another predictable swashbuckler.

REVIEWS: *Daily Cinema* 12 July 1963: 5. *Kinematograph Weekly* 4 July 1963: 27–28. *Monthly Film Bulletin* 30 (August 1963): 120–21.

ADDITIONAL DISCUSSION:

Nash, Jay Robert, and Stanley Ralph Ross. *The Motion Picture Guide, S, 1927–1983*. Chicago: Cinebooks, 1987.

484. *The Spirit of the Lake* (1910)

Italy; Cines.

A jealous spirit inhabiting an enchanted lake causes lovers, a knight and his lady, to die tragically.

REVIEW: *Bioscope* 5 May 1910: 32.

485. *The Squire and the Noble Lord* (1909)

Great Britain; Urban-Eclipse.

A squire falls in love with a village maiden, only to find that his lord lusts after the girl. When the lord discovers their love, he imprisons the squire and kidnaps the girl, whom he attempts to ravish. The squire manages to escape from prison and, in a struggle, kill his lord. The two lovers then escape into the night.

REVIEWS: *Moving Picture World* 19 April 1909: 490; 1 May 1909: 555. *Nickelodeon* 1 (May 1909): 146. *New York Dramatic Mirror* 8 May 1909: 16.

ADDITIONAL DISCUSSION:

Savada, Elias. *The American Film Institute Catalog of Motion Pictures Produced in the United States: Film Beginnings, 1893–1910*. Metuchen, N.J.: Scarecrow, 1995.

Star Knight (1985) see *El Caballero del dragon* (1985)

486. *Stealing Heaven* (1989)

Great Britain; dir. Clive Donner; Amy International-Jadran Films.

CAST: Patsy Byrne, Kenneth Cranham, Derek de Lint, Denholm Elliott, Bernard Hepton, Mark Jax, Rachel Kempson, Angela Pleasence, Kim Thomson.

Despite his vow of chastity, Abelard, director of the cathedral school at Notre Dame, falls in love with Heloïse, whose guardian and uncle (a vain nobleman and dealer in questionable relics) hopes to marry off to titled money. His plans are dashed by the scandalous romance between Abelard and his niece. With the approval of the Bishop of Paris, who worries that his university will lose its star teacher, Heloïse's uncle takes his revenge by having Abelard castrated. Abelard becomes a monk; Heloïse, a nun. Their love continues, albeit on a platonic level and at a distance, and they are reunited, along with their son, shortly before they die.

The film, which is told from Heloïse's point of view, is based on Marion Meade's 1979 novel *Stealing Heaven*. After a brief theatrical release, the film became almost immediately available on videotape. It deserves more attention than it has received. It is an effective film whose success is attributable to the performances of de Lint and Thomson as the two lovers and to the authentic look of its sets.

REVIEWS: *Films and Filming* 415 (May 1989): 44–45. *Globe and Mail* [Toronto] 28 April 1989: C4. *Hollywood Reporter* 2 May 1989: 4, 8. *Los Angeles Times* 28 April 1989: Calendar 17. *Monthly Film Bulletin* 56 (May 1989): 151. *New York Times* 28 April 1989: C14. *Sunday Times* [London] 30 April 1989: C8. *Variety* 8 June 1988: 12. *Video Review* June 1989: 60.

ADDITIONAL DISCUSSION:

The Motion Picture Guide: 1990 Annual (The Films of 1989). Evanston, Ill.: Cinebooks, 1990.

Abelard (Derek de Lint), Heloïse (Kim Thomson), and her uncle (Denholm Elliott) in a scene from Clive Donner's *Stealing Heaven* (1989).

Stephen, the King (1984) see *Istvan, a Kiraly* (1984)

Storia d'armi e d'amori (1983) see *I Paladini* (1983)

The Story of Robin Hood (1952) see *The Story of Robin Hood and His Merrie Men* (1952)

487. *The Story of Robin Hood and His Merrie Men* (1952)

Great Britain; dir. Ken Annakin; RKO Radio–Disney British Productions.

CAST: Patrick Barr, Peter Finch, Hubert Gregg, Elton Hayes, James Hayter, Michael Hordern, Martita Hunt, James Robertson Justice, Bill Owen, Joan Rice, Reginald Tate, Richard Todd.

King Richard goes off to the Crusades and appoints his brother John regent. With the aid of a new Sheriff of Nottingham, John initiates a reign of terror. When Robin Fitzooth and his father best the Sheriff's men in an archery con-test, the enraged Sheriff has Robin's father killed. Robin flees to Sherwood Forest to join a company of outlaws. Meanwhile, Richard is being held hostage and the Queen sets out with ransom money to free him, only to be robbed by Prince John's men. Robin retrieves the ransom, but not before Maid Marian, his love, is kidnapped by the Sheriff. Richard, now freed, returns to England in disguise and joins forces with Robin. The Sheriff and Prince John are defeated, and Robin and Marian marry.

While adding nothing new or unusual to the legend of Robin Hood, Annakin's film is a good example of cinematic derring-do, though it is no match for Michael Curtiz's 1938 classic version of the story, *The Adventures of Robin Hood*.

REVIEWS: *Film Music* 12 (November-December 1952): 18. *Monthly Film Bulletin* 19 (April 1952): 54. *Motion Picture Herald* 23 March 1952: Product Digest Section 1289–90. *New York Times* 27 June 1952: 18. *Picturegoer* 15 March 1952: 12–13. *To-day's Cinema* 6 March 1952: 14. *Variety* 12 December 1952: 16.

ADDITIONAL DISCUSSIONS:
Behlmer, Rudy. "Robin Hood on the Screen." *Films in Review* 16 (February 1965): 91–102.

Knight, Stephen. *Robin Hood, A Complete Study of the English Outlaw.* Oxford; Blackwell, 1994.

"Knighthood Never Had It So Good." *Life* 33 (11 August 1952): 53–54, 56, 58.

Leebron, Elizabeth, and Lynn Gartley. *Walt Disney, A Guide to References and Resources.* Boston: Hall, 1979.

Maltin, Leonard. *The Disney Films.* New York: Crown, 1973.

Nash, Jay Robert, and Stanley Ralph Ross. *The Motion Picture Guide, S, 1927–1983.* Chicago: Cinebooks, 1987.

Richards, Jeffrey. *Swordsmen of the Screen from Douglas Fairbanks to Michael York.* London: Routledge & Kegan Paul, 1977.

"Robin Hood and His Merrie Men." *Illustrated London News* 15 March 1952: 468–69.

"'Robin Hood' ... and ... Walt Disney's Merry Men!" *Cinema Studio* 6 (July 1951): 7–11.

The Story of Robin Hood and His Merrie Men. London: Walt Disney Productions, 1952. [Press book.]

Turner, David. *Robin of the Movies.* Kingswinford, Eng.: Yeoman Press, 1989.

Striely Robin Guda (1977) see *Robin Hood's Arrows* (1977)

The Strife Eternal (1915) see *Jane Shore* (1915)

488. *Svo a Jördu sem á Himni* (1992)

Iceland; dir. Kristín Jóhannesdóttir; Tiu-Tiu Films.

ALTERNATE TITLE: *As in Heaven.*

CAST: Christian Charmetant, Valdimar Örn Flygenring, Tinna Gunnlaugsdóttir, Sigrídur Hagalín, Christophe Pinon, Helgi Skúlason, Pierre Vaneck.

A young Icelandic girl walks along the shore in the late summer of 1936. Giving her imagination free rein, she conjures up events from the fourteenth century that parallel those in her own life.

This visually stunning film expertly and impressively balances the parallel medieval and modern tales it tells.

REVIEW: *Variety* 24 August 1992: 63.

ADDITIONAL DISCUSSIONS:

Cowie, Peter, ed. *Variety International Film Guide 1994.* Hollywood, Calif.: Samuel French, 1993.

Ómarsson, Thorfinnur. "Cinematic Resurgence." *Iceland Review* 30.1 (1992): 20–25.

The Sword and the Dragon (1956) see *Ilya Muromets* (1956)

489. *The Sword and the King* (1909)

United States; Vitagraph.

A medieval tyrant stabs a shepherd to death in front of the shepherd's wife and an old hag. The hag curses the tyrant, who almost immediately begins to see the ghost of the shepherd he has killed. Twenty years later, the shepherd's son avenges his father and is crowned king.

REVIEWS: *Bioscope* 9 September 1909: 27, 29. *New York Dramatic Mirror* 31 July 1909: 16.

ADDITIONAL DISCUSSION:

Savada, Elias. *The American Film Institute Catalog of Motion Pictures Produced in the United States: Film Beginnings, 1893–1910.* Metuchen, N.J.: Scarecrow, 1995.

490. *The Sword in the Stone* (1963)

United States; dir. Wolfgang Reitherman; Walt Disney Productions.

CAST: (the voices of) Norman Alden, Sebastian Cabot, Junius Matthews, Alan Napier, Ricky Sorenson, Karl Swenson, Martha Wentworth.

England needs a king, but legend has it that only he who can pull a sword out of a stone may ascend the throne. A young boy named Wart meets the magician Merlin, who agrees to educate him. Wart also becomes squire to his foster brother Kay, and when he forgets to bring a sword for his brother to use in a tournament, Wart pulls the sword from the stone, not knowing the significance of what he has just done. Named King Arthur, Wart is reassured by Merlin that he is indeed the rightful king.

Based on T.H. White's novel *The Sword in the Stone* (1938), and intended for a younger audience, this Disney film presents a cartoon version of the events of Arthur's *enfance.*

REVIEWS: *Daily Cinema* 4 (December 1963): 8. *Film Daily* 3 October 1963: 14. *Filmfacts* 6 (9 December 1963): 286–87. *Films and Filming* 10 (January 1964): 25–26; 352 (January 1984): 42–43. *Hollywood Reporter* 2 October 1963: 3. *Kinematograph Weekly* 5 December 1963: 9. *Los Angeles Times* 26 March 1983: 5. 7. *Monthly Film Bulletin* 31 (February 1964): 22. *Motion Picture Herald* 230 (16 October 1963): Product Digest Section 913–14. *New York Times* 26 December 1963: 33. *Photoplay* 21 (January 1964): 21. *Times* [London] 12 December 1963: 15. *Variety* 2 October 1963: 6.

ADDITIONAL DISCUSSIONS:

Carey, Mary. *The Sword in the Stone.* Racine, Wisc.: Whitman, 1963. [Novelization.]

Duchène, Alain, and Odile Houen. "Merlin l'en-

Wart prepares to pull the sword from the stone in Wolfgang Reitherman's animated *The Sword in the Stone* (1963).

chanteur ou le désenchantment." *Banc-titre* 40 (April 1984): 33–35.

Frank, Thomas, and Ollie Johnston. *Disney Animation: The Illusion of Life.* New York: Abbeville, 1981.

Grant, John. *Encyclopedia of Walt Disney Animated Characters.* New York: Harper, 1987.

Grellner, Alice. "Two Films That Sparkle: *The Sword in the Stone* and *Camelot.*" In Kevin J. Harty, ed. *Cinema Arthuriana, Essays on Arthurian Film.* New York: Garland, 1991.

Johnston, Ollie, and Frank Thomas. *The Disney Villain.* New York: Hyperion, 1993.

Krafsur, Richard P., ed. *The American Film Institute Catalog of Motion Pictures, Feature Films 1961–1970.* New York: Bowker, 1976.

Leebron, Elizabeth, and Lynn Gartley. *Walt Disney, A Guide to References and Resources.* Boston: Hall, 1979.

Maltin, Leonard. *The Disney Films.* Rev. ed. New York: Crown, 1984.

Nash, Jay Robert, and Stanley Ralph Ross. *The Motion Picture Guide, S, 1927–1983.* Chicago: Cinebooks, 1987.

Plas, Marc. "'Merlin l'enchanteur' de Walt Disney: du roman médiéval au conte de fées." *Les Cahiers de la cinémathèque* 42–43 (Summer 1985): 103–04.

Umland, Rebecca A., and Samuel J. Umland. *The Use of Arthurian Legend in Hollywood Film from Connecticut Yankees to Fisher Kings.* Westport, Conn.: Greenwood, 1996.

491. *Sword of El Cid* (1962)

Italy and Spain; dir. Miguel Inglesias; Alexandra Cinematografica.

ALTERNATE TITLES: *Las Hijas del Cid* and *La Spada del Cid.*

CAST: Daniela Bianchi, Roland Carey, Chantal Deberg, Sandro Moretti.

The daughters of the Cid are mistreated by their husbands whom King Alfonso orders to fight a trial by combat. The husbands, with the aid of an evil courtier, kill Alfonso and plot to divide the kingdom between them. Alfonso's son, unaware at first of his identity, defeats the husbands and the courtier, marries one of the daughters of the Cid and succeeds to the throne.

Relying overly on swashbuckling derring-do at the expense of plot continuity, this film makes little if any sense.

6575-41

(From left to right) Merlin (Mark Dingham), King Arthur (Brian Aherne) and Lancelot (Cornel Wilde) in a scene from Wilde's *The Sword of Lancelot* (1963).

REVIEWS: *Daily Cinema* 23 August 1963: 4. *Monthly Film Bulletin* 30 (October 1963): 148.

ADDITIONAL DISCUSSIONS:

Italian Production 1962. Rome: Unitalia Film, 1963.

Nash, Jay Robert, and Stanley Ralph Ross. *The Motion Picture Guide, S, 1927–1983.* Chicago: Cinebooks, 1987.

Poppi, Roberto, and Mario Pecorari. *Dizionario del cinema italiano. Vol. 3: I Film dal 1960 al 1969.* Rome: Gremese Editore, 1992.

The Spanish Cinema. Madrid: Uniespaña, 1964.

492. *The Sword of Lancelot* (1963)

Great Britain; dir. Cornel Wilde; Emblem Productions.

ALTERNATE TITLE: *Lancelot and Guinevere.*

CAST: Brian Aherne, George Baker, Mark Dingham, Michael Meacham, Jean Wallace, Cornel Wilde.

In order to marry Guinevere, the daughter of King Leodogran, Arthur must find a knight to defeat the giant who is Leodogran's champion. Lancelot accepts the challenge, mortally wounds his opponent and escorts Guinevere to Camelot. Mordred plans to murder Guinevere, but Lancelot protects her, and the two fall in love. Arthur and Guinevere marry, and at first she is loyal to Arthur. Eventually, she and Lancelot become lovers and are found out by Mordred. After Arthur banishes Lancelot and Guinevere enters a convent, Arthur is killed by Mordred, who seizes the throne. Lancelot returns to defeat Mordred, but Guinevere remains in her convent to atone for her sins.

This elaborately mounted production is clearly intended to be an intelligent adult version of the familiar story of Arthur, Lancelot and Guinevere, and it largely succeeds, though it takes some liberties with its putative source, Sir Thomas Malory's fifteenth century Arthurian compendium *Le Morte Darthur*, especially in identifying Mordred as Arthur's brother.

REVIEWS: *Daily Cinema* 3 May 1963: 5. *Film*

Richard Greene as Robin Hood (center) in a scene from Terence Fisher's *Sword of Sherwood Forest* (1960).

Daily 29 April 1963: 8. *Filmfacts* 6 (10 October 1963): 211–12. *Films and Filming* 9 (July 1963): 24. *Hollywood Reporter* 29 April 1963: 3. *Monthly Film Bulletin* 30 (June 1963): 87. *Motion Picture Herald* 229 (15 May 1963): Product Digest Section 809. *New York Times* 10 October 1963: 49. *Times* [London] 2 May 1963: 6. *Variety* 1 May 1963: 6.

ADDITIONAL DISCUSSIONS:

Coen, John. "Producer/Director Cornel Wilde." *Film Comment* 6 (Spring 1970): 53–61.

Kaminsky, Stuart M. "Getting Back to Basics with Cornel Wilde." *Take One* 5 (October 1976): 22–24.

Krafsur, Richard P., ed. *The American Film Institute Catalog of Motion Pictures, Feature Films 1961–1970.* New York: Bowker, 1976.

Lancelot and Guinevere. London: Rank Film Distributors, [1963]. [Press book.]

Lucanio, Patrick. *With Fire and Sword, Italian Spectacles on American Screens 1958–1968.* Metuchen, N.J.: Scarecrow, 1994.

Nash, Jay Robert, and Stanley Ralph Ross. *The Motion Picture Guide, S, 1927–1983.* Chicago: Cinebooks, 1987.

Parish, James Robert, and Don E. Stanke. *The Swashbucklers.* New Rochelle, N.Y.: Arlington House, 1976.

Richards, Jeffrey. *Swordsmen of the Screen from Douglas Fairbanks to Michael York.* London: Routledge & Kegan Paul, 1977.

Smith, Gary. *The Epic Film.* Jefferson, N.C.: McFarland, 1991.

Umland, Rebecca A., and Samuel J. Umland. *The Use of Arthurian Legend in Hollywood Film from Connecticut Yankees to Fisher Kings.* Westport, Conn.: Greenwood, 1996.

493. *Sword of Sherwood Forest* (1960)

Great Britain; dir. Terence Fisher; Hammer Films.

CAST: Sarah Branch, Peter Cushing, Richard Greene, Niall MacGinnis, Richard Pasco.

Robin Hood allies himself with the Earl of Newark, not knowing he is in league with the Sheriff of Nottingham to kill the Archbishop of Canterbury. Robin rescues the Archbishop and kills the Earl and the Sheriff. As reward for his service, the Archbishop marries Robin and Maid Marian.

Greene, who plays Robin, previously starred in an English-made television series about Robin Hood (1955–1959). This action-packed cinematic retelling of the legend of Robin Hood is clearly intended for a juvenile audience.

REVIEWS: *Daily Cinema* 21 November 1960: 9. *Harrison's Reports* 14 January 1961: 7. *Kinematograph Weekly* 24 November 1960: 12. *Monthly Film Bulletin* 28 (February 1961): 25. *New York Times* 26 January 1961: 32. *Variety* 11 January 61: 6.

ADDITIONAL DISCUSSIONS:
Behlmer, Rudy. "Robin Hood on the Screen." *Films in Review* 16 (February 1965): 91–102.
Johnson, Tom, and Deborah Del Vecchio. *Hammer Films, An Exhaustive Filmography.* Jefferson, N.C.: McFarland, 1996.
Knight, Stephen. *Robin Hood, A Complete Study of the English Outlaw.* Oxford; Blackwell, 1994.
Lucanio, Patrick. *With Fire and Sword, Italian Spectacles on American Screens 1958–1968.* Metuchen, N.J.: Scarecrow, 1994.
Nash, Jay Robert, and Stanley Ralph Ross. *The Motion Picture Guide, S, 1927–1983.* Chicago: Cinebooks, 1987.
Richards, Jeffrey. *Swordsmen of the Screen from Douglas Fairbanks to Michael York.* London: Routledge & Kegan Paul, 1977.
The Sword of Sherwood Forest. London: Hammer House, 1960. [Publicity manual.]
Turner, David. *Robin of the Movies.* Kingswinford, Eng.: Yeoman Press, 1989.

494. *Sword of the Conqueror* (1961)

Italy; dir. Carlo Campogalliani; Titanus Productions and United Artists.

ALTERNATE TITLE: *Rosmunda e Albino.*

CAST: Andrea Bosic, Carlo D'Angelo, Eleonora Rossi Drago, Guy Madison, Jack Palance.

At the dawn of the Middle Ages, Albino, Duke of Lombardy, defends his country against invading barbarians. But he is undone by court intrigue, his unflinching cruelty and his own daughter Rosamunda, who secretly loves the leader of the barbarians and bears his son.

As gaudy as it is gory, this film's primary interest lies in the battle of the sexes, not in the clash of warring factions.

REVIEWS: *Cinématographie française* 24 August 1963: 2. *Daily Cinema* 27 November 1963: 7. *Film Daily* 11 September 1962: 7. *Film-echo/Filmwoche* 50 (23 June 1962): 9 *Filmfacts* 5 (25 June 1963): 348. *Hollywood Reporter* 12 September 1962: 3. *Kine-*

matograph Weekly 28 November 1963: 16. *Monthly Film Bulletin* 31 (January 1964): 10. *Motion Picture Herald* 3 October 1962: Product Digest Section 667. *Variety* 19 September 1962: 6.

ADDITIONAL DISCUSSIONS:
Italian Production 1961. Rome: Unitalia Film, 1962.
Lucanio, Patrick. *With Fire and Sword, Italian Spectacles on American Screens 1958–1968.* Metuchen, N.J.: Scarecrow, 1994.
Nash, Jay Robert, and Stanley Ralph Ross. *The Motion Picture Guide, S, 1927–1983.* Chicago: Cinebooks, 1987.
Poppi, Roberto, and Mario Pecorari. *Dizionario del cinema italiano. Vol. 3: I Film dal 1960 al 1969.* Rome: Gremese Editore, 1992.

495. *Sword of the Valiant* (1983)

Great Britain; dir. Stephen Weeks; Cannon Films.

ALTERNATE TITLE: *The Legend of Gawain and the Green Knight.*

CAST: Cyrielle Claire, Sean Connery, Peter Cushing, Trevor Howard, Miles O'Keefe.

At Christmastide, a mysterious Green Knight enters Camelot and challenges everyone present to an exchange of blows with an ax. A reluctant Gawain agrees and chops off the Green Knight's head. The Green Knight offers Gawain a reprieve if within a year he can answer a riddle. Gawain sets off on a series of adventures, succeeds in answering the riddle and marries his lady love.

Somehow with this film, Weeks manages to make an even sillier version of what is arguably the finest Middle English romance, *Sir Gawain and the Green Knight,* than he did in his 1973 film *Gawain and the Green Knight.*

REVIEWS: *Cinefantastique* 15 (May 1985): 53. *Monthly Film Bulletin* 52 (May 1985): 164–65. *Starburst* 70 (June 1984): 24–25. *Variety* 5 December 1984: 17.

ADDITIONAL DISCUSSIONS:
Berry, David. *Wales and Cinema, The First Hundred Years.* Cardiff: University of Wales Press, 1994.
Blanch, Robert J., and Julian N. Wasserman. "Gawain on Film." In Kevin J. Harty, ed. *Cinema Arthuriana, Essays on Arthurian Film.* New York: Garland, 1991.
Dupuis, Jean Jacques. *Sean Connery.* Paris: Veyrier, 1986.
Munn, Michael. *Trevor Howard: The Man and His Films.* London: Robson, 1989.
Nash, Jay Robert, and Stanley Ralph Ross. *The Motion Picture Guide, W–Z, 1927–1984.* Chicago: Cinebooks, 1987.
Parker, John. *Sean Connery.* London: Gollancz, 1993.

Sean Connery as the Green Knight in Stephen Weeks's *Sword of the Valiant* (1983).

Pfeiffer, Lee, and Philip Lisa. *The Films of Sean Connery.* New York: Citadel, 1993.
Sellers, Robert. *The Films of Sean Connery.* New York: St. Martin's, 1990.
Tanitch, Robert. *Sean Connery.* London: Chapmans, 1992.

Sylvestre (1981) see *Silvestre* (1981)

496. *A Tale of the Crusades* (1908)

United States; Vitagraph.

A knight on crusade rescues his lady love from a band of thugs who intend her harm.

REVIEWS: *Bioscope* 14 January 1909: 23. *Moving Picture World* 28 November 1908: 432.

ADDITIONAL DISCUSSION:

Savada, Elias. *The American Film Institute Catalog of Motion Pictures Produced in the United States: Film Beginnings, 1893–1910.* Metuchen, N.J.: Scarecrow, 1995.

497. *Tales of Robin Hood* (1952)

United States; dir. James Tinling; Lippert Pictures.

CAST: Robert Bice, Whit Bissell, Paul Cavanagh, Robert Clarke, Wade Crosby, Mary Hatcher, Bruce Lester, Keith Richards, Tiny Stowe, Ben Welden.

The Sheriff of Nottingham has the Earl of Chester killed for refusing to pay taxes. Robin, the earl's young son, witnesses his father's murder and flees to Sherwood Forest, where, when he grows up, he forms a band to rob the rich and help the poor. To rid the shire of Robin and his men, the Sheriff promises the hand of Maid Marian, a rich heiress, in marriage to Sir Alan Beaulieu, who had been responsible for the murder of the Earl of Chester. A trap is laid to catch Robin, but he refuses to fall for the bait. With the aid of his men, Robin defeats the Sheriff and marries Maid Marian.

While this film adds nothing new to the screen tradition of Robin Hood, it does present an action-packed version of familiar material. It was originally shot for television by Hal Roach, Jr.

REVIEWS: *Kinematograph Weekly* 4 June 1953:

9. *Motion Picture Herald* 9 August 1952: Product Digest Section 1478. *To-day's Cinema* 1 June 1953: 8. *Variety* 9 January 1952: 6.

ADDITIONAL DISCUSSIONS:

Behlmer, Rudy. "Robin Hood on the Screen." *Films in Review* 16 (February 1965): 91–102.

Knight, Stephen. *Robin Hood, A Complete Study of the English Outlaw*. Oxford: Blackwell, 1994.

Nash, Jay Robert, and Stanley Ralph Ross. *The Motion Picture Guide, T–V, 1927–1983*. Chicago: Cinebooks, 1987.

Okuda, Ted. *Grand National, Producers Releasing Corporation, and Screen Guild/Lippert: Complete Filmographies with Studio Histories*. Jefferson, N.C.: McFarland, 1989.

498. *Le Tambourin fantastique* (1905)

France; dir. Georges Méliès; Star Films.

ALTERNATE TITLE: *The Knight of the Black Art*.

CAST: Georges Méliès.

In the banquet hall of a medieval castle, a knight (played by Méliès) performs a series of magic tricks for three pages in this remarkable early example of cinematic prestidigitation.

REVIEW: *Moving Picture World* 18 January 1908: 45.

ADDITIONAL DISCUSSIONS:

Complete Catalogue of Genuine and Original "Star" Films Manufactured by Geo. Méliès of Paris. New York: Star Film, [1907?].

Essai de reconstitution du catalogue français de la Star-film suivi d'une analyse catalographique des films de Georges Méliès recensés en France. Bois d'Arcy: Publications du Service des Archives du Film du Centre National de la Cinématographie, [1981].

Frazer, John. *Artificially Arranged Scenes, The Films of Georges Méliès*. Boston: G. K. Hall, 1979.

Savada, Elias. *The American Film Institute Catalog of Motion Pictures Produced in the United States: Film Beginnings, 1893–1910*. Metuchen, N.J.: Scarecrow, 1995.

499. *Tannhauser* (1913)

United States; Thanhouser Film Corporation.

CAST: James Cruze, Florence La Badie.

Princess Elizabeth of Thuringion, noted for her great beauty, is the prize in a contest between minstrels. The expected winner is Wolfram, but the unknown Tannhauser wins the contest, only to find that Elizabeth's guardian insists that she marry Wolfram. Tannhauser flees into the forest where he is enchanted by Venus. After a year, he escapes his enchantment and returns to win Elizabeth's hand. Again, he is thwarted when he is accused of blasphemy and must journey to Rome to seek pardon from an unforgiving pope, who refuses his absolution until the papal staff blooms as a tree. The miracle does finally happen, but too late, as both lovers die of grief.

This film adaptation of Wagner's famous 1845 opera *Tannhäuser* won praise for its outstanding production values.

REVIEWS: *Bioscope* 18 September 1913: 949. *Kinematograph Monthly Record* 19 (November 1913): 40–41.

I Tartari (1960) see *The Tartars* (1960)

500. *The Tartars* (1960)

Italy; dir. Richard Thorpe; Lux Film/MGM.

ALTERNATE TITLE: *I Tartari*.

CAST: Bella Cortez, Arnoldo Foà, Folco Lulli, Luciano Marin, Victor Mature, Furio Meniconi, Liana Orfei, Orson Welles.

In medieval Russia, Vikings clash with the Tartars, each of whom holds a beautiful woman hostage, when they cannot form an alliance against the native Russians. The result is a series of battles, orgies and spectacular burning sets.

Mature plays the leader of the Vikings and

Orson Welles as the Tartar chieftain Burundai in Richard Thorpe's *The Tartars* (1960).

Welles the leader of the Tartars in this often unintentionally humorous melodramatic comic strip. As a number of critics noted, both actors were obviously in this film just for the money.

REVIEWS: *Daily Cinema* 29 November 1961: 17. *Harrison's Reports* 7 July 1962: 103. *Hollywood Reporter* 20 June 1962: 3. *Intermezzo* 15 June 1961: 4. *Kinematograph Weekly* 23 November 1961: 27. *Monthly Film Bulletin* 29 (January 1962): 14–15. *Motion Picture Herald* 11 July 1962: Product Digest Section 611. *New York Times* 21 June 1962: 26. *Variety* 27 June 1962: 6.

ADDITIONAL DISCUSSIONS:
Italian Production 1960. Rome: Unitalia Film, 1961.
James, Howard. *The Complete Films of Orson Welles.* New York: Citadel, 1991.
Lucanio, Patrick. *With Fire and Sword, Italian Spectacles on American Screens 1958–1968.* Metuchen, N.J.: Scarecrow, 1994.
Nash, Jay Robert, and Stanley Ralph Ross. *The Motion Picture Guide, T–V, 1927–1983.* Chicago: Cinebooks, 1987.
Poppi, Roberto, and Mario Pecorari. *Dizionario del cinema italiano.Vol. 3: I Film dal 1960 al 1969.* Rome: Gremese Editore, 1992.
Smith, Gary A. *Epic Films.* Jefferson, N.C.: McFarland, 1991.

The Tears of Saint Peter (1995) see
Petri Tarar (1995)

501. Tennessee Ernie Ford Meets King Arthur (1960)

United States; dir. Lee J. Cobb; Ford Startime.
CAST: Danny Arnold, John Dehner, Robert Emhardt, Tennessee Ernie Ford, Alan Mowbray, Vincent Price, Addison Richards, Alan Young.

Trapped inside a time machine, Tennessee Ernie Ford finds himself transported back to England in the days of King Arthur, where he has a series of comic misadventures liberally punctuated with homespun wit. In this rare example of noted actor Lee J. Cobb's work as a director, Twain's satire loses its edge.

REVIEWS: *Variety* 18 May 1960: 39.
ADDITIONAL DISCUSSIONS:
Gianakos, Larry James. *Television Drama Series Programming: A Comprehensive Chronicle, 1959–1975.* Metuchen, N.J.: Scarecrow, 1978.
Terrace, Vincent. *Television Specials.* Jefferson, N.C.: McFarland, 1995.

502. Tesoro della foresta pietrificata (1964)

Italy; dir. Emimmo Galvi; Asteria Film.

CAST: Eleonora Bianchi, Gordon Mitchell, Luisa Rivelli, Ivo Payer, Pamela Tudor.

The outraged gods of Valhalla clash with peaceful woodsmen over a vast treasure in this loose adaptation of scenes from *The Nibelungenlied.*

REVIEWS: *Bianco e nero* 29 (May-June 1968): supplement 66. *Les Cahiers du cinéma* 179 (June 1966): 81. *Film-echo/Filmwoche* 7 (26 January 1968): 12.

ADDITIONAL DISCUSSION:
Poppi, Roberto, and Martin Pecorari. *Dizionario del cinema italiano. Vol. 3: I Film dal 1960 al 1969.* Rome: Gremese Editore, 1992.

The Teutonic Knights (1960) see Knights
of the Teutonic Order (1960)

503. Time Trackers (1989)

United States; dir. Howard R. Cohen; Concorde Pictures.

CAST: Ned Beatty, Kathleen Beller, Lee Bergere, Bridget Hoffman, Alex Hyde-White, Wil Shriner.

A group of young scientists from the year 2033 travel back in time by way of Los Angeles in the 1990s to England in the year 1146 to stop an evil sorcerer from changing the course of history.

Not much in the plot here makes sense, and the medieval material is given as short shrift as the science fiction special effects.

REVIEWS: *Daily News* [New York] 4 October 1989: 37. *Variety* 17 May 1989: 39–40.
ADDITIONAL DISCUSSION:
Biodrowski, Steve. "Roger Corman." *Cinefantastique* 19 (May 1989): 19.

The Tournament of the Golden Scarf
(1912) see Le Tournoi de l'écharpe d'or
(1912)

504. The Tournament of the Golden Tree (1914)

France; Film de Paris.

In honor of the 1468 arrival of Charles the Bold, Duke of Normandy, the citizens of Bruges stage an elaborate tournament.

REVIEWS: *Bioscope* 5 November 1914: supplement iii. *Kinematograph Monthly Film Record* 32 (December 1914): 91.

505. Le Tournoi de l'écharpe d'or (1912)

France; dir. Henri Andréani; Production Série d'Art, Pathé Frères.

CAST: Paul Franck, Léontine Massart.

Hugues, a knight, is suitor for the hand of Yolande, the daughter of the Duke de Haumont, himself married for a second time to a much younger woman, who falls madly in love with Hugues. When the knight wins the tournament and the right to marry Yolande, the duchess has her stepdaughter flung in prison. Disguised as Yolande, she meets Hugues; when he rejects her, she vows vengeance. Hugues rescues Yolande and imprisons the duchess, who dies in the same dungeon that previously housed Yolande.

REVIEW: *Bioscope* 11 January 1912: supplement iii.

ADDITIONAL DISCUSSION:

Bousquet, Henri. *Catalogue Pathé des années 1896 à 1914: 1912–1913–1914.* Paris: Henri Bousquet, 1995.

506. *Tower of London* (1939)

United States; dir. Rowland V. Lee; Universal Pictures.

CAST: Nan Grey, Ian Hunter, Boris Karloff, Barbara O'Neil, Vincent Price, Basil Rathbone.

Richard, Duke of Gloucester, eliminates everyone who stands in his way to the throne of England. This period of terror ends when Richard is crowned king, but his success is short-lived. His treasure is stolen to finance the return of the exiled Henry Tudor, who deposes Richard and ascends to the throne as Henry VII.

The story told here is perhaps best known from Shakespeare's *Richard III*, but Lee's film only nods in the direction of its Elizabethan ancestor. Instead, the tale of events during the Wars of the Roses is recast as an unfolding court intrigue punctuated by horror and suspense — all the murders are especially brutal, as lingering camera shots make abundantly clear.

REVIEWS: *Film Bulletin* 2 December 1939: 17. *Film Daily* 21 November 1939: 6. *Harrison's Reports* 2 December 1939: 190. *Hollywood Reporter* 17 November 1939: 3. *Kinematograph Weekly* 22 February 1940: 14. *Monthly Film Bulletin* 7 (31 May 1940): 76. *Motion Picture Daily* 21 November 1939: 8. *Motion Picture Herald* 25 November 1939: 43. *Motion Picture Review Digest* 4 (4 December 1939): 8; 4 (25 December 1939): 107–08. *New York Times* 12 December 1939: 37. *Rob Wagner's Script* 22 (9 December 1939): 15. *Times* [London] 6 May 1940: 4. *To-day's Cinema* 21 February 1940: 13; 15 September 1948: 12–13. *Variety* 22 November 1939: 14.

ADDITIONAL DISCUSSIONS:

Bojarski, Richard, and Kenneth Beale. *The Films of Boris Karloff.* Secaucus, N.J.: Citadel, 1974.

Buehrer, Beverley Bare. *Boris Karloff, A Bio-Bibliography.* Westport, Conn.: Greenwood, 1993.

Druxman, Michael B. *Basil Rathbone, His Life and His Films.* South Brunswick, N.J.: A.S. Barnes, 1975.

Hanson, Patricia King, ed. *The American Film Institute Catalog of Motion Pictures Produced in the United States: Feature Films 1931–1940.* Berkeley: University of California Press, 1993.

Jensen, Paul M. *Boris Karloff and His Films.* New York: A.S. Barnes, 1974.

McAsh, Ian F. *The Films of Vincent Price.* London: Barden Castell Williams, 1984.

Nash, Jay Robert, and Stanley Ralph Ross. *The Motion Picture Guide, T–V, 1927–1983.* Chicago: Cinebooks, 1987.

Nollen, Scott Allen. *Boris Karloff.* Jefferson, N.C.: McFarland, 1992.

507. *The Tower of London* (1962)

United States; dir. Roger Corman; United Artists.

CAST: Robert Brown, Joan Camden, Joan Freeman, Bruce Gordon, Sandra Knight, Richard McCauly, Michael Pate, Vincent Price, Justice Watson.

Shortly before his death, England's Edward VI names his brother Richard Lord Protector and guardian of his two sons. Richard promptly has the two young boys murdered, drifts into madness, kills his wife and is finally himself killed.

Corman's version of the 1939 film of the same title starring Basil Rathbone as Richard is even further removed from its putative source in Shakespeare. Vincent Price, who had played the role of Clarence in the 1939 film, here plays Richard in a film more indebted to the horror tales of Edgar Allan Poe than to Shakespeare.

REVIEWS: *Daily Cinema* 22 March 1967: 17. *Kinematograph Weekly* 18 March 1967: 28. *Motion Picture Bulletin* 24 (April 1967): 64. *Video Watchdog* 22 (March-April 1994): 22–23.

ADDITIONAL DISCUSSIONS:

Bourgoin, Stéphane. *Roger Corman.* Paris: Edilig, 1983.

McAsh, Ian F. *The Films of Vincent Price.* London: Barden Castell Williams, 1984.

McGee, Mark Thomas. *Roger Corman, The Best of the Cheap Acts.* Jefferson, N.C.: McFarland, 1988.

Naha, Ed. *The Films of Roger Corman: Brilliance on a Budget.* New York: Arco, 1982.

Nash, Jay Robert, and Stanley Ralph Ross. *The Motion Picture Guide, T–V, 1927–1983.* Chicago: Cinebooks, 1987.

508. *Une Tragédie à la cour de Milan*
(1912)

France; Pathé Frères and Film d'arte italiana.

ALTERNATE TITLE: *A Tragedy in the Court of Milan.*

CAST: Francesca Bertini, Giovanni Pezzinga, Gustavo Serena, Celia Zucchini.

Philip Visconti has himself declared Duke of Milan and asks his predecessor's widow, Beatrice di Tenda, to be his wife. They are married, but Philip turns his attention to one of his wife's ladies-in-waiting, Agnes del Maino, who with the help of a sorcerer persuades Philip that Beatrice has been unfaithful to him with her squire Orombello. Philip has Orombello tortured in front of Beatrice, who in fear confesses to a crime of which she is guiltless. Orombello is executed, and Beatrice dies from sorrow.

The plot of this film has some historical basis. Philip (Filippo Maria) Visconti (1392–1447) seized power in Milan in 1412 after having married Beatrice di Tenda, the widow of a noted general who had ruled the city since Philip's mother's 1404 assassination.

REVIEWS: *Bioscope* 21 March 1912: 861; 11 April 1912: supplement iii.

ADDITIONAL DISCUSSION:
Bousquet, Henri. *Catalogue Pathé des années 1896 à 1914: 1912–1913–1914.* Paris: Henri Bousquet, 1995.

A Tragedy in the Court of Milan
(1912) see *Une Tragédie à la cour de Milan* (1912)

The Tragedy of Robert the Silent, Duke of Aquitaine (1910) see *La Tragique Aventure de Robert le taciturne duc d'Aquitaine* (1910)

509. *La Tragica notte di Assisi* (1960)

Italy; dir. Raffaello Pacini; Chiara Film.

ALTERNATE TITLE: *Angelo di Assisi.*

CAST: Carlo Giustini, Evi Maltagliati, Leda Negroni, Antonio Pierfederici.

To end the division between the papacy and the Holy Roman Empire, Monaldo of Assisi, a supporter of the Pope, proposes that his niece Chiara (Clare) marry Lorenzo, a vassal of the emperor. Chiara and her sister are, however, drawn to the religious life and want to follow the teachings of Francis. With the wedding

called off, the emperor renews his war against the Pope, sending Saracen mercenaries against Assisi under Lorenzo's command. Monaldo organizes the city's defenses and kills Lorenzo, only to fall mortally wounded himself. Chiara appears before the Saracen hordes holding the consecrated host. The invaders turn back, and the city is spared by its faith.

In her own lifetime, Chiara was famous for the efficacy of her prayers. When in 1244 Frederick II sent his army, which was in part made up of Saracens, to plunder Assisi, Chiara appeared on the city's walls with the consecrated host and beseeched God to spare the city. Terror stricken, the imperial army fled.

DISCUSSIONS:
Italian Production 1960. Rome: Unitalia Film, 1961.
Poppi, Roberto, and Mario Pecorari. *Dizionario del cinema italiano. Vol. 3: I Film dal 1960 al 1969.* Rome: Gremese Editore, 1992.

510. *La Tragique Aventure de Robert le taciturne duc d'Aquitaine*
(1910)

France; dir. Ferdinand Zecca and Henri Andréani; Pathé Frères, S.A.P.F.

ALTERNATE TITLE: *The Tragedy of Robert the Silent, Duke of Aquitaine.*

CAST: Stacia Napierkowska, Louis Ravet, Madeline Roch.

Robert, the always despondent Duke of Aquitaine, falls in love with a young gypsy girl. His wife discovers them making love and has the girl thrown into a dungeon where she dies. Out of despair, Robert drinks poison and dies at the gypsy girl's side.

REVIEW: *Bioscope* 18 August 1910: 27.

ADDITIONAL DISCUSSION:
Bousquet, Henri. *Catalogue Pathé des années 1896 à 1914: 1910–1911.* Paris: Henri Bousquet, 1994.

511. *The Trial of Joan of Arc* (1962)

France; dir. Robert Bresson; Agnès Delahaie Productions.

ALTERNATE TITLE: *Le Procès de Jeanne d'Arc.*

CAST: Florenz Carrez, Marcel Darbaud, Jean-Claude Fourneau, Michel Hérubel, Roger Honorat, Marc Jacquier, André Régnier.

Joan's parents enter Notre Dame Cathedral to ask the Church to reconsider her condemnation. In a flashback, the film rehearses her trial and condemnation. In this version of her interrogation, Joan is clearly a match for the

Florenz Carrez as Joan in Robert Bresson's *The Trial of Joan of Arc* (1962). (Still courtesy of the British Film Institute.)

ecclesiastical authorities who remain divided on the question of her guilt. However, Bishop Cauchon prevails, and Joan dies at the stake refusing to renounce the rightness of her visions. Her last word is "Jesus."

Like Dreyer's 1928 film *The Passion of Joan of Arc*, this film is selective in its coverage of the events in the life of Joan of Arc, focusing just on her trial. Bresson based his screenplay on the records of Joan's trial and rehabilitation. The director's interests are narrower than those of others who have brought Joan's story to the screen. Bresson eschews general issues such as Joan's role in the conflict between Church and state in French history and presents instead a personal meditation on the possibility of good in a world overrun with evil.

REVIEWS: *Cinéma* 67 (June 1962): 94–95. *Cinématographie française* 14 April 1962: 8. *Commonweal* 81 (19 February 1965): 671. *Film-echo/Filmwoche* 42 (26 May 1962): 9. *Film français* 29 March 1963: 18. *Films and Filming* 9 (February 1963): 36. *Image et son* 152 (June 1962): 3. *Kinematograph Weekly* 14 March 1963: 22. *Monthly Film Bulletin* 30 (April 1963): 44. *Motion Picture Herald* 17 February 1965:

Product Digest Section: 236. *Movie* 7 (February-March 1963): 30–32. *New York Times* 12 February 1965: 19. *Sight and Sound* 31 (Summer 1962): 130–31; 32 (Winter 1962-1963): 37–38. *Times* [London] 23 May 1962: 15; 1 November 1962: 8. *Unifrance Film* 37 (July 1962): 13a–13b. *Variety* 30 May 1962: 6.

ADDITIONAL DISCUSSIONS:

Agel, Henri. "Sainte Jeanne d'arc." *Études* [Paris] 314 (September 1962): 262–73.

Amenguael, Barthélemy. "Les Pouvoirs de l'abstraction." *Positif* 430 (December 1996): 79–84.

Arnaud, Philippe. *Robert Bresson*. Paris: Cahiers du cinéma, 1986.

Biggs, Melissa E. *French Films, 1945–1993*. Jefferson, N.C.: McFarland, 1996.

Blaetz, Robin J. "Strategies of Containment: Joan of Arc in Film." Ph.D. dissertation. New York University, 1989.

Cameron, Ian. "Interview with Robert Bresson." *Movie* 7 (February-March 1963): 28–29.

Estève, Michel. *Robert Bresson*. Paris: Albatros, 1983.

Garrigou-Lagrange, Madeleine. "Le Procès de Jeanne d'Arc." *Téléciné* 112 (October 1963): 1–9.

Harty, Kevin J. "Jeanne au cinéma." In Bonnie Wheeler and Charles T. Wood, eds. *Fresh Verdicts on Joan of Arc*. New York: Garland, 1996.

"'Jeanne d'Arc' e l'antiteatro, colloquio con Robert Bresson." *Bianco e nero* 24 (March 1963): 9–20.

Kovacs, Yves. "Entretien avec Robert Bresson." *Les Cahiers du cinéma* 140 (February 1963): 4–10.

Krafsur, Richard P., ed. *The American Film Institute Catalog of Motion Pictures, Feature Films 1961–1970.* New York: Bowker, 1976.

Magill, Frank N., ed. *Magill's Survey of Cinema: Foreign Langauge Films.* Englewood Cliffs, N.J.: Salem, 1985.

Margolis, Nadia. *Joan of Arc in History, Literature, and Film.* New York: Garland, 1990.

Nash, Jay Robert, and Stanley Ralph Ross. *The Motion Picture Guide, T–V, 1927–1983.* Chicago: Cinebooks, 1987.

Pichonnier, Catherine. *Le Procès de Jeanne d'Arc.* [Fiche filmographique 184.] Paris: IDHEC, [1962?].

"*Le Procès de Jeanne d'Arc.*" *Avant-scène du cinéma* 408–09 (January-February 1992): 73–79.

"*Le Procès de Jeanne d'Arc.*" *Téléciné* 112 (October 1963): [Fiche 423] 1–9.

Rhode, Eric. *Tower of Babel, Speculations on the Cinema.* London: Weidenfeld and Nicolson, 1966.

Sémolué, Jean. "*Le Procès de Jeanne d'Arc* dans l'œuvre de Robert Bresson." *Esprit* June 1963: 1190–94.

Sloane, Jane. *Robert Bresson, A Guide to References and Resources.* Boston: Hall, 1983.

Thurley, Geoffrey. "Give: Sympathise: Control." *Motion* 6 (Autumn 1963): 19–24.

Vecchiali, Paul, et al. "*Le Procès de Jeanne d'Arc.*" *Les Cahiers du cinéma* 143 (May 1963): 35–49.

Young, Vernon. "Films to Confirm the Poets." *Hudson Review* 16 (Summer 1963): 255–64.

512. *Il Trionfo di Robin Hood* (1962)

Italy; dir. Umberto Lenzi; Italiana Film Buonavista.

CAST: Don Burnett, Samson Burke, Vincenzo Musolino, Gia Scala.

Robin Hood, whose band of men here includes Ivanhoe and Quasimodo, defends the interests of the absent King Richard when his brother, Prince John, attempts to steal money intended to ransom the king.

REVIEW: *Cinématographie française* 2055 (7 March 1964): 25.

ADDITIONAL DISCUSSION:

Poppi, Roberto, and Mario Pecorari. *Dizionario del cinema italiano: I Film dal 1960 al 1969.* Rome: Gremese Editore, 1992.

Tristan and Isolda (1911) see *Tristan et Yseult* (1911)

513. *Tristan and Isolt* (1979)

Ireland; dir. Tom Donovan; Clar Productions.

ALTERNATE TITLE: *Lovespell.*

CAST: Richard Burton, Nicholas Clay, Cyril Cusack, Geraldine Fitzgerald, Kate Mulgrew.

Tristan journeys to Ireland to bring back Princess Isolt as bride for his uncle, King Mark of Cornwall. After slaying a dragon, Tristan meets Isolt. As the two journey back to Cornwall, they accidentally drink a love potion and become lovers.

Burton is essentially wasted in this tepid cinematic retelling of the legend of Tristan and Isolt. Clay (Tristan) also played Lancelot in John Boorman's 1981 film *Excalibur.*

DISCUSSIONS:

Alpert, Hollis. *Burton.* Toronto: Paper Jacks, 1987.

McMunn, Meradith T. "Filming the Tristan Myth: From Text to Icon." In Kevin J. Harty, ed. *Cinema Arthuriana, Essays on Arthurian Films.* New York: Garland, 1991.

Steverson, Tyrone. *Richard Burton, A Bio-Bibliography.* Westport, Conn.: Greenwood, 1992.

The Video Sourcebook. 8th ed. Syossett, N.Y.: National Video Clearinghouse, 1986.

Willis, John. *Screen World.* [Volume 33]. New York: Crown, 1982.

514. *Tristan et Iseult* (1972)

France; dir. Yvan Lagrange; Film du Soir.

CAST: Yvan Lagrange, Claire Wauthion.

Lagrange filmed this visually striking if not always coherent retelling of the legend of Tristan in Iceland. The director characterized his film as a "visual opera."

REVIEWS: *Cinéma* 187 (May 1974): 138. *Ecran* 25 (May 1974): 68. *Image et son* 284 (May 1974): 103–04; 288–89 (October 1974): 364–65. *Kino* 9 (January 1974): 60–61. *Téléciné* 188 (May 1974): 27. *Variety* 18 July 1973: 14.

ADDITIONAL DISCUSSIONS:

McMunn, Meradith T. "Filming the Tristan Myth: From Text to Icon." In Kevin J. Harty, ed. *Cinema Arthuriana, Essays on Arthurian Film.* New York: Garland, 1991.

Payen, Jean Charles. "Le *Tristan et Iseult* de Lagrange comme un anti–Tristan." *Tristania* 4 (May 1979): 51–56.

Paquette, Jean-Marcel. "Le Derniere metamorphose de Tristan: Yvan Lagrange (1972)." In Ulrich Müller, et al., eds. *Tristan et Iseut, mythe europeen et mondial.* Göppingen: Kümmerle, 1987.

Selcer, Robert W. "Yvan Lagrange: Impressions of a Filmmaker." *Tristania* 4 (May 1979): 44–50.

Vialle, Gabriel. "Musique, la quatrième dimension." *Image et son* 29 (December 974): 10–12.

515. *Tristan et Yseult* (1909)

France; dir. Albert Capellani; Pathé Frères, S.C.A.G.L.

Tristan (Yvan Lagrange) and Iseult (Claire Wauthion) in Lagrange's *Tristan et Iseult* (1972). (Still courtesy of Film Stills Archive of the Museum of Modern Art.)

CAST: Paul Capellani, Stacia Napierkowska.
Tristan falls in love with his uncle's fiancée with tragic consequences.

DISCUSSION:

Mitry, Jean. *Filmographie universelle: tome deuxième. Primitifs et précurseurs 1895–1915. Première partie: France et Europe.* Paris: IDHEC, 1964.

516. *Tristan et Yseult* (1911)

France; dir. Ugo Falena; Il Film d'arte italiana, S.A.P.F.

ALTERNATE TITLE: *Tristan and Isolda.*

CAST: Francesca Bertini, Bianca Lorenzoni, Serafino Mastracchio, Giovanni Pezzinga.

Accompanied by his slave Rosen, Tristan journeys to Ireland to bring Yseult back to be the bride of his uncle, King Mark of Cornwall. Rosen is jealous of his master's attentions to Yseult and attempts to poison Tristan. At the last minute, the poison is changed to a love potion, which both Tristan and Yseult drink. Once back in Cornwall, the two run off and are

denounced by Rosen. Mark is moved out of pity for their youth and pardons Tristan and Yseult, but the two, realizing that they cannot overcome their love, commit suicide.

REVIEW: *Bioscope* 28 September 1911: supplement v.

ADDITIONAL DISCUSSION:

Bousquet, Henri. *Catalogue Pathé des années 1896 à 1914: 1910–1911.* Paris: Henri Bousquet, 1994.

517. *Tristan et Yseut* (1920)

France; dir. Maurice Mariaud; Nalpas.

ALTERNATE TITLE: *Tristram and Isolda.*

CAST: Sylvio de Pedrelli, Frank Heurs, Andrée Lionel.

Tristan of Cornwall defeats an Irish messenger demanding tribute, but is wounded in the effort. Put out to sea to die, he washes up on the Irish coast and is nursed by Yseut, daughter of the Irish king, who falls in love with him. Tristan sails back to Cornwall only to have to return to Ireland to bring Yseut back as bride for his uncle, King Mark. She reluctantly marries Mark, but her love for Tristan only grows, and the two run away. Caught, they are forgiven by Mark once Yseut proves her chastity by an ordeal of fire. Tristan sets sail and meets Yolande, daughter of the Duke of Brittany, who falls in love with him. Her lover mortally wounds Tristan, who sends for Yseut. She arrives too late and dies in despair.

This well-made and well-received film contained one unintentionally amusing scene: Tristan jumps from a very high tower, a distance of at least 200 feet, lands on his feet and walks away unharmed.

REVIEW: *Kinematograph Weekly* 24 November 1921: 73–74.

ADDITIONAL DISCUSSIONS:

Abel, Richard. *French Cinema, The First Wave, 1915–1926.* Princeton: Princeton University Press, 1984.

Bardèche, Maurice, and Robert Brasillach. *Histoire du cinéma.* Rev. ed. 2 vols. Givors: Martel, 1953–1954.

Fescourt, Henri. *La Foi et les montagnes.* Paris: Montel, 1959.

Landry, Lionel. "La Reconstruction historique." *Cinémagazine* 3 (14 September 1923): 368.

Tristan und Isolde (1981) see *Fire and Sword* (1981)

Tristram and Isolda (1920) see *Tristan et Yseut* (1920)

The Triumphant Hero (1910) see *Il Cid* (1910)

518. *Trollsyn* (1994)

Norway; dir. Anja Breien; Northern Lights A/S.

ALTERNATE TITLES: *Rypa i justedal* and *Second Sight.*

CAST: Bjorn Willberg Andersen, Oddbjorn Hesjevoll, Knut Husebo, Baard Owe, Reidar Sorensen, Julia Onsager Steen, Inge Steinheim.

The Black Death ravages Norway, killing everyone in a small village except eight-year old Maren. Living alone in the forest, she comes upon a group of men from a village in the next valley who become convinced that the girl has the power of second sight and can tell their futures. Maren's father, who was away when the plague struck, finally returns to claim his daughter.

REVIEWS: *Film og kino* 5 (1994): 10–11, 44. *Variety* 3 April 1995: 144.

ADDITIONAL DISCUSSION:

Norwegian Films 1995. Oslo: Norwegian Film Institute, 1995.

Trudno byt bogom (1989) see *Es ist nicht leicht Gott zu sein* (1989)

519. *True Till Death* (1912)

Spain; Hispano Films.

During the reign of Aragon's Peter I (1068–1104), a knight falls in love with a lady who will only marry him if he proves his worth. The knight succeeds, but when he is taken prisoner by the Sultan, the lady marries a rival suitor fearing the knight is dead. When the knight discovers her marriage, he dies in despair. Overcome with remorse, the lady too falls dead, and the two lovers are finally united in death.

REVIEWS: *Bioscope* 18 April 1912: 211; 30 May 1912: supplement xi. *Kinematograph Monthly Record* 1 (May 1912): 53.

520. *TV Dante* (1989)

Great Britain; dir. Peter Greenaway; Argos Films.

CAST: David Attenborough, John Gielgud, Bob Peck, David Rudkin, Joanne Whalley-Kilmer.

Using Tom Phillips's illustrations for his 1993 edition of Dante, Greenaway has fashioned a fascinating meditative television film version of the first eight cantos of *The Inferno.*

REVIEWS: *Avant-scène du cinéma* 417–418 (December 1992): 24–25. *Listener* 21 May 1987: 31; 26 July 1990: 26–27; 9 August 1990: 46. *Los Angeles Times* 31 October 1990: F12. *Television Today* 2 August 1990: 21. *Time Out* [London] 22 March 1995: 167. *Times* [London] 28 July 1990: 19.

ADDITIONAL DISCUSSIONS:

Biga, Tracy. "Cinema Bulimia: Peter Greenaway's Corpus of Excess." Ph.D. dissertation. University of Southern California, 1994.

Denham, Laura. *The Films of Peter Greenaway.* London: Minerva Press, 1993.

Iannucci, Amilcare A. "Dante Produces Television." *Lectura Dantis* 13 (Fall 1990): 32–46.

———. "Dante, Television, and Education." *Quaderni italianistica* 10 (Spring-Fall 1989): 1–34.

Jones, Derek, ed. *A TV Dante.* London: Channel 4 Television, 1990.

Liberti, Fabrizio. "L'Inferno di Peter Greenaway." *Cineforum* 290 (December 1989): 49–53.

Sanderson, Mark. "Hell on Reels." *Time Out* [London] 25 July 1990: 12–13.

Vickers, Nacy J. "Dante in the Video Decade." In Thomas J. Cachey, Jr., ed. *Dante Now, Current Trends in Dante Studies.* Notre Dame, Ind.: University of Notre Dame Press, 1995.

Wallace, David. "Dante in English." In Rachel Jacoff, ed. *The Cambridge Companion to Dante.* New York: Cambridge University Press, 1993.

Woods, Alan. *Being Naked — Playing Dead, The Art of Peter Greenaway.* New York: St. Martin's, 1997.

————. "Peter Greenaway." *Transcript* 1 (December 1994): 6–27.

The Two Crusaders (1968) see *I Due crociati* (1968)

521. Le Tyran de Jérusalem (1910)

France; dir. Camille de Morlhon; Pathé Frères, S.A.P.F.

ALTERNATE TITLE: The *Tyrant of Jerusalem.*

CAST: Berthe Bovy, Jean Jacquinet, Georges Laumonier, Léontine Massart.

Saracens led by Clorinda the Amazon defeat Christian armies marching on Jerusalem. Clorinda, who is allied with Aladin, the Saracen King of Jerusalem, nonetheless has two Christian lovers, one male and one female. The film's plot is as convoluted as it is curious.

REVIEW: *Bioscope* 11 August 1910: 29.

ADDITIONAL DISCUSSION:

Bousquet, Henri. *Catalogue Pathé des années 1896 à 1914: 1910–1911.* Paris: Henri Bousquet, 1994.

522. The Tyrant Feudal Lord (1908)

France; Gaumont.

When famine ravages the countryside, a feudal lord turns a deaf ear to the pleas of the local priest and the peasants that he offer them some relief. In desperation, the priest and peasants barge into the castle while the lord is holding a great feast. The lord orders the intruders to be executed. Their spirits return to haunt the castle and drive the lord to commit suicide.

This film garnered praise for its touching scenes of pathos.

REVIEW: *Moving Picture World* 25 July 1908: 69.

ADDITIONAL DISCUSSION:

Savada, Elias. *The American Film Institute Catalog of Motion Pictures Produced in the United States: Film Beginnings, 1893–1910.* Metuchen, N.J.: Scarecrow, 1995.

523. Tyrant of Florence (1910)

Great Britain; Urban-Eclipse.

For failing to obey the duke's every wish, a man and his wife are put to death. Years later, their now-grown daughter becomes the duke's favorite in order to poison him.

REVIEWS: *Moving Picture World* 24 December 1910: 1487; 31 December 1910: 1536. *Variety* 24 December 1910: 16.

ADDITIONAL DISCUSSION:

Savada, Elias. *The American Film Institute Catalog of Motion Pictures Produced in the United States: Film Beginnings, 1893–1910.* Metuchen, N.J.: Scarecrow, 1995.

The Tyrant of Jerusalem (1910) see *Le Tyran de Jérusalem* (1910)

The Tyrant's Heart or Boccaccio in Hungary (1981) see *A Zsarnok sziva avagy Boccaccio Magyarorszagin* (1981)

L'Ultimo Decameron (1972) see *Decameron n. 3: Le Più Belle Donne de Boccaccio* (1972)

L'Ultimo dei vikinghi (1960) see *The Last of the Vikings* (1960)

524. The Undead (1957)

United States; dir. Roger Corman; American International.

CAST: Billy Barty, Richard Devon, Val Dufour, Pamela Duncan, Richard Garland, Allison Hayes, Dick Miller, Dorothy Neumann, Aaron Saxon, Bruno Ve Sota, Mel Welles.

Hypnotized by a scientist during an experiment in regression, a prostitute awakens in the Middle Ages where in a previous life she was condemned as a witch and ordered to be beheaded at dawn. She discovers that her ancestor was framed by a real witch intent upon stealing her lover Pendragon.

This low-budget fantasy is mainly notable for being one of Roger Corman's earliest films.

REVIEWS: *Harrison's Reports* 2 March 1957: 36. *Motion Picture Herald* 16 March 1957: Product Digest Section 299. *Variety* 27 February 1957: 6.

ADDITIONAL DISCUSSIONS:

Bouroin, Stéphane. *Roger Corman.* Paris: Edilig, 1983.

di Franco, J. Philip, ed. *The Movie World of Roger Corman.* New York: Chelsea House, 1979.

McGee, Mark Thomas. *Fast and Furious, The Story of American International Pictures.* Jefferson, N.C.: McFarland, 1984.

Sir Mordred (Jim Dale) shows the "monster" (Dennis Dugan) to King Arthur (Kenneth More) and the members of his court in a scene from Russ Mayberry's *Unidentified Flying Oddball* (1979).

_____. *Roger Corman, The Best of the Cheap Acts.* Jefferson, N.C.: McFarland, 1988.

Naha, Ed. *The Films of Roger Corman: Brilliance on a Budget.* New York: Arco, 1982.

Nash, Jay Robert, and Stanley Ralph Ross. *The Motion Picture Guide, T–V, 1927–1983.* Chicago: Cinebooks, 1987.

525. *Unidentified Flying Oddball*
(1979)

United States; dir. Russ Mayberry; Walt Disney Productions.

ALTERNATE TITLE: *The Spaceman and King Arthur.*

CAST: Jim Dale, Dennis Dugan, John Le Mesurier, Ron Moody, Kenneth More, Sheila White.

With a look-alike humanoid robot in tow, a reluctant astronaut is inadvertently whisked back to King Arthur's Court to battle Mordred and Merlin on the king's behalf.

Of all the adaptations of Twain's *A Con-* *necticut Yankee in King Arthur's Court,* Mayberry's film — despite the license it takes with plot — may be truest to the humor found in the original novel.

REVIEWS: *Ecran fantastique* 11 (1979): 7. *Film Bulletin* 48 (September 1978): Review-D. *Films Illustrated* 8 (July 1979): 412. *Independent Film Journal* 82 (September 1979): 14, 55. *Monthly Film Bulletin* 46 (July 1979): 154–55. *Variety* 18 July 1979: 16.

ADDITIONAL DISCUSSIONS:

Crume, Vic. *Unidentified Flying Oddball.* New York: Scholastic Book Services, 1979. [Novelization.]

Harty, Kevin J. "Camelot Twice Removed: *Knightriders* and the Film Versions of *A Connecticut Yankee in King Arthur's Court.*" In Kevin J. Harty, ed. *Cinema Arthuriana, Essays on Arthurian Film.* New York: Garland, 1991.

Nash, Jay Robert, and Stanley Ralph Ross. *The Motion Picture Guide, T–V, 1927–1983.* Chicago: Cinebooks, 1987.

Simon, Heather. *The Spaceman and King Arthur.* London: New English Library, 1979. [Novelization.]

Thompson, Raymond H. "The Ironic Tradition in Arthurian Films Since 1960." In Kevin J. Harty, ed. *Cinema Arthuriana, Essays on Arthurian Film.* New York: Garland, 1991.

Tous les films 1981. Paris: Éditions O.C.F.C., 1982.

Umland, Rebecca A., and Samuel J. Umland. *The Use of Arthurian Legend in Hollywood Film from Connecticut Yankees to Fisher Kings.* Westport, Conn.: Greenwood, 1996.

Willis, Donald C. *Horror and Science Fiction Films II.* Metuchen, N.J.: Scarecrow, 1982.

526. *Up the Chastity Belt* (1971)

Great Britain; dir. Bob Kellett; Associated London Films and Anglo-EMI.

CAST: Graham Crowden, Bill Fraser, Frankie Howard, Roy Hudd, Eartha Kitt, Hugh Paddick, Anna Quayle.

The serf Lurkalot is unaware that he is the long-lost twin brother of England's Richard I. Lurkalot, who also sells chastity belts, follows his overlord and a ragtag crew of retainers (including assorted characters from the legend of Robin Hood) into battle to rescue the king from the Saracens who have encamped at a nightclub run by Scheherazade.

In the second of the "Up" series — *Up Pompeii* (1971) was the first — Howard, a star on the British pantomime circuit, sends up the Middle Ages in a way that today seems a bit crude and amateurish when compared with the later work of the Monty Python troupe.

REVIEWS: *CinemaTV Today* 1 January 1972: 29. *Monthly Film Bulletin* 39 (January 1972): 17–18. *Times* [London] 17 May 1971: 4.

ADDITIONAL DISCUSSION:

Nash, Jay Robert, and Stanley Ralph Ross. *The Motion Picture Guide, T–V, 1927–1983.* Chicago: Cinebooks, 1987.

527. *Utlaginn* (1981)

Iceland; dir. Agust Gudmundsson; Isfilm.

ALTERNATE TITLES: *Outlaw* and *The Saga of Gisli.*

CAST: Tinna Gunnlaugsdóttir, Arnar Jónsson, Thráinn Karlsson, Helgi Skúlason, Ragnheidur Steindórsdóttir, Thráinn Steingrimsson.

In defense of his honor, a man is forced to kill his brother-in-law. Branded an outlaw, he flees with a price upon his head.

The screenplay is adapted from the medieval saga of Gisli Súrsson. The film itself is bloody, intricately plotted and visually arresting.

REVIEWS: *Filmrutan* 27.2 (1984): 32. *Iceland Review* 24.2 (1986): 71–72. *Scandinavian Film News* 1 (November 1981): [4]; 2 (February 1983): [2–3]. *Variety* 31 March 1982: 26.

ADDITIONAL DISCUSSIONS:

Cowie, Peter, ed. *Le Cinéma des pays nordiques.* Paris: Centre Georges Pompidou, 1991.

Icelandic Films 1980–1983. Reykjavik: Icelandic Film Fund, 1983.

Nash, Jay Robert, and Stanley Ralph Ross. *The Motion Picture Guide, N–R, 1927–1983.* Chicago: Cinebooks, 1986.

528. *The Vagabond King* (1930)

United States; dir. Ludwig Berger; Paramount Pictures.

CAST: Lawford Davidson, O.P. Heggie, Dennis King, Jeanette MacDonald, Warner Oland, Lilian Roth.

In 1463, the traitorous Duke of Burgundy besieges Paris. Louis XI makes no attempt to save the city, so the vagabonds of Paris led by François Villon rise in revolt. Villon falls in love with the king's niece Katherine and rescues her from Thibault, Marshal of France, who is secretly an ally of the Duke of Burgundy. A series of ruses allows Villon to become "king" for seven days, during which time he defeats the Burgundians and Thibault and restores the good name of the monarchy. Villon's week-long rule comes with a price, his life, but the king relents when the crowds demand Villon's freedom. Once freed, Villon is reunited with Katherine.

From the 1925 musical comedy *The Vagabond King* by William H. Post, Brian Hooker and Rudolf Friml, which was in turn based on the 1901 play *If I Were King* by Justin Huntly McCarthy, this musical film version of the life of the poet and philosopher François Villon (1431–?) was released abroad as a silent film with titles and background music, in part because dubbed musicals were generally poorly received at the time.

REVIEWS: *Bioscope* 14 May 1930: 33. *Exhibitors Herald-World* 1 March 1930: 35. *Film Daily* 23 February 1930: 10. *Film Spectator* 12 April 1930: 21–22. *New York Times* 2 March 1930: 9. 5. *Photoplay* 37 (May 1930): 54. *Picturegoer* 19 (June 1930): 48, 50. *Rob Wagner's Script* 3 (26 April 1930): 11–12. *Times* [London] 7 May 1930: 14; 13 May 1930: 14. *Variety* 26 February 1930: 24.

ADDITIONAL DISCUSSIONS:

Castanza, Philip. *The Films of Jeanette MacDonald and Nelson Eddy.* Secaucus, N.J.: Citadel, 1978.

Knowles, Eleanor. *The Films of Jeanette MacDonald and Nelson Eddy.* South Brunswick, N.J.: A.S. Barnes, 1975.

Munden, Kenneth W., ed. *The American Film Institute Catalog of Motion Pictures, Feature Films 1921–1930*. New York: Bowker, 1971.

Nash, Jay Robert, and Stanley Ralph Ross. *The Motion Picture Guide, T–V, 1927–1983*. Chicago: Cinebooks, 1987.

Parish, James Robert. *The Jeanette MacDonald Story*. New York: Mason, 1976.

_____, and Michael R. Pitts. *The Great Hollywood Musical Pictures*. Metuchen, N.J.: Scarecrow, 1992.

Rich, Sharon. *Jeanette MacDonald, A Pictorial Treasury*. Los Angeles: Times Mirror, 1973.

Stern, Lee Edward. *Jeanette MacDonald*. New York: Jove, 1977.

529. *The Vagabond King* (1956)

United States; dir. Michael Curtiz; Paramount Pictures.

CAST: Kathryn Grayson, Walter Hampden, Cedric Hardwicke, Rita Moreno, Oreste, Leslie Nielsen, William Prince.

The traitorous Duke of Burgundy besieges Paris, and Louis XI makes no attempt to save the city. The vagabonds of Paris, led by François Villon, rise in revolt. Villon falls in love with the king's niece Katherine and rescues her from Thibault, Marshal of France, who is secretly a Burgundian ally. When Villon becomes "king" for seven days, he is able to save France and Louis's throne. But Villon's week-long rule ends with his being sentenced to death, until the king relents, and Villon and Katherine are reunited.

This remake of the 1930 film of the same title is notable for its lavish sets and its spectacular use of Technicolor. The score includes several new songs.

REVIEWS: *Daily Film Renter* 6 April 1956: 4. *Film Daily* 5 September 1956: 6. *Harrison's Reports* 8 September 1956: 143. *Hollywood Reporter* 30 August 1956: 3. *Kinematograph Weekly* 12 April 1956: 18. *Monthly Film Bulletin* 23 (May 1956): 59. *Motion Picture Herald* 8 September 1956: Product Digest Section 57. *New York Times* 13 September 1956: 39. *Times* [London] 9 April 1956: 3. *To-day's Cinema* 6 April 1956: 8. *Variety* 5 September 1956: 6.

ADDITIONAL DISCUSSIONS:

Guidorizzi, Mario. *Michael Curtiz, un europeo a Hollywood*. Verona: Mazziania, 1981.

Kinnard, Roy, and R.J. Vitone. *The American Films of Michael Curtiz*. Metuchen, N.J.: Scarecrow, 1986.

Nash, Jay Robert, and Stanley Ralph Ross. *The Motion Picture Guide, T–V, 1927–1983*. Chicago: Cinebooks, 1987.

Parish, James Robert, and Michael R. Pitts. *The Great Hollywood Musical Pictures*. Metuchen, N.J.: Scarecrow, 1992.

Robertson, James C. *The Casablanca Man, The Cinema of Michael Curtiz*. London: Routledge, 1993.

Thomas, Nicholas, ed. *International Dictionary of Films and Filmmakers— Vol. 2: Directors*. 2nd ed. Chicago: St. James Press, 1991.

The Vagabond King. London: Moore & Matthes, [1956.] [Pressbook.]

El Valle de las espadas (1963) see *The Castilian* (1963)

Valley of the Swords (1963) see *The Castilian* (1963)

Vanda Soldanieri (1910) see *Wanda Soldanieri* (1910)

Veiviseren (1987) see *Pathfinder* (1987)

Veliky voine Albany, Scanderbeg (1953) see *Skanderbeg* (1953)

Vem Dömer? (1922) see *Love's Crucible* (1922)

530. *La Vengeance du Prince Visconti* (1912)

France; Pathé Frères, Production Milanese Film.

ALTERNATE TITLE: *The Vengeance of Prince Visconti.*

On his deathbed, Prince Visconti instructs his young son to avenge the family honor against Ludovic the Moor, Duke of Milan. Years pass, and the young Visconti joins the army of Duke Trivulee in its siege of Milan. He is sent as an ambassador to Ludovic to sue for peace, but the duke recognizes young Visconti and imprisons him. He escapes from prison and sneaks into Ludovic's bedroom. He is about to stab him when the duke drops dead of a seizure.

This film is based partly on fact, but it seems to have borrowed its plot from another film made by Pathé in the same year, *La Fin de Louis XI*, in which the French king also dies of a seizure just as the son of a long-time rival is about to stab him. Ludovico Sforza (1452–1508), called the Moor, is perhaps best remembered as the patron of Leonardo; it was the duke who commissioned *The Last Supper*. His father was the first Sforza to reign as duke in Milan. The last Visconti duke, Filippo Maria, died in 1447, and Francesco Sforza, his son-in-law, succeeded him.

REVIEW: *Bioscope* 11 January 1912: supplement v.

ADDITIONAL DISCUSSION:

Bousquet, Henri. *Catalogue Pathé des années 1896 à 1914: 1912–1913–1914*. Paris: Henri Bousquet, 1995.

The Vengeance of Prince Visconti

(1912) see *La Vengeance du Prince Visconti* (1912)

531. Vengeance of the Vikings (1964)

Italy; dir. Mario Caiano; Nike Cinematografica.

ALTERNATE TITLE: *Erik il vichingo*.

CAST: Giuliano Gemma, Gordon Mitchell, Elsia Montés, Elly McWhite, Montgomery Wood.

In 965 A.D., the Viking king Thorwald dies, leaving his treasure to be divided equally between his sly and treacherous son Eylof and his noble nephew Erik. When Erik undertakes a long sea voyage, Eylof sends Biarni with him to kill his cousin. Erik lands in America and falls in love with a native princess, who throws herself in the path of a poison arrow meant for Erik. Having killed Biarni, Erik returns home and challenges Eylof, who falls from a cliff. Erik is named sole heir to Thorwald's treasure and his successor.

This fairly conventional costume melodrama also places among Erik's crew a Greek who introduces both the Vikings and the native Americans to the art of winemaking.

REVIEWS: *Daily Cinema* 3 July 1968: 3. *Kinematograph Weekly* 6 July 1968. *Monthly Film Bulletin* 35 (August 1968): 118.

ADDITIONAL DISCUSSIONS:

Cinéma espagnol. Madrid: Uniespaña, 1966.

Italian Production 1965. Rome: Unitalia Film, 1966.

Poppi, Roberto, and Mario Pecorari. *Dizionario del cinema italiano*. Vol. 3: *I Film dal 1960 al 1969*. Rome: Gremese Editore, 1992.

532. La Véridique et Doloureuse Histoire de Catelan le ménestrel

(1910)

France; dir. Michel Carré; Pathé Frères, S.C.A.G.L., S.A.P.F.

ALTERNATE TITLES: *Catalan, the Minstrel* and *The Minstrel*.

CAST: Roger Puylagarde, Laura Lukas.

In thirteenth-century France, King Philip wants to hear Alan, a famous minstrel in the service of his cousin Elisabeth, Queen of Savoy, perform. Knights sent to escort Alan to the French court murder and rob Alan of precious perfumes sent as a gift from his mistress for the king. When a peasant girl denounces the knights, Philip has them executed and raises a cross over the spot where the minstrel was murdered.

REVIEWS: *Bioscope* 26 May 1910: 29; 30 October 1913: supplement xi. *Moving Picture World* 31 December 1910: 1548; 14 January 1911: 88. *Pathé Frères Weekly Bulletin* 165 (26 December 1910): [8–9]. *Variety* 7 January 1911: 13.

ADDITIONAL DISCUSSIONS:

Bousquet, Henri. *Catalogue Pathé des années 1896 à 1914: 1910–1911*. Paris: Henri Bousquet, 1993.

Savada, Elias. *The American Film Institute Catalog of Motion Pictures Produced in the United States: Film Beginnings, 1893–1910*. Metuchen, N.J.: Scarecrow, 1995.

533. The Viking (1928)

United States; dir. R. William Neill; MGM.

CAST: Donald Crisp, Leroy Mason, Pauline Starke, Harry Woods.

The Viking leader Leif (called "the Lucky") and his men set sail from Norway and ravage the English coast, carrying off an English princess as a slave. After a series of adventures, they land in present-day Rhode Island, where the princess and Leif become lovers and Leif converts to Christianity.

The sets for this film, which was based on Ottilia Adelina Liljencrantz's 1902 novel *The Thrall of Leif the Lucky, A Story of Viking Days*, are as unconvincing as its plot is convoluted.

REVIEWS: *Bioscope* 3 July 1929: 43. *Film Spectator* 17 November 1928: 7. *Kinematograph Weekly* 4 July 1929: 65. *New York Times* 29 November 1928: 32. *Variety* 5 December 1928: 12.

ADDITIONAL DISCUSSION:

Munden, Kenneth W., ed. *The American Film Institute Catalog of Motion Pictures Produced in the United States, Feature Films 1921–1930*. New York: Bowker, 1971.

534. The Viking Queen (1915)

United States; dir. Walter Edwin; Edison.

CAST: Frederick Annerley, Harry Beaumont, Harry Eytinge, Mary Fuller, Charles Ogle, William West.

While she is away leading her armies in

raids upon neighboring kingdoms, Helga the Glorious, queen of one of the kingdoms of Norway, faces a rebellion at home among vassals (led by Jarl of Finskarr) unwilling to submit to a woman. Jarl is initially successful in deposing Helga, but when he becomes a cruel tyrant, Jarl is overthrown and killed, and Helga is recalled to rule her country.

REVIEWS: *Bioscope* 21 January 1915: 279. *Edison Kinetogram* 4 September 1914: Film 7722. *Kinematograph Monthly Film Record* 35 (March 1915): 83.

The Viking Women (1957) see *The Viking Women and the Sea Serpent* (1957)

535. *The Viking Women and the Sea Serpent* (1957)

United States; dir. Roger Corman; American International Pictures.

ALTERNATE TITLES: *The Saga of the Viking Women and Their Voyage to the Waters of the Great Sea Serpent* and *The Viking Women.*

CAST: Susan Cabot, Gary Conway, Abby Dalton, Richard Devon, Jonathan Haze, Brad Jackson, Betsy Jones-Moreland, June Kenny, Jay Sayer.

When their men fail to return from a hunting expedition, a group of Viking women set out in search of them. The women are shipwrecked on an island inhabited by primitive warriors who, the women discover, hold their husbands captive. The women free their husbands and set sail, only to encounter a great sea serpent which they defeat.

The critics generally — and rightly — agreed that the advertising campaign for this film featuring the provocatively posed stars was more interesting than the film itself.

REVIEWS: *Daily Cinema* 17 September 1958: 4. *Kinematograph Weekly* 18 September 1958: 28. *Monthly Film Bulletin* 25 (November 1958): 146. *Motion Picture Herald* 5 April 1958: Product Digest Section 785.

ADDITIONAL DISCUSSIONS:

Bourgoin, Stéphane. *Roger Corman.* Paris: Edilig, 1983.
di Franco, J. Philip, ed. *The Movie World of Roger Corman.* New York: Chelsea House, 1979.
Lucanio, Patrick. *With Fire and Sword, Italian Spectacles on American Screens 1958–1968.* Metuchen, N.J.: Scarecrow, 1994.
McGee, Mark Thomas. *Fast and Furious, The Story of American International Pictures.* Jefferson, N.C.: McFarland, 1984.
_____. *Roger Corman, The Best of the Cheap Acts.* Jefferson, N.C.: McFarland, 1988.

Naha, Ed. *The Films of Roger Corman: Brillance on a Budget.* New York: ARCO, 1982.
Nash, Jay Robert, and Stanley Ralph Ross. *The Motion Picture Guide, S, 1927–1983.* Chicago: Cinebooks, 1987.
Smith, Gary A. *Epic Films.* Jefferson, N.C.: McFarland, 1991.

536. *The Vikings* (1958)

United States; dir. Richard Fleischer; United Artists.

CAST: Maxine Audley, Ernest Borgnine, Eric Connor, Tony Curtis, James Donald, Kirk Douglas, Alexander Knox, Janet Leigh, Dandy Nichols, Frank Thring, Eileen Way.

Ragnar the Viking rapes the English Queen Enid. Years later, his vassals unknowingly make their son Eric a slave. When he grows up, Eric becomes the bitter enemy of Ragnar's other son Einar, especially when the two half-brothers fall in love with the Welsh Princess Morgana. The English King Aella kills Ragnar and takes Morgana prisoner. Eric and Einar set aside their differences, revenge their father and free Morgana. In a final battle, Eric defeats Einar for the hand of Morgana.

Based on Edison Marshall's 1952 novel *The Viking,* this film never misses an opportunity to show the brutality of Viking life in the ninth century. Kirk Douglas, who invested $4 million to underwrite this film, is well-cast as the villain Einar. Tony Curtis is considerably less effective as the victorious Eric.

REVIEWS: *Cine jeunes* 19 (1959): 18–19. *Daily Cinema* 9 July 1958: 7. *Études cinématographiques* 3–4 (Summer 1960): 189–90. *Extension* 53 (August 1958): 57. *Film Daily* 20 May 1958: 6. *Filmfacts* 1 (23 July 1958): 101–02. *Films in Review* 9 (August–September 1958): 402–03. *Harrison's Reports* 24 May 1958: 84. *Hollywood Reporter* 20 May 1958: 3. *Kinematograph Weekly* 10 July 1958: 21. *Le Monde* 20 December 1958: 13. *Monthly Film Bulletin* 25 (August 1958): 100–01. *Motion Picture Herald* 24 May 1958: Product Digest Section 840. *New York Times* 12 June 1958: 35. *Times* [London] 9 July 1958: 6, 10. *Variety* 21 May 1958: 6.

ADDITIONAL DISCUSSIONS:

Elley, Derek. *The Epic Film.* London: Routledge & Kegan Paul, 1984.
Hunter, Allan. *Tony Curtis, The Man and His Movies.* New York: St. Martin's, 1985.
Lucanio, Patrick. *With Fire and Sword, Italian Spectacles on American Screens 1958–1968.* Metuchen, N.J.: Scarecrow, 1994.
Medved, Harry, and Michael Medved. *The Golden Turkey Awards.* New York: Perigee, 1980.
Nash, Jay Robert, and Stanley Ralph Ross. *The*

Tony Curtis (left) as Eric and Kirk Douglas as Einar, the Viking half-brothers, in Richard Fleischer's *The Vikings* (1958).

Motion Picture Guide, T–V, 1927–1983. Chicago: Cinebooks, 1987.

Parish, James Robert, and Don E. Stanke. *The Swashbucklers.* New Rochelle, N.Y.: Arlington House, 1976.

Smith, Gary A. *Epic Films.* Jefferson, N.C.: McFarland, 1991.

Thomas, Tony. *The Films of Kirk Douglas.* Secaucus, N.J.: Citadel, 1972.

The Vikings. London: United Artists, 1958. [Pressbook.]

The Vikings. New York: Progress Lithographers, 1958. [Souvenir book.]

537. *The Viking's Bride* (1907)

Great Britain; dir. Lewin Fitzhamon; Hepworth.

When his new bride is kidnapped by a neighboring tribe, a Viking chieftain's vassals help him rescue her.

REVIEW: *Moving Picture World* 18 January 1908: 45.

ADDITIONAL DISCUSSION:

Savada, Elias. *The American Film Institute Catalog of Motion Pictures Produced in the United States: Film Beginnings, 1893–1910.* Metuchen, N.J.: Scarecrow, 1995.

538. *The Viking's Daughter, the Story of the Ancient Norsemen* (1908)

United States; dir. J. Stuart Blackton; Vitagraph.

CAST: Florence Lawrence.

Viking raiders take a Saxon prince prisoner. To her father's dismay, the Viking leader's daughter falls in love with the prince. When the Saxon rescues her from a fire, her father relents, and the two are married.

REVIEW: *Moving Picture World* 1 August 1908: 92.

ADDITIONAL DISCUSSION:

Savada, Elias. *The American Film Institute Catalog of Motion Pictures Produced in the United States: Film Beginnings, 1893–1910.* Metuchen, N.J.: Scarecrow, 1995.

Birgitta Pettersson as Karin, the young girl who is raped and murdered, in Ingmar Bergman's *The Virgin Spring* (1959).

539. *The Virgin Spring* (1959)

Sweden; dir. Ingmar Bergman; Svensk Film-industri.

ALTERNATE TITLE: *Jungfrukällan.*

CAST: Gundrun Brost, Avel Duberg, Allan Edwall, Tor Isedal, Gunnel Lindblom, Oscar Ljung, Birgitta Pettersson, Ove Porath, Axel Slangus, Birgitta Valberg, Max von Sydow.

In thirteenth-century Sweden, two stepsisters, Karin and Ingeri, set out through the forest to offer prayers to the Virgin Mary at a nearby church. They become separated, and Karin meets three herdsmen who rape and kill her. When herdsmen arrive at the sisters' farmhouse, their crimes are revealed, and Karin's father kills them after a violent fight. He then goes with his family and servants to the spot where Karin was murdered, vows to build a church of stone on the spot, and finds a stream has sprung up where his daughter's body lay dead.

By any measure, *The Virgin Spring*, like Bergman's *The Seventh Seal*, is one of the finest films set in the Middle Ages. The script by Ulla Isaksson is based on a medieval Swedish ballad, "Töre of Vänge's Daughters."

REVIEWS: *Biografägaren* 4–5 (1959): 39; 2 (1960): 19. *Les Cahiers du cinéma* 116 (February 1961): 51–53. *Chaplin* 9 (March 1960): 62. *Cinema nuovo* 143 (January-February 1960): 45–47. *Cinématographie française* 28 May 1960: 7. *Commonweal* 73 (25 November 1960): 231; 73 (2 December 1960): 245. *Daily Cinema* 5 June 1961: 8. *Film Daily* 15 November 1960: 10. *Filmfacts* 3 (9 December 1960): 277–279. *Film français* 23 (December 1960): 17. *Filmkultura* 19 (July-August 1983): 37–41. *Filmnyheter* 9–10 (1959): 1–9; 12 (1959): 1–3, 16–18; 13 (1959): 1–3, 13; 14 (1959): 1–3, 17–21; 1 (1960): 1–7, 35; 2 (1960): 15, 32–33. *Film Quarterly* 13 (Summer 1960): 43–47. *Films and Filming* 7 (July 1961): 26–27. *Films in Review* 11 (November 1960): 556–57. *Harrison's Reports* 10 December 1960: 200. *Kinematograph Weekly* 8 June 1961: 34. *Kosmorama* 46 (October 1959): 14–17. *Monthly Film Bulletin* 28 (July 1961): 92. *New York Times* 15 November 1960: 46; 20 November 1960: 2.1, 26. *Scen och salong* 3 (1960): 22. *Sight and Sound* 29 (Spring 1960): 66–67. *Times* [London] 26 August 1960: 5; 2 June 1961: 22. *Variety* 24 February 1960: 6.

ADDITIONAL DISCUSSIONS:

Björkman, Stig, et al. *Bergman on Bergman.* Trans.

Paul Briten Austin. London: Secker & Warburg, 1973.

Cowie, Peter. *Ingmar Bergman*. Loughton, Essex: Motion Monographs, 1961.

_____. *Ingmar Bergman, A Critical Biography*. London: Secker & Warburg, 1982.

_____. *Max von Sydow from* The Seventh Seal *to* Pelle the Conqueror. Stockholm: Swedish Film Institute, 1989.

_____. "Resolving the Conflict." *Motion* 1 (Summer 1961): 18–20.

_____. *World Cinema 2: Sweden*. New York: A.S. Barnes, 1970.

Donner, Jörn. *The Films of Ingmar Bergman*. Trans. Holger Lundbergh. New York: Dover, 1972.

Duprey, Richard A. "Bergman and Fellini, Explorers of the Modern Spirit." *Catholic World* 194 (October 1961): 13–20.

Durand, A. "*The Virgin Spring*." *Homiletic and Pastoral Review* 64 (June 1964): 321–27.

Dymling, Carl A., ed. *The Virgin Spring*. Stockholm: Svensk Filmindustri, 1961.

Feldman, Ellen. "Allegorical Structure in *The Virgin Spring*." *Field of Vision* 9–10 (Winter-Spring 1980): 18–21.

Gado, Frank. *The Passion of Ingmar Bergman*. Durham, N.C.: Duke University Press, 1986.

Holland, Norman A. "Bergman Springs Again." *Hudson Review* 14 (Spring 1961): 104–11.

Isaksson, Ulla. "Source of a Spiritual Spring." *New York Times* 13 November 1960: 2. 9.

_____. *The Virgin Spring*. Trans. Lars Malmström and David Kushmer. New York: Ballantine, 1960.

Lefevre, Raymond. *Ingmar Bergman*. Paris: Edilig, 1983.

Long, Robert Emmet. *Ingmar Bergman, Film and Stage*. New York: Harry N. Abrams, 1994.

Madden, David. "*The Virgin Spring*: Anatomy of a Mythic Image." *Film Heritage* 2 (Winter 1966-1967): 2–20.

Marty, Joseph. *Ingmar Bergman, une poétique du désir*. Paris: Les Éditions du Cerf, 1991.

McIlroy, Brian. *World Cinema 2: Sweden*. London: Flick Books, 1986.

Mishler, William. "*The Virgin Spring* and *The Seventh Seal*: A Girardian Reading." *Comparative Drama* 30 (Spring 1996): 106–34.

Napolitano, Antonio. "Dal settimo sigillo alle soglie della vita." *Cinema nuovo* 151 (May-June 1961): 210–18.

Nash, Jay Robert, and Stanley Ralph Ross. *The Motion Picture Guide, T–V, 1927–1983*. Chicago: Cinebooks, 1987.

Pechter, William S. "*The Virgin Spring*—The Ballad and the Source." *Kenyon Review* 23 (Spring 1961): 332–35. [Rpt. in Julius Bellone, ed. *Renaissance of the Film*. New York: Collier, 1970.]

Siclier, Jacques. *Ingmar Bergman*. Rev. ed. Paris: Classiques du cinéma, 1966.

Steene, Birgitta. *Ingmar Bergman*. New York: Twayne, 1968.

_____. *Ingmar Bergman, A Guide to References and Resources*. Boston: G.K. Hall, 1987.

Svensk Filmografi: 6, 1960–1969. Stockholm: Svenska Filminstitutet, 1977.

Taylor, John Russell. *Cinema Eye, Cinema Camera*. New York: Hill and Wang, 1964.

Wood, Robin. *Ingmar Bergman*. London: Studio Vista, 1969.

_____. "A Toad in the Bread." *Definition* 3 (1961): 26–31.

Young, Vernon. *Cinema Borealis*. New York: David Lewis, 1971.

540. *The Vision Beautiful* (1912)

United States; dir. Otis R. Thayer; Selig Polyscope.

CAST: Herbert Rawlinson, Tom Santschi.

A young monk struggles to meet the demands of the religious life. At heart, he is an artist and dreamer, and he has little inclination to carry out what he considers the menial tasks associated with his vocation. In a vision, Christ appears to him, reminding him that whatever he does for the least of his brethren he does for his savior. The young monk cheerfully and ardently embraces the rigors of the religious life.

The source for this film is Henry Wadsworth Longfellow's poem "The Legend Beautiful," a part of the poet's *Tales of a Wayside Inn* (collected 1886).

REVIEWS: *Moving Picture World* 15 June 1912: 1058; 29 June 1912: 1227.

ADDITIONAL DISCUSSIONS:

Butler, Ivan. *Religion in the Cinema*. New York: A.S. Barnes, 1969.

Lahue, Kalton C., ed. *Motion Picture Pioneer: The Selig Polyscope Company*. New York: A.S. Barnes, 1973.

Lauritzen, Einar, and Gunnar Lunquist. *American Film Index 1908–1915*. Stockholm: Akademi Bokhandeln, 1976.

Martinelli, Vittorio. "Filmographie de Francesco d'Assisi." *Les Cahiers de la cinémathèque* 42–43 (Summer 1985): 36.

541. *Les Visiteurs* (1992)

France; dir. Jean-Marie Poiré; Gaumont Buena Vista.

ALTERNATE TITLE: *Les Explorateurs Louis VI le Gros*.

CAST: Christian Clavier, Valerie Lemercier, Jean Reno, Gerard Sety.

A twelfth-century knight and his squire, accidentally transported forward in time to contemporary France, wreak havoc for their modern descendants as they try to find a medieval magician's manuscript that contains the spell that will return them to the year 1122. The knight returns and is able to undo a wrong he committed in his own time, but his ingenious squire remains behind, sending his foppish nouveau riche twentieth-century descendant back to the Middle Ages in his place.

The highest-grossing domestic film in France when it was released, *Les Visiteurs* reverses the pattern of most time travel medieval films in sending medieval people forward to modern times rather than modern people back to medieval times. The dialogue leans heavily on puns — in both Old and Modern French — that often get lost in translation.

REVIEWS: *Actualité* 18 (15 April 1993): 79. *Les Cahiers du cinéma* 465 (March 1993): 82–83. *Empire* 57 (March 1994): 34. *EPD Film* 10 (June 1993): 43. *Entertainment Weekly* 337 (26 July 1996): 35; 378 (9 May 1997): 91. *Film français* 5 June 1992: 19; 1 January 1993: 13; 29 January 1993: 7; 25 February 1993: 8; 5 March 1993: 6; 10 December 1993: 8; 17 December 1993: 8; 28 January 1994: 12; 4 March 1994: 6. *Film Journal International* 99 (July 1996): 65–66. *Film Review* [London] March 1994: 19. *Grand angle* 157 (February 1993): n.p.; 166 (December 1993): n.p. *Los Angeles Times* 12 July 1996: Calendar 12. *Le Monde* 30 January 1993: 15. *New York Times* 12 July 1996: C10. *Positif* 385 (March 1993): 50. *Première* 200 (November 1993): 82. *Séquences* 164 (May 1993): 65. *Sight and Sound* NS 4 (February 1994): 61–62; NS 4 (September 1994): 63. *Starburst* 186 (February 1994): 46–47. *Studio* [Paris] 65 (September 1992): 34–35; 70 (February 1993): 10. *Sunday Times* [London] 6 February 1994: 9. 54. *Télérama* 2248 (10 February 1993): 32–33; 2331 (14 September 1994): 138. *Times* [London] 3 February 1994: 33. *Variety* 8 March 1993: 62. *24 Images* 66 (April-May 1993): 77.

ADDITIONAL DISCUSSIONS:
Cameron-Wilson, James, and F. Maurice Speed. *Film Review 1994–1995*. London: Virgin Books, 1994.

Grant, Edmond, ed. *The Motion Picture Guide: 1997 Annual (The Films of 1996)*. New York: CineBooks, 1997.

Nevers, Camille, and Frédéric Strauss. "Entretien avec Jean-Marie Poiré et Christian Clavier." *Les Cahiers du cinéma* 465 (March 1993): 84–89.

542. *Les Visiteurs du soir* (1942)

France; dir. Marcel Carné; André Paulvé.
ALTERNATE TITLE: *The Devil's Envoys*.
CAST: Arletty, Jules Berry, Alain Cuny, Marie Déa, Marcel Herrand, Fernand Ledoux.

The Devil sends two envoys, Gilles and Dominique, condemned to hell for being selfish lovers on earth, to interfere with the betrothal of a count and Lady Anne. The two infernal envoys destroy the betrothal since the count and Lady Anne are not really in love, but Gilles finds true love in his seduction of Lady Anne and Dominique seduces Lady Anne's pious father. The Devil himself then arrives, and while Lady Anne's father willingly follows Dominique back into hell, Gilles and Anne are unswerving in their love for each other. In anger, the Devil turns them both to stone, though he cannot stop their hearts from beating.

In discussing the screenplay he wrote for this film, Jacques Prévert said that he intended the Devil to represent Hitler and that the medieval setting of the story was necessitated by the Nazi censors. The medieval settings are especially convincing and lavish.

REVIEWS: *Film Daily* 29 August 1947: 7. *Hollywood Reporter* 29 August 1947: 3. *Image et son* 55 (July 1952): 4–6. *Kinematograph Weekly* 15 August 1946: 18. *Monthly Film Bulletin* 13 (30 September 1946): 126. *New York Times* 30 August 1947: 8; 31 August 1947: 2. 4. *Sight and Sound* 15 (Spring 1946): 4–6; 15 (Autumn 1946): 96–98. *Times* [London] 9 August 1946: 8. *To-day's Cinema* 9 August 1946: 17. *Variety* 3 September 1947: 16.

ADDITIONAL DISCUSSIONS:
Bessy, Maurice, and Raymond Chirat. *Histoire du cinéma français: Encyclopédie des films 1940–1950*. Paris: Pygmalion, 1986.

Bill, Pierre. *L'Âge classique du cinéma français*. Paris: Flammarion, 1995.

Chevalier, Jacques, ed. *Regards neufs sur la cinéma*. Paris: Peuple et culture, 1953.

Chirat, Raymond. *Catalogue des films français de long métrage. Films de fiction 1940–1950*. Luxembourg: La Cinémathèque municipale de Luxembourg, 1981.

Les Éternels du cinéma francais (1930–1960). Paris: La Fondation Gan pour le cinéma, 1988.

Garbicz, Adam, and Jacek Klinowski. *Cinema, The Magic Vehicle*. Metuchen, N.J.: Scarecrow, 1975.

Nash, Jay Robert, and Stanley Ralph Ross. *The Motion Picture Guide, C–D, 1927–1983*. Chicago: Cinebooks, 1985.

Noguera, Rui, ed. *Les Visiteurs du soir*. Paris: Balland, 1974. [Screenplay.]

Perez, Michel. *Les Films de Carné*. Paris: Ramsay, 1986.

Prévert, Jacques, and Pierre LaRoche, eds. *Les Visiteurs du soir*. Paris: La Nouvelle édition, 1947. [Screenplay and critical analyses.]

Queval, Jean. *Marcel Carné*. Paris: Les Éditions du Cerf, 1952.

Stanbrook, Alan. "The Carné Bubble." *Film* [Federation of Film Societies of Great Britain] 22 (November-December 1959): 12–15.

Alain Cuny as Gilles, the devil's henchman, and Marie Déacas Lady Anne in Michel Carné's *Les Visiteurs du soir* (1942). (Still courtesy of the British Film Institute.)

Thomas, Nicholas, ed. *International Dictionary of Films and Filmmakers–Vol. 2: Directors.* 2nd ed. Chicago: St. James, 1991.

"*Les Visiteurs du soir.*" *Avant-scène du cinéma* 12 (February 1962): 1–55. [Screenplay.]

_____. *Analyses de films.* Paris: Institut des hautes études cinématographiques, 1948. (Rpt. in *Image et son* 50 [February 1952]: [insert between 10 and 11].)

The Visitors (1992) see *Les Visiteurs* (1992)

543. *Vsadnik na zolotam krone* (1982)

Soviet Union; dir. Vasily Zhuravlev; Mosfilm.

ALTERNATE TITLE: *The Man on the Golden Horse.*

CAST: Nina Agapova, Fidan Gafarov, Pyotr Glebov, Irina Malysheva, Pavel Vinnik.

In medieval Bashkiria, after years of tribal feuding, a marriage makes allies of former enemies, but not before warriors from the Evil Kingdom seek to upset the nuptials.

REVIEW: *Soviet Film* 3 (1982): 8–9.

ADDITIONAL DISCUSSION:

Tous les films 1982. Paris: Éditions Chrétien-Médias, 1983.

544. *A Walk with Love and Death* (1969)

United States; dir. John Huston; 20th Century–Fox.

CAST: Anthony Corlan, Assaf Dayan, Guy Deghy, John Hallam, Michael Gough, Anjelica Huston, Robert Lang, Eileen Murphy, Anthony Nicholls, Joseph O'Connor.

In France during the Hundred Years War, Heron, a student expelled from his university, travels to another school across a war-scarred countryside. Escaping a band of mercenaries, he finds refuge in the castle of a count and falls in love with his host's daughter, Claudia. A peasant uprising only further contributes to the civil chaos in the region; fleeing the count's castle, Claudia and Heron are alternately chased by peasants and nobles. Finally finding a moment of peace, they courageously face impending death.

As visually arresting as it is convoluted in its plot, this film, a plea against war and killing in any era, is more interested in examining the impossibility of love during a period of turbulence than it is in medieval history. The film's source, Hans Koningsberger's 1961 novel *A Walk with Love and Death*, was about the 1358 revolt of French peasants; critics saw parallels in the film to the conflict in Vietnam, the riots among French students and the civil rights movement in the United States. The film marked the screen debut of Anjelica Huston.

REVIEWS: *Les Cahiers du cinéma* 229 (May-June 1971): 59–60. *Cinema* 4 (Fall 1968): 24. *Cinéma* 156 (May 1971): 116–19. *Film Heritage* 6 (Winter 1970-71): 14–18 *Film Society Review* 6 (October 1970): 44–46. *Films and Filming* 9 (June 1963): 22–23. *Films in Review* 20 (October 1969): 511. *Hollywood Reporter* 8 September 1969: 3. *Kinematograph Weekly* 9 December 1965: 9. *Monthly Film Bulletin* 44 (February 1977): 33–34. *Motion Picture Herald* 10 September 1969: Product Digest Section 269. *New York Times* 6 October 1969: 56. *Positif* 118 (Summer 1970): 43–46. *Variety* 10 September 1969: 48.

ADDITIONAL DISCUSSIONS:

Hammen, Scott. *John Huston.* Boston: Twayne, 1985.

Kaminsky, Stuart. *John Huston, Maker of Magic.* London: Angus & Robertson, 1978.

Koningsberger, Hans. "From Book to Film — via John Huston." *Film Quarterly* 22 (Spring 1969): 2–4.

McCarty, John. *The Films of John Huston.* Secaucus, N.J.: Citadel, 1987.

Nash, Jay Robert, and Stanley Ralph Ross. *The Motion Picture Guide, W–Z, 1927–1983.* Chicago: Cinebooks, 1987.

Pratley, Gerald. *The Cinema of John Huston.* New York: A.S. Barnes, 1977.

Tozzi, Romano. *John Huston.* New York: Falcon, 1971.

545. *Wanda Soldanieri* (1910)

Italy; dir. Mario Caserini; Cines.

ALTERNATE TITLE: *Vanda Soldanieri.*

Wanda, daughter of the leader of the Guelf party, marries Ginni Soldanieri, a leader of the rival Ghibellines. Her parents try to convince her to leave her husband and have him murdered when she will not comply with their wishes. Wanda in turns leads an uprising against her parents, which fails. In despair, she commits suicide.

REVIEW: *Bioscope* 3 February 1910: 54.

546. *The Wanderer* (1991)

Great Britain; dir. Andrew Crabb and David Lewis; Crabb and Lewis Production Company.

CAST: Phil Daniels, Michael Gough, James Oliver, Imogen Stubbs, Michael York.

An Anglo-Saxon warrior cut off from his lord treads the barren English countryside. After World War I, a veteran finds himself thrown out of a mental institution. In 1990, a gay man is rejected by his lover.

Taking its cue from the anonymous Anglo-Saxon poem of the same title, this film mixes Old and Modern English dialogue to tell three parallel stories of loneliness and rejection.

Anjelica Huston as Claudia and Assaf Dayan as Heron in John Huston's *A Walk with Love and Death* (1969).

REVIEW: *Time Out* [London] 2 October 1991: 64.

ADDITIONAL DISCUSSION:
[Catalog of the] *Eighteenth San Francisco International Lesbian and Gay Festival.* San Francisco:

Frameline, 1994.

547. *The War Lord* (1965)
United States; dir. Franklin J. Schaffner; Universal Pictures.

Charlton Heston as Chrysagon and Rosemary Forsyth as Bronwyn in Franklin J. Schaffner's *The War Lord* (1965).

Niall MacGinnis, Guy Stockwell, Henry Wilcoxon.

In the eleventh century, Chrysagon, the Duke of Normandy, overruns a Frisian village whose inhabitants he is intent on converting from Druidism to Christianity. The Duke soon falls in love with a peasant girl betrothed to a Frisian villager named Marc. Claiming the ancient Druidic *jus primae noctis* (right of first night), Chrysagon beds the girl on her wedding night, but in the morning the two cannot bear to part from each other. As a result, civil strife breaks out. Chrysagon is able to put down the revolt, but he is in the end killed by Marc, the jilted bridegroom.

From Leslie Stevens's 1956 play *The Lovers,* this film is notable for its authentic-looking recreation of settings and detailed elaborate costumes.

REVIEWS: *Les Cahiers du cinéma in English* 4 (1966): 62. *Cinema* 3 (December 1965) 3 December: 49. *Cinemeditor* 15 (Fall 1965): 6. *Daily Cinema* 3 December 1965: 14. *Film Daily* 5 October 1965: 4. *Film Digest* 9 (March 1966): 17–18. *Film Quarterly* 19 (Spring 1966): 54. *Films and Filming* 12 (February 1966): 6. *Hollywood Reporter* 4 October 1965: 3. *Kinematograph Weekly* 9 December 1965: 9. *Monthly Film Bulletin* 33 (January 1966): 5. *Motion Picture Herald* 13 October 1965: Product Digest Section 386. *New York Times* 18 November 1965: 55. *Positif* 75 (May 1966): 136–38. *Sight and Sound* 35 (Spring 1966): 73–75. *Times* [London] 16 December 1965: 4. *Variety* 6 October 1965: 6.

ADDITIONAL DISCUSSIONS:

Erwin, Kim. *Franklin J. Schaffner.* Metuchen, N.J.: Scarecrow, 1985.

Lucanio, Patrick. *With Fire and Sword, Italian Spectacles on American Screens 1958–1968.* Metuchen, N.J.: Scarecrow, 1994.

Nash, Jay Robert, and Stanley Ralph Ross. *The Motion Picture Guide, W–Z, 1927–1984.* Chicago: Cinebooks, 1987.

Rovin, Jeff. *The Films of Charlton Heston.* Secaucus, N.J.: Citadel, 1977.

Warrior of Russia (1938) see *Alexander Nevsky* (1938)

548. The Warriors (1955)

Great Britain; dir. Henry Levin; Allied Artists.

ALTERNATE TITLE: *The Dark Avenger.*

CAST: Joanne Dru, Peter Finch, Errol Flynn.

Victorious in the Hundred Years War, the English take the French king prisoner. The English king, Edward I, returns to England

leaving his son Prince Edward in France to rule over Aquitaine, where Count Deville refuses to swear allegiance to the English throne. What is left of the French army rallies around Deville and the Marshal of France, Du Guesclin. When Prince Edward's beloved Lady Joan is kidnapped by the French, the Prince disguises himself as the Black Knight, rescues her, kills Deville, defeats Du Guesclin and restores peace between England and France.

This lavishly costumed swashbuckler, which borrowed its sets from *Ivanhoe* (1952), plays fast and loose with history while allowing Flynn one last rousing bit of derring-do.

REVIEWS: *Film Daily* 15 September 1955: 6. *Kinematograph Weekly* 21 April 1955: 25. *Monthly Film Bulletin* 22 (June 1955): 89–90. *Motion Picture Herald* 17 September 1955: Product Digest Section 594. *New York Times* 10 September 1955: 11. *To-day's Cinema* 18 April 1955: 8. *Variety* 11 May 1955: 8.

ADDITIONAL DISCUSSIONS:

Morris, George. *Errol Flynn.* New York: Pyramid, 1975.

Nash, Jay Robert, and Stanley Ralph Ross. *The Motion Picture Guide, W–Z, 1927–1984.* Chicago: Cinebooks, 1987.

Parish, James Robert, et al. *Errol Flynn.* New York: Cinefax, 1969.

Thomas, Tony, et al. *The Films of Errol Flynn.* Secaucus, N.J.: Citadel, 1969.

Valenti, Peter. *Errol Flynn, A Bio-Bibliography.* Westport, Conn.: Greenwood, 1984.

When Almanzor Lost His Drum (1983) see *Cuando Almanzor tocó el tambor* (1983)

549. When Knights Were Bold (1929)

Great Britain; dir. Tim Whelan; British and Dominions Production Company.

CAST: Martin Adeson, Wellington Briggs, Eli Freewin, Hal Gordon, Lena Halliday, Nelson Keys, Edith Kingdon, Miriam Seegar, Eric Bransby Williams.

A nineteenth-century British baronet finds himself transported back to the Middle Ages, where he learns a lesson about the duties of the nobility.

The screenplay is adapted from Marjorie Benton Cooke's 1906 novel of the same title.

REVIEWS: *Bioscope* 6 February 1929: 37–38. *Close Up* 5 (July 1929): 48–49.

550. When the Raven Flies (1984)

Iceland; dir. Hrafn Gunnlaugsson; F.I.L.M.

Joanne Dru as Lady Joan and Errol Flynn as Prince Edward in Henry Levin's *The Warriors* (1955).

ALTERNATE TITLES: *Flight of the Raven, Hrafninn Flygur, Korpen Flyger, The Raven Flies* and *Revenge of the Barbarians.*

CAST: Edda Björgvinsdóttir, Sveinn Eidsson, Jacob Thor Einarsson, Egill Ólafsson, Flosi Ólafsson, Helgi Skúlason.

In the tenth century, an Irish boy, Gest, wit-

nesses the murder of his father by marauding Vikings who also kidnap his sister. Fully grown, Gest tracks down the Viking brothers Thor and Erik, who squabble between themselves. Once Thor kills Erik, Gest kills Thor and rescues his sister.

The film's most obvious debt is to the Ice-

Embla (Maria Bonnevie) and Askur (Gottskálk Sigurdarson), the young lovers forced to separate, in a scene from Hrafn Gunnlaugsson's *The White Viking* (1991). (Still courtesy of Hrafn Gunnlaugsson and Filmeffekt A/S.)

landic saga tradition; its closest cinematic inspirations are, however, the spaghetti Westerns of Sergio Leone and Clint Eastwood.

REVIEWS: *Film og kino* 6 (1985): 217–18. *Hollywood Reporter* 27 March 1985: 11. *Iceland Review* 22.2 (1984): 2–3; 24.2 (1986): 71–72. *Los Angeles Times* 21 March 1985: Calendar 2; 27 March 1985: Calendar 7. *New York Times* 25 April 1985: C2. *Scandinavian Film News* 3 (May 1983): 3; 4 (April 1989): 6. *Variety* 21 March 1984: 17–18.

ADDITIONAL DISCUSSIONS:
Cowie, Peter, ed. *Le Cinéma des pays nordiques.* Paris: Centre Georges Pompidou, 1990.
Fridgeirsson, Asgeir. "The Bishop and the Actor." *Iceland Review* 29.3 (1991): 37–40.
Gunnlaugsson, Hrafn. "A Film Director's Conversion." *Cinema Canada* 113 (December 1984): 13–14.
Icelandic Films 1979–1988. Reykjavik: Icelandic Film Fund, 1988.
Jónsdóttir, Solveig K. "Once Upon a Time in the North." *Iceland Review* 25.4 (1987): 4–11.
Nash, Jay Robert, and Stanley Ralph Ross. *The Motion Picture Guide, 1986 Annual (The Films of 1985).* Chicago: Cinebooks, 1987.

Swedish Film Institute Film Catalogue. Stockholm: Swedish Film Institute, 1989.

551. *The White Viking* (1991)

Iceland; dir. Hrafn Gunnlaugsson; Filmeffekt A/S.

ALTERNATE TITLE: *Den Hvite Viking.*

CAST: Maria Bonnevie, Tomas Norström, Egill Ólafsson, Helgi Skúlason, Gottskálk Sigurdarson.

Two young lovers, Askur and Embla, are separated at their wedding feast by King Olaf of Norway, who is intent upon forcing his pagan Icelandic subjects to embrace Christianity. To save his bride-to-be, whom Olaf houses in a convent where the king falls in love with her, Askur journeys to Iceland as a Christian missionary. Askur succeeds in the conversion and in rescuing Embla.

Two versions of *The White Viking* were made, a seven-hour television series and this feature film.

REVIEWS: *Iceland Review* 28.4 (1990): 52. *Variety* 16 March 1992: 61.

ADDITIONAL DISCUSSIONS:

Cowie, Peter, ed. *Variety International Film Guide 1992.* Hollywood, Calif.: Samuel French, 1991.

Fridgeirsson, Asgeir. "The Bishop and the Actor." *Iceland Review* 29.3 (1991): 37–40.

Norwegian Films 1992. Oslo: Norwegian Film Institute, 1992.

Vikingson, Vidar. "New Venture into Viking Territory." *Iceland Review* 29.4 (1991): 22–28.

The White Viking. Oslo: Filmeffekt, 1991. [Souvenir booklet.]

Whom the Gods Wish to Destroy

(1966) see *Die Nibelungen* (1966)

Wilhelm Tell (1912) see *Guillaume Tell* (1912)

552. Wilhelm Tell (1921)

Switzerland; dir. Friedrich Genhardt; Tell-spielgesellschaft.

CAST: Otto Gebühr, Hans Marr, Erna Morena, Agnes Straub, Conrad Veidt, Eduard von Winterstein.

The theatrical troupe of Altdorfer Tell-Spiele restages Friedrich Schiller's play for the camera.

DISCUSSION:

Dumont, Hervé. *Histoire du cinéma suisse.* Lausanne: Cinémathèque suisse, 1987.

553. Wilhelm Tell (1933)

Germany; dir. Heinz Paul; Terra-Film.

ALTERNATE TITLES: *Guillaume Tell* and *The Legend of William Tell.*

CAST: Dennis Aubrey, Charles Cullum, Hans Marr, Werner Schott, Emmy Sonnemann, Conrad Veidt, Edmond Willard, Detief Willecke.

Suffering continuing indignities at the hands of their Austrian oppressors, Swiss peasants under the leadership of Tell rise up and reclaim their country.

Tedious acting combines with handsome photography in this version of the Tell story that downplays the famous incident of Tell's shooting an arrow from his son's head.

REVIEWS: *L'Echo de Paris* 10 May 1935: 4. *Motion Picture Herald* 13 July 1935: 65. *L'Œuvre* [Paris] 3 May 1935: 6. *New York Times* 2 October 1935: 27. *Variety* 2 October 1935: 16.

ADDITIONAL DISCUSSIONS:

Dumont, Hervé. *Histoire du cinéma suisse.* Lausanne: Cinémathèque suisse, 1987.

Klaus, Ulrich J. *Deutsche Ton Filme Jahrgang 1934–1935.* Berlin: Ulrich J. Klaus Verlag, 1993.

Wilhelm Tell. Berlin: Terra-Film, 1933. [Screenplay.]

Wolf, Friedrich. "Hitler's Films." *International Literature* 1 (April 1931): 135–38.

554. Wilhelm Tell (1956)

Austria; dir. Josef Gielen; Mundus-Thalia.

CAST: Erich Auer, Ewald Balser, Paul Hartmann, Judith Holzmeister, Albin Skoda.

The Burgtheater performs Schiller's play.

REVIEWS: *Filmblätter* 27 (6 July 1956): 838. *Studio* [Munich] 6 (November 1959): 11–12.

555. Wilhelm Tell—Burgen in Flammen (1960)

Switzerland; dir. Michel Dickoff; Urs-Film.

ALTERNATE TITLE: *Guillaume Tell.*

CAST: Maria Becker, Leopold Biberti, Birke Bruck, Robert Freitag, Trudy Moser, Wolfgang Rottsieper, Heinz Woester.

Dickoff covers familiar territory rather tepidly here, combining scenes from Schiller's drama with others inspired by period chronicles and records.

REVIEWS: *Filmwoche* 16 (6 May 1961): 7. *Kino-Information* 2 (15 May 1975): 6. *Variety* 11 January 1961: 6.

ADDITIONAL DISCUSSION:

Dumont, Hervé. *Histoire du cinéma suisse.* Lausanne: Cinémathèque suisse, 1987.

William Tell (1903) see *Guillaume Tell* (1903)

William Tell (1911) see *Guillaume Tell* (1911)

William Tell (1912) see *Guillaume Tell* (1912)

William Tell (1913) see *Guillaume Tell* (1913)

William Tell (1914) see *Guillaume Tell* (1914)

556. William Tell (1914)

Great Britain; Supreme Company Ltd.

In 1298, Albert of Austria orders the Swiss cantons to pay homage to him. When they refuse, he installs the traitorous Gessler as his chancellor. Gessler's soldiers occupy the cantons and place an Austrian hat atop a pole in each village, ordering the Swiss to bow before the hat whenever they pass by. William Tell, a simple mountaineer unaware of Gessler's edict, fails to bow before the hat and is sentenced to shoot an apple off his son's head with an arrow. As Gessler terrorizes the countryside, Tell leads a rebellion against him. The chancellor is killed and, in an oath of independence, the Swiss declare themselves free of Austrian rule.

William Tell's story is here retold using scenes from Schiller's famous play and passages from the medieval texts that chronicle Tell's exploits.

REVIEWS: *Bioscope* 27 August 1914: 845. *Kinematograph Monthly Film Record* 29 (September 1914) 48–50.

William Tell (1925) see *Les Origines de la Confédération* (1925)

William Tell (1949) see *Guglielmo Tell* (1949)

557. *William Tell* (1954)

United States; dir. Jack Cardiff; United Artists.

CAST: Bruce Cabot, Dave Crowly, Errol Flynn, Aldo Fabrizi, Franco Interlenghi, Antonella Lualdi, Alberto Rabagliati, Vira Silenti.

Flynn, using Schiller's play as an outline, wrote the script for this uncompleted project, which he personally helped to finance.

DISCUSSIONS:
Archer, Steve. "An Untold Tale of William Tell." *Filmfax* 38 (April-May 1993): 50–59, 98.
Morris, George. *Errol Flynn.* New York: Pyramid, 1975.
Thomas, Tony, et al. *The Films of Errol Flynn.* Secaucus, N.J.: Citadel, 1969.
Valenti, Peter. *Errol Flynn, A Bio-Bibliography.* Westport, Conn.: Greenwood, 1984.

William Tell—The Birth of Switzerland (1925) see *Les Origines de la confédération* (1925)

558. *William Tell: The Liberator of Switzerland* (1909)

Denmark; Nordisk Films.

This film tells the standard tale of Tell and Gessler. Critics commented favorably on its scenic and costume effects.

REVIEWS: *Moving Picture World* 3 April 1909: 402; 17 April 1909: 483. *New York Clipper* 17 April 1909: 258. *New York Dramatic Mirror* 10 April 1909: 15.

ADDITIONAL DISCUSSION:
Savada, Elias. *The American Film Institute Catalog of Motion Pictures Produced in the United States: Film Beginnings, 1893–1910.* Metuchen, N.J.: Scarecrow, 1995.

Wind Is My Lover (1950) see *The Mask and the Sword* (1950)

The Witch (1906) see *La Fée carabosse* (1906)

Witchcraft Through the Ages (1921) see *Häxan* (1921)

Without Fear or Blame (1988) see *Sans peur et sans reproche* (1988)

559. *Wolfshead, the Legend of Robin Hood* (1969)

Great Britain; dir. John Hough; London Weekend Productions.

CAST: Kathleen Byron, Kenneth Gilbert, Ciaran Madden, Dan Meaden, David Warbeck.

Robert Locksley, a Saxon yeoman, offends Sir Roger of Doncaster and his brother Geoffrey, both powerful Normans, when he hides a runaway serf. The Normans plot against Robin, accuse him of killing a royal stag, and condemn him as a "Wolfshead" (outlaw). Deprived of his lands, Robert flees to the forest and forms an outlaw troop. Robert kills Geoffrey in an archery contest and flees again to the forest, where others flock to his side to continue the fight against Norman oppression.

This film version of the familiar legend downplays the swashbuckling scenes common in other Robin Hood films, concentrating instead on providing a detailed portrait of life in Plantagenet England.

REVIEWS: *CinemaTV Today* 28 April 1973: 15. *Monthly Film Bulletin* 40 (June 1973): 136.

ADDITIONAL DISCUSSIONS:
Knight, Stephen. *Robin Hood, A Complete Study of the English Outlaw.* Oxford: Blackwell, 1994.
Turner, David. *Robin of the Movies.* Kingswinford, Eng.: Yeoman Publishing, 1989.

The Wonderful Adventures of Guerrin Mechimo (1951) see *Le Merav-*

(From left to right) Lyn Harding, Theresa Maxwell Conover, and Marion Davies in a scene from Robert G. Vignola's *Yolanda* (1924). (Still courtesy of the British Film Institute.)

igliose avventure di Guerrin Meschimo (1951)

Wood of Love (1981) see *Bosco d'amore* (1981)

560. *Yolanda* (1924)

United States; dir. Robert G. Vignola; Metro-Goldwyn.

CAST: Holbrook Blinn, Theresa Maxwell Conover, Marion Davies, Leon Errol, Robert Graves, Lyn Harding.

At the end of the fifteenth century, Princess Mary of Burgundy travels disguised as a commoner named Yolanda and falls in love with Prince Maximillian of Styria, himself disguised as a simple knight. Maximillian is later imprisoned but saved from execution by Yolanda.

When war with France threatens, the Duke of Burgundy betroths his daughter to the dimwitted Dauphin, but Maximillian rescues her, leads the Burgundians to victory and marries his beloved.

Adapted from Charles Major's 1905 novel *Yolanda*, this film provided Marion Davies with a vehicle for continuing to lay claim to the title of "The Queen of the Screen."

REVIEWS: *Harrison's Reports* 1 March 1924: 34. *Kinematograph Weekly* 10 April 1924: 29. *New York Times* 20 February 1924: 23. *Variety* 21 February 1924: 18.

ADDITIONAL DISCUSSIONS:

Connelly, Robert. *The Motion Picture Guide, Silent Film, 1910–1936.* Chicago: Cinebooks, 1986.

Munden, Kenneth W., ed. *The American Film Institute Catalog of Motion Pictures Produced in the United States, Feature Films 1921–1930.* New York: Bowker, 1971.

Yolande (1963) see *Iolanthe* (1963)

Yolanta (1963) see *Iolanthe* (1963)

561. *A Young Connecticut Yankee in King Arthur's Court* (1995)

Canada; dir. R.L. Thomas; Filmline International.

CAST: Paul Hopkins, Jack Langedijk, Nick Mancuso, Philippe Ross, Theresa Russell, Polly Shannon, Michael York.

Nearly electrocuted by a short in his guitar amplifier, shy suburban teenager Hank awakens stunned to find himself in King Arthur's Court. Dubbed Sir Dude, Hank retraces (with some 1990s updates) the misadventures of Twain's Connecticut Yankee, managing to save Camelot from the wiles of Morgan Le Faye.

The worst of three very bad adaptations of Twain's novel that turn the Yankee into a teenager (the other two are 1995's *A Kid in King Arthur's Court* and 1989's *A Connecticut Yankee in King Arthur's Court*), this telefilm, which first aired on Canada's The Movie Network on June 1, 1995, was rightly dismissed by Greg Quill from the *Toronto Star* as "an embarrassment to Canadian filmmaking, a fiasco from start to finish."

REVIEWS: *Arthuriana* 6 (Summer 1996): 115–18. *Globe and Mail* 1 June 1995: C1.

ADDITIONAL DISCUSSION:
Quill, Greg. "CBC Critics Best Heed a Warning from U.S." *Toronto Star* 1 June 1995: B8.

562. *Young Lochinvar* (1923)

Great Britain; dir. Will Kelino; Stoll Picture Productions.

CAST: Charles Barratt, Dorothy Harris, Gladys Jennings, Owen Nares, Nelson Ramsay, Dick Webb, Cecil Morton York.

In fifteenth-century Scotland, Lochinvar, betrothed from birth to Cecilia, daughter of Johnstone of Lockwood, falls in love with Helen, daughter of Graeme of Netherby, herself betrothed to Musgrave. Lochinvar and Musgrave quarrel, and the latter is killed by Cecilia's brother Alick. When Helen finds herself in distress, Lochinvar rescues her and carries her off to marry him.

From J.E. Muddock's 1896 novel *Young Lochinvar, A Tale of the Border Country*, itself based on Sir Walter Scott's poem "Lochinvar" (first published in 1808 as part of *Marmion*), this film

is notable for its use of the Scottish countryside to provide spectacular location shots.

REVIEWS: *Bioscope* 11 October 1923: 62. *Stoll Herald* 6 (4 February 1924): 4–5.

ADDITIONAL DISCUSSIONS:
Connelly, Robert. *The Motion Picture Guide, Silent Film, 1910–1936*. Chicago: Cinebooks, 1986.
Warren, Patricia. *The British Film Collection 1896–1984*. London: Elm Tree, 1984.

563. *The Zany Adventures of Robin Hood* (1984)

United States; dir. Ray Austin; Charles Fries Productions.

CAST: Tom Barker, Morgan Fairchild, Kenneth Griffith, Melvyn Hayes, Michael Hordern, Robert Hardy, Roy Kinnear, Roddy McDowall, George Segal, Janet Suzman.

A middle-aged Robin Hood, who dresses in drag to deliver a singing birthday telegram to his nemesis Prince John, steals from the rich and gives to the poor — *after* taking a percentage for his trouble. Maid Marian balks at keeping her vow of chastity, and Prince John merrily tortures peasants, pillages villages and lays waste to the countryside — when he is not seeing a psychiatrist. Meanwhile, King Richard is held prisoner and is in need of rescuing, which Robin and Marian plot to do.

Intended as a parody of Errol Flynn's 1938 *The Adventures of Robin Hood*, this film is reminiscent, thanks to its reliance on borscht-belt humor, of Mel Brooks's short-lived American television series *When Things Were Rotten* (ABC 1975). It is, however, amateurish in comparison to that series.

REVIEWS: *Hollywood Reporter* 22 May 1984: 8, 28. *New York Times* 22 May 1984: C16. *TV Guide* 19 May 1984: A-117.

ADDITIONAL DISCUSSIONS:
Burden, Martin. "Ivan, Ho! George Segal Is the New Robin Hood." *New York Post* 26 April 1984: 85.
Marill, Alvin H. *Movies Made for Television 1964–1980*. New York: Zoetrope, 1987.
Robinson, Jeff. "Director to Morgan Fairchild: 'I'm Shocked You're Funny!'" *TV Guide* 19 May 1984: 18–20.

564. *A Zsarnok sziva avagy Boccaccio Magyarorszagin* (1981)

Hungary; dir. Jancso Miklos; Mafilm Studio.

ALTERNATE TITLES: *Boccaccio in Hungary, Heart of a Tyrant* and *The Tyrant's Heart*.

CAST: Gyorgy Cserhalmi, Ninetto Davoli, Laszlo Galffy, Jozsef Madaras, Laszlo Markus, Teresa Ann Savoy.

Gáspár Guthi, heir apparent to the Hungarian throne, returns home from Italy, where he was reared, to find his father dead under unexplained circumstances. To unravel what has really happened, Gáspár relies upon two Italian actor friends. Their efforts uncover an elaborate Turkish plot to conquer Hungary that involves Gáspár's uncle, mother and the Hungarian Archbishop.

Based loosely on Boccaccio's *Decameron* and Shakespeare's *Hamlet,* the plot's confusion here is probably only matched by that of any audience trying to sit through this film.

REVIEWS: *Filmkultura* 17 (November-December 1981): 38–41. *Hollywood Reporter* 26 November 1982: 5. *Hungarofilm Bulletin* 3 (1967): 3–4. *Times* [London] 8 September 1981: 8. *Variety* 9 September 1981: 23.

BIBLIOGRAPHY

*In part or in whole, the following studies have previously
discussed or cataloged cinematic depictions of the Middle Ages.*

Beatie, Bruce A. "Arthurian Films and Arthurian Texts: Problems of Reception and Comprehension." *Arthurian Interpretations* 2 (Spring 1988): 65–78.

Behlmer, Rudy. "Robin Hood on the Screen." *Films in Review* 16 (February 1965): 91–102.

Blaetz, Robin J. "Strategies of Containment: Joan of Arc in Film." Ph.D. dissertation. New York University, 1989.

Les Cahiers de la cinémathèque 42–43 (Summer 1985): 1–188. (Special issue devoted to "le moyen âge au cinéma.")

Carnes, Mark C., ed. *Past Imperfect: History According to the Movies*. New York: Henry Holt, 1995.

Carpenter, Kevin, ed. *Robin Hood: Die vielen Gesichter des edlen Räubers*. Oldenburg: Bibliotheks- und Informationssystem der Universität Oldenburg, 1995.

de la Bretèque, François. "Le Choc des deux Méditerranés." *Les Cahiers de la cinémathèque* 61 (September 1994): 51–63.

_____. "La Figure de chevalier errant dans l'imaginaire cinématographique." *Cahiers de l'Association Internationale des Études Françaises* 47 (1995): 49–78.

_____. "Les Films hagiographiques dans le cinéma des premiers temps." In Roland Cosandey et al., eds. *Une Invention du Diable? Cinéma des premiers temps et religion*. Sainte-Foy: Les Presses de l'Université Laval, 1992.

_____. "Le Moyen Âge au cinéma français 1940–1987." In M. Perrin, ed. *Dire le Moyen Âge hier et aujourd'hui*. Laon: Université de Picardie, 1987.

_____. "Présence de la littérature française du Moyen Âge dans le cinéma français." *Cahiers de recherches médiévales* 2 (1996): 155–65.

_____. "Le Regard sur cinéma sur le Moyen Âge." In Jacques Le Goff and Guy Lobrichon, eds. *Le Moyen Âge aujourd'hui*. Cahiers du Léopard d'or 7. Paris: Le Léopard d'or, 1998.

_____. "Stéréotypes des marginaux et exaltation des comportements déviants dans les films à sujet moyenâgeux." *Cahiers du C.R.I.S.I.M.A.* [Centre de Recherche Interdisciplinaire sur la Société et l'Imaginaire au Moyen Âge, Université Paul-Valéry, Montpellier] 2 (1995): 9–21.

du Bus, Olivier Lefébure. "La Table ronde et ses chevaliers." *Séquences* 177 (March-April 1995): 51–52.

Dumont, Hervé. "Guillaume Tell au cinéma." *Travelling* 43 (1975): 21–29.

Durand, Jacques. "La Chevalerie à lécran." *Avant-scène du cinéma* 221 (1 February 1979): 29–40.

Elley, Derek. *The Epic Film*. London: Routledge & Kegan Paul, 1984.

Filmer-Davis, Kath. *Fantasy, Fiction, and Welsh Myth*. New York: St. Martin's, 1996.

Fraser, George MacDonald. *The Hollywood History of the World*. New York: Beech Tree, 1988.

Gorgievski, Sandra. "The Arthurian Legend in the Cinema: Myth or Legend?" In Marie-Françoise Alamichel and Derek Brewer, eds. *The Middle Ages after the Middle Ages in the English-Speaking World*. Cambridge, Eng.: D.S. Brewer, 1997.

Guibert, Pierre and Marcel Oms. *L'Histoire de France au cinéma*. Paris: CinémAction, 1993.

Harty, Kevin J. "Cinema Arthuriana: A Bibliography of Selected Secondary Materials." *Arthurian Interpretations* 3 (Spring 1989): 119–37.

_____. "Cinema Arthuriana: A Filmography." *Quondam et Futurus* 7 (Spring 1987): 5–8; 7 (Summer 1987): 18.

_____. "Cinema Arthuriana: Translations of the Arthurian Legend to the Screen." *Arthurian Interpretations* 2 (Fall 1987): 95–113.

_____, ed. *Cinema Arthuriana, Essays on Arthurian Film*. New York: Garland, 1991.

_____. "Jeanne au cinéma." In Bonnie Wheeler and Charles T. Wood, eds. *Fresh Verdicts on Joan of Arc*. New York: Garland, 1996.

Holly, Linda Tarte. "Medievalism in Film: The Matter of Arthur, A Filmography." In Jürgen Kühnel et al., eds. *Mittelalter-Rezeption III*. Göppingen: Kümmerle, 1988.

Knight, Stephen. *Robin Hood, A Complete Study of the English Outlaw*. Oxford; Blackwell, 1994.

Lacy, Norris J. "Arthurian Film and the Tyranny of Tradition." *Arthurian Interpretations* 4 (Fall 1989): 75–85.

_____, ed. *The New Arthurian Encyclopedia*. Updated paperback edition. New York: Garland, 1996.

_____, and Geoffrey Ashe (with Debra Mancoff). *The Arthurian Handbook*. 2nd ed. New York: Garland, 1997.

Lucanio, Patrick. *With Fire and Sword, Italian Spectacles on American Screens 1958–1968*. Metuchen, N.J.: Scarecrow, 1994.

MacCurdy, Marian. "Bitch or Goddess: Polarized Images of Women in Arthurian Films and Literature." *Platte Valley Review* 18 (Winter 1990): 3–24.

Margolis, Nadia. *Joan of Arc in History, Literature, and Film*. New York: Garland, 1990.

Parish, James Robert, and Don E. Stanke. *The Swashbucklers*. New Rochelle, N.Y.: Arlington House, 1976.

Prodolliet, Ernest. *Faust im Kino, Die Geschichte des Faustfilms von den Anfängen bis in die Gegenwart*. Freiburg, Switz.: Universitätsverlag Freiburg, 1978.

Richards, Jeffrey. *Swordsmen of the Screen from Douglas Fairbanks to Michael York*. London: Routledge & Kegan Paul, 1977.

Schenk, Irmbert. *Der italienische Historienfilm von 1905 bis 1914*. Bremen: Uni Bremen, 1991.

Searles, Baird. *EPIC! History of the Big Screen*. New York: Harry N. Abrams, 1990.

Smith, Gary. *Epic Films: Casts, Credits and Commentary on Over 250 Historical Spectacle Movies*. Jefferson, N.C.: McFarland, 1991.

Tarpley, Fred. "King Arthur on Film." In William E. Tanner, ed. *The Arthurian Myth of Quest and Magic, A Festschrift in Honor of Lavon B. Fulwiler*. Dallas: Caxton's Modern Arts Press, 1993.

Turner, David. *Robin of the Movies*. Kingswinford, Eng.: Yeoman Press, 1989.

Umland, Rebecca A., and Samuel J. Umland. *The Use of Arthurian Legend in Hollywood Film from Connecticut Yankees to Fisher Kings*. Westport, Conn.: Greenwood, 1996.

Wehrhahn, Jürgen. "König Artus und die Ritter der Tafelrunde." *Retro* 12 (November-December 1981): 5–13.

ꓘNDEX

References are to entry numbers unless preceded by "p." for page.
Numbers in **boldface** refer to pages with photographs.

291